Scott's Shadow

LITERATURE IN HISTORY

—————————— SERIES EDITORS ——————————

David Bromwich, James Chandler, and Lionel Gossman

The books in this series study literary works
in the context of the intellectual conditions,
social movements, and patterns of action
in which they took shape.

OTHER BOOKS IN THE SERIES

Lawrence Rothfield, *Vital Signs: Medical Realism in
Nineteenth-Century Fiction*

David Quint, *Epic and Empire: Politics and Generic
Form from Virgil to Milton*

Alexander Welsh, *The Hero of the Waverley Novels:
With New Essays on Scott*

Susan Dunn, *The Deaths of Louis XVI: Regicide and the
French Political Imagination*

Sharon Achinstein, *Milton and the Revolutionary Reader*

Esther Schor, *Bearing the Dead: The British Culture of
Mourning from the Enlightenment to Victoria*

Elizabeth K. Helsinger, *Rural Scenes and National
Representation: Britain, 1815–1850*

Katie Trumpener, *Bardic Nationalism: The Romantic Novel
and the British Empire*

Karen Chase and Michael Levenson, *The Spectacle of Intimacy:
A Public Life for the Victorian Family*

Joshua Scodel, *Excess and the Mean in Early Modern English Literature*

William Keach, *Arbitrary Power: Romanticism, Language, and Politics*

Scott's Shadow

THE NOVEL IN
ROMANTIC EDINBURGH

Ian Duncan

PRINCETON UNIVERSITY PRESS   PRINCETON AND OXFORD

Copyright © 2007 by Princeton University Press
Published by Princeton University Press, 41 William Street, Princeton,
New Jersey 08540

In the United Kingdom: Princeton University Press, 3 Market Place,
Woodstock, Oxfordshire OX20 1SY

Library of Congress Cataloging-in-Publication Data

Duncan, Ian.
Scott's shadow : the novel in Romantic Edinburgh / Ian Duncan.
p.   cm. — (Literature in history)
Includes bibliographical references and index.

ISBN-13: 978-0-691-04383-8 (acid-free paper)
1. English fiction—Scottish authors—History and criticism. 2. English
fiction—19th century—History and criticism. 3. Scott, Walter, Sir,
1771–1832—Influence. 4. Romanticism—Scotland. 5. Nationalism
in literature. 6. National characteristics, Scottish, in literature.
7. Scotland—In literature. 8. Modernism (Literature)—Scotland.
9. Edinburgh (Scotland)—Intellectual life—19th century. I. Title.
PR8601.D86 2007
823.0099411—dc22   2007061023

British Library Cataloging-in-Publication Data is available

This book has been composed in Sabon

Printed on acid-free paper. ∞

press.princeton.edu

Printed in the United States of America

1 3 5 7 9 10 8 6 4 2

Contents

❧

Illustrations

❦

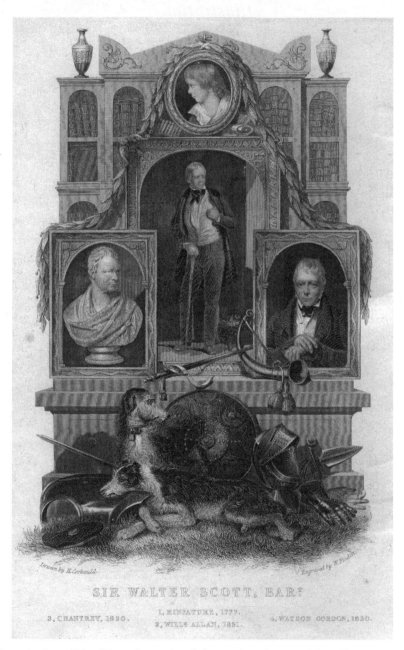

SIR WALTER SCOTT, BAR.ᵗ

Drawn by H.Corbould.   Engraved by W.Finden

3, CHANTREY, 1820.   1, MINIATURE, 1777.   4, WATSON GORDON, 1830.
2, WILᵏᵉ ALLAN, 1831.

Frontispiece: The Victorian cult of the author (see p. 281). Frontispiece
to J. G. Lockhart, *Life of Sir Walter Scott, Bart.* (London: A. & C. Black,
1896); reproduced from the Abbotsford Edition of the Waverley Novels.
Author's collection.

Preface

❦

Scott's Shadow explores the distinctive literary field that flourished in Edinburgh between 1802, the year of the founding of the *Edinburgh Review*, and 1832, the year of the Reform Bill and the death of Sir Walter Scott. In those decades Scottish publications and genres dominated a globalizing English-language market and made Edinburgh a literary metropolis to rival London. The forms, discourses, and institutions produced there shaped an imperial British culture that lasted throughout the century, long after Edinburgh's relapse to provincial status. They included definitive versions of the prose genres, fictional and periodical, that informed the nineteenth-century reading public; figureheads of an industrial mode of literary production, the professional author and entrepreneurial publisher; antithetical discourses of political economy and national culture that together would structure a Victorian liberal-conservative ideology; and that ideology's self-reflexive formal principle of fictional realism.

Current disciplinary history holds that the modern category of literature in English emerged conceptually in the Romantic period, as the fictional genres of prose, verse, and drama disaggregated from the general field of written discourse that Enlightenment intellectuals called "the Republic of Letters."[1] The Republic of Letters was, at least nominally, a cosmopolitan domain—if restricted to gentlemen—and the disaggregation of literature brought a compensatory investment with nationalist associations and ideologies as well as with a "deep" appeal to "the people." Edinburgh provides an exceptionally clear view of this general transformation, in part because of the infrastructural shift that took place from the university curriculum, matrix of the projects of Enlightenment, to an industrializing literary marketplace, in the publishing boom of the first quarter of the nineteenth century.

This book focuses on Scott, the dominant figure in literary Edinburgh, and on the novel, the genre that made modernization and national life its themes, in the decade or so from the end of the Napoleonic wars to the publishing crash of 1825–26. Scott's novels saturated the British fiction market, outselling all other novels combined; their claim on the cultural authority of the Enlightenment human sciences, as well as their artistic prowess, helped win them an overwhelming critical prestige; and their author stood at the center of the regional network of Tory patronage in unreformed Scotland.[2] This unprecedented ascendancy makes the reassessment of Scott's achievement critical for any understanding of the larger scene and period, and it provides the organizing topic of *Scott's Shadow*.

Accounts of Scott's famous invention, the historical novel, have typically specified historicism as its key component, as though Scott chose to write history in the guise of fiction. *Scott's Shadow* takes seriously the invention's other term, fiction: the quality that differentiates the novel from other narrative genres, such as history, and renders its formal autonomy in the period.[3] Scott's historicization of fiction elicits not fiction's absorption into history but its full categorical emergence, which made possible the Victorian primacy of the novel as a representation of national life. Elsewhere I have shown how the eighteenth-century revival of vernacular, premodern, and indigenous cultural forms supplied a repertoire for that representation, under the sign of romance.[4] In these pages I shall argue that philosophical authority for the claim on fiction as the medium for reality, instead of its antithesis, was developed in Scottish Enlightenment empiricism. Hume's *Treatise of Human Nature* provided a theoretical basis for that "fundamental practice of modern ideology—acquiescence without belief, crediting without credulousness,"[5] that would find its technical realization in the Waverley novels.

Scott's centrality in early nineteenth-century Edinburgh constitutes him as the figure I call "Scott's shadow." The term refers not only to Scott's influence, and the turbulent formation of Scottish Romanticism as a force field of that influence, in which other writers were compelled to accept, refuse, or work through their configuration as shades of Scott. It designates Scott's own presence in the field, which was not reducible to any of his various public, private, and secret personae—not even to that of the Author of *Waverley* and his avatars, refracted through the formal anonymity of the "Great Unknown." "A shadow—and an impersonal author is nothing better—can cast no shade," equivocates the "Eidolon, or Representation, of the Author of Waverley," in one of his manifestations in a series of novel prefaces published at the height of the Scottish fiction boom in the early 1820s.[6] Bearded in the recesses of Constable's shop, publishing powerhouse of the Waverley novels and the *Edinburgh Review*, the Eidolon considers the question: What is an author? Refuting Adam Smith, this shadow affirms "that a successful author is a productive labourer" whose "bales of books" should not "be esteemed a less profitable part of the public stock than the goods of any other manufacture." At the same time, authors should aspire to a professional ideal: "the lawyer who pleads, the soldier who fights, the physician who prescribes, the clergyman . . . who preaches, without any zeal for their profession, without any sense of its dignity, and merely on account of their fee, pay, or stipend, degrade themselves to the rank of sordid mechanics . . . it is the same thing with literary emolument" (14). Constable's shop opens onto one of those subterranean interiors of the Edinburgh Old Town, a "labyrinth of small dark rooms, or *crypts*" (4), at the center of which ("a vaulted room, dedicated to secrecy and silence") the Eidolon makes his unashamedly worldly apology, assuming the double guise of garrulous humdrum gentleman and sublime archetypal phantasm—a "*magna parens*," as "closely veiled and wimpled" as Spenser's hermaphrodite demiurge Nature (5). Scott's frank location of his authorial function at the core of a capitalist mode of literary production discovers it as an underworld of occult procreative powers.[7]

This complex, self-baffling recognition, at once demystifying and remystifying, differentiates Scott's Edinburgh from the later nineteenth-century literary field analyzed by Pierre Bourdieu. In Flaubert's Paris, according to Bourdieu, the imaginary autonomy of the work of art relies on an antithetical inversion of the political economy of industrial capitalism.[8] Fiction in the Age of Scott, however, asserts its peculiar character in terms of a ghostly relation to the market, to "reality": one of doubling or repetition—haunting—rather than transcendence. What Bourdieu calls "the charismatic rupture between art and money" has not yet opened in Edinburgh in the early 1820s; on the contrary, a newly totalizing convergence of art and money generates charisma.[9] Or rather, charisma is generated by the immanence of the rupture in the convergence, as art and money uncannily double one another. The Edinburgh post-Enlightenment bloomed around a complex of anxieties about the institutional relation of literature to politics and commerce (Bourdieu's "field of power") in the wake of the French Revolution, which moved a succession of attempts to define a separate public sphere, prefiguring, although still far from enunciating, a domain of aesthetic autonomy. The *Edinburgh Review* sought to revive the Republic of Letters within the marketplace and at the same time to raise it above industrial conditions by claiming professional distinction, and thus scientific and judicial disinterestedness, for literary work—as Scott's Eidolon insists. The Tory writers at *Blackwood's Magazine* accused the *Edinburgh Review* of debauching literature with politics under the cloak of that claim, and countered it with the appeal to a profound conception of national tradition, which accommodated, in turn, their own, more aggressive politicization, the bad faith of which was not so much disavowed as acted out in a relentlessly ironic and satirical infestation of periodical writing with fictional devices. The Blackwoodians conscripted Scott's historical fiction as the solemn template for their imperial ideal of national culture, recasting the nineteenth-century public as a reading nation that consumed romance as history.

Massively influential, the Blackwoodian takeover of Scott for a Romantic cultural nationalism retains currency today, in disparaging characterizations of the Waverley novels as tools of a factitious "invention of Scotland," a delusional substitution of romance for real history.[10] Such accounts mystify Scott's fictional practice by severing it from its Humean roots, as I show in chapter 2. It was their professedly inauthentic status as works of fiction that allowed Scott's novels to float above local partisan alignments (however embroiled their author) and invoke a national public, as some of Scott's liberal opponents, including William Hazlitt and Harriet Martineau, would acknowledge. Fictional status, reflexively insistent in Scott's writing, provided for the doubled consciousness—of a skeptical disillusionment from reality and a sentimental attachment to reality as illusion—rehearsed in the self-representation of the Eidolon of the Author of *Waverley*. *Scott's Shadow* restores to view this Humean legacy, characterized as Romantic irony or a proleptic postmodernism in some of the most acute recent Scott criticism.[11]

Scholars have sought to analyze the reenchantments of literature as it shifts into industrial production in the Romantic age. Deidre Lynch evokes the Romantic library as haunted enclosure of "a strange time of posthumousness," vibrant with telepathic yearnings between readers and ghostly—dead or absent—authors.[12] Contemporary authors in Scott's shadow testified to a more troublesome haunting of the scene of writing. "The mighty spirit of the Magician has already so filled the labyrinth of Romance, that it is not easy to venture within its precincts, without feeling his influence," murmured one of Scott's fainter disciples.[13] More ambitiously, James Hogg wrote the Magician into his own romances in a bold series of attempts to command or exorcize that influence. Scott's preternatural dominion over so condensed and layered a terrain as Romantic Edinburgh intensified the strife of authorial "position takings" that internally structure a literary field.[14] The second part of *Scott's Shadow* looks in detail at the rival projects of Scottish fiction by Hogg, John Galt, Christian Johnstone, and others, as well as Scott's responses to them, that proliferated in the 1820s, composing a major episode in the history of British fiction as well as a major scene of British Romanticism. While some of those other projects and careers have returned to view, most spectacularly Hogg's, *Scott's Shadow* undertakes the first comprehensive critical study of them.[15]

Romantic-period Edinburgh has been all but invisible in modern literary studies. Recent scholarship has begun to address the interrelation of national, regional, and imperial sites of production in the cultural history of the long eighteenth century, and to reevaluate the Scottish contribution to the projects of British Romanticism.[16] *Scott's Shadow*, aligning itself with and owing much to these studies, differs from them in sustaining an intensive focus on the Edinburgh post-Enlightenment. Its focus is more local and period-specific than that of Katie Trumpener's *Bardic Nationalism*, the authoritative recent treatment of British fiction in the period, which ranges across a century of Irish, Welsh, English, and North American as well as Scottish writing and an array of nationalist genres besides the novel. *Scott's Shadow* departs from *Bardic Nationalism* in making Scott's centrality its topic, rather than displacing it—a move which, while recovering hitherto overshadowed alternative projects, tends to reconstitute the Great Unknown as a kind of dark matter in the Romantic universe. Ina Ferris's *The Achievement of Literary Authority*, the other influential study of Scott's novels and their local contexts, examines the impact of *Waverley* in relation to the *Edinburgh Review* and early Irish national tales as well as the rival fictions by Hogg and Galt that issued through the *Old Mortality* controversy. *Scott's Shadow* revisits that terrain, but weights its inquiry towards the postwar periodical matrix of *Blackwood's* and a more comprehensive examination of Scottish novels and careers.[17] Much of the revisionary work that has followed Ferris and Trumpener seeks to dismantle the trope of Scott's originality by celebrating dissident and precursor projects of national and historical fiction, eclipsed by the global media triumph of the Waverley novels and their Victorian monumentalization.[18] Valuable, indeed necessary as that work has been, it has not always avoided a reductive or zero-sum accounting of the oppositions on which it mounts its case. Understanding originality and influence as dialectically productive conditions and effects of literary work, *Scott's Shadow* attends to the generative rather than restrictive force of Scott's impact on prose fiction in the Romantic period.

Chapter 1 of *Scott's Shadow* sketches an archaeology of the Edinburgh literary field and Scottish fiction that provides a formal introduction to the book. Besides the rise of the Scottish novel, the postwar decade (1815–25) saw the rise of *Blackwood's Edinburgh Magazine*: the archetype of Romantic miscellanies, wellspring of nonnovelistic fictional experiments and regional base camp for alternative projects to the Waverley novels. *Blackwood's* accommodates the belated theorization of a "Scottish Romanticism" in the form of an aesthetic ideology of cultural nationalism, which provides the topic of the second chapter. Chapter 3 contextualizes Scott's achievement with a discussion of the Scottish school of domestic national fiction that took its cue from Maria Edgeworth. Chapter 4 turns to Scott, and to the critical consensus that has cast Scott's novels as the ideological engines of an Anglo-British internal colonialism. The chapter reorientates the discussion of Scott by examining Scott's own reorientation of *Waverley*, and of the progressive plot of Enlightenment stadial history (i.e., a history articulated by stages of economic and social development), in the later Highland romance *Rob Roy*. Chapter 5 discovers the philosophical source for Scott's work of fiction in Humean empiricism.

The second half of the book looks at the field of influence constituted by "Scott's shadow" in rival projects of Scottish fiction in the early 1820s, focusing on the entangled projects of Hogg, Galt, and Scott himself. Chapter 6 revisits, through Hogg's career, the sociology of the Edinburgh literary scene and its mixed culture of patronage, commerce, and professionalism analyzed in the first chapter. The chapter reads Hogg's inset allegories of his relationship with Scott as he turned from ballad-based poetry to novel-length prose fiction, as well as the outrageous fictionalization of an all-too-organic Hogg in *Blackwood's*. Chapter 7 reads Hogg's novelistic (or counternovelistic) experiments with the forms and figures of popular tradition. These express, through tropes of cannibalism and the upright corpse, an increasingly resolute resistance to the ideology of Enlightenment progress and the cultural historiography of loss and salvage that Hogg associated with Scott. Hogg's resistance to the scheme is so violent that it demands a different critical vocabulary, and I have drawn on psychoanalytic theories of incorporation and the uncanny as offering the best entry into his work. John Galt, the subject of chapter 8, offers the converse case: where Hogg claimed a rival position by repudiating Scott's dialectic of improvement, Galt seeks a more rigorous fictionalization of Enlightenment conjectural history, undisfigured by residual artifices of romance. Yet, after all, Galt found himself struggling with allegorical and romance plotting, and with the large-scale novelistic forms associated with Scott, in his most ambitious works. Chapter 9 offers a summation of the themes of *Scott's Shadow* in the triangulation of masterpieces by Galt, Hogg, and Scott from 1823–24. If *Redgauntlet* offers a virtuoso reaffirmation of Scott's aesthetic of Romantic skepticism, set against Galt's formal and ideological revision of historical romance in *Ringan Gilhaize*, Hogg's *Private Memoirs and Confessions of a Justified Sinner*—the astounding terminus to which several preceding chapters have been tending—obliterates both positions. Chapter 10, a coda, tracks the dissolution of the literary field of Scottish Romanticism through three stages: Christian Johnstone's 1827 novel *Elizabeth de Bruce*, which registers the saturation and exhaustion of the genre; the outbreak of liberal magazines in Edinburgh around the 1832 Reform legislation and Scott's death, which, among their proclamations of signs of the times, attempt to redeem the Waverley novels from Tory bondage for a progressive "spirit of the age"; and lastly, Carlyle's programmatic disintegration of the literary and ideological forms of the Edinburgh post-Enlightenment (the novel, conjectural history, national culture, common life) in that climactic specimen of *Blackwood's*-style serial, fusing fiction with cultural critique, *Sartor Resartus*.

It has taken me far longer than it should have done to write this book, and I have accumulated many debts along the way. First thanks must go to my resourceful and meticulous research assistants, Nick Nace and Slavica Naumovska, who have prevented many inaccuracies, great and small.

Princeton University Press has blessed me with a succession of astonishingly tolerant editors: Bob Brown, Mary Murrell, and latterly Hanne Winarsky, who has seen the project to completion with apparently imperturbable patience and good humor. I thank Kathy Cioffi, the most scrupulous and discreet of copyeditors, and an exemplary production team at Princeton under Ellen Foos. The editors of the Literature and History series—David Bromwich, James Chandler, and Lionel Gossman—encouraged this project from the very start. I could not have wished for better press readers, as supportive as they were exigent, than Ina Ferris, Susan Manning, and the anonymous third reviewer. I owe a particular debt to Jim Chandler and to Douglas Mack, who also read the entire MS, and have been models of unstinting generosity as well as inspiration over the years. My greatest thanks go to my best critic, Ayşe Agiş, for her intellectual companionship and love.

Research on *Scott's Shadow* has been supported by fellowships and grants from the Smart Family Foundation, the College of Arts and Sciences, and the Whitney Humanities Center at Yale University; from the Barbara and Carlisle Moore endowment and the Oregon Humanities Center at the University of Oregon; and from the Committee on Research of the Academic Senate and the Division of Arts and Humanities at the University of California, Berkeley. A grant from the National Endowment for the Humanities supported a visiting fellowship at the Institute for Advanced Studies in the Humanities at the University of Edinburgh, where I began my research; I was also able to pursue my work as a short-term guest of the Programme in Modern Scottish Thought at the University of Edinburgh, the Noted Scholars Program at the University of British Columbia, and the Department of Literature at the University of Konstanz. I thank my hosts, friends and colleagues-for-a-season, Peter Jones, Penny Fielding, Cairns Craig, Miranda Burgess, and Silvia Mergenthal. I am also grateful to the staff of the university libraries at Yale, Oregon, and Berkeley, the British Library, the National Library of Scotland, the Edinburgh City Libraries, and the Edinburgh University Library.

It is a particular pleasure to acknowledge friends, colleagues, students, and teachers at the English departments where I have been lucky enough to have taught and studied while at work on this book. In New Haven, besides names already mentioned, Dick Brodhead, Jill Campbell, Elizabeth Heckendorn Cook, Kevin Dunne, Lynn Enterline, Elizabeth Fowler, Paul Fry, Suzanne Fusso, Sara Suleri Goodyear, Lanny Hammer, Geoffrey Hartman, John Hollander, Suzanne Keen, Jacques Lezra, Victor Luftig, David Marshall, Linda Peterson, Martin and Mary Price, Lawrence Rainey, Claude Rawson, Patricia Spacks, Howard Stern, Gordon Turnbull, Lynn Wardley, Sandy Welsh, Laura Wexler, Sarah Winter, Suzanne Wofford, and Mark Wollaeger all had an impact on this work in ways of which they may never have been aware. The Yale diaspora has kept other friendships warm: David Hensley, David Kaufmann, Maggie Kilgour, Scott Klein, Steven Meyer, Sophia Padnos, Leah Price, Jahan Ramazani, and Jennifer Wagner-Lawler. I salute the generosity and enthusiasm of friends, former colleagues, and dissertation students in Eugene: Liz Bohls, Ken Calhoon, George Cusack, Dianne Dugaw, Rachel Foster, John Gage, Sarah Goss, Roland Greene, Clare Lees, Randy McGowen, Paul Peppis, Amanda Powell, Tres Pyle, Eric Reimer, Bill Rossi, David Sandner, Steve Shankman, Dick Stein, Richard Stevenson, Tom Tracy, Bianca Tredennick, Julian Weiss, Molly Westling, George Wickes, Harry Wonham, and the late Carlisle Moore. Here in Berkeley I thank Janet Adelman, Mark Allison, Ann Banfield, Kelvin Black, Mitch Breitwieser, Janet Broughton, Anne-Lise François, Cathy Gallagher, Steve Goldsmith, Kevis Goodman, Jared Greene, Rae Greiner, Dori Hale, Nick Howe, Priya Joshi, Lewis Klausner, Celeste Langan, Jennifer Miller, Kent Puckett, Padma Rangarajan, Sue Schweik, Monica Soare, George Starr, James Turner, Leslie Walton, and Alex Zwerdling.

Extramurally, I thank the friends and collaborators on various projects that have fed into this book: Leith Davis and Janet Sorensen, Gill Hughes, Ann Rowland and Charles Snodgrass, and Murray Pittock. My work has been nourished over the years by the communities of scholars of Scott and Hogg, Scottish studies, studies in the novel, Romanticism, and the nineteenth century. Some of them have read or heard parts of this, and some of them said helpful things they will no doubt have forgotten: besides those I have mentioned above, they are Ian Alexander, Sharon Alker, Steven Arata, Nancy Armstrong, Alyson Bardsley, John Barrell, Guinn Batten, Ian Baucom, John Bender, David Brewer, Marshall Brown, Margaret Bruzelius, Jim Buzard, Joe Carroll, Siobhan Carroll, Claire Connolly, Robert Crawford, Janette Currie, Jenny Davidson, David Duff, Hans de Groot, Simon Edwards, Mary Favret, Peter Garside, Luke Gibbons, Denise Gigante, Suzanne Gilbert, Nancy Goslee, Evan Gottlieb, Tony Hasler, David Hewitt, Bob Irvine, Catherine Jones, Jon Klancher, Andrew Lincoln, Alison Lumsden, Deidre Lynch, Caroline McCracken-Flesher, Jerry McGann, Maureen McLane, Ken McNeil, Richard Maxwell, Franco Moretti, Nicholas Phillipson, John Plotz, Fiona Robertson, the late Jill Rubenstein, Meg Russett, Mark Schoenfield, Jonah Segal, Clare Simmons, David Simpson, Katie Trumpener, Graham Tulloch, Enrica Villari, Tara Wallace, and Matt Wickman.

Parts of the work in progress were delivered as lectures and papers at various institutions, conferences, and symposiums over the last dozen or so years. I thank my hosts and colleagues, in addition to those already named, especially Jonathan Allison, Kevin Gilmartin, Greg Kucich, Jill Heydt-Stevenson, Loretta Innocenti, Catherine Kerrigan, Michael Moses,

Thomas Pfau, and Charlotte Sussman. In recent years I revised the manuscript in balmy circumstances on the southwest coast of Turkey, and I have to thank visiting family and friends for their forbearance while I shut myself away for the large part of the day: Hamish and Maureen Duncan; Rory, Victoria, Fern, and Aeneas Duncan; Godfrey Bird; Saime Ünlüsoy; and Fethiye Çetin.

Shorter versions of the "A King and No King" and "The Modern Athens" sections of chapter 1 and part of the "Scottish Romanticism" section of chapter 2 have appeared in *Romantic Metropolis: The Urban Scene of British Culture, 1780–1840*, edited by James Chandler and Kevin Gilmartin (Cambridge: Cambridge University Press, 2005), 45–64; part of chapter 2 also appeared as "*Blackwood's* and Romantic Nationalism" in *Print Culture and the Blackwood Tradition, 1805–1930*, edited by David Finkelstein (Toronto: University of Toronto Press, 2007), 70–89; a version of chapter 4 appeared as "Primitive Inventions: *Rob Roy*, Nation and World System" in *Eighteenth-Century Fiction* (2002): 81–102, and an excerpt from chapter 5 appeared in a special issue (edited by Lene Østermark-Johansen) of *Angles on the English Speaking World* 3 (2003): 63–76; the "Suicide's Grave" and "Organic Form" sections of chapter 6 and the "Magical Realism," "Upright Corpse," and "Resurrection Men" sections of chapter 7 appeared in a series of articles in *Studies in Hogg and His World* (1993–98); and a few pages of the "Post-Enlightenment Postmodernism" section and all of the "Authenticity Effects" section in chapter 9 appeared as "Authenticity Effects: The Work of Fiction in Romantic Scotland" in *SAQ* 102, no. 1 (2003): 93–116. I am grateful to the editors and publishers for permission to reprint the revised versions in this book. I thank the Trustees of the National Library of Scotland for permission to publish excerpts from manuscript and printed materials in their holdings, and the Edinburgh Central Library and the National Galleries of Scotland for permission to reproduce the images.

Part One

Chapter 1

❧

EDINBURGH, CAPITAL OF THE
NINETEENTH CENTURY

How high the situation of poor Scotland . . . in arts, in arms, and in literature—her universities every year more crowded—her philosophers advanc-
ing with so proud a career in the field of science—her little junta of accomplished men in the first literary journal that ever appeared in any country,
giving law to the republic of letters—her moralists improving—her poets
delighting the world.
    —Christian Isobel Johnstone, *The Saxon and the Gaël; or,*
The Northern Metropolis (1814)

The poets, the orators, and the lawyers, of the flat Boetian region of the
dull and muddy Thames, being under the influence of the envious spirit
of conscious inferiority, make a point of rarely noticing the pre-eminent
endowments of the northern Athenians. . . . The whole English people, the
Irish, and all Europe, are chagrined at the superiority of the wise and
learned of Edinburgh; yea, every other town that participates in the intellec-
tualising keenness of the Scottish air, turns the sharpness of its wits against
the pretensions of the provincial capital.
    —John Galt, *Glenfell; or, Macdonalds and Campbells.*
An Edinburgh Tale of the Nineteenth Century (1820)

The tartan robe (which has got into vogue in France and Flanders) adorns
the London fair ones; the border and other minstrelsy delight the lovers of
literature; the Scottish novels turn the heads of the readers of light matter,
and even those of the second class are found to amuse their perusers; the
stage teems with imitations and representations from the former.
    —Felix MacDonogh, *The Hermit in Edinburgh: or, Sketches of*
Manners and Real Characters and Scenes in the Drama of Life (1824)

A KING AND NO KING

In the early afternoon of 14 August 1822, the yacht *The Royal George*
with its naval and civilian escort cast anchor off the Edinburgh port of
Leith. Heavy rain postponed the King's landing until the following day.

At about half past two on 15 August, a naval barge drew alongside the royal yacht, bearing, among other dignitaries, the home secretary, Robert Peel, and Sir Walter Scott, whose baronetcy had been gazetted on George IV's accession to the throne two years earlier. "Sir Walter Scott!" exclaimed the King; "The man in Scotland I most wish to see! Let him come up."[1]

No reigning monarch had visited Scotland since its incorporation into the British state at the Treaty of Union in 1707. Under Scott's careful management, the "King's Jaunt" unfolded as a fortnight-long pageant of antique ceremonies—most of which were made up for the occasion.[2] Here, in one of the centers of the European Enlightenment, Scott staged the sovereign's relation to "the ancient kingdom of Scotland" as the primitive, patriarchal relation of a Highland chieftain to his clan. The return of the king conjured up a vanished social formation. At the height of a new wave of forced clearances of tenantry to make way for sheep, Scott wrote to Highland landlords exhorting them to bring their traditional "tail" of kilted and armed retainers, and published a pamphlet instructing gentlemen attending the Grand Ball at the George Street Assembly Rooms to wear "the ancient Highland costume." The King himself appeared at his Holyrood Levee in an extravagant outfit (it cost £1,354. 18s. 0d.) of scarlet philabeg, jewelled weapons, and pink satin drawers. George was wearing the Royal Stuart plaid of his own grandfather's dynastic rival. With lavish insistence, the pageantry of the royal visit kept alluding to the last occasion on which Edinburgh had been visited by a claimant to the throne of Scotland—an outlaw one. Seventy-seven years earlier, for a few momentous days in September 1745, Prince Charles Edward Stuart had occupied the city with an army composed largely of Highlanders, whom many of the inhabitants regarded as savage banditti.

Commentators then and since have deplored the King's Jaunt as a garish travesty—the iconographic investiture of the British monarchy, as well as Scotland's postnational identity, with a bogus, retro-Jacobite, Highland pageantry. Much of that commentary has satisfied itself with denouncing the phoniness of Scott's "invention of Scotland" as a nation of Highlanders and Jacobites doing homage to a Hanoverian king.[3] But in identifying the gouty ageing dandy, legitimate George, with the defeated but glamorous Chevalier, in dressing metropolitan Scotland in the robes of its desolated Gaelic hinterland, in redeeming a lost national cause for a modern imperial triumphalism, Scott was far from being the dupe of an antiquarian nostalgia. This was no deluded abolition of modernity for a regression to misty origins. Scott was assembling a gaudily up-to-date national spectacle that relied on the availability of sovereignty—its mystic link with the past decisively broken—as a sign among other signs that gathered its meaning in public circulation and consumption.

The political purpose of the Jaunt was clear at the time. The King's Scottish excursion followed a visit to Ireland the previous year: no doubt the tour of the Celtic provinces would endow the monarch with a measure of public dignity in the wake of the Queen Caroline scandal. In Scotland, the mass spectacle of sovereignty and reciprocal loyalty symbolically repaired the rifts of post-Union history: not just the dynastic conflict of the preceding century, but more recent civil tensions. Postwar recession and unemployment had driven the struggle over constitutional reform, muted for two decades by anti-Jacobin repression and war with France, to crisis pitch. Government spies, dragoons, and magistrates had put down working-class unrest in the western Lowlands only two years earlier, with exemplary ferocity. A journalistic warfare waged between Edinburgh and Glasgow Whigs and Tories set gentlemen as well as hacks (the difference was not always evident) at one another's throats in libels, lawsuits, brawls, and duels—James Stuart of Dunearn had shot dead Sir Alexander Boswell, son of the biographer, as recently as March 1822. The Scots Tory administrative junta, vexed by the clamor for reform, was attempting to shore up its legitimacy by laying claim to a transcendental national interest. In staging the royal visit as a mass loyalist pageant, Scott and his collaborators sought to replicate the outbursts of public festivity that had greeted the news of Napoleon's defeat in the spring of 1814 and again the following year after Waterloo.[4] Some of the devices of these victory celebrations—parades, fireworks, illuminations, allegorical transparencies, the lighting of a beacon on top of Arthur's Seat—were repeated in 1822 (not always successfully: rain made the beacon a damp squib). The most suggestive of these recyclings was a double one: the adoption of Jacobite tokens such as the white cockade and tartan. In 1814–15 these had expressed solidarity with the House of Bourbon, restored to the French throne after a cataclysmic interlude. In 1822 they identified the once-revolutionary House of Hanover with the anciens régimes restored across Europe at the Congress of Vienna. The King's Visit staged the spectacle of legitimacy itself as a neoabsolutist politics: in William Hazlitt's sardonic phrase, "ingrafting the principles of the House of Stuart on the illustrious stock of the House of Brunswick."[5]

The most elaborate of the loyalist accounts of the Visit took the form of a commemorative "Royal Number" of the vanguard Tory organ *Blackwood's Edinburgh Magazine*. Christopher North's closing sonnet "To the King" (printed in red capital letters) follows a three-act episode of the satirical dialogue series "Noctes Ambrosianae," which shamelessly identifies the interests of the sovereign with *Blackwood's Magazine*. Mr. Blackwood and his literati descend upon a local farmhouse. "This is maist as gude's a visit frae the King himself," cheers the Gudeman. His wife praises the magazine: "Siccan a buik I never read afore. It gars ane laugh, they

canna tell how; and a' the time ye ken what ye're reading is serious, too—
Naething ill in't, but a' gude—supporting the kintra, and the King, and
the kirk."[6] An item by the premier *Blackwood's* author of the day illustrates, however, the complexity of responses to the King's Jaunt even
within the Tory camp.

The title of John Galt's comic sketch, "The Gathering of the West,"
mocks the strategy of Scott's pageant. Instead of the Gathering of the
Clans, that topos of Jacobite revival, Galt narrates an invasion of Edinburgh by the citizens of its great industrial rival, the economic powerhouse of Scottish modernity as well as of "the radical distemper which
lately raged in the west"[7]—Glasgow and its outlying ports and burghs.
Galt recounts how "the whole west began to move": "all the roads from
Glasgow to Edinburgh were like so many webs of printed calico, stamped
with the figures of coaches and carriages, horses and noddies, men,
women, and children, and weavers from Paisley, who had abjured reform" (317). The Radicals butchered after the "Battle of Bonnymuir" had
been weavers from Strathaven and Greenock (where Galt spent part of his
childhood), not far from Paisley. In Galt's simile, the energies of popular
resistance now feed the loyal mass movement without, however, being
completely digested by it. The modern labor of weaving that constitutes
the fabric of national patriotism, "like so many webs of printed calico,"
remains visible, and does not quite yield to the image it suggests, the dominant image of the Jaunt: tartan plaid. In Edinburgh, in the following chapter, the visitors behold "writers [solicitors] and writers' clerks . . .
trembling in the breeze, dressed in the Celtic garb, that their peeled, white,
ladylike legs might acquire the healthy complexion of Highland boughs"
(317). Galt's satire ends up confining itself to a harmless, indeed, healthy
regional animosity and submitting to the general tone of celebration, but
only after it has made its own distinctive—"western"—claim on the occasion. Rather than an ancient nation centered in Edinburgh, the King represents a modern commercial empire in which Glasgow's interests are crucial: "free trade and loyalty beget ease and affluence" (327).

The Scottish Whigs and Tories vied with one another to define the
meaning of the Jaunt, contending whether its spectacles of mass enthusiasm showed that sovereignty descended from the King or rested with the
consent of the people. Outright derision, much of it scurrilous, poured
from the Radical press in London.[8] Nor was a disillusioned view confined
to the opposition. An impeccably ironical account of the royal visit turns
up where it might perhaps be least expected, fifteen years later, in the
monumental biography of Scott by John Gibson Lockhart—former
Blackwood's fire-eater, now respectable editor of the *Quarterly Review.*
"Before this time," Lockhart reminds his readers, "no Prince of the house
of Hanover was known to have touched the soil of Scotland, except one,

whose name had ever been held there in universal detestation—the cruel conqueror of Culloden, —'the butcher Cumberland.' "[9] Lockhart understood very clearly what his father-in-law had been up to. The national humiliation marked by 1745 and its aftermath was to be healed through a ceremonial and comic reenactment. Lockhart saw, however, that what he called "Sir Walter's Celtified pageantry" alluded only secondarily to the historical event of Jacobite occupation. Before that, it referred to the literary medium that had given the '45 its mythic shape in the modern imagination. Scott's first novel *Waverley* (1814) had represented Charles Edward's Edinburgh sojourn as the moment when the Jacobite dream of a recaptured Scottish royalty achieved its greatest brilliance, above all as an evanescent series of civilian and military spectacles. Accordingly, referring to Daniel Terry's theatrical adaptations of the Waverley novels as well as his assistance in planning the royal visit, Lockhart calls Scott's management "a sort of grand *terryfication* of the Holyrood chapters in *Waverley*; —George IV, *anno ætatis* 60, being well contented to enact 'Prince Charlie,' with the Great Unknown himself for his Baron Bradwardine" (7:50). Scott staged the Royal Visit as the reenactment of a fictional representation of a historical event, the Jacobite project of restoration he had already exposed as theatrical, "romantic," and historically inauthentic, in *Waverley*.[10] Charles Edward was, after all, a Pretender: his own performance the hapless, ghostly repetition of a Scottish sovereignty that had exited the stage of history with the removal to London of his ancestor James VI one hundred and forty years earlier. Jacobitism could only reiterate, with the blindly literal insistence of a tragic protagonist, the loss of a sovereign presence that the Stuart kings themselves had belatedly defended with the principle of Divine Right. Instead of the king's body (or its constitutional supplement, a parliamentary assembly), national order resided now in Edinburgh with the problematically textual institution of the law—as several Scottish novels, notably Scott's *The Heart of Mid-Lothian* (1818) and Galt's *The Entail* (1822), would propound.

Lockhart narrates George IV's ceremonial reenactment of Charles Edward's attempt to replicate a lost ancestral sovereignty as a succession of tragedy by farce. Scott, treasuring the glass in which the King has toasted him, forgets he has it stowed away in a pocket until he sits down on it; the poet Crabbe, Scott's houseguest, finds himself surrounded by Gaelic-speaking Highlanders and stammers away at them in French ("what he considered . . . the universal language," 7:55); best of all the King, in full Highland fig at Holyrood, confronts "a figure even more portly than his own, equipped, from a sudden impulse of loyal ardour, in an equally complete set of the self-same conspicuous Stuart tartans." This is the London alderman Sir William Curtis, whose "portentous apparition cast an air of ridicule and caricature over the whole of Sir Walter's Celtified pageantry"

(7:64–65). Lockhart follows contemporary caricatures in making Sir William the King's "heroic *doppel-ganger*," the mirror image of an inauthentic Scotch Majesty.[11] The absurd alderman exposes the King's own status as a facsimile, bound to the inorganic, metaphysically empty spatial and temporal axes of duplication and repetition. Duplication and repetition: sovereignty's modern origin is no divine Logos, nor any natural bond, but literary production in the mode of mechanical reproduction: industrial print technology. A genealogy showing George as legitimate heir of the Stuarts was duly got up for the occasion and circulated in the loyalist press. Scott's pageant reiterates the more spectacular topoi of the Romantic literature that flourished in Scotland in the decades since 1746: not just the meteoric transit of a Pretender (*Waverley*) but the dubious revival of extinct ancestral origins (James Macpherson's *Fingal*) and the metaphysically disastrous proliferation of the Double (James Hogg's *Private Memoirs and Confessions of a Justified Sinner*).

Lockhart wavers between describing the King's Jaunt as a blatant confection, its artifice plain to see ("the extent to which the Waverley and Rob Roy *animus* was allowed to pervade the whole of this affair," 7:58), and as "a hallucination" that had "completely . . . taken possession" of spectators and participants (7:67). He describes, in short, the ambiguous subjectivity effect of a work of fiction, which takes possession of the imagination while the reader goes on knowing that it is just a fiction. Lockhart recognizes, even as he mocks, Scott's sophisticated staging of a disenchanted, thoroughly textualized figure of sovereignty in a modern commercial culture. Lockhart's treatment, along with the range and complexity of contemporary responses to the event, must complicate the gesture of ideological exposé with which the royal visit is typically dismissed: as though it is enough to denounce the "inauthenticity" of an occasion of which inauthenticity was the point. Observing the King's coronation at Westminster the previous year, Scott had been impressed by the ideological power of such public spectacles of invented tradition.[12] The inauthenticity—the alienation, portability, and recursiveness—of the signifiers of sovereignty, ancestry, territoriality, and legitimacy was a chief end of the pageant, not its inadvertent by-product.[13]

THE MODERN ATHENS

The royal visit reflected the civic confidence of an Edinburgh that showed itself off as a national metropolis more than a century after Scotland had lost the last of its institutions of sovereignty. The city was not only tartan decked for the occasion, dressed in the trophies of a North British "internal colonialism," but more durably adorned with the edifices and monuments of an imperial classicism. The adoption of James Craig's plans for a New Town in 1767 had initiated a sixty-year boom of construction and civic improvement, fuelled by the Edinburgh Town Council's combination of visionary enthusiasm and deficit spending. By the early nineteenth century Edinburgh's professional and gentry elite had deserted the medieval city, huddled precipitously around the Royal Mile, for the townhouse-lined piazzas of the South Side and the boulevards spreading beyond the North Loch. This was the post-Enlightenment era of "The Modern Athens," unfolding lavishly in the completion of Robert Adam's palatial frontage on Charlotte Square (commissioned in 1791 but interrupted by the French wars), the extension of the New Town in the Raeburn and Moray estates to the northwest of Princes Street (1813–22), and a series of splendid public works, from the Regency triumphalism of Waterloo Place (1815–19) to civic temples such as William Playfair's Royal Institution (now the Royal Scottish Academy) on Princes Street itself (1822–26). The Leith docks, too, had been improved and beautified (1806–17), at a cost that would hasten the city's bankruptcy in 1833.[14] This spectacular, monumental, and imperial urban landscape, dominated by the work of William Playfair and Thomas Hamilton, exploiting the unevenness and sheer verticality of the city's topography, marked a shift from the rational, horizontal, rectilinear conception of Craig's residential New Town. The city magistrates encouraged the change, commissioning William Stark (1814) and, on Stark's death, his student Playfair (1819) to develop Calton Hill and the adjacent lands. Calton Hill, its romantic prospects newly illustrated by J.M.W. Turner, was the site of ambitious plans for a monumental acropolis crowned with an observatory (1818), model temples to Robert Burns (1830) and Dugald Stewart (1831), a Nelson memorial (1807–16), Hamilton's Royal High School (1825–29), and a National Monument (1822–29), the foundation stone of which was laid during the royal visit.[15] The staging of the visit revealed all this to be something more grandiose than regional civic pride. Edinburgh was promoting and redefining itself as a new kind of national capital—not a political or commercial metropolis, but a cultural and aesthetic one.

Henry Cockburn attributed the postwar civic improvements to a spirit of emulation fired by national victory and renewed access to the Continent:

It was the return of peace that first excited our attention, and tended to open our eyes. Europe was immediately covered with travellers, not one of whom . . . failed to contrast the littleness of almost all that the people of Edinburgh had yet done, with the general picturesque grandeur and unrivalled sites of their city. It was about this time that the foolish phrase, "The Modern Athens," began to be applied to the capital of Scotland; a sarcasm, or a piece of

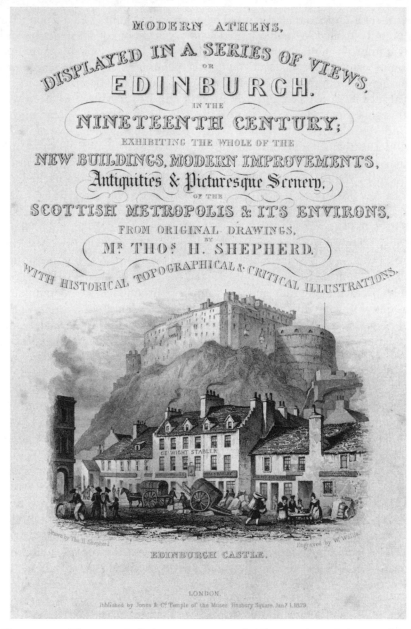

Figure 1.1. The post-Enlightenment era of "The Modern Athens," from T. H. Shepherd, *Modern Athens: Displayed in a Series of Views, or, Edinburgh in the Nineteenth Century* (1829), title page. Courtesy of Edinburgh City Libraries.

Figure 1.2. The Regency triumphalism of Waterloo Place—with the National Monument in the background, from Shepherd, *Modern Athens*. Courtesy of Edinburgh City Libraries.

Figure 1.3. Calton Hill, its romantic prospects newly illustrated by Turner, from Walter Scott, *Provincial Antiquities and Picturesque Scenery of Scotland* (1820). Courtesy of Edinburgh City Libraries.

Figure 1.4. The site of ambitious plans for a monumental acropolis. An imaginary view of Calton Hill "with the national Monument as it would appear if completed." Courtesy of Edinburgh City Libraries.

affected flattery, when used in a moral sense; but just enough if meant only as a comparison of the physical features of the two places. . . . There were more schemes, and pamphlets, and discussion, and anxiety about the improvement of our edifices and prospects within ten years after the war ceased, than throughout the preceding one hundred and fifty years.[16]

The antiquarian James Stuart seems to have been the first to compare the physical settings of Edinburgh and Athens in 1762, although, as Cockburn suggests, the epithet "Modern Athens" did not become widely current until after Waterloo.[17] Cockburn's discomfort with the "foolish phrase" stems from its association with the Whig cultural ascendancy of the *Edinburgh Review*, with which Cockburn himself was linked. Peacock makes it the boast of the mulish modernist Mr. MacQuedy in *Crotchet Castle* (1831): "Morals and metaphysics, politics and political economy, the way to make the most of all the modifications of smoke, steam, gas, and paper currency; you have all these to learn from us; in short, all the arts and sciences. We are the modern Athenians."[18] In the year of the Royal Visit, the Tory wits of *Blackwood's Magazine* poured scorn:

> In the days of Smith, and Hume, and Robertson, we were satisfied with our national name, and so we were during a later dynasty of genius, of which old Mackenzie still survives; but now-a-days, when with the exception of Scott, yourself North, and myself, and a few others, there is not a single man of power or genius in Edinburgh, the prigs call themselves *Athenians*! Why, you may just as appropriately call the first Parallelogram, that shall be erected on Mr Owen's plan, the Modern Athens, as the New Town of Edinburgh. . . . We are Scotsmen, not Greeks. We want no Parthenon—we are entitled to none. There are not ten persons in Edinburgh—not one Whig I am sure, who could read three lines of Homer "*ad aperturam libri.*" There are pretty Athenians for you! Think of shoals of Scotch artisans, with long lank greasy hair, and corduroy breeches, walking in the Parthenon![19]

Edinburgh's title to Athenian glory was a topic of lively controversy. Descriptions and illustrations of "picturesque Edinburgh" formed an aesthetic hinge for the turn from a "Classical" to a "Romantic" city, secured by the accession of a sublime vocabulary. The political terms of this shift involved the displacement—bitterly contentious—of an oligarchic and republican ideal of citizenship based on civic virtue, developed in the moral philosophy of the Scottish Enlightenment and sustained by the Edinburgh reviewers, to an aesthetically based cultural nationalism promoted by the *Blackwood's* literati.

Partisanship and scandal inflame the many books, pamphlets, essays, and reviews published about Edinburgh in the second and third decades of the nineteenth century. Lockhart's *Peter's Letters to His Kinsfolk*

(1819) founds a Tory cultural politics on the critique of Scottish public figures and institutions, while the anonymous *Edinburgh: A Satirical Novel* (1820) scarcely glances up from its trough of scurrilous gossip, and Felix MacDonogh's *The Hermit in Edinburgh* (1824) offers "Sketches of Manners and Real Characters and Scenes" in "Edina, the pride of the North."[20] The city's metropolitan pretensions come under hostile scrutiny in Robert Mudie's *The Modern Athens: A Dissertation and Demonstration of Men and Things in the Scotch Capital* (1825). Mudie (the son of a Tayside weaver) had attempted to exploit the postwar vogue for Scottish novels in *Glenfergus* (1820), which was respectfully reviewed but by no means a hit on the scale of Scott or even Hogg (with whose *Winter Evening Tales* the publishers coupled it in their advertisements).[21] Since 1820 Mudie had been working in London for the radical *Morning Chronicle*, and he returned north to cover the royal visit for the paper. A first, obsequiously exhaustive spin-off, *A Historical Account of His Majesty's Visit to Scotland* (which went through four editions in 1822), preceded the polemical *Modern Athens*.

In *The Modern Athens*, Mudie argues that Edinburgh's civic prominence constitutes an illegitimate claim on national representation. He fastens his critique upon a semantic shift in the term "nation":

> [T]he idea of building a national monument for Scotland, or in other words, a monument for the Scottish nation, may seem a work not of supererogation merely, but of folly; because the Scottish nation, so far from running any risk of becoming extinct and being forgotten, is in a very lively and flourishing state; and there are no people that, wherever they may go, cherish so carefully and proclaim so loudly, the praise of their country, as the Scotch.[22]

In rehearsing a traditionally English complaint about the infestation of office-hunting Scotchmen, Mudie pitches a reductively local, tribal sense of "nation" against the newer, conceptually more ambitious usage forged through the Napoleonic wars as an ideological shield against revolutionary republicanism. The clannish advancement of the Scots throughout the imperial state and civil apparatus, bragging all the while of a regional distinctiveness they have opportunistically abandoned, precludes their larger claim on a British national identity—and on the status of Edinburgh as a British metropolis. Mudie insists on a literal construction of sovereignty as a condition that has definitively lapsed for Scotland with the Union. Edinburgh's current pretensions take the form of a cultural nationalism that is no more than a deluded attempt to compensate for that political loss: "she is in herself not only the capital of Scotland, but all that Scotland has localized as an apology for a king; and therefore, besides assuming the consequence due to a royal seat, she puts on the air of royalty itself, and worships her own shadow in the mirror of the passing time" (162). A "widowed metropolis" unable to renounce the vanities of lost youth, Edinburgh has locked herself into a narcissistic and fetishistic circuit of pure representation. The result is a grotesque confusion of categories: "the Athens, taking her nominal and her real situation into the account, is both metropolitan and provincial" (163). What Mudie names but refuses to recognize is a new kind of nationality, a "nominal" one, which inheres in publicly circulated representations rather than in a determinate territory, body, or bloodline. By commanding a certain symbolic capital, a province can indeed claim metropolitan status in a new kind of imperial polity: one not bound by political borders but diffused across the globe in mainly maritime lanes and links of trade, secured by naval power. By 1815 the Scots had "thoroughly and systematically colonized all areas of the British empire from commerce to administration, soldiering to medicine, colonial education to the expansion of emigrant settlements," from Canada and the Caribbean to India.[23]

Mudie focuses his critique on the projected National Monument on Calton Hill. Plans to commemorate Scotland's contribution to the victory over Napoleon with some sort of monument were floated as early as 1817. Both Scott and Cockburn were among the promoters who appealed, in the year of the King's visit, for a public subscription of £42,000 "to erect a facsimile of the Parthenon" in Edinburgh. Construction began in 1826, four years after the laying of the foundation stone, but ceased when funds ran out in 1829, leaving the skeletal fragment that frames the east end of Princes Street today.[24] In 1819–20 *Blackwood's Magazine* devoted a series of articles to the controversy surrounding the Monument and the attendant issues of Edinburgh's civic improvements and national status. The first of these, "On the Proposed National Monument at Edinburgh" (July 1819), sets out with exemplary clarity the new ideology of an imperial cultural nationalism developed at *Blackwood's*.[25]

The writer, the younger Archibald Alison, deprecates "a want of the due sense of the importance of the proposed edifice on national character" on the part of those who think that a monument in London will suffice "since the two kingdoms have now been so long united into one great empire" (377). On the contrary, the empire's moral and political welfare requires the cultivation of its ancient national distinctions. Alison combines the argument, most cogently made by Adam Ferguson, that the political competitiveness of small republics supplies the most favorable conditions for the exercise of patriotism, with the counterargument that such states are also most vulnerable to political turbulence; an extensive empire maintains better order and security, but at the cost of authoritarian centralization. However, "the union of three kingdoms promises to combine for this country the advantages of both these forms of government without the evils to which either is exposed": the Pax Britannica will be preserved from despotic stagnation by "the rivalry of the different nations of whom the empire is composed" (379). To maintain this dynamic balance, each nation must cultivate the remembrance of a distinctive identity located in the past:

> It is quite right that the Scotch should glory with their aged sovereign in the name of Britain: and that, when considered with reference to foreign states, Britain should exhibit an united whole, intent only upon upholding and extending the glory of that empire which her united forces have formed. But it is equally indisputable that her ancient metropolis should not degenerate into a provincial town; and that an independent nation, once the rival of England, should remember, with pride, the peculiar glories by which her people have been distinguished. Without this, the whole good effects of the rivalry of the two nations will be entirely lost; and the genius of her different people, in place of emulating and improving each other, will be drawn into one centre, where all that is original and characteristic will be lost in the overwhelming influence of prejudice and fashion. . . . The city and the nation which have produced David Hume, and Adam Smith, and Robert Burns, and Henry Mackenzie, and Walter Scott, would cease to exist; and the traveller would repair to her classical scenes, as he now does to Venice or Ferrara, to lament the decay of human genius which follows the union of independent states. (379)

The national obsolescence of Scotland, its consignment to a "classical" antiquity, can be prevented by cultivating that past, by converting the foundation of national identity from politics to culture. The National Monument will "fix down, in a permanent manner, the genius of Scotland to its own shores" (380), replacing evanescent oral tradition as the modern medium of public virtue. To locate national distinction in the past, the ideal time of dead ancestors and lost origins, is to divert it from the contentious arena of contemporary politics. Thus national identity is split between a political and economic dimension (imperial Union) and a supplemental cultural one (national distinctiveness). Where once political competition generated the ancient republics (according to Ferguson), and economic competition has generated modern commercial society (according to Adam Smith), now culture is the medium of that national-subject-tempering activity of "emulation and rivalry."

The division of ideological labor magically recovers Edinburgh's status as a national metropolis—asserting it as a natural rather than historical endowment, fixed by canons of taste:

> [W]hile London must always eclipse this city in all that depends on wealth, power, or fashionable elegance, nature has given to it the means of establishing a superiority of a higher and more permanent kind. The matchless beauty of its situation, the superb cliffs by which it is surrounded, the magnificent

prospects of the bay, which it commands, have given to Edinburgh the means of becoming the most *beautiful* town that exists in the world. (385)

The modern topos of Edinburgh's beauty is born in the conversion of the old language of a strategic, military, and commercial eminence to the new language of an aesthetic eminence:

> And thus, while London is the Rome of the empire, to which the young, and the ambitious, and the gay, resort for the pursuit of pleasure, of fortune, or of ambition, Edinburgh might become another Athens, in which the arts and the sciences flourished, under the shade of her ancient fame, and established a dominion over the minds of men more permanent even than that which the Roman arms were able to effect. (385)

Alison recommends the Parthenon of Athens as the ideal model for the National Monument, on the paradoxical grounds of its being devoid of national associations: "this impression [of beauty] would be far greater, just because it arose from a style of building hitherto unknown in this country" (384). Lacking, in other words, the divisive political associations of national history, "the work of Phidias" can represent pure aesthetic form. (Although the Monument would remain unfinished, this Hellenic ideal was realized in Hamilton's Royal High School on the southern flank of Calton Hill.) The condition for an authentically national feeling turns out to be the suppression of actual specific, local, or traditional markers of national identity.

Edinburgh's status as cultural metropolis turns out to reside not in its fabric of civic institutions but in a natural ensemble of vistas, prospects, and panoramas, composed in the trained aesthetic sensibility of an observer. Edinburgh's beauty of setting had become a commonplace with the closing of the Continent in the French wars and the development of domestic tourist itineraries. The appreciation of the city as a panorama coincided with the formal invention of the device. In June 1787 an Edinburgh portrait painter named Robert Barker patented "an entire new contrivance or apparatus, called by him *La Nature à Coup d' Œil,* for the purpose of displaying Views of Nature at large." Barker's 360-degree paintings of the prospects from Calton Hill and the steeple of St. Giles's went on display in the city.[26] A dozen years later, Sir John Stoddart—friend of a not-yet-famous Walter Scott—began to apply the aesthetic canons of Edmund Burke and William Gilpin, hitherto trained on wild or rustic landscapes, to the view of Edinburgh:

> I shall not easily forget the singular impression, which I received, on first crossing the North Bridge, and beholding the strange contrast between the New and Old Town, the mixture, or rather confusion, of hill, and rock, and valley, with churches, and houses, and other works of art piled together, as

it were, in a chaotic mass. The effect, at the first view, is equally unfavourable to the poet, and to the painter, neither of whom can work to advantage on scattered parts, which have no uniting principle. Yet the very circumstance of its being so entirely out of all rule, gives an interest to the general view; and after a short observation, the different parts arrange themselves into numerous picturesque combinations.[27]

Stoddart's paragraph mimes the transition from a Neoclassical to a Romantic aesthetics, in which sublimity gains over beauty as the dominant principle of the picturesque.

In another two decades the conversion was complete. Even the truculent Mudie would grant his narrator sensations of "sublimity" and "witchery" in the view from Holyrood Palace (*Modern Athens*, 49–55). In *Peter's Letters to His Kinsfolk*, Lockhart gives an account of Edinburgh as the aesthetic site of an imperial nationalist ideology that encodes the Tory politics promoted in *Blackwood's Magazine*. The narrator admires the city's "sublimity of situation and scenery":

Edinburgh, even were its population as great as that of London, could never be merely a city. Here there must always be present the idea of the comparative littleness of all human works. Here the proudest of palaces must be content to catch the shadows of mountains; and the grandest of fortresses to appear like the dwellings of pigmies, perched on the very bulwarks of creation. Everywhere—all around—you have rocks frowning over rocks in imperial elevation, and descending, among the smoke and dust of a city, into dark depths such as nature alone can excavate. The builders of the old city, too, appear as if they had made nature the model of their architecture. Seen through the lowering mist which almost perpetually envelops them, the huge masses of these erections, so high, so rugged in their outlines, so heaped together, and conglomerated and wedged into each other, are not easy to be distinguished from the yet larger and bolder forms of cliff and ravine, among which their foundations have been pitched. There has been a certain gloomy indistinctness in the formation of these fantastic piles, which leaves the eye, that would scrutinize and penetrate them, unsatisfied and dim with gazing.[28]

Edinburgh's civic forms are at once miniaturized and magnified by the natural landscape in which they are embedded, filling a vertical, hierarchical, Gothic space of "imperial elevation" and "dark depths." The spectator is left disoriented, "unsatisfied," before a vision of power characterized by a blurring of the boundaries between art and nature. Aesthetic consolation—a pleasure recovered from abasement—resides, however, in the very "indistinctness" that yields the intimation of an organic principle of totality. The visitor climbs Calton Hill: "It seems as if you had not quitted the city, so easy is the ascent; and yet where did streets or city ever afford such a prospect! The view changes every moment as you proceed; yet what grandeur of unity in the general and ultimate impression!" (1:11). If Lockhart's Edinburgh sublime follows (and vulgarizes) a Kantian aesthetic scheme, the political analogy comes from Burke.[29] The city's prospects disclose (to the properly disciplined observer) the counterrevolutionary vision of a national constitution folded in the timeless order of nature. Meanwhile Lockhart avoids using the title "Modern Athens," presumably because of its republican associations.

A POST-ENLIGHTENMENT

Literary fame, still more than civic improvement, made plausible the idea of Edinburgh as Modern Athens, even in the twilight of a heroic age of Scottish philosophy. In Cockburn's summary, the appearance of the *Edinburgh Review* "elevated the public and the literary position of Edinburgh to an extent which no-one not living intelligently then can be made to comprehend"; its publisher "made Edinburgh a literary mart, famous with strangers, and the pride of its own citizens"; and Scott's romances "threw a literary splendour over his native city, which had now the glory of being at once the seat of the most popular poetry, and the most powerful criticism of the age."[30] Scotch novels and Scotch reviewers were the most brilliant constellations in a northern literary galaxy which included—besides the historical romance and critical quarterly—a professionalized intellectual class, the entrepreneurial publisher, the nationalist ballad epic, and the monthly magazine. If not all absolutely original, here these genres and institutions acquired their definitive forms and associations, and a prestige they would bear throughout the nineteenth century. Their potent ideological distillations, political economy and cultural nationalism, informed a British imperial hegemony long after the fading of the city's literary splendor. Edinburgh, the seat of the Tory political establishment known as the "Dundas despotism," thus occupies, in its character as capital city of modern literature, the threshold of what we are used to reading as a Victorian story of world empire.

The year 1802 saw the publication of the first number of the *Edinburgh Review*, founded by a quartet of ingenious Whig lawyers who had been blocked from preferment under the Pitt-Dundas regime, as well as a two-volume collection of traditional ballads, *Minstrelsy of the Scottish Border*, edited by their Tory colleague and coeval Walter Scott. The *Edinburgh Review* was financed by an ambitious bookseller, Archibald Constable, who also had a share in the *Minstrelsy* and would remain the principal publisher of Scott's works until his own and Scott's ruin in 1826. Constable's "vigorous intellect, and liberal ideas have not only rendered his native country the mart of her own literature, but established there a Court of Letters, which must command respect, even from those most inclined to dissent from many of its canons," Scott paid tribute, well after his own defection.[31] Commentators then and since have credited Constable with enacting the functional conversion of the eighteenth-century bookseller into the modern entrepreneurial publisher.[32] Whether or not they have exaggerated the change, Constable played a key role in the institutional transformation of Scottish literature after 1800, in which it devolved from the academic infrastructure of the Lowland Enlightenment to an industrializing marketplace. As Edinburgh became the nation's main publishing center besides London, the curricular genres of moral and natural philosophy gave way to the booksellers' genres that would dominate the nineteenth-century trade—periodicals and novels. The *Edinburgh Review*, first of the great critical quarterlies, established the authoritative forum of cultural commentary for the age. Its Tory rival the *Quarterly Review* (1809) was also in large part a Scottish project, founded by a renegade Edinburgh reviewer (Scott) in collusion with a second-generation emigrant Scots publisher (Murray), and planted in London for the sake of proximity to government.[33] In postwar Edinburgh the politically revanchist but culturally avant-garde *Blackwood's Edinburgh Magazine* (1817) revitalized the genre of the monthly miscellany for a more determinately middle-class readership. If the Romantic magazine became, as one scholar contends, "the preeminent literary form of the 1820s and 1830s in Britain," *Blackwood's* led the way, its innovations of style and format copied by political opponents (John Scott's *London Magazine*) as well as fellow travelers (William Maginn's *Fraser's Magazine*).[34] In 1832 the Reform legislation encouraged several new, liberal Edinburgh periodicals, the most consequential of which were a monthly, *Tait's Edinburgh Magazine*, a Radical riposte to *Blackwood's*, and *Chambers's Edinburgh Journal*, which successfully inaugurated the cheap-but-respectable weekly miscellany aimed at tradesman and artisan readers.

Meanwhile, in the aftermath of the Napoleonic wars, the Scottish novel on national and historical themes became one of the leading genres of European Romanticism. In 1819 one reviewer sums up the "important change" that has taken place "within these few years in the general taste and literature of Scotland": in a strange reversal of "the usual progress of the human mind," the "grave and metaphysical propensities of our countrymen" have succumbed to a "rage for works of fancy."[35] The novel, according to another commentator, has assumed the role of epic to represent "the different modes of national existence . . . in modern times."[36] Scott had held the wartime role of national minstrel for a half-dozen years, outselling all rivals (even Byron) in the genre of long verse-romance his success established. In 1814, with the anonymous publication of *Wa-*

verley, the "Wizard of the North" refashioned himself as "the Great Unknown," the dominant author of the age, who "sold more novels than all the other novelists of the time put together."[37] The Scottish Novels (to give them their contemporary title) fixed all the general trends in British Romantic fiction publishing recently summarized by Peter Garside: the displacement of poetry by the novel, the novel's heightened definition as a genre, the professionalization of production and marketing, the standardization of format for new works (three volumes, post-octavo, 31s. 6d. the set), and even a masculine takeover of what had been understood to be a feminine kind of writing.[38]

As well as boosting a general increase in British novel production in the decade after Waterloo, Scott's success fuelled the local takeoff in Edinburgh fiction publishing. Scotland had accounted for a mere 0.5 percent of all novels published in the British Isles in the first decade of the nineteenth century; this figure rose to 4.4 percent in the following decade and to 12 percent in the 1820s, reaching 15 percent, or 54 out of 359 titles, in the peak years 1822–25—a rate of growth far steeper than the national average.[39] William Blackwood arose as Constable's chief rival in novel as well as periodical publishing, attempting to take over Scott (with the first series of *Tales of My Landlord*, 1816) and going on to become the most prolific publisher of fiction in Edinburgh (bringing out twenty-seven titles between 1820 and 1826, versus Constable's twenty-one).[40] Blackwood's list established a distinctive profile of fiction on Scottish national and regional themes, some of which (e.g., tales by Hogg and Galt) first appeared in *Blackwood's Edinburgh Magazine*. Itself experimenting with fictional devices, the magazine wove formal as well as thematic and ideological ties with the novel that were more intimate than could be maintained by the austere quarterlies. Critics have identified a Blackwoodian school of Scottish fiction in competition with Scott's, characterized by comic and sentimental depictions of regional, especially rural or small-town settings and manners, and sensational "terror tales," which flourished in the years (from 1820) when Scott himself turned from the making of modern Scotland to more exotic horizons.[41] The chief fiction writers associated with Blackwood were Hogg, Galt, Lockhart, John Wilson, David Macbeth Moir, Thomas Hamilton, and Susan Edmonstone Ferrier (the only one not also a contributor to the magazine). Such was the house's prestige that even a writer so antipathetic to its politics as Christian Isobel Johnstone would publish her best novel there (*Elizabeth de Bruce*, 1827). In the early 1820s Hogg and Galt emerged as the most original authors of Scottish prose fiction besides Scott, masters of the distinctive genres developed in the Blackwood orbit, regional tale and fictitious autobiography (although Hogg published his novel-length works away from Blackwood).

The rise of an Edinburgh publishing industry and the reorientation of Scottish writing to periodicals and fiction justify the framing of a distinct period, a "post-Enlightenment," for the literary history of the early nineteenth century. Scholars have argued that the French Revolution and Waterloo supplied British Romanticism with historiographic paradigms of rupture and closure that framed a new kind of historical consciousness. That consciousness apprehended the historicity of the present, understood as itself part of a chronological order, a period.[42] Scots writers articulated their period consciousness by looking back at the preceding epoch, the half-century from the 1745 rising to the recent French wars covered in the first trilogy of "Waverley novels," in which the drastic if uneven modernization of Scottish life provided a material context for the Enlightenment conception of history as wholesale social change.[43] They characterized their "last purely Scotch age" in terms, usually nostalgic, of vanishing manners and customs, but were also keenly aware of the transformations in literary genres and modes of production. "[T]here were men of literature in Edinburgh before she was renowned for romances, reviews, and magazines," Scott reminded readers (not without irony) in an 1827 retrospect of the Enlightenment philosophers.[44]

The Edinburgh post-Enlightenment may conveniently be divided into three phases, of which the rise of Scottish prose fiction and *Blackwood's Magazine*—the topic of this book—occupies the middle, postwar decade (1814–25). The first stage (1802–13) is constituted by the wartime ascendancy of the *Edinburgh Review* and a vogue for national ballad collections and ballad-based metrical romances (from *Minstrelsy of the Scottish Border* to Hogg's *The Queen's Wake*). The third stage lasted from the 1826 crash through the death of Scott, the Reform Bill, and the bankruptcy of the Edinburgh Town Council in the early 1830s: a terminus marked by a flowering of liberal periodicals and a dearth in the quality and quantity of Scottish fiction. Besides ruining Scott and Constable, the crash damaged the wider networks of British publishing and depressed the market for new novels into the next decade.[45] When the industry recovered in the 1840s, literary production was decisively London based, including the management of the major Edinburgh periodicals, although the city's printing presses kept their national, even imperial preeminence due to the supply of well-educated cheap labor in Lowland Scotland. Two major works signalize the end of the Edinburgh post-Enlightenment. Lockhart's *Memoirs of the Life of Sir Walter Scott, Bart.* (1837–38) made up the epoch's literary monument. An antithetical limit, parodic and deconstructive, is drawn in Carlyle's antinovelistic magazine serial and pseudo-memoir *Sartor Resartus* (1833–34), which darkly figures its author's departure from Scotland as well as undoing the symbolic complex of national bildungsroman installed two decades earlier with *Waverley*.

In the shadow of a counterrevolutionary world war, literary production in Edinburgh was linked to the politics of the Whig and Tory party establishments. Pre-Reform Scotland, in Cockburn's vivid if tendentious account, was "not unlike a village at a great man's door": with "no popular representation, no emancipated burghs, no effective rival of the Established Church, no independent press, no free public meetings, and no . . . trial by jury," patronage was "really all the government that the country then admitted of."[46] Thirty-three electors (out of a population of 160,000) comprised the Edinburgh Town Council, controlled by a Westminster-appointed proconsular manager. An almost uninterrupted half century of Tory government after 1782 ensured the virtual dynastic rule of the Dundas family, who had well-nigh absolute disposal of Scottish jobs and appointments. Anti-Jacobin repression in the mid-1790s, more ruthlessly efficient in Scotland than in England, provoked a crisis of ideological legitimation in the institutions of civil society and effectively shut down the so-called Scottish Enlightenment. Scottish judges jailed and transported leaders of "Friends of the People" while chilling admonitions were issued to Girondist professors like John Millar and Dugald Stewart as well as to plebeian hotheads like Burns. Tightening its monopoly over patronage and institutions (including university appointments), the regime saturated public life with a counterrevolutionary surveillance and closed off all space of political debate: "*As a body to be deferred to*, no *public* existed."[47] Cockburn goes on to credit the *Edinburgh Review*, founded as an organ of polite, moderate, antirevolutionist but proreform liberalism in the brief respite from wartime regimentation opened by the Peace of Amiens, with inaugurating the fitful, contentious rebuilding of a Scottish public sphere in the long dusk of the Dundas despotism. "[It] was only through the press that [party] intolerance could be abated, or our policy reformed."[48]

Politics thus hastened, if it did not solely drive, the commercial devolution of the Scottish Republic of Letters. The transition took the form, at first, of a displacement of Enlightenment cultural formations into "the press" rather than their replacement with something new. The Edinburgh reviewers, Scott as well as Jeffrey, Brougham, and Horner, were trained at the premier academic institutions of late-Enlightenment Edinburgh—the High School, University, and Faculty of Advocates. The Scottish legal and educational systems, their national distinctiveness preserved by the articles of Union, had supplied Lowland Scotland with a strong foundation of civic institutions that supported a liberal, professional culture of intellectual work and literary production, independent (to a limited but effective degree) from both the state and market, although enmeshed in regional patronage networks. This civic infrastructure differentiated the Scottish republic of letters from its more thoroughly commercial English counterpart in the "Age of Johnson."[49] Dustin Griffin has insisted that, far from there occurring any "sudden change from a patronage economy to a literary marketplace" in eighteenth-century England, the period "is characterized by overlapping 'economies' of patronage and the market-place."[50] With patronage regulating political life in pre-Reform Scotland still more strongly than in England, the "overlapping economies" of liter-ary production are correspondingly densely entangled. Patronage frames the professional culture of polite letters in the Scottish Enlightenment and post-Enlightenment, differentiating it from the more thoroughly market-based professional culture that would emerge later in nineteenth-century Britain. Optimally, the Scottish republic of letters was constituted by a productive relation between the professions and the market. The adja-cency of the larger English trade, with new colonial markets looming be-yond, provided a dynamic opening for eighteenth-century Scottish literary production; but while such philosophical blockbusters as *The Wealth of Nations* or the histories of Hume and Robertson were produced for the British trade, they were incubated in the Scottish universities (and at acces-sory institutions such as the Speculative Society and Faculty of Advocates' Library). The Scottish men of letters, nearly all of them professors or placed ministers, provided intellectual capital for the "loose-knit printing and publishing syndicate[s]" of London-based Scots booksellers (Strahan, Millar, Cadell) and their Edinburgh associates.[51]

Prompt to exploit the crisis of legitimacy in the Scottish institutions of civil society after 1800, Constable translated these Enlightenment condi-tions of authorship into the genres of the market. He was able to reclaim the tradition of a professional rather than merely commercial class of men of letters by paying unprecedentedly high fees to his editors and contribu-tors: an investment that saved their status as gentlemen and, conversely, cast the publisher himself as an enlightened patron rather than a trades-man. Constable and the Edinburgh reviewers were thus able to reconfig-ure, in the early nineteenth-century press, a functional equivalent of the cultural authority of the Enlightenment philosophers.[52] Authorship be-came, following the cue of the *Edinburgh Review,* a professionalizing for-mation—closing the circuit between professional career and literary pro-duction established in eighteenth-century Scotland. "The lawyer of former days was esteemed irrevocably lost to his profession, if he meddled with literature," Scott wrote in 1819, looking back at his father's genera-tion: "But now the most successful professional men are both aspirants after, and dispensers of, literary fame; and there is spread throughout society at large a more general tinge of information and good conversa-tion than is to be met with elsewhere."[53] This professionalized literary culture, prototypical of later developments in Victorian Britain, thus con-stitutes itself upon a potent, uneven combination of "modern" and "tradi-

tional" elements—an industrializing, globalizing market involving vola-
tile new financial mechanisms of capitalization and credit as well as new
technologies and circuits of production and distribution, patronage networks entangled with tribal, collegial, and partisan loyalties, and the Enlightenment academy's mixed ethos of public spirit, meritocracy, and corporate privilege.

Scottish literary production after 1800 dialectically combines a reorientation from the academy to the market with an elevation of the commercial genres of periodical and fiction to civic, indeed national, dignity, as
these assume the professional ethos of Enlightenment together with its
philosophical themes. The *Edinburgh Review* opened a new public domain of literary and scientific culture, which it defined in professional,
judicial terms as a disciplinary court of judgment and evaluation rather
than a marketplace of information and opinion. Jeffrey and his fellow
advocates convened a critical equivalent of the Court of Session, a literary
reinvention of the old Scottish Parliament-House. The ideological project
of the *Edinburgh Review* was to provide a scientific basis for Reform by
yoking opposition policy to Scottish Enlightenment political economy.[54]
At first, this agenda was not especially divisive, since it appealed to an
intellectual heritage shared by Edinburgh Whigs and Tories alike. The
Edinburgh Review could claim to represent a civic and national interest
rather than a party-political one, as it seemed to revive the Moderate,
Old-Whig consensus of the Scottish Enlightenment that had been torn
apart in the anti-Jacobin reaction.[55] Scott, although a Tory, was a contributor alongside Jeffrey and his set, because they were all products of that
tradition; they had all, for instance, attended the lectures of Dugald Stewart, the Edinburgh professor of moral philosophy and most influential
interpreter of Enlightenment thought for the new generation.

But the neomoderate consensus proved too fragile to survive the resumption of war against France. In 1809 Scott broke with the *Edinburgh
Review* over its refusal to support British intervention against Napoleon
in Portugal and Spain, and instigated the progovernment *Quarterly*. Its
critics began to accuse the *Edinburgh Review* of a blatant politicization
of the literary field, in the teeth of any claims to liberal disinterestedness.
Christian Johnstone's characterization (in 1814) of a "little junta of accomplished men . . . giving law to the republic of letters" casts the *Edinburgh Review* as a mirror image of the Dundas Despotism it opposes. The
politicization of Edinburgh literary culture—immanent in the patronage
system—would erupt in the decade after Waterloo, when the ideological
resources mobilized in the cause of wartime patriotism recoiled upon a
domestic situation of economic recession, high grain prices, mass unemployment, and growing agitation for reform. In Edinburgh a series of
public occasions—university appointments, assemblies to petition parlia-

ment, antislavery meetings, banquets in honor of Burns and Fox—became battlefields between the entrenched Tory administration and the Whigs, as the star of Reform rose in the south.[56] The periodical press became the main arena of this conflict, constituting indeed (in Jon Klancher's account) a new kind of national public sphere—one splintered by competing claims and interests.[57] The *Edinburgh Review* was the official platform of opposition policy in the country, but however obnoxious, it was at least socially respectable, a rival gentlemen's establishment. It was soon apparent that the quarterlies were too ponderous to fight the kind of guerrilla war the postwar terrain required. The advent of a Whig weekly newspaper in Edinburgh, the *Scotsman* (January 1817), provoked the outbreak of *Blackwood's*, instantly scandalous for the ferocity of its attacks on Whigs and "Cockneys." In the years from the so-called "Radical war" of 1819–20 to George IV's visit, the literary feuding boiled over into verbal and physical violence, much of it inflamed by *Blackwood's* and the irregulars of the Tory press.

Blackwood's momentous achievement was the construction of a "Romantic ideology" to oppose the neo-Enlightenment liberalism of the *Edinburgh Review*, which it denounced for Jacobin tendencies of skepticism and materialism. *Blackwood's* equipped Tory politics with a counter-Enlightenment aesthetic ideology of cultural nationalism shaped by the magazine's innovative mixture of literary forms and discourses, among them fiction. Although the quarterlies had condescended to review novels, beginning with Maria Edgeworth and then Scott, they tended to maintain a neoclassical suspicion of fiction as such; *Blackwood's*, in contrast, not only published fiction in varying styles and formats but juxtaposed poems and tales with essays and reviews, rather than segregating them as had been the practice in earlier magazines, and introduced fictional devices into nonfictional articles. Hybrid works of serial fiction and cultural criticism, notably *Peter's Letters to His Kinsfolk* and the "Noctes Ambrosianae," gave especially potent expression to the *Blackwood's* marshalling of cultural nationalism against Whig political economy. Ideological contest took the form of an antagonism between literary genres and discourses that would frame the British debate about modernity well into the twentieth century.

This set of political, commercial, and generic antagonisms—Whig versus Tory, Blackwood versus Constable, review versus magazine, essay versus fiction, political economy versus national culture—had important consequences for the development of the Scottish novel. Ina Ferris shows how the Waverley novels set themselves above the ruck of common fiction by claiming a share in the "literary authority" of the quarterlies, and thus a measure of critical respectability, through Scott's synthesis of romance with Enlightenment historicism as well as the alignment of his authorial role with the *Edinburgh Review*'s professional ethos.[58] The keenest of the *Blackwood's* critics, Lockhart, attacked the professional culture of the *Edinburgh Review*, arguing that its commercial basis drove a fatal wedge between the reviewers' claims to judicial disinterest and their praxis of a partisan politics. Instead of extending the critique to Scott's poems and novels, Lockhart appropriated them for the rival camp on the basis of their successful occupation of an aesthetic high ground of national representation. In an argument Lockhart developed in *Peter's Letters to His Kinsfolk*, Scott's totalizing representation of Scottish historical life fitted him to become the figurehead of the new Tory cultural nationalism formulated in the pages of *Blackwood's*.

Lockhart was able to base this symbolic appropriation on a wider platform than Scott's role as literary viceroy of the Dundas despotism and patron of several *Blackwood's* authors, including his future son-in-law. Politics did not settle everything: Scott made a business decision to return to Constable when Blackwood mishandled *Tales of My Landlord* in 1817. The "overlapping economies" of patronage and the market are part of a larger historical complex. Tory in his politics but ideologically a product of the Whig Enlightenment, Scott stood between the literati of his own generation (Jeffrey and the Edinburgh reviewers) and the Young Turks at *Blackwood's*, strong enough to encompass both sides rather than fall between them. The Author of *Waverley* could personify the "moderate" Enlightenment ethos that the *Edinburgh Review* had revived and then forfeited with its parti pris, and plausibly (although far from uncontroversially) represent a national culture in all its historical variety and complexity. The Author of *Waverley* could play that role more plausibly, certainly, than Sir Walter Scott of Abbotsford, client of Dundas and Buccleuch patronage and backer of Tory periodicals from the high-toned *Quarterly* to the blackguardly *Beacon* and *Sentinel*. Crucial here was the status of the novel as the ascendant genre of national life.

In the early nineteenth century, according to Clifford Siskin, the novel triumphed over periodical genres to become the normative literary form of middle-class culture, since novels rhetorically unified a modern reading public, in their invocation of national life, whereas magazines and reviews politicized its social divisions.[59] Edinburgh was the decisive site for this development and the Waverley novels its decisive agent. It is a version, after all, of the story Scott's novels are supposed to tell—the (Humean) history of a modernizing nation formation out of the bitter clash of factions, out of "politics" and "ideology" as such. Just as crucial to the cultural work done by Scott's novels as their topical assumption of Enlightenment historicism, in this light, is their powerful, categorical investment in the rhetoric of fiction, abstracted and historicized under the title of "romance." Fiction is the discursive category that separates novels from history, from periodicals and other kinds of writing, in its designation of a strategic difference from reality—a distance or obliquity in the relation between narrative and world, a figurative disguise or darkening of the real—in contrast to the referential immediacy that charges the very premise of periodical publication.

More thoroughly than a book of poems, with its subscription list and dedication to a patron, a novel belongs to the market and the reading public convened there. And in contrast to a review's or magazine's explicit intervention and position taking in the historical here and now, a novel lays itself open to imaginative appropriation by different communities and interests and for divergent intentions. But the corollary of this is that, for the same reason, fiction tends to occupy a fugitive, unreliable, duplicitous, even resistant relation to any determinate identity or stance in the world. In other words, this designation of the novel's special quality— its fictionality—opens rather than closes the question of its relation to historical and political contexts. Lockhart's appropriation of Scott (in *Peter's Letters*) shifted from critical appreciation of the work of fiction to a cult of the author, around whom cultural authority could be reassembled in the fully counter-Enlightenment mode that Carlyle would later call "hero-worship." At the same time, this Tory Romantic apotheosis required the amputation of Scott's own roots in the culture of Enlightenment, which Lockhart identifies with the skeptical philosophy of David Hume. In Lockhart's account, Scott's is a charismatic authority that compels his readers' belief, just as Scott's novels supply a necromantic medium for historical truth and national spirit.

Nevertheless it was Hume who provided the philosophical justification for Scott's combination of history and romance. The Humean trajectory of enlightenment traces a skeptical dismantling of the metaphysical foundations of reality and their replacement with a sentimental investment in "common life," intermittently recognized as an imaginary construction of reality ratified by custom. Thus *Waverley* narrates not just the emergence of modern civil society through the final conquest of an ancient regime but a Humean dialectical progression from metaphysical illusion through melancholy disenchantment to a sentimental and ironical reattachment to common life. Reflexively insistent upon their fictional status, Scott's novels activate skepticism rather than faith as the subjective cast of their reader's relation to history, which includes, in the logic of metafictional reflection, the reader's own historical situation. Following Hume, Scott made fiction the performative technique of a liberal ideology—an ideology that stakes its modernity on the claim of having transcended primitive modes of belief (superstition and fanaticism) through a moral and cognitive abstraction from the submerged life of history, the blind rage of politics.

Scott's novels commanded a cultural centrality—a national representa-
tiveness—in post-Enlightenment Edinburgh that the reviews and magazines, because of their partisan alignment, could not claim. That centrality
overlays, but is not reducible to, their author's location at the center of the
Scottish network of Tory patronage and his quasi-monopolistic control of
an Edinburgh apparatus of literary production by the early 1820s. These
topological relations remained as stressed as the moral relations between
Sir Walter Scott, the Author of *Waverley*, and the secret partner in Ballantyne and Company. Accordingly, Lockhart's claim on Scott as author
breaks down the division of labor encoded in Scott's anonymity: between
the person, involved in webs of patronage and influence, and the novels,
convening a national reading public in the open forum of the market.
The identification of Scott's works with a Tory Romanticism required
a measure of symbolic violence that did not go uncontested. Although
Lockhart went on to secure (and modify) his account of Scott with his
great biography (the genre that canonically closes a circuit between life
and works), other voices challenged it—some, in a reciprocal symbolic
violence, collapsing the works into their author, flattening the Waverley
novels into a pageantry of Tory prejudice, and others, more ambitiously,
reopening the categorical difference between them.

The critique of Scott as national author appeared as early as Jeffrey's
review of *Marmion* (1808), which deplored the faulty patriotism of a
poem celebrating Scotland's worst military defeat as well as the poet's
Tory prejudices.[60] After 1818 the complaint informs a sharper scrutiny of
Scott's cultural authority as grey eminence of the Dundas despotism,
blamed for abetting the hooliganism of the Tory press. William Hazlitt's
commentary provides a locus classicus for the conjunction of admiration
of Scott's art with detestation of his politics. "His works (taken together)
are almost like a new edition of human nature. This is indeed to be an
author!"[61] Their author's magnanimity makes "the political bearing of
the *Scotch Novels* . . . a considerable recommendation to them": "The
candour of Sir Walter's historic pen levels our bristling prejudices . . . and
sees fair play between Roundheads and Cavaliers, between Protestant and
Papist. He is a writer reconciling all the diversities of human nature to
the reader" (231). Hazlitt goes on, however, to sever this myriad-minded
author from the Scott who intervenes in contemporary politics, a move
that requires a radical division of agency within the author function. Hazlitt picks up a slighting allusion to the "Peterloo massacre" in *Ivanhoe*,
in which Scott likens the crowd assembled to witness Rebecca's fate to a
modern "meeting of radical reformers" who are liable for whatever harm
may befall them:

> He is indeed so besotted as to the moral of his own story, that he has even
> the blindness to go out of his way to have a fling at *flints* and *dungs* (the

contemptible ingredients, as he would have us believe, of a modern rabble) at the very time when he is describing a mob of the twelfth century—a mob (one should think) after the writer's own heart, without one particle of modern philosophy or revolutionary politics in their composition, who were to a man, to a hair, just what priests, and kings, and nobles *let* them be, and who were collected to witness (a spectacle proper to the times) the burning of the lovely Rebecca at the stake for a sorceress, because she was a Jewess, beautiful and innocent, and the consequent victim of insane bigotry and unbridled profligacy. And it is at this moment (when the heart is kindled and bursting with indignation at the revolting abuses of self-constituted power) that Sir Walter *stops the presses* to have a sneer at the people, and to put a spoke (as he thinks) in the wheel of upstart innovation![62]

The great work of the Author of *Waverley* is interrupted by another figure, the censorious editor "Sir Walter," whose intrusion occurs subsequently to the time of composition: he "*stops the presses.*" Sir Walter's reactionary sneer, the emanation of a local, historically contingent subjectivity, breaks the sympathetic circuit between author and reader ("when the heart is kindled and bursting") that constitutes the authentic medium of "human nature" and "the *Spirit of the Age.*" At the end of his essay Hazlitt turns to that historically contingent domain to denounce the political corruption of "the finest, the most humane and accomplished writer of his age": "who took the wrong side, and defended it by unfair means," and "associated himself with and encouraged the lowest panders of a venal press."[63]

Scott's death, coinciding with Reform, inspired a reprise of Hazlitt's critical strategy, the separation of Scott's politics from his art, by Radical feminist critics. Christian Johnstone (in *The Schoolmaster*) and Harriet Martineau (in *Tait's*) sought to reclaim Scott's achievement for a liberal and progressive spirit of the age. The Waverley novels are the property of all mankind, not just of a party interest. Now that the Tory regime is falling into the past, they can belong, at last, to the nation's future.[64] Scott's opponents shared a commitment to the novel as a representation of national life that should exceed local, social, and political differences to enfold a greater reading public. They reaffirm the genre that Scott set in place, even while they might criticize him for inadequately realizing it.

SCOTCH NOVEL WRITING

The general name of these works, "the Scotch novels," will always indicate an era in our literary history, for they add a new species to the catalogue of our native literary productions, and nothing of the same nature has ever been produced any where else. . . . [T]he Scotch novels, as they are the first of their class, so they are inimitable—perfectly, hopelessly inimitable for the time to come. . . . [W]e pronounce that the Scotch novels must remain alone, forming their own class, which is a new one in literature, and which they may be considered to have both commenced and finished. We should much sooner expect another author equal to the Paradise Lost, than another equal to Guy Mannering and Rob Roy.[65]

In the early 1820s, in William St. Clair's only slightly hyperbolic summary, "Scott and his partners achieved an ownership of the whole literary production and distribution process from author to reader, controlling or influencing the initial choice of subjects, the writing of the texts, the editing, the publishing, and the printing of the books, the reviewing in the local literary press, [and] the adaptations for the theatre."[66] This "vertical and horizontal concentration of media ownership" was accompanied by a bewildering dispersal of the Author of *Waverley* across the literary field, refracted through the figure's formal anonymity. The uncannily prolific Great Unknown, dashing off novel after novel alongside his other, professional and public and domestic careers, already constituted himself as Scott's Shadow. "A shadow—and an impersonal author is nothing better—can cast no shade," declares "the Eidolon, or Representation, of the Author of Waverley" in the preface to *The Fortunes of Nigel* (1821).[67] But shades of Scott's shadow were everywhere. In the preface to *The Monastery* (1820) the Eidolon had ruefully observed the renegade career of one of them, Jedediah Cleishbotham, who "misbehaved himself so far as to desert his original patron, and set up for himself," in an inauthentic "New Series" of *Tales of My Landlord*. Challenged in the press by John Ballantyne, the publisher called the Scott consortium's bluff: "The Fourth Series, collected and arranged by Jedediah Cleishbotham, is no more spurious than the First, the Second, or the Third."[68]

Scott's saturation of the literary field, in the view of some contemporaries, was symptomatic of a degradation of originality—the literary value that the Author of *Waverley* was supposed to typify—by the pressure of commerce or politics. Sarah Green's burlesque *Scotch Novel Reading* (1824) mocks the dissolution of the author function into a generic, quasi-mechanized Scotch Novel industry. Writing under the anti-Blackwoodian pseudonym "A Cockney," Green complains of a Scottish invasion of English literature: "We have been now, for some years, inundated with showers of Scotch novels, thicker than the snow you see falling." The blame for the blizzard lies less with Scott himself (grudgingly acknowledged to be a superior author) than with a proliferation of cheap knockoffs: Green's heroine "never reads any novels than *Walter Scott's*; though no-one, but herself, seems really to know who the deuce it is that scribbles away so fast."[69] That proliferation cancels the original distinction of an achievement so facilely mass-reproduced, so that Scott himself sinks to being one of his own imitators, and conversely any display of originality by a Scotch novelist, such as James Hogg, may stamp him as just another of Scott's brand names.[70]

Francis Jeffrey's 1823 *Edinburgh Review* article "Secondary Scottish Novels" implies that politics is the force that thwarts originality and condemns the new generation of Tory literati to mechanical reproduction of their master. Jeffrey discusses titles by Galt, Lockhart, and Wilson, mainstays of Blackwood's list in the early 1820s; in addition, Wilson and Lockhart performed editorial roles at *Blackwood's Magazine*, and Galt was rumored to.[71] He ignores other authors who are Scott protégés, even those with strong claims to consideration such as Ferrier (who did not publish in the magazine) and Hogg (no longer a Blackwood author). These Blackwood products are mere copies of a "great prototype."[72] "In intimating that we regard them as imitations of the inimitable novels, — which *we*, who never presume to peep under masks, still hold to be by an author unknown, —we have already exhausted more than half their general character." By respecting the decorum of anonymity, Jeffrey keeps intact Scott's status as original author—in order to draw the contrast with his followers, lapsed under the laws of the market. "In the arduous task of imitating the great novellist [*sic*], they have apparently found it necessary to resort to the great principle of division of labour; and yet they have not come near to equal the work of his single hand": Galt develops Scott's comic vein, while Wilson and Lockhart exaggerate his pathos (160).

Politics also moved John Scott, editor of the *London Magazine*, to condemn the "bad precedent" set by the *"mystery as to the authorship"* of what were evidently works by Sir Walter Scott. "The example given by the author of the Scotch Novels in this respect, is leading to a fashion of hoaxing and masquerade, in regard to authorship, which must degrade, and is degrading, the character of our literature": the worst offenders being "the Veiled Conductor of Blackwood's Edinburgh Magazine" and his avatars—"Z.," "Wastle," and "Peter Morris"—disguises worn by Wilson and Lockhart.[73] This virulent pullulation of shadows corrupts the originality, "co-extensive . . . with nature itself," that the editor of the *London Magazine* had only a few months earlier granted to his namesake, in a panegyric on the singular and unrepeatable genius of the Author of *Waverley*: "The general name of these works, 'the Scotch novels,' will always indicate an era in our literary history, for they add a new species to the catalogue of our native literary productions, and nothing of the same nature has ever been produced any where else. . . . [W]e pronounce that the Scotch novels must remain alone, forming their own class, which is a new one in literature, and which they may be considered to have both commenced and finished."[74]

Indeed few novels were published in Scotland before that "era in our literary history" opened by *Waverley* in the late summer of 1814.[75] Garside and Schöwerling list barely a dozen titles from 1800 through 1813, the most notable of which are Elizabeth Hamilton's *The Cottagers of Glenburnie* (1808) and Mary Brunton's *Self-Control* (1811; Brunton's *Discipline* appeared five months after *Waverley*). Reviewers assigned Brunton's and Hamilton's works to a tradition of female-authored domestic fiction reaching from Frances Burney through Maria Edgeworth, who gave the tradition its "national" (Irish) development, and Hannah More, who supplied an evangelical didacticism.[76] Scott himself differentiated this tradition from his own, and hailed Susan Ferrier (daughter of a fellow Clerk of Session) as its local adept, the Scots equivalent of Edgeworth in Ireland and Jane Austen in England. Ferrier admired Hamilton and Brunton (as well as More, Edgeworth, and Austen), and began her first novel, *Marriage*, under their aegis in 1810.[77] Despite the anterior presence of the tradition, Ferrier remained its only notable practitioner in Scotland after 1814. Brunton died in childbed in 1818, leaving the didactic fragment *Emmeline*. The only other Scottish Romantic woman novelist to enjoy significant success, Christian Johnstone, kept her distance from domestic fiction, mocking it by literalizing it, in a quasi-fictional guide to domestic economy (*The Cook and Housewife's Manual*, 1826), or combining the depiction of Scottish manners (in *Clan-Albin*, 1815, and *Elizabeth de Bruce*, 1827) with the more dissident Irish mutations of the national tale practiced by Sydney Owenson and Charles Maturin—to the extent that Johnstone might be claimed as an Irish novelist, much as Edgeworth might be claimed as a Scottish one.

Marriage was one of two titles with which Blackwood launched the movement of "secondary Scottish novels" in 1818, the other being a set of tales by Hogg, *The Brownie of Bodsbeck*. Although Hogg claimed (plausibly) he had written it earlier, *The Brownie* appeared as a popular riposte to Scott's treatment of the Covenanters in *Old Mortality*, the main work in the first series of *Tales of My Landlord*. This was the title with which Blackwood first challenged Constable in the field of Scottish fiction publishing at the end of 1816, after moving his premises from the Old Town to fashionable Princes Street. When he lost Scott back to Constable a year later Blackwood began his aggressive, no doubt compensatory investment in other authors (and in his magazine). *Tales of My Landlord* opened a path for the characteristically "Blackwoodian" fiction that followed. Compared with the studiously approximate settings of his first three novels, Scott emphasizes a more decisively regionalist representation of national life in the medium of a set of "tales." "To his loving countrymen," goes the dedication, "whether they are denominated Men of the South, Gentlemen of the North, People of the West, or Folk of Fife, these Tales, illustrative of ancient Scottish manners, and of the Traditions of their Respective Districts, are respectfully inscribed."[78] The most gifted of the Blackwood authors would develop this emphasis, making regional identity (the traditions of their respective districts) the foundation for their own claims upon originality. Hogg's tales—*The Brownie of Bods-beck* and its successors, *Winter Evening Tales* (1820), *The Shepherd's Calendar* (1829), *Altrive Tales* (1832)—root their narrative matter and manner in the popular traditions of the Scottish Borders, centering on Ettrick but ranging from Berwick to Dumfries. Galt conceived of his characteristic fiction as a series of "Tales of the West," emanating from and representing Glasgow and Ayrshire as a world socially and culturally distinct from Edinburgh.[79] Hogg and Galt gave the tale its most striking formal development, the first-person fictional memoir grounded in local patterns of experience and discourse (developed, in Galt's case, from Edgeworth's *Castle Rackrent*). Galt had his imitators in the vein, such as David Moir (*Mansie Wauch, Tailor at Dalkeith*, 1824), Andrew Picken (*Tales and Sketches of the West of Scotland*, 1824), and Thomas Hamilton (*The Youth and Manhood of Cyril Thornton*, 1827). The novels and tales of Lockhart and Wilson, who also emerged, like Galt, from the West (but via Oxford), forgo regional specificity for typical rather than particularized provincial settings, drawing upon the moral-evangelical tradition.

Blackwood's Edinburgh Magazine became the leading British forum for publishing nonnovelistic kinds of prose fiction in the 1820s, establishing the modern short story as a genre and developing a range of experimental styles and formats, including serialization (Galt's *The Ayrshire Legatees* and *The Steam-Boat*, 1820–21; Moir's *Mansie Wauch*). As well as mixing fictional with nonfictional articles, the magazine infiltrated its essays and reviews with fictional devices such as disguised or fictitious contributors and narrative and dramatic frames. Ethnographic sketch and satirical mock-autobiography graduate insensibly into outright works of invention, with historical and imaginary characters jostling each other on the page. The most elaborate of these Blackwoodian para- or pseudofictions included Lockhart's novelized anatomy of the Scottish cultural scene, *Peter's Letters to His Kinsfolk* (1819), and the symposium series "Noctes Ambrosianae" by Wilson, Lockhart, Maginn, and others (1822–35).

Mere copies, spin-offs and outright rip-offs of the Waverley novels tended to issue elsewhere: the spurious series of "Tales of My Landlord" (1820, 1821) and "Tales of My Landlady" (1818) in London, or *Walladmor* (1825), a German fabrication posing as a translation from Scott retranslated or rather refabricated into English by Thomas De Quincey.[80]

Scott imitation at its most mechanical can be found in the novels of Sir Thomas Dick Lauder, brought out by Scott's publisher Constable: *Lochandhu: A Tale of the Eighteenth Century* (1824), *The Wolfe of Badenoch: A Historical Romance of the Fourteenth Century* (1827).[81] In a "Preliminary notice" to the latter, Lauder addresses critics who have accused him of "being an imitator of the Great Unknown." The apology confirms the charge: "In truth, his greatest anxiety has been to avoid intruding profanely into the sacred haunts of that Master Enchanter. But let it be remembered, that the mighty spirit of the Magician has already so filled the labyrinth of Romance, that it is not easy to venture within its precincts, without feeling his influence."[82] The figure of the magician or enchanter revives the antique, astrological sense of "influence," emanations from the stars, as though the Author of *Waverley*, unnameable, ineffable, occupies the station that the ascendant (Romantic) conception of literary influence has granted the illustrious dead. If modern English literature is haunted by Shakespeare and Milton, the labyrinth of Scottish romance is haunted (stranger still) by a living author.

Blackwood provided the base where an ambitious novelist might claim to be something better than an "imitator of the Great Unknown," if by no means outside the eldritch zone of his influence. In 1821 Galt wrote to his publisher:

> For although the Legatees is apparently my first Scottish work, the fact is that the Pastor [*Annals of the Parish*] was begun many years ago, and before Waverley appeared I wrote to Constable proposing to execute a Scottish story. It is also a curious coincidence, that long before the appearance of the Lay of the Last Minstrel, I, then very young, in sending some trifle to the Scotch magazine mentioned my design of executing a series of historical ballads & dramas from Scottish history—What a cursed fellow that Walter Scot has been, to drive me out of my old original line.[83]

Galt told the story of his proposal at greater length in his *Autobiography* (diplomatically muting the snarl against Scott). Cold-shouldered by Constable, he shoved the manuscript into a drawer, and rediscovered it several years later when setting his papers in order: the similarity with Scott's famous account of the hatching of *Waverley* (itself a redaction of the Gothic-antiquarian "found manuscript" topos) rather undermines the point being made.[84] Several other Scots authors besides Galt claimed to have written or conceived a work of fiction on national themes before or around the appearance of *Waverley*. Some of them had also taken their proposals to Constable. In May 1813, buoyed by the success of his romantic ballad sequence *The Queen's Wake*, Hogg offered Constable a collection of Scottish rural tales, most of them adapted from his magazine the *Spy* (1810–11); but Constable was not interested, and Hogg's fiction did not begin to appear in book form until several years later. Ferrier had begun writing *Marriage* as early as 1810, although it too would not be published until 1818. Lockhart wrote to Constable five months after *Waverley* announcing the completion of a novel, "The Romance of the Thistle": "I am sensible that much has been done of late years in the description of our national manners, but there are still, I apprehend, many important classes of Scotch society quite untouched."[85] In the summer of 1814 Mary Brunton was completing the third volume of *Discipline*, with its Highland idyll, when *Waverley* came out: "The worst of all is, that I have ventured unconsciously over Waverley's own ground, by conveying my heroine to the Highlands!"[86] In her preface to *Clan-Albin* (1815) Christian Johnstone claimed that "the first half of this Tale was not only written but *printed* long before the animated historian of the race of Ivor had allured the romantic adventurer into a track, rich, original, and unexplored, and rendered a second journey all but hopeless."[87] And Mary Johnston's preface to *The Lairds of Glenfern; or, Highlanders of the Nineteenth Century* (published in London, 1816) anticipates charges that she has imitated "those exquisite delineations of Scottish scenery and manners which have lately appeared, under the titles of *Waverly* [*sic*], *Discipline*, &c." with an avowal that "the whole of the first, and great part of the second volume, have been written nearly four years."[88]

Christian Johnstone tempered her declaration of independence by dedicating the second edition of *Clan-Albin* to Scott, while Brunton expressed her admiration of *Waverley* and *Guy Mannering* in her correspondence. Galt's *Autobiography* conceals any private resentment at Scott's success beneath fulsome praise, including two eulogistic poems (which are so bad, however, as to arouse suspicion that the author's characteristic irony may be at work). Even authors who happened not to be protégés of Scott could not help but acknowledge his ascendancy. All concurred in viewing the publication of *Waverley* as (in John Scott's phrase) "an era in our literary history"—an event that opened up the field of Scottish fiction, but at the same time colonized it with a particular model of historical romance. Scott's presence and example were unavoidable, especially for those novelists who would assert their own originality. Not surprisingly, we find them reckoning with that presence—with Scott's cultural centrality, his social and literary influence—in their own works of fiction.

Several novels, for instance, feature characters who are engrossed in reading Scott. Old Mr. Ramsay in Ferrier's *The Inheritance* (1824) disdains the modern trash of novels—until one day, "in a paroxysm of ennui," he takes up *Guy Mannering* and finds himself addicted: "In short, Uncle Adam's whole being was completely absorbed in this (to him) new creation; while, at the same time, he blushed even in private at his own weakness in filling his head with such idle havers, and indeed could never have held it up again if he had been detected with a volume in his hand."[89] Scott's art is so potent as to enchant even the antiromantic (although Uncle Adam's susceptibility is index to his buried but potent sensibility). Galt's first canonical Scottish tale, *The Ayrshire Legatees*, contrasts the Rev. Charles Snodgrass's fashionable enthusiasm for the newly published *Ivanhoe* with the response of another naïve reader, the small-town minister Dr. Pringle, to what he conceives to be "a *History of the Rebellion*, anent the hand that an English gentleman of the name of Waverley had in it." The doctor's acceptance of the book as an authentic chronicle encourages one of his correspondents to speculate whether "Waverley's *History of the Rebellion*" might not be "another doze o' the radical poison in a new guise."[90]

Robert Mudie's *Glenfergus* (1820) introduces the fair Amelia "accompanying the gifted Gilfillan in his march to Stirling," while her sister Flora ("all romantic affectation, and fine sentiment") strums her harp.[91] The scene combines the reading of *Waverley* with a second type of representation, the inclusion of characters derived from Scott's novels. Baillie Nicol Jarvie's widow makes a pompous appearance in Galt's masterpiece *The Entail* (1823); readers had last encountered her as the servant girl Mattie, whose marriage to Jarvie was foretold at the end of *Rob Roy* (1818). Since reviewers of *Rob Roy* were giving Scott credit for putting Glasgow on the literary map, Galt's appropriation of one of his characters issues a rebuke to that claim, sharpening the Glasgow-Edinburgh rivalry articulated elsewhere in *The Entail*.[92] The hero of an earlier novel, *Sir Andrew Wylie* (1822), shares his name with an offstage character in *Rob Roy*, while the title of a chapter in Galt's *Blackwood's* serial (and *Ayrshire Legatees* sequel) *The Steam-Boat*, "A Jeanie Deans in Love" (August 1821), acknowledges the provision of a type rather than the actual character. A servant girl goes to London to petition the Duke of York to grant a commission to her lover, a ne'er-do-well who rejects her anyway, so she marries another suitor: Galt's conclusion supplants romance with irony.[93] Galt startles the reader of *Rothelan* (1824) with the insertion of a chapter called "Redgauntlet"—containing a variant of one of the interpolated tales in Scott's eponymous novel. Johnstone's *Cook and Housewife's Manual* (1826) begins as though it is a Waverley novel, a sequel to *Saint Ronan's Well* (1824), before settling into the business of recipes and instructions. Alongside Scott's nabob Peregrine Touchwood and landlady Meg Dods, Johnstone brings in the English epicure Dr. Redgill from Ferrier's *Marriage*. The blending of characters from different sources, as well as of different genres, echoes the satirical dialogue series "Noctes Ambrosianae" (then at the height of its popularity in *Blackwood's Magazine*), in which more- and less-fictionalized versions of "real" persons of the day (Lord Byron, the English Opium-Eater, the Ettrick Shepherd,

Christopher North) rub shoulders with characters out of novels—including Galt's Sir Andrew Wylie and Leddy Grippy from *The Entail*, one of very few female voices to speak in the series. Galt himself, in the late fictional memoir *Bogle Corbet* (1831), has his protagonist encounter "the afterwards justly renowned Cyril Thornton" on the road from Glasgow to London. This is not a Scott character, for once, but the eponymous hero of Thomas Hamilton's 1827 novel, which had paid tribute to Galt's inventions in its pages. Galt extends the roman-fleuve technique of his own "Tales of the West" to encompass a Glasgow school of fiction in competition with Scott's.[94]

Meanwhile Hogg devised *The Three Perils of Man* (1822) as a special-effects-packed "prequel" to *The Lay of the Last Minstrel* (1805). Hogg's Border romance narrates the demonic apotheosis of the mighty wizard (and Scott ancestor) Michael Scott, who haunts Scott's poem; still more presumptuously, it called its hero "Sir Walter Scott" until Scott made Hogg change the name in proofs.[95] This contentious instance opens onto yet another type of Scott allusion—episodes in which Scott is introduced into the fiction in propria persona (although usually kept offstage). Early in Hogg's next novel *The Three Perils of Woman* (1823) the Border farmer Daniel Bell describes Scott sitting at his post in the Court of Session and recalls his childhood exploits on his grandfather's farm at Sandyknowe; Scott was not amused. The "Editor's Narrative" that closes the anonymous *Private Memoirs and Confessions of a Justified Sinner* (1824) alludes to Scott, without however naming him, and brings onto the page instead his son-in-law, "L——t," together with a truculent shepherd called "Hogg." Again, the episode extends the literary game-playing of *Blackwood's* serials such as the "Noctes Ambrosianae" or Galt's *Steam-Boat*. Thomas Duffle, the narrator of *The Steam-Boat*, catches sight of "an elderly man, about fifty, with a fair gray head, and something of the appearance of a gausey good-humoured country laird" while attending the coronation of George IV in London. Mrs. Pringle (of *The Ayrshire Legatees*) identifies him as the "Author of Waverley," whose "most comical novel" was mistaken by her husband for "a true history book"; he converses affably with Galt's characters, although little relishing Duffle's tirade against the "old tyrannical House of Stuart." Later Duffle meets another literary lion, "the great Odontist," "whose genius and talents . . . make such a figure in Blackwood's Magazine."[96] This too was an actual person, an ordinary Glasgow dentist named James Scott, whom the *Blackwood's* wits had turned into modern culture's first instance of media-manufactured virtual celebrity. The "Small Known" ended up embracing the role *Blackwood's* had invented for him, claiming the magazine's songs and squibs as his own. In *Elizabeth de Bruce* (1827) Christian Johnstone sends the pious minister Gideon Haliburton, incensed by a slur on the reputation of Presbyterian heroine Jenny Geddes, to denounce the editor of the newly published *Minstrelsy of the Scottish Border*. Scott and his companions (by now embedded in an earlier historical moment) charm Gideon out of his wrath with the assistance of draughts of champagne—innocents are as susceptible to social cheer as they are to romance.

These representations of and allusions to Scott, some of which will be revisited in the following chapters, articulate a complex mixture of responses: emulation, homage, critique, mockery, defiance, rejection. The authors who (as these examples suggest) were most intensely engaged with working through Scott's influence were also the most original, Hogg and Galt. Their high-profile interventions in the so-called *Old Mortality* controversy, inflamed by criticisms of Scott's depiction of the Covenanters by evangelical reviewers and Scott's defense of his art in the *Quarterly Review*, have drawn the attention of modern critics. *Old Mortality* applies the *Waverley* plot of a "moderate" hero embroiled in rebellion and threatened by extremists on both sides to the religious civil wars of the late seventeenth century. The evangelicals denounced Scott's Moderatism as a partisan rather than neutral stance, and deplored the corruption of history by fiction.[97] Hogg and Galt published Covenanter historical novels contesting Scott's. Both take pains to undo Scott's conflation of Presbyterian enthusiasm with an archetypal revolutionary fanaticism, as well as to counter Scott's formal aesthetic of historical and fictional distantiation with their very different narrative investments in memory and "reenactment."[98] Hogg stresses the natural piety of the regional community in *The Brownie of Bodsbeck*, while Galt draws a distinction between the popular zeal of the Scottish Reformation and its terrorist remnant, warped by government persecution. Galt explicitly designated *Ringan Gilhaize* as a riposte to Scott, rebuking the "levity" of his treatment of "the defenders of the Presbyterian Church," although the novel appeared a half-dozen years after *Old Mortality* and on the heels of Galt's own series of "local theoretical histories" of the eighteenth-century West. (One of the inset tales in *The Steam-Boat*, "The Covenanter," has a trial run at the refutation of *Old Mortality* in 1821.) Douglas Mack has argued that Hogg's *Confessions of a Justified Sinner* responds, in turn, to Galt's representation of the "fanaticism of former days" in *Ringan Gilhaize*. Galt's challenge may also have stimulated Scott's return to the canonical form of the "Scotch novel" in 1824, *Redgauntlet*: a work contemporaneous with Hogg's masterpiece, and uncannily doubling its formal as well as thematic features (which include uncanny doubling).[99]

The web of responses and exchanges, provocations and revisions, extends, in other words, beyond the conspicuous topic of Claverhouse and the Covenanters. The major novels in the first two series of *Tales of My Landlord* stand out, even more than *Waverley*, *Rob Roy*, or *Ivanhoe*, as the works that challenged Scott's rivals. Their ripostes clarify the division of Scott's sequence of Scottish historical novels according to major political themes, the armed resistance movements of revolutionary Presbyterianism and counterrevolutionary Jacobitism, which (Paul Hamilton argues) Scott had begun by casting (in *Waverley*) as equivalent fanaticisms.[100] The great novels in which Scott narrates the political and cultural legacies of the Covenant in Lowland Scotland, *Old Mortality* and *The Heart of Mid-Lothian*, provide touchstones for the Blackwoodian development of the "secondary Scottish novel." *Old Mortality* represents history at zero degree, in the civil crisis that Carl Schmitt and Giorgio Agamben call "the state of exception." *The Heart of Mid-Lothian* revisits the failure of Presbyterian revolution a generation later. As the novel shifts focus from the veteran Covenanter, the rigidly righteous patriarch David Deans, to his two daughters, it displaces the public plot of civil insurrection onto a domestic crisis of maternity and sisterhood. That crisis gains allegorical density as it reveals the scandalous place of the female body in the modern symbolic order of the nation. Jeanie Deans's pilgrimage redeems popular Presbyterianism by domesticating and feminizing it—relocating it from a political to a moral arena. At the same time, the novel explores the instability of those distinctions and the legal and symbolic structures founded on them.[101]

The evidence of Galt's fiction shows *The Heart of Mid-Lothian* to have been the Scott novel he recognized as posing an especially formidable challenge. *The Provost* (1821) recombines key themes and episodes—popular riot, fornication and infanticide, women's silence—from *The Heart of Mid-Lothian*, while his most ambitious work, *The Entail*, takes on Scott's novel wholesale, with its family chronicle focused on a legal crux that encodes a national-scale social and moral crisis. Hogg's experiments in book-length prose fiction in the early 1820s unfold a serial quarrel with Scott, culminating in that alarming parody of post-Enlightenment historical romance *The Private Memoirs and Confessions of a Justified Sinner*. These works contest not just the subject matter but the terms of each other's achievement. The formal technique of *Ringan Gilhaize*, a triple-generation amplification of the first-person voice of fictional memoir, carries Galt's political theme, the popular experience of modernization as a "long revolution," and so challenges the narratology as well as historiography of Scott's skeptical Moderatism. And both Scott's and Hogg's recourse to fragmented, heterogeneous narratives as well as to the theme of "fanaticism" in their masterworks of 1824 answer, in turn, Galt's challenge, in very different ways—with Hogg's juxtaposition of fictional memoir and editorial framework also taking aim at Scott.

Clearly a zero-sum accounting of these rivalries—the conception of one achievement as trumping or cancelling another—cannot do justice to the creative wealth of Scottish novel production in Edinburgh in the fifteen years after Waterloo, especially during its height in the early 1820s. Hogg and Galt wrote their best work in response to Scott's, turning from their characteristic experiments in nonnovelistic prose fiction ("tales") to address the three-volume national historical romance that *Waverley* and its successors had made canonical. And Scott's work, far from hardening into the official monolith implied by the title "the Waverley Novels," itself kept mutating, deftly responsive to developments in Scottish fiction (as well as in English, Irish, and Continental European literature). To read these novels together is to understand intertextuality not as an arbitrary or abstract collocation of texts but as a force field of local conditions of production and reception—a charged proximity of works, authors, publishers, and reviewers in a relatively confined political economy. If the critical category of influence has lost some of its currency since Harold Bloom's work in the 1970s, the loss should not obscure the insights Bloom brought to the work of writing, such as his insistence on influence as a dialectically productive dynamic and on originality as a site of contest. The Bloomian concentration on psychodrama can be productively enlarged (unlikely as the conjunction might seem) through Pierre Bourdieu's sociology of the "literary field":

> [The literary field] is a force-field acting on all those who enter it, and acting in a differential manner according to the position they occupy there . . . and at the same time it is a field of competitive struggles which tend to conserve or transform this force-field. And the position-takings . . . are not the result of some kind of objective collusion, but rather the product and the stake of a permanent conflict.[102]

Scott's Shadow treats influence, the subjective field of "position taking," as the historically dense, overdetermined medium in which literary value becomes legible. Its dynamics are psychological but also social, political (informed by Scott's roles as patron and grandee), and commercial (the imperative to be similar but different with which novels, like other commodities, compete for market share).

The coordinates of influence and position taking trace the contours of "a gendered literary landscape." As Adriana Craciun insists, "patronage and membership in a literary circle were central to literary publication in Romantic-period Edinburgh," and these institutions were overwhelmingly controlled by men.[103] The masculine cast of 1820s Edinburgh literary life, with its high-energy competitive intimacy, becomes explicit in the "Noctes Ambrosianae." The convivial dialogues rehearse an extended metacommentary on the Edinburgh literary scene, which they represent in the guise of a private party at a tavern—a sentimental apotheosis of the clubs and societies that incubated masculine literacy of all classes,

from weavers and field workers to lawyers and professors, in Enlightenment Scotland.[104] The "Noctes" offers the symposium of Tory good fel-
lows as a fantastic allegorical masquerade of the commercial and patronage structures of the Scottish culture industry. Conversation unfolds
through a succession of whisky-fuelled, testosterone-charged feats of
boasting, brawling, and singing of songs: a festive counterblast to the
Whig junta of the *Edinburgh Review*. The rarity of female voices at the
feast glosses the phenomenon mentioned earlier, the relative weakness of
the feminine tradition of domestic fiction in Scotland. Ferrier was practi-
cally its sole representative after Scott's advent and Brunton's death, as
well as the only woman novelist published more than once by Blackwood.
Garside and Schöwerling show an even stronger correlation in Scotland
between the net rise in novel production and the proportional decline in
female authorship that characterize British publishing as a whole in the
decade up to 1825.[105] Their findings confirm recent critical accounts of
the rhetorical accession of masculine "authority" over feminine "romance" in the early reception of Scott's novels, and those novels' internal
allegories of a male encroachment on aboriginal female powers.[106] In this
regard the boisterous and sentimental masculinism of the "Noctes Ambrosianae" follows the cue of the *Edinburgh Review*, which (it seems)
returned the eighteenth-century term "blue-stocking" to derogatory currency in the first quarter of the nineteenth century.[107]

Not just Scott's example, then, but the patronizing and professionalizing ethos that framed it, the larger cultural legacy of the Scottish Enlightenment, contributed to a relative exclusion of women authors from the
literary boom in Edinburgh. (Scotland was the source of the two most
influential female conduct books of the later eighteenth century, William
Fordyce's *Sermons for Young Women* and John Gregory's *A Father's Legacy to his Daughters*.)[108] Brunton and Ferrier, gifted as they were, anxiously avoided public visibility and any claim to professional status:

> I would rather, as you well know, glide through the world unknown, than
> have (I would not call it *enjoy*) fame, however brilliant. To be pointed at—
> to be noticed and commented upon—to be suspected of literary airs—to be
> shunned as literary women are, by the more unpretending of my own sex;
> and abhorred as literary women are, by the pretending of the other! —My
> dear, I would sooner exhibit as a rope dancer—I would a great deal rather
> take up my abode by that lone loch on the hill.[109]

Brunton wrote these sentences in a letter to Eliza Izett shortly before the
publication of *Self-Control*.[110] According to a family tradition Ferrier kept
the composition of *Marriage* a secret from her censorious father and read
the completed manuscript to him without telling him what it was, confess-
ing her authorship only after he told her how much he enjoyed it. The

anecdote, as Ferrier's biographer admits, "bears a suspicious likeness to the well-known story of Miss Burney."[111] Ferrier was paid a copyright fee of one thousand pounds for her second novel, *The Inheritance*, and the still-more-impressive sum of seventeen hundred pounds for *Destiny* (1831). Despite this, she refrained from representing herself as a professional author. Scott liked to praise Ferrier and her compatriot Joanna Baillie for having conversation and manners "without the least affectation of the bluestocking."[112] After *Destiny* Ferrier would write no more novels although she lived until 1854.

Christian Johnstone, the most versatile of the Scottish women writers, presents the contrasting case of a successful professional career. De Quincey—writing in Johnstone's own periodical *Tait's*—paid tribute: "Mrs Johnstone, of Edinburgh, has pursued the profession of literature—the noblest of professions, and the only one open to both sexes alike—with even more assiduity, and as a *daily* occupation; and, as I have every reason to believe, with as much benefit to her own happiness, as to the instruction and amusement of her readers: for the petty cares of authorship are agreeable, and its serious cares are ennobling."[113] Johnstone's forays into prose fiction were framed by her experience as a journalist, first at the *Inverness Courier* and later at a succession of Edinburgh Radical magazines. She was able to sustain this career by standing behind her husband, master printer John Johnstone, whose name appears on the title pages of the magazines she edited. When *Elizabeth de Bruce* did not meet with the success anticipated, Johnstone gave up writing Scottish novels—*Elizabeth de Bruce* registers the form's exhaustion—for the magazine genres of tale, essay, and review. She did her most influential work as chief author and de facto editor of *Tait's Edinburgh Magazine*, where she assumed the editorial privilege of patronage, publishing some of the late work of Hogg and Galt, and fostering younger writers such as Robert Nicoll, who dedicated his poems to her.[114]

Not that male novelists proved any more effective, or even as effective, when it came to managing a career. Despite the ideological prestige of professionalism in post-Enlightenment writing and publishing, the historical practice of a literary profession, in the shape of a career, was always precarious. The nexus between patronage and commerce that sustained authorship would often fail, undone by the surge and recoil of market forces. Scott concealed his authorship under his professional identities as Sheriff and Clerk of Session, and beneath his authorship concealed another identity, partner in Ballantyne & Co., chained to an unstable network of credit and deficit. The crash of his fortunes was triggered by a speculation in hops by Constable's London associate Robinson. Scott's subsequent struggle to write his way out of debt might have constituted an ethical redemption, but it also killed him, setting a cautionary example to authors for the rest of the century. Discouraged by cold publishers and carping reviews, Hogg retreated from novel-length fiction (and book-length poems) after 1824, and reverted to the magazine genres with which he had launched his career. Hogg never emerged from financial insecurity, and his failed investment in a farm at Mount Benger echoes the grander folly of Abbotsford. Galt led the most frankly entrepreneurial of all these careers: writing across a miscellany of fiction and nonfiction genres, striking a characteristic vein of Scottish tales in the early 1820s but then moving away from it, in alternation with nonliterary ventures, notably colony-building in Upper Canada. His experience of economic downturn included a spell in a debtors' prison. When Galt wrote his memoirs, he brought out two different versions—an *Autobiography* devoted to his business career and a separate *Literary Life*. With this avocational schism Galt formalizes the Scottish topos of the "divided self" that subsequent critics have read into the careers of his contemporaries: "Ettrick Hogg" and "Edinburgh Hogg," a Scott sentimentally split between Hanoverian-Enlightenment improvement and Tory-baronial nostalgia.[115] Lockhart and Wilson were able to keep up professional careers as men of letters, thanks to their editorial positions (like Johnstone's) at major periodicals; but they also gave up writing fiction, as the market for Scottish novels declined through the 1830s.

Chapter 2

❧

THE INVENTION OF NATIONAL CULTURE

The essence of all nationality, however, is a peculiar way of thinking, and conceiving, which may be applied to subjects not belonging to the history of one's own country.
    —J. G. Lockhart, *Peter's Letters to His Kinsfolk*

A SCOTTISH ROMANTICISM

The historicizing retrospect of the post-Enlightenment, defining the present through reflection on the recent past, informs not only the Scottish novels of national history and manners and the attention paid to antiquarian and biographical "remains" in the Edinburgh periodicals but also a distinctive genre of cultural memoir. Along with John Galt's remarkable fictional autobiographies (*Annals of the Parish, The Provost*), Henry Cockburn's *Memorials of His Time* and Robert Chambers's *Traditions of Edinburgh* are the outstanding examples of a combined discourse of "civic and personal memory" that registers (in Mark Phillips's description) a newly felt "historicization of everyday life."[1] "The change from ancient to modern manners, which is now completed, had begun some years before this, and was at this period in rapid and visible progress," wrote Cockburn of the age of Scott and the *Edinburgh Review*: "It was the rise of the new town that obliterated our old peculiarities with the greatest rapidity and effect."[2] The postwar wave of monumental building seemed to mark a period. The polite classes looked across the chasm of the North Loch, from the comfort and elegance but also "hollow silence of the new town,"[3] to the Old Town they had left behind. "The ancient part of EDINBURGH has, within the last fifty years, experienced a vicissitude scarcely credible to the present generation. What were, so late as the year 1775, the mansions of the higher ranks, are, in 1823, the habitations of people in the humblest degrees of life": Chambers opens *Traditions of Edinburgh* (1824) by noting the opening and closing dates of the era of modernization. He adds, sounding a characteristic note: "The contemplation of this change is at once melancholy and gratifying."[4]

No nostalgia for Auld Reekie softens the most ambitious of the contemporary dissertations on Edinburgh. John Gibson Lockhart's *Peter's Let-*

ters to His Kinsfolk (1819) trains an acerbic critical attention on the present, which it frames polemically as a "period," a post-Enlightenment. More precisely, Lockhart diagnoses the failure of the present to have fully emerged as a new era of Scottish cultural history, shedding the worn-out rags of eighteenth-century thought to assume the spirit of the age that will later be named "Romanticism." Neglected outside the field of Scottish literary studies, *Peter's Letters* offers the first programmatic account of the ideological formation of a romantic cultural nationalism in Great Britain.[5] It articulates the doctrinal emergence of a modern aesthetic conception of national culture, polemically defined against an Enlightenment discourse of skeptical reason, and realized through the symbolic techniques of romance revival.

Glasgow born and bred, a Snell Exhibitioner at Balliol, disappointed by the failure of a fellowship to follow his first-class degree, Lockhart came to Edinburgh in 1815 to study law.[6] Together with fellow briefless advocate and Scots Oxonian John Wilson, he fell in with the rising publisher William Blackwood, who set both young men to work at his new monthly magazine. In the summer of 1817, Blackwood bankrolled Lockhart's trip to Germany where he scouted the advance guard of the counter-Enlightenment recently popularized by Madame de Staël.[7] Lockhart followed in the footsteps of Coleridge, who had visited Germany in his radical youth but was at this moment harnessing German metaphysics to the cause of church and state in two *Lay Sermons* (1816–17). From Friedrich Schiller and, especially, Friedrich Schlegel, whose *Geschichte der alten und neuer Literatur* (1812) he translated on his return to Scotland, Lockhart derived the cultural theory with which he would scourge Edinburgh's literary establishment in the early numbers of *Blackwood's Edinburgh Magazine*. In May 1818 this enfant terrible—notorious for the savagery of his attacks on Whigs and "Cockneys"—was introduced to Scott, who had discreetly supported the new magazine while maintaining an official neutrality in the contest between Blackwood and his old publisher Constable. Impressed by Lockhart's account of the German literary scene, Scott drew him into his patronage network. In October, Lockhart and John Wilson visited Scott's country house at Abbotsford, where Lord Melville was among the company. Anxious that this gifted protégé should distance himself from the scandalous orbit of *Blackwood's*, Scott offered Lockhart the historical portion of the *Edinburgh Annual Register*, which he was too busy to continue himself. *Peter's Letters to His Kinsfolk* appeared the following year. Lockhart's first book, a testament to the maturity and respectability that ought to accompany the new association with Scott, performs an elaborate homage to his future father-in-law, beginning with its titular echo of Scott's quasi-fictional account of a tour to the field of Waterloo, *Paul's Letters to His Kinsfolk* (1816). As the ceremonial centerpiece of *Peter's Letters*, Lockhart recreates his visit to Abbotsford, casting Scott as the tutelary genius of an ancestral Scottish culture.

Peter's Letters to His Kinsfolk combines Schlegel's schema of national literary history and (behind that) Schiller's "aesthetic education" with the counterrevolutionary tropes of an organic constitutionalism devised by Edmund Burke. Lockhart applies this (Coleridgean) synthesis of German theory and Burkean politics to the topos of a Scottish, rather than English, national culture. In so doing, no doubt paradoxically, *Peter's Letters* founds the modern tradition of nationalist critiques of Scottish culture. Twentieth-century thinkers inveterately hostile to Lockhart's Tory Union- ism have tended nevertheless to repeat its main rhetorical strategy, which brings a Scottish tradition to light by exposing its deficiency in relation to a naturalized English standard.[8] Adopting and extending Schlegel's anti- Enlightenment polemic, Lockhart brands a modern school of "speculative philosophy" or "Scotch metaphysics," running from Hume to the *Edin- burgh Review*, as the inauthentic version of a national culture. Lockhart rejects popular Presbyterianism on the same grounds, as an alien, divisive cultural force. The new nationalist ideal of a mystic secular totality, com- bining past, present, and future generations, relies on a polemical repudia- tion of the Whig tradition that empirically constituted much of modern Scottish cultural history. As so often seems to be the case, the foundational speech act of national tradition is a sentence of banishment.

With this rejection of the modern past, the post-Enlightenment epoch of Scott's novels and *Blackwood's Magazine* comes into critical focus as the opening of a new cultural stage or period.[9] The *Blackwood's* essay "On the Revival of a Taste for our Ancient Literature" (published be- tween Lockhart's Schlegel translation and *Peter's Letters*) summarizes the preceding half-century of British antiquarian and poetic revival as evi- dence of a modern "revolution of sentiment," echoing Schlegel's account of "a mighty change" in European literature flowing out of Germany and Great Britain.[10] The critique of the Enlightenment supplies the dialectical fulcrum for a new—"Romantic"—ideological formation, as it adapts the radical cultural themes of an earlier generation (the elevation of sentiment over reason, the location of collective identity in an ancestral past) and applies them to the case of Scotland. (It also involves the misrecognition of those themes insofar as they are products of the Enlightenment culture under attack.) *Peter's Letters to His Kinsfolk* prescribes a nationalist cul- tural politics in which culture absorbs politics and an aesthetic investment in tradition constitutes national identity. Following Schiller, paving the way for Carlyle, Lockhart personifies national tradition in the authoritar- ian archetype of the "hero as man of letters," whom we engage in pious reverence rather than critical dialogue. The great man restores, in his own example, the organic relation between individual and society that constitutes national character. Lockhart represents his patron Scott as the incarnation of national tradition: a synthesis of antiquary and bard, impresario and necromancer. Scott appears to have authorized Lockhart's representation, which would turn out to be decisive in the later fortunes of his reputation.[11] In certain key respects, however, Lockhart's version of Scott is a misconstruction—severing him, for instance, from the Enlightenment philosophical matrix he shared with the Edinburgh reviewers. Scott's role emerges through a systematic clouding of the distinction between antiquarian discovery and scientific historicism, on the one hand, and invention, *poesis*, fiction making, on the other. Lockhart casts Scott, in short, as an up-to-date, technically sophisticated, successful version of James Macpherson. By their author's uncanny ability to channel the inner, spiritual truth of historical experience, inaccessible to mere (Whig) historicism, Scott's poems and novels realize the revivalist project botched in the "Poems of Ossian."

Scott's career straddled a major shift in Edinburgh literary politics from the Moderate Whig, neo-Enlightenment regime of the *Edinburgh Review* to the new Romantic Tory dispensation of *Blackwood's Magazine*. The transition carries a paradigmatic force in the pitting of political economy—the scientific project of the *Edinburgh Review*—against the Blackwoodian reaction formation, based in part on an ideological reduction of Scott and his works, of national culture. This contest of establishment ideologies, articulated by the Edinburgh periodicals, gives institutional definition to the discursive opposition between social science and "culture" that opens with the Lake poets' repudiation of Malthus and runs through the modern tradition of British cultural criticism, from J. S. Mill's essays on Bentham and Coleridge to Raymond Williams's *Culture and Society*.[12] In Scotland in 1819 that epochal shift appears as an effect of a political antagonism, the ideological reproduction of party strife across the institutions of literature. *Peter's Letters* participates in a larger debate in the Edinburgh periodicals about the social status and function of "literature" in relation to what were perceived, in the aftermath of the French Revolution, as the dangerously totalizing forces of politics and commerce in modern society. The debate traces the disintegration of the eighteenth-century idea of a "Republic of Letters," supposed to regulate civil society, and its replacement with the new figure of national culture, conceived of as a domain separate from—undetermined by, indeed transcending—politics and commerce. With the conceptual inadequacy of particular institutions to sustain it, however, this new domain is founded upon the equivocal figure of the Author of *Waverley*, a shadowy entity who stands at once inside and outside public life and the marketplace, whose power is simultaneously that of mechanical reproduction and demiurgic creation. Scott functions as an allegorical figure for industrial production, reimagined as magical invention in its character as symbolic production, at the opening of the nineteenth century.

FROM POLITICAL ECONOMY TO NATIONAL CULTURE

Perhaps the best known legacy of the Scottish Enlightenment theory of modernity remains the concept of a liberal domain of civil society separate from the state, above all an economic domain constituted by market exchange. Civil society was clearly, as Tom Nairn and others have suggested, a historical figure for the advancement of an eighteenth-century Scottish professional class that realized itself, thanks to the Union, in a social space removed from the state apparatus of court and parliament.[13] The institutions that sustained this elite—the Church of Scotland, the universities, and the law—bore a distinctively Scottish identity preserved by the articles of Union. Together they constituted the emergent public sphere, the field of civil society, that Jürgen Habermas distinguishes from the field of the state.[14] Not only were they the vessels of a national distinctiveness but already, in effect, they established an official order of "culture," a complex sign- and value-producing system regulating social life and constituting it as a meaningful totality. The prototypical discourses of culture had their formal origins in the innovative branches of Scottish academic philosophy, with its simultaneous tendency towards a disciplinary specialization of the curriculum and ambition to construct a unified "science of man," as well as in the antiquarianism that was increasingly the avocation of Scots intellectuals.[15] James Chandler has argued that the Scottish theorization of "uneven development," in the work of John Millar, Adam Smith, and William Robertson, opened up a discursive field of culture constituted by the intersection of history and ethnography.[16] In Enlightenment Scotland, the conceptual materials of culture were institutionally assembled but not yet ideologically mobilized, not yet theorized as "culture": largely because they occupied the relatively autonomous domain of civil society, separate from the state and governed by supposedly apolitical processes of economic and moral "improvement."

The French Revolution threw this model of modernity into crisis. Establishment intellectuals in Britain, Whigs as well as Tories, interpreted the Revolution as a catastrophic saturation of the whole of social life by politics. In Cockburn's words, "Everything, not this or that thing, but literally everything, was soaked in this one event."[17] The Revolution (and anti-Jacobin reaction) challenged intellectuals to reexamine the relations between politics and other forces of social change, the relations of those forces to their own practice, and the institutional status of the Republic of Letters in a modern commercial society. Upon this challenge the *Edin-*

burgh Review was founded. The first article of the first issue, Francis Jeffrey's review of Jean-Joseph Mounier's *On the Alleged Influence of the Philosophers on the French Revolution*, grasps the nettle of the political function and responsibility of literary intellectuals. Mounier's book gives Jeffrey the opportunity to respond to Tory accusations that "a new description of men, . . . the political Men of Letters"[18] created the moral climate for the outbreak of Revolution. Jeffrey defines the Revolution as an immensely complex event whose primary causes were economic and political rather than cultural or ideological. Nevertheless, the very fact that "events are always produced by the co-operation of complicated causes" ensures that literary utterances will bear political meaning in spite of the intentions of their authors.[19] The sheer structural complexity of modern society tends to subvert the autonomy of any formation within it, including the Republic of Letters; all parts exert influence, however obliquely, on one another. Accordingly, as Biancamaria Fontana has argued, the *Edinburgh Review* promotes the rational infusion of the public sphere with political ideas as a project of scientific management. Political economy (the discursive formation that came to be associated with the *Edinburgh Review*) represents a rationalizing realignment of politics with the socioeconomic forces of modernization, designed to forestall an irrational eruption—a revolutionary return of the repressed.[20]

At the same time, the *Edinburgh Review* expresses an uneasy awareness of its own contingent status within the conditions it diagnoses. The complexity of the modern social field threatens a disintegration of knowledge and agency, an uncoupling of intentions from consequences, a separation between ethics and politics, in what is an institutional predicament as well as—or before—it is an epistemological one. The philosophes may have "facilitated and promoted the revolution" even though "their designs were pure and honourable." "They failed by a fatality which they were not bound to foresee; and a concurrence of events, against which it was impossible for them to provide, turned that to mischief which was planned out by wisdom for good" (Jeffrey, "Mounier," 11). Upon what vantage point, what social base, can literature reclaim moral agency? Taking up the question in a review of Germaine de Staël's "On Literature, Considered in Its Relationship to Social Institutions" (1813), Jeffrey diagnoses the corruption of the republic of letters by its subjection to market forces (following the critique of modernization in Adam Ferguson's *History of Civil Society*). Commercial society has reduced literature and science to commodities, available to everyone without labor of invention or research in the proliferation of periodicals, encyclopedias, and cheap reprint editions in the wake of the 1774 *Donaldson v. Beckett* copyright ruling:

But nothing, we conceive, can be so destructive of all intellectual enterprize, and all force and originality of thinking, as this very process of the reduction of knowledge to its results, or the multiplication of those summary and accessible pieces of information in which the student is saved the whole trouble of investigation, and put in possession of the prize, without either the toils or the excitement of conquest.[21]

Market-driven technologies of reproduction and circulation threaten to make obsolete the intellectual work of the consumer as well as of the producer. Even the commercial availability of the great literature of the past in modern editions makes it "cheap and vulgar in [the public] estimation." This industrialization of culture takes part in the larger process by which a "manufacturing system" restructures traditional occupations and social relations, generating an underclass to regulate the cost of labor: tenant farmers (a highly literate class in eighteenth-century Lowland Scotland) become factory workers who in turn become illiterate paupers, a modern caste of men without culture, ideologically as well as economically disenfranchised from civil society. "Enthusiasm" and "enchantment," traditional modes of identification with a symbolic order, give way to a restless, groundless, consumerist desire.[22]

The problem, of course, is that the *Edinburgh Review* participates in the conditions it analyzes. It is only the most eminent of the mercenary machines that are reducing literature to a paper currency. On the one hand refusing ancien régime tropes of aristocratic privilege and leisure (cf. the eighteenth-century *Rambler, Idler, Lounger*), the *Edinburgh Review* had to claim for itself a social profile that was not, on the other hand, merely commercial or democratic. The response, if not solution, to the predicament was to reformulate it as a problem of authority. The notorious judicial strictness of the *Edinburgh Review* (advertised in its motto, *Judex damnatur cum nocens absolvitur*, and in its founding promise "to be distinguished, rather for the selection, than for the number, of its articles") exalts critical judgment as the faculty that restores intellectual agency and distinction in a "leveling" age. As the *Edinburgh Review* enters the industrial marketplace of an expanding reading public, it stakes out a monopolistic enclave within which it attempts to regulate that marketplace by reinstating a hierarchy of cultural value. Ina Ferris has demonstrated the gender/genre equation of this discourse of authority: masculine qualities of judiciousness and rigor distinguish the new literary order from a feminized decadence of fiction. And Jon Klancher has shown how the new middle-class periodicals, from the *Edinburgh Review* to *Blackwood's*, forged a common strategy, the pedagogical reconstruction of reading as a subject-forming mode of interpretive labor.[23] I emphasize a more obvious point, the *Edinburgh Review*'s sociological claim on a class position and an institutional base independent from the leveling flux of the market with its promotion of the faculty of judgment, the disinterested ideal of the Scots legal profession. The signature trope of judicial authority invokes the specific, local site of the Edinburgh Court of Session, which, occupying the former Scottish Parliament House, represented the modern substitute for a defunct national sovereignty in post-Union North Britain.[24] Just as the law regulates civil society, so will the *Edinburgh Review* institute a literary legislature. Many of the reviewers actually were advocates, members of the elite class in Edinburgh society, so that the assumption of judicial authority marks the *Edinburgh Review's* epochal, and controversial, institution of a modern professional literary sphere.[25] Constable's handsome fee of 25 guineas per sheet defined contributors as neither aristocratic dilettanti nor Grub Street hacks but professional gentlemen. Anonymity was a concession sufficient to ensure that the reviewer retained his caste. All the same, the resort to such a cloak suggested uncertainty or vulnerability, and Jeffrey (in particular) worried constantly whether his role as editor (with a salary of £300 a year) exposed him to the contamination of trade.[26]

Tory critiques by Scott and Lockhart expose the instability of this Whig-establishment professional formation of cultural authority. The difference between them helps us read the narrative of epistemic change I am tracing. Scott largely shared the old, Moderate Whig ideology of the Edinburgh reviewers, although he belonged to the rival party. Lockhart, like Scott, was a Tory, but—a generation younger—he was at work forging a new, counter-Enlightenment ideology at *Blackwood's*. Scott's position reveals the uneven, nonhomologous relation between politics and ideology, the motor of discursive change in this history, and accounts for the complex, ambivalent cultural-historical significance ascribed to him, in his own time and afterwards. Scott's essay "On the Present State of Periodical Criticism," published in the *Edinburgh Annual Register* in 1811 (two years after he helped found the Tory *Quarterly Review*), expresses an allegiance to the institutional innovation of the *Edinburgh Review* that is in awkward tension with his recent political quarrel with it.

Scott narrates the history of periodical journalism in the eighteenth century as a decline from heroic individualism into commercial bondage: "Each of the leading English reviews, though originally established by men of letters, had gradually fallen under the dominion of the publishing bookseller," until "the reviewer, like a fee'd barrister, sacrificed his own feelings and judgement to the interest of the bookseller his employer."[27] Scott describes the overthrow of this regime by the *Edinburgh Review* in mock-heroic tropes of colonial conquest, apocalypse, and Jacobin revolution:[28]

From these soothing dreams, authors, booksellers, and critics were soon to be roused by rattling peals of thunder; and it now becomes our task to shew how a conspiracy of beardless boys innovated the venerable laws of this lenient republic of literature, scourged the book-sellers out of her senate-house, overset the tottering thrones of the idols whom they had set up, awakened the hundred-necked snake of criticism, and curdled the whole ocean of milk and water, in which, like the serpentine supporter of Vistnou, he had wreathed and wallowed in unwieldy sloth for a quarter of a century. Then, too, amid this dire combustion, like true revolutionists, they erected themselves into a committee of public safety, whose decrees were written in blood, and executed without mercy. (142)

Scott's (unusually extravagant) irony aims at the vexed relation between politics and cultural forms which is under discussion—it expresses the awareness of a contradiction but the inability to imagine it otherwise. Scott applauds the Edinburgh reviewers' cultural revolution, and his analysis of the new dispensation of a professional independence for authors is astute. But he goes on to lament "the strain of party feeling, which visibly infects those articles of general literature with which politics have least to do"—to the extent that what used to be idiosyncratic and extraneous "prejudices" have become systemic (160). "The Edinburgh Review once asserted an independence of public manners and party leaders, as absolute as their adjuration of bookselling management" (163): invoking a homology between the two kinds of "independence," economic and political, Scott denounces the *Edinburgh Review* for betraying the institutional project of professionalization. The failure of political neutrality threatens to unravel the fabric of economic independence, and thence to subvert the entire structure of liberal professionalism.

Writing in an early number of *Blackwood's*, Lockhart takes up Scott's complaint: "The English [i.e., British] Reviewers are of the opinion of Pericles, that politics are, or should be, the subject of every man's writings."[29] But Lockhart simply cuts the knot between politics and professional disinterestedness, the mandate of a judicial or statesmanlike authority, by denying that there is any professional disinterestedness in the case: reinstating the political-economic homology in its negative form. The reviews are partisan because they are commercial. Echoing Burke's indictment of the Jacobinism of provincial lawyers as well as Scott's analysis of the eighteenth-century periodical regime, Lockhart assails the *Edinburgh Review*'s claim on a professional-gentlemanly register as merely rhetorical—these paper Lords of Session are only advocates for hire after all: "The mercenary transitions of a barrister are but a bad preparation for the gravity of a judge" (675). Lockhart exploits Jeffrey's diagnosis of a commercial literary culture to accuse him of prostituting his own superior talents to "the diseased and novelty-hunting appetites of superficial readers":

> He can very easily persuade them that nothing is worth knowing but what they can comprehend: that true philosophy is quite attainable without the labour of years, and that whenever we meet with anything new, and at first sight unintelligible, the best rule is to take for granted that it is something mystical and absurd. (675–76)

Lockhart's attack exposes the instability of professionalism as a social figure in this moment of its ideological formation—a determined assault can push it back down into the abyss of "trade."[30]

In this combat over the institutional relations of literature to politics and the marketplace, we can interpret the formation *avant la lettre* of the Victorian (humanist and pedagogic) concept of culture, and its genealogical link with the moral philosophy of the Scottish Enlightenment.[31] In particular, the more conservative prognostications of Hume and Ferguson, with their powerful ambivalence about commercial society, continue to inform the argument. The prototypical appearance of a professionalized literary production in the *Edinburgh Review* marks an institutional reconfiguration of Enlightenment discourse as it descends from the traditional site of the academy (locked up by Tory patronage) into the marketplace, and claims autonomy over its own production there. Together, the sociological trope of professionalism and the aesthetic trope of critical judgment begin to constitute an etiology of disinterested value. But just as military conflict is supposed to accelerate certain kinds of infrastructural and technological development, so an ideological conflict accelerates cultural and generic transformations, in the "hot chronology" that Chandler ascribes to the period.[32] The politically driven challenge to the *Edinburgh Review* and its tropes of legitimacy in the periodical war precipitated the ideological figure of a secular site of absolute value more radically, if in the end ambiguously, aloof from the arena of social processes defined by political economy.

Effective opposition to the *Edinburgh Review* required, thus, a discursive and formal articulation—defining an alternative relation between literature and society—in addition to the assertion of a rival politics. The genre of monthly miscellany assumed by *Blackwood's* (ostensibly in rivalry with Constable's *Edinburgh Magazine*, and provoked by the appearance of a pro-Reform newspaper, the *Scotsman*) provided a nimbler and fitter medium for intervention in cultural debate, addressing the expanding population of middle-class readers, than the stately quarterlies, whether Whig or Tory. This formal and class-based rather than strictly political determination is evident in Radical critiques that reiterated the Blackwoodian stance, from James Mill's complaint (in the first number of the utilitarian *Westminster Review*, 1824) that the *Edinburgh Review* and *Quarterly* alike represent an "aristocratic" hegemony, to the Reform-era remark in *Tait's Edinburgh Magazine* that the "Whig Coterie" of the *Edinburgh Review* had founded, "if anything, a Tory publication."[33] *Blackwood's* proved remarkably effective at harnessing dissident, antiestablishment critical energies, in apparent contradiction to its Tory politics. The magazine even stole its figurehead from the Radicals, audaciously flaunting on its cover the portrait of George Buchanan, the patron saint of early-modern Scottish republicanism and founding theorist of the Whig doctrine of contractarian government and the "right of resistance." An early leading article praises Buchanan as a master of patriotic satire: "the wit of Buchanan, how sorely soever it tortured its contemporary victims, was exerted by him for noble purpose."[34] Stripped of his politics, Buchanan is turned into a mascot of nationalist rhetorical prowess, a proto-Lockhart.

Jon Klancher describes the technique by which the variegated styles and genres of the miscellany produce the figure of a transcendental subject—a "national mind":

> [S]uch a writing machine will produce a self-reflexive, desiring reader conscious of the expansive mental power that extrudes through his reading of any particular content. ... Shaping the *Blackwood's* reader demands an inexhaustible panoply of stylistic resources so that it can demonstrate a "power of thought" which is doubled and redoubled in an endless intellectual exertion.[35]

Blackwood's discourse, in other words, transforms the restless and recursive, "metaphysical" modality of modern desire into a purposive dynamic of intellectual labor. But "endless intellectual exertion" remains a rhetorical illusion, the mirroring effect of a florid and opaque stylistics rather than of critical reason, and subjectivity remains solipsistically confined within the temporality of an individual act of reading. The question remains open as to the objective, collectively acknowledged figure that will accommodate this endless intellectual exertion—lest it turn outwards to (say) politics.

"The real and radical difficulty," as Jeffrey had acknowledged, "is to find some pursuit that will permanently interest, —some object that will continue to captivate and engross the faculties."[36] The very first number of Blackwood's *Edinburgh Monthly Magazine* (preceding its scandalous mutation into *Blackwood's Edinburgh Magazine*) featured a series of articles ("On the Sculpture of the Greeks," "On Greek Tragedy") that rehearse a Schillerian argument for substituting aesthetics for politics as the modern discipline of national virtue. The Attic theater "was not merely a place of public amusement, but rather a temple for the purification of the national manners, and the worship of the gods." Now, in a commercial, cosmopolitan, protodemocratic age, the arts are all the more important "in a *moral* point of view, for the animation of virtue and of patriotism."[37] Works of art acquire the status of relics of ancestral excellence—effigies of a lost organic relation between individual subject and national community. Contact with them becomes an act of reverence in which the psyche is replenished with the virtue they contain. Still, it is far from apparent how modern literary production, bought and sold in the market and fragmented by partisan conflict, can reproduce this sacralizing function. Lockhart takes up the question, but does not answer it, in his essay on periodical criticism: "It is a bold thing to compare Shakespeare with a Reviewer; but if ever the world shall possess a perfect Reviewer, be assured that he will bear, in many respects, a striking resemblance to this first of poets. Like him he will be universal—impartial—rational."[38] Such a figure is not at present to be found. Nor does Lockhart's critique of reviewing culture (lacking as it does any institutional analysis) stake out an alternative, "universal—impartial—rational," position for *Blackwood's* and its own discourse. Lockhart's persona, the "Baron von Lauerwinkel," deplores the politicization of culture in the two great quarterlies and exhorts the reviewers to mend their ways—without any admission that his magazine is escalating the same bad process.

Lockhart found an answer in the cultural nationalism promoted in Germany by Friedrich Schlegel. Schlegel argued at the beginning of his *History of Literature* that the transformation of literary culture at the end of the eighteenth century brought the recovery of an integrated national character out of the abyss of skepticism opened by the philosophical reasoning of Hume, Rousseau, and Voltaire. Schlegel read this skepticism as the intellectual symptom of a modern social fragmentation, in terms derived from Schiller and reminiscent of Adam Ferguson: "A separation . . . between the men of letters and the courtly society, and again between both of these and the common people, is destructive of all national character."[39] The *Blackwood's* review of Lockhart's translation ("by far the most rational and profound view of the history of literature which has yet been presented to Europe") did not hesitate to apply Schlegel's diagnosis to the case of "England" (i.e., Great Britain), identifying "the host of periodical publications"—the *Edinburgh Review* implicitly foremost among them—as vectors of the destructive Enlightenment legacy of "metaphysical restlessness":

> It is a melancholy fact, that a single generation of abstract reasoners is enough to vitiate the pedigree of national sentiment and association; and although the ancient literature and history remain, they cannot resume their influence so extensively as before. Perhaps, in England, nothing has contributed so much as the host of periodical publications to obliterate sentiment, and substitute metaphysical restlessness in its place.[40]

Schlegel proposed a solution. Literature, reinterpreted "in its widest sense, as the voice which gives expression to the human intellect—as the aggregate mass of symbols in which the spirit of an age or the character of a nation is shadowed forth" (1:274), may reconstitute the nation both as a collectivity and at the level of individual psychology, as it recombines the alienated faculties of reason and sentiment. "The formation of a national character requires a combination of all those powers and faculties, which we too often keep distinct and isolated" (1:7). Literature may resolve the ideological predicament of modernity, in other words, and reconstitute a fragmented national identity, by itself representing, and so performatively reintegrating, the vital, totalizing bond between nation and psyche.

"A FAST MIDDLE-POINT, AND GRAPPLING-PLACE"

Lockhart and his fellow reviewers mystified the relation of *Peter's Letters to His Kinsfolk* to its periodical matrix, in a strategy that included pseudonymous disguises for Lockhart's authorship ("Peter Morris," a Welsh physician) and his political views ("William Wastle," an antiquarian laird), and even a pretence that the first edition of *Peter's Letters* was a second edition. In fact *Peter's Letters* made its first appearance in the pages of *Blackwood's Magazine*, which serialized substantial extracts in the numbers of February and March 1819 under the pretext of reviewing the hard-to-find first edition (allegedly printed in Aberystwyth).[41] Such mystification, part hoax and part publicity stunt, was a *Blackwood's* technique, integral to the magazine's innovative commercialization and politicization of reviewing culture. In its pages Lockhart and his cronies transformed the abstract, anonymous, judicial elitism of the Edinburgh reviewers into the masquerade of a boisterous coterie of "personalities," and used for satirical armor the authorial cloaking devices given currency by the Waverley novels. *Peter's Letters* pretends, moreover, to occupy a position outside the dirty war of the periodicals, even while reinforcing a Blackwoodian party line—it makes a feint of including *Blackwood's Magazine* and even Lockhart himself in its critique of Edinburgh literary circles.[42]

Lockhart represents his native Scotland in the character of a Welshman addressing English readers. The protagonist as stranger, adapted from *Waverley* and Irish national tales, supplies the ethnographic figure of a "participant-observer" who may render the objective field of national culture as a total, closed set of social and symbolic relations. As James Buzard argues, the device of the participant-observer resolves the "hermeneutic circle" problematic of ethnographic interpretation, which requires at once an entry into the cultural field, in order to understand its internal relations, and a stance outside it, in order to see it as a whole—as a "culture."[43] Lockhart derives the autoethnographic disguise of his protagonist, the Scotsman-as-Welshman, from Smollett's epistolary novel *Humphry Clinker* (1771), the early prototype of Romantic national fiction, and beyond that from an older (Elizabethan) discourse of British nationalism. The Welsh Briton typifies an originary ethnicity—a primitive Britishness—that has been so thoroughly colonized that it can now function smoothly as a naturalized representative of the modern United Kingdom. In other words, the subject belongs to a modern national culture by virtue of an original historical alienation within it. In this way nationality is made the badge or trophy of empire, the sign of a specifically imperial formation of subjectivity in the modern state. The ancestral depth of the protagonist's subjection equips him, moreover, to read the inner fragmentation that constitutes Scotland's present failure of national identity.

This judgment relies on an all-important relocation of national character from the empirical, ethnographic domain, where it is found to be defective, to its mystic supplement and synecdochic totality, tradition: a virtual construct (something else or more that constitutes wholeness) which restores the lost homology between individual and nation. Lockhart's fiction yields the powerful crux of the Unionist ideology of nationality: that a national culture is the product of an imperial tradition, and Scotland can only reclaim its integrity once it becomes the synecdoche for Anglo-British empire. The integrated Briton Peter Morris interprets (for "English" readers) a ruinous Scotland in the ideal shadow of a tradition defined, as it turns out, by Anglo-British tropes of cultural hegemony. The dissociation diagnosed as a psychological attribute of the tradition is an invention of the critic, who splits the actual tradition in order to invoke a lost, mystical whole. Here, the nationality that Scotland by itself cannot provide is supplied by English models. Oxford, rather than the Scottish universities, preserves "the steady and enduring radiance of *our* national past."[44] And despite the corrosive skepticism of the *Edinburgh Review*, "an immense majority of the people of Scotland" are still "enlightened patriots—men who understand the value of national experience, and venerate those feelings of loyalty and attachment to the more formal and external parts of the English constitution"—that is, the "Glorious Revolution" constitution Scotland acquired at the Union (2:139).[45]

Lockhart amplifies his earlier analysis of periodical journalism to denounce the Whig "temper," manifest in an ideological feedback loop between the "mad and ferocious scepticism" of the Edinburgh reviewers and the "vulgar and envious insolence" of middle-class dissenters. In this light (according to Morris's informant Wastle), Jeffrey and the Whig literati are "the legitimate progeny of the sceptical philosophers of the last age" (2:128). Lockhart mounts a sustained critique of the intellectual culture of the Scottish Enlightenment, personified by David Hume, through-out the first volume of *Peter's Letters*, which he summarizes in an essay on Scottish literature and national tradition that concludes the second volume. The essay contains nearly all the themes that reappear in twenti-eth-century Scottish nationalist criticism: the linguistic division between written English and spoken Scots, the social gulf between literati and folk, and even the castigation of "Puritanism," as well as Enlightenment skepti-cism, as alienating doctrinal systems. Lockhart imports Schlegel's scheme to found, in effect, the nationalist topos of the Scottish literary tradition, the notorious "Caledonian Antisyzygy" or dissociation of sensibility, in its classic definition of a split between intellect and feeling.[46]

> The generation of Hume, Smith, &c., left matters of feeling very much unex-plored, and probably considered Poetry merely as an elegant and tasteful appendage to the other branches of literature, with which they themselves were more conversant. Their disquisitions on morals were meant to be the vehicles of ingenious theories—not of convictions of sentiment. They em-ployed, therefore, even in them, only the national intellect, and not the na-tional modes of feeling. (2:360)

Although Hume's genius fitted him "for seizing and possessing an exten-sive dominion over Scottish intellect," the "defect of feeling in his compo-sition" (a term that conflates writing and character) disabled an authenti-cally national representation:

> He was very nearly the *beau ideal* of the national understanding, and had he stood in any thing like the same relation to some other parts of the national character, without all question he might have produced works which would have been recognized by them as complete pictures of their mode of thinking and feeling, and which would, therefore, have obtained a measure of influ-ence exactly coincident with the extent of their national existence. (1:85)

Hume not only promoted, through his influence, the splitting of national tradition, but personified it in his own literary character: "in spite of all that nature and art could do, the devil has been too strong for David; and the Prince of Sceptics has himself been found the most potent instrument for diminishing, almost for neutralizing, the true and grave influence of the Prince of Historians" (1:88).[47] Riven by a psychomachia between radi-cal philosopher and conservative historian, Hume becomes a character in a fable by James Hogg. This metaphysical cleft within the self constitutes the cultural schism of the nation between cosmopolitan literati and pious folk. Restoring the homology between individual and collective in the diagnosis of a division within each of them, Lockhart thus integrates the dismembered tradition at the level of critique. The critique, in other words, constitutes the nation as a virtual or ideal term by perpetuating the division as its empirical foundation.

In an analysis of the Scottish university curriculum, Lockhart appeals to history as the discipline that can unite the severed faculties: "If philosophy (strictly so called) grapples chiefly with our reason, and the Fine Arts with our feelings and imagination, History, on the other hand, claims a more universal possession of us, and considers the whole man, and all the powers of his soul, as alike within her controul" (1:165). Lockhart harnesses the traditional content of an Enlightenment historicism ("the outward and visible effects, which the various modifications of society and education have already produced upon man") to a new spiritual technique of *Bildung* or subject formation:

> [History is] the only study which presents to all our endeavours and aspirations after higher intellectual cultivation, a fast middle-point, and grappling-place, —the effects, namely, the outward and visible effects, which the various modifications of society and education have already produced upon man, his destinies, and his powers. (1:163)

Here and elsewhere Lockhart's word "grapple" designates the process (interpellation) by which the individual mind is joined to a collective ideological formation.

Above all, as Schiller had recommended, the new technique of culture is aesthetic. Its interpretive strategy yields "the link and bond of connection which fastens the whole mighty structure together": whole person and whole nation (1:165). Schlegel, once more, had defined history as a "national consciousness, expressing itself in works of narrative and illustration."[48] Lockhart's election of history as spiritual technique, rather than register of information, anticipates Macaulay, Carlyle, and even Emerson:

> History . . . when she is not confined to the mere chronicling of names, years, and external events, but seizes and expands before us the spirit of great men, great times, and great actions, is in herself alone a true and entire philosophy, intelligible in all things, and sure in all things; and above all other kinds of philosophy, rich in both the materials and the means of application. The value of the fine arts, in regard to the higher species of mental cultivation, is admitted by all whose opinion is of any avail. But even these, without that earnestness of intention, and gravity of power, which they derive from their connection with the actual experience of man, his destiny, and his history—would be in danger of degenerating into an empty sport, a mere plaything of the imagination. The true sense and purpose of the highest and most admirable productions of the imitative arts, (and of poetry among the rest,) are then only clearly and powerfully revealed to us, when we are able to transport

ourselves into the air and spirit of the times in which they were produced, or whose image it is their object to represent. (1:164)

As cultural technique, the study of history recovers—or creates—a spiritual identity with a lost past, abolishing the material differences between then and now. The act of "transport" also abolishes the distinction between history as a condition of representation and history as an object of representation: the reader is at once inside and outside the text. This hermeneutic sublime is antithetical to the scientific historicism of the Enlightenment, which measured diachronic differences ordered by synchronic analogies within a materialist developmental continuum. The past provides that mystic foundation of the transcendental subject, the imaginary Archimedean point from which the present may be criticized as well as inhabited. "The remembrance of the great *past*, —the knowledge of its occurrences and its spirit, is the only thing which can furnish us with a fair and quiet point of view from which to survey the *present*— a standard by which to form just conclusions respecting the comparative greatness or littleness of that which passes before our eyes" (1:165). Once more, we read the formulae of a Victorian pedagogy of culture and tradition at their moment of transmission and assembly.

Peter's Letters is explicit enough about the aesthetic strategy of interpretation that underwrites its autoethnographic ruse. The participant-observer, standing back from the empirical text of culture, can read it, criticize it, and imaginatively complete it, because he occupies the viewpoint of tradition, an ideal construct that belongs to him rather than to the natives of the scene. In Peter Morris's visit to a country sacrament at the conclusion of the third volume, the narrator descends, at last, among the folk. His aloofness from the ceremony enables him to harmonize its parts and situate it teleologically in a tradition, thereby reconstituting it virtually and synecdochally as an epiphany of national character. Such a meaning is emphatically not available to the people he observes:

> In surveying these pious groupes [*sic*], I could not help turning my reflections once again upon the intellectual energies of the nation to which they belong, and of whose peculiar spirit such a speaking example lay before me. It is in rustic assemblages like these that the true characteristics of every race of men are most palpably and conspicuously displayed, and it is there that we can best see in multiplied instances the natural germs of that which, under the influence of culture, assumes a prouder character, and blossoms into the animating soul and spirit of a national literature. (3:326)

The scene exhibits, in other words, a potentiality which the reader finds completed in the virtual medium of national literature. This completion substitutes the communicants' expectation of salvation as the purpose of the sacrament. "Culture," in its old meaning of cultivation, improvement, education, at once alienates the scene (from "culture," an empirical way of life belonging to the natives) and brings it into its own (as "culture," the property of our reading, the "soul and spirit of a national literature"). Accordingly, the meaning of the sacrament has to be rescued from the doctrinal hold of Presbyterian theology:

> You would have seen (for who that has eyes to see, and heart to feel, could have been blind to it?) that the austerities of the peculiar doctrinal system to which they adhere, have had no power to chill or counteract the ardours of that religious sentiment which they share with all that belong to the widespread family of Christians. (3:332)

Once again, theory is detached from sentiment in order for the latter term to signify a restored totality. In the present case the "doctrinal system," which happens to be that of the main radical and reforming tradition in early modern Scottish history, is an attribute of the relative insensibility of the natives of the scene, while "religious sentiment" turns out to be an aesthetic property of the connoisseur who can view and appreciate "the orderly and solemn guise of [the people's] behaviour," "the deep and thrilling harmony of their untaught voices," "the low and affecting swell of [the psalm's] own sad composing cadences."[49]

Not only does Lockhart expropriate popular religion for his version of national tradition by throwing out its doctrines and reducing it to a repertoire of forms and impressions, but he subjects "national literature" itself to a similar colonizing operation. The virtual, teleological projection of national literature takes place upon an allusive evocation of its empirical manifestation in the works of Robert Burns, who haunts the scene. The first volume of *Peter's Letters* had featured a rescue of Burns's reputation from Whig misprision to make it one of the modern cornerstones of a national literature. Now Morris examines the faces in the crowd "to see if I could trace any countenance resembling that of Burns" (3:329), who had demonstrated "that within the limits and ideas of the rustic life of *his* country, he could find an exhibition of the moral interests of human nature, sufficiently varied to serve as the bread and sure foundation of an excellent superstructure of poetry" (3:330–31). But the Burns embedded in an actual social history is a vexing character. He had already turned the field sacrament into a literary property in one of his masterpieces, "The Holy Fair." Peter Morris admits that the verification of Burns's description in "The Holy Fair" is a principal motive for his visit. Lockhart, who would play a decisive role in Burns's posthumous canonization, was troubled by "The Holy Fair": far from inculcating a tender reverence, the poem unleashes an exuberantly lewd and satirical depiction of the country sacrament. "That the same man should have produced the 'Cottar's Saturday Night' and the 'Holy Fair' about the same time," Lockhart later wrote, "will ever continue to move wonder and regret."[50] The historical Burns, in short, was another schizoid figure, like Hume, and his admission to national tradition requires some surgical adjustment.

Lockhart's representation of the field sacrament corrects Burns's most vivid account of popular life by, in effect, transforming "The Holy Fair" into "The Cotter's Saturday Night"—the showcase of a pious peasantry for gentle readers. Lockhart takes the logic of the participant-observer some steps beyond the poet of the "Cotter." The aesthetic mode of representation, having banished doctrine as the source of piety, replaces it with a past emptied of social meaning—and of life:

> There was a breath of sober enduring heroism in [the psalm's] long-repeated melancholy accents—which seemed to fall like a sweet evening dew upon all the hearts that drank in the sacred murmurs. A fresh sunset glow seemed to mantle in the palest cheek around me—and every old and hagard [sic] eye beamed once more with a farewell splendour of enthusiasm, while the air into which it looked up, trembled and was enriched with the clear solemn music of the departed devout. It seemed as if the hereditary strain connected all that sat upon those grassy tombs in bonds of stricter kindred with all that slept beneath them—and the pure flame of their Christian love derived, I doubt not, a new and innocent fervour from the deeply-stirred embers of their ancestral piety. (3:333–34)

"Ancestral piety" signifies death instead of the dogmatic zeal of Presbyterian forefathers, in an extended allusion (via Gray's "Elegy") to the narrator's meditation on the peaceful graves of long-dead Covenanters in the opening chapter of *Old Mortality*.[51] As Lockhart glosses it, his favorite among Scott's novels has made the Covenanting heritage safe ("a new and innocent fervour") for the national tradition by purging it of its political energies and turning it into an object for aesthetic contemplation. Absence and death constitute tradition, the mystic bond of connection between generations. Yet there is something unwholesome about this covenant with the dead. Lockhart's purple prose metamorphoses the erotic vitality of Burns's Holy Fair into a hectic, vampirical illusion—"a fresh sunset glow seemed to mantle in the palest cheek around me"—as it relegates "enthusiasm" to "a farewell splendour."

Thus Lockhart's construction of national culture performs the dismemberment of the empirical body of tradition that is its critical theme. Lockhart invokes history as the discipline that constitutes a national culture; but the past recovered is an ideal one, a spectral dimension parallel to the record of actual utterances, events, and deeds. Such history is, in fact, a romance revival, which converts the scientific representation of an ancient other, in an evolutionary relation to ourselves, to an imaginary identification with ancestral origins separated from us by death—but which we will join in our death.

"PATRIARCH OF THE NATIONAL POETRY OF SCOTLAND"

The romance-revival tropes of tradition converge upon the figure of Scott, "Patriarch of the National Poetry of Scotland" (2:351), in the extended account of the visit to Abbotsford that closes the second volume of *Peter's Letters to His Kinsfolk*.[52] Lockhart's election of Scott as national author coincides with a major crux of Scott's literary career, between the last of the great sequence of Scottish novels (*Tales of My Landlord, Third Series*, June 1819) and a new romance of Anglo-British imperial origins, *Ivanhoe* (December 1819). This gives Lockhart's account of Scott's Scottishness a timely (however contingent) retrospectiveness. It also marks a turning point in the cultural politics of the postwar and Scott's role in them. *Peter's Letters* solemnizes a takeover of Scott for the new *Blackwood's* ideology, quite as much as it predicts a shift of affiliation on Lockhart's part from the Mohawks of *Blackwood's* to the Laird of Abbotsford.

Peter Morris's journey to Abbotsford and tour of the countryside, guided by his host, allegorize the subject's induction into national culture. An initially "bare and sterile" landscape begins to blossom with "picturesque" features, including relics of a feudal past. Literary and historical associations condense around the estate. Scott informs Morris that he is "treading on classical ground—that here was *Huntly Burn*, by whose side Thomas the Rhymer of old saw the Queen of Faery riding in her glory" (2:318). Scott conducts a cognitive remapping in which the strange scenery becomes uncannily familiar. Its national associations, recognized from the reading of Scott's poetry (and mediated through an echo of Wordsworth's), make it more profoundly homely than would any merely personal remembrance:[53] "The name of every hill and every valley all around is poetical, and I felt, as I heard them pointed out one by one, as if so many old friends had been introduced to my acquaintance after a long absence, in which I had thought of them all a thousand times" (2:320). Scott's nation-forming authority resides in his joint character as interpreter and proprietor: Scotland, Abbotsford, and Scott's poetry all stand for one another. His ability to reanimate the landscape by reviving (or creating) its national associations, for Morris and for us, is inextricably tied up with his role as landlord. The figure of the Laird as genius loci is a striking variant of the national-tale convention, carried over into *Waverley*, which casts the native informant and national spirit as an heiress whom the visiting protagonist ends up marrying. All the more so that this would constitute the author's, Lockhart's, biographical plot. Sophia

Scott herself makes no appearance in *Peter's Letters*, which surrounds the patriarch with his feudal retainers.[54] Here, the appearance of the national father-in-law announces the summation of the historical process of Union. His private ownership of national tradition is the very condition that makes it available, through his works, in the modern domain of the reading public.

Lockhart elides distinctions between real and imaginary property, and between Scott's poetic inventions and the ballads he has collected in *Minstrelsy of the Scottish Border*: all rightfully belong to the author whose national representation conflates ownership, transmission, interpretation, and creation into a single organic function. That organic function allegorizes the "ownership of the whole literary production and distribution process" consolidated by Scott and his partners at around this time, a "close vertical and horizontal concentration of media ownership" that renders Scott's authorship and the "reading nation" together as the sublime form of the market.[55] Scott's recitation of verses from "The Battle of Otterbourne," one of the *Minstrelsy* ballads, reveals "the true stamp of Nature on the Poet of Marmion" (2:303), in a fusion of proprietary authorship with oral tradition. Despite the concern of *Marmion* with a knight who betrays his rank by a deed of forgery (thus advertising, as Jeffrey complained, the poem's own modern, post-Ossianic status as a forgery),[56] Lockhart also—accordingly—elides, or rather restructures, the vexed distinction between authentic and fake manifestations of national tradition. The recital of the Border ballad (included in the *Minstrelsy* as a national rival to Percy's version in *Reliques of Ancient English Poetry*)[57] gives way to a more incongruous performance:

> While I was thus occupied, one of the most warlike of the Lochaber pibrochs began to be played in the neighbourhood of the room in which we were, and, looking towards the window, I saw a noble Highland piper parading to and fro upon the lawn, in front of the house—the plumes of his bonnet—the folds of his plaid—and the streamers of his bag-pipe, all floating majestically about him in the light evening breeze. (2:304)

Lockhart confronts the flagrantly inauthentic—Ossianic—tendency of the imperial fiction of nationality. Scott's project must be justified:

> It is true, that it was in the Lowlands—and that there are other streams upon which the shadow of the tartans might fall with more of the propriety of mere antiquarianism, than on the Tweed. But the Scotch are right in not now-a-days splitting too much the symbols of their nationality; as they have ceased to be an independent people, they do wisely in striving to be as much as possible an united people. But here, above all, whatever was truly Scottish could not fail to be truly appropriate in the presence of the great genius to

whom whatever is Scottish in thought, in feeling, or in recollection, owes so large a share of its prolonged, or reanimated, or ennobled existence. The poet of Roderick Dhu, and—under favour—the poet of Fergus Mac-Ivor, does well assuredly to have a piper among the retainers of his hospitable mansion. (2:305)

"Mere antiquarianism" weighs far less than the poetic imagination that forges an essential unity ("whatever is truly Scottish") out of the dispersed figures of regional, ethnic, and political difference. Indeed historical fragmentation, extending to the loss of sovereignty, is the precondition of the modern imperial fiction of nationality. Civil war yields the most powerful "manifestations of national mind"—in Shakespeare's history plays, "the more than dramatic Clarendon" and *Waverley* and *Old Mortality*—since there "all the various elements of [the nation's] character, religious and political, [are] exhibited in their most lively fermentation of sharpness and vigour" (2:352–53). Lockhart stops short of acknowledging that what binds such fragmentary "elements" into a national whole is the modern medium of commerce, designated by Scott's proprietary performance as best-selling author. Sales figures make these fictions authentic for being the index of a collective imaginary investment or "belief."

To further deflect the charge of inauthenticity Lockhart introduces Scott's Radical neighbor, the Earl of Buchan, as a parody of the Laird of Abbotsford. The earl's "devices" at Dryburgh—a modern chain-link bridge, a "huge colossal statue of Sir William Wallace, executed in staring red free-stone," a pompous bust of the earl himself—cater to the low taste of "Cockney visitants." The statue even accommodates "a pot-house, where a rhyming cobler [*sic*], one of the noble Lord's many protegees, vends odes, elegies, and whisky, for his own behoof, and the few remaining copies of that charming collection, 'the Anonymous and Fugitive Pieces of the Right Honourable the Earl of Buchan,' for behoof of his patron" (2:329). Very much according to the logic of tourism analyzed by Buzard, Lockhart displays a vulgar, commercialized foil for the more exclusive sign of culture—the "authenticity effect"—at Abbotsford.[58] Structurally the earl's devices resemble Scott's, and Lockhart's own. An exhibition of plaster-cast busts features Homer, "Mr Watt of Birmingham, the inventor of the steam engine," General Washington, Sir Philip Sidney, "Shakespeare—Count Rumford—Dr Matthew Baillie—Charles James Fox—Socrates—Cicero—and Provost Creech of Edinburgh," and so on, culminating in "a rueful caricature of the Ettrick Shepherd" (2:331–32). To jeer at bad taste is to acknowledge good, and so this ludicrous miscellany (a botched attempt at a Whig pantheon) justifies rather than undermines the "propriety" of the national cultural bricolage at Abbotsford.

Morris crowns the account of his visit with an essay on national literature in which Scott occupies the station elsewhere granted to Burns:

> At a time when the literature of Scotland—and of England too—was becom-
> ing every day more and more destitute of command over everything but the
> mere speculative understanding of men—this great genius seems to have been
> raised up to counteract, in the wisest and best of all ways, this unfortunate
> tendency of his age, by re-awakening the sympathies of his countrymen for
> the more energetic characters and passions of their forefathers. (2:348)[59]

Scott enacts the program of aesthetic education that Lockhart had described under the rubric of history, decisively establishing it as a technique
of historical romance. The national author "grapples boldly with the feelings of his countrymen" (2:361), "making them acquainted with the various courses of thought and emotion, by which their forefathers had their
genius and character drawn out" (2:350).

He transports his readers by a genial force. His, not theirs, is the sublime agency of sympathetic reawakening. In Scott's recital of the ballad
of Otterbourne, Lockhart describes the process at work. First, like a vatic
medium, Scott undergoes a physiognomic transformation, as the verse
possesses *him*:

> It seemed as if one single cadence of the ancestral strain had charm enough
> to transport his whole spirit back into the very pride and presence of the
> moment, when the White Lion of the Percies was stained and trampled
> under foot beside the bloody rushes of Otterbourne. The more than martial
> fervours of his kindled eye, were almost enough to give to the same lines the
> same magic in my ears; and I could half fancy that the portion of Scottish
> blood which is mingled in my veins, had begun to assert, by a more ardent
> throb, its right to partake in the triumphs of the same primitive allegiance.
> (2:303–4)

The romance revival is oddly qualified by the time it reaches its audience:
"almost enough to give to the same lines the same magic in my ears . . . I
could half fancy." Ours can only ever be a partial imitation or reflection
of the author's transport, as though his mediumship shields us from the
violence of the energy he channels. "Primitive allegiance" remains, for the
reader still more than the listener, a representation realized by the heroic
labor of an author, whose authentic connection with his sources is part
of his performance. The reader is not required, in other words, to believe
in the romantic illusion—but to believe in the author's belief in it. What
Lockhart's enthusiastic rhetoric mimes as a doubled or intensified belief,
supplanting the Humean skepticism refashioned in Scott's fictions, viti-
ates itself into a removed and pretended belief, the reader's submission to
an authorial show of force.

After all, too much of the primitive allegiance of a portion of Scottish blood might blow the Anglo-British body apart. The tropes of horror fiction are never far away. It is a necessary condition that the material of national culture lie in the past, dead and broken, in order that the interpreter's art retrieve and reassemble it. But it never is quite made whole or brought back fully to life. It continues to lack, in the aesthetic mode of perception, the lifeblood of social and political meaning. The romance revival is a Frankenstein operation:

> The eye, and the voice, and the words, and the gestures, seem all alike to be the ready unconscious interpreters of some imperial spirit, that moves irresistibly their mingled energies from within. There is no effort—no semblance of effort—but everything comes out as is commanded—swift, clear, and radiant through the impartial medium. The heroes of the old times spring from their graves in panoply, and 'drink the red wine through the helmet barred' before us. . . . [T]hese are all alike, not names, but realities—living, moving, breathing, feeling, speaking, looking realities—when he speaks of them. The grave loses half its potency when he calls. His own imagination is one majestic sepulchre, where the wizard lamp burns in never-dying splendour, and the charmed blood glows for ever in the cheeks of the embalmed, and every long-sheathed sword is ready to leap from its scabbard, like the Tizona of the Cid in the vault of Cardena. (2:314)

Lockhart's rhapsodic evocation of Scott's art as mansion of an imperial spirit decays into the Gothic scenario of a crypt infested with zombie warriors. Even the allusion to Burke (the sword ready to leap from its scabbard) is one that marks the historical demise of chivalry, the catastrophe of the old regime, in the downfall of Marie Antoinette. The echo of Burke's lament is drowned by the reference to a grotesque incident in Southey's translation of *The Cid*, in which a tourist tries to plunder a souvenir from the embalmed body of Spain's epic hero and is rebuked by the corpse itself.[60] It is as though the reanimation of the past reveals ourselves as inauthentic, unreal, spectral: "The ambiguous and contradictory nature of the modern *nation* is the same as that of vampires and other living dead: they are wrongly perceived as 'leftovers from the past'; their place is constituted by the very break of modernity."[61] Scott appears, in Lockhart's epiphany, arrested—just at the point of transport—in a deconsecrated yet haunted temporality, a "time of the nation" that is neither past nor present, living nor dead. The sublime vision of national culture declines into the contaminated aesthetic mode of the uncanny.

Chapter 3

✣

ECONOMIES OF NATIONAL CHARACTER

DIRT

"National" difference is put to work, formally and ideologically, in the first Scottish novel published in Edinburgh, Elizabeth Hamilton's *The Cottagers of Glenburnie* (1808).[1] *The Cottagers of Glenburnie* specifies its Scottish setting with the protoethnographic rhetoric of a "thick description" that particularizes regional manners, dialect, and household objects. Mrs. Mason, a virtuous widow, comes to live at the village of Glenburnie, where the domestic economy is typified by a family named MacClarty—"MacDirty." Dirt, in fact, constitutes the vivid details of village life:

> The walls were substantial; built, like the houses in the village, of stone and lime; but they were blackened by the mud which the cart-wheels had spattered from the ruts in winter; and on one side of the door completely covered from view by the contents of a great dunghill. On the other, and directly under the window, was a squashy pool, formed by the dirty water thrown from the house, and in it about twenty young ducks were at this time daubling.[2]

Inside the cottage the hospitable Mrs. MacClarty serves tea. Her hands, sooty from stirring the fire, leave black thumbprints all over the butter. In vain Mrs. Mason attempts to eat: "the disgust with which she began, was so augmented by the sight of the numerous hairs which, as the butter was spread, bristled up upon the surface, that she found it impossible to proceed" (147–48).

Contemporary readers fastened upon this aspect of the tale. Scots readers "must blush at the nastiness and indolence which [the author] so well depicts," wrote the *Critical Review*, and hope in future to be "indebted to the literary labours of Miss Hamilton for more cleanliness in the inns."[3] North British nastiness was a commonplace of eighteenth-century travel writing, summed up in James Boswell's anecdote of Samuel Johnson flinging his lemonade out of the window after an Edinburgh waiter puts sugar in it with greasy fingers.[4] More than a satirical ornament, dirt is a structural principle of the rhetoric of regional specificity in *Cottagers of*

Glenburnie. It provides the texture—bristling up upon the surface—of a world of particular, localized phenomena, of sense impressions and material surfaces, that we associate with literary realism, in a novel otherwise parsimonious with descriptive detail. Dirt is not only, in Mary Douglas's anthropological definition, "matter out of place," a material excess in the order of culture; in Hamilton's novel it also constitutes the metonymic excess, the unnecessary and therefore validating detail, that Roland Barthes called the "reality effect."[5]

Mrs. Mason cleans up Glenburnie, directing a liberal, evangelical program of economic, moral, and above all hygienic improvement.[6] She reforms the cottagers' manners, teaches them how to increase household productivity, and instigates a physical cleansing of domestic spaces and bodies. The last of these improvements is the one most consequential for the reader, since it sweeps and scrubs away the metonymic foreground, the "local color," that fixes our imagination to the novel's world. When we read that "the village presented . . . a picture of neatness and comfort" (397) we know that there is nothing more to be told. Here, then, arises a conundrum. The dirt that gets cleaned up is the stuff that gives the tale its savor, its humor, its distinctiveness—that constitutes, in opposition to its didactic program, its aesthetic enjoyment. John Galt, voyaging in Sicily, walked into a shop "kept by the very prototype of Mrs. Maclarty, of Glenburnie."[7] The squalid natives, not the worthy missionary, stuck in readers' minds. They personified a regional difference from the metropole designated as Scottish (as opposed to British) "national character."

The Cottagers of Glenburnie inaugurates, for Scottish fiction, the paradox of regional difference recently identified with the nation-forming project of the historical novel: "to represent internal unevenness," in Franco Moretti's summary, "and then, to *abolish* it."[8] Glenburnie seems to be located in the Highlands, and it is hard not to read Mrs. Mason's hygienic intervention as an idealized, compensatory version of the Clearances—the forced migration of populations in the name of improvement—at the very moment that these were entering an intensified, violent phase on the Sutherland estates. *Cottagers of Glenburnie* shows that the abolition of internal unevenness was on the agenda of national fiction before *Waverley*, publication of which coincided with the worst of the Sutherland Clearances in 1814. Scott's historicization of regional difference would make it conceptually available as "culture" in the ethnographic sense: the way of life and value system of a local society, embedded in the economic conditions of a specific developmental stage. That historicization invoked a global narrative of modernization, at least in *Waverley*, which subjected regional difference to a dialectic of loss and salvage—the material destruction of a traditional culture followed by its sentimental and aesthetic reconstitution, as a property of polite connoisseurs. Lockhart drew on this loss-and-salvage model for the full-scale ideology of cultural nationalism analyzed in the previous chapter. This chapter traces the vicissitudes of regional difference in the Scottish tradition of national fiction that preceded *Waverley* and preceded the conceptual transformation of national character into national culture.

Cottagers of Glenburnie exemplifies the pre-Romantic meaning of "culture" as the antithesis of a national character anchored in a local way of life: culture as cultivation, or economic and moral improvement, requiring the abolition of original conditions under the slogan of their reformation. Hamilton's novel is closely aligned with the more ambitious Irish novels of Maria Edgeworth, who first combined a "Scottish" philosophical plot of economic improvement—the motor of modernization—with a private plot of moral improvement, refined in the "Burney school" of English domestic fiction, to produce national character as a major crux in British literature. Edgeworth established what James Buzard has called the "metallurgical metaphor according to which national culture and identity must pass through the cauldron of alienation in order to become their better selves."[9] This metaphor or, rather, scheme (drawn from Puritan conversion narrative) would govern the post-Enlightenment Scottish fictions of national character, earning Edgeworth the right to be acknowledged as a modern founder of the Scottish school. The plot of improvement through alienation retains its hold even on the Romantic revaluation of national character as ethical source or aesthetic resource, as the examples of Mary Brunton and Susan Ferrier show later in this chapter.[10] Scott's intervention in this story, I shall argue, accompanies the historical recognition of a regional social difference as "culture" with a formal recognition of the novel itself as a discrete aesthetic medium. National fiction before Scott bears a didactic program that disciplines not only its characters but its readers, by activating an aesthetic enjoyment (in local color) which it then suppresses and disavows (as dirt). Edgeworth, characteristically rigorous, has her fiction proclaim its own abandonment as a condition of attaining its pedagogic goal. Scott's novels, however, develop an ideological work that takes place through an aesthetic enjoyment identified with the categorical autonomy of fiction itself, no longer subservient to some other, programmatic discourse, such as religious doctrine or political economy. The antagonisms that structure Hamilton's and Edgeworth's tales—between national character as (Scottish) local origin and national character as (British) product of improvement, between aesthetic and moral terms of value—reappear in the case study that closes this chapter, John Galt's disconcertingly frank attempt to reconcile the poles of origin and improvement in an economic allegory of national character, *Sir Andrew Wylie*.

Katie Trumpener has drawn a distinction between the early Irish national tale and Scott's historical novels, according to which the national tale curates a coexistence of Celtic and metropolitan regions within a utopian geography of cultural difference, while the historical novel predicates a developmental collapse of such differences upon their status as successive historical stages.[11] Trumpener's distinction favors the "Bardic," sentimental, philo-Jacobin branch of national fiction inaugurated by Sydney Owenson in *The Wild Irish Girl* (1806) over the satirical, reformist, liberal-conservative branch inaugurated by Maria Edgeworth in *Castle Rackrent; An Hibernian Tale* (1800). Yet the latter would prove more consequential for Scottish fiction, since Edgeworth's Irish tales establish not only the nineteenth-century literary repertoire of national character but the plot of a Scottish alienation from it. *Castle Rackrent* opens the formal contradiction between a regionally grounded national identity and the liberal project of improvement, and signalizes it (more explicitly than Hamilton) as a crux of imperial state formation.[12] Edgeworth also explicitly associates improvement, as a pedagogic and an economic project, with the modernizing disciplines of the Scottish human sciences. "She had so much in common intellectually with leading writers of the Scottish Enlightenment," writes Marilyn Butler, "that she needs to be grouped with them as well as with the ungathered tradition of Irish writing after Swift."[13] The present study groups Edgeworth with the Scottish tradition of post-Enlightenment national fiction that she can be said to have founded.

Castle Rackrent installs the key conventions of regional writing: the thick description of manners and traditions, artifacts, antiquities, and landscape features; the transcription of dialect; and the analytic view of a local economy against the horizon of modernization. These compose the material base of a regional representation that Edgeworth's tale relegates to the past:

> The editor hopes his readers will observe that these are "tales of other times": that the manners depicted in the following pages are not those of the present age: the race of the Rackrents has long since been extinct in Ireland. . . . There is a time, when individuals can bear to be rallied for their past follies and absurdities, after they have acquired new habits, and a new consciousness. Nations as well as individuals gradually lose attachment to their identity, and the present generation is amused rather than offended by the ridicule that is thrown upon its ancestors. . . . When Ireland loses her identity by an union with Great Britain, she will look back with a smile of good-humoured complacency on the Sir Kits and Sir Condys of her former existence.[14]

Ireland's future in the British Union will bring "new habits and a new consciousness" at the price of a loss of national identity. That loss constitutes the new consciousness, in the form of a satirical disavowal of the past that justifies a cheerful acceptance of its passing.

Castle Rackrent plots loss of national identity through a family history of ruin and extinction. Edgeworth unfolds this history through a radically modernist narratology determined by principles of material contingency and accidental causality (in contrast to Romantic providence or Gothic fatality), which Galt would develop in his Scottish fiction of the early 1820s. The tale abounds in notations of material detail that represent the encroaching reality of a money economy, against which successive Rackrent delusions of feudal entitlement founder: the seizure of Sir Patrick's body for debt; Lady Murtagh's parsimony; Sir Kit's calling for household furnishings that the widow has taken away with her, as though "all those things must come of themselves" (72). Edgeworth develops an analogous rhetoric of accidental causality which shapes the most developed narrative sequence, that of Sir Condy. Condy tosses a coin to decide whom he will marry, he cannot obtain light or fire because a horse wants a shoe, Thady overhears a crucial conversation while he is replacing a broken windowpane with a slate, and so on. Materiality and accident converge in the brilliant final pages, when rumor magnifies Lady Rackrent's car crash into a false report of her death. An earlier episode epitomizes the narrative method. Sir Kit's wife suffers "a sort of fit," and the news spreads "that she was dead, by mistake"; neighboring ladies to whom Sir Kit has been paying court show his letters to their brothers, and Sir Kit is obliged to fight a series of duels. "He met and shot the first lady's brother; the next day he called out the second, who had a wooden leg; and their place of meeting by appointment being in a new ploughed field, the wooden-leg man stuck fast in it" (81). The vivid, apparently gratuitous circumstances of the wooden leg and the ploughed field produce the narrativity of accident and the associated "reality effect"—figured, in a miniature allegory, as an irresistible traction of the material world, a sticking in the dirt. The real is that contingent material excess that clogs human intention. The happy outcome of one duel—Sir Kit and the wooden-leg man go home to dinner together—is capsized in the next: "unluckily, after hitting the tooth-pick out of his adversary's finger and thumb, he received a ball in a vital part, and was brought home, in little better than an hour after the affair, speechless on a hand-barrow, to my lady" (81).

Castle Rackrent sets out the formal problem implicit in *Cottagers of Glenburnie*. The old, unregenerate national character is the ingredient that confers value (both aesthetic and commercial) on Edgeworth's tale—it gives it its humor, its originality and distinction. *Castle Rackrent* subsumes national character into the emanation of a voice, narrating from within the local scene, belonging to the family steward Thady Quirk. The lack of formal closure between Thady's *récit* and the tale's enlightened editorial frame produces an ironical resonance between both discourses, rather than (as the Edgeworthian editor would like to insist) a sublation of one of them (the local) into the other (the imperial).[15] A large-scale narratalogical, historiographic, and ideological conundrum occupies the gap between tale and frame: How shall Ireland graduate from the sorry conditions exposed in Thady's narrative to the utopian horizon of Union? What political and economic developments can sustain the "new consciousness" of a comic acceptance of, rather than regret for or rage against, the loss of national identity?

The conundrum provides the scheme for Edgeworth's second Irish novel, *Ennui* (1809), an innovative synthesis of the regional satire of *Castle Rackrent*, the satire of "fashionable life" developed in the Burney tradition of female bildungsroman, and the sentimental allegory of Union as a marriage plot pioneered in Owenson's *Wild Irish Girl*. With this synthesis *Ennui* provides the template, more sophisticated than Hamilton's rudimentary reform plot, for the Scottish tradition of national fiction. The Anglo-Irish Earl of Glenthorn narrates his progress from decadent cosmopolitan aristocrat to British professional gentleman. These conditions fall before and after the local terrain of a "Hibernian," indigenous Irish identity, traversed by Glenthorn in the course of the tale. The novel begins by diagnosing "ennui," the moral disorder of the old regime, as the melancholic symptom of a lack of national character: to suffer from ennui is to be adrift in the unnatural topology and temporality of fashionable life. Glenthorn's cure begins when he travels to his Irish estate, where he encounters "national character" as an unaccustomed phenomenological pressure of materiality and contingency. The description of the ramshackle hackney chaise that carries him into the country spectacularly inaugurates the rhetoric of national character, in the mode of *Castle Rackrent*, as a recalcitrant material excess. Glenthorn's journey into Ireland and his adventures along the way supply an invigorating friction of objects and accidents that chafes him out of his ennui, through salutary (Swiftian) fits of anger and laughter (176), into a state of moral purposiveness.

Once he arrives at his estate, however, Glenthorn relapses into false consciousness, which Edgeworth represents in a technique (subsequently developed by Scott) of literary-historical stylization. The first view of Glenthorn Castle as a Gothic setting out of Ann Radcliffe underlines Glenthorn's misprision of his sojourn there as a retro-feudal idyll, soon given political bite by his resort to the models of Enlightenment despotism in an ineffectual attempt to impose his authority. The cottage of his old nurse Ellinor O'Donoghoe, the first object of his improving ambition, exemplifies the Hibernian condition of a wasteful material redundancy. Edgeworth's description amplifies one of Hamilton's Glenburnie set pieces to establish the "dirty cottage" as a long-standing topos of regional realism:

We came to Ellinor's house, a wretched-looking, low, and mud-walled cabin; at one end it was propped by a buttress of loose stones, upon which stood a goat reared on its hind legs, to browse on the grass that grew on the house-top. A dunghill was before the only window, at the other end of the house, and close to the door was a puddle of the dirtiest of dirty water, in which ducks were dabbling. At my approach there came out of the cabin a pig, a calf, a lamb, a kid, and two geese, all with their legs tied; followed by turkeys, cocks, hens, chickens, a dog, a cat, a kitten, a beggar-man, a beggar-woman with a pipe in her mouth, children innumerable, and a stout girl with a pitch-fork in her hand; all together more than I, looking down upon the roof as I sat on horseback, and measuring the superficies with my eye, could have possibly supposed the mansion capable of containing. (186)

Matter out of place indeed. Glenthorn has the cabin repaired and redecorated—but MacClartys are no match for O'Donoghoes:

Her ornamented farm-house became, in a short time, a scene of dirt, rubbish, and confusion. There was a partition between two rooms, which had been built with turf or peat, instead of bricks, by the wise economy I had employed. Of course, this was pulled down to get at the turf. The stairs also were pulled down and burned, though there was no scarcity of firing. (199)

Waste matter rather than raw material, Irish dirt is charged with a regressive, entropic force.

Glenthorn's interventions remain futile until he submits to the guidance of his estate manager, a Scotsman named M'Leod. Citing Adam Smith's *Wealth of Nations*, promoting gradual progress through programs of tenant education and market-based reform, M'Leod personifies the values and precepts of the Scottish Enlightenment. His lessons prevail across the remainder of the novel, in which Glenthorn gives up his estate and fortune and then earns them back by becoming a lawyer, a typically North British professional formation. For "Ennui" to be respelled as "Union" the Irish, it seems, must follow the Scots' example. This North British solution is proposed elsewhere in the tale, in the emigration of Cecil Devereux and Lady Geraldine to India: the provincial elites from the former "Celtic" nations can reclaim metropolitan status by devoting themselves to overseas colonial administration.

Thus *Ennui* casts national improvement as a Scottish topos and Scotland as Ireland's future. The Lowland Enlightenment is the source of discourses and institutions of modernization, foremost among them political economy, professionalism, and the law, which submit the materiality of national character to a rationalizing and moralizing program of disciplinary abstraction. The Smithian discourse associated with M'Leod is one that requires the rhetorical and cognitive sublimation of material objects into a complex abstraction of relations of exchange value. The logic of abstraction governs the various branches of Smith's analysis of modern civil society, in which, for instance, the "passions originating in the body" are rarefied into harmonious relations of imaginary sympathetic exchange.[16] Native speech forms, analogously, undergo disciplinary refinement into the literacy-based "grammar of empire," a pedagogy that notoriously required the purging of "Scotticisms"—the linguistic dirt ("clarty," "fash") of *Cottagers of Glenburnie*.[17] Hume's essay "Of National Characters" remarks on the condition won through this purification: "the ENGLISH, of any people in the universe, have the least of a national character; unless this very singularity may pass for such."[18] That singularity marks England's historical achievement of a mixed constitution and civil and religious liberties. Developing Hume's thesis, John Millar's *On the Origin of the Distinction of Ranks* formulates an antithesis between the linear axis of historical progress and the lateral one of national character:

> It has even happened that nations, being placed in such unfavourable circumstances as to render them long stationary at a particular period, have been so habituated to the peculiar manners of that age, as to retain a strong tincture of those peculiarities, through every subsequent revolution. This appears to have occasioned some of the chief varieties which take place in the maxims and customs of nations equally civilized.[19]

The diachronic impulse of improvement is universal and purposive, while national "peculiarity" is the accidental byproduct of periods of stagnation. Millar's scheme clarifies the opposition between an Enlightenment trajectory of "culture" as progress and a naturalized condition of national character that is little more than an inert customary residue.

Ennui discloses the violence that underwrites the liberal, pedagogical, and ethical renunciation of a residual national character, although it blurs the disclosure by representing the violence as autotelic, the evidently natural tendency of an abject, perverse, unimprovable Irishness toward (literally) spontaneous combustion. In a startling plot twist Glenthorn discovers Irish identity as his own genetic inheritance: he is the son of a Catholic peasant, switched at birth with the true Earl, his foster brother. The materialization of Irishness in his own body obliges the ci-devant Glenthorn to sublimate his newfound origins, as well as the remnants of aristocratic ennui, through the discipline of professional training, thus proving that character is the product of education rather than birth. Yet this is not enough. Glenthorn Castle decays into squalor once the Earl's peasant family moves in, fulfilling the early portent of Ellinor's cottage. At the very end of the novel the feckless drunkard son burns down the building, together with himself, in a last, lethal accident that clears the way for the hero to repossess the estate—cleansed now of incorrigible residues of national character. Glenthorn's progress, the painstaking moral reformation of old habits and identities, requires for its completion the physical elimination of a base Irishness figurally congealed into waste matter.

The ethical contradiction between the solutions so disconcertingly yoked together—enlightened pedagogy and extermination—takes effect as a violent formal contradiction within the novel, which tears itself in two between competing narrative modes of a Scottish historiography of gradual, incremental, rationally accountable progress and a wild Irish romance of catastrophic reversals and revolutionary redistributions of property and identity.[20] This violence is directed not just against the novel's form but against the reader:

> If, among those who may be tempted to peruse my history, there should be any mere novel readers, let me advise them to throw the book aside at the commencement of this chapter; for I have no more wonderful incidents to relate, no more changes at nurse, no more sudden turns of fortune. I am now become a plodding man of business, poring over law-books from morning till night, and leading a most monotonous life[.] (305)

It seems we are forced to renounce the genre and its pleasures whether we keep reading or not.

The Scottish school of national domestic fiction, as though in acknowledgment of Edgeworth's appeal to Scottish philosophical authority, would take up the satirical combination of "national tale" and "tale of fashionable life" founded in *Ennui*. However Edgeworth deconstructs in advance, by splitting it into metaphoric and literal trajectories, the influential solution her combination provides: what Buzard calls (apropos of its declension in Victorian bildungsroman) "the refining-fire model of national imagining," in which local origins—and the primitive pleasures of fiction—are a moral dross, purified in the flame of an exemplary progress.[21]

PURITY

Edgeworth invents a satirical plot in which national character is reconstituted through a strenuous, even violent course of revulsions. Sydney Owenson's *The Wild Irish Girl* (1806) establishes a rival, "Romantic" plotting of national character as a pure origin that supplies an alternative set of values to those of a corrupt metropolis. The scheme was pioneered by Smollett in *Humphry Clinker* (1771), which contrasts the "sophistication" of fashionable Bath and London (provoking the most nauseating

renditions of nastiness in British fiction) with the moral and aesthetic purity of the "Highland Arcadia" discovered on the banks of Loch Lomond.
Drawing more systematically on the late-eighteenth-century repertoire of
"Bardic Nationalism," Owenson makes the Celtic hinterland the seat of
virtue and learning—of "culture" as the spirit of an indigenous civilization (although still a "Classical," aristocratic rather than popular formation). Desire rather than revulsion moves the hero's progress ("enthusiasm for Ireland assumes the character of sublimated or deferred sexual
longing"): disciplinary authority emanates not from a dour Scotch manager but from the Milesian Princess Glorvina, whose pedagogy glows with
a sentimental and erotic as well as intellectual charisma.[22]

The Scottish school of domestic national fiction that succeeded *Cottagers of Glenburnie* takes up Owenson's sentimental revaluation of national character to imagine a feminized version of the Highland Arcadia
that contains the moral sources of improvement rather than the material
conditions abolished by it. The aura of a redemptive premodernity or
prehistory is if anything enhanced by the region's contemporaneous economic and demographic collapse. Flourishing at the close of the Napoleonic wars, Scottish domestic tales stage the Highlands as an opening of
utopian possibility out of the cataclysm of European states. With the striking exception of Christian Johnstone's *Clan-Albin* (1815), which explores
the world-historical conditions of that opening in a dialectic between internal and external colonialisms (Ireland, the Highland Clearances, North
American settlement) made visible through imperial war with France,
these novels make regional difference the private enclave, preserved from
history, of a virtuous domesticity that repairs the faults of fashionable life.
The most formally accomplished works in the tradition, Mary Brunton's
second novel *Discipline* (1814) and Susan Ferrier's first novel *Marriage*
(1818), follow *The Wild Irish Girl* in making the Highlands the destiny
for a conjugal reformation of gender relations, the didactic burden of the
marriage plot. In other respects both novels pursue the satirical antithesis
between national character and fashionable life developed by Edgeworth.
The instability of the blend of models, satirical and romantic, expresses
these works' critical struggle with their program, especially Ferrier's. Restoring the feminine progress plot of domestic fiction, Brunton and Ferrier
send their heroines (and, in the satirical opening of *Marriage*, an anti-
heroine) from London to a Highland marriage via a course of moral refinement.[23] Reaffirming the Enlightenment protocol of culture as improvement, in an ambivalent dialectic of domestication, the Highland settlement represents at once a retreat from the world, the historical domain
of social relations, and an exemplary transformation of those relations
within the private politics of marriage.[24]

Brunton's Ellen Percy grows up in metropolitan luxury, loses her father and fortune, and makes her way north: at first to Edinburgh, where she is obliged to work for a living and is briefly confined in a lunatic asylum, at last to the Highlands. There, suitably chastened, she marries the novel's Mr. Knightly figure, who for his part has undergone a metamorphosis from the austere West India merchant Mr. Maitland to the glamorous chief of Glen Eredine, Henry Graham. As Ellen approaches the Highlands, the new setting condenses in the thick description of landscape and manners, ballasted with words and phrases in Gaelic and extensive ethnographic footnotes, in one of which the author feels moved to attest to the reality effect: "the only merit which the Highland scenes in Discipline presume to claim, is, that, however inartificially joined, they are all borrowed from fact."[25] At first the onset of local color does not fail to include an allowance of dirt: "the earthen floor, as well as an oaken table, which stood in the middle of it, was covered with the *debris* of cheese, oat-cakes, and raw onions, intermixed with slops of whisky" (3:201). The traveller's topos of North British nastiness registers a liminal disgust as Ellen enters the country, but that passes once she settles in Glen Eredine.[26] Later, Ellen visits Cecil Graham's cottage and finds it poor and smoke stained, but decent. Smoke, the metonymy of a material sublimation as well as of the domestic hearth, is a recurrent figure in Brunton's Highlands: a fragrantly ethereal form of dirt, at least outside cities. "Beyond, in a sheltered valley, the evening smokes floating among the copse-wood alone betrayed the hamlets, concealed by their own unobtrusive chastity of colouring" (3:213): the sentence delicately echoes the close of Virgil's first Eclogue. That poem, which celebrates the settlement of civil war veterans on farms expropriated for their use, achieved a peculiar resonance in the Highlands after 1746: "Guglielmus Cumbriae Dux nobis haec otia fecit," read the inscription on the foundation stone of the Duke of Argyll's grand new castle at Inveraray.[27]

The density of descriptive reference signalizes our entry into a zone of cultural difference, and not, as in *Cottagers of Glenburnie*, of cultural lack: characterized, however, once Ellen is inside this world, by the sublimation rather than materialization of premodern social and economic relations. Culture inheres in a magical economy of autopurification. Ellen's epithets for Glen Eredine, "the native land of strong attachment" (2:281) and "the land of imagination" (3:230), specify a sentimental and metaphoric, rather than literal and genetic, field of anthropological gravity. Her subjunctive invocations of the trope of fostering, associated with the sentimental modernization of Highland kinship in Scottish Romantic fiction, further displace the "native" relations it invokes: "in less than a week, I was as much at home as if I had been born in Glen Eredine" (3:216); "I was as much domesticated at Eredine as if I had already been a daughter of the family" (3:231).[28] The imaginary valence of Ellen's (and our) attachment to a primitive kinship network generates the effect of a "total domesticity," in Peter Womack's phrase, extolled in her rapturous peroration:

> But far beyond my own walls extend the charities of kindred. Many a smoke, curling in the morning sun, guides my eye to the abode of true, though humble friends; for every one of this faithful romantic race is united to me by the ties of relationship. I am the mother of their future chieftain. Their interests, their joys, their sorrows, are become my own. (3:275–76)

A biologically real relation, motherhood, is named after all (although projected into a future beyond the text) as the key to the new regime. The ideologically soft fantasy of an organic community sustained by maternal bonds of love and trust relies, however, on the hard figure of a hereditary ruler that the mother is pledged to reproduce.

The domestic economy of Glen Eredine shimmers between traditional and modern formations, somewhat inconsistently with the acknowledgment of a post-1745 historical setting. In Edinburgh, Ellen learns "how much the innovations and oppressions of twenty years had defaced the bold peculiarities of Highland character; how, stripped of their national garb, deprived of the weapons which were at once their ornament, amusement, and defence, this hardy race had bent beneath their fate, seeking safety in evasion, and power in deceit" (2:293–94). Such knowledge remains confined to Edinburgh and is effectively forgotten once Ellen enters the Highlands. A discreet, sentimentally tempered program of improvement maintains the organic community at Glen Eredine. Henry Graham's benevolent plans for the estate, like M'Leod's in *Ennui*, are "minute and practicable, rather than magnificent":

> No whole communities were to be hurried into civilization, nor districts depopulated by way of improvement; but some encouragement was to be given to the schoolmaster; bibles were to be distributed to his best scholars; or Henry would account to his father for the rent of a tenant, who, with his own hands, had reclaimed a field from rock and broom; or, at his expense, the new cottages were to be plastered, and furnished with doors and sashed windows. (3:194)

The capital for these improvements comes, presumably, from the fortune Maitland has made in the West Indies, rather than from Glen Eredine rents. In a further displacement, we learn of Maitland's vigorous opposition to the slave trade: somehow he has accumulated the profits that support the Highland estate without recourse to the atrocious exactions of plantation slavery (in which Scotsmen played a prominent part).[29] This makes the economic basis of the regime at Glen Eredine curiously fugitive and insubstantial. "Feudal habits were extinct; and the days were long since gone, when bands of kinsmen, united in one great family, repaid hospitality and protection with more than filial veneration and love,"

Ellen assures the reader (3:223). A few pages later, however, she observes "the tenantry of Glen Eredine, assembled to cut down the landlord's corn; a service which they were bound to perform without hire. Yet never, in scenes professedly devoted to amusement, had I witnessed such animating hilarity as cheered this unrewarded labour" (3:226–27). It seems feudal habits are not quite extinct after all, or rather, that they persist outside the material frame of a feudal economy as a form of play, mirroring the landlord's prerogative of leisure: a free labor rewarded by its own affective surplus of "animating hilarity."

This free labor stands, alongside Maitland's slavery-free West Indian wealth, for the invisible, sanitized, magical productivity that sustains Glen Eredine. One of the key tropes of the Highland Arcadia—perhaps the key trope of its sublimation of material conditions—free labor formally cancels the basis of regional representation in a historical economy that Edgeworth established in *Castle Rackrent*: turning *Castle Rackrent* into the satirical demystification of this solution *avant la lettre*. As Scott put the case in his 1816 review of "Culloden Papers," the opening of the Highlands to a money economy, following the suppression of the clans, completed the region's transmutation from a historical reality vested in local social relations into a "faery ground for romance and poetry, or subject of experiment for the professors of speculation, political and economical."[30] Of the Waterloo-era proponents of the Highland Arcadia, only Johnstone in *Clan-Albin* works out a historical narrative of redemptive modernization which locates the source for a providential mode of production in the vision of a global sentimental commonwealth that transcends its violent imperial origins. In the novel's address to a very immediate social crisis, comprising the "massive demobilization and a flow of poverty-stricken migrants from the countryside" as well as the passage of the Corn Laws in 1815,[31] the war veterans who resettle the emptied glen (echoes of Virgilian pastoral again) receive economic assistance from the former natives, who have emigrated to Canada and prospered there; they send home their surplus grain until the new Highlanders are able to institute agricultural improvements and support themselves. Johnstone provides the logic of sublimation that sustains the Highland Arcadia with a contemporary map, extending from Ireland through Spain to North America, which shows, in effect, that the material sources of national character now lie abroad, in the imperial reaches of a modern world system.

BEAUTY

In Susan Ferrier's *Marriage* the benevolent Mrs. Douglas narrates the improvement of the Highland estate of Lochmarlie by a variant of "free labor":

When we first took possession of this spot, it was a perfect wilderness, with a dirty farm-house on it; nothing but mud about the doors, nothing but wood, and briers, and brambles beyond it; and the village presented a still more melancholy scene of rank luxuriance, in its swarms of dirty idle girls, and mischievous boys. I have generally found, that wherever an evil exists, the remedy is not far off; and in this case, it was strikingly obvious. It was only engaging these ill-directed children, by trifling rewards, to apply their lively energies in improving instead of destroying the works of nature, as had formerly been their zealous practice. In a short time, the change on the moral as well as the vegetable part of creation became very perceptible: the children grew industrious and peaceable; and, instead of destroying trees, robbing nests, and worrying cats, the bigger boys, under Douglas' direction, constructed these wooden bridges and seats, or cut out and gravelled the little winding paths that we had previously marked out. The task of keeping everything in order is now easy, as you may believe, when I tell you the whole of our pleasure-grounds, as you are pleased to call them, receive no other attention than what is bestowed by children under twelve years of age.[32]

As in the case of Ellen Graham at Glen Eredine, Mrs. Douglas's status as the landlord's wife effects a displacement of the masculine registers of history and political economy. More rigorously than Brunton, Ferrier follows the logic of that displacement into an aesthetic discipline of domestication, in which taste defines the authority of a sublimated—symbolic, now, rather than literal—maternity. The relation of mother and child (as opposed to master and man) licenses play rather than work as the activity that transforms Lochmarlie from "a perfect wilderness, with a dirty farm-house on it" into "pleasure-grounds." The aesthetic conversion produces a scenic register of "matchless beauty":

> Before them lay the dark blue waters of Lochmarlie, reflecting, as in a mirror, every surrounding object, and bearing upon its placid transparent bosom a fleet of herring boats, the drapery of whose black suspended nets, contrasted with picturesque effect the white sails of the larger vessels, which were vainly spread to catch a breeze. (93–94)

The view discloses, in trim stylization, the suspension of economic activity—present in the scene but becalmed—as the condition of its "picturesque effect." Instead the landscape reflects "as in a mirror" its own status as a metonymy of Mrs. Douglas's virginal-motherly body ("bearing upon its placid transparent bosom . . . drapery . . . vainly spread"). Mrs. Douglas's beauty, unutilized as an erotic resource in the domestic economy, since she has borne no children, is poured instead into the landscape.

Lochmarlie offers a corrective contrast to the nearby estate of Glenfern. There the ladies' monopoly on domestic work deprives their tenants of productive employment. While they scold "half the poor women in the parish for their idleness, the bread was kept out of their mouths, by the incessant carding of wool and knitting of stockings, and spinning, and reeling, and winding, and pirning, that went on amongst the ladies themselves" (40). Their implacable industriousness deprives the ladies of the conditions of aesthetic enjoyment, leisure, and spectatorial distance that prevail at Lochmarlie. There is neither time nor room at Glenfern for the exercise of taste, the faculty through which character is purified and a proper domesticity established in Ferrier's fiction.[33]

The contrast between Glenfern and Lochmarlie complicates the larger satiric contrast between the Highlands and London that structures *Marriage*. Mrs. Douglas's domain provides a dialectical fulcrum for the turn from a double-barreled satire of provincial squalor and fashionable vanity à la Edgeworth, which takes up most of the novel, to an idyllic Highland settlement à la Brunton in the closing chapters. The early view of Lochmarlie, establishing its aesthetic credentials as the beautiful Highlands, punctuates the satirical narrative of a spoilt London belle's entry into Scottish provincial life. Lady Juliana's first view of Glenfern reads like a burlesque of Radcliffe's description of the heroine's approach to Udolpho:

> [J]ust at that moment they had gained the summit of a very high hill, and the post-boy stopping to give his horses breath, turned round to the carriage, pointing at the same time, with a significant gesture, to a tall thin grey house, something resembling a tower, that stood in the vale beneath. A small sullen looking lake was in front, on whose banks grew neither tree nor shrub. Behind, rose a chain of rugged cloud-capped hills, on the declivities of which, were some faint attempts at young plantations; and the only level ground, consisted of a few dingy turnip fields, enclosed with rude stone walls, or dykes, as the post-boy called them. It was now November; the day was raw and cold; and a thick drizzling rain was beginning to fall. . . . "What a scene!" at length Lady Juliana exclaimed, shuddering as she spoke; "Good God, what a scene! I pity the unhappy wretches who are doomed to dwell in such a place! and yonder hideous grim house; it makes me sick to look at it." . . . "Hooss!" replied the driver; "ca' ye thon a hoose? thon's gude Glenfern Castle." (9)[34]

The style of antiromance disappointment, with its lowering refusal even of a Gothic sublime, carries a reality effect absent from the idealized register of Lochmarlie, down to the speech and gestures of the driver. The main setting for the first volume of *Marriage*, Glenfern establishes the satirical version of Scotland as a realist norm. Its comic details of household disorder, fixed in the empirical register of a welter of particular sensory impressions, amplify the descriptive mode of *Glenburnie* and *Castle Rackrent* in a range of synesthetic effects. Lady Juliana experiences Glenfern as a nightmarish immersion in Scotch manners, expressions, clothes, objects, noises, tastes, and smells, from squalling bagpipes to "old cheese and herrings" at breakfast (30). The Scottish sequence mirrors the more conventional metropolitan satire of the remaining volumes. As Scotland is a hell to Lady Juliana, so is London a hell, or more strictly speaking a purgatory, to her Highland-bred daughter Mary. The crucial difference is that Mary undergoes the ordeal of a virtuous soul in a wicked world, while Scotch vulgarity mocks, even as it mortifies, the moral vulgarity of highborn Lady Juliana.

Yet after all *Marriage* closes much like *Discipline*, with the heroine's marriage to a Highland gentleman (Colonel Lennox), amid a now aesthetically purified scenery:

> [H]er feelings arose to rapture when Lochmarlie burst upon her view, in all the grandeur, beauty, and repose of a setting sun, shedding its farewell rays of gold and purple, and tints of such matchless hue, as no pencil can e'er imitate—no poet's pen describe. Rocks, woods, hills, and waters, all shone with a radiance that seemed of more than earthly beauty. (466)[35]

Here is abstraction indeed: casting even such material features as are named in the Platonic mode of general categories. Glenfern, and the satirical representation of Highland life as a chaos of redundant sense impressions, seem comprehensively transcended. Mary can view a sublime Lochmarlie because she has undergone moral sublimation through a series of disciplinary displacements from a native origin fixed in the perverse figure of the mother. Abandoned by Lady Juliana, Mary is brought up by Mrs. Douglas, who has herself submitted to a course of erotic renunciation—seeking refuge in a companionate marriage (and Highland exile) in order to suppress a forbidden passion. Mrs. Douglas's self-denial, informing her child rearing and pedagogy, braces Mary for the milder refinement of her trials in London. More decisively than Brunton, Ferrier channels national character into the ethical category of personal character, which she fixes in the scheme of a sanitizing alienation from genetic, especially maternal, origins. If fathers are not much good in *Marriage*, mothers—biological mothers—are worse: the logic overrides even the sentimental value that accrues to the hero's blind mother, whose passive-aggressive interference stalls the courtship plot.

This (Puritan) ethical discipline via an abstraction from origins yields aesthetic fruit in the precocious refinement of Mary's taste. In turn, the heroine's formation as an aesthetic subject fills the gap opened by her genetic alienation and reconstitutes her as exemplary national figure. The formation of her taste "on the wild romantic scenery of the Highlands" (253) grants Mary a critical distance from English standards that boosts her immunity to fashionable corruption:

[T]o Mary's eyes, the well dressed English rustic, trudging along the smooth path, was a far less picturesque object, than the bare-footed Highland girl, bounding over trackless heath-covered hills; and the well preserved glossy blue coat, seemed a poor substitute for the varied drapery of the graceful plaid. (254)

The act of aesthetic judgment casts Mary not as the Highland girl, the native of the scene, but as the refined spectator who can view the girl— image of her own childhood self—as a "picturesque object." The faculty of taste, in other words, also fixes a critical distance from the Highland world in which Mary has grown up. The narrator calls her "the refined yet unsophisticated child of nature" (198) in an attempt to split the difference between metropolitan sophistication and a refinement or cultivation which is yet congruent with "nature," or rather, reconstitutes nature as a pure aesthetic object. It is easy to parse the contrast with the vicious taste of Mary's mother and sister (and other sophisticated types, such as the habituées of Mrs. Bluemits's salon); less so the contrast with the coarse taste of her Glenfern aunts, who have also grown up, after all, amid romantic Highland scenery. The logic of sublimation makes the difference. The Highland setting exerts a beneficial influence on Mary, unlike her aunts, precisely because it remains for her *scenery*, a repertoire of aesthetic forms attached to Mrs. Douglas's model settlement, rather than a social-historical habitat, in which the natives (her aunts) are unreflectively embedded.

With a saintly patience Mary puts up with her aunts, the incorrigible representatives of Scotch vulgarity and unwitting scourges of her mother. Jacky, Grizzy, and Nicky, mired in the trivial particularities of daily life at Glenfern, personify the satirical version of national character as a muddy coagulation of the local and the customary. Together with their domineering neighbor Lady Maclaughlan and the Edinburgh dowager Violet Macshake they form a cast of eccentric elderly ladies who represent— more forcefully than any of the men—traditional Scottish character in *Marriage*. These ancient Scotswomen are also more potent than their southern equivalents (Mrs. Down Right, Mrs. Pullen, Mrs. Bluemits, et al.), generic types exhausted by their one-note satiric function.[36] Ferrier grants her Scots ladies a vitality that exceeds their typological frame of vulgarity or eccentricity. Lady Maclaughlan's entry into the story releases a cascade of bizarre descriptive detail that anticipates Flaubert's description of Charles Bovary's school cap:

Out of this equipage issued a figure, clothed in a light coloured, large flowered chintz raiment, carefully drawn through the pocket holes, either for its own preservation, or the more disinterested purpose of displaying a dark short stuff petticoat, which, with the same liberality, afforded ample scope for the survey of a pair of worsted stockings and black leather shoes, something resembling buckets. A faded red cloth jacket, which bore evident marks of having been severed from its native skirts, now acted in the capacity of a spencer. On the head was a stupendous fabric, in the form of a cap, on the summit of which was placed a black beaver hat, tied *à la poissarde*. (43)

This is not so much unfashionable as antifashionable, a sublime tastelessness rather than bad taste. The excess of detail marks, in Lady Maclaughlan's case, a reversal of the ratio between character and environment that governs the Glenfern aunts: a disquieting moral excess, not without a pathos the more potent for its confinement to exterior signs: "in spite of her ridiculous dress and eccentric manners, an air of dignity was diffused over her whole person, that screened her from the ridicule to which she must otherwise have been exposed" (45).

Metonymic detail overflows its satirical matrix to make a perverse claim on moral authority, at the close of the marriage plot, licensed by the program that was meant to improve it out of sight. The aunts remain—they hold forth to the very end—as permanent exhibits in the gallery of comic types. Their sheer persistence has turned into a virtue: unlike the unstable creatures of fashion they are reliably, however murkily, true to themselves. More striking is the functional conversion of Lady Maclaughlan. The early part of the novel casts her as a burlesque witch, another comic instrument of Lady Juliana's scarification, brewing vile potions in an "enormous kettle" in her "laboratory" at the top of a tower (104–5). In the final chapter she emerges as an authentic wise woman. Like her London avatar, witty Lady Emily, she foresees the end of the marriage plot: "I know all," she admonishes Mary, "I wished you to marry him" (463). More than that: she helps make it happen, managing a Highland backstory (about an ancient family feud) that pops up at the last moment, vestigial but nonetheless forceful enough to block the resolution for a few pages. Any remaining embarrassments are removed by the convenient death of Lady Maclaughlan's own marital appendage Sir Sampson, the most grotesque and least human of all the novel's characters, on the wedding day. In a final speech Miss Grizzy credits Mary with having "had a hand in dear Sir Sampson's death," and congratulates her on her succession to the occult arts of Lady Maclaughlan's laboratory (468). It seems that these old Scotswomen may still command a residual magic.

More generously than *Cottagers of Glenburnie* or *Ennui*, *Marriage* saves room for those unimproved national characters whose quirks and crotchets give the fiction its spice—acknowledges, even, that they supply the main savor for many readers. Ferrier's unimproved characters embody a resistance (however local and limited) to the ascendant regime of taste, with its tendency to polish characters to an interchangeable surface, described by Leah Price (and thus constitute more interesting works than her critique admits).[37] Such characters are rarer in Ferrier's later novels. *The Inheritance* (1824), her second, features the most recalcitrant of them all, the old-fashioned, misanthropic country laird Adam Ramsay. At first "Uncle Adam" takes the stage as another type, a Juvenalian reduction of the book's satirical tendency, the vehemence of whose contempt for the world reconstitutes its imaginary power over him.[38] As the story unfolds, however, his voice (he is the novel's main Scots speaker) becomes the medium of a rugged integrity, revealing his true character as a "national" descendant of the eccentric, embittered but virtuous Albany in Burney's *Cecilia* or the Man of the Hill in *Tom Jones*. When the heroine Gertrude "love[s] with all the delusion of romance" (2:203–4) it is Uncle Adam who is perceptive enough to be disappointed in her. Better than the sentimental heroine (whose disciplinary plot is squeezed into the last few pages), Uncle Adam fulfils the positive side of the antinomy between primitive virtue and metropolitan mores that organizes *The Inheritance*. The London excursion in the final chapters produces the most schematic critique of "the arbitrary and capricious mechanism of the fashionable world" (3:79) to be found in any of these novels. The "unceasing whirl" of fashionable life, the "vortex of elegant dissipation" (3:85), revolves around "the nameless *je ne sai quoi*" (3:77) that structures metropolitan desire. Against this fantastic system, Scots character—embodied in Uncle Adam—promises, at least, a reassuringly stable, solid world of *things*.

ENJOYMENT

Ferrier completed *Marriage* after reading the early Waverley novels, and no doubt Scott's example informed her combination of the two modes, satiric and aesthetic, of representing national character.[39] Edward Waverley's first view of Tully-Veolan, like Lady Juliana's of Glenfern, reiterates an Edgeworthian, Hamiltonian stress on the poverty and dirt of the outlying clachan:

> In a few favoured instances, there appeared behind the cottages a miserable wigwam, compiled of earth, loose stones, and turf, where the wealthy might perhaps shelter a starved cow or sorely galled horse. But almost every hut was fenced in front by a huge black stack of turf on one side of the door, while on the other the family dung-hill ascended in noble emulation.[40]

The view is sentimentally cleansed by the end of the novel. The general crisis of civil war mobilizes traditional virtues of allegiance that (it seems) have lain latent in this squalor, as the tenants rally around their hunted landlord. The manor is ransacked and then restored, but the hamlet stays out of sight, forgotten, at the end of the story. Throughout the central action of the novel, Tully-Veolan—the present-tense scene of regional social difference—has been displaced by Waverley's excursion into the Highlands, through which such difference can be reconfigured as a doomed historical anteriority. In plotting a historical as well as moral and aesthetic logic of improvement, nevertheless, Scott collectivizes national character as the quality of a traditional society, a whole way of life, rather than of an exemplary individual: even as its destiny consists in a translation to the aesthetic forms of "tradition" and "culture," salvaged from the wreck as trophies for the polite hero and the novel's readers.[41]

Scott's subsequent novels vary, sometimes radically, the allegory of salvage through which culture is produced in *Waverley*, not least when they turn away from the Highlands. Scott claimed to have founded *The Antiquary*, the "domestic" novel in his early trilogy, on the conventional antithesis between the customary life of regional communities and the restructuring impetus of plot, now associated (the novel is set in 1794) with revolution rather than improvement. This is crucial: a fully modern recuperation of local social difference as culture takes place when it can be cast as a bulwark against revolution rather than as a roadblock to improvement. In the preface to *The Antiquary* Scott reviews the Enlightenment account of national character as a residual byproduct of uneven development:

> I have . . . sought my principal personages in the class of society who are the last to feel the influence of that general polish which assimilates to each other the manners of different nations. Among the same class I have placed some of the scenes, in which I have endeavoured to illustrate the operation of the higher and more violent passions; both because the lower orders are less restrained by the habit of suppressing their feelings, and because I agree with Mr Wordsworth, that they seldom fail to express them in the strongest and most powerful language. This is, I think, peculiarly the case with the peasantry of my own country, a class with whom I have been long familiar.[42]

In a Romantic reversal of the Enlightenment scheme, the author now values the gritty particularity of national character over the "general polish" of modernization. (The formula persists as late as James Frazer's 1890 preface to *The Golden Bough*.) Scott also reverses the classical hierarchy that granted "the higher and more violent passions" and "the strongest and most powerful language" to royalty and aristocracy: modern literature locates passion and eloquence, markers of the prestige genre of tragedy, with the premodern class of "peasantry." The narrative that follows (as I show in chapter 5) balks the onward flow of plot, and dissipates the tragic force of catastrophe, for a dense capillary enfolding of the materi-

als—antiquities, dialect, custom and tradition, loyalty and obligation—
that constitute a national culture, a regionally grounded way of life.

The "peasantry" play a limited part in *The Antiquary*; the Words-
worthian promise of Scott's preface is more faithfully redeemed, for example, in the Border tales of James Hogg. Scott's revision of the Hamil-
ton-Edgeworth topos of the poor people's dirty cottage is all the more
forceful, nevertheless, for its adherence to the decorum of polite ethnography. This unprepossessing interior will turn out to house the core of memory and information in the novel, its archive of the tragic potential of
plot. All of which is a distraction from the scene's authentic interest:

> We must now introduce our reader to the interior of the fisher's cottage men-
> tioned in chapter eleventh of the first volume of this edifying history. I wish
> I could say that its inside was well arranged, decently furnished, or tolerably
> clean. On the contrary, I am compelled to admit, there was confusion, —
> there was dilapidation, —there was dirt good store. Yet, with all this, there
> was about the inmates, Luckie Mucklebackit and her family, an appearance
> of ease, plenty, and comfort, that seemed to warrant their own sluttish prov-
> erb, "The clartier the cosier." (210)

Scott renders "dirt good store" as the very medium of culture, rather than
its lack, through a crucial recognition of the natives' enjoyment of their
way of life. The MacClartys' equivalent enjoyment at Glenburnie was
nothing more than indolence, a vacancy waiting to be filled by middle-
class purposiveness. But these Mucklebackits are nothing if not hard-
working—they risk death plying their trade—and their enjoyment carries
a moral force. They utter the sharpest gloss, in any Romantic novel, on
the logic of abstraction and reification that improvement brings: "it's no
fish ye're buying—it's men's lives" (89). "The clartier the cosier": the
narrator acknowledges the mysterious subjective substance of collective
identification that makes up what Slavoj Žižek calls the "national Thing":
"something accessible only to us . . . present in that elusive entity called
'our way of life,' " immanent in "the way our community organizes its
feasts, its rituals of mating, its initiation rituals, in short, all the details by
which is made visible the unique way a community *organizes its enjoyment.*"[43] The narrator acknowledges this enjoyment without making it
transparent to us—it is dirt, therefore unassimilable—at the same time as
he insists on its equivalence with middle-class values: "an appearance of
ease, plenty, and comfort."

The scene is not simply reconstituted as an aesthetic object by our social
distance from it, then, since the narrator makes the natives' enjoyment
of their world a condition of our enjoyment of his representation. Their
enjoyment, no doubt, secures that distance by reassuring us that this set
of poor people (a family of fisherfolk, not hand-loom weavers) entertains

no disagreeable wish to change their (and our) condition. Nevertheless the reflexive structure of the enjoyment remains critical. With the recognition of an aesthetically productive opacity, Scott formally designates the work of fiction itself as the medium of an enjoyment that does not fall under a pedagogic sentence of renunciation.

TRAFFIC

Eclipsed after 1815 by Scott's historical novels, the national domestic tale reappears, in strange mutation, in John Galt's *Sir Andrew Wylie of That Ilk* (1822), published at the height of the vogue for Scottish fiction in the early 1820s. Eschewing the historicization of Scottish life opened up by Scott and pursued in Galt's own *Annals of the Parish* and *The Provost*, *Sir Andrew Wylie* resumes the domestic tale's address to the problem of national character as a problem of character as such, in the singular, typical, and ethical sense. Instead of following the feminine displacement into an aesthetic register, à la Ferrier, Galt returns the plot of an "entrance into the world"—that is, the market—to a male protagonist. The national character as self-made man: *Sir Andrew Wylie* struck many readers as being in the worst possible taste. "I have not read 'Sir Andrew Wyllie' [*sic*]," Ferrier herself protested, "as I can't endure that man's writings, and I'm told the vulgarity of this *beats print*."[44] Henry Mackenzie complained that Galt had "got among a Rank & class of men, of whose manners & language he seems perfectly ignorant, & has therefore drawn a picture as devoid of truth as of taste."[45] If earlier novels waver between a satirical representation of national character as dirt and a romantic representation of it as pure source or transcendent telos, Galt narrates its formation in a money economy. The historical position of *Sir Andrew Wylie*, looking back at an earlier phase of Scottish fiction from the other side of *Waverley*, allows it to reflect—with a clarity unmatched in British Romantic fiction—upon the structural constitution of novelistic character, along with its analogue culture, as a sublimation of the commodity form: in Deidre Lynch's phrase, "the repository of a value that is valuable in the absence of relations of exchange" yet is produced through those relations.[46] *Sir Andrew Wylie* represents national character as the dialectical product of primitive virtue and exchange value—and the story goes to unsettling lengths before it makes origins, in the end, trump exchange.

Sir Andrew Wylie recounts the wonderful self-making of a Scots lad o' pairts in London. Andrew enters parliament and the highest social circles, becomes a baronet, and returns home in triumph to marry the laird's daughter. This version of a popular Scottish fable (from Smollett's *Roderick Random* to Alasdair Gray's *The Fall of Kelvin Walker*) allegorizes, with optative force, Galt's own career as a successful author of Scottish fiction in a metropolitan rather than regional literary market, in which the triumph of his works over rival forms depends upon the claim on an authentic representation of national character. *Sir Andrew Wylie* thus reflects on the larger fortunes of Scottish fiction at its zenith in the early 1820s. London, more decisively than Edinburgh or Glasgow, constitutes Galt's achievement as one of national character, a writing that derives aesthetic status, the exchange value of its originality, from its difference from the standardized products of the metropolitan core. Accordingly, the novel casts London no longer simply as the alien medium of "fashionable life" (although it remains that) but also as the market to which Andrew must go in order to realize his own value.

Character, the repository of an original virtue, is Andrew Wylie's prime asset and the engine of his advancement. An only child and orphan, he is brought up in an old-fashioned Ayrshire village by his maternal grandmother, "one of those clachan carlins who keep alive among the Scottish peasantry the traditions and sentiments which constitute so much of the national character."[47] Andrew may not acquire this cultural capital passively, like an inheritance; he has to work for it. From an early age the boy sedulously cultivates the sources, interests, and affections from which national character blooms. He keeps company with "travelling tinklers, blue-gowns [and] old soldiers" and frequents the "firesides of the gash and knacky carles and carlins of the village" (1:27; the language mimics the organic milieu). At Edinburgh studying law, he continues to savor "the knacky conversation of old and original characters" (1:58), until he perfects for himself "a happy vernacular phraseology which he retained through life, and, with those who had a true relish of character, was enjoyed as something as rare and original as the more elegant endowment of genius" (1:8). Later, Wylie's London friends marvel "that he should have retained his Scottish accent so perfectly" even at the height of his career. It cannot be a social residue, a dirt of origins, for "he appears to have always cherished his national affections upon principle" (3:262)— he could have washed his speech of Scotticisms, presumably, had he wished to. On his return to Ayrshire, Wylie easily resumes "the broad accent of his boyish dialect," since "he had carefully and constantly preserved it"— even though he has picked up "a few terms and phrases purely English" as well as a "considerable purity of language" (i.e., grammar, 3:130). Andrew's Scottishness is an identity at once original and chosen, maintained through a painstaking labor of conservation and performance.

National character is thus available for appreciation by connoisseurs ("those who had a true relish of character"), including the reader, but only because Wylie has first relished and cultivated it himself. In London, it supplies the "gusto" or aesthetic aura that grants him access to circles from which rank ought to exclude him. The Earl of Sandyford, diverted by Andrew's "originality," invites him to a masquerade, where Andrew is self-assured enough to maintain his provincial persona. "This simple reply was received as original humour, and much amused the high-bred assemblage, by both its gusto and familiarity. Sir Timothy Knicketty, the connoisseur, who was of the party, declared it was truly à la Teniers" (1:132). At once an original virtue and an effect produced in performance, national character enables Wylie (like his author) to outperform metropolitan styles and genres, commercially exhausted into a sheerly mechanical conventionalism. (This prowess is represented by Wylie's ability to resolve the hackneyed plots of three-volume Regency fiction.) Galt's hero exemplifies the modern technology of character theorized by Adam Smith in The Theory of Moral Sentiments and Lectures on Rhetoric and Belles-Lettres. He practices a self-fashioning through acts of rhetorical and sentimental exchange with other selves in civil society, with the notable difference from Smith's prescriptions that Wylie maintains his Scottish origins as the foundation of his performance, rather than anglicizing his manners and speech. Sir Andrew Wylie illustrates with impressive clarity Janet Sorensen's argument that Scottish participation in the eighteenth-century standardization of English entailed the alienation and abstraction of Scots as well as English in order to produce these as (respectively) organic and imperial forms of national language. Galt's novel offers, however, a redemptive inversion of the case of Smollett, as analyzed by Sorensen: "In detaching linguistic and cultural identity from spatial locations, Smollett makes it available to Scots and English alike. Core/periphery spatial distinctions give way to distinctions of linguistic competency and, finally, taste—which are in turns distinctions of class."[48] As Mackenzie and Ferrier complained, Sir Andrew Wylie upsets taste and class distinctions in replanting national character on a linguistically demarcated regional soil.

As Wylie enjoys his first London season, the narrator reassures us that "his simplicity remained invincible to the blandishments of pleasure, and the sterling worth of his character raised him more and more in the estimation of Lord Sandyford." "I have hitherto lived among machines," exclaims Lord Sandyford, "but this is a human being" (1:146). In Wylie, as Francis Hart comments, "provinciality of character has become virtually a force of natural magic."[49] Simplicity and sentiment are realized, not corrupted, in the imperial mart; organic virtue and exchange value guarantee one another. All the same, the ethical form of a contradiction vexes the story. Andrew's fine friends begin to wonder at "a degree of system in the simplicity of his manners": "beneath his simplicity he has not only the slyness of a fox, but the ambition of an ancient personage too shocking to be named to ears polite" (3:99, 100). After all Wylie is prompt to exploit his simplicity, ingratiating himself with his betters and establishing an ascendancy over them. Himself a man of feeling, he elicits sentiment in others—as though his surplus fills up their deficit—and then manages it. "[A]ctuated by gratitude and affection," he brings about a reconciliation between Lord Sandyford and his wife, quite aware, however, "that in their happiness he had obtained a fulcrum for the engines that were to raise his own fortune" (2:300). Wylie lends money to a former school friend who has wasted his fortune, but under humiliating conditions, taking control of his friend's life and redefining their relationship to one between patron and client. Galt's narrative, not just the view of baffled friendship, keeps glimpsing the shadow of a will to power investing Andrew's performance. This ethical disturbance issues in the novel's marriage plot, a narrative supplement that retroactively rewrites the psychic energy of the hero's rise so as to invest it with moral authenticity.

Andrew's friends can only satisfy their suspicions of a foxy slyness and devilish ambition beneath his simplicity by digging even deeper, to posit a "romantic motive at the bottom of the principles by which he has been so long and so constantly actuated" (3:101). The "national affections" Wylie has cherished must encompass "some rustic beauty [who] had early interested him" (3:263). The rustic beauty exists; she is Andrew's childhood playmate Mary Cunningham. The narrator has assured us that simplicity is the original medium of the children's affection, preceding the alienating onset of sexual and social desire: "They were themselves unconscious of the tie with which simplicity had innocently linked them together—and being as yet both free from the impulses of passion, they felt not the impediments which birth and fortune had placed between them" (1:24). The reiteration of this early love towards the end of the novel reaffirms simplicity as the authentic core of Wylie's character, the germ of an affection that redeems a career that, up until now, had seemed in no need of a sentimental economy of redemption. Wylie has striven so hard and climbed so high, after all, for a childhood sweetheart.

Close to his goal, Andrew experiences a surprising, if momentary, ethical crisis. The "acquiescence of another's will and affections" makes courtship unexpectedly challenging. Andrew suspects that Mary loves another—the former school friend, Charles Pierston, he has reduced to a client. At first this provokes a chivalrous impulse: "I can prove that I wasna unworthy of her love." He'll bring Charles back from India and give him his own estate and fortune so that he will be able to marry Mary. But Wylie's romantic resolution is short-lived. He goes on to meditate, more interestingly, that Mary is not the only woman he might think of. "She's neither so bonny nor so blithesome as fifty others I hae seen." In other words, he begins to regard her in the light of a commodity, as belonging to a marriage market. He protests: "I'll ne'er take a portion of a divided heart" (3:226–27). The desire of a rival produces the beloved in the light of an exchange value; but in this case—contrary to René Girard's theory of mimetic desire and the nationalist variant described by Ian Dennis—it threatens an alienation of the hero's affection, generated before desire and the market.[50] As it turns out, Andrew will not have to take his love to market, since no rival stands between him and Mary after all. What the narrator calls "habitual affection" fulfils itself in their union.

Their union stands as a rebuke to the conventional trajectory of the Scot who makes his fortune in London and stays there. It seals Galt's revision of the national allegory of union with the assertion of a regional domestic bond—reaching across a local difference of rank—instead of a cross-regional, British one. Nevertheless, as the novel moves towards its conclusion, symbolic energy drains away from Andrew and Mary to gather around the humors and crotchets of Mary's father, the Laird of Craiglands. The cranky old gentleman, not despite but because of his reactionary whims, ends up being the repository of national character more convincingly than Andrew himself. He plays the same anomalous role as Adam Ramsay in *The Inheritance* or the elderly Scots ladies in *Marriage*—showing us that the anomaly is structurally fundamental to these stories. The old laird's death generates a pathos that overwhelms the comic closure of the marriage plot. With the return home Galt's narrative regresses to an elegiac emphasis on the elder generation, as it celebrates a whimsical patriarch whose passing signifies an extinction of national character. Failing to sustain the argument that an original virtue can reproduce itself without loss of aura in the marketplace, the novel backs into nostalgia after all. It is telling that the last of Galt's Blackwoodian sequence of "Tales of the West," far from being a sequel to *Sir Andrew Wylie* (*Sir Andrew in Upper Canada . . .*), takes up the manuscript found among the Laird's papers after his death: "a most full account of all manner of particularities anent the decay of the ancient families of the West Country." This would be published, bowdlerized without Galt's consent, as *The Last of the Lairds* in 1826.

Chapter 4

❧

MODERNITY'S OTHER WORLDS

SCOTT'S HIGHLANDS

The Highland piper on the banks of the Tweed: in *Peter's Letters to His Kinsfolk* Lockhart follows Scott's own adaptation of the tropes of "picturesque tourism" to represent national manners to a modern reading public.[1] Contemporaries picked up on the association between Scott's fiction and an ascendant tourist industry. Writing in his periodical the *Spy* in 1811, James Hogg made fun of the vogue for viewing Highland scenery through the lens of *The Lady of the Lake*:

> Whoever goes to survey the Trossacks, let him have the 11th, 12th, and 13th division of the first canto of the *Lady of the Lake* in his heart; a little Highland whisky in his head; and then he shall see the most wonderful scene that nature ever produced. If he goes without any of these necessary ingredients, without one verse of poetry in his mind, and "Without a drappie in his noddle;" he may as well stay at home; he will see little, that shall either astonish or delight him.[2]

A few years later, the *Edinburgh Magazine* complained of "steam-boat parties of cockneys" invading the Highland setting of Scott's latest novel: "all the world of tourists have been pouring from every corner of the kingdom to visit [Rob Roy's] cave."[3]

Lockhart's version of Scott—conflating the Author of *Waverley* with the Laird of Abbotsford, fusing Scotland's historical and legendary geography with Scott's fictional settings—retains critical currency today, with a censorious emphasis falling on the false consciousness of a wholesale ideological program. Scott's fiction is an "invention of tradition" or "invention of Scotland" that folds the modern nation into the defeated Jacobite Highlands; tourism and historical romance compose the symbolic arm of an Anglo-British "internal colonialism."[4] The destruction of clan society after Culloden provided the historical condition not just for domestic national unity but for a modern literary tradition, founded by James Macpherson's "Poems of Ossian" in the early 1760s. *Fingal* and *Temora* established a new cultural station of inauthenticity, somewhere between translation and forgery, as the address of an invented tradition in modern

letters. Antiquarian reconstruction and poetic fantasy combine to produce the image of a vanished ancestral nation, glamorously remote and
strange. Modern cultural historians, especially, follow Lockhart in casting
Scott as "a second M'Pherson" who perfected the invention of tradition—
the reduction of Gaeldom to the trophy of a nostalgic pseudonational-
ism—with a plausible historicism and a virtuoso rhetoric of fiction.[5]

The account of Scott as master ideologue of internal colonialism con-
verges with Benedict Anderson's claim on the particular efficacy of the
novel in producing the "imagined community" of the modern nation. As
its narrative invokes a temporal simultaneity across the diverse spaces and
populations of the national territory, the novel synchronizes its reader's
subjectivity with a calendrical order of "homogeneous, empty time," in
an imaginary standardization that marches with projects of political,
legal, and economic rationalization.[6] The ideological force of Scott's novels lies in their explicit representation of modernization as an overdetermined historical process, in which a complex set of social and psychic
transformations comes to bear on an inevitable outcome: here and now,
the real world, the commercial society of the post-1707 United Kingdom.
The historical novel consummates the novel's historical agenda by making
it its theme. Recent criticism of Romantic fiction, modifying Anderson,
attends to the imperial, globalizing force field of the emergent modern
world system as the political-economic crucible of nationalist ideologies.
Internal and external forces of colonization, acting upon domestic as well
as foreign peripheries within the reach of empire, together produce the
modern nation-state; romantic national tales and historical novels reflect
on the assimilation of Scotland and Ireland into the Union as at once
condition and consequence of British imperial ventures overseas. Romantic writing expresses the historical immanence of "universal empire"
through its "fascination . . . with the pre- or anti-modern (Nature, the
colonial realm, the Orient)," constructing a dialectical opposition between the "virtual form" of a planetary political economy and the "fractured, disjointed, and disruptive temporalities" of those other spaces
that fall under empire's shadow.[7] These poles of representation—universal empire and the naturally or culturally differentiated settings found
at the margins and interstices of modernity—organize the imaginary
geography of Romantic nationalism. The "tidal wave of modernization"[8]
reveals chronotopic difference—the temporal as well as spatial layering
of distance from the metropolis—as the condition it is in the process of
overwhelming.

The nation-forming project of the historical novel, in Moretti's phrase,
is "to represent internal unevenness, no doubt; and then, to *abolish* it."[9]
The relation between the abolition of internal unevenness and its representation in the potent synecdoche of a regionally based "national charac-

ter" constituted the ideological problematic, rather than simply the agenda, of Scottish fiction before Scott's entry into the field. The previous chapter traced the shift of that problematic from an Enlightenment understanding of "culture" as economic and moral improvement (requiring the abolition of unevenness) towards the Romantic conception of it, analyzed in its fully ideological articulation in chapter 2, as medium for the preservation of "unevenness" in aesthetic forms of value. The present chapter brings critical pressure to bear on the consensus that views the Waverley novels as the instrument of an imperial ideology of official nationalism. The impulse to read Scott's novels as closing down the formal and political potentialities of Romantic-era fiction has made it harder, perhaps, to attend to all that they opened up—as though their author's counterrevolutionary politics must have determined a general dynamic of closure.[10] Yet opening up, rather than closure, characterizes the revolutionary impact of these novels on the nineteenth-century literary field, and here I shall explore that opening.

Scott's narrative of national formation, according to a powerful recent analysis, converts a spatial or geographical order of difference into a temporal, historical difference governed by the teleology of modernization. This conversion, formally established in Scottish Enlightenment philosophical history, defines the world-historical epistemic project summarized by Reinhart Koselleck: "The geographical opening up of the globe brought to light various but coexisting cultural levels which were, through the process of synchronous comparison, then ordered diachronically."[11] Cultural differences fall into a receding, insatiable past. In Waverley, the hero's (and the reader's) enchanted discovery of Highland clan society signals its translation from a remote place to the remote time of a vanishing premodernity. The contemplation of this lost world converts our disaffection from the imperial violence of modern state formation into a luxurious, aestheticized melancholy. Sentimental distance is secured by Scott's highlighting of the techniques of inauthenticity, the devices of "translation and tourism" (in James Buzard's phrase) that mediate the reader's, as well as the protagonist's, historical difference from the Gaelic world, such as the portrait of the English hero wearing Highland dress unveiled in the last scene of Waverley. Such devices encode the formation of a distinctively modern kind of national subjectivity, in which the knowledge of our alienation from authentic cultural identities accompanies our privileged repossession of them as aesthetic effects.[12]

Modern criticism of Scott's Highland romances, referring almost exclusively to Waverley, insists upon this elegiac cadence. Whether they evoke nostalgic enchantment or a more ironical self-fashioning, Scott's Highlands are the scenery of a lost world locked in the past. Scott himself reflects upon the elegiac, posthistorical construction of the Highlands in an article, "Culloden Papers," published two years after *Waverley* in the *Quarterly Review*. He traces the modern history of the Highlands to its contemporary terminus in the Clearances, the landlords' eviction of unprofitable tenantry to make way for sheep farming. Contrary to some accounts of his views, Scott admits a somber protest against the human costs of economic development. History comes to an end as a landscape is emptied of human lives and made into a blank page for competing discourses of "speculation":

> [I]n but too many instances, the glens of the Highlands have been drained, not of the superfluity of their population, but of the whole of their inhabitants, dispossessed by an unrelenting avarice, which will one day found to have been as short sighted as it is unjust and selfish. Meanwhile, the highlands may become the faery ground for romance and poetry, or subject of experiment for the professors of speculation, political and economical. —But if the hour of need should come—and it may not, perhaps, be far distant—the pibroch may sound through the deserted region, but the summons will remain unanswered. The children who have left her will re-echo from a distant shore the sounds with which they took leave of their own—Ha til, ha til, ha til, mi tulidh! —"We return—we return—we return—no more!"[13]

Against the rival claims of romance and political economy—both of which will be aired in a new novel with a Highland setting, *Rob Roy*— Scott poses the practical question (barely a year after Waterloo) of the future supply of those warriors who have defended the nation overseas since the elder Pitt raised Highland regiments in the Seven Years' War. The primitive skills of the colonized, as soldiers or as colonists in their turn, should be a valuable resource in the progress of empire. In adverting to a dynamic part still to be played by Highlanders in the nation's destiny, understood as an ongoing imperial history, Scott warns of the futility of elegy—even as he continues to sound it.

Scott's citation of the Gaelic lament "Cha till mi tuilleadh" alludes to Christian Isobel Johnstone's national tale of the Highland Clearances, *Clan-Albin*, published a few months after *Waverley* and reviewed in the *Quarterly*, April 1815. *Clan-Albin* traces the contemporary diaspora of Highlanders across the emergent world system when profiteering landlords, clearing their estates for sheep, force their tenants to choose between Canadian emigration and service in the French wars. Modern imperial war, waged on a planetary scale, turns out to generate a centripetal counterbalance to colonial dispersal. Mass mobilization provides for a new kind of communal framework by throwing together different subject peoples, uprooted from their native villages, who forge empire-wide networks of sentimental allegiance. At the end of the novel, veterans from all over Britain (not just the Highlands) return from victory in Spain to settle the evacuated glens. Ina Ferris aptly characterizes this countercolonization, repairing the disastrous clearances and reinventing the organic community, as a work of liberal utopian bricolage.[14] Meanwhile the Canadian settlers, thriving in their transplanted Clan-Albin, renew their bond with the homeland—not by coming back ("we return no more") but by sending surplus grain for famine relief, until their successors are able to institute agricultural improvements. World empire generates its own solution, in globalizing networks of colonization and capital, to the local disruptions and displacements of its start-up phase. Although as a novel Clan-Albin is a ramshackle affair, it unfolds an ideologically prescient vision of imperial commonwealth.

Johnstone's utopian declension of the dialectics of colonialism within a modern world system provoked Scott to look again at the end of Waverley, with its consignment of the clans to a romantic past and obliteration of their historical present. Scott's allusion, in "Culloden Papers," to the clearance episode early in Clan-Albin ("this the glen whose every echo was ringing—'We return, we return, we return no more!' ")[15] transmits the pathos evoked by Johnstone but refuses her utopian solace. Instead, the "re-echo" of the Gaelic lament forebodes a desolate future not just for the Highlands but for the larger national community. Scott's view of the historical effects of eviction and emigration recalls Samuel Johnson's more than it does Christian Johnstone's. Johnson's Journey to the Western Islands of Scotland (1775), the first major literary reckoning with the state of the country after 1746, offered a melancholy prognosis of Highland depopulation as symptom of an irreparable national decay, not an imperial strengthening—a premonition of the country's failure to enter commercial modernity, against the grain of Johnson's ideological commitment to such a destiny.[16] Scott's reiteration of the elegiac cry admits a critique—Johnsonian, Tory, melancholic—of the consolations offered both by Clan-Albin, looking hopefully to the future, and his own Waverley, looking back at the past.

The review of "Culloden Papers" should upset the critical tendency to make Waverley stand for Scott's work as a whole, a tendency that recasts chronological priority as a typological priority and reduces the novel to a fixed template of aesthetic and ideological effects. Until recently even Scott specialists have been inclined to brand Rob Roy, written and published the following year, a mere "Waverley novel," a repetition of the pattern that fails to sustain the first novel's formal and thematic coherence.[17] Yet Rob Roy remained the most popular of the Scottish romances well into the twentieth century; and while it may be the case that readers preferred a blurred reproduction to the original, it seems likelier that their enthusiasm registers a critical difference. Jane Millgate has argued that Scott's novels require the alert reader to interpret them in relation to one another, as an unfolding series of formal and thematic variations.[18] Falling between discrete series in the early succession of novels—the first trilogy "by the Author of Waverley," the *Tales of My Landlord*—the place of *Rob Roy* would not at first have been perspicuous to Scott's readers. It might have taught them to read through the apparent discontinuity (of period and setting) marked by *Ivanhoe*, the title with which the "Author of Waverley" resumed his career two years later; while the appearance of *Redgauntlet* (1824) would at last constitute *Rob Roy* as the middle work, after all, in a dispersed trilogy of Jacobite romances. Millgate points out that Scott draws attention to his return as the Author of *Waverley* in *Rob Roy*, revisiting not just the earlier novel's Highland setting but its basic plot of a romantic young Englishman, estranged from his father and profession, who ventures north into Scotland and becomes embroiled with Jacobite rebels and Highland outlaws. This revisitation highlights a revisionary rethinking (rather than hapless repetition) of the earlier work in order to reopen, rather than seal shut, the project of national historical romance. Scott disassembles the screen of "homogeneous, empty time" upon which the narrative equation between modernization and nation formation might be projected. Neither a national nor a historical novel in the sense established by *Waverley*, *Rob Roy* gives its readers a different kind of imaginative access to a British modernity constituted internally as well as externally by its imperial practice: limning the unrecognizable forms of the present rather than offering a consolatory flight to the past.

TOPOLOGIES OF MODERNIZATION

Scott developed his historical scheme from the conjectural historicism of the Scottish Enlightenment, which theorized cultural difference as the effect of historical difference articulated along a universal developmental axis—the set stages of social evolution from savage tribalism to commercial society, formulated by Adam Smith in his *Lectures on Jurisprudence* in the early 1760s and developed by (among others) John Millar, Adam Ferguson, and Smith himself in *The Wealth of Nations*.[19] James Chandler argues that this Scottish sociological history provided Romantic historicism with its fundamental principle of anachronistic or anatopic unevenness within the smooth calendrical time of modernization.[20] The Scottish formulation of "comparative contemporaneity" goes on to generate the Marxist thesis of uneven development (*Ungleichzeitigkeit*) and its variants: Ernst Bloch's nonsynchronism, Koselleck's noncontemporaneity, Raymond Williams's typology of residual, dominant, and emergent formations, Fredric Jameson's sedimentation. Bloch's and Koselleck's accounts of noncontemporaneity, in particular, show us how the concept might yield the obverse of the linear historicism it is invoked to serve: since the epistemic horizon of modernity that allows a recognition of "the same" cultural stage existing at different times also necessitates the recognition of different cultural stages—different temporalities—inhabiting, and alienating, "the same" historical moment. The violent contemporaneities produced by imperial modernization remain latent within the negative term, noncontemporaneity, that covers them—awaiting their uncanny recognition at any disturbance of the rationalizing order of history:

> In such a framework, one can describe peoples of two different historical moments as belonging to the same state of civilization: in this case the same state of "rudeness and barbarism." Nonetheless, being in the state of barbarism in the "present state of the globe" and being in the state of barbarism in some past "state of the globe" will *not* be quite "the same," in Millar's analysis, because of the different *global circumstances* of such states of a nation. . . . Indeed, one could not in the same sense even speak of the "state of the globe" in relation to the barbaric state of polished nations. The "globe" would signify differently in different times.[21]

The "globe" makes its appearance, as a specifically modern condition of knowledge, through the disjunctive contemporaneity of which noncontemporaneity is the rationalizing inflexion, in the juxtaposition of different cultural "states" rather than in the comparison of one particular state with "universal history." In other words, the historical recognition of modernity itself—commercial society in its world-imperial range—renders the synchronic field of a radical contemporaneity: the present, imbued with strange shadows of the past and of unknown futures through the globalizing mechanisms of contact, exchange, and circulation by which it is constituted.

The argument that Scott's historical novel reproduces the program of Scottish Enlightenment historicism takes its cue from a famous passage in the last chapter of *Waverley*.[22] Scott frames his narrative with a meditation on the modernization of Scotland in the period since 1745:

> There is no European nation which, within the course of half a century, or little more, has undergone so complete a change as this kingdom of Scotland. The effects of the insurrection of 1745, —the abolition of the heritable jurisdictions of the Lowland nobility and barons, —the total eradication of the Jacobite party, which, averse to intermingle with the English, or adopt their customs, long continued to pride themselves upon maintaining ancient Scottish manners and customs, commenced this innovation. The gradual influx of wealth, and extension of commerce, have since united to render the present people of Scotland a class of beings as different from their grandfathers, as the existing English are from those of Queen Elizabeth's time.[23]

Scott identifies the political movement of Jacobitism with a vanished Scottish cultural past, which the preceding narrative (despite the reference to "Lowland nobility and barons") has located especially in the Gaelic Highlands.[24] Secondly, Scott aligns the perspective of his narrator and his reader with the temporality of the historical process of modernization, an alignment signalled in the novel's subtitle: "'Tis Sixty Years Since." The title of this last chapter, "A Postscript, which should have been a Preface," spells out the character of a retrospect that sets the terms through which the preceding narrative is to be interpreted.[25]

   Rob Roy, however, undoes the rhetorical hinges which articulate that historicist certainty. With the loss of the temporal coordinate, "sixty years since," the tale comes adrift from the linear chronicle of modernization. The "extraordinary mistake" made by Lukács, in dating the action of *Rob Roy* (1715) several decades after that of *Waverley* (1745), expresses a profound if inadvertent insight into the later novel's scrambling of the scheme of Enlightenment historicism.[26] Scott refuses the teleological viewpoint of a narrator-editor able to offer us a postscript so sure of itself that it ought to have been a preface. *Rob Roy* is narrated in the first person by a protagonist who "never comes into imaginative possession of himself," or of the story he tells.[27] Frank Osbaldistone fails to give us final access to the meaning of the events he relates; neither his own life nor the public history with which it intersects arrange themselves into a clear pattern in his telling. Resisting the generic imperative of bildungsroman, the narrative never fully emerges from a subjective condition that Scott himself diagnoses as male hysteria. Frank finds himself unmanned by eloquent Amazons: Diana Vernon, whose more authentic "frankness" thwarts his callow lovemaking, and then, at the heart of the story, the terrifying matriarch Helen McGregor, who destroys life in front of his helpless, fascinated gaze. These figures block the course of a masculine heterosexuality that seeks its cue in protective fathers, friendly elder brothers, nurturing mothers, maidens obedient to male desire. The adventure culminates not in any clarity of action or self-realization but in a remarkable sentimental "paroxysm."[28] Diana bids Frank farewell "*for ever*":

> Heaven knows, it was not apathy which loaded my frame and my tongue so much, that I could neither return Miss Vernon's half embrace, nor even answer her farewell. The word, though it rose to my tongue, seemed to choke in my throat like the fatal *guilty*, which the delinquent who makes it his plea knows must be followed by the doom of death. . . . I felt the tightening of the throat and breast, the *hysterica passio* of poor Lear; and, sitting down by the wayside, I shed a flood of the first and most bitter tears which had flowed from my eyes since childhood. (386)

In the 1780s William Cullen, the influential professor of medicine at Edinburgh, had revived the ancient uterine diagnosis of hysteria as a primarily
female sexual disturbance, partially reversing the early modern theorization of "hypochondria" as a nervous imbalance afflicting both men and
women. Right at the stage where, by the logic of bildungsroman, Scott's
hero ought to have realized his masculine agency, he experiences instead
the internal irruption of an archaic female organism—a drastic, psychosomatic state of "noncontemporaneity."[29]

Scott uncouples the identification of Jacobitism with Highland culture
and blocks both terms from attaining a synecdochical equivalence with
"Scotland." The uncoupling makes possible the framing of a new discursive category: the primitive. It is new in that Scott separates the primitive
from the past as the product of a linear, teleological historicism, although
only after he has evoked the past as a discursive stage through which his
narrative may activate the primitive and its uncanny contemporaneity.
Rob Roy adumbrates the primitive as a category invented by modern
culture to allegorize itself: a quality or agency intrinsic to the operations
of modernity, but troped as alien to it, moving outside the domestic ideological field of civil society. Rob Roy thus dramatizes an internal cleft in
the conception of the modern secular collectivity within which the novel
circulates, and to which its readers (and its by now transnational machinery of production and reception) belong.

Peter Womack has argued that the wild Highlands and their inhabitants
only become visible—valuable—once modernity frames them as figures
for its own past, the condition it has extinguished in order to become
what it is.[30] But here Scott offers something different from an elegiac surmounting, in that the primitive sheds the trappings of its pastness, its
own discursive origin, as soon as it begins to circulate in the narrative. A
division of symbolic labor in Rob Roy allots the past to that figure now
split off from the Highlander—Jacobitism, or the figure of the past as
ideology—in order that the primitive may embody another temporal
scheme. Scott drives a wedge between two disciplinary categories, anthropology and history, as they emerge from the matrix of the Enlightenment
human sciences where they tend to be joined together. Rob Roy asserts
its generic distinction as a novel in this opening of a gap between the
categories. It teases apart the discursive and disciplinary bindings of a
rationalist synthesis of the sciences to claim a different kind of imaginative
space, one that is not the less a domain of knowledge. In this opening,
with its notorious effects of opacity, irrationality, and incoherence, Scott's
novel asserts its own modernity, its own contemporaneity. Here the novel
claims a cognitive mastery peculiar to itself, rather than justifying fiction
as the didactic bearer of some other kind of truth—such as, for instance,
political economy.

INSIDE AND OUTSIDE THE WEALTH OF NATIONS

In *The Wealth of Nations* Adam Smith founded a new discourse of modernity. The famous first chapter closes with an oblique reflection upon the phenomenon of chronotopic unevenness in an immanent world system. Besides expounding the formal principle of a modern economy— the division of labor—Smith establishes the rhetorical conditions of his discourse. He does so by testing its limits: limits that are on the one hand discursive and rhetorical, and on the other hand geographical and anthropological. The implicit question of who shares in the wealth of the nation measures the extent to which the nation itself might constitute an intelligible category.

By means of the division of labor, writes Smith, "a general plenty diffuses itself through all the ranks of society."[31] This general diffusion of plenty turns out to be an imaginary, indeed ghostly condition, realized in the act of reading about it (foreshadowing Anderson's account of the imagined community). It consists in a convergence of globalized metonymic relations, so that the most ordinary everyday object can no longer be conceived as an effect of its phenomenological circumstances, bound to a particular space, visible and tangible against a local ground. Instead it is haunted by an intricate and far-flung network of processes of production and distribution:

> Observe the accommodation of the most common artificer or day-labourer in a civilized and thriving country, and you will perceive that the number of people of whose industry a part, though but a small part, has been employed in procuring him this accommodation, exceeds all computation. The woollen coat, for example, which covers the day-labourer, as coarse and rough as it may appear, is the produce of the joint labour of a great multitude of workmen. The shepherd, the sorter of the wool, the wool-comber or carder, the dyer, the scribbler, the spinner, the weaver, the fuller, the dresser, with many others, must all join their different arts in order to complete this homely production. How many merchants and carriers, besides, must have been employed in transporting the materials from some of those workmen to others who often live in a very distant part of the country! How much commerce and navigation in particular, how many ship-builders, sailors, sail-makers, rope-makers, must have been employed in order to bring together the different drugs made use of by the dyer, which often come from the remotest corners of the world! (22–23)

The day laborer's woollen coat is no longer just a coat, but a singular, contingent node in a dynamic topology of relations that is—if we trace it far enough—worldwide in its extent. This potentially global topology disintegrates national boundaries as well as the local scene. The perception of such a topology—and of the nature of commodities in a modern economy—requires a special kind of vision, a new kind of discursive mapping, for it to become apparent: an inexhaustible power of metonymy, correspondent to the inexhaustible dynamism of the market. The political economist, Smith himself, aims to provide that mapping: "insisting that society constitutes a *system* visible only to the moral philosopher cum political economist."[32]

The end of Smith's commercial-metonymic sublime takes an odd turn. The smoothly inexorable diffusion of the discourse predicates a homogeneity of "opulence" across all the classes of society. The nation, internally homogenized, secures and stabilizes the scheme. Any economic unevenness between master and worker is a phenomenological illusion which vanishes in the philosophical lens, since the invisible complex relations that signify wealth invest the laborer's coat just as they do the sumptuous garb of royalty:

> Compared, indeed, with the more extravagant luxury of the great, [the day laborer's] accommodation must no doubt appear extremely simple and easy; and yet it may be true, perhaps, that the accommodation of an European prince does not always so much exceed that of an industrious and frugal peasant, as the accommodation of the latter exceeds that of many an African king, the absolute master of the lives and liberties of ten thousand naked savages. (23–24)

Smith affirms the comparative equality of property relations within the national society by invoking a violently exploitative differentiality found outside it: outside Europe, outside civilization and modernity, in Africa. Smith admits this external difference covertly, in another register, that of simile; for it requires little reflection to see that African savagery is nevertheless part of the political economy of the nation, if we trace the metonymic chain far enough. As Smith knew perfectly well, mid-eighteenth-century Glasgow's commercial wealth was founded on the Chesapeake tobacco and (increasingly) West India sugar trades, and thus on slavery.[33] The deflected recognition of that fact occurs here across a syntactical suppression: the European subject (the merchant or citizen who, in Lowland Scotland at any rate, has supplanted Smith's feudal dyad of prince and peasant) *is*, in effect, "the absolute master of the lives and liberties of ten thousand naked savages," whether he owns plantations, has shares in the trade, or consumes sugar or tobacco. Through an analogic skewing, Smith's scheme admits the violent synchronicity of different historical stages—feudalism, savagery, and a suppressed modernity—linked by "savage" political relations of dominance, in the global economy of modern commercial society.

It is unlikely that this distortion, both of Smith's syntax and of the representation of the political economy, marks a "repression" of slavery on Smith's part—its relegation to the text's political unconscious. Later in *The Wealth of Nations* Smith condemns slavery for being economically inefficient, in a critique that would furnish a powerful argument for the antislavery movement. What is at issue is a structure of representation, in the relation of a normative, domestic order (the economic, political, and moral relations that constitute the nation) to another, alien, exterior horizon—one of archaic, savage political relations—which nevertheless permeates the former. Smith's prose admits the shadow of a rhetorical threat: once a system of relations becomes total—global—it reduces all analogies, equivalences between terms inside and outside the system, to homologies: equivalences within the system. Modernity, far from abolishing the difference between civilization and barbarism, preserves it—produces it—inside itself, in a relation of perpetual violence.

Rob Roy opens with a ceremonial duel between commerce and romance. The contest, associated with a filial resistance to paternal discipline, replays another topic—the debate between romance and history—familiar from *Waverley*. Frank Osbaldistone would rather be a poet than succeed his austere father as head of the family firm. But Scott's narrative charges commercial enterprise with the peril and glamour of romance, and sets up the merchant as the proper hero of modern society. Frank's poetry, by contrast, is a dead letter, imitation in the most lifeless, literal sense. Like the youthful Scott, he is translating Ariosto, replicating the forms of the ancien régime in a kind of cultural Jacobitism. Incapable of understanding the dynamic energies of modernity, Frank only dutifully repeats the Smithian maxim: "[Commerce] connects nation with nation, relieves the wants, and contributes to the wealth of all; and is to the general commonwealth of the civilized world what the daily intercourse of ordinary life is to private society, or rather, what air and food are to our bodies" (75). It will take another kind of romance than Frank's verses to be adequate to the forces of connection and circulation that mesh together—and so categorically constitute—nation, world, ordinary life, private society, and our bodies. The romance form of modernity is the novel, exemplified by the book we are reading. It is one of the many subtleties of *Rob Roy* that its poet-*manqué* narrator, in contrast to its author, never quite becomes aware of his vocation as a novelist. Frank does not think of his contemporary, Daniel Defoe, who combined a literary career as "the father of the novel" with the role of economic and political agent, involved, among other enterprises, in the forging of a new multinational state through the Union of Scotland and England; but Scott alludes to him more than once, and makes him the source for the novel's account of the rising economic energies of Glasgow.[34]

MODERNITY'S OTHER WORLDS

The reader encounters a scientific analysis of history according to Scottish principles of political economy two-thirds of the way through *Rob Roy*, after hundreds of pages in which the historical referent for this historical novel has been all but inscrutable. The analysis is offered by the Glasgow merchant and magistrate Nicol Jarvie, who is the novel's spokesman for an ascendant sociology of commerce, legality, and civic virtue, as well as being the proprietor of a West-India plantation, and thus of slaves (295).[35] Jarvie rehearses the Smithian account of modernity that identifies it with mercantile capitalism and the institutions of a post-1688 national economy: the Stock Exchange, colonial free trade, a national debt. Anticipating a genre that might be called (after Sir John Sinclair's great economic and demographic survey of 1791–99) "the statistical account of Scotland," Jarvie explains the state of the Highlands and the coming rebellion as products of a dynamic relation between population, productivity, and credit. The overpopulated Highlands have become a kind of third-world debtor economy within the new British state, and a national credit collapse will drive the clans into insurrection. Far from marking a resurgence of ancient cultural loyalties, the Jacobite rising is determined by the fluctuations of a modern, imperial economy across a political geography of underdevelopment (300–307).

Jarvie's statistical account appears to occupy a position of authority in *Rob Roy*, identical with the perspective of modernity from which we are reading, and made possible by the very site from which Jarvie, quasi-prophetically, speaks: Glasgow, where Adam Smith—at the time Frank is supposed to be narrating, in the mid-1760s—is delivering the university lectures on jurisprudence out of which will emerge *The Wealth of Nations*. The analysis explains not only historical events but also the novel's private plot, in which Frank's wicked cousin steals the firm's assets, provoking a nationwide financial panic and the Jacobite counterrevolutionary attempt. (We also learn that a credit squeeze lies behind Rob Roy's career in banditry.) Economics would seem to furnish the definitive discourse of the historical novel as well as of history itself, and Jarvie's historical position would seem to grant him the clarity and certainty denied to the novel's first-person narrator.

Scott frames this historical position and its scientific authority within the familiar narrative schema of a tour through the nation that articulates its internal differences. The act of framing, however, historicizes the discourse of historical explanation and deprives it of universal authority. Frank sets out on a northern journey across a series of regional sites, each of which represents a different historical relation to national modernity.

The story opens in London: less thickly described place than abstract premise, the center of the new United Kingdom and its expanding empire. Then the narrative settles, for what seems an inordinate length (chapters 5–18), at a country estate in Northumberland, before moving on to Glasgow (chapters 19–26) and at last the Highlands (chapters 27–36). Respectively, these are the settings of a rustic feudalism (the crucible of Jacobite intrigue), commercial protomodernity, and prefeudal, "savage," clan society. The novel's settings represent not just geographically distinct spaces but anthropologically distinct stages, very much according to Enlightenment conjectural history. We might expect this arrangement of settings to map the historicist scheme exemplified in *The Wealth of Nations*, so that clan society, feudalism, and commerce will describe a developmental progression in which the obsolescence of one stage—its pastness—guarantees the succession of the next. The Northumberland chapters seem to bear this out, their alternating styles of satire and Gothic consigning the feudal, Catholic, and Royalist culture of Jacobitism to a superseded past. The comedy of regional manners, perfected by Maria Edgeworth in *Castle Rackrent*, marks the residual character of a backwoods feudalism. Sir Hildebrand's sons are not characters, inhabitants of the new discourse of the novel, psychologically individuated by the complex specificity of a modern economy. They are types: generic cases of booby-squire decadence, barely distinguishable by their respective humors. Such a representation has nowhere else to go but to record their extinction, which it does in a suitably absurdist key at the end of the novel. As Frank lingers at Osbaldistone Hall, a different stylization of feudal obsolescence takes over, this time drawn from the Gothic novels of Horace Walpole and Ann Radcliffe. Gothic aligns the Jacobites, especially Die's father, not just with psychological themes of repression and sublimation but with a more drastic condition of ghostliness.[36] Both styles, the satiric and the Gothic, suggest a fated fall into the past.

The story's move north into Scotland, however, undoes the teleological certainty—the conviction of pastness—encoded in the Northumberland chapters, and with that the ordering of regional cultural differences along a linear chronology. Scotland is not represented as a unified territorial and cultural entity, a nation, since it is split between the very different worlds of Glasgow and the Highlands; nor, crucially, is it situated as provincial or as past in relation to metropolitan England. The Glasgow of *Rob Roy* is hypermodern and Gothic: the setting for Jarvie's "statistical account" and encomium to commercial society, as well as for a hair-raising series of nocturnal, carceral, and labyrinthine adventures. Glasgow, set just below the Highland line, exemplifies the principle of a contrast of cultures and epochs embodied in Rob Roy himself: a figure like "Robin Hood in the middle ages," as Scott explains in his 1829 introduction, "blending the wild virtues, the subtle policy, and unrestrained license of an American Indian," yet "flourishing in Scotland during the Augustan age of Queen Anne and George I," "within forty miles of . . . a great commercial city, the seat of a learned university" (5). Here Scott specifies the Border topos—the geographical adjacency of different epochs, the historical simultaneity of different worlds—that animates his fiction.[37] However in *Rob Roy* the juxtaposition of savage and commercial stages obliterates instead of clarifying their relation as each other's past and future. Despite their official opposition, savagery and commerce sustain rather than cancel one another, constituting the uncertain, cryptic field of the present.

By the end of *Rob Roy* it will have become clear that particular systems of meaning and value may not always prevail outside the cultural sites where they are produced. The situational specificity that gives Jarvie's "statistical account" its authority—its Glaswegian provenance—also defines its limits. While it is never falsified, the analysis exerts no enlightening force throughout the rest of the narrative. Jarvie's cognitive mastery vanishes (unlike those primitive impulses, his courage and loyalty) once he and Frank enter the Highlands, already denominated in his account "a wild kind of warld by themsells" (300). As the two men cruise on Loch Lomond, Scott gives them set-piece reactions to the scenery: Jarvie speaks for economic improvement, Frank for romantic appreciation (415–16). Jarvie's scheme of development seems grotesquely inappropriate, the crude vision of an economic colonialism that expresses no more than the Glasgow Bailie's provincial foible. This is not just because Frank's aesthetic view seems more authentic, reflecting what he conceives to be the Highlanders' own relation to their setting—"the natural taste which belongs to mountaineers, and especially to the Scottish Highlanders, whose feelings I have observed are often allied with the romantic and poetical" (410). Frank is narrating his adventures in the mid-1760s, the age not just of Adam Smith but of Macpherson's "Ossian" translations, Walpole's Gothic tale, the aesthetic vogue for the sublime, and dissertations on the natural taste of clans and tribes by Hugh Blair and Adam Ferguson. In other words, Frank's aestheticism is no less modern than Jarvie's utilitarianism, and not simply because it yields a prediction of the region's economic future as a destination for picturesque tourism. The two discourses—romance and political economy—persist alongside each other to constitute the contemporary literary culture of Scott's readers, in the Waverley novels, Edgeworth's tales, and the *Edinburgh Review*. Our act of reading acknowledges a romantic aesthetic that is *more* modern than the raw utilitarianism of the primitive stage of capitalism for which Jarvie speaks, since the novel, the up-to-date form of romance, is able to dramatize both perspectives. In contrast to the transcendental authority of a "postscript which should have been a preface," the political-economic analysis remains embedded within the relative cultural spaces of Scott's narrative, framed by it rather than framing it. Scott turns the historicist scheme of Enlightenment political economy against itself, and at the same time fulfils it, by representing the temporal unevenness of the discourses of which the novel is composed, not just of the sites it represents.

This may seem especially paradoxical in the Highland chapters, since the narrative keeps invoking the anthropological equation of Gaelic clan society with a "savage" tribalism, especially of North American Indians, that was one of the set pieces of Enlightenment conjectural history.[38] Rob's kinsman Dougal resembles "a very uncouth, wild, and ugly savage, adoring the idol of his tribe" (258), the Highlanders are "the natives" (324, 345), Mrs. MacAlpine's hut is a "hospitable wigwam" (394). Scott gives this savagery a different kind, not degree, of relation to modernity from that of a Jacobite retro-feudalism. Clan culture enjoys a defiant autonomy rather than a fated obsolescence; it may look marginal and lawless in the eyes of Glasgow or London, but it is the center of its own world, and governed by its own laws. If feudalism and Jacobitism constitute the British nation's socioeconomic and political past, the Highlanders evoke a different order of ancestral relationship to modernity: the order of the primitive. The object of a nascent science, anthropology, the primitive signifies an origin morphologically immanent in modernity—disavowed but persistent—rather than a superseded developmental stage. Charged with original virtues—bravery, loyalty, pathos, but also murderous rage[39]—the primitive belongs to the present as well as to the past, even if it must shift in disguised or (in current jargon of state) deniable forms.

Rob Roy the character embodies the category of the primitive in the tale that bears his name. The outlaw recurs across the narrative's different sites in a sequence of metamorphic appearances and disappearances, gradually uncloaking his shape as Frank and the reader approach his "native heath," the terminus of this revelation being our glimpses (never more than fragmentary) of his wild body. In the Glasgow jail, Frank observes Rob Roy's freakishly broad shoulders and long arms:

> I afterwards heard that this length of arm was a circumstance on which he prided himself, that when he wore his native Highland garb, he could tie the garters of his hose without stooping; and that it gave him great advantage in the use of the broadsword, at which he was very dexterous. But certainly this want of symmetry . . . gave something wild, irregular, and, as it were, unearthly, to his appearance, and reminded me involuntarily, of the tales which Mabel used to tell of the old Picts who ravaged Northumberland in ancient times, who, according to her tradition, were a sort of half-goblin half-human beings, distinguished, like this man, for courage, cunning, ferocity, the length of their arms, and the squareness of their shoulders. (273)

Over the Highland line, Rob's appearance "in the dress of his country" allows Frank to notice the "fell of thick, short, red hair, especially around his knees, which resembled in this respect . . . the limbs of a red-coloured Highland bull" (374). While the allusion to "the old Picts" may echo the account of the MacGregors as the last pure-blooded specimens of "the ancient Celtic race" in one of his sources, Scott develops Rob Roy's primitivism in terms opposite from those of racial purity.[40] Rob is native yet "unearthly," "half-human" and "half-goblin," but also part animal, simian and bull-like: the tropes for his elemental or aboriginal status are not just mixed but contradictory. Through this figure Scott imagines a heretic or outlaw identity at human and cultural origins, both in the miscegenation of categories (human, animal, demonic) and in the appeal to heterodox discourses, folkloric (goblins as the aboriginal inhabitants of the country) and biological (beasts as human ancestors).

Rob Roy's goblinlike power to shift his shape and appear or disappear at will enrolls him within the traditional discourse of "folklore," albeit newly recovered under an anthropological rubric. More striking are the glimpses of him as a kind of anthropoid ape—broad-shouldered, long-armed, covered in a red pelt—and the allusion to a conspicuously new and heterodox scientific hypothesis of subhuman origins. Edinburgh in the late Enlightenment (until the 1830s) was the British institutional center for pre-Darwinian theorizing about human origins, and Scott would have been familiar with the polygenetic thesis of Lord Kames, as well as the notorious claims of Lord Monboddo (ridiculed by Samuel Johnson) that the orangutan was a human subspecies that only lacked speech. This is the kind of ape that Rob Roy resembles. The Romantic vogue for the orangutan—a figure on the threshold of humanity, language, and culture—extended through Scott's own late romance, *Count Robert of Paris*, Peacock's *Melincourt*, and tales by Hogg and Poe.[41] When, in the Northumberland episode, Die Vernon refers to "the Ourang-Outangs, my cousins" (152), the metaphor is absorbed in its satiric context as a joke forecasting the cousins' extinction. But in Rob Roy's case primitivism signifies a rough vitality and cultural integrity ("honour"), the opposite of a destiny of extinction: he is quintessentially a survivor, triumphant over the proscription of his clan. Scott makes the point that Rob dies peacefully in bed long after the end of the adventure, in defiance of Jarvie's prophecy that he will be hanged.

This makes for a striking contrast with *Waverley*, where Scott had identified the failure of the Jacobite rising with the historical end of clan society, ceremonially marked by the state trial and execution of the chieftain Fergus Mac-Ivor. Thanks also, in part, to the earlier novel, Scott's readers knew about the end of the clans; but in this tale they survive, the secret sharers of an imaginary present, strengthened rather than depleted by their station outside the law. Rob Roy's physical energy, his talent for action, puts him at an opposite pole to the wraithlike figures of the Jacobite nobility. He enjoys a preternatural ability to turn up in any scene, or scenario, without being confined to it. Breaking in and out of the story at its crisis points, he inhabits a recursive rather than linear, interruptive rather than continuous, narrative time. Far from typifying the vulnerable savage incarcerated in his "other time" by Western anthropology,[42] this primitive prefigures late-nineteenth-century biological fantasies of organic vitalism and "eternal return." Adept in all cultural sites and roles, the master of appearances and languages, Rob is expert, above all, in the modern arts of commerce and negotiation, which may extend to robbery and homicide—who better than a freebooter should thrive in the new economy? The wild Highlander is also the archetype of economic man, since the new age requires an ideological recovery of "natural man" at the same time that actual savages are being figured into the expanding horizon of an imperial economy. (Mungo Park, the African explorer, had been Scott's friend and neighbor in the Borders.) That is just what theorists of capitalism-as-modernity have wanted to insist, whether they formulate the original principle of human nature as a propensity to exchange or barter (*The Wealth of Nations*) or as an insatiable desire (Ferguson's *History of Civil Society*, Millar's *Origin of the Distinction of Ranks*).

If Scott's novel endows Highland savagery with a specific historical context, it is unmistakably, if only partially, that of colonial empire. More explicitly than just about any other Scott novel, *Rob Roy* represents the Highlands as a colonial frontier. The tale's single episode of military violence follows the historical-romance convention of dramatizing a clash between different worlds, but it is significant (again, in contrast to *Waverley*) that the ambush of Thornton's troop by Helen MacGregor does not belong to the history of the Jacobite rising. This overthrow of disciplined redcoats by a rabble of wild "natives" (most of them women and youths, led not by Rob Roy but his fearsome wife), complete with barbaric atrocity, belongs to the theater of colonial resistance rather than of national history. For Scott's readers, the military role of Highland regiments in the British army would have compounded the episode's allusive force; only a few years earlier, in Wellington's Peninsular campaign, such troops had supported mountaineer guerilla fighters against the Napoleonic empire (a conjunction dramatized by Johnstone in *Clan-Albin*). Scott revives a traditional rhetoric of Highland savagery to insist not on the obsolescence but on the contemporaneity of these figures, "the indispensable atavistic natives," as Womack calls them, "in the Victorian triumph of peace and progress."[43] Here, though, complicating the formula, Scott emphasizes the MacGregors' ferocious resistance to the military and legal apparatus of the state. These Highlanders may not be drafted. Rob Roy's support of Frank, like his kinship with Jarvie, remains private, covert, illicit, unaccountable.

Through the figure of the up-to-date primitive we glimpse instead the shadow of a world system, a sublime, dynamic, outlaw field of force that exceeds the official, public, enlightened boundaries, historical and ideological as well as territorial, of civil society and the nation-state. We intuit, darkly, that the British condition of modernity does not after all consist of an internally unified, civilized "nation," the product of an evolutionary graduation of discrete historical stages. It consists of a global network of uneven, heterogeneous times and spaces, lashed together by commerce and military force, the dynamism of which is generated by the jagged economic and social differences of the local parts. This sublime imperial dynamism, rather than their elegiac absorption by the modern state, invests the aesthetic glamour of the Highlanders in *Rob Roy*.

Rather than opening a window onto the past, Scott's novel shows us the obscure, occult, bewildering shapes and forces of the present—a present not yet amenable to the perspective of historical analysis, and so more authentically sensed through the symbolic techniques of romance. The historicity of the world system becomes legible in the novel's derangement (but not its obliteration) of an Enlightenment historicism by primitive forms and figures. Far from disabling storytelling from the power to represent modernity, Scott's reactivation of these primitive forms produces the cognitive fitness of the novel as the genre of modern life. This fitness relies on those effects that are most notoriously novelistic, least reducible to other discourses: the disclosure of relations and connections through the formal turns of plot (coincidence, reversal, doubling) and symbol (metaphor, allegory); the evocation of psychic states of anxiety, dread, wonder, bafflement, hilarity, longing, all part of the complex of strange pleasures that fiction affords, but officially dismissed from the faculty of cognition. Nassau Senior, the first professor of political economy at Oxford, deplored the plot of *Rob Roy* as a "mass of confusion and improbability":

> The author himself, as he goes on, finds himself so thoroughly involved in the meshes of his plot, that seeing no legitimate extrication, he clears himself at last by the most absolute, we had almost said the most tyrannical, exercise of the empire which authors must be acknowledged to have over their personages and events, which we recollect, even in the annals of that despotic class of sovereigns. C'est un vrai coup d'état—and one which we should have expected rather from an Asiatic writer, than from a novelist "in this free country."[44]

Scott's novel enthralls its readers in the barbaric political psychology of world empire rather than admitting them to the rational transactions of civil society, as a British novel should do. "Despotism is a legitimate mode of government in dealing with barbarians," John Stuart Mill, the great Victorian exponent of civil liberty in the tradition of Smith and Senior, would later declare: "providing the end be their improvement."[45] To be enthralled by *Rob Roy*—as hundreds of thousands of readers have been enthralled—is to find oneself outside the narrative of modernity as a "free country," and with no sure prospect of improvement.

Chapter 5

❦

THE RISE OF FICTION

SEEING NOTHING

National character is not to be found in London. The novels discussed in chapter 3 set the thick description of regional manners in Ireland or Scotland against the moral vacancy of "fashionable life." For David Hume, a characterological blankness at the metropolitan core signified the gloss of plenty rather than the gape of lack, in England's achievement of liberty and a mixed constitution: "the ENGLISH, of any people in the universe, have the least of a national character; unless this very singularity may pass for such."[1] Anti-Jacobin polemic of the 1790s associated Englishness with a robust resistance to abstract categories and metaphysical systems, founded on the irreducible particularity of felt life.[2] Hume, in more ironical vein, contends that "'tis almost impossible for the mind of man to rest, like those of beasts, in that narrow circle of objects, which are the subjects of daily conversation and action"—except "in *England*," where "honest gentlemen" are so engrossed in their "domestic affairs" and "common recreations" that they "have carried their thoughts very little beyond those objects, which are every day expos'd to their senses."[3] In England everyday life absorbs those immersed in it, whereas subjects marked by an ethnic or cultural difference, like Hume himself, are obliged to reflect on their doubled relation to national identity as North Britons and Scots. These associations set the terms for the remarkable identification of England with "provincial life" in mid-Victorian fiction, from *Cranford* to *Middlemarch*. The province situates an England whose circumference is nowhere and whose center is everywhere—even if the center might not hold very far beyond the 150 miles or so from London that marks the range of Jane Austen's "3 or 4 Families in a Country Village."[4]

Writing in the flush of his success as a new novelist, Scott hailed *Emma* (1816) as the model of "a style of novel [that] has arisen, within the last fifteen or twenty years," distinguished by "the art of copying from nature as she really exists in the common walks of life, and presenting to the reader, instead of the splendid scenes of an imaginary world, a correct and striking representation of that which is daily taking place around him."[5] This modern novel is distinguished by its rendition of what Scott calls "the common walks of life" or "the paths of common life"—the habitat of "the middling classes of society" who constitute a national reading public. The author of *Emma* narrates "such common occurrences as may have fallen under the observation of most folks," and her characters "conduct themselves upon the motives and principles which the readers may recognize as ruling their own and that of most of their acquaintances" (231). In Scott's carefully indirect formulations, "common life" is a medium at once transparent and opaque. Its surface texture of events "may have fallen under" our observation—but we do not actually observe them until the novel shows them to us. Absorbed in everyday life, we overlook the "motives and principles" that regulate its practice—until the novel holds them up for our recognition.[6]

Austen describes the world of her novel in two separate but analogically linked set pieces in which the heroine goes on a walk and looks at a view. Late in the story, Emma visits Mr. Knightley's manor at Donwell. She and her party wander about the grounds:

> [T]hey insensibly followed one another to the delicious shade of a broad avenue of limes, which stretching beyond the garden at an equal distance from the river, seemed the finish of the pleasure grounds. —It led to nothing; nothing but a view at the end of a low stone wall with high pillars, which seemed intended, in their erection, to give the appearance of an approach to the house, which never had been there. Disputable, however, as might be the taste of such a termination, it was itself a charming walk, and the view which closed it extremely pretty. . . . It was a sweet view—sweet to the eye and the mind. English verdure, English culture, English comfort, seen under a sun bright, without being oppressive.[7]

The insensible, indirect rambling that characterizes Emma's path is set in implicit contrast to a French, formal, absolutist style of gardening and the kinds of approach it governs. The walk's resonantly negative termination—"It led to nothing; nothing but a view," "the appearance of an approach . . . which never had been there"—nevertheless yields something. It yields a general, abstract quality of national setting: "English verdure, English culture, English comfort." Englishness, modifying the suggestive series of abstractions (verdure, culture, comfort), turns out to be the view's sweet and formless content, its curiously rich and potent quality of "nothing."

Readers may remember an earlier episode in which the heroine, "seeing nothing," looks at a view. Emma and Harriet go shopping in the village:

> [W]hile [Harriet] was still hanging over muslins and changing her mind, Emma went to the door for amusement. —Much could not be hoped for from the traffic of even the busiest part of Highbury; —Mr Perry walking hastily

by, Mr William Cox letting himself in at the office door, Mr Cole's carriage horses returning from exercise, or a stray letter-boy on an obstinate mule, were the liveliest objects she could presume to expect; and when her eyes fell only on the butcher with his tray, a tidy old woman travelling homewards from shop with her full basket, two curs quarreling over a dirty bone, and a string of dawdling children round the baker's little bow-window eying the gingerbread, she knew she had no reason to complain, and was amused enough; quite enough still to stand at the door. A mind lively and at ease, can do with seeing nothing, and can see nothing that does not answer. (241)

Once again, "nothing" yields the vision of a substantial reality, which consists this time of a detailed description of local, particular activities and objects. The narrative context, a shopping expedition, specifies the category, "traffic," that governs the spectacle. The nothing Emma sees includes the circulation of persons, commodities, and correspondence, and the union of all degrees of local society in a prosperous consumption of the fruits of an imperial economy, from the "tidy old woman" with her full basket to the children eyeing the gingerbread. So comfortable is Highbury that signs of dirt and poverty, far from needing to be swept out of sight, can confidently be relegated to "curs." This is what Glenburnie and the other Scottish and Irish clachans should look like once the process of Anglo-British absorption is complete.

The view of everyday life in the village and the view of "English culture" at Donwell inform and sustain each other, under the shared rubric of "nothing," to supply Austen's representation of the world to which her characters belong. They articulate, to be sure, the ideological theme of a national society constituted upon a harmonious conjunction between a modern economy based on imperial trade and a traditional social hierarchy based on inherited property. "Nothing" refers not only to the everyday domain of traffic: it also refers, obliquely or metaphorically, to that reality's governing abstraction, embedded in naturalized forms and qualities, English verdure, culture, comfort. Nothing names the immanence of the system in an invisible cause that sustains and regulates these conjunctions and circulations. Emma, by virtue of her caste and intelligence, is able to perceive this invisible cause, "seeing nothing," by constituting commerce as a view, in a motion that faithfully reiterates the reflexive form of exchange: seeing "nothing that does not answer." While Harriet is submerged in the blind life of traffic, Emma rises above it for an aesthetic appreciation allied with the ethical constancy of a mind that can regulate its own enjoyment. At the same time, it is by no means clear that we can define this viewpoint as Emma's—as (according to the emergent convention of free indirect style) the experience of a particular subjectivity. "In the paradoxical form of an impersonal intimacy," writes D. A. Miller,

Austen's style "grants us at one and the same time the experience of a character's inner life as she herself lives it, and an experience of the same inner life as she never could."[8]

THE SPHERE OF COMMON LIFE

Both the positive term "nothing" and the problematic of reflection emerge from Humean empiricism, the most rigorous and subtle description of a reality evacuated of metaphysics in modern British philosophy. "Nothing" denotes the absence of divine agency and transcendental forms of meaning from the world (such as metaphysical causality)—and thus the abyss behind appearances disclosed by the skeptical work of reason. "Nothing" also designates the phenomenological substance that covers up that abyss: the imaginary fabric of "customary conjunctions" or habitual associations that make up our positive knowledge of the world. "[All] our reasonings concerning causes and effects are deriv'd from nothing but custom," Hume insists; "belief is more properly an act of the sensitive, than of the cogitative part of our natures" (234). Custom alone—repetition and habituation—produces the effects of continuity and consistency that knit together an intelligible, familiar world and our identity in it. In the famous set piece that concludes the first book of the *Treatise on Human Nature*, Hume makes it clear that this secondary domain of the phenomenal world holds sway by virtue of its being held in common. The philosopher recovers from the alienation wrought by his skeptical understanding by turning again to "the common affairs of life":

> I dine, I play a game of backgammon, I converse, and am merry with my friends; and when after two or three hours' amusement, I wou'd return to these [philosophical] speculations, they appear so cold, and strain'd, and ridiculous, that I cannot find in my heart to enter into them any farther.
>
> Here then I find myself absolutely and necessarily determin'd to live, and talk, and act like other people in the common affairs of life. (316)

Intercourse with others, "the commerce and society of men" (317), supplies the substance of common life. The world is recharged with the sentimental positivity of social exchange.

In Hume's wake, Adam Smith devoted his career to analyzing the domains and disciplines that organize the "sphere of common life" (*Treatise*, 318), such as moral psychology, rhetoric, jurisprudence, and political economy. Smith discovers *exchange* as the structural principle of social life, which reaches its culmination in commercial society. Economic exchange (commerce), linguistic exchange (conversation), and sentimental exchange (sympathy) provide the mechanisms of mediation and continuity that sustain the empirical world. In *The Theory of Moral Sentiments* Smith describes a white noise of affective gratification through which common life keeps itself going:

> It is decent to be humble amidst great prosperity; but we can scarce express too much satisfaction in all the little occurrences of common life, in the company with which we spent the evening last night, in the entertainment that was set before us, in what was said and what was done, in all the little incidents of the present conversation, and in all those frivolous nothings which fill up the void of human life. Nothing is more graceful than habitual cheerfulness, which is always founded upon a peculiar relish for all the little pleasures which common occurrences afford. We readily sympathize with it: it inspires us with the same joy, and makes every trifle turn up to us in the same agreeable aspect in which it presents itself to the person endowed with this happy disposition.[9]

Such language, mixing registers of excess and scarcity, describes a reality that is customary and continuous, reproduced by microscopic transactions of exchange, so smoothly as to go unremarked; a subconscious sympathetic medium that "makes every trifle turn up to us," or reflexively constitutes the texture of everyday life as present and self-evident.

Smith's language also calls attention to the absence of a metaphysical ground and its replacement by something else, a phenomenal background. The transactions of "commerce and society" are "frivolous nothings" that "fill up the void of human life": we glimpse the abyss of skepticism through Smith's bourgeois *sprezzatura*. Why nothings, why a void? Because Humean skepticism posits this continuous, habitual world of ordinary relations as a fiction. "The memory, senses, and understanding," Hume insists, are "all of them founded on the imagination" (313). The imagination fills in the gaps between discrete "impressions" and weaves phenomena into an intelligible text of experience. Articulating the relations of resemblance, contiguity, and causality that constitute (in Susan Manning's phrase) its "grammar," the imagination produces the necessary illusions of spatial and temporal continuity, and of subjective as well as objective identity.[10] The identity of an object over time is a "fiction of the imagination" (251); "we have a propensity to feign the continu'd existence of all sensible objects; and as this propensity arises from some lively impression of the memory, it bestows a vivacity on that fiction; or in other words, makes us believe the continu'd existence of a body" (259). "The identity, which we ascribe to the mind of man, is only a fictitious one, and of a like kind with that which we ascribe to bodies" (306–7).

This imaginary production of reality is customary—habitual and social—rather than solipsistic; its great work of fiction, common life, is an ongoing, collective project, consensually shared and reproduced. Hume reflects on this condition in the passage from the *Treatise* cited above, in which the author recapitulates his philosophical argument in a confessional drama of crisis and recovery. The reflection looks back, in particular, to the key discussions of skepticism with regard to the reason and senses (pt. 4, chaps. 1 and 2), in which Hume outlines a progress of enlightenment:

> In considering this subject we may observe a gradation of three opinions, that rise above each other, according as the persons, who form them, acquire new degrees of reason and knowledge. These opinions are that of the vulgar, that of a false philosophy, and that of the true; where we shall find upon enquiry, that the true philosophy approaches nearer to the sentiments of the vulgar, than to those of a mistaken knowledge. (272)

False philosophy furnishes the existential crisis of a total (Pyrrhonian) skepticism, while true philosophy, which Hume calls a "moderate scepticism" (273), attends the sympathetic reinvestment in custom and common life. Hume's threefold "gradation" inserts a dialectical difference between this philosophical return to common life and a blind submission to it. Moderate skepticism may be closer to a vulgar acceptance of common life than to a false-philosophical rejection of it, but it is not the same as it. "Carelessness and in-attention alone can afford us any remedy," temporarily at that, for the chronic "malady" of "sceptical doubt" (267–68). Hume's irony separates the intellectually refined inattention earned through skeptical doubt from the undifferentiated inattention of those who never doubt. Nor is that inattention a terminus, since philosophical attention frames it. Donald W. Livingston characterizes the Humean movement between skeptical reason and natural (i.e., sympathetic and customary) belief, or common sense, as a dialectical progression. "Common life, as Hume understands it, is an object of thought only for a philosophical consciousness that has passed through the exacting route of philosophical self-doubt."[11] Reflection situates the philosopher "both within and without the world of common life": although immersed in the tide of custom, passion, and prejudice, he is able (by virtue of his knowledge that these are not facts but interpretations) to leverage its practices and beliefs against each other.[12] To engage in critical reflection is not to escape "the reign of custom," as another commentator puts it: "rather we use custom to correct custom," in the hope of being able to tell the difference between those "principles which are permanent, irresistible, and universal"—the grammar of the imagination—and those "which are changeable, weak, and irregular"—mere ideology, imagination's ephemeral vocabulary.[13]

Hume's is a form of negative dialectic, in that it produces neither a simple return to philosophical innocence nor a horizon of enlightenment that transcends the common and the customary. There is no delivery from what Hume characterizes as an organic, psychosomatic rhythm of tension and relaxation. If nature drives the philosopher to seek refuge in social cheer, nature will also eventually, just as surely, drive him to resume his researches—since the motive for philosophical inquiry, the desire to think through the veil of custom, is no less pleasure oriented. Truth arises neither in alienated reflection nor in forgetful habituation, nor in some cognitive synthesis of the two, but in the temporal oscillation between them. "A true sceptic will be diffident of his philosophical doubts, as well as of his philosophical conviction; and will never refuse any innocent satisfaction, which offers itself, upon account of either of them" (320). Instead of a higher wisdom, Hume's conservative skepticism offers (with ironical modesty) a peculiar enjoyment in the lesson that "pleasure" drives the turn to philosophical reflection as well as the return to common life.[14]

Hume reformulates his dialectical scheme in an account of what he calls the hypothesis of "the double existence of perceptions and objects" (264), the strategy by which thoughtful persons reconcile their reflections with the practice of everyday life:

> This philosophical system . . . is the monstrous offspring of two principles, which are contrary to each other, which are both at once embrac'd by the mind, and which are unable mutually to destroy each other. The imagination tells us, that our resembling perceptions have a continu'd and uninterrupted existence, and are not annihilated by their absence. Reflection tells us, that even our resembling perceptions are interrupted in their existence, and different from each other. The contradiction betwixt these opinions we elude by a new fiction, which is conformable to the hypothesis both of reflection and fancy, by ascribing these contrary qualities to different existences; the *interruption* to perceptions, and the *continuance* to objects. Nature is obstinate, and will not quit the field, however strongly attack'd by reason; and at the same time reason is so clear in the point, that there is no possibility of disguising her. Not being able to reconcile these two enemies, we endeavour to set ourselves at ease as much as possible, by successively granting to each whatever it demands, and by feigning a double existence, where each may find something, that has all the conditions it desires. (265)

This is not merely an ideological delusion entertained by other, mystified thinkers. Hume's irony, characteristically, implicates himself and his readers in the "monstrous" conceit he exposes. The "new fiction" allows us to "elude" the contradiction opened up by reflection—not by closing the contradiction but by mentally inhabiting it, in the equivocation between reflection and belief. Consciousness, "feigning a double existence," becomes doubled itself—at once interrupted and continuous, renewing the commitment to an illusion upon the alienated knowledge of its illusoriness. Recognition of its fictive status makes the difference between this "philosophical system" and Hume's metacommentary. Once more, the recognition does not deliver us to a point of cognitive unity outside the system. Instead it affords us a view—intermittent, itself subject to the temporal logic of "double existence"—of our condition inside it. Our sentimental investment in common life and in the authority of custom is framed by the fitful, uneven knowledge of their fictiveness.

This doubled consciousness—oscillating between alienated reflection and absorption in the illusory surfaces of life, mediating rather than re-solving a radical contradiction, generative of a melancholic enjoyment—characterizes the subjective effect of a work of fiction: at the very moment when fiction, negotiating between the ideologically prestigious domains of knowledge and belief, begins to claim rhetorical autonomy in mid-eighteenth-century Great Britain.

THE RISE OF THE NOVEL AND THE RISE OF FICTION

Hume's philosophical career coincides with a literary development dis-cussed in recent historical criticism of the novel in eighteenth-century Brit-ain: the midcentury emergence of what Catherine Gallagher calls "the novel's most important formal trait: its overt fictionality."[15] Fictionality, in Gallagher's account, "does not precede but is rather coterminous with the rise of the novel" (164). It acquires categorical definition with the rhetorical access of "self-consciousness" that J. Paul Hunter ascribes to the form at midcentury.[16] Lennard Davis, refuting the traditional geneal-ogy that makes "romance" the novel's ancestral genre, separates the ori-gins of the novel altogether from the category of fiction. He describes, instead, the matrix of what he calls a "novel/news discourse" in early modern culture: the novel disguises itself with the referential rhetoric of "news" so as to evade the censure attached to the category of fiction, associated with a falsification of religious or (increasingly) scientific or-ders of truth. This commits the early novel, in Davis's words, to the "in-herent doubleness and reflexivity" of "an ambiguous form—a factual fic-tion which denied its fictionality and produced in its readers a characteristic uncertainty or ambivalence as to whether they were reading something true or false."[17] By the middle decades of the eighteenth cen-tury, however, certain novelists (notably Henry Fielding) grew confident enough to affirm the fictional status of their work, while nevertheless re-taining the "doubleness and reflexivity" attached to the genre.[18] Abandon-ing the disguise of fact, fiction guarantees the moral truth of its representa-tions with a rhetoric of probabilistic verisimilitude.[19] Gallagher argues that "overt fictions . . . became both more strongly marked and more positively valued in the mid-eighteenth-century than they had been pre-

viously" due to changes in copyright law and the consequent "birth of
the author-proprietor, whose property claims might rest on his or her 'faculty of invention,' " as well as the development of a discourse of sympathy
that privileged readers' subjective identification with fictional characters.[20] Meanwhile, according to John Bender, the claim upon a "guarantee
of factuality" in the natural sciences "increasingly required the presence
of its opposite, a manifest yet verisimilar fictionality in the novel."[21] These
rather different (although not necessarily exclusive) explanations converge upon a strong, overdetermined recourse by British novelists to a
rhetoric of fiction in the middle decades of the eighteenth century, as they
certify the hold of their representation on social life. Fictionality marks a
more assured appropriation of the real rather than an evasion or denial
of it, while realism, reciprocally, becomes "the code of the fictional."[22]

Wolfgang Iser has also identified the second half of the eighteenth century as the era when a distinctively secular rhetoric of "the fictive" began
to take hold in European literary culture. Iser characterizes the fictive—
in terms that should by now appear familiar—as "an operational mode
of consciousness," "an act of boundary-crossing which, nonetheless,
keeps in view what has been overstepped" and thus "simultaneously dis-
rupts and doubles the referential world."[23] In the modern era fiction
comes to designate a cognitive engagement with reality rather than, as in
Platonic or Christian conceptions, the falsification of a reality guaranteed
by metaphysical forms of truth. Iser grants Hume a pivotal if ambiguous
role in the theoretical conversion of fiction "from a form of deception to
a basic constituent of cognition" in British empiricist philosophy: "Instead of criticizing fiction, he used it as an instrument of criticism, and he
turned the traditional negative view of it against the supposed laws of
cognition. This signals a new use of fiction, even if once more it exploits
the negativity of past uses."[24]

My present argument makes a stronger claim than Iser's for the importance of Hume's contribution to the history of the novel—a contribution
that spread from Scotland to the North Atlantic literary world through
Scott, whose work fully realizes Humean principles. In affirming the epistemological primacy of the imagination, endowing it with a socially productive and normative function, Hume establishes the philosophical matrix for the ascendancy of fictional realism in modern British literature.
Humean empiricism generates a "novelistic" model of the imagination
that will pose a fertile alternative to the Kantian-Coleridgean "lyric"
model, associated (in modern academic criticism) with English Romantic
poetry, which casts the imagination as trace of an alienated transcendental
cognition.[25] Hume's philosophical legitimation of the fictive as an "authentic" representation of common life, since common life is a consensually reproduced fiction, coincides chronologically with the affirmation of

fictionality in a cluster of major English novels, from *Tom Jones* to *Tristram Shandy*. Fiction, traditionally stigmatized as inauthentic for its divergence from truth or fact, becomes the mode of representation best fitted to render the "nothing" that is the empirical domain of common life: first, because that "nothing" has gone unremarked by the historical record; and second, because that domain is itself already fictive, an intersubjective representation sanctioned by custom.

Nevertheless, these philosophical and novelistic realizations of the fictive do not yet fully converge. There remains a gap between Hume's theory and the theory and practice of the eighteenth-century English novelists. As Iser notes, Hume continues to repeat the "negative" associations of fiction, in his thoroughly conventional pronouncements on poetic genres—even as Hume's general epistemology grants fiction a critical force as the mental medium of common life. (It falls to the perhaps unlikely initiative of Jeremy Bentham—Scott's contemporary—to elaborate a full-blown theory of "the fictive.")[26] Conversely, as Everett Zimmerman argues, novelists continue to invoke the authority of a nonfictional discourse, namely history, despite their assumption of a rhetoric of fiction. The novels of Richardson, Fielding, and Sterne "constitute themselves as sharing a border with history and thus impute to themselves some kind of referentiality, however attenuated."[27] History is the category that occupies the gap between the philosophical theory of fiction and its novelistic realization in the second half of the eighteenth century. Hume himself, when it came to writing narrative, turned to history and not the novel—in acceptance of the customary, hierarchical difference between them—as the legitimate discourse of common life, "the inclusive fiction that constitutes our social world and enables our understanding of it."[28]

Narrative constitutes a formal bond between the eighteenth-century novel and historiography which is more intimate than the novel's relation to other discourses that have been identified as its dialectical contraries, such as natural science and political economy.[29] The border shared by history and fiction, like all borders, is a site of crossings, of traffic and intercourse, as well as of demarcation and dispute. Mark Salber Phillips demonstrates an intensive preoccupation with the representation of manners and everyday life—the stuff of the novel—on the part of eighteenth-century historians, especially in Scotland, as they enlarge the scope of their writing to account for a more complete range of human experience. Their narrative experiments draw upon novelistic forms and techniques, notably those of "sentimental reading": Phillips emphasizes "the importance of sympathy, not only as the basis of social relations, but also as the essential bond that shapes the way readers enter into and experience a text."[30] Hume himself supplied mid-eighteenth-century British fiction with an influential discourse of sympathy.[31] Appropriately, though, it was the author of *The Theory of Moral Sentiments* who developed the age's most sophisticated analysis of literary techniques of sympathetic interpellation, in his lecture course on "Rhetoric and Belles Lettres." Smith prescribed a set of tropes for the writing of history—particularity, mixed character, "indirect" representation—which codify a technical repertoire for the novel as it would eventually be practiced (especially) by Scott.[32]

The formal proximity of history and the novel, drawing on each other's methods and strategies, brings into relief an intensifying rivalry between them for prestige and market share. Lionel Gossman points to the later eighteenth century as the era when historiography revoked its membership in the general category of "literature"—formerly inclusive of all kinds of written discourse, now increasingly associated with "poetic and figurative writing"—and began to claim the methodology and status of a scholarly discipline.[33] The novel is corespondent in that divorce. As novelists call their works "histories" in a bid for legitimacy they bring a skeptical, destabilizing pressure to bear on the textual conventions by which history makes its truth claims, threatening to reduce it philosophically to the status of just another fiction (however officially sanctioned). The threat drives historians, in turn, to claim scientific norms of evidence in the attempt to set their work apart from mere invention.[34] The scientific and disciplinary hardening of history—its separation out of the literary field—assists the dialectical clarification of the rejected term, fiction, which thus comes to characterize the "literary" itself.

That dialectical definition is accelerated, certainly, by the epoch-breaking shock of the French Revolution, the event that recast history in the mode of crisis—both as collective lived experience and as rationalizing account of that experience—and brought in its wake a catastrophic perturbation of all narrative categories. Scott's historical novels, published in the aftermath of the Revolutionary and Napoleonic wars, at once exemplify and thematize the formal emergence of fiction in British literary history. Scott's historicism distinguishes his fiction, at the same time, from the formalist claim on aesthetic value with which, according to several critics, "literature" emerges as an autonomous category in the Romantic period.[35] The Waverley novels, as Zimmerman rightly insists, demarcate fiction alongside history rather than annexing one discourse to the other: "Scott claims both historical and fictive elements and accepts their essential division even as he joins them"; "Although Scott's combination of history and fiction subsumes the interrogation and emendation of history characteristic of eighteenth-century fiction, it also differentiates itself from history and from other realistic novels that merely simulate history."[36] The invocation of history precipitates a reflexively distinct work of fiction that sets the novel apart from other narrative genres, such as memoir and history, and defines its place and function in modern culture.

Fiction, in short, moves from idea to substance as it becomes the dominant principle and identifying term of a literary genre. John Bender notes that perhaps the first usage of "fiction" as a synonym for novel or romance occurs in the title of John Dunlop's *History of Fiction*, published in the same year as *Waverley*.[37]

Meanwhile, the term that marks the ideological border between history and fiction also designates the crux of Hume's philosophy: the subjective index of knowledge and truth, the term of interpellation, *belief*. Before turning to the dialectical realization of fiction and history in Scott's novels, my argument will trace the vicissitudes of Hume's account of belief in Scottish Enlightenment moral philosophy.

FICTION AND BELIEF

The epistemological argument of the *Treatise of Human Nature* gives us Hume's original contribution to literary theory, not his conventional pronouncements on fictional genres. As Scott complained, "David Hume was no good judge of poetry; had little feeling for it; and examined it by the hackneyed rules of criticism."[38] The field opened up by Hume would be colonized neither from the high road taken by Lord Kames, whose aesthetic theory grants fiction a para- or pseudo-ontological force and licenses a kind of armchair quixotism, nor from the low road of Thomas Reid's "Common Sense" philosophy, which reinstates the traditional antithesis between fiction and reality. According to the received intellectual history, Reid's refutation of Humean skepticism was decisive in Great Britain for the next hundred years (the epoch of literary realism), while Hume's most radical exposition of his argument, the *Treatise of Human Nature*, remained an esoteric document until the twentieth century. The dispute between Reid and Hume flared up again in Edinburgh during the period of the Scottish Waverley novels, however, with Reid's authority challenged and Hume enjoying something of a revival. Reid himself was as much Hume's disciple as he was his adversary, and his own work as well as the subsequent debate ensured that the terms of Hume's philosophy remained in circulation. Indeed, Reid's decision to advert to the *Treatise,* as the most uncompromising expression of the arguments he sought to refute, gave that work the public currency it had failed to achieve by itself. That currency was kept up by Reid's student Dugald Stewart, who began a partial rehabilitation of Hume, pursued more aggressively by Stewart's successor Thomas Brown.[39] Humean theory would find its fullest realization in Scott's novelistic practice—a practice that continuously produces its own theoretical reflection, through and alongside the fictional recreation of historical scenes and events.

Hume's formal account of fiction takes shape around the topic of belief, the ideological crux of his argument, where he addresses the border fiction shares with history.[40] Hume defines belief as "a lively idea related to a present impression" (147; cf. 144), which is different in degree, not in kind, from other ideas: "nothing but *a more vivid and intense conception of any idea*" (169; emphasis in original). Fiction assumes categorical form in a discussion of "the influence of belief . . . on the imagination" (170), in which Hume turns to theorizing the literary uses of history. Interestingly, history is subordinate to mythology in the "poetical system of things":

> Poets have form'd what they call a poetical system of things, which tho' it be believ'd neither by themselves nor readers, is commonly esteem'd a sufficient foundation for any fiction. We have been so much accustom'd to the names of MARS, JUPITER, VENUS, that in the same manner as education infixes any opinion, the constant repetition of these ideas makes them enter into the mind with facility, and prevail upon the fancy, without influencing the judgment. In like manner tragedians always borrow their fable, or at least the names of their principal actors, from some known passage in history; and that not in order to deceive the spectators; for they will frankly confess, that truth is not in any circumstance inviolably observed; but in order to procure a more easy reception into the imagination for those extraordinary events, which they represent. (171)

Sketching in effect a rationale for historical fiction, Hume inverts the usual didactic ratio that makes fiction an agreeable vehicle for historical truth. Here, history is the vehicle: the record of what is accepted as true helps accustom the reader, suspending the judgment, to the tropes of fiction, so that these can "enter into the mind" and "prevail upon the fancy."[41]

History makes familiar—it provides a shared referential framework for—the figures of romance: a process that does not, however, oblige readers to mistake romance for reality. The fiction maintains its generic visibility:

> 'Tis evident, that poets make use of this artifice of borrowing the names of their persons, and the chief events of their poems, from history, in order to procure a more easy reception for the whole, and cause it to make a deeper impression on the fancy and affections. The several incidents of the piece acquire a kind of relation by being united into one poem or representation; and if any of these incidents be an object of belief, it bestows a force and vivacity on the others, which are related to it. The vividness of the first conception diffuses itself along the relations, and is convey'd, as by so many pipes or canals, to every idea that has any communication to the primary one. This, indeed, can never amount to a perfect assurance; and that because

the union among the ideas is, in a manner, accidental: But still it approaches
so near, in its influence, as may convince us, that they are deriv'd from the
same origin. (171)

The historical data signify within a unified system of associations that
constitutes the "poem or representation," infusing all the other terms with
the "force and vivacity" that attend our recognition of their factuality.
They provide the vital substance that gives body to a formal scheme; while
the formal (Aristotelian) "union" of the system of associations is the condition that makes it legible as a "poem or representation," a text that
can be read. Hume says that the "accidental" construction of "the union
among the ideas" differentiates it from being received with "a perfect
assurance." According to his general thesis, though, such a union is by
definition "accidental" in its constitution, a set of associations naturalized
(granted the appearance of necessity) by custom. A system of relations
becomes intelligible, and acquires schematic or symbolic status, by virtue
of the artifice that binds it into a union. In a work of fiction that artifice
remains legible, ritualized, itself part of the text; "absolute belief or assurance" takes hold (we might extrapolate) once custom, via repeated usage,
has worn the artifice into transparency so that it is no longer noticed, and
the "union" comes to seem a necessary rather than accidental condition.

Hume's last sentence admits an anxiety about the proximity of fiction
and belief in the continuum of representation: how near may a fiction
approach belief before it takes it over—reveals its system of associations
to be accidental and conventional rather than necessary and natural?
Here, of course, the ideological scandal of Hume's philosophy, its corro-
sion of the foundations of religious truth, stresses the argument. Hume
returned to worry over the relation in an appendix to the third volume of
the *Treatise*. He strains to find the terms to reconcile what his theory holds
to be a difference in degree with what experience (sentiment, custom,
prejudice) insists is a difference in kind:

> An idea assented to *feels* different from a fictitious idea, that the fancy alone
> presents to us: And this different feeling I endeavour to explain by calling it
> a superior *force*, or *vivacity*, or *solidity*, or *firmness*, or *steadiness*. This variety
> of terms, which may seem so unphilosophical, is intended only to express
> that act of the mind which renders realities more present to us than fictions,
> causes them to weigh more in the thought and gives them a superior influence
> on the passions and imagination. Provided we agree about the thing, 'tis need-
> less to dispute about the terms. (146; emphasis in original)

Hume wavers between assurances that the distinction is "conformable to
everyone's feeling and experience" and protestations that he cannot (yet)
find a philosophical language to express it. Belief, so deeply embedded in

custom that it lies beyond analytic reach (or daring), marks a limit of his discourse, a point at which it will not close.

Hume thus falls back on a more conventional assertion (again, inserted in the appendix) that "the *feelings* of the passions are very different when excited by poetical fictions, from what they are when they arise from belief and reality" (173). In an interesting passage (inventing, in effect, the problematics of reception theory), he tests the distinction between romance and history by imagining them as different ways of reading the same text:

> If one person sits down to read a book as a romance, and another as a true history, they plainly receive the same ideas, and in the same order; nor does the incredulity of the one, and the belief of the other hinder them from putting the very same sense upon their author. His words produce the same ideas in both; tho' his testimony has not the same influence on them. The latter has a more lively conception of all the incidents. He enters deeper into the concerns of the persons: represents to himself their actions, and characters, and friendships, and enmities: He even goes so far as to form a notion of their features, and air, and person. While the former, who gives no credit to the testimony of the author, has a more faint and languid conception of all these particulars; and except on account of the style and ingenuity of composition, can receive little entertainment from it. (147)

Hume relies on a weak characterization of romance reading to secure his point; even though the description of "a more lively conception" and a "deeper" identification suggests the sentimental subjectivity of reading that the novel will shortly own, following in part from Hume's own promotion of sympathy as the imaginary medium of social relations. Hume has abandoned the structural account of "a poem or representation" he had sketched earlier, in which a formal unity of relations constitutes the representation, and fictiveness resides in the sign of an artificial and "accidental" construction. To sketch, once more, the logic of that suggestion: the effect of fiction resides in the evidence of an artificial and accidental construction—that is to say, a work of fiction is a representation that keeps visible its accidental rather than necessary construction by giving ritual form to its own artifice. After all, it is custom that decrees the visibility of these signs, and thus whether a particular book is read as romance or history: "custom" meaning not so much one person's habit, now, as the traditional consensus of a community. Yet Hume's thought experiment presupposes a radically individual act of reading, as though the book circulates outside of any institutional conditions and conventions, and an individual rather than collective force of custom.

Hume falls back, then, from fiction to history. Elsewhere, critics such as Hugh Blair continue to insist that "fictitious histories" can be justified solely on didactic grounds: "They furnish one of the best channels for conveying instruction, for painting human life and manners, for showing the errors into which we are betrayed by our passions, for rendering virtue amiable and vice odious."[42] Lord Kames in his *Elements of Criticism* (1762), the most elaborate attempt to codify an aesthetic science in eighteenth-century Scotland, rushes in where Hume had feared to tread. Kames enthusiastically grants fiction an imaginative dominion over history, by virtue of its technical command of the "vivacity of ideas," but in doing so he obliterates the crucial dialectic between absorption and reflection—the double consciousness—activated in Hume's theory.[43] In a discussion of the "Emotions Caused by Fiction" Kames coins the term "ideal presence" to characterize the subjective effect of a work of fiction.

> In contradiction to real presence, ideal presence may be properly termed *a waking dream*; because, like a dream, it vanisheth the moment we reflect on our present situation. . . . [T]he reader's passions are never sensibly moved, till he is thrown into a kind of reverie; in which state, forgetting that he is reading, he conceives every incident as passing in his presence, precisely as if he were an eye-witness. . . . [I]f, in reading, ideal presence be the means by which our passions are moved, it makes no difference whether the subject be a fable or a true history: when ideal presence is complete, we perceive every object as in our sight; and the mind, totally occupied with an interesting event, finds no leisure for reflection. (1:68, 69, 70)

Kames describes a state of total mental absorption which cannot brook reflection, since reflection breaks the illusion. This is, in short, the quixotic reading—the weak romanticism—conventionally disavowed in the modern tradition of the British novel. Ideal presence, like memory, suspends the passage of time: "in a complete idea of memory there is no past or future; a thing recalled to the mind, with the accuracy I have been describing, is perceived as in our view, and consequently as existing at present" (1:67). Reflection, conversely, activates time—it breaks the spell by imposing a fatal afterwards.[44] Hume's conception of a "true" philosophical relation to the fictive medium of common life, in contrast, follows a resolutely narrative insistence on the temporal succession of states of reflection and absorption. Kames's theory undoes its purportedly strong construction of the literary imagination by opposing it both to common life and to reflection, which together constitute an undialectically dense force of the real. While Humean reflection breaches common life, Kamesian reflection restores it, casting fictional belief as a fragile ontological nostalgia.

Hume's disciple and adversary Thomas Reid made the question of belief central to his celebrated "confutation" of Humean skepticism, confirming its status as a crux. In *An Inquiry into the Human Mind* (1764) Reid characterizes Hume's achievement as having exposed to view the "abyss of scepticism" that always subtended "the ideal system" of Descartes and Locke. Reid attacks Hume's argument that all our knowledge proceeds from the imagination: "But when I look within, and consider the mind itself . . . if it is indeed what the *Treatise of Human Nature* makes it, I find I have been only in an inchanted castle, imposed upon by spectres and apparitions."[45] In other words, Hume's philosophy is the opposite of the Enlightenment natural history or science of man it purports to be—it is a Gothic romance. (Reid alludes maliciously to Hume's protestation, in the appendix to the *Treatise*, that the ideas of belief "take faster hold of my mind, than the ideas of an inchanted castle," 673.) The first principle of Hume's argument, that the "simple apprehension" of an idea precedes the formation of any belief in it, "appears to me all fiction, without any foundation in nature" (Reid, 29): such a theory can insist on the sovereignty of the imagination only by virtue of its own status as a product of the imagination. Reid thus reaffirms the traditional dichotomy between truth and fiction that he blames Hume for having destabilized. Far from expressing only a more intense degree of imaginative "vivacity," belief is an original, intrinsic faculty of human nature, "a simple act of the mind," irreducible to other terms or operations (30). The evidence of our senses is authentic, and skeptical reflection inauthentic, a delusion, just another fiction—the professional deformation of philosophers out of touch with common life.

The argument that belief is an authentic mode of perception because skepticism is counterintuitive, a melancholic delusion, keeps falling back, however, into the terms already dramatized by Hume—as a problem of pathos rather than logic—in the conclusion to book 1 of the *Treatise*. Reid must still show that belief may express the apprehension of an objective, stable structure of reality, a natural or authentic relation with some thing that lies deeper than custom: "Nature hath established a real connection between the signs and the things signified; and nature hath also taught us the interpretation of these signs; so that, previous to experience, the sign suggests the thing signified, and creates the belief of it" (190). Reid locates this "real connection" in what he calls "natural signs," the prelinguistic gestural and expressive repertoire of the human body, which must be the same through all ages and cultures. Later, in the first of the *Essays on the Intellectual Powers of Man* (1785), he grounds it in a universal grammar or "general structure of language."[46] (At its most sophisticated, Reid's argument anticipates neo-Darwinian or sociobiological explanations: sincerity and belief, the forms of an instinctual attachment to objective truth, are adaptive characteristics of humans as "social creatures": *Inquiry*, 193–95.)

Reid's controversion of Hume's account of belief, more effectively than Kames's mystifying exaggeration of it, clarifies the age's most refined account of the status of fiction in the theoretical conditions of a secular, realist representation. Where Reid wishes to reassert an organic standard of empirical reality, guaranteeing truth and belief, against which fiction can be reckoned as a cognitive error or delusion, mere "romance," Hume theorizes a foundational role for fiction and the imagination in the work of representation that constitutes all knowledge. Hume's case, that all representation is a fiction, a *poesis*, since all experience is mediated through the imagination, provides a stronger and more comprehensive theoretical base for fiction than any that had appeared hitherto, delivering it from the sentence of inauthenticity, of categorical opposition to reality. It licenses Scott's own fictional practice, with its deconstruction of the opposition between history and fiction and dialectical reconstitution of their difference in a suspension of empirical realism in the medium of romance. Humean skepticism rather than Kamesian quixotism or Reidian common sense—or, more properly, Humean skepticism as the persistent condition or inescapable horizon of Reidian common sense—provides the philosophical framework for the fiction of the Scottish post-Enlightenment.

Despite Reid's influential intervention, the controversy over Humean skepticism was far from being settled in the early decades of the nineteenth century. Its persistence as an unresolved problem or theoretical scandal, investing the political and ideological disputes of the generation following the French Revolution, marked it as one of the philosophical limits of what could be claimed about reality and its representations. There is no question that Reid's correction of Hume took hold institutionally. Reid's academic eminence in the moral philosophy chair at Glasgow (where he succeeded Adam Smith in 1764) and, no less crucially, the pedagogy of his student Dugald Stewart (professor of moral philosophy at Edinburgh, 1784–1810, where his students included Scott and the Edinburgh reviewers), made Reidian "common sense" the philosophical correlative of the Whig Moderate hegemony of the late Enlightenment in Scotland.[47] Common sense itself thematized consensus, finding the standard of reality in a "universal agreement, among the learned and the unlearned, in the different ages and nations of the world."[48] Such a standard will always remain provisional to the extent that it is empirical, statistical and quantitative: the universality of the agreement corresponds with the record so far, up to the present case. The "problem of induction" implied by Hume, that no necessity dictates that a future element may *not* agree, remains open.[49]

As the political shock of the French Revolution broke up the Moderate consensus in Edinburgh, so the specter of Hume kept having to be invoked and exorcized, and the authority of Reid's answers began to falter. The postwar brought a revival of Hume in Edinburgh, with the publication of a second edition of the *Treatise on Human Nature* in 1817, and a rehabilitation of Hume's arguments in the university lecture course on moral philosophy—at least, until John Wilson assumed the chair in 1820. As we saw in *Peter's Letters to His Kinsfolk*, Tory loyalists could simply dismiss Hume, without the trouble of engaging his arguments, as a kind of sanguine Scots Voltaire, the impish parent of a Whig ideology now tainted with Jacobinism and infidelity. The debate among the philosophers, however, returned Hume's critique to currency and ensured that it continued to challenge the solutions Reid had laid down. Since the debate is little known, I shall give a brief account of it.

The first serious public controversy over cultural politics in Edinburgh since the anti-Jacobin crackdown of the mid-1790s broke out in 1805, anticipating the culture wars to come. John Leslie's appointment to the chair of mathematics at Edinburgh University was fiercely contested by the Moderate clergy and Tories, on the grounds that Leslie subscribed to Hume's theory of causation (and "all the moral consequences which that cunning sceptic deduced from it").[50] Although Leslie's appointment was confirmed after a few months, the controversy seethed into the following year. A philosophical argument in Leslie's defense appeared in the form of "Thomas Brown's fine metaphysical spear,"[51] a pamphlet titled *Observations on the Nature and Tendency of the Doctrine of Mr Hume, Concerning the Relation of Cause and Effect*. Brown's strategy, here and later in his career, is to recover Hume's epistemological thesis but deny the moral consequences imputed by his adversaries. The argument develops a distinction made by Stewart, between physical and metaphysical modes of causality (in *Elements of the Philosophy of the Human Mind*, 1792), but casts off Stewart's conciliatory tone to mount a counterattack on Reid. Brown argues that Reid unwittingly reinforces Hume's argument that cause and effect cannot be discovered a priori; where Reid disagrees, on the grounds that Hume therefore denies "power" (i.e., agency), he lapses into a misunderstanding. After all Hume's is "a mild and moderate scepticism, which suffers us to take shelter in a first principle of intuitive belief."[52] The deconstruction of causality remains a purely logical operation that does not threaten the ethical foundations of belief and agency.

In 1810 Stewart resigned from his teaching duties, and Brown took over as Conjoint Professor of Moral Philosophy. The appointment was objected to by the Tories, on the grounds of Brown's liberal views, but confirmed thanks to influential patronage. Brown's *Lectures on the Philosophy of the Human Mind*, published in the year of his death (1820), engage more thoroughly with "Dr Reid's supposed confutation" of Hume.[53] Brown devotes one of his lectures (vol. 1, no. 27) to cutting Reid down to size. However estimable, Reid has been overrated in Scotland, thanks to "the influence of his academic situation" and the "moral and religious objects which he uniformly had in view" (342)—in other words, his institutional status as Moderate bulwark against Humean and Jacobin infidelity. Reid's high standing is also due to "the eloquence of his illustrious Pupil, and Friend, and Biographer," Brown's own teacher Dugald Stewart.[54] In any case, Brown argues, the orthodox Reid and the skeptic Hume both agree that "no argument of mere reasoning . . . can prove the existence of an external world; [and that] it is absolutely impossible for us not to believe in the existence of an external world" (1:358). The difference is one of emphasis—Reid asserts the positive force of belief, Hume the negative force of reason. Despite his assent to Reid's contention that belief is a primary act of the mind, Brown reinstates Hume's argument that the difference between fiction and belief is one of a degree of intensity of subjective conception, regulated by custom and consensus, rather than of kind. Brown revives Hume's more subtle, dialectical stance and refutes the dichotomy Reid substituted for it.

Brown's career, occupying the Edinburgh chair of moral philosophy between the Moderate Whig Stewart and ultra-Tory Wilson in the decade of the Scottish Waverley novels, expresses the persistence of Hume's controversial argument, its investment with the political and ideological contests of the age, and the cutting edge Hume's thought continued to bear as Reid's authority foundered with the Moderate consensus it had supported. Brown's confutation of Reid's confutation, folding it back into Hume's more comprehensive system, reaffirms the sovereignty of the imagination as the faculty through which reality is apprehended, although in a conciliatory mode that rejects atheist conclusions, and, waiving the charge of inauthenticity, grants fiction its philosophical license as a representation of the world. Reid's philosophy had stripped fiction of its legitimacy once more, by upholding the traditional distinction that opposed it to the categories of reality and truth. Brown's reconciliation of Reid with Hume, reinstating Hume's epistemology but warding off its alleged ethical and political consequences, renders the difference between truth and fiction as one of subjective, if intersubjective, emphasis: an authentic representation is a fiction established by force of custom.

HISTORICAL FICTION

At times of historical crisis, writes Lionel Gossman, the "tension between the requirements of system and those of change" that informs all narrative genres may "become acute enough to become itself the principal theme of narrative works. At such times history may come to be associated . . . with the singular, the unexpected, the unsystematic," while fiction reimagines order and convention.[55] The French Revolution remains the archetypal modern instance of a general perturbation in the categories of history and fiction. Just such a scrambling of generic lines takes place in its Scottish Romantic representations, from Scott's historical novels to Carlyle's antinovelistic assumption of the techniques of fiction for revolutionary history. The shockwaves of Revolution broke up Scotland's Moderate consensus and the cultural forms associated with it. Revolution opened the possibility—eventually the necessity—of a counterhistoriography of violent discontinuity, perpetual crisis: recasting the outline of history from "homogeneous, empty time," the even (if rubble-strewn) gradient of improvement, to the jagged peaks and gulfs of *Jetztzeit*, "time filled by the presence of the now."[56] If Carlyle's *French Revolution* represents the most thoroughgoing attempt, in British historiography, to make a revolutionary form for revolutionary history, Scott—writing in the shadow of the event— sought to contain revolution's apocalyptic potential, to fold it back into "the continuum of history" (Benjamin, 261), in part by displacing it into the past, and in part by investing it with the tropes of fiction: the Humean medium of the conventional, the customary, the everyday. The containment holds, of course, its dialectical reversal, in the investment of fiction with the revolutionary disturbances of contemporary history.

Scott's invention of historical fiction involves, dialectically, the specification of history—the new force and density of which is registered in ways that have been well described by twentieth-century criticism—and also of fiction: a specification that brings the abstraction of both history and fiction (given its historicist title "romance") as discursive categories. *Waverley* and its successors do not just fictionalize history—representing the events, figures, forms, and forces that constitute history in the medium of the novel. They historicize fiction as an institution, a set of material forms and social practices, which includes as its paradigmatic modern case the novel itself and our act of reading it. *Waverley* makes the gesture of foundation for the series: a referential and allusive cut to the past that exposes the embedded, sedimented archive of British fiction. *Waverley* combines an internal allegory of the emergence of the novel as the genre of modern life from premodern traditions of ballad, epic, allegory, and romance with a thematic revisitation of 1745, the historical moment not just of the last ancien régime insurgency but also of a prior national formation of the novel—an English one, Fielding's in *Tom Jones*.[57] Both moves bear paradigmatic force for a later literary historiography that traces the "rise of the novel" out of romance, modelling the ascendancy of a modern social order, and designates the 1740s as the horizon at which (in the work of Richardson and Fielding) the novel can be said definitively to have risen.

Waverley thus writes 1745 as the double horizon, opening onto its own present moment, of a rise of the novel and an end of history, and marks both developments with an accession of fictionality—designating fiction as the mode in which we imaginatively inhabit the present. The novel is set in the age of Hume as well as Fielding: in its cut back to 1745 *Waverley* poses itself as the dialectical sequel to the *History of England* as well as to *Tom Jones*, subsuming their cultural work in its condition as historical romance. Scott's novels are Humean in their history and politics: they share with Hume's *History* the ethos of a moderate or conservative skepticism, the combination of Whig narratology and Tory sentiment, the detachment from party faction, the critique of fanaticism, and a recognition of the authority of custom.[58] They are Humean in more than the sum of these parts. History and politics yield a narrative technique elucidated in recent commentary on Hume's historiography. Glossing Hume's remark, "My views of *things* are more conformable to Whig principles; my representations of *persons* to Tory prejudices," David Wootton argues that Hume aligns his history with "disinterested" historical agents whose commitment to the public good compels them to "[fluctuate] between the factions." Principled moderates who change sides, like Falkland and Clarendon, are the true heroes of the *History of England*. These wavering heroes, rather than some transcendental horizon outside historical process, situate an "objective" and critical historiographic viewpoint.[59] Such virtuous equivocation counters the fanaticism that Hume diagnoses as an exclusive identification with political faction—and thus, a blind immersion in historical process. Hume translates the ethical detachment from sectarian politics gained by this identification to the aesthetic trope of "historical distance" which, according to Mark Phillips, governs his narrative epistemology. The volumes on the Stuarts, which Hume wrote first, "[seek] a kind of historical distance that would allow the turbulent epoch that closed in 1688, 'sixty years since', to be accepted and transcended." Phillips's quotation of the subtitle of *Waverley* recognizes what Hume bequeathed to Scott: a historiographic ethos of aesthetic detachment that allows the free play of sympathy and so predicts the liberal horizon of our reading.[60]

Waverley coordinates different developmental narratives into a complex whole: the Humean national history of emergence from a violent factional past to the liberal horizon of civil society; the bildungsroman of a personal progress from adolescent illusion through sentimental and moral crisis to mature settlement; and the literary allegory of the rise of the novel. This developmental complex rehearses the Humean dialectic between reason and imagination, skeptical alienation and sympathetic absorption, that governs an enlightened relation to common life. Like Hume's philosopher, young Waverley must move from a "vulgar" confusion of reality with the figures of the imagination, through disorientation and disenchantment, to a reconnection with common life—set at the horizon of civil society and our own act of reading, at the end of the story. To recast the dialectic in the philosophical terms of belief: Scott's novel engages the Kamesian lure (and Ossianic error) of reading as a mode of reverie, of total imaginative absorption in an illusion of presence that cancels the line between fiction and history, by setting it within a Humean sequence of romantic absorption, disillusioning reflection, and a sentimental return to common life that at once reaffirms its historical necessity and recognizes its fictionality. The comic conclusion of *Waverley* establishes a skeptical, melancholy, and aesthetic distance from historical reality that nevertheless (and hence the melancholy) accepts the authority as well as inauthenticity of that reality, parsed as the authority of custom.[61]

AFTER HISTORY

Thomas Brown made Humean principles safe for a liberal or neomoderate conservatism in the wake of the anti-Jacobin alarms that consolidated the Tory hegemony in Edinburgh, on behalf of a generation of intellectuals (Scott's, Jeffrey's) that wanted to distance itself from the extremity of that reaction as well as from the radicalism it had opposed. The most elaborate expression of a "mild" or conservative skepticism in Scotland during Brown's tenure can be found in *The Antiquary* (1816), Scott's first novel after Waterloo, the events of which take place in the mid-1790s, during the first crisis of the war against revolutionary France. The antiquary Jonathan Oldbuck, "too little of an aristocrat to join the club of Loyal True Blues, and too little of a democrat to fraternize with an affiliated society of the *soi disant* Friends of the People," defends the early tendencies of the Revolution against the Tory fanaticism of Lord Glenallan, somewhat in the vein of Scott's teacher Dugald Stewart.[62] Inevitably Oldbuck falls foul of both parties for recommending "quiet and moderate measures" to tranquillize domestic unrest (283–85). Scott advertised *The Antiquary* as the last in a trilogy of "fictitious narratives, intended to illustrate the manners of Scotland at three different periods," from 1745 to the threshold of the present (3). The contrast with his next major novel—which appeared seven months later (December 1816), with a new publisher and a new set of authorial and editorial personae—could hardly be more striking. "The end of war, which is the condition for a retrospect on its unfolding as a narrative of violent ruptures and collective delusion," writes Jerome Christensen, "coincides with the foreclosure of a future that is anything more than that condition of normal change which Immanuel Wallerstein has described as the characteristic temporal modality of modern liberalism."[63] *The Antiquary* submerges historical plotting, at "the end of history," in the pacific medium of "normal change," the temporality of common life. *Old Mortality*, however, set in the abyss of civil war preceding the "British Revolution" of 1688, is Scott's most sustained narrative of the "violent ruptures and collective delusion" that characterize Benjamin's "time filled with the presence of the now," or what Carl Schmitt and Giorgio Agamben call the "state of exception," the political abolition of common life. The passage to our own horizon of reading, securing the book's status as a work of fiction, takes place through a sequence of alienation effects which renders the temporal relation between its past and our present as a catastrophic breach of form.

Strikingly for a work composed mere months after Waterloo, *The Antiquary* unfolds its epiphany of national solidarity through the mock-heroic narration of a conflict that does not take place. The inhabitants of a harbor town on the northeastern coast of Scotland put aside their local differences and rally to defend their homeland against a French invasion. It turns out that the alarm has been set off by a bonfire of mining equipment, not a warning beacon, and no armada appears. The false alarm is the crowning instance of a series of nonevents that articulates the plot of *The Antiquary*. Jonathan Oldbuck expects that his young friend Lovel will compose an epic poem on the successful repulse of a foreign invasion by ancient Scots patriots; not only does Lovel not write the *Caledoniad*, but (as he protests) "the invasion of Agricola was *not* repelled" (107). The German swindler Dousterswivel involves the credulous Sir Arthur Wardour in an excavation for nonexistent treasure. The same principle determines the secret-within-a-secret of the Gothic, aristocratic plot that leaks out across the last volume. The tragic guilt that has paralyzed the Glenallan family stems from acts of incest and infanticide that turn out not to have been committed. The lost heir, Lovel/Nevil, was not even born out of wedlock. Frauds and hoaxes proliferate throughout the novel's texture of allusion as well as in its plot: the Ossian affair, the genealogy of early kings of Scotland.

In *The Antiquary* Scott undertakes what might be called the Shandyfication of historical romance, glossing his earlier fiction and its cultural themes in a self-reflexive and metafictional novel in which "nothing happens." At the same time, *The Antiquary*, of all Scott's novels, is the one most devoted to a representation of common life—the thick description of an everyday social surface of manners and conversation. The author's "Advertisement" apologizes for a discrepancy between this aspect of the fiction and its plot: "I have been more solicitous to describe manners minutely, than to arrange in any case an artificial and combined narration, and have but to regret that I felt myself unable to unite these two requisites of a good Novel" (3). Critics of *The Antiquary* have been only too ready to accept the invitation issued by this characteristic rhetoric of self-depreciation.[64]

It is not so much that *The Antiquary* has no plot; the narrative bustles, rather, with an intensive activity of plotting that comes to nothing—at least, nothing that is not thoroughly conventional and so foreseen from the start. (E. M. Forster on the opening sentence: "[Lovel] is the hero or Scott would not call him genteel, and he is sure to make the heroine happy.")[65] The ideological charge of this rhetoric becomes unmistakable in the final chapters, where the historical event that does not happen in the summer of 1794 is a French invasion.[66] The invasion scare diverts the threat of political unrest at home, represented by the Jacobin Club at Fairport, and identifies revolution as the event that must on no account take place. Revolution represents at once the archetypal form of a plot (peripeteia) and the content of a heroic historical narrative that severs the present from the past ("blasts open the continuum of history") and flings it open to futurity. The negative recognition of revolution as historical futurity determines an effect that many commentators have noticed, the novel's elaborate and complex concern with the past as the direction of interest, sentiment, and meaning.[67] The past is safe, paradoxically, because it is the domain of a Humean skepticism. *The Antiquary* keeps playing on the uncertain borders between what has always happened and what never happened, in its skeptical rehearsal of antiquarian debates about the Ossian epos, the ancient kings of Scotland, the ethnicity of the ancient Scots, even the ditch that Oldbuck claims is a Roman ruin and Edie Ochiltree insists is modern. Again and again, scrupulous inquiry—culminating in Oldbuck's legalistic redaction of the Glenallan family history to "a regular and authenticated form" (273)—involves the demystification of a past event or else a positive recognition of its fictional status.[68]

Scott makes the thick description of regional manners represent a profound, organic inertia of common life that resists the totalizing force of historical change.[69] Manners encode a long afterlife of feudal relations of obligation and deference, decayed from political and legal bonds into residual modes of custom and sentiment—released, in other words, from politics into nature. This is the modality of a present that already belongs to the past, and a past that flows into the present: a condition that preempts its radical transformation. Accordingly (in contrast to *Emma*, which situates the reader inside its society), *The Antiquary* frames common life as an anthropological and antiquarian field of representation. Reiterating a commonplace of conjectural history's uneven development thesis (as we saw in chapter 3), the novel's preface identifies its principal characters as belonging to that "class of society who are the last to feel the influence of that general polish which assimilates to each other the manners of different nations" (3). National character resides most distinctively among the common people because, in effect, they belong to a still-living past. This past, then, is the reverse of that time of ruin and extinction, broken off from history, in which the depressive aristocrats (the Glenallans) immure themselves. Scott's novel redefines an organic, continuous, multitudinous present-past that overflows the factitious temporal schemata of "artificial" plotting.

It is a measure of the turbulence of the ideological crisis navigated in *Old Mortality* that Scott makes common death, not common life, the restorative figure of an organic time released from history. The novel's introductory chapter invokes the Humean topos of historical distance in the elegiac setting of a country churchyard:

> Death has indeed been here, and its traces are before us; but they are softened and deprived of their horror by our distance from the period when they have been first impressed. Those who sleep beneath are only connected with us by the reflection that they have once been what we now are, and that, as their reliques are now identified with their mother earth, ours shall, at some future period, undergo the same transformation.[70]

The lapse of secular time dissolves political differences (and all distinctions of identity) into the death that is at once history's natural by-product and the process that turns history into nature.

The narrative that follows sinks us in the period of "horror" where death is suffered and inflicted. Of all Scott's novels this most thoroughly commits itself to the pressure of the historical event, distilled to agonistic essence in sequences of challenge, combat, torture, execution. *Old Mortality* traces the political escalation and ideological radicalization of a regional insurgency towards full-scale civil war and revolution, the novel's anxiously deferred, at once feared and wished-for, apocalyptic horizon. The British Revolution of 1688, the modern domestic settlement that frames the final chapters, displaces the more radical and violent mode of revolution activated in the preceding narrative, which has returned—via the recent world-historical convulsion in France—to haunt Scott's generation. *Old Mortality* is British fiction's most compelling exploration of what Agamben (after Schmitt and Benjamin) calls the "state of exception," the state's suspension of law and the norms of civil society under a declaration of political emergency.[71]

The tale's opening sequence dramatizes an ideological colonization of local customary life by state power, one of the symptoms of which is an "invention of tradition," the wappenschaw and game of the popinjay. Domestic manners and everyday social forms (not only forms of worship) are mobilized by a fatal accession of political consciousness. National politics invests, in short, what ought to have remained *unconscious*—private life, custom, second nature, the realm of "nothing"—with the stress of intention and struggle. The ethical product of the politicization of everyday life under the state of exception is fanaticism. Fanaticism, in the novel's diagnosis, expresses a violent conscription of the dense life of custom into allegorical schemes and figures. Ideological identification sublimates the particularities of lived experience into a totalizing, singular, and instantaneous meaning. In its fiery vapor arise such specters as the terrorist preacher Habbakuk Mucklewrath, the most radical—scarcely human—of the novel's cast of fanatics: a "ghastly apparition, which looked more like the resurrection of some cannibal priest, or Druid, red from his human sacrifice, than like an earthly mortal" (181). With his claim on charismatic agency Mucklewrath conjures open a temporal abyss in the continuum of history. The atavism of the Covenanters coincides with their role as advance guard of modernity, staking claim on an apocalyptic futurity rather than on the past. True to his allegorical status, Mucklewrath pushes forward the clock hand to accelerate the hour of Morton's death (265).

Scott binds his narrative in an iron logic of causality in which all acts (including speech acts: prayers, oaths, toasts), however "private" their motives or contexts, have deadly consequences. Morton shelters his father's old companion Burley for a night; twenty-four hours later he is condemned to death for it. A series of reciprocal vows and pledges articulates the plot, at once invoking and deferring the sentence of death, which hangs over Morton's head for the rest of the story. Evandale saves Morton's life, and Morton saves Evandale's, twice. The gesture, with its logic of sacrificial substitution ("he shall not die, if I should die in his place!" 108), predicts that one of them will be killed, and Evandale duly is at the end of the tale; but not before Morton falls (more heavily) into the role of sacrificial victim. At the nadir of his adventures Morton is doomed by his own party. The Covenanters wield typology to interpret the historical event and license their agency: "He hath burst in like a thief through the window; he is a ram caught in the thicket, whose blood shall be a drink-offering to redeem vengeance from the church, and the place shall henceforth be called Jehovah-Jirah, for the sacrifice is provided" (261). The apocalyptic rendering of history collapses the tropes of distance, a collapse reinforced in Scott's "sensational" (proto-Blackwoodian) rhetoric of horror:

> His destined executioners, as he gazed around on them, seemed to alter their forms and features, like the spectres in a feverish dream; their figures became larger, and their faces more distorted; and, as an excited imagination predominated over the realities which his eyes received, he seemed surrounded rather by a band of demons than of human beings; the walls seemed to drip with blood, and the light tick of the clock thrilled on his ear with such loud, painful distinctness, as if each sound were the prick of a bodkin inflicted on the naked nerve. (264)

As relations of spatial separation (regulated by the eye) disintegrate, the ear—organ of sensory immediacy—registers the traumatic pressure of "time filled with the presence of the now."

A few chapters later, we read the opposite effect: an explicit reassertion of distance that unhinges "the unities of time and place":

> It is fortunate for tale-tellers that they are not tied down like theatrical writers to the unities of time and place, but may conduct their personages to Athens and Thebes at their pleasure, and bring them back at their convenience. . . . Craving, therefore, the privilege of my cast, I entreat the reader's attention to the continuation of the narrative, as it starts from a new æra, being the year immediately subsequent to the British Revolution. (286)

For the first time, at this late stage, the narrator reflects upon his performance as a "tale-teller." (He had opened *Old Mortality* by characterizing it as a compilation from historical tradition.) The reference to "theatrical writers" masks the more momentous contrast between tale-tellers and historians, since the ostentatious breach of the unities is itself a theatrical device, as in the choral intervention of Time midway through *The Winter's Tale*. (The apology recalls, also, the Author of *Waverley*'s resort to the device in *Guy Mannering*, the most "romantic" of his early novels.) Here the temporal chasm in the narrative, marking the "new æra" opened by the British Revolution, brings a release from the historical logic of civil war, the formal correlative of which is the fatal causality of plot. Previously, under that logic, such a release has been associated with "romance," the fragility and futility of which is marked by its historicization (as when the narrator differentiates the present novel from "the laborious and long-winded romances of Calprenede and Scuderi," 19–20). Thus, the first, bold resort to a romance redemption fails when Tam Halliday overhears Jenny Dennison's plan for Morton's escape: in romances, guards are obligingly deaf. Edith then summons her uncle under the pretence of requesting a volume of *The Grand Cyrus*, but his intercession also fails to rescue Morton; only Evandale's activation of the logic of sacrificial substitution proves effective. Now, in the new dispensation, Morton may return (ghostlike) from exile and reclaim his love, upon a last flurry of violent action—novelistic, rather than historical, as it ties up the plot's private strands.

A more startling repetition of this temporal and formal breach comes with a "Conclusion" that delivers us to the far threshold of the modern era: the present time, our own activity of reading. Here, we find, the authority of custom is quite literally fictive. The narrative dissolves to the screen of its conventional reception in a dialogue between the narrator, Peter Pattieson, and local mantua maker Miss Martha Buskbody, a typical connoisseur of novels, who has read "through the whole stock of three circulating libraries in Gandercleuch and the next two market towns" (349). Miss Buskbody insists that Pattieson wrap up his plot—accounting for even the minor characters—according to the moral and aesthetic formulae of the day. Pattieson's (and Scott's) compliance mocks at the same time as it obeys the authority of custom. In Humean terms a moderate skepticism, which we are party to, has more in common with a "vulgar" acceptance of fictional convention than it does with a "false philosophy" that would debunk the romancing of history altogether.

Scott's fade to the fiction's institutional conditions—as an item of the general class of novels and the stock of circulating libraries—reaffirms the principles of distance and mediation, in a skeptical counterweight to the elegiac reflection in the country churchyard with which the story opened. The coda of alienating shocks, disintegrating "the Tale of Old Mortality" as it enters our own moral atmosphere, reverses the synchronization of the narrative with our time of reading that occupies the last paragraphs of *The Antiquary*. That novel's continuous temporality overflows the end of the story to absorb not just the principal characters but the reader too:

> People talk of a marriage between Miss MacIntyre and Captain Wardour, but this wants confirmation.
>
> The Antiquary is a frequent visitor at Knockwinnock and Glenallan-house, ostensibly for the sake of completing two essays, one on the mail-shirt of the Great Earl, and the other on the left-hand gauntlet of Hell-in-Harness. He regularly enquires whether Lord Geraldin has commenced the Caledoniad, and shakes his head at the answer he receives. *En attendant*, however, he has completed his notes, which, we believe, will be at the service of any one who chuses to make them public, without risk of expence to THE ANTIQUARY. (356)

Reaffirming the key of an urbane and leisured skepticism, the synchronization folds our present back into the novel's tranquil continuum. The characters live on forever in their open-ended time of common life, where we (who must die) are privileged (if only intermittently, each time we read the book) to join them.

Part Two

Chapter 6

✣

HOGG'S BODY

To those who are unacquainted with the pastoral scenes in which our author was educated, it may afford some amusement to find real shepherds
actually contending for a poetical prize, and to remark some other peculiarities in their habits and manners.
—Scott's introduction, "Memoir of the Life of James Hogg," 1807

O Mr Scott, Mr Scott, thou wilt put me stark mad some day.
—Hogg, *A Tour in the Highlands in 1803*

ETTRICK SHEPHERD

One of the set pieces in *Peter's Letters to His Kinsfolk* is provided by the
second triennial Burns dinner held in Edinburgh on 22 February 1819.
Complaining that Burns has become a hostage of the Whig literati, Dr.
Morris sets out to rescue him for the *Blackwood's* camp. He reports John
Wilson's eulogy of James Hogg, "the Ettrick Shepherd":

> [W]hat homage could be so appropriate to the Manes of Burns, as that which
> sought to attain its object by welcoming and honouring the only worthy suc-
> cessor of his genius? I wish I could recall for your delight any portion of those
> glowing words in which this enthusiastic speaker strove to embody his own
> ideas—and indeed those of his audience—concerning the high and holy con-
> nection which exists between the dead and the living peasant—both "sprung
> from the very bosom of the people," both identifying themselves in all things
> with the spirit of their station, and endeavouring to ennoble themselves only
> by elevating it. It was thus, indeed, that a national assembly might most effec-
> tually do honour to a national poet. This was the true spirit for a commemo-
> ration of Robert Burns.[1]

Dead and living peasant share the endeavor to ennoble themselves by
elevating the spirit of their station rather than its material conditions.
They earn their title to national character by purifying their humble origin
of any ambition to change it. But for Hogg, no less than for Burns, literature bore the promise of worldly advancement.

Hogg was at the height of his literary career. Following the success of his poem *The Queen's Wake* (1813), he had recently turned to historical fiction with *The Brownie of Bodsbeck* (1818). In these works he sets aside the folk persona of "the Ettrick Shepherd" and announces himself as "James Hogg." In moving from the pastoral forms of ballad and lyric through a more ambitious national poetry and thence to the epic form of the historical novel, Hogg was following the classical path of a literary career as remade by Scott. But while his biographical origins as a Border shepherd might have served as a guarantee of authenticity for dialect songs and ballads, the editors and reviewers who monitored the literary market-place would invoke those origins to disqualify Hogg's attempts to write in metropolitan genres. In *Peter's Letters* Lockhart continues to identify James Hogg as the Ettrick Shepherd, a regional folk poet, and this would remain his official persona for a century after his death. When Sheriff Scott rode over the moors to meet him in 1802, "Jamie the poeter" was a local celebrity who had published a small volume, *Scottish Pastorals*, at his own expense in Edinburgh the previous year. Scott found him to be "a wonderful creature for his opportunities, which were far inferior to those of the generality of Scottish peasants," Burns not excepted—pastoral societies, according to Enlightenment stadial history, being more primitive than agricultural ones. Viewing Ettrick Forest for the first time, Scott is said to have pronounced it "a savage enough place, a very savage place."[2] All the same, the Ettrick Shepherd was a literary confection from the start. Hogg's early Highland Tour letters (1802) depict the Vale of Ettrick as—far from "savage"—a rural center of civilization where sports, music, and oral poetry make conditions "elegant and agreeable" for "those who can relish such a life."[3] In contrast, Hogg's autobiographical preface to *The Mountain Bard* (1807) stresses the material privation of the author's early years in order to produce the narrative of a triumphant progress from rustic poverty, toil, and illiteracy toward metropolitan fame.

Hogg's accounts of his career negotiate a compromise between the authenticity of pastoral origins and the obsolescence of oral tradition in a market economy, where the identity of an author is bound by copyright, the legal nexus of name, text, and property. *The Queen's Wake* comments ruefully on the risks of tradition, viewed definitively from outside:

> Woe that the bard, whose thrilling song
> Has poured from age to age along,
> Should perish from the lists of fame,
> And lose his only boon, a name.[4]

The traditional topos of elegiac consolation—translation of dead poet into genius loci—falls back into the communitarian current of oral cultural origins: "The song is saved, the bard is lost" (37). But name and fame are everything now in a literary culture in which songs are bought and sold as printed texts. Evidently the way forward would be to enclose popular tradition and turn it into private property, as Scott was doing with *Minstrelsy of the Scottish Border* and the ballad-based verse romances that followed.

Hogg lived out, across his career, the structural contradiction of "national character" discussed in chapter 3 of *Scott's Shadow*. The affixing of a literary career to the bardic figure of the Ettrick Shepherd clarified the crux as one of cultural origins, already schematized in a historiography which at once valorized the poet as voice of a primordial stage of society close to nature and depreciated him as an uncouth relic doomed to extinction by the logic of economic and cultural improvement. Hogg's hold on his title grew precarious as he entered the Edinburgh literary mart, where the "Ettrick Shepherd" would come to designate the opposite of an author's control of his own name and property. Hogg blithely participated in the early campaigns and promotions of *Blackwood's Magazine*, in which the Ettrick Shepherd played a key part, that of the naïve poet (in a Schillerian typology) guaranteeing the Tory claim on national tradition.[5] But it turned out that the Ettrick Shepherd would realize most value when alienated from the original proprietor. The August 1819 issue of *Blackwood's* carried a long article by Lockhart, expanded in the following number into "The Tent," in which various authorial and editorial avatars—including Christopher North (John Wilson) and Dr. Morris of *Peter's Letters*—celebrate the "Glorious Twelfth" with a patriarchal holiday on the Earl of Fife's estate. They are joined by a clownish but kindly figure, fount of pawky folk wisdom and impromptu lyrical flights, the Ettrick Shepherd. "I think it is excellent sport," was Hogg's own verdict: "and very good natured sport beside."[6]

"The Tent" (its stale whiff of coterie heartiness recalling yesteryear's school magazine) marks the ceremonial enrolment of the Ettrick Shepherd in the Blackwoodian mythology. Wilson especially would go on to make the Shepherd into a full-blown "national character"—perhaps the most famous in British Romanticism—in the symposium series "Noctes Ambrosianae." The casting of Hogg as Tory mascot did not go unchallenged. Hogg's friend James Gray wrote a set of articles celebrating his life and works in Constable's *Edinburgh Magazine*, the local rival to *Blackwood's*, in 1818. Two years later the *London Magazine* and the *Scotsman* (the newspaper of record of the Edinburgh Whigs) were mounting a campaign to rescue Hogg from the "Mohock Magazine": "His name is taken as a cover for malignity of which he is incapable. . . . In the black catalogue of offences committed by this worthless gang against decency and principle, there is perhaps nothing so atrocious as their conduct to Mr Hogg."[7] By the late 1820s, nevertheless, it seemed that the marvellous peasant-poet was a fiction wholly owned and produced by Wilson and his subsidiaries, to the embarrassment of the still-struggling author and private person, James Hogg, who would try with limited success to wrest his public identity back from them.[8] The reduction of the Shepherd to a commodity, a brand name or trademark, accompanied his symbolic apotheosis as an organic national character—most bizarrely in a series of dramatic epiphanies, in the pages of *Blackwood's*, of his wild body. Before turning, in the last part of this chapter, to read Wilson's rhapsodic fantasies of an all-too-organic Hogg, I shall trace Hogg's own representations of his entry into the Edinburgh literary system, mediated by his relationship with the most powerful figure in that system: the wizardlike patron, Scott.

HOGG'S SCRAPES

By 1819 the Ettrick Shepherd was already a veteran of the culture wars, enlisted in the *Blackwood's* camp since its mobilization two years earlier. Although Lockhart and Wilson would deny him the credit, Hogg claimed to have originated the idea of a monthly magazine that would break the hegemony of the *Edinburgh Review,* and he drafted the "Ancient Manuscript Translated from the Chaldee" with which *Blackwood's* opened its guerilla campaign of personal satire in October 1817.[9] Nine months before the Burns dinner Hogg found himself involved in one of those "affairs of honour" that were becoming only too characteristic of Edinburgh literary life. Scott tells the tale to the Duke of Buccleuch:

> Two mornings ago about seven in the morning my servant announced while I was shaving in my dressing room that Mr Hogg wishd earnestly to speak with me. He was usherd in & I cannot describe the half startled half humourous air with which he said scratching his head most vehemently "Odd Scott here's twae fo'k's come frae Glasgow to provoke *mey* to fight a duel"—"A duel" answerd I in great astonishment "And what do you intend to do?"— Odd I lockd them up in my room & sent the lassie for twa o' the police & just gied the men ower to their charge—"and I thought I wad come & ask you what I should do wi' Douglas for he's at the Turf coffee house."[10]

Hogg had been conscripted as bodyguard in an exchange of thrashings between William Blackwood and John Douglas, editor of the Whig *Glasgow Chronicle.* When the *Chronicle*'s account of the fracas compared Hogg to a shop porter, Hogg published a statement that he frequented society to which Douglas would not be admitted even as a waiter, and here were Douglas's seconds calling him out. In the event, Hogg was unable to press charges and he retreated to his cottage in the Borders, nervous about further violence. "Now although I do not hold valour to be an essential article in the composition of a man like Hogg," confides Scott to his Grace, "yet I heartily wish he could have prevaild on himself to swagger a little had it been but on the speculation that the Glasgow Chronicler might have fled the first." Scott clearly relishes the episode's incongruities of social pretension—these brawls annihilate whatever gentlemanly status they are meant to defend. But if the Whig Douglas is a blackguard, honest Hogg can never rise above the mock-heroic. His rustic dialect sets off the urbanity of Scott's conversation with his "clan chief" (and while Scott has a manservant, Hogg must send out "the lassie" for the police). It is not so much that Scott's own performance here is seamless as that Hogg constitutes its (richly embroidered) seam: reassuring both Scott and Buccleuch that the present author does indeed belong to gentlemanly society rather than a mob of scribblers.

Social farce spills over into literary criticism. In deploring Hogg's want of prowess Scott takes the trouble to damn his recently published *Brownie of Bodsbeck*:

> His Tales which is a worse scrape than his retreat before this second Bell-the-Cat Douglas are not liked. He has slanderd Claverhouse to please the Cameronians who never read novels & therefore will not be pleased. The verses to Lady Anne are the best of the volume. I hope she will not take his defection in Chivalry to heart too much—it was after his defeat that Don Quixote meditated being a shepherd which serves to show that the scrip & staff have nothing to do with the duello.

Scott's mockery poses a tactful apology. The *Brownie* was dedicated to the eldest daughter of the Duke, the wing of whose patronage Scott had coaxed over Hogg; in 1815 the late Duchess had bequeathed the poet the Altrive property to which he has just fled. Scott is responding to a risk that their patron might take offence at Hogg's involvement in public brawls and at his antiaristocratic burlesque of Claverhouse in *The Brownie*. Scott strategically praises the dedicatory poem, which performs an acceptably complex and delicate negotiation of traditional folk identities. The poet is no radical; in fact these scuffles are proof of a robust if reckless anti-Whiggery. Scott's rhetorical management of a quite complicated patronage relation, in which he triangulates himself between Buccleuch and Hogg on the patron's side, commits him, then, to expressing contempt for his friend at the same time as he is doing him a kindness. Nor does the contempt negate the kindness: theirs was a bond, in Karl Miller's words, "which difference of class tended to strengthen and define, as well as to impair."[11]

Hogg's scrapes prove he is least of all fit for the heroic enterprise of epic representation exemplified by *Old Mortality*, Scott's controversial novel of Claverhouse and the Covenanters. Scott's implausible claim that Hogg "slandered Claverhouse to please the Cameronians" recalls the recent attacks on *Old Mortality* in the *Eclectic Review* and *Edinburgh Christian Instructor*, evidence that the legacy of the Covenanters was alive and well in Scottish radical and evangelical circles.[12] Yet Hogg was a *Blackwood's* man whose tale of the killing time reproduces Scott's ideological strategy of a moderatism that corresponds with natural human feeling, as I shall argue in the next chapter. Rank makes the crucial difference. The compassion Hogg's farmer hero feels for the persecuted Covenanters suggests an alliance against oppressive government based on a nascent class sympathy rather than on religious or political ideology. Scott's hero is a gentleman, which means that although he may side with the radical Whigs he will never become one of them; his performance of a code of manners held in common with his royalist adversaries (including Claverhouse) ensures his eventual survival. Scott's dismissal of *The Brownie* detects a "new" class formation, a shared social resentment that might bind together ex-shepherds and radical weavers, behind Hogg's attack on Claverhouse—and a confusion of motive that disqualifies Hogg's pretensions to compete with Scott as a historical novelist. Above all, Scott resists a view of Hogg that implicates the beholder. By writing a historical tale about Claverhouse, Hogg has presumed an equivalence (if not an equality) with Scott—an equivalence constituted by a national culture defined by the literary marketplace: as though the difference between them will be measured henceforth solely by sales figures. Everything in the passage drives against the recognition of Hogg in the part of peer and rival, as merely another author. Scott would take part in the patrician mockery of "the great boar of Ettrick" carried on by Lockhart and Wilson, even as he continued to support Hogg with advice, interest, money, and affection. Witnesses testify to Scott's magnanimity, his lack of jealousy of fellow authors, and certainly he had little reason to worry about Hogg's impact on his own sales or fame. Something more subtle is at stake: the degree to which Scott felt his own identity to be defined in the relationship between them.

Hogg's memoir of Scott was published within two years of the latter's death. Scott's reputation was at once a national treasure, his family's and publishers' prime asset, and (in the wake of the Reform Bill) a political debating point; accordingly, the memoir proved controversial. It spurred Lockhart, at work on the official biography, to fury. The ground of offence was the levelling tendency of that very familiarity with which the memoir advertised itself. The risk as well as value of the modern (post-Boswellian) figure of the biographical subject lay in the biographer's sale of private character for public consumption. In his own *Memoirs of the Life of Scott* Lockhart perpetuates many of his father-in-law's strategies of self-authentication and self-elevation, to the extent of representing the "tragic flaw" of a would-be-lordly disdain for the commercial realities of a literary career. (Scott fully inhabits the noble genre with his fall.) Lockhart does more, however, than etch in acid Scott's social distance from the vulgar middlemen and mechanics (the Ballantyne brothers, Hogg) who were his familiars. He represents them (especially John Ballantyne) as parodies of Scott, grotesque doubles, thereby exorcizing certain potentialities that might otherwise cloud our view of the author as hero. So Lockhart's Hogg is the theriomorphic clown of the "Noctes Ambrosianae" whom no literary title can gentrify. The familiarity he claims (sprawling tipsily on a sofa at Castle Street, haranguing Lady Scott as "Charlotte") is farcically boorish.[13]

Lockhart's biographical authority was strong enough to eclipse Hogg's account of a complex friendship between a forthright, shrewd, affectionate narrator and a kindly but also temperamental and domineering Scott. Nineteenth-century accounts of the relationship, such as Margaret Oliphant's, tended to follow Lockhart in bias (if not in detail) and reiterate a stark hierarchical difference between the two authors. Scott remains unfailingly gracious in his efforts to assist the shepherd, whose peasant character is spoilt by poetic fame into absurd and self-thwarting displays of presumption. Scholars engaged in the modern revaluation of Hogg, in contrast, have found Scott wanting. Unwilling or unable to appreciate Hogg's originality, Scott discouraged and misdirected him.[14] Useful as it has proven in the recovery of Hogg's reputation, the revisionist view mystifies Scott's influence by reading it in sheerly negative terms. Zealous to reclaim Hogg as original genius, it takes too little account of the social and dialogical construction of such genius, Scott's as well as Hogg's; it yields instead the Romantic myth of Hogg as victim of a literary system that remained external to him, and overlooks Hogg's vigorous agency in entering that system, taking part in it, and using its terms. Literary influence, rather, is the social and psychological medium in which Hogg wrote himself into being. Enthralled as he remained by Scott's seemingly irresistible example and authority, Hogg worked out his literary identity (a literary identity that was never solely his) in a complex, strenuous dialectic of emulation and resistance, in which—in the last analysis—the act of resistance cannot be separated from the act of emulation.

Hogg's memoir of Scott is all the more moving for its registration of tensions and anxieties within their friendship. The narrative moves in associative circles rather than chronologically, as though the author is mulling over a relationship he does not quite yet fully understand, trying to reconcile discordant elements.[15] While Hogg the narrator warmly affirms the affection and respect between the two men, the anecdotes he selects tend to dramatize moments of contention—disappointments, discourage-ments, snubs. We read of a Scott who is generous with advice and money yet "shy and chary of his name and interest,"[16] who praises Hogg's literary ventures yet also discourages them. In dialogue with Scott, Hogg sometimes dramatizes himself (arguing about their prose tales and the traditions upon which they are based) as the Ettrick Shepherd, whose "broad homely way" contrasts with Scott's imperiously polite dialect much as in Scott's own representation of their talk; and sometimes he gives himself a proud formal English equal to Scott's (quarrelling about their public ranking of one another as poets). Each voice is conventional, rhetorically fitted to the cultural authority Hogg claims in the scene (the authenticity of popular tradition; the judgment of the literary public). The pattern of the friendship is exemplified in a well-known incident: their estrangement because of a literary dispute is healed when Hogg falls ill and Scott can intervene, once more, as loving protector, paying his medical bills.[17]

It turns out then that familiarity, the modern figure of a sentimental affinity between private selves, coincides with and can only be sustained by a traditional relation of patronage and dependency. Hogg's admiration of Scott is enthusiastic but uneasy:

> He was truly an extraordinary man; the greatest man in the world. What are kings or Emperors compared with him? Dust and sand! And unless when connected with literary men the greater part of their names either not remembered at all or only remembered with detestation. (*Anecdotes of Scott*, 66)

Such praise admits a protest as it turns the hierarchy of patronage upside down, recalling the criticism of Scott's "devotion for titled rank" which opens the memoir. In each case of contention that he relates in the *Familiar Anecdotes*, Hogg represents his own literary enterprise as encroaching in some way upon Scott's, threatening to define both authors as constituted in equivalent terms by the market. He goes ahead with his periodical the *Spy* despite Scott's discouragement (58–59), and when he presumes to judge Scott's poetic rank in its pages (as "perhaps" below his own) they exchange cross words (48–50). When they wrangle over the depiction of Claverhouse in *The Brownie of Bodsbeck*, Hogg tells Scott that his version is a great deal more "true" than "your tale o' Auld Mortality" (50–52). Scott complains that in *The Three Perils of Man* Hogg has "ruined one of the best tales in the world," but subsequently copies it in his own *Castle Dangerous* (52). Elsewhere, Hogg recounts how his "poetical repository," a projected benefit anthology, fell through after Scott refused to contribute to it, so he turned it into a book of parodies ("Memoir," 39–41). The more famous name will not stoop to collaboration or stand beside his peers in the marketplace. Whenever the two encounter as authors, Scott, no longer affable, bends heavy brows on the presumptuous shepherd.

These scenes of rivalry and rebuke follow Hogg's commitment to a professional literary career in 1810, after his failure to set up as a farmer on the profits of *The Mountain Bard*. The principal, defining tension of the friendship between Scott and Hogg can be traced in the confusion of a relation between patron and client with one between potential equals, commercial rivals—the latter constituting a "new" subjectivity that neither author would find himself willing or able to sustain.

MEN OF LETTERS

It was then I commenced a Spy upon the manners, customs, and particular characters of all ranks of people, and all ranks of authors in particular.
—*The Spy*

In his autobiography Hogg recounts his discovery that once he has set out on a literary career he cannot return to pastoral origins:

Having appeared as a poet, and a speculative farmer besides, no one would now employ me as a shepherd . . . and for a whole winter I found myself without employment, and without money, in my native country; therefore, in February 1810, in utter desperation, I took my plaid about my shoulders, and marched away to Edinburgh, determined, since no better could be, to push my fortune as a literary man. It is true, I had estimated my poetical talent high enough, but I had resolved to use it only as a staff, never as a crutch; and would have kept that resolve, had I not been driven to the reverse. ("Memoir," 23)

Three years earlier, Scott's interest had secured Hogg the attention of Constable and a list of subscribers for *The Mountain Bard*. Now he recalls Scott's favorite precept ("I determined that literature should be my staff, but not my crutch")[18] in a concerted attempt to establish himself in the Edinburgh literary field. Hogg's most audacious bid was to edit a weekly magazine, the *Spy*, as though his personal progress were to recapitulate the formation of civil society in the *Spectator*. Hogg wrote most of the paper himself, and he donned a succession of authorial masks, including the Addisonian ("Urbanity, however, is itself a duty"), as well as that of the "Nithsdale Shepherd" John Miller, come to make a literary career in the capital.[19] Hogg's main editorial persona, Mr. Spy, is a figure of polymorphic potentiality in the urban scene, with no identity apart from those he acquires by observation: by no means the impartial spectator of Enlightenment philosophy, ethically regulating the social field, "but an alienated outsider who is not accountable to anyone," occupied in a primitive accumulation of moral capital.[20]

Such a figure was well suited to the social milieu within which Hogg put together his magazine. Gillian Hughes's recent edition of *The Spy* opens a window onto a thriving "alternative if not counter culture" (in Susan Manning's phrase) to the gentlemanly establishment of Scott, Jeffrey, and the lawyer-literati of the *Edinburgh Review*, one composed of "printers, schoolteachers, physicians, working farmers" and (not least) women writers.[21] Excluded from political representation in unreformed Scotland, these circles fostered oppositional views and sympathies. Two of Hogg's collaborators, Robert Anderson and James Gray, hosted influential literary salons in Edinburgh in the years before Scott's ascendancy; Gray and his wife Mary, who together wrote the bulk of contributions not by Hogg himself, had been close friends of Burns in his last years at Dumfries, thus providing a living link between the poets. Such company encouraged a democratic understanding of the literary market as a medium for open competition and social advancement as well as for the dissemination of information and ideas. From the *Spy* through the publication of his breakthrough work *The Queen's Wake*, this "somewhat radical alternative Edinburgh" provided Hogg with an alternative base to the patronage network of Scott, and an alternative conception of a career, although it would soon be eclipsed by Scott's consolidation of "literary authority" in postwar Edinburgh and the formation of *Blackwood's*.[22] A dissenting, lower-middle-class literary culture would resurface in the Edinburgh radical and liberal magazines and allied projects encouraged by the 1832 Reform Bill. Meanwhile, the arch-Tory *Blackwood's Magazine* owed much of its success to its ability to harness subaltern and dissident cultural energies, casting itself as an antiestablishment counterblast to the elite quarterlies, so that the contradiction between the Hogg of the *Spy* and the Hogg of *Blackwood's* may be more apparent than actual.

The Spy failed after a run of one year. Hogg fell back on his original persona:

> . . . that a common shepherd who never was at school, who went to service at seven years of age, and could neither write nor read with accuracy when twenty, yet who, smitten with an unconquerable thirst after knowledge, should run away from his master, leave his native mountains, and his flocks to wander where they chose, come to the metropolis with his plaid wrapt round his shoulders, and all at once set up for a connoisseur in manners, taste, and genius, has certainly much more the appearance of a romance than a matter of fact. Yet matter of fact it certainly is, and such a person is the editor of the Spy.[23]

It was the romance he would be stuck with. The editor represents his entry into literary society as no polite negotiation but a row between plebeian gate-crasher and bouncers at a select club:

> From the boldness of such an attempt by an illiterate person, it will naturally be expected, that the Spy should make some acknowledgements, if not absolutely cringe to the critics; but the truth is, he expects only such mercy as an intruder deserves, either to keep his ground by main force, or be kicked out of the premises of genius and learning, bruised and maimed. —He whose confidence in his own merit invites him to meet, without any apparent sense of inferiority, those who flattered themselves with their own dignity, may justly be considered as an insolent leveller, impatient of the just prerogatives of rank and wealth, eager to usurp the station to which he has no right, and to confound the subordinations of society; and who would contribute to the exaltation of that spirit which even want and calamity are not able to restrain? (518)

Mr. Spy had laid out the complaint in an earlier issue. The outsider's analysis is valuable for its shrewd reductiveness:

> [T]he *business* of literature in this country is monopolized by a few individuals, out of whose hands it is impossible at present to recover it, and without whose sanction to a work, no bookseller will publish it, neither will the public peruse it. Works of literature are become much like bank notes, they must be issued by certain firms, else they will not pass current. These firms keep the reviews under controul; reviews are at present the rage, and magazines in disrepute; the nation, sensible that the reviewers are men of superior abilities, condescend to be directed by them, without taking the private interests of a party, whose rights these reviewers are bound to support, at all into question; and thus the whole business goes on mechanically. . . . The literary taste, of Scotland in particular, being thus ruled by a very few, who are formed into two parties, unless you can get enlisted into one or other of these corps, you cannot so much as get a chance of appearing in public. (120–21)

Hogg's critique is more acute than Tory polemics against an *Edinburgh Review* hegemony, with which it has some affinities. In his contemporaneous essay on periodical criticism in the *Edinburgh Annual Register* (discussed in chapter 2), Scott locates the booksellers' despotism with an ancien régime overthrown by the Edinburgh reviewers, who liberated authors from the corruptions of patronage and raised their status from hacks to professionals; all the same, he deplores the infiltration of party spirit into this newly won territory.[24] Hogg's Spy complains, in contrast, that the rank and patronage structures of Old Corruption remain in place, if anything fortified by the new monopoly of the reviews, and that they are congruent with party-political interest. The historical progress high-lighted by Scott—a professional gentlemen's revolution—is invisible from this perspective. In the shock of his intrusion the outsider apprehends the political and institutional force field of the literature industry as far differ-ent from the free space of chameleonic role playing, individual mobility, and self-fashioning that its ideology advertised. Meanwhile the Spy's cri-tique has a prophetic poignancy, since Hogg would see himself doomed to a parodic version of the career he describes: complaining at once that an elite conspiracy has impeded his access to a free market where he might compete on equal terms, and that Scott's interest has not advanced him far enough.

The satire of Scott's poetic reputation by another of Hogg's personae, Giles Shuffleton, amplifies the complaint against the "stranglehold on Scottish literature, as poet, critic, and patron of his impoverished fellow-authors" that Scott already seemed to be exercising by 1810.[25] In the com-ing years the consolidation of literary authority that accompanied Scott's apparent "horizontal and vertical concentration of media ownership"[26] would exacerbate the sense of a monopolistic control over Edinburgh literary life, strengthened by the war between parties. The quasi monop-oly reinforced an ideology of patronage that was all too consonant with the political condition of Edinburgh, with its government-appointed ad-ministration and powerful professional elites. Constable and Scott may have glimpsed the industrial dimensions of an expanding literary market in 1825, issuing in *Constable's Miscellany* and the "Magnum Opus" edi-tion, but they preferred to behave like feudal barons, presiding over net-works of influence, while failing in the end to command the machinery of capital and credit they had set in motion.[27] Scott's shrewd remarks about the periodical trade contrast strangely with the unmarketable proj-ects in which he involved his firm, including the *Edinburgh Annual Regis-ter*.[28] He would insist on construing his relationship to the Ballantynes, boyhood friends, and to authors of Ballantyne projects such as John Leyden and Henry Weber, in terms of patronage rather than business. Scott also saw himself as the patron of his publishers, and was touchy about defending this status. "I am really tired of being supposed to receive favours when I am in fact conferring them," he growled to James Ballan-tyne in the thick of the dispute that cost Blackwood and Murray the future series of *Tales of My Landlord*.[29] The author's appropriation of the pa-tronage position clashes ludicrously with the claims put upon it by the publishers themselves. Although he himself never quite attains this sta-tus—the image of the shopkeeper cudgelled by rivals clings too much about him—Blackwood admired Murray for making publishing "a liberal profession, and not a mere business of pence." Significantly, such "privi-lege" came from association with the likes of Byron and Scott.[30] To these golden decades (1805–25) belong the anecdotes of princely publishers handing out thousands of guineas to lordly authors who would condescend to accept them. Lockhart, with characteristically satirical hindsight, identifies the tension among these categories—patron, author, publisher—in his anecdote of a complacent Constable marching up and down in his rooms exclaiming, "By G——, I am all but the author of the Waverley novels!"[31]

"So much for bookselling the most ticklish and unsafe and hazardous of all professions scarcely with the exception of horse-jockeyship."[32] These imaginings were attempts to master a coherent identity in an economic condition of drastic uncertainty and instability. The years surrounding the 1826 ruin are littered with failures, including those of Hogg's publishers George Goldie, who fell in the shudder of 1813 (the same that drove Scott and the Ballantynes back to Constable), and James Cochrane, who went down in 1832. Hogg too remained double bound by the entangled discourses of patronage and commerce. As Peter Garside has argued, in moving from the residual patronage form of subscription poetry to prose fiction Hogg sought a popular triumph such as Scott enjoyed, and believed that it would be his if only his wares were allowed fair access to the market.[33] He persisted in blaming his publishers for the failure of that success to materialize—they must have exercised a form of negative patronage, behind which might be glimpsed the shadows of Scott and his gentlemen protégés Lockhart and Wilson. And at same time Hogg felt compelled to press his reliance upon Scott, asking him for his advice and interest, complaining that he was in the end not patron enough. Hogg wished the systems of patronage and the market to reinforce one another and sustain his career, as they appeared to do for Scott, but it seemed rather as though they combined to keep him down.

BORDER MINSTRELS

Hogg's patron, as well as mentor, critic, censor, friend, Scott occupied the senior role so consistently that it is easy to forget he was the younger man (by one year). Scott haunts Hogg's writings, in the crucial years of his literary career, as a preternatural figure of authority and influence. At the same time, in the struggle to claim his own place, Hogg plays a more spirited part than that of client. The next two sections of this chapter follow the confrontations Hogg rehearsed with the shadow of Scott across his career: first, in the establishment of a poetic persona on the terrain of Border tradition (1807–13), as Hogg moved from a subjective position of client to rival, and then in the more vexed turn to novel-length prose fiction in the early 1820s. Here we can witness the emergence of the mod-

ern, Romantic conception of literary influence: from a relation homologous with patronage to a lonely and bitter struggle over originality, the
value that at once precedes the formation of a literary market and yet is
realized there. The case of Scott and Hogg demystifies the official conception of influence as a struggle with the mighty dead—showing it as a
competition for profit and prestige in a closed economy—and at the same
time realizes its uncanniness, with a living author standing in the role of
ghostly patriarch.

When Scott and Hogg first met, in 1802, it was Hogg who could claim
higher poetic authority. For all of the éclat of the newly published *Minstrelsy of the Scottish Border*, Hogg stood closer to the traditions upon
which it drew. His maternal grandfather, Will o' Phaup, was "the last man
of this wild region, who heard, saw, and conversed with the fairies," while
his mother, Margaret Laidlaw, was "a living miscellany of old songs."[34]
Scott might claim a genealogy of Border barons but he was a bourgeois
incomer, an Edinburgh lawyer's son. Scott's office as Sheriff-Depute of
Selkirk gave him the opportunity to carry out his ballad-gathering expedi-
tions, his name for which, "raids," evokes an indigenous ancestry (of
Border reivers) as well as an outsider's expropriation. Hogg touches the
latter association in reporting his mother's famous rebuke: "[T]here war
never ane o' my sangs prentit till ye prentit them yoursel', an' ye hae spoilt
them awthegither. They were made for singing an' no for reading; but ye
hae broken the charm now, an' they'll never be sung mair."[35] William
Laidlaw, who brought the poets together, comments on the hereditary
"fear and respect" with which the Border folk regarded their sheriffs;
so stable a social difference made it possible for them to meet as fellow
connoisseurs.[36] "I am surprized to find that the songs in your collection
differ so widely from my mother's," Hogg had written, with a clear infer-
ence as to which were better.[37] Hogg was a crucial collaborator on the
third volume of the *Minstrelsy*, and the assistance Scott gave him with his
own literary projects was fair reciprocation. The first of these projects
was the 1802 Highland tour Scott encouraged Hogg to undertake for
Constable's *Scots Magazine*, and introduced as "really and unaffectedly
the production of a shepherd of Ettrick Forest."[38] Soon Scott was helping
Hogg with his own ballad collection *The Mountain Bard* (1807)—getting
him a publisher and subscribers, correcting texts, seeing the volume
through the press. Robin MacLachlan comments that their friendship
"was never closer" than at this early stage of both men's literary careers,
when poetic fellowship encouraged them to play with a certain heartiness
the parts of Border sheriff and "your faithful [or poor, or grateful] shepherd."[39] But as Hogg's reliance upon Scott's offices for getting him into
print became evident, and as Scott's fortunes took off, the bias of patronage prevailed over any claim to literary equality. "Now my dear sir I can

do nothing without you," writes Hogg in 1807: "I am just like the old pagans who when they could do no better ran to their gods for redress."[40]

This mighty patron appears to the shepherd in a dream, in an episode near the end of the Highland tour that foreshadows the visitations of a demonic tempter in the *Confessions of a Justified Sinner*. Solitary and dejected, Hogg broods over the purpose of the tour, clearly a metaphor for the literary career upon which he is embarking. He questions what profit or pleasure may be gained in venturing so far from his roots: "Sure it is not only *vanity* but *vexation of spirit*."[41] Then he falls asleep. (The tour is written up as a series of letters to Scott.)

> I thought I was sitting in my chamber at Dalnacardoch by a window that looked toward the south, and writing to you of mountains and plains of unspeakable grandeur and beauty, when you suddenly entered behind me. I held you out the letter, telling you that was the way you sometimes did with me; but without making me any answer to that purpose, you began to up-braid me for my irresolution, and wondered how I could so soon relinquish an enterprise of which I seemed so fond. I then went over the above arguments with some warmth, which you quite disregarded, and were busy all the time adjusting your dress, which was much more magnificent than ever I had before seen it; yea, so *braw* were you, that had it not been for your voice and gait I could not have recognized you. No sooner had I finished than you left the room, telling me peremptorily to proceed, and depend on your promise that I never should repent it.[42]

Exhorted by this sumptuous eidolon, the custodian of theologically dubious aesthetic values, Hogg proceeds into the wilderness, which may be at once the symbolic space of the sublime, promising the poet's worldly elevation, and the allegorical space of a spiritual perdition. "Nor have I yet repented," he writes to Scott: "Don't think, my dear sir, that this is a story; it is just as true as a preaching, and I have since been induced to look to you as my guardian angel." Elsewhere Scott functions as spell-binding author of the shepherd's progress, whirling him through dizzying changes of scene and rank. One night he is couched among "dying wives, crying children, pushing cows, and fighting dogs"; the next, "in the splendid dining-room in the Castle of Inveraray, surrounded by dukes! lords! ladies! silver, silk, gold, pictures, powdered lacqueys, and the devil knows what! O Mr Scott," for this seems a translation more infernal than heavenly, "Mr Scott, thou wilt put me stark mad some day."[43]

"There is no publishing a book without a patron."[44] In dedicating *The Mountain Bard* to the "Sherriff of Ettrick Forest, and Minstrel of the Scottish Border," Hogg formally launched his career in the track of Scott's, and attached himself to Scott's patronage network. Hogg had devoted the first letter of the 1802 tour to a description of Ettrick Forest celebrating the dominion of the Scotts of Buccleuch. Shortly after that Scott was interceding on his behalf with the Earl of Dalkeith. Hogg dedicated *The Forest Minstrel* (1810) to the Countess (who would bequeath him his Altrive property), just as Scott had dedicated *The Lay of the Last Minstrel* to her husband (1805). In a letter to Scott shortly after publication of the *Lay*, Hogg included himself in the imaginary feudal community evoked in that poem:

> My ancestors farmed the lands of Fauldshope &c. under the Scotts of Harden or Oakwood even so early as the time of their residence at Kirkhope, and for several ages, even until the family lost these lands. They were noted for strength, hardiness, and a turbulent disposition; and one of them named William was Hardens chief champion, and from his great strength and ferocity was nick-named *the Wild Boar*.[45]

The claim was important enough that Hogg published it in the notes to *The Mountain Bard*, for it announces the principal strategy with which he would situate his poetic authority in relation to Scott's. With the acknowledgment of feudal subjection he may pretend to an equality in prowess and a share in these lands, forfeited through some ancestral mishap, that are now so powerfully mythologized as the estate of the Scotts.[46] In the event, the poets' sole future collaboration as peers would take place through one of Scott's ad hoc feudal revivals, the grand "Wappenschaw" or football match between Yarrow and Selkirk at Ettrickhaugh in December 1815, for which both bards contributed songs.[47] Here was a ceremonial enrollment of the Ettrick Shepherd in the legendary border domain Scott had made his own—and on Scott's terms.

On other occasions, however, Hogg would claim that fabulous territory for himself. The "Ballads, in Imitation of the Antients" that make up *The Mountain Bard* rehearse a more complex engagement with the figure of Scott than simple gratitude or obeisance. Hogg certainly would have recognized the verses that Scott interpolated into some of the traditional ballads in the *Minstrelsy*. Egregious among such interpolations was Scott's own name, as though the editor were justifying his enclosure of Border tradition by forging an ancient title to it. In "Jamie Telfer of the Fair Dodhead" Scott changed the heroes from Elliotts to Scotts and inserted stanzas featuring the ancestral septs of Harden and Buccleuch, an innovation repeated in "The Sang of the Outlaw Murray."[48] Two of Hogg's ballads in *The Mountain Bard*, "Gilmanscleugh" and "The Fray of Elibank," take up this ancestral history of the Scotts. "Gilmanscleugh: Founded upon an Ancient Family Tradition" recounts a feud between the Scotts of Harden (Scott's ancestors) and the Scotts of Gilmanscleugh which leads to the ascendancy of the former. The tale effects a pathetic reconciliation in the poem's present, in which the Harden patriarch takes in the beggarly scion of Gilmanscleugh in return for a pledge of feudal service:

> A Scott shou'd ay support a Scott,
> When sinking to decaye,
> Till over a' the southlan' hills
> We stretch our ample sway.[49]

Under cover of a complimentary anecdote about Scott hegemony (bloody and devious, however) Hogg expresses the fantasy by which he would make these feudal scenarios his own: service to a more fortunate patron is the means to recovering a lost, original relation of peerage. The client is also an apprentice, who expects to become master in his turn.[50] "The Fray of Elibank" offers a more insolent variant. Young Wattie o' Harden (Scott's ancestor) calls upon his favorite champion, stout Willie o' Fauldshope (Hogg's), to join him in a reiving expedition, in contravention of the law-and-order policy of their chieftain Buccleuch. In the course of the raid young Harden cannot keep up with the exuberant charge of the Wild Boar and falls into the hands of the enemy. Harden only escapes hanging by agreeing to marry his captor's ill-favored daughter. She proves however to be "a prudent, a virtuous, and sensible wife," and "muckle good blood frae that union has flowed"—including that of the present Sheriff of Ettrick (*Mountain Bard*, 64). The Hogg character bursts out of the tale with an uncontainable feral energy, leaving Scott's bogged down in a generic residue of ironical worldliness and prudent domesticity.

As Scott attains the front rank among European poets (with *The Lady of the Lake*) and Hogg makes his way in literary Edinburgh in 1810, we find Hogg prosecuting a series of startlingly brisk criticisms of his friend's reputation in the early numbers of the *Spy*. In the "Mask of Scottish Poets" Giles Shuffleton complains of the "wild and uncouth" fashion of Scott's Muse, and predicts that posterity will not endorse the contemporary preeminence trumpeted by Scott's claque of supporters (Hogg, *Spy*, 13–14, 100–104). "Malise's Journey to the Trossacks" satirizes the fashion for the scenery of *The Lady of the Lake*—suggesting that Scott's celebrity is as much a touristic as a literary phenomenon. In the last number of the *Spy* (provoking the quarrel related in *Familiar Anecdotes*), Hogg replied to what he took to be Scott's slighting reference to him in the *Edinburgh Annual Register* (as gifted but mired in "vulgarity") by accusing Scott of inflating his own reputation in anonymous periodical puffs (517).

Hogg highlights bardic rivalry with Scott in his national poem *The Queen's Wake*, published in the year Scott was offered and turned down the title of Poet Laureate (1813). *The Queen's Wake* is an extended meditation on the topic of a national culture, the kinds of poetry that might claim to represent it, and the various provincial and metropolitan identities that constitute it.[51] In the poem's frame, Hogg reflects on the state of his literary career. Defying "cold winds of adversity" he reclaims his poetic vocation: "I've found my Mountain Lyre again."[52] In the past few years of literary toil in Edinburgh, marked by the failure of the *Spy*, he had lost touch with the sources of his genius, but now he returns to his native countryside. Hogg resumes the character of Ettrick Shepherd as a figure inflected by the metropolitan idea of a national literary tradition, in which he claims a central rather than marginal place. In the fable of *The Queen's Wake* the Scottish bards compete in a festival to celebrate Queen Mary's return from France. One of them is a humble shepherd from Ettrick, ragged and dejected, bearing the motto *Naturae Donum*. He wins second prize, which he boldly redefines: "Your cottage keep, and minstrel lore, — / Grant me a harp, I ask no more." Not the hand-me-downs of patronage and antiquarianism, in short, but original genius: "a harp of old renown . . . framed by wizard of the wild" which grants the solitary poet access to fairy visions (168).

The first prize, the golden harp of Queen Mary, falls to the bard of a Highland Gaelic tradition. Hogg recounts the modern fate of that tradition: after the '45, and the extinction of the northern bards, the harp, "Defaced of all its gems and gold, . . . Back to Dunedin [Edinburgh] found its way" (168). With his recent triumph, *The Lady of the Lake*, Scott now laid claim to the "Harp of the North." In "Mary Scott" a youthful Border bard narrates another of those rather discreditable ancestral feuds of the Scotts, reconciled this time by way of the poisoning and wonderful revival of the eponymous "flower of Ettrick."[53] In short, more than one avatar of Scott appears to give the shepherd a run for his money—as Wordsworth noticed when he praised the "Witch of Fife," "Kilmeny," and the "Abbot Mackinnon" but complained that "in too many places [*The Queen's Wake*] recalls Mr Scott to one's mind."[54] The shepherd's opponents represent a generic Scots minstrelsy, an anthology of traditions, regions, and genres, such as Scott has been engrossing in his recent claim to the title of national poet. Hogg acknowledges his rival's status (by awarding his own persona second place) at the same time as he overbids it (enclosing all these kinds, and more, in his own *Queen's Wake*).

Thus diffused, the contest with Scott is relegated to the frame of the poem. The figures of the poetic career with which it begins derive, after all, from Scott: minstrel singing before fair patroness from the *Lay of the Last Minstrel*, wintry weather of adversity from *Marmion*, harp from *The Lady of the Lake*. Most recently and provokingly, in *The Vision of Don Roderick* (1811), Scott had urged the insufficiency of the old Border themes for a subject of national poetry in the present crisis of war against France; fairy tales and "feuds obscure" are only fit for "grey-hair'd shepherds" to sing.[55] The rivalry comes into focus in the "progress of poetry" of the final pages of the *Wake*, where Hogg traces the descent of the shepherd's harp into modern times. The deftly varied series of Bangour, Ramsay, Langhorne, Logan, and Leyden ("Thrilling the heart of Indian maid, / Beneath the wild banana's shade") culminates in the advent of "Walter the abbot," whose powerful art revives the ancient Border chivalry and lures back the fairies to their haunts. Finally, the shepherd inserts himself into the line—in a vexed relation to Walter that shifts from patronage to rivalry. At first, wondering at the shepherd's natural gift, Walter generously directs his minstrelsy. Friction comes when, "to native feelings true," the shepherd claims an art of his own:

> When by myself I 'gan to play,
> He tried to wile my harp away.
> Just when her notes began with skill,
> To sound beneath the southern hill,
> And twine around my bosom's core,
> How could we part for evermore?
> 'Twas kindness all, I cannot blame,
> For bootless is the minstrel flame;
> But sure, a bard might well have known
> Another's feelings by his own!   (171–72)

Poetic rivalry is born in a sentimental scenario of jealousy and betrayal— a passionate triangulation of Scott, Hogg, and (vaguely feminine) harp. The plaintive line, "How could we part for evermore?" refers to Hogg and his art, but also to the rift between Hogg and Scott. And Hogg's claim that Scott should not be blamed since "bootless is the minstrel flame" suggests that Scott's discouragement was kindly meant, in that a poetic calling can bring no earthly advantage, and that "the minstrel flame" burns, like love, regardless of propriety. In *Familiar Anecdotes* Hogg explained that the passage alluded to Scott's attempt to get him a place as bailiff on a nobleman's estate, which turned out to be contingent upon Hogg promising "to put my poetical talent under lock and key forever!"[56] Although the incident took place early in their relationship, at a time when Scott was exerting himself to satisfy Hogg's request for such a position, Hogg felt insulted by the advice. After publication of *The Queen's Wake* he wrote to Scott: "I can never however get quit of the idea that you wished to discourage me from ever touching the harp more You were rather explicit on that head sometimes I know I durst not for my life show you any thing for fear of the most humiliating mortification."[57] In the hard years of his attempt to establish himself in Edinburgh, Hogg's recollection of this lack of faith rankled into a sense of betrayal. Scott would intervene on Hogg's behalf, once again, to assist with the publication of a new quarto edition of *The Queen's Wake* in 1817–18. Strikingly, this was to be a subscription edition: Hogg's most successful title was reverting to the conditions of patronage.[58]

At the conclusion of the "progress of poetry" in the *Wake*, Walter the abbot deserts his native land, bearing the "Caledonian harp of yore" "far to other kingdoms." Hogg refers here to *The Vision of Don Roderick*, in which the Mountain Spirit bids the poet forsake the "decay'd ... old traditionary lore" of the Borders for the "romantic lands" of Iberia, "Where wonders wild of Arabesque combine / With Gothic imagery of darker shade, / Forming a model meet for minstrel line."[59] Walter's apostasy allows the shepherd to assert, not without defiance, his own possession of that native ground: "That harp he never more shall see, / Unless 'mong Scotland's hills with me" (*Queen's Wake*, 172). With *The Queen's Wake* Hogg lays claim to a national poetry that Scott appears to have forsaken (*Rokeby*, his latest, is set in England).[60] Not much more than a year later, however, Scott returned to Scottish ground in the seemingly invincible character of the Author of *Waverley*.

THE SUICIDE'S GRAVE

"The great Hogg found his lair at Abbotsford on Friday," Scott informed a correspondent in August 1823, "Lockhart bringing him here like a pig in a string, for which the lady of the mansion sent him little thanks, she not thinking the hog's pearls (qu. Perils) an apology for his freedoms."[61] Not the least of those freedoms was Hogg's evocation of Scott himself at the opening of his new novel *The Three Perils of Woman*. The Border farmer Daniel Bell is sending his daughter Gatty to be educated in Edinburgh. Warning her against the affectation of English over "our own good, full, *doric tongue*," Daniel cites the example of "my good friend Wattie Scott," whose father was his father's lawyer. Daniel describes Scott at his post at the Court of Session: "[I]f ye see a carl that sits always with his right shoulder to you, with hair of a pale silver grey, a head like a tower, braid shoulders, and long shaggy e'e-brees—the very picture of an auld, gruff Border Baron, —that's Wattie Scott."[62] Daniel goes on to recall Scott's juvenile exploits at his grandfather's farm in the Borders: "he was a bit hempy callant, wi' bare legs, and the breeks a' torn off him wi' climbing the linns and the trees for the nests o' corbie-craws and hunting-hawks" (12). This fictional reminiscence annoyed Scott, with its reminder that his paternal grandfather was a sheep farmer like James Hogg, as well as its glossing over the reason for his childhood residence at Sandyknowe, convalescence from the polio that lamed him. Nevertheless the Wattie

Scott evoked by Daniel is a wonderfully reassuring figure. Genius loci of polite Edinburgh and the ancient Borders, he personifies fortune in the city and a national character composed of a harmonious compact between traditional patriarchal values and modern civility. The tribute recalls the bond between another lawyer and client, advocate Pleydell and Liddesdale farmer Dinmont, representing just such a compact in Scott's *Guy Mannering* (1815). Now Hogg discloses the author of *Guy Mannering* in the role of lawyer-baron who dispenses influence: a complex cultural power comprising personal, social, and political as well as textual authority. A rhetoric more urgent than literary allusion hints at a possibility of Sir Walter's direct intercession in the plot of *The Three Perils of Woman*. Much as Scott has intervened as a patron in Hogg's career, or as a censor in his texts, will he now be called upon to protect the heroine, or to straighten out the love intrigue that follows? It is as if Scott himself, a historical figure in a work of fiction, might perform something like the providential mediation carried out by the Duke of Argyle in *The Heart of Mid-Lothian*.

The startling directness of this manifestation—a referential apocalypse of the patron figure—signals a crisis in the field of influence. The crisis unfolded through Hogg's attempt to rival Scott in the national historical novel during the peak years of Scottish fiction (1821–24). Hogg's collections of "rural and traditionary tales of Scotland," contemplated as far back as 1811, had appeared in separate sets, *The Brownie of Bodsbeck* (Blackwood, 1818) and *Winter Evening Tales* (Oliver & Boyd, 1820). The novella-length *Brownie of Bodsbeck* treats the same historical topic, the late-seventeenth-century Covenanter insurgency, as *Old Mortality*, published also by Blackwood fifteen months earlier. Hogg insisted he had written the greater part of *The Brownie* "long ere the tale of 'Old Mortality' was heard of"; it seems likely that a version of it formed part of his stock of rural tales, and that he revised it in light of the controversy that flared around *Old Mortality* in 1817.[63] The commercial disappointment of *The Brownie*, for which Hogg blamed his publishers, was compounded by its reception as a crude imitation of Scott's masterpiece. The more favorable reception of *Winter Evening Tales* encouraged Hogg to produce a succession of highly ambitious, experimental, extended works of prose fiction in the early 1820s. All three titles (published by Longman) engage in a critical argument with the forms of national fiction that dominated the market, especially the synthesis of those forms mastered by Scott. The literary and cultural themes of the argument will form the topic of the next chapter. Here I will trace the appearance of shadows of Scott in Hogg's novel-length works, where they focus a growing antagonism towards the institution of Scottish fiction that Scott personified.

In 1820 Hogg hailed the news of Scott's baronetcy in verses that pretended to bury any hatchet he might have brandished in *The Queen's Wake*:

> Long brook thy honours, firm to stand
> As Eildon rock; and that thy land
> The first e'er won by dint of rhyme,
> May bear thy name till latest time;
> And stretch from bourn of Abbot's-lea
> To Philhope Cross, and Eildon Tree,
> Is the heart's wish of one who's still
> Thy grateful Shepherd of the Hill![64]

Hogg bows in acknowledgment of Scott's title to that estate he continues to occupy in the dependent station of shepherd. A protest lurks, however, in the allusion to "Eildon rock," Hogg's simile for the durability of Scott's honors, which Border folklore held to have been split in three by the black arts of a Scott ancestor, the warlock Michael Scott. This event, recalled in Scott's *Lay of the Last Minstrel*, appears at the heart of the three-volume "romance of Border chivalry" that Hogg had been working on since 1819. In *The Three Perils of Man* we see the figure of Scott shivered into at least three parts, metamorphosed by the art he strives to command, felled from the station of author to a set of allegorical ciphers.[65]

Hogg's publisher rejected his Border romance, as he complained to Scott in June 1821, on the grounds that it "must draw down comparisons with the romances of the author of Waverley and manifestly to its disadvantage these being made the criterion of judging of merit."[66] Once again Hogg appealed for Scott's interest: "merely by promising to Constable, Murray, Longmans or any you please to go over my new work either in proof or M.S. —I felt long ago when I took you up as my pattern and master in literature that without you I could not do."[67] Scott was disconcerted when he found out just what kind of a pattern he was making in his protégé's work. Hogg had taken over the sacred property of Scott's name and genealogy, and that of his clan chief Buccleuch, to make "Sir Walter Scott the first baron of Rankleburn" a prominent figure in the story. Hogg reluctantly gave way before Scott's protest and changed the name in proof (to Sir Ringan Redhough).[68] Clearly, as Douglas Gifford notes, Hogg meant to recapitulate his earlier *Mountain Bard* mode of compliment to his "master and benefactor" by celebrating the prowess of Scott's forefathers and those of his feudal chief, and so the tale begins with the prophetic theme of Scott supremacy in the Borders. But after *The Brownie of Bodsbeck* it would be hard to ignore the usurping thrust of a compliment that claimed not just Scott's literary territory and themes but his own ancestry for an audacious recasting of ancient Border romance.

The allegory of originality in *The Three Perils of Man* yields the most elaborate of all Hogg's representations of his "pattern and master in literature." Alongside the rechristened Sir Walter Scott of Rankleburn and the wizard Michael Scott, Hogg sets another Scott ancestor, Watt of Harden, alias Charlie Scott of Yardbire. These wraiths of Scott are linked by a thematic concern with relations of service and mastery, communion and bondage. The frame plot of the stalled siege of Roxburgh hinges on a point of honor between the Earl of Douglas and Sir Ringan, who holds back from intervention lest it define him as the Douglas's vassal rather than peer. The dilemma is resolved jointly by the diplomacy of the Douglas, who courteously addresses Sir Ringan as a fellow chieftain, and by Sir Ringan's obedience to the oracle his embassy brings back from Aikwood: "Rise not against feudal union, / No advance but in communion" (337). In these terms the "feudal union" between Sir Ringan and Charlie Scott, head of the Aikwood embassy, proves exemplary. Although Sir Ringan is Charlie's chief he treats him like an equal, and Charlie goes on to earn the equality in title, becoming Sir Charles Scott and the wealthy husband of Lady Jane Howard.

The alternative declension of patronage—the one that occupies Hogg's touchstone register of magic realism in *The Three Perils of Man*—is a dire relation of servitude. Independence remains an inadmissible term, the infernal delusion that covers slavery. In Blackwoodian vein Hogg makes the Devil a Radical, hailed by his imps as "patriot spirit" and the first "of all great reformers" (294). "By his principle of insubordination to established authorities," Satan gloats over a notably Napoleonic Michael Scott, "I yet hope to bring all mankind to my own mind and my own country" (291). Aikwood, a Hellish Abbotsford, is the site of that "liberty" (292) which is a relation of dominion and thraldom without communion. The metamorphoses that take place there are sports of an absolute power. Although Michael Scott may transform people, animals, and even the face of Scotland for his bleak amusement, he is the Devil's bondsman. In an apocalyptic showdown the Master proves his book lore of elemental science to be equal to the powers of Hell; but he has overdrawn his resources. After trouncing the infernal dragon come to fetch him he falls from a great height to his death.

The "Scottish magician" or "Wizard of the North" was, of course, the spectacular public persona of Scott's poetic supremacy. In the "Translation from an Ancient Chaldee Manuscript" Hogg introduced Scott as "the great magician who dwelleth in the old fastness, hard by the river Jordan, which is by the Border," to whom the rival publishers Constable and Blackwood apply for interest.[69] He gives both parties the same noncommittal answer, encouraging Blackwood and discouraging Constable: a mischievous gloss on Scott's authority in Edinburgh literary politics, officially neutral but influential behind the scenes. Scott would understand his art, like Michael Scott's, to be at once mastery and vassalage:

> He who limits his expense within such bounds as a professional income, however small, can afford him, is independent both of the bookseller and the public, and may, if he has talents, by writing what he likes and when he likes, be the conjuror who commands the devil instead of the witch who serves him.[70]

In Hogg's fable he who commands the devil also serves him, and may find equivocal release in ruin. Michael Scott, figure of the sublime in the tale, achieves mastery at the hour of his death, affirming his autonomy in a blaze of negation, like Byron's Manfred. This Scott personifies a Romantic ideology of art as triumph of the will; nor does Hogg shrink from the Nietzschean declension, that such a figure would "rather will *nothingness* than *not* will."[71]

The blatantly biographical invocation of "Wattie Scott" early in *The Three Perils of Woman* opens a trajectory opposite to the fantastic proliferation of Scotts in *The Three Perils of Man*. Scott never enters the action of the novel, nor, despite the promise of a wise potency, does he contribute anything to its plot. He remains offstage: an influence that fails to circulate. The only other brief glimpse of him is related by Gatty in one of her letters home. She observes Sir Walter at the theater: "He did not look often at the players, but when he did he made his lips thin, and looked out at the tail of his eye, as if he deemed it all a joke" (40). Scott as a figure of Olympian detachment, satirically aloof from the show, resembles Hogg's own shifty persona of Mr. Spy more than he does (say) the impartial spectator of Adam Smith's civic ethos of sympathy. Gatty's sketch, less reassuring than her father's reminiscence, hints that the persona of strength and balance may maintain itself by an essential withdrawal, a slyness.

The Three Perils of Woman models the withdrawal of Scott's influence as a drastic decentering of the gravitational field of Scottish fiction. Its vertiginously turning "circles" (as Hogg calls his chapter divisions) yield no position of spectatorial impartiality, no still point to which a stable aesthetic might be rooted, but a queasy oscillation among tones, genres, and discourses, "by turns pathetic and horrific, farcical and grotesque, and finally harrowing to a degree unmatched in any fiction of the period."[72] Commentators have read the crisis of "Peril the First" as, variously, a psychological analysis of the dilemmas of repression, an exhibition of morbid physiology, and a religious allegory.[73] Perils the Second and Third, compressed into the final volume, revisit the foundational topic of Scottish historical romance, the 1745 Rebellion, only to dissolve the scenario of national reconciliation drawn in *Waverley* by insisting on what the end of Scott's novel left out: Culloden and its aftermath. "There were many things happened to the valiant conquerors of the Highlands in 1746 that were fairly hushed up, there being none afterwards that dared to publish or avow them," interjects Hogg's narrator: "For my part, I like to rake them up whenever I can get a story that lies within twenty miles of them" (332). His rakings-up come more and more to resemble excavations of the terrain of war crimes.

The last pages of *The Three Perils of Woman* are outrageous not only for their narrative of atrocities committed against civilians by government troops but for their derangements of literary decorum. The tragic confusions of the heroine's quest are interrupted by some grisly slapstick between the sexton Davie Duff, who is collecting severed ears for bounty, and a doctor, who amuses himself by lopping off Davie's ears and handing them to him: "The thing was so suddenly and so deftly done, that the poor beadle could scarcely believe he had received any injury, but, holding the two severed ears in one hand, he put up the other to his temple, the blood whizzed against it" (395). Two paragraphs later: "Alas! unhappy Sarah! To what a scene art thou come!" By the end of the tale the narrator can declare, on the one hand, of some knockabout business involving an attempt to rifle Sarah's corpse, "the scene that then occurred for a short space was too ludicrous to be described at the close of a tale so lamentably unfortunate in all its circumstances"; on the other, "Is there human sorrow on record like this that winded up the devastations of the Highlands?" (406–7). Hogg confirms no single literary register, or compound of registers, as adequate to represent the violence inflicted on ordinary human life that underlies great historical events. The thematic correlative, a harmonious national identity, is the fiction Hogg's "Series of Domestic Scottish Tales" refuses to deliver. As Antony Hasler argues, the work's reversal of the chronology of historical progress—it circles back from contemporary Edinburgh to 1745—tracks its undoing of the literary progress from domestic tale to historical novel that constituted the dominant form of modern national fiction achieved by Scott (introduction," xxxiii– xxxix). Viewed through the perspective of the post-Culloden disasters that close *The Three Perils of Woman*, the "Wattie Scott" invoked at its opening looks like into an empty figurehead.

More disquietingly than any of Hogg's works yet, *The Three Perils of Woman* articulates a protest against the aesthetic of historical fiction established in *Waverley* as well as its author's seemingly inescapable field of influence.[74] Between *The Three Perils of Man* and *The Three Perils of Woman*, Hogg moved from high-spirited installation of an alternative romance synthesis to a disintegration of the modern Scottish novel that seems meant to baffle and dismay its readers. Besides the Waverley novels, as Hasler and Douglas Mack have shown, Hogg takes aim at a softer target, John Wilson's collection of tales *Lights and Shadows of Scottish Life* (1822), which seek to neutralize evangelical piety in the medium of conservative pathos.[75] Wilson devoted his review of *The Three Perils of Woman* in *Blackwood's* (October 1823) to a bizarre attack on Hogg's literary character. This was the culminating offence in a pattern of mockery and rejection by Hogg's peers at *Blackwood's*. A dozen years after his diagnosis of its elitist and partisan character in the *Spy*, and despite considerable if inconsistent success, Hogg felt increasingly closed out from the Edinburgh literary establishment. His attempt to make his own way as a novelist in Scott's wake had met with commercial and critical failure, and relations with the *Blackwood's* set had deteriorated. Several commentators have suggested that Hogg's travails with the "two devils" Wilson and Lockhart inform *The Private Memoirs and Confessions of a Justified Sinner* (1824), Hogg's devastating terminal essay in the genre (this time, the one-volume "accursed memoir" that had a brief vogue in the mid-1820s).[76] That Wilson and Lockhart would turn out, in their different ways, to be Scott's heirs (Lockhart his son-in-law and literary executor, Wilson by the late 1830s the ascendant power in Edinburgh literary life) made Hogg's case all the more poignant: of the same generation as Scott, edged out by the younger men, never, finally, to be admitted on equal terms.

The demonic theme of the *Confessions of a Justified Sinner* comprises, from this perspective, not only a nightmarish sibling rivalry but bondage to a mysterious potentate who tenders the delusive promise of a glorious career. Wringhim's supposition that his formidable friend and patron must be "no other than the Czar Peter of Russia . . . travelling through Europe in disguise"[77] casts the politics of influence in the sinister formation of enlightened despotism. And just as the early chapters of *The Three Perils of Woman* invoked Scott in propria persona, James Hogg himself, the famous shepherd-poet of Ettrick, makes a startling appearance in the editorial narrative that closes *The Private Memoirs and Confessions of a Justified Sinner*. Hogg is named as the author of a letter to *Blackwood's Magazine* (August 1823) that describes the marvellously preserved remains of a hundred-year-old suicide, exhumed and then buried again at a remote Border location. Curiosity piqued, the editor and his friends seek out Hogg at Thirlestane fair, but he declines to guide them on the grounds that he has to attend to business. The literary gentlemen go on anyway and raid the grave for souvenirs, one of which is the memoir we have been reading.

The shadows of more than one author fall upon this last episode.[78] The James Hogg who refuses to assist in the literary enterprise, speaking unintelligible dialect, appears to be a genuine Ettrick Shepherd: "Od bless ye, lad! I hae ither matters to mind. I hae a' thae paulies to sell, an' a' yon

Highland stotts down on the green every ane; an' then I hae ten scores o' yowes to buy after" (170). *Yowes* and *paulies* are sheep, hinting at a reclamation of Hogg's own virginal name ("unshorn yearling") from the English association with which the literati liked to mock him. He takes back his folk identity from the *Blackwood's* wits to utter a gruff rejection of the unseemly business of exhuming the traditions of his countryside for public amusement—even while that is what, as anonymous author of *The Private Memoirs and Confessions of a Justified Sinner*, he has been doing all along. The shrewd integrity of the Shepherd's refusal places him at an ethical pole opposite to the fiction's divided and outcast protagonist, at the same time that it separates him no less decisively from the authorship which is the occult identity in these pages of James Hogg.

Another author is conspicuous by his absence at the suicide's grave. The old college friend "Mr. L——t" who leads the editor to Hogg must be John Gibson Lockhart, who procures a pony and the services of William Laidlaw from his famous father-in-law. The "romantic and now classical country" through which they ride is Sir Walter Scott's (169), not least because Scott's writings have made it classical, the property of an official literary tradition. This excursion into Scott Country reverses the symbolic homecoming sketched in *Peter's Letters to His Kinsfolk*. The hilltop grave of the "*lost sinner*" is located on land owned by the Duke of Buccleuch, and not, as Hogg's letter misleadingly claimed, at a point where three estates meet (165, 170). These names of landlords, genealogies of Scott, efface that of James Hogg, whose neighborhood in fact this is: Fall Law is one of the stark hills behind St. Mary's Loch and Altrive farm in the Vale of Ettrick. The ancestral ground of the Scotts, the heritage claimed in *Minstrelsy of the Scottish Border* and *The Lay of the Last Minstrel*, is now the desolate site of Hogg's self-cancelling—a nameless grave which yields a baffling confessional fragment.

ORGANIC FORM

> I have been trying my hand on a *Noctes* for these two or three days but Wilson has not seen it as yet I fear it will be all to re-write. I *cannot* imitate him and what is far more extraordinary I cannot imitate myself.[79]

John Wilson dances on the grave of Hogg's reputation in his notorious *Blackwood's* review of *The Three Perils of Woman*. The alleged excesses of Hogg's writing provoke excesses of Wilson's own:

> It is indeed this rare union of high imagination with homely truth that constitutes the high character of his writing. In one page, we listen to the song of the nightingale, and in another, to the grunt of the boar. Now the wood is

vocal with the feathered choir; and then the sty bubbles and squeaks with a farm-sow and a litter of nineteen pigwiggins. . . . Now enters bonny Kilmenie, or Mary Lee, preparing to flee into Fairy-land, or beat up the quarters of the Man in the Moon; and then, lo and behold, some huggered, red-armed, horny-fisted, glaur-nailed Girrzy, removing on the day before term, from the Hen-coop to the sign of the Kilt, on an advance of six shillings on the half-year's wage. Never was there such a bothering repast set down before the reading public by any other caterer. . . . If you suffer your plate for a single moment to escape from the shelter of your bosom, a hundred to one but you see one of the Tweeddale Yeomanry licking it up with a tongue half a yard long, and as rough as a bison's.[80]

The reader seeks in vain for anything like this bacchanalia in *The Three Perils of Woman*. Glaur-nailed Girrzy and the bison-tongued yeoman are the reviewer's inventions. The riotous hotchpotch of style and substance, troped as Hogg's intractable *hoggishness*, energizes Wilson's own writing, obsessed with monstrous physical forms. It is not long before the novel, the ostensible object of the review, is displaced by the body of its author:

What with his genius, and what with his buck-teeth; what with his fiddle, and what with his love-locks lolling over his shoulders as he gaed "up the Kirk," tastily tied with a blue ribbon; what with his running for prize-hats up the old avenue of Traquhair, "with his hurdies like twa distant hills," to the distancing of all competitors; and what with his listering of fish and grewing of mawkins, a gentler and more irresistible shepherd was not to be found from Moffat to Mellerstain. (428)

The tone of this writing is hard to place. It wants to be contemptuous, and is not lacking in a bullying affection; it is also exhilarated by the vision of the "gentle and irresistible shepherd" with his shameless pretensions to being minstrel, sportsman, and lover. Wilson's rhetoric mimes an excessive, comic outrage at the usurpation of pastoral conventions by an actual shepherd, and something else besides: beyond the burlesque roar, an overtone of yearning. The desire to crush Hogg, to put him down, is so exaggerated as to have the opposite effect, of celebrating him, building him up, into a mythic figure—the Comus of Scottish letters. This obscene shepherd presides over the imaginary barnyard of Wilson's review, heaving and teeming with anarchic life, like some pansexual nature spirit, whose avatars include the bison-tongued yeoman and the sow with her "nineteen pigwiggins."[81]

Wilson takes up a satirical equation of Hogg with his body that was already well established in Edinburgh literary circles by the early 1820s. Such rhetoric embeds the Shepherd—even as he tries to rise in his career—in the base materiality of social origins. The present chapter concludes, following Hogg's allegories of his relation to his great friend and patron, by looking at the symbolic expropriation of not just his name but his body by his peers at *Blackwood's*. The logic of that expropriation turned full circle, beyond the conversion of the Ettrick Shepherd into a token for other authors' traffic, to a full-blown reinvention of organic form. Wilson, carrying the game to its strangest length, transforms the figure of Hogg from a merely hoggish body, notable for its brutish physiognomy, to something more potent: a sexualized "wild body," the bearer of a spectacular virility.

An early instance of the hoggish body appears at the Burns Dinner in *Peter's Letters to His Kinsfolk*, with which this chapter opened. Dr. Morris is gratified by how well the Ettrick Shepherd suits his part:

> [T]he external appearance of the man can have undergone but very little change since he was "a herd on Yarrow." His face and hands are still as brown as if he lived entirely *sub dio*. His very hair has a coarse stringiness about it, which proves beyond dispute its utter ignorance of all arts of the friseur; and hangs in playful whips and cords about his ears, in a style of the most perfect innocence imaginable. His mouth, which, when he smiles, nearly cuts the totality of his face in twain, is an object that would make the Chevalier Ruspini die with indignation; for his teeth have been allowed to grow where they listed, and as they listed, presenting more resemblance, in arrangement, (and colour too,) to a body of crouching sharp-shooters, than to any more regular species of array.[82]

Lockhart establishes the two features that identify Hogg's physiognomy: the Shepherd's long hair, transformed from gracefully luxuriant to coarse and stringy, and his irregular, jutting teeth—emblems of bestial appetite and oral aggression, the tusks of the Boar of Ettrick. Sarah Green's burlesque *Scotch Novel Reading* (1824) pays tribute to the forcefulness of Lockhart's description—and to the peculiar frisson of having the imaginary features of an author, that shadowy figure "behind" the text, emerge into visibility. Seduced by fashionable Scottish fiction, Green's heroine falls in love with the Ettrick Shepherd: "She saw, in imagination, the sunny ringlets floating over the rosy cheek of poor Hogg." But she receives a disillusioning shock when she reads Dr. Morris's description in *Peter's Letters*. Hogg's physiognomy is bound up, as in Wilson's review of *The Three Perils of Woman*, with the English reading of his name: "when she found that The Ettrick Shepherd was named Hogg, her grief was beyond all bounds."[83]

Nor was the figure of Hogg as hoggish body limited to the Blackwoodians. This chapter has traced the appearance of Scott as a figure in Hogg's fiction. More conjectural is the presence of Hogg in Scott's. In *Ivanhoe* (1820) Scott may have paid a compliment to Hogg, de haut en bas, in the person of Gurth the swineherd, the hoggish shepherd of his English romance of chivalry. Gurth's valor and loyalty to Ivanhoe earn him his manumission from serfdom; internal bonds of fealty replace the slave's collar. Thus Scott rehearses the roles of patron and "faithful shepherd" with which he and Hogg had commenced their relationship, and even provides for a scenario of modest advancement. Three years later, following the homage to Scott in *The Three Perils of Man* and contemporaneously with the disturbing cameo in *The Three Perils of Woman*, the hero of *Quentin Durward* encounters a fearsome lord of misrule called "the Wild Boar of the Ardennes." The Wild Boar exhibits a hideously divided physiognomy: the upper part of his face consists of "an open, high, and manly forehead, broad ruddy cheeks, large, sparkling, light-coloured eyes, and a nose hooked like the beak of an eagle," while the lower part is disfigured by "an unusual thickness and projection of the mouth and upper-jaw, which, with the huge projecting side-teeth, gave that resemblance to bestial confasciation, which . . . procured for him the name of the Boar of the Ardennes."[84] This creature commands a revolutionary violence that degrades men to beasts—not only himself and his mob but the venerable Bishop of Liège, poleaxed like an ox in the shambles. The Wild Boar's leadership of a popular rebellion glosses his title as chief of a "swinish multitude," Edmund Burke's epithet for an insurgent populace in the *Reflections on the Revolution in France*.[85] Philo-Jacobin authors defiantly embraced Burke's slur, and it informs the Tory jeers at Hogg's name—stigmatizing the pretensions of a peasant who will not stay confined to his station. In this context Hogg's own assumption of the ancestral persona of the Wild Boar, "whetting his dreadful tusks," strikes a recalcitrant if not mutinous pose.

The most elaborate representation of Hogg in the 1820s, the Shepherd of the "Noctes Ambrosianae," gives us a more complex creature. Contesting the view that the "Noctes" simply traduce Hogg as a "boozing buffoon," J. H. Alexander argues that its authors—Wilson especially— make of the Shepherd a richly symbolic, even mythic figure, the personification of a Romantic ideology of organic vitalism: he embodies "nonintellectual and instinctive" energies, a "sane and healthy" imagination, "an intensely physical response to experience."[86] Although "the Shepherd with his noble buck teeth, displayed in all their brown irregularity," makes his appearance in the Lockhartian precursor series "Christopher in the Tent" (August–September, 1819), and shows up in an early "Noctes" written jointly by Lockhart, Maginn, and Wilson, he really comes into focus once Wilson takes over the series in 1825. Hogg's body becomes the vessel of a wonderful vitality, evident in gargantuan feats of appetite— many episodes take place around lavish banquets and potations, which themselves furnish much of the conversation. More strikingly, the Shepherd embodies a natural, instinctual masculine sexuality: never more so than when he takes his clothes off.

In "Noctes" 34 (July 1827) Tickler and the Shepherd go sea bathing. Hogg immediately gets "mother-naked," boasting that he never bothers with underwear:

> As for mysell I never wear drawers, but hae my breeks lined wi' flannen a' the year through; and as for thae wee short corded under-shorts that clasp you like ivy, I never had ane o' them on syn last July, when I was forced to cut it aff my back and breast wi' a pair o' sheep-shears, after having tried in vain to get out o't every morning for twa months.[87]

As Hogg shows off in the water, Tickler pays tribute to his comeliness:

> You look more irresistible than you imagine. Never saw I your face and figure to more advantage—when lying on the braes of Yarrow, with your eyes closed in the sunshine, and the shadows of poetical dreams chasing each other along cheek and brow. You would make a beautiful corpse, James. (109)

The Shepherd spins an elaborate fantasy of being embraced by a Mermaid: a passage that shifts from a delicate eroticism ("Something—like a caulder breath o' moonlicht—fell on my face and breast, and seemed to touch all my body and my limbs") to a vivid if predictable sexual horror ("slimy and sliddery as the sea-weed . . . hech, sirs! hech sirs! the fishiness o' that kiss!" 110). The grotesque and bestial body returns in the form of the Mermaid; sexuality is exteriorized, alienated, as an obscene feminine aggression. Otherwise, it seems to be necessary to the scenario that some ladies show up to be thrilled by the spectacle of Hogg's nakedness. When a Steamer draws near, with "a bevy of ladies on deck," Tickler predicts "fainting from stem to stern, in cabin and steerage" (111). By this time a kindlier totem animal, the acceptable figure of the Shepherd's virility, has joined them: "MR NORTH'S GREAT NEWFUNLAN' BRONTE!"— Wilson's Newfoundland retriever Bronte, who swims about barking ecstatically.

The other major episode of heroic nudity occurs in the Shepherd's tall tale of his adventure with the Bonassus, a wild ox or bison. Hogg infuriates one of these animals by practicing blasts on a cow horn; presumably it mistakes him for a sexual rival. Charged by the enraged beast, Hogg once more takes off his clothes:

> I appeared suddenly before him as naked as the day I was born—and sic is the awe, sir, wi' which a human being, *in puris naturabilis*, inspires the maddest of the brute creation, (I had tried it ance before on a mastiff,) that he was a' at aince, in a single moment, stricken o' a heap[.][88]

The naked Shepherd hops on the bull's back, and there ensues a comic-epic wild ride. Once again, Hogg's body has to be exhibited to a scandalized female gaze: he encounters "three gig-fu's o' leddies," one of whom however, "a bonny cretur—leuch as if she kent me, as I gaed by at full gallop—and I remembered haeing seen her afore, though where I couldna tell" (671). The momentary erotic recognition, an exchange of glances that registers physical presence but not name or social station, acknowledges the triumphalism of Hogg's naked ride on bull back.

These episodes render Hogg as a mythic figure of primitive male sensuality—a figure of, to use a term coined a hundred years later by Wyndham Lewis, "the Wild Body." Even so, Wilson's narratives are only able to produce that figure by splitting off and externalizing its "hoggish" property, genital sexuality, which reappears in the form of a monster with which the Shepherd is forced to struggle. Equally conventionally, the Mermaid represents a feminine sexual threat. Her embrace brings a loss of control and consciousness, issuing in lonely postcoital disgust: "there I was sittin' in the cave, chitterin' like a drookit cock, and nae mermaid to be seen or heard; although, wad ye believe me, the cave had the smell o' crabs, and labsters, and oysters, and skate, and fish in general, eneuch to turn the stamach o' a whale or a sea-lion."[89] Hogg's combat with the Bonassus, however, brings a reunion of male body with phallic beast in the parade of a triumphant, satyrlike virility.

To compose the icon of a primitive virility, the male body is split off from and then rejoined to its wild sexuality through a confrontation with monsters and totem animals. This logic points us toward a further symbolic predicament, the division of Wilson himself as authorial subject. In his review of The Three Perils of Woman, Wilson justifies his sketch of Hogg's physiognomy by taking exception to Hogg's prior depiction of Wilson himself—a "self" in which the features of John Wilson and his magazine persona, Christopher North, are superimposed. Wilson begins with a testy allusion to the vignette of himself in Hogg's "Memoir of the Author's Life" (already abused by Wilson in a review in 1821): "In his 'Own Life,' he describes his friends by 'hair like feathers,' and 'nails like eagle-claws,' and so forth, which is all very proper and pretty portraiture." Wilson goes on: "More than once hath he scoffed at our crutch and our rheumatiz; and, from these and sundry other hints, we presume he wishes us to favour the public with a caricature of himself in an early Number."[90] Here speaks North, Wilson's main avatar in Blackwood's, a lame, decrepit old man, grotesquely at odds with the biographical legend cultivated by Wilson as early as his Oxford student days. Tall, strong, and graceful, endowed with his mother's fairness, Wilson excelled in athletic and field sports—notably (to cite the running heads of his daughter's 1863 biography) "Walking Feats," "Cock-Fighting—Pugilism—Leaping"—as well as boozing, brawling and seducing lower-class women.[91] It is hard not be impressed by the thoroughness of Wilson's expulsion of this aggressively muscular and heterosexual masculinity from his literary self-performance, even before his appointment to the chair of moral philosophy at Edinburgh in 1820, when he was forced to clean up his act. In the event, Christopher North is only able to recover his author's exuberant youthful fleshliness via the oral gratification of second childhood, in the heroic gourmandizing at Ambrose's, or else in the medium of memory, as a lost innocence. A later series of *Blackwood's* sketches, "Christopher in his Sporting Jacket" (1828), looks back nostalgically on a boyhood spent hunting, shooting, and fishing in the Paisley countryside, amusements that as often as not involve the wanton destruction of pets and livestock belonging to local farmers.

Wilson's Shepherd, however, lacks cruelty. His masculinity expresses itself, without sense of contradiction, in a lyrical tenderness and sympathy, even at the heights of knockabout farce or superhuman whisky consumption. Wilson projects this richly sensitive virility onto the Shepherd instead of claiming it as his own; the virtues he lends Hogg in the "Noctes" are not virtues that belong to his own authorial performance, despite his reputation for physical prowess. At the same time this Not-Self, the Ettrick Shepherd, is to some extent Wilson's invention and so his property, and throughout the "Noctes" we find him asserting his control over the figure: making North overwhelm the Shepherd with flights of oratory, turning Hogg into an obedient interlocutor in Socratic dialogues, and putting Wilson's own views into his mouth. In one episode (no. 42, April 1829) Hogg, exasperated by North's inattention, flings a glass of toddy in his face and provokes a boxing match. His lameness notwithstanding, North floors the Shepherd with a scientific blow under the ear, and then magnanimously colludes in the fiction that the Shepherd was the winner. The author feels so anxious that he has to throw a punch through his persona to remind Hogg (and the reader) who really is the strong man here. This brawling registers how far the performance is getting out of control—and how far the loss of control is its point.

After the grotesque flourishes that introduce the review of *The Three Perils of Woman*, Wilson goes on to admit that Hogg's exhibitions of sexuality ("coarse, but potent; hairy, but headlong") may look almost respectable when set beside those of the detested Hazlitt, whose *Liber Amoris* (1823) had just been published:

> Now, our most excellent friend, the Shepherd, would not have allowed himself to have been jilted like the New Pygmalion. He would have made love, not like a small, fetid, blear-eyed pug, but like a big curly Newfoundlander, who had broken his chain, and bounced like a rocket out of his kennel upon the beauty of Southampton-Row. . . . James is a man, and that is well known among friend and foe alike all over the Forest; but silly Billy was taken up

for an indecent exposure of his person, and acquitted solely on the ground, that the New Pygmalion was incapable of any misdemeanour implying manhood. (428–29)

Anticipating future "Noctes," Wilson represents Hogg's reckless phallic brio through the medium of a totem animal: metamorphosing Hogg into his beloved Newfoundland, Bronte. The Shepherd is redeemed from hoggishness into doggishness—and an animal that happens to be Wilson's property, just as Wilson closes the review by asserting a proprietary concern in the literary career of James Hogg: "It is impossible to know you, James, and not to love and admire you. . . . But you know little or nothing of the real powers and capacities of James Hogg" (437). We see that Hogg *is* Wilson's dog, or at any rate that Wilson wants him to be—his innocent, sensual, animal part, his body.

The function of Hogg as Wilson's body expresses a symptomatic cleavage in Wilson's writing which has been well noted by critics. Andrew Noble draws attention to the schism between "melancholic fine-feeling" and "manic, animal high spirits" which he reads as the symptom of a pathologically "fissile" personality.[92] Wilson's official, high style, when he is writing as Christopher North, is a primary source of the most overwrought effects of Victorian sentimentalism. At its best it looks towards the finer unreadability of Pater (in *Marius the Epicurean*): "To Amy Gordon, as she chanted to herself, in the blooming or verdant desert, all these various traditional lays, love seemed a kind of beautiful superstition belonging to the memory of the dead."[93] This style insistently performs the disembodiment that is its preferred thematic content. Wilson's fiction offers a parade of triumphs of repression and sublimation issuing, more often than not, in ailing, wasting bodies and lachrymose deathbed scenes.[94] Although Wilson's programmatic sentimentalism gestures back to Henry Mackenzie, still alive as the grand old man of the Edinburgh post-Enlightenment and figurehead of the Blackwood school, commentators perceived it as an appropriation of feminine rhetorical resources: "a Female Wordsworth is the designation of this author," sneered Henry Crabb Robinson.[95] For so ostentatiously manly an author, feminization, like North's lameness, would signify a high-minded castration—a literary equivalent of the disciplinary self-mutilation practiced by certain religious sects.

The stylistic virile body missing from these performances is Scots, the language of national popular life, gendered masculine where it abounds in the "Noctes Ambrosianae," the expression of Wilson's other side of "manic, animal high spirits." Henry Cockburn—a critic far from disposed in Wilson's favor—praised the "Noctes" for exhibiting "the best Scotch that has been written in modern times."[96] This best Scotch, Wilson's best writing, issues most eloquently from the mouth of the Ettrick Shepherd. Noble describes the "Noctes" as the product of "a more genuine symbiosis with Hogg's genius than Wilson would ever admit to."[97] Symbiosis, though, is not quite the right term for these psycho-rhetorical strategies of self-division attended by a jealous, bullying appropriation of the Other, who has become the narcissistic image of a lost, pure, better self. Some critics have read the Shepherd in the "Noctes" as the figure of a traumatic dissociation of identity for Hogg, reproduced (for example) in the thematics of doubling in the *Confessions of a Justified Sinner.*[98] The subject of a division of identity or loss of self is surely, rather, the author of the figure, John Wilson. Wilson may have gone out of his way to insist that the Shepherd was his invention, his property, his dog: an identity no longer belonging to the unworthy original. But Wilson's very insistence reiterated the designation of this authentic, organic, unalienated self, his own natural true genius, as not himself but another—as the Ettrick Shepherd, James Hogg. In this way the alien career of the Shepherd in the "Noctes Ambrosianae" rehearses a Hoggian revenge upon Wilson.

The powerful convergence of figures of male sexuality and masculine authority in early-nineteenth-century Edinburgh is a legacy of the precocious professionalization of Enlightenment literary culture, further modernized in the culture wars that raged after 1815 and stiffened by the authoritarian and rivalrous discourses of patronage and the market. One consequence of this professionalization, well noted by Scottish historians and critics, was a class distinction written into the division between vernacular Scots, increasingly designated the oral language of a residual peasantry, and English, the literary language of an imperial elite. Under Wilson and Lockhart *Blackwood's* redefined the social style of national literature towards Victorian norms of middle-class gentility. The new gentility, despite a tendency to regress to eighteenth-century bouts of swaggering, claimed the distinguishing virtues of piety and propriety, including a self-righteous sexual propriety. The language of cultural authority was increasingly a language that obliterated its origins not just in speech and locality but in the body.[99]

Wilson's claim on Hogg as Burns's heir, with which we began, took part in a more general, contentious refashioning of Burns's image as National Bard in the generation after his death, one of the persistent themes of which was a debate over the poet's sexual character. Francis Jeffrey complained of Burns's "licentiousness" or unruly virility, and a correspondent lack of "chivalry," the temper of a masculine politeness defined by self-restraint.[100] In the case of Wilson's Hogg, however, something else is at stake in the sexualizing of the peasant poet's body besides the distinction between boor and gentleman. By the 1820s Edinburgh literary politics were beset by an institutional exaggeration of gendered relations of paternal control, dynastic succession, oedipal conflict, and sibling rivalry. The formidable fatherly authority of Scott presided over a fierce warfare between the ascendant young Tories and their Whig elders, complicated by intense, tangled, often bitter relationships of friendship, competition, collaboration, and betrayal. The *Edinburgh Review* Whigs had set a characteristic style of professional authority, the militant enhancement of an Enlightenment language of cosmopolitan, abstract judicial reason. The Blackwoodian nationalist reaction followed Scott's appropriation of the feminine cultural territory of romance to mobilize the domestic discourses of sentiment, piety, propriety, and local specificity, remaking them into the ideological constituents of a new bourgeois gentility. This rhetorical strategy reinforced the exclusion of actual women writers and intellectuals, the unfeminine "Bluestockings," from the masculinist construction of literature as a profession. Wilson, an exemplary rather than anomalous case, enacted in his writing a correspondent expulsion of the differential signifier of male sexuality, the virile body. He chose James Hogg, the Ettrick Shepherd, to be the bearer of his rejected body, regaining access to its outcast wild innocence through authoritarian strategies of repossession and coercion. Hogg's body—the avatar of that national body, the people ("a swinish multitude")—would be readmitted to the convivial table of the Blackwoodian boys' club, but under strict conditions of patronage and supervision. Nevertheless Hogg, even cast as Wilson's phantasmatic, alienated corporeal being, triumphed over them all with displays of an organic energy, at once fierce and tender, they had exiled from themselves.

Chapter 7

๖๕

THE UPRIGHT CORPSE

And if it is in death that the spirit becomes free, in the manner of spirits, it is not until then that the body too comes properly into its own. For this much is self-evident: the allegorization of the *physis* can only be carried through in all its vigour in respect of the corpse. And the characters of the *Trauerspiel* die, because it is only thus, as corpses, that they can enter into the homeland of allegory. It is not for the sake of immortality that they meet their end, but for the sake of the corpse.
   —Walter Benjamin, *Origin of the German Tragic Drama*

THE MOUNTAIN AND FAIRY SCHOOL

"Dear Sir Walter," Hogg boasts, "ye can never suppose that I belang to your school o' chivalry? Ye are the king o' that school but I'm the king o' the mountain an' fairy school which is a far higher ane nor yours."[1] As both authors' careers took them beyond Border minstrelsy Hogg could disdain the cool medium of antiquarian historicism preferred by his rival:

> A great number of people now-a-days are beginning broadly to insinuate that there are no such things as ghosts, or spiritual beings visible to mortal sight. Even Sir Walter Scott is turned renegade, and, with his stories made up of half-and-half like Nathaniel Gow's toddy, is trying to throw cold water on the most certain, though most impalpable, phenomena of human nature.[2]

Scott had concluded *Letters on Demonology and Witchcraft* (1830) with the impious hope "that the grosser faults of our ancestors are now out of date," even though "every generation of the human race must swallow a certain measure of nonsense."[3]

Elsewhere, however, Scott makes "superstition," or local traditional belief, the crux of his own aesthetic. He praises Ann Radcliffe, "first poetess of romantic fiction," for having sounded new psychological depths in modern readers, composed of "curiosity and a lurking love of mystery, together with a germ of superstition"—a mixture of anthropologically universal and historically residual structures of feeling that becomes unstable as the analysis proceeds.[4] What kind of imaginative investment can enlightened readers make in the figures of an "out of date" reality? Claiming a preference for Horace Walpole's bold avowal of supernatural machinery over Radcliffe's retroactive rationalization, Scott charges authors who "compound betwixt ancient faith and modern incredulity" with evading rather than solving the crux (116). Nevertheless such a compound might be "most artful" insofar as it renders the formal equivalent of a Humean moderate skepticism: balancing the "childlike" desire of readers to have everything explained against a connoisseurial pleasure in what stays "hidden and mysterious"—the aesthetic condition of the symbol (116, 118). It is the desire for a total rationalization that is naïve, the mirror image of blind faith.

Hogg's tales characteristically turn upside down Scott's "compound betwixt ancient faith and modern incredulity." "Adam Bell" (1820) opens with a laird leaving his Annandale estate in the autumn of 1745; one morning a few days later his housekeeper is startled by his apparition; he is not heard of again until a witness recalls a moonlit duel in Edinburgh, sixteen years later, and his description of the slain duellist tallies with the missing laird. The narrator alludes to, rather than lays out, romantic and historical explanations of the sequence of events, but neither works properly. According to local lore a daylight wraith is supposed to presage "very long life" rather than sudden death, and Bell's fate has no evident connection with the Jacobite rebellion. The duel appears to promise a resolution, some version of poetic justice (as it does in novels from *Clarissa*, 1748, to *St. Ronan's Well*, 1823), but it lacks the aesthetic satisfaction of exact synchrony. Bell's wraith appeared before or after but not at the very hour of his death. We are left with a swarm of questions: "But who the person was that slew him, how the quarrel commenced, or who it was that appeared to his housekeeper, remains to this day a profound secret, and is likely to remain so, until that day when every deed of darkness shall be brought to light."[5] Understanding founders in the gap between reason and empirical evidence:

> This tale, which may be depended on as in every part true, is singular, for the circumstance of its being insolvable either from the facts that have been discovered relating to it, or by reason. . . . But the causes which produced the events here related, have never been accounted for in this world; even conjecture is left to wander in a labyrinth, unable to get hold of a thread that leads to the catastrophe. (75)

No Humean return to common life may stabilize this bewilderment. The tale's unsettling force comes from its breaching of a cognitive space between traditional and scientific phenomenologies that it finds opaque, impenetrable even by our act of reading. Hogg reverses the dialectic of fictional recognition at work in Hume and Scott: the opening between skepticism and faith, far from admitting a friendly daylight, floods the mind with darkness.

The category of the supernatural, according to Emile Durkheim, "does not appear until late in the history of religions." It depends on a modern scientific conception of nature to which it is antithetical: "In order to say that certain things are supernatural, it is necessary to have the sentiment that a *natural order of things* exists, that is to say, that the phenomena of the universe are bound together by necessary relations, called laws."[6] If Durkheim specifies the categorical modernity of the supernatural, Freud, in his famous essay "The Uncanny," sketches its historical development across three cultural stages: a primitive animism which admits no distinction between natural and supernatural phenomena, represented in the anthropological register of *Märchen* or folktales; late-archaic to early-modern religious models of a middle earth regulated, sometimes visited, by agents of a higher order; and the modern, empirical, and positivist "world of common reality." The last stage accommodates the "uncanny," a distinctively modern structure of feeling formed dialectically through the natural historicism of the Enlightenment.

Freud characterizes the uncanny as the subjective experience of a gash in the naturalized texture of everyday life. It comprises a psychological and aesthetic set of threshold disturbances: "the impression of automatic, mechanical processes at work behind the ordinary appearance of mental activity," the "doubling, dividing and interchanging of the self," a confusion between the real and the imaginary or symbolic, and (above all) the recurrence of an old, familiar figure that has been alienated from the conscious mind through a process of repression.[7] Freud distinguishes between an ontogenetic version of the uncanny, the compulsive reiteration of repressed infantile complexes, and a phylogenetic—racial or cultural—uncanny, the persistence of "primitive" mental habits in modern life. He contrasts the "actual repression of some content of thought and a return of this repressed content," which takes place within the individual psyche, with the "cessation of *belief in the reality* of such a content," which is determined by the social, ideological work of a civilized "surmounting" of "animistic beliefs" (247–48). Surmounting differs from repression in its pedagogic enlistment of the will and reason: a distinction that by no means relieves the experience of cultural succession (the progress of civilization), on the part of individuals or communities, from exterminating depths of violence. Earlier, Freud has conceded that the referential content of the cultural uncanny appears to be death rather than survival (242). Quite as much as its ontogenetic equivalent, the cultural uncanny signifies the disruption of a temporality of development by the recurrence of a superseded stage. Such a recurrence is the echo or shadow of an always-incomplete act of repression, the violent disjunction upon which an evolutionary order turns out to be founded.

Positivist accounts of the modern "survival" of archaic cultural forms are commonplace, from Victorian anthropology to Marxist sociology. Ernst Bloch's "non-synchronous contradiction" develops Marx's account (in the *Eighteenth Brumaire*) of the tactical reanimation or reinvention (rather than residual persistence) of figures of the past in times of drastic social change, to invoke a teleological continuity into the future.[8] This utopian promise invests, for example, the "Highland Arcadia" of the Scottish national tales produced at the close of the Napoleonic wars, discussed in chapter 3. At the same time, a romance revival may underwrite the extinction of the traditional form of life it salvages as an aesthetic trophy or talisman for the modern ideological assembly of a national culture.[9] In this light the uncanny is the sign of a botched or failed romance revival: in which, far from inspiring the present with a future vitality, the reappearance of a dead past mirrors (like Banquo's ghost) the deathliness of the present, the compulsive repetition of an original murder. While Enlightenment natural historicism relies on schemes of developmental continuity, the uncanny is the subjective figure of a violent discontinuity at the transition between historical orders.[10] The spectral persistence of ancient forms beyond the cessation of their social life unsettles the linear, evolutionary unfolding that shapes the progressive narrative of modern history. At the same time, the uncanny is an intensified effect of that same unfolding, since evolutionary development abolishes an absolute distinction between past and present, making them immanent in one another, distinguishable only by degrees.

Freud's tripartite scheme itself exemplifies an Enlightenment historiography of stadial development, even as its last stage, the vantage point from which this history is viewed, frames its subjective collapse. And just as that developmental history was crafted in Enlightenment Scotland, so the uncanny appears as a key topic in Scottish Romanticism, where it condenses the problematic of evolutionary discontinuity and cultural disintegration.[11] From Macpherson and Burns to Scott and Hogg, the uncanny marks the crux—hinge or gap?—between the diachronic axis of history and the synchronic axis of culture that together structure modern national identity: the spectral repetition, in the aesthetic medium of romance, of the imaginary life of a social world abolished in the forward drive of progress. If Scottish history casts modernity as a succession of disjunctions and dismemberments (the Reformation, the Acts of Union), the Romantic ideology of national culture, as we saw in chapter 2, promises the eternal recurrence of a spiritual unity that wipes out the division between past and present (as well as contemporary social divisions) even in its reiteration of the figures of historical loss. This aesthetic salvage of tradition made Scotland the conspicuous, poignant topos of a popular and organic national culture in the symbolic geography of European Romanticism. The discourse of cultural nationalism efficiently internalized the uncanny as its symptom, the expression of a core psychosis. The modernist trope for the predicament of Scottish identity, the "Caledonian Antisyzygy" and its variants, conforms impressively to Freud's diagnosis of "a doubling, dividing and interchanging of the self."[12] But the uncanny was not simply given to the authors of Scottish Romanticism as the fatal flaw of an already installed (genuine or delusional) national culture. It marks various recognitions of the status of national culture as a historical problem rather than a solution—an ascendant, potent, disputed, and unstable ideological formation.[13]

In the discussion that follows, I find psychoanalytic theory to yield the best instruments for interpreting Hogg's resistance to the narrative forms of historicism, socialization, and the ideology of modernity he found himself confronting in post-Enlightenment writing, above all in the novels of Scott. Hogg's representations of the uncanny, unmatched for their range and sophistication, deploy all three of the historical mentalities defined by Freud, disclosing especially the first and last as modern, romantic constructions. His novel-length experiments of the early 1820s range from the "magical realism" of *The Three Perils of Man*—in which natural and supernatural forces contend in the same world—to the abysmal cracks in common life that crazy-pave *The Three Perils of Woman* and *Private Memoirs and Confessions of a Justified Sinner*. In those works Hogg undoes the national dialectic between history and culture and makes the uncanny the topos of culture as such, both in its "primitive," traditional states and under the material and ideological stresses of modernization. Magical realism, while ostensibly defending the authenticity of traditional modes of expression and cognition, unfolds a crisis in the categories of culture no less powerfully than does the uncanny in its technical (Freudian) sense. Before looking at these two modes, I shall turn to the problematic compromise with the historical novel, and its logic of what Freud would call "surmounting," in Hogg's first extended work of prose fiction.

LEAGUES AND COVENANTS

The Brownie of Bodsbeck, like *Old Mortality*, narrates the ordeal of a neutral hero who shelters persecuted Whigs and is arrested by government dragoons in the "killing time" of the late 1670s and 1680s. These similarities highlight such drastic formal divergences (of style and tone, narrative structure and technique) as to suggest, indeed, the deliberate production of a distinct kind of fiction, a "mountain and fairy school" of historical romance. Responding to Scott's disapproval, Hogg justified his representation of "the times and the existing characters" in terms not of doctrine or principle (invoked by Scott's evangelical critics, and by Galt in the opening pages of *Ringan Gilhaize*) but of fidelity to local tradition:

> It is the picture I hae been bred up in the belief o' sin' ever I was born and I had it frae them whom I was most bound to honour and believe. An' mair nor that there is not one incident in the tale—not one—which I cannot prove from history to be literally and positively true.[14]

Truth and history are grounded in local custom—in the stories, proverbs, and anecdotes a community tells about itself, with which it constitutes its collective memory and generates itself through time. *The Brownie of Bodsbeck* expresses a formal fidelity to the narrative practices of such a tradition, in sharp tension (as a number of critics have noted) with Scott's national historical novel. Ina Ferris describes a "loose, anecdotal narrative" which foregrounds "the telling rather than the representation of experience" and rejects linear temporality (the unified time of national history) for a digressive, circular, multiple narrativity grounded on a "specificity of place."[15] Hogg's tale is articulated across a spatial cluster (rather than series) of narrative occasions, which fail or refuse to cohere into the grand dialectical form of the historical novel and its trajectory of a synthetic literary subject.

Hogg's regionalism in *The Brownie* confounds the imperial topography of periphery and center upon which a state-based national history might rely. Where Scott's Gandercleugh, the narrative platform of *Tales of My Landlord*, might in a range of ironies be called "the navel . . . of this our native realm of Scotland" (the navel is a site of origins but also of a severed connection),[16] Hogg's Ettrick farming community is quite unself-consciously the center of the world, the metonymically dense local ground of an essential humankindness sustained by domestic relations and rural labor. Viewed from this ground, the contending political forces of state history appear as alien invasions of common life. The king's dragoons undertake an enemy raid of the familiar countryside, the Covenanter refugees an eldritch haunting of it. Their irruptions paralyze daily life and drain the local economy, like a malignant spell.

If the Covenanters assume the elemental identities of Border folklore (such as the eponymous Brownie), Clavers, the personification of state power, is altogether Satanic: "the violation of all the tender ties of nature was his delight."[17] Hogg cunningly diminishes Clavers's allegorical status by turning him into just another figure from local tradition—the wicked gentleman who takes advantage of country lasses, the kind of devil who can be outfoxed by canny peasants. The principal figure from the register of "national history," in short, is emptied and remolded by the tropes of "folklore," despite the violence of his assault. Hogg's principal comic device in *The Brownie* is the trouncing of the plots of aristocratic oppressors by a vigorous folk energy, both in the scenes in which government inquisitors are baffled by shrewdly impenetrable dialect, and in capsizings of generic decorum such as the following. Clavers and a fellow officer are molesting the daughter of the hero, Walter Laidlaw, when he bursts in to grab both gentlemen, like puppies, by the scruffs of their necks:

> "Wha ir ye, I say, ye useless weazel-blawn like urf that ye're?"
>
> The haughty and insolent Clavers was stung with rage; but seeing no immediate redress was to be had, he endeavoured to pronounce his dreaded name, but it was in a whisper scarcely audible, and stuck in his throat—"Jo—o—o Graham," said he.
>
> "Jock Graham do they ca' ye? —Ye're but an unmannerly whalp, man. And ye're baith king's officers too! —Weel, I'll tell ye what it is, my denty clever callants; if it warna for the blood that's i' your master's veins, I wad nite your twa bits o' pows thegither." (52–53)

The comedy of physical force is staged as a contest of idioms, in which Claverhouse is so generically reduced (in the grip of a folkloric giant) that he cannot pronounce his own dreaded name. Hogg insists throughout on calling him Clavers, "as he is always called by that name in the country" (14)—a dialect term glossed by Scott himself (in his 1830 notes to *Old Mortality*) as "signifying, in common parlance, idle chat."[18]

This dramatic schema is confirmed at the end of the story with the return of Walter Laidlaw unscathed from the Edinburgh treason trials. Walter's own voice takes over the narration, confirming a comic triumph of "common parlance." His homecoming makes a striking contrast with the fate of Scott's hero in the last volume of *Old Mortality*. Morton has to witness the judicial torture and butchery of his former comrades in arms (who had themselves sought his death), endure a long exile, and return at last as a kind of ghost, haunting the scenery of his former life. Hogg's Walter plays the part, rather, of Morton's servant Cuddy Headrigg, who saved himself by acting the stolid peasant unmoved by politics; only Walter more forthrightly wields the voice of a regional community unspoilt by nation-making ideologies. In the rejoicing after the trial we glimpse the spontaneous generation of a broader (protonational) solidarity around this outspeaking of local identity:

> Weel, when I came out to the closs at the back o' the prison, a' the fock croudit about me; an' *he* shook hands wi' me; an' the young chaps they hurra'd an' waved their caps, an' cried out, Ettrick Forest for ever! —Auld Braid-Bonnet for ever, —hurra! An' I cam up the Lawn-Market, an' down the Bow, wi' sic an army at my tail, as I had been gaun away to fight Boddell-Brigg owre again. (142)

For a moment Walter seems to march at the head of a popular insurrection that he compares with the late rebellion. He ducks out of it, however, and we realize that the point of the parade is to replace, rather than turn into, an ideologically mobilized popular rising. Highlanders and Edinburgh mob alike cry "Ettrick Forest forever!" to celebrate, after all, the security of a neighborhood to which a man may go home.

The efficacy of Walter's speech to the Court of Session relied upon something else besides the formal authenticity of dialect:

> G——d d——n the hale pack o' ye, do ye think that auld Wat Laidlaw's a whig, or wad do aught against his king, or the laws o' his country? They ken little about him that say sae! . . . had I ony twa o' ye on the Chapelhope-flow thegither, if ye dared to say that I was a whig, or a traitor to my king, I wad let ye find strength o' arm for aince. (141)

As in the model for this outburst, Evan Dhu's challenge to the court at the treason trial in *Waverley*, loyalty is the flower of a traditional society, blooming spontaneously from family through landlord to king. The kindly interest of his "master Drumelzier" (a figure hitherto absent in the story) facilitates Walter's return (142). The good nation is characterized by a benign, hierarchical equilibrium of protection and neglect. The libertarian space of Hogg's traditional countryside in *The Brownie of Bodsbeck* is politically guaranteed by a quasi-feudal paternalism identified with a natural order of human relations and set apart from the turbulence of state history. Hogg takes over from *Old Mortality* the representation of civil war as an internecine conflict between state and people rather than between dynasties or parties, the symptom of which is an encroachment of ideology upon a local way of life. The difference between them is apparent in each novel's deployment of feeling, the ethical figure for a socially based human nature, in relation to historical process.

In both novels the private yet universal ethical imperative of "humanity," defined by sympathetic feeling, justifies the hero's falling on the wrong side of the law. Scott, more suspicious of the category's social production, overdetermines Morton's motives. Morton shelters Burley out of piety to the memory of his father as well as natural compassion, and soon enough frustrated ambition and disappointed love are added to resentment of the excesses of arbitrary government in driving him to the rebel cause.[19] Within this psychological complex, the political principle (of constitutional liberty and the right of resistance) is nevertheless clearly marked, Scott's point being (as well as to excuse Morton's rebellion) that such principles are always realized in local, mixed predicaments. The modern site of human nature, "private life," is founded no longer in natural origins but produced through a difficult resistance to the dangerous politicization of manners, of everyday life, that characterizes the replacement of feudal ties with nation-forming ideologies. Later Morton angers the Covenanters by assisting the prisoner Evandale. This time his humanity is modulated by the Royalist ethic of chivalrous self-sacrifice, and once more his motives are complex and private (Evandale is his rival in love). Scott thus deftly illustrates the utopian ideological synthesis of Morton's Moderatism, struggling to be born in a nation beyond one defined by political contention, as human nature may look forward to its accommodation in a modern, economically dynamic formation of civil society afforded by the 1689 settlement.

In *The Brownie of Bodsbeck* Hogg's dramatization of natural human feeling, through the mouth of Walter Laidlaw, relies upon a blunt dismissal of, rather than negotiation with, institutionally specific, theologically dense political claims:

> I dinna gie a bawbee about your leagues, and covenants, and associations, for I think aye there's a good deal o' faction and dourness in them; but or I'll desert a fellow-creature that's oppressed, if he's an honest man, and lippens to me, od, I'll gie up the last button on my breast. (23)

At the end of the novel Walter commends his daughter Katharine for taking "the side o' human nature; the suffering and the humble side, an' the side o' feeling, my woman." (163) The side of human nature is found in a structure of persecution in which politics as such is the oppressive force; feeling is suffering (and Christian and feminine), produced by the antagonism of an external power. Scott is careful to depict the Covenanters too in the role of persecutors, and in defeat they remain sublime (i.e., politically dangerous) rather than pathetic. His example of compassionate womanhood, Bessie McClure, succors the wounded Tory Evandale. But Hogg's Covenanters arouse compassion insofar as defeat has admitted them to a "side of human nature" further removed from the bitter ironies of historical meaning.

"The side of human nature" and "feeling" takes the place, accordingly, of a perilous political solidarity; for Hogg's Borderers remain immune to the ideological radicalization of the western Whigs, despite a shared experience of government tyranny. They are immune because, for them, history does not mean modernization. "Leagues, and covenants, and associations" exert no appeal to Borderers still enfolded in a more ancient covenant, the primitive ecology of their community and customs. And here we reach the crux of Hogg's romantic aesthetic in *The Brownie*: in the second of its interlaced plots, the supernatural being that protects the cottagers' ancient way of life turns out to be a modern fake.

For if, as Ferris writes, "Covenanter and Cavalier alike are alien in their ideological approach to experience" (192), there is a crucial difference in each party's alienness. Clavers's role as Devil, the universal adversary of

Presbyterian theology, confers upon that theology the legitimacy of a common culture of popular religion, shared by those he persecutes. As they go to ground the Covenanters become a different kind of demon: creatures more ancient and familiar, emanations of the local landscape, pagan elementals or nature sprites. The Brownie of Bodsbeck, the last of the Border goblins, is uncanny in the technical sense of something native and familiar now lost or forgotten, grown strange. In his weird appearances we glimpse the distorted shadow of a cultural origin nested in the natural world, a pre-Christian autochthony with no clear boundary between nature and supernature. The Brownie is "a being without any definitive form or feature" (160), unfigured (in that he represents an origin) as well as disfigured (in that he represents that origin's loss). The Brownie's nocturnal reign over Chapelhope brings about the wonderful restoration of the traditional economy that has been disrupted by the civil wars. Brownie is a tutelary sprite who protects the cottagers from harm and labors in their fields, magical patron and servant at once. More particularly, he is a guardian of virginity, and his mysterious intercourse with Katharine invests her with an allegorical aura, making her the figure of a threatened cultural purity. Under the pressure of national historical crisis, it seems, the old georgic world survives intact, underground, in uncanny guise, until the natural order of peacetime resume. The representation of rural labor as the economic site of a covenant between the natural world and human society is perhaps the dominant trope of georgic. Here it is set off by the profane tyranny of the Royalist troops (extorting oaths of loyalty by violence) and, far less emphatically, the fanaticism of the Covenanters themselves (alluded to but not depicted in Hogg's tale).

With the resumption of peacetime, and the return of Walter to his farm, the Brownie is exorcized in a gust of rational explanation. There are no fairies or goblins after all; only human devices, historical effects. Hogg belatedly invokes the Enlightenment aesthetic of romance revival, typified by Scott, which requires—before it can be bought back as an aesthetic effect and thus a rational possession—the epistemological undoing of the covenant that has sustained (and in crisis has rescued) an ancient cultural heritage. In the Waverley novels, uncanny figures tend to be elegiac portents of the passing of a traditional society (the Bodach Glas in *Waverley*, Alice's ghost in *The Bride of Lammermoor*), while it is part of the scheme of historical irony in *Old Mortality* that the Covenanter leader Burley, having outlived his epoch, becomes at the end of the novel both pagan nature demon and the devil of his own theological fantasy, as if in the new dispensation all old bogies are the same sort of anachronistic nuisance. The historical guise of Hogg's demonic Covenanter, a mutilated victim of the wars, makes Brown/Brownie a more moving figure of historical disturbance than the conspiring maniac to which Burley is reduced, for all the superior technical bravura of Scott's last chapters. Here too, nevertheless, rational explanation brings an end to old mysteries, a view from outside the tradition, the triumph of an enlightened knowledge. So, Hogg's narrator concedes, the "evening tale" may give form to something universally latent and "primitive" in the self, rather than a distinct cultural reality:

> The truth was, that the phantoms of superstition had in a measure fled with the shadows of the night, which they seldom fail to do. They, indeed, remain in the bosom, hid, as it were, in embryo, ready to be embodied again at the fall of the long shadow in the moon-light, or the evening tale round the fading embers[.] (153)

Hogg rehearses a quintessentially modernist formula of "surmounting" as psychological internalization.

On the one hand, then, national history, far from being an inexorably linear and universal development that reorganizes all of human life, is a momentary disturbance (however violent) of perennial tasks and customs determined by natural rhythms and seasonal cycles. Historical events are a kind of occasional, memorable natural disaster, like the storms Hogg writes about in his "Shepherd's Calendar" sketches.[20] On the other hand, the narrator of *The Brownie of Bodsbeck* steps back to cast a cool eye on the obsolescent "superstitions" of his country—not so much in the narrative voice, which keeps seeking refuge in the language and technique of local narrators, as in the plot, which makes the formidable revenants of rural mythology turn out to be impersonators from that same alien dimension of national history against which the traditional culture is posed as an authentic covenant.[21]

Hogg's ambivalence is finely stated in the dedicatory verses to Lady Anne Scott, which articulate a modern, elegiac stance toward "the mountain music heard no more" (178). To imagine a primitive covenant of fairy time is to recall its loss:

> To list the songs such beings sung,
> And hear them speak in human tongue;
> To see in beauty, perfect, pure,
> Of human face the miniature,
> And smile of being free from sin,
> That had not death impress'd within.
> Oh, can it ever be forgot
> What Scotland had, and now has not!

Hogg comes very close here to investing his fairy world with a political allegory of national independence. It is miniaturized, in one of the classic tropes of nostalgia,[22] and contained in the visionary turn for which the poet of "Kilmeny" was celebrated. "If there's a land, as grandsires tell, / Where Brownies, Elves, and Fairies dwell"—it will no longer be found on this earth.

MAGICAL REALISM

If *The Brownie of Bodsbeck* was perceived to be following in the track of *Old Mortality*, despite claims it was written earlier, in *The Three Perils of Man* Hogg produced what Hollywood would call a "prequel" to the romance with which Scott first claimed mythopoetic dominion over the Scottish Border. Scott preemptively secured the role of national bard against rivals by casting himself as "the Last Minstrel," a figure without coevals, let alone successors. Hogg's audacious solution in *The Three Perils of Man* was to situate himself before rather than after the Last Minstrel. In narrating the legendary prehistory to *The Lay of the Last Minstrel* Hogg subverts the antiquarian concept of the source, according to which chronological priority defines originality, and unfolds an alternative topology of cultural origins.

The years of composition of *The Three Perils of Man*, 1819–21, coincide with a crux in the career of the Author of *Waverley* which Hogg's work does not fail to register. Given the innovation of its Gothic setting, one of the most striking aspects of *Ivanhoe* is its determinedly enlightened tone, and the renunciation even of such ambiguous supernatural machinery as had operated in some of the Scottish Waverley novels. Its successor *The Monastery* is set in the sixteenth-century Borders and, by contrast, features an all-too-active spook, the White Lady of Avenel, a device generally blamed for the author's first major public disappointment. Scott defended the White Lady with the claim that she was real enough in the mentality of a local culture, and so he had undertaken to represent her— producing the interesting, Hoggian anomaly of a historical novel about the transition from Catholicism to Protestantism in which the liveliest agent is a doggerel-chanting banshee. For once Scott's Border sprite might have upbraided Hogg's (in *The Brownie*) with equivocation. Perhaps the relative failure of *The Monastery* provoked Scott to object that in *The Three Perils of Man* Hogg had spoilt "the best tale in the world" with a mess of "witchcraft and diablerie."[23] Witchcraft and diablerie, however, constitute the strong counteraesthetic—an early postmodern magic realism—with which Hogg challenges Scott's school of chivalry.

Hogg glosses the relation between his romance and Scott's, and rewrites the relation between nature, supernature, and history that proved problematic in *The Brownie of Bodsbeck*, in a meditative interlude quite late in the *The Three Perils of Man*. The narrator revises the Enlightenment allegory of cultural progress as a disenchantment of the world, versions of which can be found in Scottish writing from Blair's "Critical Dissertation upon the Poems of Ossian" (1763) to Scott's *Letters on Demonology and Witchcraft* (1830). Hogg's narrator assumes the editorial voice, made familiar in Scott's novels, of the enlightened historian, but in order to confound that voice's sentence of scientific surmounting. Instead of affirming a progression of cultural stages from superstition to reason, Hogg describes a clash of rival enchantments. He evokes the "aboriginal" culture of the Borders as a domain of natural magic—a world wild and fallen, far from idyllic, but nevertheless habitable:

> The land was the abode of the genii of the woods, the rocks, and the rivers; and of this the inhabitants were well aware, and kept within locked doors, whose lintels were made of mountain ash, and nightly sprinkled with holy water. Cradle and bed were also fenced with cross, book, and bead; for the inmates knew that in no other way could they be safe, or rest in peace. They knew that their green and solitary glens were the nightly haunts of the fairies, and that they held their sports and amorous revels in the retiring dells by the light of the moon. . . . But these were the natural residenters in the wilds of the woodland, the aboriginal inhabitants of the country; and however inimical their ways might be to the ways of men, the latter laid their account with them. There were defences to be had against them from holy church, which was a great comfort.[24]

Human settlers have achieved a delicate coexistence with the forest's elemental spirits. The advent of the wizard Michael Scott brings an alien invasion and colonization, characterized as a fall from nature into art:

> But ever since Master Michael Scott came from the colleges abroad to reside at the castle of Aikwood, the nature of demonology in the forest glades was altogether changed, and a full torrent of necromancy, or, as Charlie Scott better expressed it, of *witchcraft*, deluged the country all over, —an art of the most malignant and appalling kind, against which no fence yet discovered could prevail. . . . [The Borderers] dreaded the spirits of the old school, the devil in particular; but of the new prevailing system of metamorphoses they had no comprehension. (323–24)

The anterior ecology of natural magic belongs to Hogg, poet of the old school, while "the new prevailing system of metamorphoses" foreshadows the literary empire—the scholarly, alienated demonology—of a modern Master Scott. Hogg's magical realism rewrites the script of Enlightenment historicism so that cultural succession no longer appears in the light of a universal law of progress from illusion to reality. Power, not truth, determines the conquest of one magical regime, naturalized by custom, by another, possessed of a technological virulence.

The Three Perils of Man resists this conquest by proposing a critical alternative to the elegiac model of national historical romance. Scott's *Lay of the Last Minstrel* founds literary modernity upon the passing of an oral traditional culture of heroic song. Penny Fielding summarizes the Enlightenment dictum that "the oral is always other: of writing (speech), of culture (the voice of nature), of the modern (a pre-modern past)." As literature's antithetical origin, the primeval chaos out of which it arose, orality has to be "more valuable dead than alive"—its death, indeed, is a necessary condition.[25] Scott's romance revisits the scene of that cultural death to heal its trauma. Healing means accepting the fact of death, as part of a natural process: the act of restoration that transforms loss into continuity turns out to be a rite of mourning. But what room at the ceremony is there for James Hogg, who staked his career on the modern viability of popular tradition? His work enacts a persistent refusal to mourn, even when it confronts the supposedly incontrovertible evidence of death. *The Three Perils of Man* turns out to be less concerned with the fact of death (and with the figure of the corpse) than with the symbolic logic through which death is produced, circulated, and consumed as a trope of cultural formation. Hogg's narrative takes up the conventional figure of an orality that marks the origins and outside of culture and splits it into opposite yet interlocked tropes of narration and cannibalism. Against Scott's mourning or "introjective" account of the relation between modernity and a premodern imaginary, Hogg represents a melancholic, devouring, or "incorporative" account of that relation, which insists on a material violence, rather than a sublime absence, at the limits of culture.

The Three Perils of Man juxtaposes two main narratives: a prolix, tonally unstable historical romance, the siege of Roxburgh, and an extended supernatural adventure, the embassy to Aikwood. The formal disposition of these narratives (one inside the other, opening and closing each other) sets up a scheme of inside and outside, elaborated in a set of symbolic equivalences. At Roxburgh the Scots want to get into a castle inside which the English are perishing of famine, while at Aikwood the characters want to get out of one where they find themselves threatened with the same fate. Each of these predicaments hosts a ritual masculine competition for a female prize: at Roxburgh a contest of chivalric prowess for the princess Margaret, at Aikwood a tale-telling contest for the maiden Delany. And each contest proposes the abominable event of a human sacrifice. The tale-telling competition has a double stake: if the best narrator wins the maiden, the worst must forfeit his body to feed his starving companions. At Roxburgh, the Scottish commander has told the English that unless they surrender the captive, Lady Jane Howard will be exposed "in sight of both hosts, [and] compelled to yield to that disgrace which barbarians only could have conceived; and then . . . have her nose cut off, her eyes put out, and her beauteous frame otherwise disfigured" (68). In both cases the sacrificial turn outrages the decorum under which reading—our conventional relation to the story—takes place. The atrocity threatened against Lady Jane upsets the genre containing the siege narrative, chivalric romance as revived and authorized by Scott, who argued that, whatever its extravagances, chivalry at least instituted a reverence for women. Scott made the claim in his "Essay on Chivalry," written for the 1822 Supplement to the *Encyclopaedia Britannica*; Hogg here presses to extremes the preoccupation with sexual conquest and sacrifice already fictionalized in *Ivanhoe*.[26]

The tale-telling contest locks together the topoi of narration and cannibalism. Fielding argues that the episode gives the romance's own narrative and cultural status an allegorical prominence, scrambling the categorical distinctions between (oral) narrative performance and (textual) narrated event.[27] Hogg's representation of oral performance brings a brilliant mimicry of literary and vernacular registers, in a sardonic reprise of the scenario of *The Queen's Wake*, with its poetic tournament for the role of national minstrel.[28] Narrative orality devolves into another kind of orality: a cannibal rite. Storytelling is the opposite or alternative to cannibalism—its substitute, its sublimation: while we are telling each other tales we are not devouring each other. Yet storytelling is also continuous with cannibalism: it produces the identity of the victim. With this ambivalent structural relation to the practice that constitutes its outside or other, storytelling becomes a figure for culture itself, an apparatus of sublimation and regulation that binds men together in sociable amusement even as it selects who gets the girl and who will get eaten.

In so framing the act of narration, *The Three Perils of Man* turns upon a pervasive mythology of cultural foundation, analyzed by Maggie Kilgour, in which communion and cannibalism represent opposite valences of a primal rite of incorporation. Demarcating the physiological threshold between inside and outside, these constitute the set of symbolic oppositions between culture and its other: art and nature, civilization and savagery, human and beast.[29] This binary system is given a psychoanalytic and linguistic inflexion by Nicolas Abraham and Maria Torok, who (building on the literature of mourning and melancholia) distinguish between two types of internalization in relation to loss, introjection and incorporation.[30] Introjection designates a normative path of psychic development, in which the self comes to terms with loss through the process of mourning. Mourning converts loss into language, through which absence can be recognized, abstracted, and internalized, made part of a fortified, outward-directed self. The empty mouth fills itself with words: at first the inarticulate cry of its deprivation and then language addressed to and exchanged with other selves. The language produced through mourning is social, dialogical, and—in its character of a substitution for the original loss—metaphoric or figurative. Narration, the consensual exchange of stories, represents an optimal realization of this social and figurative conception of language.

Incorporation, which is structurally equivalent to Freud's uncanny, represents a pathological blockage of the introjective process. It is a "fantasy of nonintrojection" (126): the melancholic symptom of a denial of loss, a refusal or inability to mourn. Instead of recognizing loss through figurative abstraction as a constitutive condition of the self, the self projects its loss onto the external world as the fantasy of a missing thing outside itself. "In order not to have to 'swallow' a loss, we fantasize swallowing (or having swallowed) that which has been lost, as if it were some kind of thing" (126). Blockage takes the form of a linguistic breakdown:

> As the empty mouth calls out in vain to be filled with introjective speech, it reverts to being the food-craving mouth it was prior to the acquisition of speech. Failing to feed itself on words to be exchanged with others, the mouth absorbs in fantasy all or part of a person—the genuine depository of what is now nameless. The crucial move away from introjection (clearly rendered impossible) to incorporation is made when *words* fail to fill the subject's void and hence an imaginary thing is inserted into the mouth in their place. . . . Born of the verdict of impracticable introjection, the fantasy of incorporation appears at once as its regressive and reflexive substitute. This means of course that every incorporation has introjection as its nostalgic vocation. (128–29)

Abraham and Torok insist that *"the crucial aspect of these fantasies of incorporation is not their reference to a cannibalistic stage of development, but rather their annulment of figurative language"* (132; emphasis in original). Incorporation represents a "demetaphorization," a collapse into the literal and objective, a *"fantasmatic destruction of the act by means of which metaphors become possible: the act of putting the original oral void into words"* (132; emphasis in original). "Hostile external forces" (136) must have inflicted the trauma that renders loss unspeakable, unassimilable except in the melancholic rehearsal of fantasies of cannibalistic ingestion. It is the effect of an objective historical violence.

I do not mean to read Scott's and Hogg's romances as symptomatic instances of the truth of psychoanalytic theory. Rather, the work of Abraham and Torok, as it explicates a psychic topology joining mourning and melancholia, the generation of figurative language and the fantasy of cannibalism, illuminates the argument between *The Lay of the Last Minstrel* (thematically preoccupied with mourning and melancholia) and *The Three Perils of Man* (thematically preoccupied with narration and cannibalism), both of which investigate the foundation of modern literary romance upon the figure of a primordial, supernatural orality. "Introjection" and "incorporation" designate alternative structures of feeling within a collective formation, such as a national culture, predicated on a loss of origins. Both terms express a psychic relation to a historical process, modernization, interpreted as a disconnection from an ancestral world felt to be past, vanished, buried, but therefore available for commemoration or revival. Does a modern romance raise the past in order to mourn it, confirming its death, or in order to bring it back to life, defying the sentence of death? Scott's script of mourning casts the reanimation of the past as a fantasy of incorporation succeeded by the rite of introjection—a mischievous phantom conjured up to be exorcized so that real life may move forward; while Hogg's script of reanimation exposes introjection as a repressive fantasy in its turn—a performative utterance that goes on killing the life it mourns.

In his *Blackwood's* elegy for Princess Charlotte, subject of a Princess Diana–style frenzy of public mourning in 1817, John Wilson evokes a necrophiliac intensity of grief as the emotional medium for national unity: "Grief has disclosed the secret heart of the people. . . . The distinctions of society are forgotten; and we are privileged by nature to embrace Her in the grave."[31] Theories of nationalism have not overlooked the function of mourning as a performative rite of modern national subjectivity. "No more arresting emblems of the modern culture of nationalism exist than cenotaphs and tombs of Unknown Soldiers," writes Benedict Anderson.[32] The Tomb of the Unknown Soldier provides for a disciplinary focus—a regimentation—of a modern, secular, anonymous, corporate identity, "the people," assembled in the shadow of death: its own death, the industrial mass death promised by modern war. Nor should we forget the civilian analogues of the unknown soldier, the representatives of a collective, ancestral, anonymous life supposed to be dead and buried: such as the unknown poet, the bard or minstrel, blank vessel of a silenced oral tradition and an extinct way of life. Scott himself, rising in his career as modern national minstrel during the Napoleonic wars, aligns the poetic project of romance revival with the themes of national crisis and mourning in time of war in the introduction to canto 1 of *Marmion* (1808). Only after the war do we find him adopting, with a more comprehensively popular genre of national fiction, the persona of "the Great Unknown."

The title and narrative frame of *The Lay of the Last Minstrel* expound a preoccupation with cultural lateness and the passing of ancient traditions. The poem's plot, at the same time, feints deviously around the necromantic power of a buried ancestral book. Frame and plot articulate two possible fates of romance in modernity, in a dynamic, chiastic relation to each other: the lay or song, breathing but transient, embodied and mortal, in the mouth of the last singer at the end of a tradition; and the book or text, not so much dead as buried alive, undead in fact, waiting for reanimation each time its pages are opened.[33] If the former is associated with what passes away and is mourned, the latter corresponds to the "encrypted" figure of the swallowed but unabsorbed, secret and traumatic object of loss, in Abraham and Torok's incorporative scheme: that past which refuses to pass and returns to unsettle the present. Scott's poem yokes together the elegiac and uncanny, or introjective and incorporative, valences of a historical present constituted upon an expired origin. As we read, we see that the two modes work together, with the introjective or mourning agency dialectically surmounting the incorporative to perform a joint exorcism of the past—laying it to rest—in the service of a renovated and (to adapt Susan Stewart's usage of the term) "distressed" modernity.[34] In this way Scott defines the ambiguous status of his own poem: it is a printed text, a book, in a modern commercial society, which mimics the manners and covets the political energies of an ancient, feudal, and heroic oral culture ("the unpremeditated lay": premeditated enough, however, for the epithet to have been lifted from the revolutionary bard Milton).

Dedicated to his "clan chief," Scott's poem tells a tale in which "the last of all the Bards . . . / Who sung of Border chivalry" performs before an ancestral Duchess of Buccleuch.[35] The minstrel narrates the exhumation of the sorcerer Michael Scott's magic book, and the consequent escalation of a national feud to a crisis that, however, can be resolved: a wedding can take place, alliances be forged, life go forward. "Revolution" has dispossessed the bard of his courtly function, felling minstrelsy from high art to vulgar commerce.[36] But the present scene of patronage holds the promise of a revival. When the bard sings for the Duchess he changes from the "Last" to "the LATEST MINSTREL," whose self-positioning at the end of a tradition might yet win him fashionable currency in a new one. This dialectical self-consciousness, the advertisement of its status as a fiction, marks the saving difference between Scott's minstrelsy and (its major precedent) Macpherson's, whose elegiac layerings empty out the cultural sites of production and reception.[37]

Michael Scott, entombed before the action begins, represents the opposite case, a verbal art charged with a magic of origins. This ancestral Scott commanded the sublime language of the natural world, "The words that cleft Eildon hills in three"—words so dangerous that "to speak them were a deadly sin" and "[a] treble penance must be done" even "for having but thought them" (canto 2, line 8). Robbed from the grave, the wizard's "Book of Might" remains alive and potent, on no account to be opened. The transgressive reader of this forbidden text is the changeling dwarf Gilpin Horner:

> A moment then the volume spread,
> And one short spell therein he read:
> It had much of glamour might;
> Could make a ladye seem a knight
>
> . . . .
>
> And youth seem age, and age seem youth:
> All was delusion, nought was truth.   (3.9)

The "Book of Might" bears an imaginary grammar of metamorphosis (*Might*, power in the subjunctive); it is the source of romance tricks of distraction and delusion, as the rest of the tale bears out. The book provokes its reader to a compulsive behavior of deceptive shape-shifting, attended by the refrain, "Lost! lost! lost!" until the shade of the departed wizard himself intervenes to snatch "the elvish page" away with him, beyond the grave.[38] Reader (Gilpin), text (Book of Might) and author (Michael Scott) appear together only as they perform a sublime disappearing act on the stage of the historical reconciliation that they have helped bring about. The onlookers left on the scene vow the renunciation of such risky magic. The poem ends with a "Hymn for the Dead" and the minstrel's settlement in a climate of pastoral elegy. In short, the poem closes itself down—and its unruly psychic and narrative energies—by a series of effects of distantiation, elegiacally keyed as rites of mourning, in order to bring us to an enlightened, settled present (Sheriff Scott at Ashestiel, under the wing of Buccleuch).

We read the most concentrated instance of the poem's elegiac turn in the topos of the death of the poet:

> Call it not vain; they do not err,
>   Who say, that when the poet dies,
> Mute Nature mourns her worshipper,
>   And celebrates his obsequies.   (5.1)

There follows a catalogue of figures of mourning nature, marked as conventional ("Who say"). But then, remanding the anxious denial with which the meditation began, the minstrel turns upon the pathetic fallacy to reconstitute it at a double remove:

> Not that, in sooth, o'er mortal urn
> Those things inanimate can mourn;
> But that the stream, the wood, the gale,
> Is vocal with the plaintive wail
> Of those, who, else forgotten long
> Liv'd in the poet's faithful song,
> And, with the poet's parting breath,
> Whose memory feels a second death.   (5.2)

The elegiac grammar of romance is a double negative. They do not err who say that nature mourns the dead poet; only it is not nature itself that mourns, since its objects are mute and inanimate, but the figures of cultural memory that are the poet's inventions, lamenting their extinction at the end of a tradition—"a second death." Maiden, knight, chief, "All mourn the Minstrel's harp unstrung, / Their name unknown, their praise unsung" (5.2). The landscape echoes with the lamentation of a double passing, of an ancient way of life and of the poetic representation of that life. This echo, translated into print (as a literary convention), condenses Scott's own present act of romance revival.[39] His minstrelsy is "latest" because it is "last" after all.

With its techniques of synesthetic and elegiac mediation, *The Lay of the Last Minstrel* represents a cultural program in broad correspondence with the psychoanalytic scheme of introjection. Scott's poem establishes the project of romance revival as the rite of mourning a cultural past, via the exorcism of incorporative phantasms of traumatic disturbance, in order to make settled the modern present. By converting a lost world of social relations into literary figuration and literary tradition (so marking it as lost) the modern poet consigns loss, as a category of experience, to the past, and secures it for the present in the aesthetic faculty of the imagination.

In Hogg's *Three Perils of Man*, Michael Scott is formidably alive, until we read an eyewitness account of his apotheosis in the final pages. Although the story closes with the interment of the undead wizard and his black book, its tendency is the opposite of elegiac: these wild old tales belong to here and now. Hogg's narrative frame refuses the teleology of historical stages, with its hierarchy of cultural forms, addressed (however ambivalently) in Scott's romances. Set loosely in the fourteenth century, conflating different historical incidents and characters, Hogg's romance reinterprets "history" not as an objective chronology of modernization but as a subjective, legendary dimension, at once deep past and unsettlingly present. These events are ancient and modern, real and fantastic, all at once. In Hogg's most striking technique, analogous to twentieth-century magic realism, natural and supernatural effects occupy the same narrative dimension, the same ontological register—neither is more real than the other. In contrast to the nation-forming genre of the historical novel, magical realism is a "postcolonial" romance genre, autoethnography's epic mode; it represents the synchronous interpenetration of different cultural systems without ordering them in an epistemic hierarchy.[40] *Three Perils of Man* unfolds less in historical time than in a fantastic cultural space, Hogg's marvellous Borders, as in Scott the figural topography of a transformation of possibilities, represented by disguise and metamorphosis. But Hogg empties this symbolic field of the historical teleology that would make it transitional toward some future national order. Although the historical plot of the siege of Roxburgh frames the magical plot of the embassy to Aikwood, the two narratives occupy a nondialectical relation of contiguity rather than succession, encircling rather than superseding or contradicting one another. Indeed, the magical plot produces the most dense and vivid rhetoric of "realism" in Hogg's prose, as an empirical, materialist register of sensation and appetite.

Distilled to its essence in the tale-telling contest, the thematic content of this prose is hunger and violence. Here indeed orality, the occasion of narration, falls under the sentence of a black-comic "demetaphorization." The triumph of Hogg's realism comes in Gibbie Jordan's tale of Marion's Jock, a perpetually hungry boy who devours one of his master's sheep and murders his master. The story of this cannibal shepherd is one of human life stripped to an extremity of poverty and servitude in a rural setting that might just as well be twenty-first- as fourteenth-century. The tale inverts not only the scheme of a Christian allegory of sacrament (the good shepherd offering up his own body to grant his flock eternal life) but its spiritualizing register. Hogg writes a starkly materialist parable of original sin as a contest between nature (appetite) and law (property). Jock's appalling hunger is produced by a series of privations and prohibitions, beginning, suggestively enough, with a "constant battle" for oral satisfaction waged between him and his mother (215). As those prohibitions ascend the hierarchy of law the appetite grows more monstrous, until it becomes absolute, swallowing not just all objects but all other desires and affects, including—in the central episode of the murder of the goodman's ewe lamb—the sentimental and erotic:[41]

> Jock was seized with certain inward longings and yearnings that would not be repressed. He hesitated long, long, and sometimes his pity awoke, —but there was another natural feeling that proved the stronger of the two; so Jock at length took out his long knife and unsheathed it. Next he opened the fleece on the lamb's throat till its bonny white skin was laid bare, and not a hair of wool to intervene between it and the point of his knife. He was again seized with deep remorse, as he contemplated the lamb's harmless and helpless look; so he wept aloud, and tried to put his knife again into its sheathe, but he could not. (221–22)

In the ensuing argument over the tale's merits, Michael Scott himself interprets its "moral": "The maid Delany is the favourite lamb, whom he wishes you to kill and feast on in the same delicious manner as did the hero of his tale; and I am the goodman whom you are to stick afterwards, and fairly make your escape" (230). All appetites merge in a primal devouring. Just as the lamb is eroticized by the somatic comprehensiveness of the boy's hunger, so has desire for the maid Delany grown carnivorous.

All drives, in extremis, become reflexes of an original hunger, the drive to fill an empty mouth. Even the distinction between winning and losing is abolished for the female body that is the contest's prize. Tam Craik's anthropophagous lust is the obverse of the poet's fanciful adoration, just as the violation of Lady Jane Howard at Roxburgh (another ritual devouring) is to be prelude to the wedding of the princess Margaret. Delany has been brought to Aikwood as a gift for the sorcerer (along with the boy Elias, whom the story forgets); the repeated attempts of the ogreish seneschal Gourlay to drag her to his lair confirm her status as prey. So much for the subtitle of Hogg's romance, advertising women as the second peril of man. A misogynist dismemberment comes to pass in Gibbie Jordan's vision of the witches' weddings, in which the unlucky brides are blasted, crushed, and torn to pieces in their diabolical intercourse.

Otherwise, the narrative violence remains largely rhetorical against its female characters, discharging instead upon a series of presumptuous servants. To be a vassal, even more than to be a woman, is to be prey. Bound over to the Master's service, Gibbie endures an interminable, nightmarish metempsychosis:

> I was stabbed as a salmon, hunted as a roe-buck, felled as a bull, and had my head chopped off for a drake. The dinner was made up of me. I supplied every dish, and then was forced to cook them all afterward. It was no wonder that I could not partake of the fragments of the meal. (450)

Here the dominant themes of the romance's "system of metamorphoses"—sorcery, bondage, famine, homicide—clench together. Cannibalism is the drastic final term in the figural sequence of metamorphosis and metempsychosis, for with it the lineaments of the human are once and for all torn away. Michael Scott dismisses the embassy by transforming Charlie Scott and his companions to an "outrageous drove" of bellowing bulls—which turns out to supply the solution to the siege of Roxburgh. Disguised thus the Scottish soldiers are finally able to enter the castle: "If we but walk on all four we will pass with hungry men for oxen in a dark night" (395).

Cannibalism marks the boundary at which humanity undoes itself in an absolute convergence of domination and appetite—the point at which, indeed, domination produces appetite as its original effect, the effect of a privation. Other boundaries, those of narration, are threatened with disintegration, as cannibalism marks a malign complicity between taleteller and audience:

> "I wish ye wadna always turn your green een on me that gate when you speak about your fat flesh," said Gibbie. "I assure you, mine is neither like beef, nor mutton, nor venison; and, what is more, you shall never taste it. I appeal to

you all, masters and friends, if this man has not fairly fallen through his tale."

"I suppose it must be very like veal, then," continued Tam; "and if so, I have seen a joint of cold veal very excellent meat, more especially that adjoining the white gristly part; with a little salt, a man can eat a great deal of that without being anything the worse."

"My masters, I do protest against the carnivorous looks of the story-teller," rejoined Gibbie; "they make ane feel so queerly. It is as if he were tearing my flesh quick from the banes with his teeth. And I call you to note that he has sticked a story, which, from the beginning, is no story." (266)

Gibbie protests against the failure of the tale as a drastic failure of sublimation. As the narrative falls apart, narrator and audience are to tear each other with their teeth.

The ill-favored Tam Craik has turned out, furthermore, to be none other than Marion's Jock, the cannibal shepherd of Gibbie's story. This disconcerting metamorphosis exemplifies a second, antithetical way in which narrative frames are breached: when figures in the tale turn into persons in the audience. This is an old romance device, displayed in the later chapters of the first part of Don Quixote, where characters from the apparently digressive interpolated tales start showing up at the inn. The compulsively serial narrative of Don Quixote's monomania expands into a fabric that knits together different spaces and times and plots, marvellously repairing the gaps and losses of human experience (without any therapeutic effect, unfortunately, on the Don himself). The recognition of oneself in another's story, the recovery of a lost relation out of storytelling: these are tropes for the thaumaturgic power of a narration that restores the alienated identity of its reader, listener, or even teller. In The Three Perils of Man the sufferers in the Friar's gloomy tale turn out to be the parents of Delany, while the babe saved from burning in Charlie Scott's tale is the poet. Narration becomes a benign magic, cancelling its own borders for the restoration of those primitive relations that are the foundations of human identity.[42]

Thus a devotion to mere figures has conjured back lost bodies after all. "Every incorporation has introjection as its nostalgic vocation," according to Abraham and Torok (128), and this romance magic would appear to express such a nostalgia. Psychoanalytic transference, the modern clinical version of a process of recovery through narration, will insist on the fictive or metaphoric, not literal, quality of the recognition it elicits: to comprehend the story we have been living is at best to comprehend its status as a story, if we would be released from its compulsive sentence. But "the recuperative magic of incorporation" (Abraham and Torok, 114), with its literalizing spell, is the wishful schematic reverse of that other terminus of storytelling, the cannibal orgy, with its closure upon the vulnerable body—as in those metamorphoses where poor Gibbie must preside at the killing, cooking, and eating of himself. Cannibalism for Gibbie means not an end of narrative but its hellish endlessness. His metamorphic slippage along the food chain enacts an interminable and tormenting displacement in which he is unable even to coincide with himself by consuming himself. As the narrator of this adventure, he appears to be the opposite of that ideal of the author who may control the figures of identity and desire in his story—an ideal associated in the case of Scott, as Susan Manning has argued, with a stable self-interest based on the moderation of appetite.[43] Here, instead of a magical substitution of its figures with real bodies and relations, narrative enacts a compulsive repetition of the loss it is supposed to compensate.

It may not be possible to close down or step outside some stories, since they may have no afterwards or outside. They may not be dismissed to the other time of the past. *The Three Perils of Man* turns the apparatus of narrative framing to an opposite effect from Scott's in the *Lay*, using it to scramble the temporal distinctions between a narrative past and present, and to insist upon the interminably recurring liminality of the narrative act, in the doubled or divided "now" of telling and reading. Hogg's frames prescribe their own transgression in a perilous inclusion of the reader,[44] an abolition of distinctions and distances, and the threat of a materialist reduction to bodies and drives: that is, we have not transcended any of those conditions, least of all the violence upon which the order of culture is founded. The theoretical language available to Hogg for this was not, of course, psychoanalytic, but theological; instead of the exotic term incorporation, he would have acknowledged the Presbyterian trope of "carnality." The carnal brings together in one word the condition of being in the flesh, the life of the senses, the bloody appetite to devour, and the secular, material, unsanctified state that is the dominion of idle tales and vain romances. Thomas Boston, Minister of the Gospel at Ettrick, writes in 1720:

> Lions make not a prey of lions, nor wolves of wolves; but men are turned wolves to one another, biting and devouring one another. Since Cain shed the blood of Abel, the earth has been turned to a slaughter-house; and the chase has been continued since Nimrod began his hunting; on the earth, as in the sea, the greater still devouring the lesser.[45]

Boston gives the orthodox version of the effect that Abraham and Torok call "demetaphorization": "Doth not the carnal mind naturally strive to grasp spiritual things in imagination; as if the soul were quite immersed in flesh and blood, and would turn every thing into its own shape?"[46] *The Three Perils of Man* glosses the lesson in its characters' metamorphosis into cattle: art, supreme refinement of "the carnal mind," is the deception of appetite, a ruse and a temporary off-putting, rather than a transcendence. Here, though, the theological absolutism of Boston's scheme is lacking. Narration and devouring are oral acts that define the limits of formation and dissolution in a carnal society: a fellowship of tales and a violence that reduces your fellow to prey. *The Three Perils of Man* exposes the reciprocity of these limits, the way these acts depend on each other to define each other, as well as their vital, precarious, if merely temporal difference. That is to say, Hogg situates narrative—the ceremonial time of a breathing space, the linguistic act that sustains social relations—within a perilous political economy of competition, dominance, and devouring.[47] Far from consigning it regretfully to a legendary past, Hogg's narrative tells over and over again, although as black comedy rather than tragedy, the violence that remains culture's condition: not right here or now, perhaps, but never far away.

THE UPRIGHT CORPSE

Hogg's most striking figure of the uncanny is the upright corpse. The botched revival of the past raises a lifeless body animated by an alien, unnatural, and inscrutable power.[48] *Winter Evening Tales* (1820), bearing the subtitle *Collected among the Cottagers in the South of Scotland*, is a miscellaneous collection of tales, sketches, ballads, and fragments: the raw ingredients of national-historical romance and of the ensemble the ethnographer will call "culture." Strikingly, Hogg refuses to assemble these parts into any kind of a totality. The first, most internally heterogeneous of the tales, "The Renowned Adventures of Basil Lee," brings its modern, deracinated, opportunistic narrator into a series of collisions with "superstition" on the primitive isle of Lewis. The encounter with a troop of phantom warriors pitches Basil into a baffling cognitive and historical interim:

> I make no pretensions to account for this extraordinary phenomenon, but the singular circumstance of its being visible only from one point, and no other, makes it look like something that might be accounted for. I can well excuse any who do not believe it, for if I had not seen it with my own eyes, I never would have believed it. But of all things I ever beheld for wild sublimity, the march of that troop of apparitions excelled—not a day or a night hath yet passed over my head, on which I have not thought with wonder and awe on *the Visit of M'Torquille*. (52)

If it is too late for belief it is also too early, as it were, for a scientific explanation, in which the phenomenon might turn out to be, in a curiously technical sense, a matter of perspective. (In "Welldean Hall" the ghost rudely refutes a clergyman's materialist diagnosis of him as "a penumbra, [proceeding] from some obtuse reflection," 448–49). Meanwhile the present accommodates the threshold sensation of romance revival: a purely aesthetic, ideologically undetermined "wonder and awe" at a spectacle of "wild sublimity."

The following supernatural adventure yields an aesthetic effect that is the reverse of a sublime elation. Basil visits an old peasant woman supposed to be haunted by the ghost of her son. Sharing her vigil, he sees what appears to be "the corpse of her son sitting directly opposite her" (56). Livid, wrapped in its dead clothes, mumbling unintelligibly, the figure appears as an animated corpse and not (like the providential wraiths in other Hogg tales) as the fetch of a once-living person. The return of the dead wears a repellently literal aspect. The uncanny effect is manifest in a weird possession of the spectator by the spectacle: "The old woman's arms were stretched out towards the figure, and her face thrown upwards, the features meanwhile distorted as with extatic agony" (56). This "extatic agony"—the image of death—is in turn infectious, and Basil falls into "a stupor, like a trance, without being able to move either hand or foot." When he comes to, he finds the old woman actually in her death throes. Another hour passes, and he is disturbed by "a rustling in the bed where the body lay":

> On looking round, I perceived with horror that the corpse was sitting upright in the bed, shaking its head as it did in the agonies of death, and stretching out its hands towards the hearth. I thought the woman had been vivified, and looked steadily at the face; but I saw that it was the face of a corpse still; for the eye was white, being turned upward and fixed in the socket, the mouth was open, and all the other features immoveably fixed for ever. (57)

Whether or not it was a dream, Basil comments, "There was a tint of spiritual sublimity in the whole matter." But the episode is striking for the opposite effect: a contagious circuit between subject and object, like a parody of the moral philosophers' account of sympathetic exchange,[49] in which psychic blackouts alternate with the reanimation of corpses—bodies visited with motion but not spirit. At the center of the circuit is a literal death, and the old woman's corpse is the only evidence that remains. For the materialist self of Hogg's persona a weird insistence of physical bodies, not of any spiritual entity, constitutes the uncanny experience, as though in a rehearsal of his own death.

Some of the details here, in particular the corpse that sits upright, anticipate the bizarre culmination of "Peril First" in *The Three Perils of Woman* (1823). That episode is prefigured by an early crisis in which the heroine, Gatty Bell, falls in a swoon so profound that the onlookers think she is dead. When her lover, an Edinburgh medical student, attempts to revive her, the signal of her return to life is "a torrent of blood" that drenches them both.[50] In the second volume, after a comic plot of lovers' errors has gone horribly awry, Gatty prophesies her own death, suffers a mysterious decline, and appears indeed to have passed away. When her lover approaches the bed on which she is laid out, an occult power of sympathy convulses the apparently lifeless body with muscular spasms:

> The body sprung up with a power resembling that of electricity. It did not rise up like one wakening out of a sleep, but with a jerk so violent that it struck the old man on the cheek, almost stupefying him; and there sat the corpse, dressed as it was in its dead-clothes, a most appalling sight as man ever beheld. (200)

The "ghastly automaton" (201) with "the dead countenance of an idiot" burbles unintelligibly (200). The scene communicates the horror of a mechanistic pseudolife, an animation unendowed with reason or sensibility: "No human heart could stand this; for though the body seemed to have life, it was altogether an unnatural life; or rather, the form seemed as if agitated by some demon that knew not how to exercise or act upon any one of the human powers or faculties" (200). The comatose woman is confined in an asylum, where "in due time" she gives birth to a son. In Freudian language, something "new and alien" has turned out to be something "old and familiar" indeed—a maternal body.

New and alien: Gatty is animated by "a power resembling that of electricity"—the mysterious vital current replicated in galvanism. Public experiments upon the cadavers of executed felons by Luigi Galvani's nephew Giovanni Aldini attracted popular attention and scientific debate in Great Britain in the first three decades of the nineteenth century. "The trunk was thrown into strong convulsions," Aldini describes one electrocution: "the shoulders were elevated in a sensible manner; and the hands were so agitated that they beat against the table which supported the body."[51] Other accounts mention corpses sitting upright and striking bystanders. Proponents of galvanism made claims for its medical efficacy in treating "cases of torpor in persons afflicted with melancholy madness" and those "in which life is not extinguished, but its influence on the animal organization merely suspended."[52] Could life, then, be reduced to a material substance, an electric fluid immanent in organic structure? Galvanism was just one current (phrenology was another) in a rising tide of scientific materialism that found its British institutional center in Edinburgh, until the founding of London University (on Scottish principles) in the 1830s. The postwar politicization of literature and science exacerbated the association of organic materialism with political radicalism, an association that grew increasingly fractious in the decade preceding Reform.[53] The Blackwood's wits, as might be expected, denounced the phrenologists and radical materialists, such as the soon-to-be infamous anatomist Robert Knox. The "Noctes Ambrosianae" represent the Ettrick Shepherd lapping up Christopher North's pious diatribes:

> *North.* If this be true, then, all that is really deficient in our conception of Spirit is that which it could not by any possibility include, namely, the image of an impression on sense!
>
> *Shepherd.* Let the materialists answer that. That's a bane for them to mumble till their jaws are sair.[54]

Yet Hogg himself was an Edinburgh maverick, more like Knox than he was like the Oxford men Wilson and Lockhart. He had taken part in an extracurricular debating society while moving in democratic circles a decade or so earlier.[55] The Ettrick Shepherd turns out to be imaginatively more attuned to the intellectual currents of advanced modernity, including radical materialism, than any contemporary Scots author.

In *Frankenstein* (1818) Mary Shelley depicts the generation of reason and sentiment as well as animal vitality from physical sources; social pressures of neglect and persecution warp the new being into criminality.[56] In Hogg's scenes of reanimation the intellect remains absent and the body moves with an insensate, mechanical energy. Yet such energy is sufficient, in Gatty's case, for the gestation of a child. The body without spirit is a maternal one, the deficiency far from impairing (quite the contrary) its occult powers of procreation. Hogg's representation insists on the biological materiality of the body as not only alien and monstrous but untransfigurable, even (or especially) in its generative power. Biology itself, in Foucault's sense of a new epistemic formation, has not yet become legible.[57] The appearance of these carnal origins brings a blankness, disgusting rather than sublime; aesthetic distance cannot regulate a crisis that shakes the most intimate property of the self. It is not so much, then, that Hogg is to be understood as endorsing or refuting a materialist view of life, or that his tales are allegorical expositions of scientific issues, or even that in deploying these figures he is much concerned with their technical or institutional specificity. Hogg uses the heat rather than light generated by the current scientific ferment for his own literary purpose of a revisionary disturbance of the genres of national fiction. In these uncanny moments the foundational categories of life are represented as in crisis, their natural stability and continuity suddenly overthrown, and it is the crisis itself rather than any solution that grips the imagination. Lacking spirit, reason, or voice, the reanimated corpse is a body reduced to a thing, a horrifying nexus of matter and force.

Old and familiar: Valentina Bold has drawn attention to Hogg's use of oral-traditional tropes and patterns in the episode of Gatty's illness.[58] "Ancient" and "modern" leak into one another to produce a frightening opacity—an animated but mindless corpse, a cancelling overlay of cultural codes. The narrator issues a standard disclaimer:

> In what state she then was, it will never be in the power of man to decide. The issue turned out so terrible, that the whole matter has always appeared to me as much above human agency as human capacity; if any can comprehend it from a plain narration of the incidents as they succeeded one another, the definition shall be put in their power; but farther I take not on me to decide. (196–97)

The strangeness of the present—the up-to-date milieu of the first of Hogg's "Series of Domestic Scottish Tales"—is expressed in a freakish revelation of archaic forms. Gatty's friends cannot decide whether they are witnessing a case of "mere animal existence" or one of demonic possession (202). Her condition suggests the parodic inversion of a typological life-in-death: she continues for three days and nights in her automaton state before relapsing into a "vegetable" coma, a reduction to the body which is the opposite of a resurrection. Three years later, after a further threshold period of three days and nights, Gatty just as mysteriously revives.[59] Meanwhile, "in due time this helpless and forlorn object was safely delivered of a son, without manifesting the slightest ray of conscious existence, or even of experiencing, as far as could be judged, the same throes of nature to which conscious beings are subjected" (204). The disturbing quality of the episode bears upon its narrative centrality. What was a curious incident in "Basil Lee" invests the heroine of Hogg's domestic Scottish tale to unmake not only her but, by synecdoche, the genre of which she is protagonist.

From its inception in the Irish novels of Edgeworth and Owenson to its Scottish versions, including the transformation to historical romance effected in *Waverley*, the "national tale" had relied upon the teleological figure of a female body as reproductive vessel for the domestic union of historical antagonisms. That female body supplies the natural source and cultural property that together guarantee the crucial effects of lineal descent, historical continuity, and a synchronization of the different registers of organic, domestic, and national-historical time. *The Three Perils of Woman* follows Edinburgh novels such as Brunton's *Discipline* (1814) and Ferrier's *Marriage* (1818), both of which culminate in the heroine's proper union with an ideal modern gentleman who is also—like Gatty's beau M'Ion in *The Three Perils of Man*—a Highland chief. Hogg also aims at the appropriations of this tradition by Wilson (in *Lights and Shadows of Scottish Life*) and Scott. *The Heart of Mid-Lothian* is exceptionally ambitious in its complication of the feminine domestic matter at the core of Scott's own transformation of the genre; here, too, the maternal body appears as a foundational categorical problem for the allegory of national identity before it can become a solution.[60]

Absent from *The Three Perils of Woman* (disorientingly fractured into "series" and "circles") is the retrospective ethical certainty, maintained through a continuity of first-person narration, that attends the heroine's progress in *Discipline*, even during her delirium and incarceration in an Edinburgh insane asylum. The most disconcerting rupture here, however, is that of the bond between social and natural or organic time, as if, unregulated by the networks of collective consciousness, the body may generate a tempo of its own. The terrible jarrings of genre and history that constitute the last volume of *The Three Perils of Woman*, set in the wake of Culloden, are the narrative issue of this scandalous reduction of the domestic national heroine. Hogg dismantles not just the domestic national tale but its developmental mutation into Scott's historical romance. Gatty's is only the first in a series of bodies that "remain recalcitrantly and terrifyingly corporeal." Peril Second plays the "recurrent transgression of boundaries between bodies, and between living and dead" as a graveyard farce, with David Duff the sexton and Peter Gow the smith tumbling on top of each other in an open grave.[61] Peril Third discloses a nightmarish aftermath, out of Brecht or Hasek, of the genre established by *Waverley*. Foreshadowed in the strange trances and reanimations of the earlier "circles," Hogg's post-Culloden landscape is ghastly with unburied and living dead, among them another maternal heroine, the unfortunate Sally Niven. When a scavenger gropes in her bosom for gold, "the dead woman seize[s] him by the hand with a frightened and convulsive grasp, setting her nails into his wrist" (406). Revived, her wits gone, she haunts the sites of massacre, "rocking and singing over the body of a dead female infant" (407). The novel closes upon the figure of the mother, bereft and traumatized, as animated corpse.

RESURRECTION MEN

In 1828 Dr. Robert Knox found himself at the epicenter of the Burke and Hare scandal, accused of stocking his dissecting theater with the cadavers of murder victims. "It is an ugly business altogether, James," North gloats to the Shepherd in the "Noctes" of March 1829; "far worse than the Chaldean MS."[62] Hogg puts grave robbery, a resurrection that raises only the dead, at the end and origin of the *Private Memoirs and Confessions of a Justified Sinner* (1824), a novel richer than any other in the repertoire of uncanny effects:

> One of the young men seized the rope and pulled by it, but the old enchantment of the devil remained, —it would not break; and so he pulled and pulled

at it, till behold the body came up into a sitting posture, with a broad blue bonnet on its head, and its plaid around it, all as fresh as that day it was laid in![63]

The unresponsive body provokes a desire that turns violent:

One of the lads gripped the face of the corpse with his finger and thumb, and the cheeks felt quite soft and fleshy, but the dimples remained and did not spring out again. He had fine yellow hair, about nine inches long; but not a hair of it could they pull out till they cut part of it off with a knife. They also cut off some portions of his clothes, which were all quite fresh, and distributed them among their acquaintances, sending a portion to me, among the rest, to keep as natural curiosities. Several gentlemen have in a manner forced me to give them fragments of these enchanted garments: I have, however, retained a small portion for you, which I send along with this, being a piece of his plaid, and another of his waistcoat breast, which you will see are still as fresh as that day they were laid in the grave. (168)

Hogg alludes to the allegorical burden of romance revival as the loving resurrection of a buried and dismembered national culture, associated with a textual corpus and a genius loci, meant to replenish the ruined imaginative life of modernity.[64] Here, in grisly burlesque, antiquarian research cannot animate the dead body it unearths—only despoil it in a necrophiliac traffic of "curiosities."

In *Peter's Letters to His Kinsfolk* Lockhart had elected Scott as national resurrection man:

The grave loses half its potency when he calls. His own imagination is one majestic sepulchre, where the wizard lamp burns in never-dying splendour, and the charmed blood glows for ever in the cheeks of the embalmed, and every long-sheathed sword is ready to leap from its scabbard, like the Tizona of the Cid in the vault of Cardena.[65]

The grave loses only half its potency: the act of revival never brings its subjects all the way back to life, instead rendering them as undead things, infused with an alien energy, in the eye of critical reflection. In the "Dedicatory Epistle" to *Ivanhoe*, Scott compares the "Scottish Magician" (himself) to Lucan's witch Erichtho, "at liberty to walk over the recent field of battle, and to select for the subject of resuscitation by his sorceries, a body whose limbs had recently quivered with existence, and whose throat had but just uttered the last note of agony." The contrast with the "English author," obliged to compose his subjects from "the dust of antiquity," emphasizes—as James Chandler points out—the recent date of civil war in Scottish history, just beyond the reach of living memory, and thus the more proximate violence upon which "the classical form of the historical novel" is founded.[66] The field traversed by the Scottish magician looks a lot like the post-Culloden landscape of *The Three Perils of Woman*. Glancing back as he turns from Scottish to English history, the Author of *Waverley* acknowledges a resurrection that perpetuates the "agony" it was supposed to cure. Mirroring Lockhart's figure of the undead, representing a failure of the past to return fully to life, Scott's acknowledges a past that has never been laid properly to rest.

The end of *Confessions of a Justified Sinner* brings a more drastic desublimation of the scenario of revival. Instead of the raising of a national body or spirit, we witness (through the Editor's pruriently literal gaze) a noisome regurgitation of ransacked, half-rotten fragments:

> A number of the bones came up separately; for with the constant flow of liquid stuff into the deep grave, we could not see to preserve them in their places. At length great loads of coarse clothes, blanketing, plaiding, &c. appeared; we tried to lift these regularly up, and on doing so, part of a skeleton came up, but no flesh, save a little that was hanging in dark flitters about the spine, but which had no consistence; it was merely the appearance of flesh without the substance. (171–72)

Organic unity, Romantic ideology's powerful theme of a transhistorical continuity, is reduced to the slime of decomposition. As readers, accessories after the fact, we are left with a still more unsettling relic, the sinner's text, riven with tropes of doubling and fragmentation. "It was a bold theme for an allegory," the Editor surmises, "and would have suited that age well had it been taken up by one fully qualified for the task, which this writer was not" (175). If *The Three Perils of Woman* closed with an ideological collapse of national allegory onto the figure—the maternal body—it had posed as its end and origin, *Confessions of a Justified Sinner* closes with a technological collapse of allegory itself as a culture-making symbolic system. Such a collapse is in its turn allegorical. Modern allegory, according to Benjamin, condemns its characters to death because it is only in death that "the body comes properly into its own," only in the corpse that the world as a materialist natural order is fully revealed to us.[67] With this dour revelation Hogg leaves his modern Editor: for whom, his imagination unable to reach beyond a baffled apprehension of dead things, it is no revelation at all.

Chapter 8

❧

THEORETICAL HISTORIES OF SOCIETY

[I]t is not in this age that a man of ordinary common sense would enter into competition, in recreative stories, with a great genius who possessed the attention of all, I mean Sir Walter Scott.
—John Galt, *Autobiography*

What a cursed fellow that Walter Scot has been, to drive me out of my old original line.
—Galt, letter to William Blackwood, 30 January 1821

LOCAL THEORETICAL HISTORY

John Galt, the other major talent among the Blackwoodians besides James Hogg, also found himself having to reckon with the ascendancy of the Waverley novels. One way of setting limits to Scott's influence was to identify his work with a stock-in-trade of literary convention, into which Galt's own practice sometimes lapsed by default. The claim on an "originality" rooted outside convention, and outside Edinburgh literary-professional culture, allowed Galt to deny a relation of competition with Scott. The "radical defect" of *The Spaewife*, a rambling historical novel of intrigue at the court of James I, consists in its resembling "too much the work of Sir Walter Scott, with whom I never placed myself consciously in any rivalry." Galt adds: "Excellence is his characteristic, and, if I may say so, originality is mine."[1] The contrast between "originality" and "excellence"—conventional artistry—expresses the rivalry Galt has disavowed, like the proposal (coolly received by Blackwood) to combine his separate works in a grand *Tales of the West*, a regional riposte to Scott's *Tales of My Landlord*. It was at this time, at the zenith of his success with Blackwood in the early 1820s, that R. P. Gillies recalls Galt boasting "that his literary resources were far greater in extent than those of Sir Walter Scott or any other contemporary."[2]

Scott's achievement precipitated Galt's "originality" as the term of his difference in the literary market. To defend that originality Galt laid claim to a more substantial principle than competition, since Scott's commercial and critical success would always define competition in his terms. James

Hogg's originality was framed (more and more restrictively) by the canons of Enlightenment historiography, which identified it with premodern cultural conditions; Galt, lacking primitivist credentials, had to locate originality elsewhere. Galt's social origins in "the West," Scotland's commercial and industrial heartland, necessitated no critical distance from the principles of Enlightenment philosophy, which recast "origins" as a universal human motive (desire, ambition) instead of a location in the past. Galt's account of his originality, accordingly, reappropriates Enlightenment philosophy from historical romance and makes it authorize a very different conjunction of Scottishness, history, and fiction.

In his *Autobiography* Galt characterizes his difference from Scott as a distinction in narrative mode and genre:

> It may be necessary to explain here, that I do not think the character of my own productions has been altogether rightly regarded. —Merely because the incidents are supposed to be fictitious, they have been all considered as novels, and yet, as such, the best of them are certainly deficient in the peculiarity of the novel. They would be more properly characterised, in several instances, as theoretical histories, than either as novels or romances. . . . Many, I am very free to allow, have vastly surpassed my endeavours in the historical novel, but I do not think that I have had numerous precursors, in what I would call my theoretical histories of society.[3]

Galt sets his work apart from "novels or romances," in particular "the historical novel," by laying claim to an alternative discourse he calls "theoretical history." Reasserting the traditional antithesis between romance and history, Galt refuses to acknowledge the dialectical and deconstructive play between them in the Waverley novels, which are thus reduced to the inauthentic pole of romance. Theoretical history is pledged to the truth effects of reason, experience, and common sense: instead of "the wild and wonderful," Galt declares, "my wish is to be estimated by the truth of whatever I try to represent" (1:230–31). The opposition to romance ensures that this truth emerges as a didactic principle: "I considered the novel as a vehicle of instruction, or philosophy teaching, by example, parables, in which the moral was more valuable than the incidents were impressive" (2:210). Galt reverts, in effect, to the early modern, prenovelistic narratology—associated with his technical model Defoe—that Lennard Davis calls "factual fiction," which preceded the novel's formation through the assumption of fictionality.

Galt derives the term "theoretical history" from Scottish Enlightenment philosophy, where it denotes, after all, a kind of fiction.[4] In his biography of Adam Smith, Dugald Stewart coined the term to define the method of inductive reasoning by which a philosopher may project a hypothesis beyond the record of empirical data:

In examining the history of mankind, as well as in examining the phenomena of the material world, when we cannot trace the process by which an event *has been* produced, it is often of importance to be able to show how it *may have been* produced by natural causes. . . . To this species of philosophical investigation, which has no appropriated name in our language, I shall take the liberty of giving the title of *Theoretical* or *Conjectural History*; an expression which coincides pretty nearly in its meaning with that of *Natural History*, as employed by Mr Hume[.][5]

Stewart describes the experimental method of modern science, devoted to unfolding the laws of a universal nature that governs human perceptions, motives, and actions as well as physical processes. The philosopher proposes an invention that may not coincide with the recorded evidence, but reproduces a paradigm abstracted from that evidence. As Mary Poovey argues, the formulation of conjectural history was meant to resolve the epistemological scandal of induction that followed Hume's installation of "fiction making . . . at the heart of both the idea of society and theorizing about society." Theoretical history is a licensed kind of fiction, regulated—as novels themselves were beginning to claim they were—by emergent canons of probability.[6]

Scott would certainly have recognized "theoretical history" as a term applying to his own novelistic practice, and he appeals to its principles in the prefatory matter to *Waverley* and *Ivanhoe*. Since human nature is the same everywhere and at all times, its laws will inform the most exotic settings and extraordinary turns of event. Turn of event is the principle Galt invokes to distinguish his brand of theoretical history from Scott's romantic hybrid: "A consistent fable is as essential to a novel as a plot is to a drama, and yet those, which are deemed my best productions, are deficient in this essential ingredient" (2:219). The formal principle of romance, "the peculiarity of the novel," that Galt eschews is an extended, complex, unified plot (mythos). Instead, in practice, Galt cleaves to a trompe-l'oeil mimicry of those secular narrative forms, admitted to the fold of historiography in the late Enlightenment, that have transmitted the historical record without the conspicuous imposition of a plot: memoir, anecdote, local annals or chronicle, the "statistical account."[7] These forms converge in the work that Galt instantiates as "theoretical history," *Annals of the Parish* (1821); although *Annals* turns out to be entangled in plot and allegory, and Galt's companion fictional memoir, *The Provost* (1822), offers a stricter realization.

A sequence of episodes in *The Provost* shows Galt disassembling and recombining Scott's most elaborate, allegorically charged work of romance plotting, in *The Heart of Mid-Lothian* (1818). The ninth chapter of *The Provost*, "An Execution," condenses the infanticide plot of *The*

Heart of Mid-Lothian; the following chapter, "A Riot," recalls Scott's impressive opening scenes (even to the detail of the mob's emitting "a frightful yell, and rolling like the waves of the sea").[8] The order of chapters reverses the order in which these events are narrated by Scott, but restores their chronology, straightening out Scott's "artificial" temporal loop.[9] Galt's realignment also strips away the thematic and symbolic links Scott forges between the cases of riot and infanticide,[10] leaving no connection between them beyond the arbitrary one of sequence. (The infanticide case inspires compassion among the townsfolk but not criticism of the law's injustice; while the riot breaks out in protest against "a heinous trespass on the liberties and privileges of the people," 33.) Galt's infanticide chapter plots a set of antithetical coordinates to *The Heart of Mid-Lothian*. Here the unmarried mother is indisputably guilty of killing her child, its body is discovered beside her, and she is condemned and hanged without reprieve. Galt names the wretched girl "Jeanie," after Scott's heroine Jeanie Deans, the sister of his novel's condemned mother Effie; but Galt's Jeanie is in some respects more like Effie's double, Madge Wildfire—she is mentally retarded and has a disreputable mother who comes looking for her in prison. Galt's condensation of Scott's several figures into one reverses the romance technique of allegorical doubling with which Scott generates his complex plot and resolves its ethical and ideological dilemmas: this unfortunate girl has no sister to plead her case before a higher power, no proxy to perish in her stead. The inscrutable silence of Galt's Jeanie, in prison and at her trial, combines Effie's failure "to communicate her situation" with Jeanie Deans's refusal to bear false witness. Here, though, the silence remains a blank. It does not hide a significant utterance that, if only spoken, would resolve or save. It covers, rather, a pathos terrible for being meaningless. The trial and execution generate intense but temporary feeling—pity for the witless victim—but no expansive machinery of plot. There is, however, a late narrative sequel (chapter 29) in which the dead girl's missing male relative turns up. Instead of the absconded lover or lost son, as in *The Heart of Mid-Lothian*, this is Jeanie's brother, who left town after her death to enlist in the army and now reappears with his regiment. The captain is ostracized by his fellow officers when they find out that his sister was hanged for child murder, until all is put right by a gracious word of recognition from "His Lordship." This nobleman's intercession recalls the Duke of Argyle's in *The Heart of Mid-Lothian*, but here it resolves a local sentimental crisis rather than redeeming an allegorically resonant tragedy. The meaning of Jeanie's death is not at stake; hers is an empty silence. Galt withholds Scott's romance plotting, which transforms events and changes their significance as they are viewed at different stages of the narrative.

Galt correctly identifies plot as a necessary ingredient of Scott's historical romance, and the formal element that separates romance from history.
For Scott, romance is the cultural instrument through which "nature"
may be apprehended. Just as fiction—following Hume—is the medium of
common life, its conventions encode the *mentalité* of a traditional society,
inaccessible in historical modernity save through these conventions, as
"romance." The artificiality or conventionality of romance, ritually
marked in its plots, reveals not that it is false but that it is a shared, continuous work of human invention. The recurrence of certain artificial forms,
conveying psychological meaning across cultural and historical gaps, expresses recurrent structures of feeling and so is powerful evidence of an
abiding human nature. By a double logic, articulated in the philosophical
debate between Humean skepticism and Reidian common sense that continued to agitate post-Enlightenment Edinburgh, this conventionality at
once marks romance plotting as a kind of universal grammar of the
human imagination, representing nature more reliably than the echolalia
of raw, individual experience; and exposes it, all the same, as a fiction: a
human invention with no formal legitimacy outside its own devices.

By rejecting plot Galt contends, in effect, that the skeptical turn of
Scott's romance dialectic negates its claim on common sense. The representation of truth is falsified by the overarching presence of artifice and
convention—the ritual insistence that this is "just a fiction." To abide in
plot is to occupy an intensely ideological and catastrophic relation to history. As this chapter and the next will show, Galt associates romance
plotting with submission to an obsolescent—yet also apocalyptic and revolutionary—mode of allegorical meaning, and a negative, fatalistic determination of human agency. Just as (Thomas Brown pointed out) Reid's
critique rehearses a weak misreading of Hume's account of agency and
belief, Galt comes to problematize his own dismissal of plot, and to recover, through a critical dialogue with Scott's fiction, its function as a
critical instrument for exploring the problematics of ideology, agency, and
belief in historical narrative.

At the height of his success in the early 1820s Galt shifted the form of
theoretical history from anecdotal and annalistic fictional memoir into
the arena of rivalry with Scott, and of a more thorough reckoning with
his work, in the three-volume national and historical novel. If *Sir Andrew
Wylie* interrogates national character as the term of Galt's success in a
literary market defined by the plot-intensive three-volume novel and by
London rather than Edinburgh as metropolitan field of reception, Galt's
best novels, *The Entail* and *Ringan Gilhaize*, work out a complex philosophical debate with Scott's most ambitious historical fiction in the early
series of *Tales of My Landlord*. In each Galt assumes a "consistent fable"
so as to represent the ideological ambition of protagonists who impose

their agency on history by identifying it with a written master plot, the text of law or scripture, only to become tragically determined by the allegorical structure of meaning they have invoked. We even find Galt's weaker novels of the mid-1820s, such as the incoherent and tedious *The Spaewife* and the coherent but tedious *The Omen*, thematizing the work of plot as disastrous fatality rather than romantic providence.

Galt's affirmation of theoretical history by way of a refusal and then critique of romance, identified with the conventions of an extensive artificial plot, makes for a striking contrast with Hogg, whom we found subverting the Enlightenment scheme of theoretical history in order to reclaim the critical force of "traditionary" narrative modes. These authors differentiated themselves from Scott by taking opposite sides of the dialectic between romance and history activated in Scott's fiction, in each case dismantling Scott's synthesis by rejecting the antithetical discourse. This triangulation sketches a plan of competition and influence in a regional center, Edinburgh, at the moment of intensive formation of a capitalist mode of literary production. Scott's ascendancy, a formidable combination of artistic prowess, commercial dominance, and cultural authority, obliged ambitious authors to respond to his example and define their work in relation to his. Hogg and Galt responded minimally to one another;[11] instead, their artistic relation is mediated through Scott, whose work makes available the positions they occupy in relation to him and to each other. The economy of this triangulation is Darwinian, charting the "objective" effects of proximity and competition in a closed institutional economy. It schematizes uneven development on a local scale, inflecting different historical positions and generic possibilities in a dialectical and critical simultaneity. Their regional and social origins provided Hogg, the Ettrick shepherd, and Galt, Clydeside entrepreneur, with a valuable critical distance from the literary-lawyer culture of Scott's Edinburgh. While this distance certainly did not constitute their remarkable literary skills, it gave them direction and edge. Hogg takes the "primitive" work of romance to magic-realist and postmodernist conclusions. Galt, rejecting "fable" as obsolete rather than archaic, a deadweight of convention, instantiates (with unprecedented rigor) that bourgeois empirical realism celebrated by Ian Watt and other critics as the authentic mode of the modern novel, and for which Defoe is the touchstone (as he is for some of Hogg's experiments in fictional memoir, notably "Renowned Adventures of Basil Lee" and "Some Remarkable Passages in the Life of an Edinburgh Baillie"). Needless to say, the contemporaneity of this empirical realism with the declensions of "naïve" and "sentimental" romance practiced by Hogg and Scott, and the dialogic implication of all of them within each author's work, troubles any account of it as progressive or ascendant, beyond the values ascribed by the practitioners themselves.

If theoretical history eschews romance in the name of "truth," how may it justify its own status as a fiction? Galt said he intended *The Provost* "to exhibit a local theoretical history, by examples, the truth of which would at once be acknowledged."[12] "Theoretical" means fictional in the sense of typical or exemplary; theoretical history is a register of hypothetical instances unfolding general laws. The exemplary status of the case reconciles a contingent difference from the historical record with a typical congruence with it. This typicality is not typological, or allegorical; that is to say, it does not depend on the mediation of an invisible, absolute pattern of events, encoded in a master plot, informing local experience. The romance plot that Galt has rejected presumes an obsolete mode of allegory for its justification. Instead, theoretical history relies on an empirical, inductive, statistical mode of exemplarity, for which Reid's common-sense philosophy provides a theoretical basis. Reid argues that our knowledge of reality is secured by a universal, instinctive ground of common sense, manifest in the expressive repertoire of "natural signs" produced by the human body and in a universal grammar or linguistic structure.[13] As the word "common" suggests, the criterion for truth is quantitative rather than archetypal: truth is the aggregate measure of instances within the empirical set rather than the impress of a Logos from outside it. It is the statistical effect of a consensus of shared characteristics. The claim of universality can only ever be provisional, however, since it falls under the "problem of induction" installed in the empiricist account of reality by Hume: the problem, in Poovey's summary, that "one cannot know in advance of observation that instances yet to be observed will resemble those the philosopher has seen."[14]

A fiction is "true," accordingly, to the extent that it is probable—that is to say, it resembles (it reproduces a selected set of characteristics of) events which are known to have taken place. Its status as a fiction, its difference from those events, lies in its contingent, empirical specificity— the fact that this particular set of events is known not to have taken place (or rather, not known to have taken place). Recognition of fictional status becomes problematic, since it depends on the reader's familiarity with the historical record rather than a grammar of conventions. It is important that the reader recognize the example's status as a fiction, in order to perceive the principle, the truth, that it represents: "to exhibit a local theoretical history, by examples, the truth of which would at once be acknowledged." Galt's work requires a strenuous and delicate work of discernment, in which the reader apprehends a truth-bearing fiction by distinguishing it on the one hand from the historical record and on the other hand from mere romance. In practice such a status turned out to be precarious. Galt recalls how he conceived *Annals of the Parish* as "a kind of treatise on the history of society in the West of Scotland during the reign of King George the Third; and when it was written, I had no idea it would ever have been received as a novel."[15] Its readers redefined the book "as a novel"—another effect of Scott's power in the market—despite the author's conception of it as "a kind of treatise." (Scott himself registered an appropriate caution when he recommended the *Annals* to Joanna Baillie as "a most excellent novel, if it can be calld so.")[16] Conversely, anecdotes abound of readers who took the *Annals* for fact rather than fiction, and this seems to have been a widespread reaction.[17] Both avenues of reception divert us from the recognition of truth, displacing it on the one hand for the merely fictional, that is, false, conventions of romance, and on the other for the distracting contingencies of data.

Galt's first popular success, the magazine serial *The Ayrshire Legatees* (1820–21), also hoodwinked some readers into believing in the actuality of its cast of characters. The confusion fits the work's miscellaneous form, in which, reviving the epistolary travelogue of Smollett's *Humphry Clinker*, Galt combines fictitious characters and their adventures with current events such as George IV's coronation and the Queen Caroline trial. In an internal set piece, *Ayrshire Legatees* mocks the instability of the categories of fact and fiction, romance and history, in the field of reception. Dr. Pringle, a small-town Church of Scotland minister, takes up what he conceives to be "a *History of the Rebellion*, anent the hand that an English gentleman of the name of Waverley had in it."[18] Ignoring Scott's ostentatious deployment of "fable," the doctor accepts the book as an authentic chronicle: "it was wonderful interesting, and far more particular, in many points, than any other account of the affair I have yet met with; but it's no so friendly to Protestant principles as I could have wished." Mr. Craig, one of the auditors of Dr. Pringle's letter back in the parish, surmises darkly that "Waverley's *History of the Rebellion*" must be "another dose o' the radical poison in a new guise" (8). The joke goes against Pringle as a naïve reader, unaccustomed in his saintly simplicity to what the world recognizes as the conventions of romance; but it also raises questions about the political and ideological meanings carried by those conventions, and the conditions under which those conventions and those meanings become legible. If Mr. Craig's secondhand misprision itself performs a "radical" inversion of Dr. Pringle's complaint about Waverley's Jacobitism, the complaint stands: fiction as such opens up an indefinite imaginary terrain, not so much opposed to "Protestant principles" as lying outside them, and outside the various political alternatives which lay claim to it, depending on the particular community, with its local culture of literacy and values, that constitutes the work's reception.

Galt's anecdote about reading *Waverley* makes for a more skeptical account of the work of convention and the status of fiction than perhaps might be expected from a rejection of novelistic plotting in the name of truth. Before his success with *The Ayrshire Legatees* Galt had tried a broad range of genres, including the long poem, periodical essay, tragedy, travelogue, biography, and novel, of which the novels, *The Majolo*, *Glenfell*, and *The Earthquake* (the last written before *The Ayrshire Legatees* although published in its wake), were notably unsuccessful. With *The Ayrshire Legatees* Galt invented a kind of fiction—serial, topical, anecdotal, stylistically and tonally heterogeneous—suited to the miscellaneous format of *Blackwood's Magazine*, and he followed it with one-volume "autobiographies" and further Blackwoodian miscellanies over the next couple of years. (Hogg complained that *Annals of the Parish* ought to have been published in miscellaneous, i.e., magazine, format rather than as a book, since it wasn't really a novel.)[19] At Blackwood's prompting, Galt also turned to the high-earning and prestigious form of the three-volume "Scotch novel," beginning with *Sir Andrew Wylie* in 1822. *Sir Andrew Wylie* has become the locus classicus in a tradition of criticism, following the author's own commentary and that of his modern biographer and editor Ian Gordon, that has characterized Galt's career as a struggle to maintain artistic integrity against the corrupting pressure of market-sanctioned conventions exemplified by the Waverley novels. This account represents *Sir Andrew Wylie* in particular, but also *The Entail*, as disfigured by varying degrees of accommodation to these conventional pressures, urged upon Galt by Blackwood, whose demands for a three-volume novel driven by an "interesting" plot forced Galt out of his original vein.[20] The romantic dichotomy between original genius and alienating market scarcely fits the Smithian representation of commerce in Galt's own theoretical histories, or his general view of his career as a series of entrepreneurial ventures among which literature by no means came foremost. Galt's complaints about the constraints of the market have led commentators to underestimate or ignore the ways in which dominant conventions, and the force of Scott's example, constituted a creative challenge rather than a prohibition. These were the conditions for Galt's most ambitious work in *The Entail* and *Ringan Gilhaize*, both of which undertake a disciplinary reckoning with the Scottish historical novel.

EXEMPLARITY: *ANNALS OF THE PARISH*

Annals of the Parish, the work Galt most elaborately justified as original, works out a new, modern rhetoric of typology, what might be called an empirical or statistical typology, in relation to an older allegorical mode. Allegory claimed to provide a view of a cultural system by plotting a discursive position outside that system—hence *allos*, other—whereas the new typology does not transcend the world it represents. Galt imitates the genre of the parish register or chronicle, given canonical form in *The Statistical Account of Scotland*. He dismantles "fable" for a series of interwoven anecdotes, episodes, and micronarratives which carry an exemplary force: the small and the local typify a larger collective or totality. The narrative is given unity by the scheme of autobiography, the narrative of a singular subjectivity occupying a definite place and time.

Galt associates allegorical typology with the "simplicity" of his narrator, the parish minister Micah Balwhidder. Balwhidder justifies his narrative by drawing attention to certain correspondences between his ministry and the reign of George III:

> In the same year, and on the same day of the same month, that his Sacred Majesty King George, the third of that name, came to his crown and kingdom, I was placed and settled as the minister of Dalmailing. . . . [E]verybody spoke of me and the new king as united in our trusts and temporalities, marvelling how the same should come to pass, and thinking the hand of Providence was in it, and that surely we were pre-ordained to fade and flourish in fellowship together; which has really been the case[.][21]

This seems comically presumptuous and literal-minded, inviting the reader to occupy an ironical—skeptical, enlightened—position somewhere over the narrator's head. The correspondence between parochial and national levels of event appears confined to a naïve mode of allegory, which must be read satirically. "[W]hat happened in my parish," the minister later confirms, "was but a type and index to the rest of the world" (186). By this stage, however, the reader will have come to agree with Balwhidder: events in the parish are indeed typical, representative of larger historical processes such as the extension of overseas empire, the development of trade and industry, the diffusion of commodities and information, the appearance of new social and ideological formations. Balwhidder sums up these processes as "the great changes in my day and generation—a period which all the best informed writers say, has not had its match in the history of the world" (201). These parochial events do, then, constitute a meaningful totality; the record of them brings history into formal visibility as an unprecedented epoch of "changes." Balwhidder's typological language is after all able to apprehend a complex, revolutionary process of modernization, by virtue of its impulse to make connections between local and global levels of event and meaning, "the political condition of the world felt in the private concerns of individuals" (175).[22]

These correspondences express a different, nonallegorical scheme of representation, one that works by metonymy and homology rather than by metaphor and analogy. On the one hand, Balwhidder understands his relation to George III to be one of symbolic equivalence mediated by a third, invisible master plot, "the work of a beneficent Providence" (4), which both of them typify. On the other hand, the correspondence between "the political condition of the world" and "the private concerns of individuals" takes the form of a set of complex connections brought about by the circulation of persons and objects in an expanding, industrializing, imperial economy. The appearance of a turtle in the parish, sent via Glasgow from the Caribbean to supply a local magnate's feast, illustrates "to what lengths a correspondence had been opened in the parish with the farthest parts of the earth" (184). There is no invisible, external master narrative ordering these correspondences—no work of an author, no plot: just the materiality of the connections themselves, as far as they can be traced. Yet the author of the *Annals* asserts no functional contradiction between the old typological rhetoric and this materialist, metonymic account of modernity à la Adam Smith. Balwhidder's concern with the analogies between himself and George III appears as a residual crotchet, harmless and amusing, that clarifies rather than obscures the general view, the truth of history.[23]

Balwhidder's typological rhetoric is rooted in his religious faith, and as such expresses his connection with the Covenanting past—the cultural heritage of the Presbyterian church in Ayrshire. The opening pages of the *Annals* perform a delicate ideological negotiation between this past and the present, a negotiation to which Galt will return in *Ringan Gilhaize*. Balwhidder prefaces the chronicle by quoting from his own retirement sermon, in which he exhorts his younger parishioners "to look to the lives and conversation" of their parents, who enjoyed peace and prosperity following their forefathers' armed struggle against government persecution in the late seventeenth century. Balwhidder reaffirms the Covenanters' "divine right of resistance," and opposes it not only to the doctrine of "passive obedience" under the Stuarts but to the "hypothetical politics" of contemporary Radical reformers; in other words, the true political legacy of the Covenant lies with a vigilant moderatism rather than with the radicalism currently laying claim to it. In the narrative that follows, we learn that Balwhidder was installed in his ministry by patronage, against the active resistance of the parishioners; he finds himself in the middle—unwittingly, on the wrong side—of the same historical clash between popular autonomy and gentry authority in church government of which the "killing times" were the heroic epoch. Eventually he is able to conciliate his parishioners by his exemplary conduct as much as by his orthodoxy. In other words, Balwhidder reprises the kind of historical subject position canonized in the Waverley novels—most pertinently, here, in *Old Mortality*: that of the moderate who finds himself in the midst of a social conflict, caught on the "wrong" side, but whose destiny it is to carry forward a scenario of reconciliation, and exemplify an ethical station fit for modern life, in which private sentiment takes the place of militant doctrine and party loyalty. That Galt locates this moderate subjectivity closer to popular Presbyterianism than to the gentry does not alter its structural resemblance with Scott's scheme.

Balwhidder's religion, his link with an older hermeneutic tradition, remains valuable as it gives historical substance to his moral character. His acuteness and accuracy of feeling, fostered by that religion, allow him to function as a reliable observer and narrator of historical process, despite the quaintness or narrowness of his theoretical opinions. Indeed, those opinions, as they represent his concrete ties to a moral tradition, reinforce rather than contradict the larger vision. Galt thus unfolds a delicate kind of irony through Balwhidder. We are not, after all, admitted to a superior viewpoint which invalidates or corrects the narrator's; on the contrary, his integrity of feeling is the necessary vehicle that, as it provides us with moral instruction, conducts us to an enlarged view of historical process. *Annals of the Parish* initiates, thus, the topic of Galt's finest work in its representation of the imaginary relation to social history and cultural systems that we call ideology.

Moral sentiment provides the regulating principle—as motive or outcome—of the episodes, or microplots, that make up the human texture of the *Annals*. Here and elsewhere Galt proves himself to be by far the subtlest exponent of the neo-Mackenzian revival of "feeling" in post-Enlightenment Edinburgh, promoted vigorously in *Blackwood's Magazine*; he is less blatantly "ideological" than Lockhart and (especially) Wilson. At issue is the rational and moral efficacy of sentiment in the face of *accident*, the modern version of fortune and, as pure event unleashed from the order of plot, the most threatening aspect of the change that constitutes history. In the absence of a connected plot Galt's narrative is full of accidents, which acquire meaning in the opportunities they afford for sentimental and moral performance. Mrs. Malcolm, the virtuous widow, is the book's model of pious and rational feeling, as she suffers all the vicissitudes of fortune—including the death in war of her firstborn son—with exemplary patience. Those in whom feeling gives way to impetuosity tend to be accident-prone, the newfangled version of "fey": in flinging themselves into the current of events they risk loss of agency against the prospect of mastery. The accident that brings Lord Eglesham into the chronicle (he falls off his carriage onto a dung heap) bears good fruit for Balwhidder and the parish, thanks to the opening it provides for the operation of his lordship's benevolence. The accident that takes him out of it—he is shot dead in a quarrel with a poacher—marks his own licentious and "thoughtless" (105) tendencies as well as, more decisively, the character of his killer (in Balwhidder's suggestive phrase, a man "hurried out of himself," 104). Mr. Cayenne, the principal agent for modernization in the parish, is the personification of a passionate impetuosity; yet his rashness marks an epistemic synchrony with the boom-and-bust rhythm of the new world system. As he grows into the local community, we find him adapting to the canons of sentiment, and eventually taking over the kindly patronage once exercised by the gentry, supplying the poor with grain in time of famine. To be sure, since he sells it to them rather than gives it away, Mr. Cayenne profits from his benevolence, but thereby he exemplifies with particular clarity the (Smithian) reconciliation of a traditional social and moral function with a new economic one, the "invisible hand" of providence in the market. We see that the profit motive need not be incommensurate with public welfare. The flow of sentiment in these cases shows that modernization entails no dehumanization, no necessary loss of virtue, no fall into anomie. Kindness and domestic virtue persist, indeed flourish, throughout these social convulsions. Balwhidder's chronicle thus bears witness to an essential continuity and stability in everyday life at the level of moral sentiment. The unprecedented epoch of change remains comprehensible in human terms. In the absence of a theodicy, a sentimental morality guarantees even—especially—accident with its sufficient reason.

Balwhidder's understanding of historical process as a system of metonymic correspondences grows as the narrative proceeds. His most elaborate meditation on the "great changes" he has been recording unfolds, in terms reminiscent of Smith's commercial sublime in the first chapter of *The Wealth of Nations*, a complex vision of the changing structural relations between a local society, bounded by personal experience, and a larger political and economic system that is not just national but global in its extent.

> Through all the wars that have raged from the time of the King's accession to the throne, there has been a gradually coming nearer and nearer to our gates, which is a very alarming thing to think of. In the first, at the time he came to the crown, we suffered nothing. Not one belonging to the parish was engaged in the battles thereof, and the news of victories, before they reached us, which was generally by word of mouth, were old tales. In the American war, as I have related at length, we had an immediate participation, but those that suffered were only a few individuals, and the evil was done at a distance, and reached us not until the worst of its effects were spent. And during the first term of the present just and necessary contest for all that is dear to us as a people, although, by the offswarming of some of our restless youth, we had our part and portion in common with the rest of the Christian world; yet still there was at home a great augmentation of prosperity, and every thing had thriven in a surprising manner; somewhat, however, to the detriment of our country simplicity. By the building of the cotton-mill, and the rising up of the new town of Cayenneville, we had intromitted so much with concerns of

trade, that we were become a part of the great web of commercial reciproci-
ties, and felt in our corner and extremity, every touch or stir that was made
on any part of the texture. (197)

The historical processes of modernization—the imperialist expansion of
trade, industrial revolution—have changed the very terms of space and
time by which locality is constituted. Balwhidder describes a "coming
nearer and nearer" of remote contingencies until they penetrate the everyday life of the parish; events that were once "old tales" have become close
and personal. He and his readers witness the collapse of a traditional
distinction between horizons of knowledge: one of them immediate, proximate, concrete, present to the senses, measured by the pace of daily life,
the other temporally as well as spatially distant, invisible and intangible,
abstract. Province and world are inextricably enmeshed together in a total
system, a "great web"—the image stays close here to its source in the
industrializing work of weaving. The web is also the original figure of
textuality (texere, "to weave"), and thus of Galt's own project of representation: by means of an intense scrutiny of the local to register the patterns of a global process of change. The new forces of commerce and
industry have literally rewoven the world, to the extent of producing the
terms in which we apprehend it.

Strikingly, Balwhidder specifies this historical process as a diffusion of
the conditions of war, "gradually coming nearer and nearer to our gates,"
investing the here and now. The Seven Years' War, the war of American
independence, and lastly the epochal struggle against revolutionary
France: an increasingly global theater distinguishes this modern imperial
warfare from the bitter civil conflicts of the preceding century. In the chapter of Annals of the Parish that follows, we see how the war comes home
to destroy local lives, not by military violence but by one of those spas-
modic contractions to which the new economy is prone. The local cotton
mill fails, the spinners and weavers are thrown out of work, and the owner
and overseers ruined. True to the logic of metonymic connection, the
cause of the failure is identified as the war, in the form of the Napoleonic
blockade. The community comes to understand, however, that this kind
of disaster is inherent in the new economy, beyond the official contingency
of wartime: "we saw that commercial prosperity, flush as it might be,
was but a perishable commodity." The insight is absorbed didactically by
Balwhidder's advice to the workmen to lay by part of their wages against
such reverses in the future, and indeed they go on to start a Savings Bank.
But the suggestion that capitalism is itself a kind of war—a global system
homologous with war, requiring foreign conquests for its advancement
but also reproducing the conditions of war at home in a sequence of ruinous collective disasters—comes into disturbing focus in the narrative of
some real casualties that closes the chapter.

Balwhidder relates the "very melancholy case" of the English overseer, a decayed gentleman, who responds to the crash by committing suicide together with his wife (or does he murder her before killing himself?). The episode is narrated, typically of such case histories in the *Annals*, in the sentimental mode, here reminiscent of the closing verses of Gray's "Elegy, Written in a Country Churchyard":

> Some days after he was seen walking by himself with a pale face, a heavy eye, and slow step—all tokens of a sorrowful heart. Soon after he was missed altogether; nobody saw him. The door of his house was however open, and his two pretty boys were as lively as usual, on the green before the door. I happened to pass when they were there, and I asked them how their father and mother were. They said they were still in bed, and would not waken, and the innocent lambs took me by the hand, to make me waken their parents. I know not what was in it, but I trembled from head to foot, as I was led in by the babies, as if I had not the power to resist. Never shall I forget what I saw in that bed * * * * * * (200)

With these victims the war has indeed come home, asserting its global presence in the innermost sanctum of domesticity, the marriage bed. This setting for the catastrophe, laid open to the gaze of both children and outsider, gives a disturbing, even unwholesome charge to the sentimental topos of the children's innocence before death (as in Wordsworth's lyrical ballad "We Are Seven"). The figure of those unseen parents, mysteriously "asleep," their state too shocking to be told (as though the reader, too, is a child, or less than a child, since the children's innocence seems to have screened them from the horror in the bed), suggests a traumatic condensation of one primal secret (the sacred space at the center and origins of a secularized private life) onto another (the ruin that is systole of the new economy). The metonymy is on the verge of yielding—since this remains only suggestive—an allegorical connection. The pressure of this allegorical connection makes itself felt as a negation, in the abrupt syntactic discontinuity, words broken off into a trail of asterisks. It is at the point when the correspondence between national and local collapses into—that is to say, analogically or metaphorically translates itself to—a correspondence between public and private lives, that the possibility for allegory reemerges. Allegory awaits at the traumatic limit of the metonymic scheme of representation, investing a correspondence that scheme cannot or will not make, offering its totalizing account of a system seen as though from the outside. The modern economy is causally moved by war, and may indeed require war for its worldwide expansion, but more, worse: it is itself a kind of war, blasting with its accidents even the domestic prosperity it has created. The blighted marriage bed, the children "on the green before the door": for such a mode of symbolic connection we would have to turn to Blake. It is all the more striking that the chapter, making and not making these connections, occupies the classical position of the catastrophe in the order of the *Annals*, despite the author's refusal of plot. It is the last significant event in the community, followed by only two more chapters, after which the narrative is effectively over. Not just the shadow of allegory but the shadow of plot invests the global vision opened by Balwhidder's chronicle.

IDEOLOGY: *THE PROVOST*

In *Annals of the Parish* we glimpse the precariousness of a formal conjunction between allegory and metonymy as interpretive schemes of correspondence, and through this the precariousness of the moderate, liberal-conservative account of history as an intelligible conjunction between material change and moral continuity summed up in the term "improvement." The containment of allegory inside a metonymic historical realism, as the minister's residual mode of belief, an ideological content which by virtue of this containment informs and validates the objective order, casts the ominous shadow of its reversal: the possibility that allegory, occupying the dominant ideological position by virtue of its moral content, may in turn contain history as its explanation. Such a reversal is precipitated by the catastrophic spasms to which the new order is prone, the kickings of a gestating plot, so that disorder and disaster characterize the narrative's secret, apocalyptic insight: capitalism as the end of history by virtue of its correspondence—via the imperialist figure of globalization, or systemic totalization—with war.

The Provost, Galt's companion theoretical history, cleaves more chastely to a "statistical" technique for narrating the truth of modern history, refusing an alignment of its chronology with symbolic plot schemes such as allegory or romance. This remarkable achievement of a metonymic realism expresses the different social identity of its narrator, who as ettling merchant and three-time mayor of an Ayrshire burgh bears a historical agency far closer to the economic forces of modernization than does Balwhidder, rooted in the faith of his rural ministry. Provost Pawkie experiences historical process in the categorical mode of local town politics, which, in his perspective, supplies the content of history, the secular medium in which human agency expresses itself. Pawkie's career is one long, vigilant effort to align his will and interests with objective economic and social developments—to master them, by prompting or initiating them, or else, he comes to realize, by following them so adroitly that he appears to be their guide, and so is able to benefit over any short-term setbacks. Provost Pawkie is thus in a position to interpret historical process—to abstract it as an intelligible form or category—in terms of an *intention*, as though history indeed coincides with his own agency, and the agency of his class. This interpretation is summed up in the ideological keyword improvement. On the first page, the "manifold improvements" in the burgh over the last fifty years move the editor of *The Provost* to read the memoirs of the official who presided over them: "a series of detached notes, which, together, formed something analogous to an historical view" of public affairs during his tenure. The memoir concludes with the Provost's own pious assertion "that really the world is gradually growing better, . . . and the main profit of the improvement will be reaped by those who are ordained to come after us" (152), where "improvement" resonates richly between the words "growing better" and "profit."

We might expect Galt's narrative—ironically containing Pawkie's—to grant the reader a satirical view of this improvement, as the self-serving slogan of a conniving small-town bourgeoisie. This is so, except that the satire does not condescend to Pawkie by reducing him to a case apart from ourselves. Galt's irony implicates the reader in his protagonist's position—he speaks for a historical process in which author and reader participate too. *The Provost* is Galt's subtlest treatment of the imaginary relation to social history and cultural systems that we call ideology, and which, initiated in *Annals of the Parish*, provides the topic of his best work. Both *Annals of the Parish* and *The Provost* follow Maria Edgeworth's *Castle Rackrent* in making fictional memoir the refined narrative instrument for exploring the subjective horizon of human understanding and feeling in relation to an objective historical horizon of social and economic change.[24] Edgeworth establishes an ironical distance between the enlightened viewpoint represented in the editorial frame of *Castle Rackrent* and the local viewpoint of its enclosed narrator, the family retainer Thady Quirk. This ironical distance is inflected, as an internal doubleness, within the enclosed narrative itself, giving rise to the so-called "Thady problem," in which critics have contended variously that Edgeworth's narrator is touchingly naïve, mystified by his feudal role as servant to the degenerate Rackrents; or else that he is odiously sly, manipulating the role so as to install his own son in the succession to the estate.[25] Both and neither of these options are true; or rather, Thady's structural position does not admit of the subjective distinction implied, between "inside" and "outside" an ideological formation that we (standing with the editor) may read as an illusion, as false consciousness. The triumph of Edgeworth's irony is that it represents Thady's subjectivity as historically dense, whole, and true to the contradictory position it may occupy.

If Balwhidder represents a naïve avatar of Thady and Provost Pawkie a sly one, the latter's case comes structurally closer to Edgeworth's irony. The work of ideology in *Annals* is easier to read. Balwhidder, a country minister, understands himself as observing rather than participating in historical process. His subjective distance from history produces allegory as the narrative articulation of that distance, even as the history he relates is one in which distances and separations metonymically implode, to reconstitute history as a global force field of exchanges and transformations. The gap between his religious faith (which licenses his allegory) and a secular account of the world allows the reader, in turn, to claim an ideological distance from Balwhidder—in order then to accept his narration as morally and sentimentally authentic. Abolishing these gaps and distances, *The Provost* produces a more devious relation between the narrator's understanding of his role and what we understand to be the objective course of events. Unlike Balwhidder, Pawkie views himself as a participant in the historical process he describes; he seeks a rhetorical closure between his intention and history. The difference between subjective and objective forms of historical agency generates the narrative's irony; but this is not always legible as a contradiction. It overlaps with, but does not map exactly, the temporal and grammatical difference between Pawkie's role as narrator, recalling and reflecting upon events, and his role as protagonist in them.

It is hard to improve upon Katie Trumpener's account of the relation between human agency and historical change in *The Provost*:

> Historical change appears to be partly the result of deliberate attempts to alter the organization and character of social life and partly the indirect effect of such manipulations, the self-perpetuation and proliferation of changes once they have been introduced. On the most visible level, change appears as an incidental (even unintended) byproduct of the growing ambition and insecurity of small-time operators, who find themselves reorganizing social life to protect the economic interests of an already-prospering middle class. . . . But once they have set in motion the new social apparatus, it not only maintains and perpetuates itself, constantly justifying the expansion of its own scope and operations, but also renders increasingly invisible the human agency that put it in place. . . . Galt's novel masterfully presents both the human agency by which social change is effected (demonstrating clearly whose interests are served and whose repressed) and how the machinery of change, once put into operation, camouflages this agency as the movement of history, freeing the manipulators to appear, even to themselves, as public benefactors.[26]

Contemplating the close of his career, Pawkie can afford a principled repudiation of bad old ways. He draws a qualitative distinction between then and now in which he looks down even on his former self. Where once he governed, he admits, "with a sort of sinister respect for my own interests," now, "standing clear and free of the world, I had less incitement to be so grippy." Even this pragmatic reassessment quickly gives way to an idealist one: his superior probity is due to his having "lived to partake of the purer spirit which the great mutations of the age had conjured into public affairs" (133–34). Improvement floats free of ambition and stratagem to become an impersonal teleological force, with which his own career has happened to coincide.

Pawkie does not retroactively impose that teleology across his narration. As readers we follow the improvisatory motion of his acts and trace their moral unevenness; we share his own oscillating insights into his motives and the meaning of events. Late one night during the war Pawkie is roused from his bed by the officer of a press-gang, come to show him his warrant and commission. "I did not like this Englification and voice of claim and authority," Pawkie protests, and he pleads with the lieutenant to defer his work until the next morning, "for the love of peace and quietness" (67). But the officer cannot wait, and the press-gang advances with "the noise of a dreadful engine" (68). As a local man, Pawkie empathizes with "the poor chased sailors" and their families: "I could na listen to the fearful justice of their outcry; but sat down in a corner of the council-chamber, with my fingers in my ears" (68). But since he is chief magistrate, the people believe he must have been party to the raid by signing the press warrants, and they stone his house. Afterwards Pawkie is able to obtain government compensation for the damage, realizing a tidy profit, by representing himself as having suffered "all owing to the part I had taken in [the government's] behalf" (69). Here Galt makes Pawkie occupy (once more) the canonical, Waverley-hero position, caught in the midst of a social conflict, only to execute a satiric inversion of it. Where Waverley or Morton finds himself on the side of an uprising through a combination of accident, principle, other people's management, and a self-reflexive overflow of sympathy, Pawkie finds himself enlisted on the side of state power, very much against his fellow feeling. Where Waverley, in particular, is reconciled with the authorities by a work of plotting that retroactively removes his agency from the historical action, Pawkie is able to claim government benefit by retroactively inscribing his agency onto the position in which he found himself. Galt plays on the relation between subjective or personal agency (one's intention, motive, will) and objective or social agency (one's deeds, or, more subtly, their abstraction in the social position and function one occupies). Pawkie comes out ahead by rewriting his subjective in terms of his objective agency, recognizing the latter as the term of historical truth—as the officer did when he showed Pawkie his commission, and as the mob did when they attacked his house. Yet, at the time of the event, Pawkie resented the officer as the figure of a colonizing alien power, "Englification," and felt keenly for the harried townsfolk. The organic ties of affection and sympathy that constitute his subjectivity are not written out of the story, just as they do not cancel his opportunistic accommodation to the course of events—or vice versa. He is, according to the occasion, both sly and sincere.

Praising Galt's technique, many readers have been content to echo Coleridge:

> [In] the unconscious, perfectly natural, Irony of Self-delusion, in all parts intelligible to the intelligent Reader, without the slightest suspicion on the part of the Autobiographer, I know of no equal in our Literature. . . . In the Provost a similar *Selfness* is united with a *Slyness* and a plausibility eminently successful in cheating the man himself into a happy state of constant Self-applause.[27]

Felicitous though this is, it suggests that Galt opens up an epistemological and ethical position outside the narrator's self-understanding, from which the intelligent reader is able to judge it as "self-delusion." But Galt's irony does not, except in a few local instances, allow the reader to dismiss Pawkie as self-deluded—or, at any rate, as more deluded than we are ourselves. Halfway through the memoir, reflecting on the passing of Old Corruption, Pawkie addresses the problem of horizons of historical understanding:

> I have endeavoured, in a manner, to be governed by the spirit of the times in which the transactions happened, for I have lived long enough to remark, that if we judge of past events by present motives, and do not try to enter into the spirit of the age when they took place, and to see them with the eyes with which they were really seen, we shall conceit many things to be of a bad and wicked character, that were not thought so harshly of by those who witnessed them, nor even by those who, perhaps, suffered them; while, therefore, I think it has been of a great advantage to the public to have survived that method of administration . . . I would not have it understood that I think the men who held the public trusts in those days a whit less honest than the men of my own time. The spirit of their own age was upon them, as that of ours is upon us, and their ways of working the wherry entered more or less into all their trafficking, whether for the commonality, or for their own particular behoof and advantage. (74)

Pawkie evokes "the spirit of the age" to question the idea of moral progress: ethically speaking, men are pretty much the same now as they have always been. To judge one age by another's standards is an error. Morally there is no improvement, except in the illusory mistaking of stratagem, or local custom, for universal principle. The irony of course invests the speaker—in effect Pawkie admits that he is as corrupt as his old rival Bailie M'Lucre—but, more disconcertingly, it invests the reader too. The spirit of our age, and our own historical situation and agency, are drawn into the reflection.[28] We may be no better, even though we are reading this book; nor are we (necessarily) worse.

PLOT: *THE ENTAIL*

Galt explores the ideological relation to history through competing modes of accidental, fatalistic and providential plotting in his most ambitious works, *The Entail* (December 1822, dated 1823) and *Ringan Gilhaize* (May 1823). In these Galt abandons the single-volume fictional memoir for the full-length novel, which he makes the vehicle for a critical argument with the genre of national historical romance practiced by Scott. While *Ringan Gilhaize* (discussed in the next chapter) narrates the ideological origins of Scottish modernity in the Reformation and Covenant, *The Entail* takes on the post-Union history of Scotland, the great topic of Scott's 1814–19 Scottish novels as well as Galt's own local theoretical histories. Aimed from the empiricist and antiromance mode of theoretical history, *The Entail* utters its powerful critique of the Scott novel through the device of formal imitation. Its three volumes, narrated in English and in the third person by an Edinburgh-trained literary lawyer, articulate family and national history through a plot of conflicts of inheritance and sibling rivalry.

However, Galt's attempt to sustain an alternative historical realism changes direction in its final stages, where the work of plot turns from the ironic and tragic mode of critique to a comic resolution. Experimentally, problematically, *The Entail* reproduces the (itself experimental and problematic) romance form it began by refusing. Ian A. Gordon, following the author's own testimony, has led the way in deprecating the third volume of *The Entail* as padded with extraneous matter, "alien to the run of the earlier narrative," forced upon Galt by the demands of the market in the person of William Blackwood.[29] Such an explanation, begging the question of why Galt might have resorted to the particular solutions he did (as though Blackwood, not Galt, were the author of the interpolated matter), reiterates even as it ignores what Scott had established as a convention, the "final volume problem," in the work that is the principal model for *The Entail*: Scott's most ambitious novel of eighteenth-century Scottish life, *The Heart of Mid-Lothian*.

Galt develops and complicates the revisionary replotting (or deplotting) of Scott's novel that occupied three chapters in *The Provost*. Like *The Heart of Mid-Lothian*, *The Entail* follows three generations of a family under the shadow of a patriarch obsessed with a lost historical cause (David Deans; Claud Walkinshaw), it is set in a Lowland city and its surrounding villages, and narrated in an initial style of social realism. In

each novel the most vital character—acceding to the status of heroine—
is an initially unprepossessing rustic maid, later wife and mother. Both
novels thematize the law as the ruling discourse of post-Union Scotland,
regulating private as well as public relations but thus coming into deadly
conflict with "organic" ties and values; both feature a central trial scene.
And both novels play on the "Highland settlement" solution of Scottish
domestic fiction by executing a last-act swerve to a Highland setting, associated with the 1745 rebellion, and invested with romance tropes foreign
to the realism of the opening.

To note these likenesses is to emphasize rather than diminish the originality of Galt's achievement, making it visible as the outcome of a close,
rigorous working-through of Scott's great work. In contrast to *The Heart
of Mid-Lothian*, Galt massively expands and intensifies the domain of
social realism: purifying it of the various romance and other genre elements that inhabit Scott's narrative from its inception, so that the Highland romance appears more problematically, perfunctorily alien, and en-
larging its share of the text, partly by a diachronic extension of the
narrative. Where Scott concentrates on a single, although complex and
protracted, crisis in the lives of the middle-generation Deans sisters and
their lovers in the 1730s and (in the Highland sequel) 1740s, Galt gives
equal time to three generations of Walkinshaws.[30] In the final romance
Galt broadens and generalizes the critique of Scott by bringing into focus
the Jacobite theme associated with earlier novels, notably *Waverley*. The
most significant difference is thematic, however, in the contrasting treat-
ments of an inheritance plot that sets "natural" kinship relations against
the letter of the law. Galt replaces Scott's topic of infanticide or "concealment of birth," allegorizing a systemic failure of patriarchal authority
across public and private life, with the entail, the utterance of a compulsive patriarchal intention that blights its children. Scott's scheme of a
usurping matriarchy countered by the virtue of a peasant-class heroine
turns into a muddling interference by headstrong old women (heralded
by an incursion of the formidable widow of Scott's Nicol Jarvie from *Rob
Roy*), with Galt's Leddy an exuberant parody of Jeanie Deans—rising to
heroine status, this time, following her marriage to a Dumbiedikes.

The Entail traces the Walkinshaws across the eighteenth century, from
the aftermath of the Darien disaster (an attempt to establish a Scottish
colonial emporium in Central America, the failure of which precipitated
the Union) to the French wars on the eve of the present (and at the chronological terminus of the Waverley novels, in *The Antiquary*). Public history
appears in a strictly commercial register, befitting the decorum of a Smithian account of modernity, until the Highland-romance swerve in the last
volume. Claud Walkinshaw's obsession with recovering the family estates
lost in the Darien speculation drives the novel's plot as a traumatic econ-

omy of repetitions of that original loss, inflicted by the very will to replenish it. Claud forbids his eldest son from marrying Bell Fatherlans after her father is ruined in the 1772 Ayr Bank crash, and Charles's defiance of his father provokes the first and most violent of the novel's acts of disinheritance. Political events such as the Union and the '45 are mentioned well after they have taken place, as belonging in the past, or else, in the case of the "rebellion in America," as occasions for "the anxieties of merchants" (169). Only in the last volume, with the excursion to the Highlands, does a different kind of history—military, political, "national"—come to bear on the family plot. Otherwise, faithful to the protocols of theoretical history, Galt's narrative tracks domestic social and economic changes with quiet exactitude. We hear about "the first four-wheeled gentleman's carriage started in Glasgow" (31), the oligarchic ascendancy of "the general merchants of the royal city" (109, 209), the regional diffusion of the "general spirit of improvement" in estate management (205) and landscape design (220), and we even catch a portentous glimpse of the Muirkirk Iron Works (245). As for the abstract or "metaphysical" system that codifies this world: in Claud's own words, "we're no now in a state o' nature but in a state o' law" (58), meaning (after Adam Smith's *Lectures on Jurisprudence*) the apparatus of contract and property law that regulates the complex socioeconomic relations of modernity.

Galt's narrative of a postnational, commercial, private society regulated by property law offers, then, a resolutely modernist version of historical fiction, eschewing political history as well as romance tropes and topics—as though these are all residual forms belonging to a receding past. The theme of the entail binds family history and inheritance to Claud's obsession with property accumulation, coded in the family name, Grippy (grasping, avaricious). Galt pioneers a distinctively nineteenth-century kind of novel, the family chronicle or dynastic anatomy of middle-class ascendancy, amplified (in British fiction) by Trollope and exhausted by Galsworthy, along with the systematic critique of the law and property, manifest in inheritance plots and themes of a "metaphysical" obsession with accumulation, perfected by Dickens. Galt also establishes, for Victorian and Modernist fiction, a Romantic antithesis between this economic regime and naturalized values of kindness and sexuality. The minister, Mr. Kilfuddy, denounces Claud's "unnatural inclination to disinherit your first-born" (36); too late, Claud feels the moral effects of his violation of the right of primogeniture: "I stiffled the very sense o' loving kindness within me" (150).

The problem with Claud's motive is that it is *not* merely acquisitive; it is not a productive mode of desire that accumulates property as a means to increase wealth, and it consequently falls outside the dynamic of improvement. The editor moralizes, "avarice with him was but an agent in the pursuit of that ancestral phantom which he worshipped as the chief, almost the only good in life" (76). Closing the ideological circuit between loyalty to an ancestral ground and a modern desire for property as capital investment, Galt reveals these motives as deformations of one another, in what Alyson Bardsley recognizes as a critique of the Scott "romance of property."[31] It is not that the romance motive is falsified by exposure of its true identity as a desire for property—there is no question as to Claud's terrifying sincerity. Rather, the romance motive falsifies the property motive by a regressive distortion that inverts its capacity to be productive. Romance denotes the "metaphysical"—ideological—misrecognition of property through a nostalgic desire for lost origins rather than a productive desire for wealth. At the same time, the entail violates the historical principle of natural succession (primogeniture) that it is supposed to secure, since the attempt to make the property inviolate in written form fetishizes it—turning *it* into the subject of the genealogy, promoting the inheritance over the heir. This commercial inversion of the patriarchal relation corrupts it just as surely as a feudal nostalgia makes commerce barren.

The entail itself, as Mark Schoenfield argues, represents the attempt to sustain an ancient patriarchal right in a modern legal form: "a grant binding heirs through a legal device to the same degree that feudal law had bound them, but in the terms of the new commercial society."[32] As (in effect) a literary revival of a premodern cultural form, the entail exemplifies an institutional complicity between Scots law and the literary movement of Scottish Romanticism. The theme accommodates the narrator's critique (he is himself a lawyer) of the "eloquence" and "metaphysical refinement" of Edinburgh advocates, trained in Rhetoric and Belles Lettres. "Mr Threeper opened the business in a speech replete with eloquence and ingenuity, and all that metaphysical refinement for which the Scottish bar was then, as at present, so justly celebrated. Nothing . . . could be more subtile, nor less applicable to the coarse and daily wear and tear of human concerns," however much endowed with "charming touches of sentiment, and amiable pathetic graces" (187–88). This is, in short, another kind of romance, an aesthetic discourse askew from the texture of common life. (The setting is the late 1770s, by which time Hugh Blair had instituted his Belles Lettres course as part of the Edinburgh legal curriculum.)[33] Galt makes the law appear an ominous alien intrusion: the fool Watty marvels at his first sight of "a haudthecat . . . that gangs about the town o' Embro, walking afore the Lords, in a black gown, wi' a wig on'ts head" (180). He will soon have good cause to bemoan "yon awfu' folk wi' the cloaks of darkness and the wigs o' wisdom frae Edinboro' " (203). *The Entail* articulates a sharp critique, from the empirical-realist perspective of a West-country merchant class, of an Edinburgh *noblesse du robe* which misrecognizes commercial society through its promotion of an ideology of feudal nostalgia. This (crypto-Jacobite) Edinburgh ascendancy includes not just the law but the literary culture which disciplines the city's professions and institutions, exemplified by the cultural industry of romance revival—a nexus personified by the Edinburgh reviewers, Scott, and the chief Blackwoodians Lockhart and Wilson.

Edinburgh's cultural ascendancy is also exemplified in the three-volume national historical romance, practiced by Scott and promoted by Blackwood. As Schoenfield demonstrates, Galt makes the entail the paradigm as well as substance of the novel's plot—the essential principle of historical romance. The entail provides the "narrative structure" that drives Galt's theoretical history in an allegorical direction. It expresses the father's attempt to bind family history to his will in a written form: determining the lives of his descendants by an appeal to the "ancestral phantom," he applies a deadly pressure of past and future, like a temporal vice, to the here and now.[34] Galt admits the work of plot into his theoretical history, in short, by containing it thematically as a fatal scheme, a teleological desire for origins that works itself out in a systematic, overdetermined contradiction of human agency. Invoked as an instrument of human agency, Claud's will, the entail inevitably exceeds and overrules it—precisely as it represents a romantic attempt to make history coincide with human agency by writing it down as law. Claud's accession to tragic status, and acquisition of moral sublimity, accompanies his belated recognition of this subversion, as he is foiled by a series of last-minute accidents. The entail as plot principle of a fatal mystification of agency, then, represents at once a negative, ironical realization of the demystified model of historical process described (in the case of *The Provost*) by Trumpener—in which a rational agency or intention proceeds to mask its activity as impersonal historical process—and a parodic inversion of the providential work of plot in a Scott novel.

Against the form of agency encoded in the entail, a teleological nostalgia that corrupts human intention, Galt poses an alternative, objective, recalcitrant narrative modality of contingency and accident. Galt called this kind of narrative, in his tentative, obscure first novel of Scottish manners *Glenfell*, a "Northern Comedy of Errors"; Maria Edgeworth provided him with its strong form, developed (as we saw) in *Annals of the Parish*.[35] Accidental narrative simulates the pressure of chance or coincidental events and other people's intentions, which, as they remain radically other, individual, and independent, countermine the claims of a single master will. This is the narrative mode of common life: the empirical, material domain of here and now, everyday circumstance, the medium in which "life goes on." The entail itself must work through this accidental modality, by which it thwarts not just its objects (disinherited Charles, non compos mentis Watty, defrauded James) but its subjects, who invest their intentions in it—so confirming the subjective effect of fatality, a systematic negation of human agency, most starkly manifest in the event of death. All the novel's deaths, except maybe Claud's own, are "accidents" that have ironical plot effects, associated with the upsetting of plans or expectations. Claud's shameful concealment of the disinheritance of his eldest son makes possible the cluster of ironical misunderstandings that blocks his repentant dying wish to provide for Charles's family: the Leddy is jealous of an infringement of her "rights" (162), while Watty refuses to sign because he fears he is being cheated of his birthright. At the end, the birthright is restored to Charles's children through a complicated chain of error and misapprehension. Objectively, Galt's accidental narrative deconstructs the ideological effects of agency, including the negative effect of fatality, projected in the entail. Among these deconstructed effects is the antithesis between the entail's influence and "nature." Although legislated by the entail, Watty's marriage to Betty Bodle happens to rest on the "habitual affection" (79) engendered between them. Far from being blighted by the entail's sentence, their affection enjoys an accidental flowering—wonderfully depicted in the comic set piece of the wedding party—perhaps because both parties are innocent, subjectively detached from the entail. The conjugal idyll is destroyed by an accident, Betty's death in childbirth, and a further accident, the death of the surviving daughter, delivers Watty himself—now parodying his father's obsession with inheritance—to the logic of the entail and the sentence of the law.

Accident upsets the intentions invested in the entail and exposes them as romantic delusions. Galt thus expresses the work of plot in the tropes of antiromance, encoding the ethical critique of Claud's obsession but also the formal critique of Scott's historical novel. The hero's origins reprise the satirical opening of *Waverley*: chapbook fables of social ascent fix in Claud the desire to redeem "the hills and lands of his forefathers" (5). Claud's three sons, romantic Charles, "natural" Watty, and commercial George, represent different ideological formations of post-Union civil society, none of which constitutes an adequate principle of virtue. Each expresses the traumatic mutation of a prior parental loss and obsession. George occupies the last term in the series, after romance and nature, but he is merely the negative response to the first two, and the dull shadow of his father's grippiness: a "design and purpose" devoid of romance idealism and thus of psychological complexity and moral sublimity. He personifies a demystified economic motive, reduced to bleak self-interest, split off from the moral imagination proposed in Smith's philosophy as the ethical aspect of improvement. Firstborn Charles brims over with imagination, in the modern aesthetic sense, and its traditional motive, romantic love; but these too bear the exaggerated, pathological character of reaction formations, determined by the moral distortion of a previous generation (in the person of his maternal grandmother). As in the case of Henry Mackenzie's "Man of Feeling" (rather than the virtuous subject of Enlightenment moral philosophy), Charles's sensibility, including his attunement to the natural world, is the index of a practical impotence in worldly affairs. Lastly, Watty the "natural" is only so on condition of his idiocy, which is what the word means in Scots. Galt grants Watty a capacity for gaiety, pathos, and affection, but unfortified by reason he too is corrupted by the entail. Watty's example disturbs the romance convention of the "natural" as a sympathetic link between the hero and the traditional world, a vessel of providence or fate. All three elements of the ideological synthesis in Scott's novels—nature, commerce, romance—remain fragments, able only to cancel each other out.

Meanwhile, as Bardsley and others have noted, Galt's inheritance plot at once invokes and rebuffs the dynastic allegory, aligning Scotland's loss of sovereignty with the disinheritance of the Stuarts, mobilized for the national historical novel in *Waverley*. The moral failures of Charles, "his father's darling chevalier," and George, cold-hearted Hanoverian citizen, mock the national allegory's dialectic of improvement. This refusal identifies the dynastic and political category of the nation with Claud's "ancestral phantom" and the lack it perpetuates: mystified Jacobite romance, demystified Hanoverian self-interest, and an idiotic cult of nature.[36] Galt rehearses theoretical history's—and capitalism's—reduction of the nation to a contingent ideological category in a global development of economic and social formations, and suggests (through the critique of Scott) that the desire to recover national origins expresses a fatal, nostalgic misprision of modern conditions that blocks any authentic ideological synthesis.

Galt's critique of Scott's national romance goes on, however, to problematize its own project as a historical novel, as well as the form it is critiquing. *The Entail* admits after all the aesthetic and ideological matter of national fiction for a comic resolution in which the birthright is restored to Charles's son, James, who marries the daughter of a Highland Jacobite family: reaffirming the ancient right of primogeniture, now associated with a historically purified Jacobitism. Galt's turn into Highland romance situates the positive appearance, at last, of a political and military register of national history, as both the war against revolutionary France and the 1745 rising enter the narrative together. Frazer of Glengael, the father of James's betrothed, buys back the family estate that was forfeited after Culloden. Unlike Claud, he is able to recover his ancestral lands through the marketplace without moral compromise. A loyal subject, he has given up his father's Jacobitism; his generation is able to free itself from nostalgic ideology, doubtless because it has been purged by political defeat. In 1793 Frazer helps James get a commission in the army and they travel to Glengael to raise recruits. As he approaches the estate, James notices rows of "green spots" like "the graves of a race that had been rooted out and slaughtered": these are "the scites of cottages, which the soldiers of the Duke of Cumberland's army had plundered and burnt in the year Forty-five" (306). There is no hint of any subsequent—land-lord-perpetrated—clearance. Instead, the patriotic bustle of recruitment promises a revival of the desolated glens. Now that Frazer has redeemed the estate, his tenants can participate in a wider national history under his leadership. Galt observes the modern historical production of "the nation" as a defensive strategy in time of imperial crisis: ancient loyalties, politically neutralized and commercially enfranchised, can be recalled in service of the state. The raising of Highland regiments is infused with a "Jacobite" spirit detached from its historical origins, its license renewed by the counterrevolutionary emergency as a primitive emblem of patriotic loyalty. Loyalist, sentimental-Jacobite counterrevolutionism, then, consti-tutes the synthetic stage of a historical dialectic, synchronized with the third generation of Walkinshaws, that forms the threshold of the pres-ent.[37] Highlanders of Jacobite stock provide an exogamous infusion of imagination and virtue (a "Highland spirit" of "romance and enthusi-asm," 222) that could not be sustained within the family line, morally blasted by Claud's deed of entail. The Highland gentry transmit the ideo-logical temper that qualifies James (whose name alludes to the Jacobite cause as well as to the Jacob/Esau story) for resumption of his birthright and historic role.

Galt imitates not just the last-act swerve into Highland romance of *The Heart of Mid-Lothian* but the ideological solution which that novel in turn reprises from *Waverley* and the domestic national tales of the post-war, *Discipline* and *Clan-Albin*. *The Entail* follows *The Heart of Mid-Lothian* in taking up the scenario of a utopian resettlement of the glens expounded in *Clan-Albin*, except that *The Entail* (like *Waverley*) glosses over the clearances in its emphasis on the '45 as the catastrophic terminus of Highland history. Galt, however, retains Johnstone's emphasis on war-time patriotism and mobilization as the generative context for the nation-alist cult of the Highlands. By making explicit the historical conditions of this cultural solution in the 1790s counterrevolutionary emergency, he identifies it as the crucible of national historical romance.

Galt's historicization of Highland romance is accompanied by discon-certing reverberations of parody and inauthenticity. The third volume of *The Entail* introduces a set of stock conventions of national romance: the Highland tour, an "astrologising" spaewife, the sublime set piece of the usurper George's providential death by shipwreck. (This ostentatiously "literary" episode—rehearsing the Lucretian topos of safe spectatorship of a storm at sea—may recall another fateful accident, George Staunton's murder by his savage son at the end of *The Heart of Mid-Lothian*.)[38] The narrative at once authorizes and mocks the "sybiline pretensions" (256) of the spaewife Mrs. Eadie. "[T]he agency of death can alone fulfil the vision," she intones, in what turns out to be an accurate forecast (256). She makes strong claims over the order of plot: her gift of second sight, the "inspiring mantle of her maternal race" (340), reveals the "mysterious link between the fortunes of your family and mine" (213) that the narrative will endorse, however perfunctorily. The narrator's reference to Ossian, the touchstone for discredited Highland romance, invites the reader to share the Lowland characters' embarrassed snickers: "She had dreams of the most cheering augury, though all the incidents were wild and funereal; and she interpreted the voices of the birds and the chattering of the magpies in language more oriental and coherent than Macpherson's Ossian" (300). When a barnyard mooing interrupts her "Pythian" raptures, the narrator seems to agree with her husband that "the bathos of that cow was quite irresistible" (301).[39] Yet Mrs. Eadie's visions and premonitions turn out, as in a Scott novel, to be true.

Galt also discredits the Highland romance by running his ironical and accidental Lowland narrative alongside it, fortified by the presence of Claud's widow, the Leddy, who emerges as the dominant character of the last third of the novel. The Leddy scoffs (hilariously) at the romantic ideology of a desire-based individualism, assumed in the intrigues of George's sly daughter Robina, as no more than the fume of modern literary fashion: "ganging to see Douglas tragedy," "the puff-paste love o' your Clarissy Harlots," "Damon and Phillis, pastorauling at hide and seek wi' their sheep" (223), "the shape and glamour o' novelles and Thomson's Seasons" (230). Yet romantic individualism constitutes the virtuous principles of the lovers James and Ellen. With her garrulous pretensions, down to a claim upon "the second sight o' experience" (298: just a few pages before Mrs. Eadie's vaticinations), the Leddy stands as the parodic, bourgeois counterpart to Mrs. Eadie, the rival matriarch of the tale's conclusion. Dividing the honors of resolution between them, Mrs. Eadie and the Leddy speak—unstoppably, ludicrously but in the end authoritatively—for opposite narrative principles. If Mrs. Eadie's prophetic gift is confirmed in George's shipwreck, the Leddy's ridiculous conceit in her own legal acumen actually undoes the last link in the entail's chain of disinheritance and restores the birthright of her eldest son.

The Leddy's triumph confirms the accidental, etiological, agency-crossing mode of narrative, which resumes once the characters return from their Highland excursion. George's death, which exhibited a sublime providential agency when it took place in the Highlands, falls back under the dominant, humdrum modality of accident once it enters legal process in the city. Indeed, the event appears to have advanced the cause of justice and right resolution of the entail no further. James's birthright remains alienated by an unlucky conjunction of error and concealment: no one seems to understand that the property should now revert to the heirs of the eldest son, except for George's son-in-law, his father, and their lawyer, who conspire to keep the information a secret. A chain of accidents, set off by the Leddy, exposes the truth and brings about the restoration of the estate. The Leddy threatens to go to law to recover compensation for her earlier hospitality to the false heirs; what looks like another comic turn, an entertaining display of her eccentric humor, propels the remainder of the plot. Afraid that her obstinacy might draw attention to the cover-up, the usurpers pay her off, only for the payment, so excessive and hastily granted, to perform that very function when it is mentioned at a dinner party. The Leddy herself obtains the vital information from a lawyer who assumes that her having been paid off must mean that she is in on the secret, and lets it slip. That the Leddy claims all the credit for the restoration, boasting of her profound legal wisdom, underscores the unwitting nature of her interference.

Galt makes his accidental narrative the medium for the Leddy's apotheosis as a "character."[40] She can emerge as an agent of resolution, a "force of nature" advertised by linguistic exuberance and an invincible self-conceit, on condition of her effectual disjunction from the (masculine) claims to agency encoded in the entail. She is always quick and obstinate to claim her interest, but she knows nothing about it—she responds impulsively to its effects rather than pretending to direct it. The Leddy's interference in the inheritance plot, at its various crises, works consistently at cross purposes with her own interest, when she thwarts her husband's dying wish, connives in having Watty declared legally incompetent, and spoils George's dynastic plans by promoting the union between Robina and Walkie. Yet the fact that she is incapable of holding a long-term rational intention—of maintaining a *plot*—is what constitutes her integrity as a character and justifies her final authority in the scheme of events. The novel closes with her death and the reading of her will, in which she at last exerts a whimsical control over legal forms and the turns of plot. The *Blackwood's Magazine* gang mischievously resurrected the Leddy in a number of the "Noctes Ambrosianae" (June 1823), claiming that by killing her off Galt had inadvertently participated in a "hoax." In doing so they pay homage to her status as a character who exceeds the closure of plot and is indeed independent of any mere text that might contain her, and vital enough to overthrow her author's intentions. So forceful is her appearance that she routs the impudent Blackwoodians ("in the greatest panic and consternation").[41]

Galt learned Aristotle's lesson that an ending, still more than a beginning and a middle, makes a plot. His tragicomedy of errors, personified at last by the Leddy, reiterates its incompatibility with national historical romance. Yet even as it mocks and disavows the romance it collaborates with it to forge the novel's resolution. Our historical perspective makes it possible to imagine a different outcome, in which the property remains alienated, sunk perhaps in an abyss of lawsuits, and the son of a cadet branch of the family (Walkie and Robina) goes on to make his own fortune, say in Canada. But *The Entail* is the tragic correction of *Sir Andrew Wylie*, rather than *Wylie* being a comic preemption of *The Entail*. The thrall of the inheritance plot would be felt across the century, through *Great Expectations*, the Featherstone episode of *Middlemarch*, and Trollope's ironical fable of disinheritance in *Mr. Scarborough's Family* (1883).

Chapter 9

✣

AUTHENTICITY EFFECTS

[T]hou, my best of friends, hast the highest knack at making histories out of nothing. . . . All that happens to thee gets a touch of the wonderful and the sublime from thy own rich imagination.

        —Scott, *Redgauntlet*

I come now to the most important period of my existence, —the period that has modelled my character, and influenced every action of my life, —without which, this detail of my actions would have been as a tale that is told, —a monotonous *farrago*, —an uninteresting harangue—in short, a thing of nothing.

        —Hogg, *Private Memoirs and Confessions of a Justified Sinner*

POST-ENLIGHTENMENT POSTMODERNISM

Reflecting upon its own procedures, and upon the materials, contexts, and preoccupations of Scott's art, *The Antiquary* highlights the retrospective station it occupies at the end of a trilogy of novels on the making of modern Scotland. The retrospective and self-reflexive stance is resumed with still greater virtuosity in *Redgauntlet*, Scott's late revisitation of the genre of Scottish historical romance established a decade earlier in *Waverley*. *Redgauntlet* advertises its retrospect through a striking reiteration of, in particular, the Jacobite and family plots of *Waverley* and *Rob Roy*. Like those works *Redgauntlet* thematizes its status as a historical romance, a compound of fiction and history, with a difference that has been made much of in recent criticism: the historical event unfolded in *Redgauntlet*, the secret return of Charles Edward Stuart for a last attempt at counterrevolution in the summer of 1765, never took place. It is the Author of *Waverley*'s invention.[1] The novel accordingly suspends the final, tragic conflict between ancient and modern orders toward which its plot has been driving. The Hanoverian general refuses to recognize the Jacobite conspirators as historical agents; everybody agrees to be "friends"; the story fades into an imperturbable light of common day. Nothing happens: the famous ending of *Redgauntlet*, with its comic yet melancholy convergence of fiction and nonevent, dazzlingly replays the Humean logic of conservative skepticism at work in *The Antiquary*.

Redgauntlet: A Tale of the Eighteenth Century was published in Edinburgh by Constable in June 1824. That same month James Hogg's last novel, *The Private Memoirs and Confessions of a Justified Sinner*, was published in London by Longmans (but printed in Edinburgh). The simultaneous appearance of the two works remains cryptic. Each is its author's last exercise in the genre of modern Scottish historical novel, and his most elaborate and subtle performance. Both novels feature a formal division of the protagonist (an epistolary narration divided between two heroes in Scott, a metaphysical splitting of Hogg's sinner) and of the narrative (between memoir and editorial narrative in Hogg, letters, journal, and impersonal narrative in Scott). Both represent sentimental and political divisions within the family, articulated through masculine relations of paternal authority, filial obedience and resistance, fraternal friendship and rivalry. Specifically, both develop a "two brothers" plot in which the alienated stepbrother, his paternity clouded in mystery, is drawn into a conspiracy by a charismatic stranger, the issue of which is "fanaticism," a deadly ideological excess. Both novels explore the cultural distance between metropolitan Edinburgh and its rural-traditional hinterland. And, in a remarkable amplification of the narrative division, both novels present themselves as heterogeneous collections of stories, languages, documents, and genres, including letters, journals, editorial narratives, and inset oral tales of Scottish "folklore." Each work insists upon its condition as a book, an artifact that grants a sheerly material unity to a miscellany of styles and sources by the circumstance of their being bound together.[2]

Their extreme degree of self-reflexivity has encouraged critics to read these novels through a late-twentieth-century, more-or-less-postmodernist vocabulary.[3] Such readings beg the question of literary-historical specificity posed by the novels' simultaneous appearance. "Possible links between the composition of *Redgauntlet* and *Confessions of a Justified Sinner* are frustratingly obscure," notes Fiona Robertson, in a discussion of their shared preoccupation with "ripping up auld stories."[4] Despite the authors' former intimacy, it is unlikely that either was privy to the other's work in progress. Hogg had come to resent his exclusion from the inner circle in which Scott admitted his identity as the Author of *Waverley*; while Scott had not been involved in Hogg's work after his proof-stage intervention in *The Three Perils of Man*. The editors of the Edinburgh Edition contend that "*Redgauntlet* was conceived in imaginative secrecy," while Peter Garside shows how Hogg kept the production of the *Confessions* under wraps, concealing his authorship and entrusting the text to a particular printer so as to prevent the interference his work had suffered in the past.[5]

One way of thinking about this literary-historical convergence is to historicize the novels' rhetoric of reflexivity—the signature of an aesthetic that Jerome McGann has called, regarding Scott, "Romantic Postmodernity."[6] Both *Redgauntlet* and *Confessions of a Justified Sinner* position themselves as post- and meta- in relation to a prominent discourse of modernity, glossing also their status as final essays in a genre. *Tristram Shandy* aside, tropes of reflexivity characterize an earlier moment of the English novel, the first decade of the eighteenth century: the historical era of the opening of modernity (1688–1707), as our authors understood it, and of the formation of the novel as modernity's typical genre.[7] The recurrence of similar devices a century later in Scottish "tales of the eighteenth century" marks a historicizing difference; since anachronism, as James Chandler has shown, is itself a historicizing trope, developed in Scottish Enlightenment theorizations of uneven development.[8] The rhetoric of reflexivity articulates a metahistorical doubling, history squared. Both *Redgauntlet* and the *Confessions of a Justified Sinner* set themselves in critical relation to the ten-year-old tradition of Scottish historical fiction as well as to its topic, the era of modernization, the century from the Treaty of Union to the wars with Revolutionary France—an era distinguished by the rise of the Scottish Enlightenment human sciences, which abstracted modernity into written discourse as a philosophical and historical category. Jerome Christensen has argued that British intellectuals viewed the end of the Napoleonic wars as an epoch, analogous to the end of the cold war in our time—an "end of history" characterized by a closing of alternative political possibilities and the triumph of a liberal ideology of "normal change." Certainly some of Scott's novels narrate a complex, dialectical act of closure, in which historical strife yields to civil society, as they look back across an era of modernization that has reached its period.[9] The postmodernism of *The Antiquary* coincides with its appearance not just at the end of a trilogy of novels about the emergence of modern Scotland but mere months after Waterloo, that thunderous epilogue to the generation-long struggle over a new world order. In a strictly technical sense, then, we might call *Redgauntlet* and *Confessions of a Justified Sinner* postmodern. They situate themselves on the far threshold of an identifiable historical stage of modernity, constituted by the literary genres and discourses that make it intelligible as such, including the one, the historical novel, that has defined it—historicized it, mythologized it— as a modern period.[10] Two elements combine to produce the effect of postmodernity: the cultural visibility of a period or stage of modernization, marked by a productive discourse of modernity; and a writing that thematizes its condition at the end of that stage by representing itself in a reflexive relation to what it brings into relief (by the act of reflection) as a modern tradition.

Self-positioning in relation to tradition is more explicit in *Redgauntlet* as it reflects back on the sequence of Scottish novels of the first five years of Scott's career as a novelist. In the five years since, the Author of *Waverley* has relinquished the making of modern Scotland in tales of the long eighteenth century for historical romances with "Gothic" British and Continental settings, while a proliferation of secondary Scottish novels has settled the field. Scott's return to the form is mediated through those rival fictions and their consolidation of a tradition in his wake. This return occupied two stages, the first an exercise in the feminine genre (as Scott himself saw it) of national domestic fiction, in *Saint Ronan's Well* (1823). The second stage, Scott's reclamation of his own masculine province of historical romance, is inflected by the appearance in 1823 of Galt's *Ringan Gilhaize, or The Covenanters*, a novel that takes aim at Scott's most controversial fictionalization of Scottish history, *Old Mortality*, reviving a debate that had raged in the postwar years of 1817–18. The programmatic challenge posed by *Ringan Gilhaize* precipitates Scott's meditation in *Redgauntlet* on his own aesthetic and ideological principles and the status of the tradition he has done so much to establish.[11]

In contrast, *Private Memoirs and Confessions of a Justified Sinner* claims a terminal rather than teleological position at the end of the modern tradition of Scottish historical fiction. Following the critical and commercial failure of *The Three Perils of Woman*, the *Confessions of a Justified Sinner* marks the end of its author's attempt to compete in the genre made prestigious and profitable by Scott. Henceforth Hogg would concentrate on magazine tales and poetry (more because of the retraction in the market for novels after 1825 than because of a loss of ambition, however).[12] Several commentators have noted the critical and parodic reflection upon the Scott model of historical fiction in the *Confessions of a Justified Sinner*.[13] Douglas Mack has made the interesting case that Hogg was also responding to *Ringan Gilhaize* in his novel, which Mack reads as a late, decisive entry in the debate about the legacy of radical Presbyterianism that had flared up around *Old Mortality* and which Hogg himself had joined in 1818 with *The Brownie of Bodsbeck*.[14]

All three novels interrogate the Enlightenment philosophical solution of a moderate or conservative skepticism, explored in the Waverley novels of 1814–19, through a Virgilian thematic of *piety* that combines questions about ideology, authority, paternity, and cultural reproduction in the imperial narrative of national formation through civil war. *Ringan Gilhaize* reinvents historical fiction contra Scott and Hume by ventriloquizing belief as the foundation of narrative agency and interpretation, restoring its strong theological term, faith. The novel rejoins historical to metaphysical causality in the figure of the Covenant, which predicates the temporal renewal of that sublime, revolutionary, and apocalyptic moment when divine purpose reclaimed national history in the Scottish Reformation. In a striking formal equivalence, the single narrator of *Ringan Gilhaize* transmits a genealogy of paternal speech as the medium of history as he relates the successive stories of his grandfather, his father, and himself. In his *Autobiography* Galt drew attention to the feat as his most original and laborious achievement. It is certainly the most extreme of his technical solutions to the challenge of writing historical fiction. Paternal word and filial will make up a continuous, unified cause in the subjectivity of piety. Ringan's own story, however, unfolds the tragic issue of this revolutionary history. Persecuted, his family destroyed, reduced to melancholy solitude, he becomes a Covenanter version of "the last man," realizing apocalypse in the act of assassination. The close of the narrative represents his devoted agency, vessel of the precious heritage of the word, as enacting a fatal script rather than embodying a living patriarchal speech. No less than Scott or Hogg is Galt committed to separating the heroic epoch of revolutionary Presbyterianism from a legacy of Radical politics in the present. He maintains the sublime authenticity of the Covenant by representing its tragic fall into modernity: enthusiasm hardens and embitters into fanaticism.

Scott's and Hogg's novels take up the conception of faith as the epistemology of a patriarchal culture, powerfully reaffirmed in *Ringan Gilhaize*, in order to confront its crisis in historical modernity. The figure of this crisis is the Gothic one of a broken or contaminated patrimony, yielding uncanny rather than sublime effects, with its formal correlative in tropes of narrative and textual fragmentation. The breach affords the subjectivity that Hume called "philosophical melancholy and delirium," a combination of radical skepticism with a masculine pathos of solitary dejection. Both novels also find the crisis to be the foundation of modern literary representation, and of their own narrative possibility, in their insistent reflection upon their status as fictions—askew from belief—or as texts—material precipitates of a lost Logos: representations, alike, of a modernity disjointed from cultural origins. The skeptical problematic of belief informs the crisis of reproduction of a patriarchal Logos, then, on two symbolic registers, both carried over from the Scottish Enlightenment discourses of modernity. One is an epistemological problem of authenticity, the topos specifying (since Macpherson's "Ossian") the vexed status of literature as the medium of cultural transmission between past and present, ancestral origins and modernity, tradition and individual genius. The other is an ethical and ideological problem of fanaticism, or a piety grown excessive—unnatural, monstrous, demonic—in the light of modernity. Ringan Gilhaize's piety turns murderous as he is stripped of kinship relations. In *Redgauntlet* and the *Confessions of a Justified Sinner*, alienated sons rediscover the lost father's word as an uncanny and fatal compulsion. Both novels stress the sexed and gendered terms of the allegory of culture as sublimated homosocial reproduction (or, in the language of Enlightenment moral philosophy, sympathy) that has informed modern national tradition. Their scenarios of intense friendship threatened by patriarchal violence (Scott), of perverse ratios of sympathy and antipathy (Hogg), expose the melancholy structure of masculine heterosexuality as the dominant subjective formation of historical modernity.[15]

Redgauntlet answers *Ringan Gilhaize* by reaffirming the skeptical and aesthetic basis of historical fiction, throwing into relief Galt's challenge to Scott's romanticism. Returning in *Redgauntlet* to *Waverley* and *Rob Roy* (novels "by the Author of Waverley") rather than to *Old Mortality* and *The Heart of Mid-Lothian* ("Tales of My Landlord"), Scott reaffirms Jacobitism over popular Presbyterianism as the exemplary topos of national historical conflict—the antagonistic ideology, reactionary and doomed, in the dialectic of modernization. The reaffirmation once more collapses a revolutionary challenge into a counterrevolutionary one. Scott's riposte involves a reckoning not only with the thematics of historical belief—recast in the familiar, enlightened topics of fanaticism and fatalism—but with its narrative form. The insistently materialist, discontinuous, and heterogeneous narrativity of *Redgauntlet* enacts a brilliant rebuttal of Galt's bravura performance of a monologic patriarchal voice as the medium of historical virtue. Scott's novel selects the figure of the labyrinth—a progress downward and roundabout rather than forward and up—as its formal analogue to the Humean logic of association, the "grammar of the imagination," in an episode in which one of the protagonists explicitly associates his descent into a labyrinth of subterranean passages with the structure of the lawsuit in which he has been involved.[16] In *Redgauntlet*, melancholy alienation is cured by the progression—downward, backward, sideways, and around, but a progression nonetheless—through the ("Jacobite") uncanny rediscovery of lost paternity in the form of a fanatical authority, ("Whig") passive resistance in the form of a skeptical refusal to engage the father's terms, and (by this quintessentially Humean negative dialectic) resolution into a conventional surface of everyday life, the positive epistemology of "nothing."

Where Scott reaffirms Humean skepticism along a labyrinthine historical dialectic, *The Private Memoirs and Confessions of a Justified Sinner* tracks its fall into a bottomless irony. Hogg represents fanaticism as the radical consequence of a modern anomie, or loss of a world in which belief can be natural, and thus as the monstrous double—profoundly impious—of an alienated skepticism. It is the epistemic surplus that corresponds to skepticism's deficit.[17] The enlightened editor's diagnosis of "the rage of fanaticism in former days" loses its historicist confidence once the sinner tells his story. Robert Wringhim represents his antinomian rampage as an acting-out of "philosophical melancholy and delirium" rather than as a reconnection with an ancient faith. Early in his memoir, the Moderate Presbyterian minister Blanchard praises religion as "the bond of society on earth, and the connector of humanity with the Divine nature," adding: "there is nothing so dangerous to man as the wresting of any of its principles, or forcing them beyond their due bounds."[18] Belief, in the Moderate view, is the subjective form of a social cohesion that represents in turn the link between humanity and "the Divine nature"; its objective form is a traditional interpretative community that sets doctrinal principles within "due bounds." The novel locates this "organic," customary culture of naturalized belief, from which the Wringhims' antinomian sect and the editor's metropolitan college circle are alike estranged, in Scottish rural society.[19] The Wringhims' sect conforms to Hume's account of political parties: "Parties from *principle*, especially abstract speculative principle, are known only to modern times, and are, perhaps, the most extraordinary and unaccountable *phænomenon* that has yet appeared in human affairs" (even Hume's diction anticipates Hogg's).[20] No less than the editor's antiquarianism is antinomianism an "invention of tradition." It keeps itself going, accordingly, by reiterating its foundational act of alienation, "splitting the doctrines of Calvin into thousands of undistinguishable films" (12). This invention is mirrored in the broken materiality of Hogg's text. While *Redgauntlet* finally recedes into a comic condition of fiction which is the field of reading, that is, our own subjective, sociable intercourse with Scott's work, the *Justified Sinner* sinks both reader and author in (to use Reid's phrase) "the abyss of scepticism"—literally a grave—that turns out to define the story's obdurately bounded, textual state.

Redgauntlet bothered Galt sufficiently for him to insert a chapter into his next historical novel, *Rothelan*, titled—bluntly—"Redgauntlet."[21] The narrator offers an ironically humble correction to "one of the most flagrant departures from fact in all the renowned pages of the GREAT UNKNOWN" (2:105). He takes aim at Scott's inset tale of the Redgauntlet family curse, related by the dark uncle Hugh Redgauntlet or Herries. There, in a novel otherwise devoted to breaking up the convention, Scott parodies the *Ringan Gilhaize* technique of a sublime patriarchal monologue commemorating historical origins. In *Redgauntlet*, the lost father's satanic substitute reveals the paternal speech act to be one that sows death: "It was said that his father cursed, in his wrath, his degenerate offspring, and swore that, if they met, he should perish by his hand" (190). Paternal authority reproduces itself in the discontinuous structure of a fatal repetition of antagonistic violence: the son reiterates the paternal will by rebelling against the father, and, in a hideous literalization of genetic imprinting, the father stamps on the son's brains. Galt parodies Scott's parody by reinserting the mother into the genealogy:

> Our author agrees with Mr Herries as to the state of Dame Margery, when she heard that her husband's horse's-hoof had trampled out the brains of their son, but he does not say that she was then prematurely seized with the pangs of labour, and died in childbed, leaving the child, to which she gave birth, "distinctly marked by the miniature resemblance of a horse-shoe" on the forehead. On the contrary, so far from being prematurely seized with the pangs of labour, he particularly states, that she went her full time, and that she was only in the fifth month when informed of the fatal catastrophe. He then describes, in the most affecting manner, the shock which she received, and how, during all the remainder of the pregnancy, she could think of nothing but the terrible impress of the horse's-hoof on the brow of her beloved first-born; which constant meditation, in the opinion of the midwife, mysteriously produced the awful sign. (2:107)

We are reminded of the normative absence of the mother, as both reproductive body and thinking and feeling subject, from these scenarios of cultural origin and transmission—Galt's in *Ringan Gilhaize* as well as Scott's.[22] The dissolution of a Gothic paternal history into a burlesque register of maternal, domestic, and sentimental bathos effectively disavows Galt's own as well as Scott's commitment to the melancholy myth of culture, although by misrepresenting Scott's as a tragic rather than a comic rendition. Galt's resort to postmodern skeptical game playing reaffirms the Scott mode he had set out to refute.

REVOLUTIONARY HISTORY

Ringan Gilhaize shivers with solitary, hurried, covert journeys. Desperate secret missions open and close the book: Grandfather Gilhaize's espionage adventures along the Fife coast, Ringan's long walk to assassinate Claverhouse at Killiecrankie. In between, Galt's narrative quickens in a series of tense escapes in which the protagonist races to and fro across country in flight from persecuting authorities.

Galt maximizes that narrative element in which Scott's heroes enact the pressure of historical causality: the "flight across the heather," the motion of going to ground, that Scott bequeathed to the later tradition of Scottish historical romance (Robert Louis Stevenson, Neil Munro, John Buchan).[23] The hero comes into his own—responds authentically to the revealed force of history—as captive and fugitive. Typically he flies across unknown country, falsely accused of treason, unwittingly sharing the plight of those on the wrong side of historical power: his agency aloof from the meaning of events (yet expressing their essential, deadly truth) as he invests it in the pure motion of escape. But in *Ringan Gilhaize* the hero's wild journey accompanies a transparent relation to a public pattern of events. It expresses the fierce coincidence of his agency with the historical plot in which he finds himself. Like Scott's, Galt's hero comes to consciousness in the midst of a historical conflict; unlike Scott's, his response is to embrace the cause without wavering, to ride the conflict by acting in it. Grandfather Gilhaize takes a diversion to avoid an enemy agent, only to run right into him: "seeing it was so, and could not be helped, he put his trust in the Lord, and resolved to swerve in no point from the straight line which he had laid down for himself."[24] Gilhaize's decision enunciates an ethically strong—pious and virtuous—version of the opportunistic model of agency Galt had drawn in *The Provost* and *Sir Andrew Wylie*; it also echoes the providentialist self-justification of the assassins of Archbishop Sharp, who were looking for someone else when they ran into him, articulated by Burley in the novel at which *Ringan Gilhaize* takes aim, *Old Mortality*. Even when he finds himself on the wrong path, Galt's hero never equivocates—in schematic contrast to Henry Morton, the principled hero of *Old Mortality*. More decisively and conscientiously than most of Scott's protagonists, Morton enlists in the cause of rebellion; yet his motives are clouded with private reasons, and he finds himself divided, ethically and sentimentally closest to his Cavalier rival Evandale, repelled by the ferocity of his Whig confederates. No such inward conflicts perturb the Galt hero in *Ringan Gilhaize*, whatever other distresses he may endure. No matter what divagations he may resort to topographically, morally he will always keep to "the straight line which he had laid down for himself."

History is transparent to these men: they see clearly where the true cause is, and are certain it will prevail, whether through the great work of Reformation, or by the advent of William of Orange, which brings this century and a half of revolution to a close. Ringan clamps his agency to the coming political denouement: "I, from that time, began to think it was only through the instrumentality of the Prince of Orange . . . that my vow could effectually be brought to pass" (288); "when Thomas Ardmillan sent me, from Mynheer Bentinck, the Prince's declaration for Scotland, . . . I was the first in Scotland to publish that glorious pledge of our deliverance" (310). Like his grandfather Ringan keeps his will synchronized with the movement of history, troped as a complex unity of speech act and writing: making a vow, redeeming it by publishing it. The moment of uprising is the spontaneous assertion, fiercely exultant, of an entire community:

> We could not stop at what we had done; —we called on those who had been
> brought to thrash the corn to join with us, and they joined; —we hastened
> to the next farm; —the spirit of indignation was there before us, and master

and man, and father and son, there likewise found that the hilts of their fathers' covenanted swords fitted their avenging grasps. We had now fired the
dry stubble of the land—the flame spread—we advanced, and grew stronger
and stronger. The hills, as it were, clapped their hands, and the valleys
shouted of freedom. From all sides men and horse came exulting towards us;
the gentleman and the hind knew no distinction. The cry was, "Down with
tyranny—we are free and we will make free!" (183)

This must be the most exhilarating description of revolutionary insurgency in nineteenth-century British fiction. The individual actors hurry to
keep up with a general will—"the spirit of indignation"—that blazes
ahead of them, unifying all distinctions of individual temper, generation
and social rank in a rapturous apocalyptic transparency (authorized by
the echo of Psalm 98). Resistance is a *calling* that "publishes" itself in
contagious proliferation across the community.

Faithful to this transparency, Galt's novel unfolds the reason of history
in an ongoing debate about the limits of authority and the rights of the
subject. Whig precepts of "the divine right of resistance" versus "passive
obedience" (143–45), contractual versus absolutist models of sovereignty
(238), are urged again and again: Galt spells out the political and ethical
principles of historical agency in an implicit critique of Scott's technique
of complication and equivocation. Galt also aims this reason of history
at current political conditions, distinguishing the principled resistance of
the Covenanters from Jacobin sedition: the Covenant is a spiritual, not a
temporal, league, provoked by an interference in matters of conscience
and so quite different from the "speculative spirit of political innovation"
that led the English parliament to kill the king (159).

Repeatedly, confidently, Galt's protagonists align their acts and intentions with a transcendental will that shapes the plot of history. Providence
means more than a capacity to rationalize the direction of events after
they have happened. In the case of Ringan's grandfather, it brings an ex-
trasensory receptiveness to the darker vibrations of history: only "the wisdom which is of this world" misguides him from paying heed to a series
of premonitions on the night of Darnley's murder (115). The transparency
of history, in other words, the detection of a providential cause in the
movement of events, requires a prophetic gift. "It cannot be that ancient
iniquities will be much longer endured," cries old Gilhaize; "Nature has
burst asunder the cords of the Roman harlot, and stands in her freedom,
like Samson, when the spirit of the Lord was mightily poured upon him,
as he awoke from the lap of Delilah" (50). (Micah Balwhidder's sallies in
Annals of the Parish are fading embers of this bonfire.) The act of uprising
is prepared by exegesis. When Gilhaize approaches Kilwinning, "the
abbey with its lofty horned towers and spiky pinnacles, and the sands of

Cunningham between it and the sea, . . . seemed to him as if a huge levia-
than had come up from the depths of the ocean and was devouring the
green inland" (52). At the preparations for the Spanish invasion, "his
imagination was kindled with some dreadful conceit of the armada, and
he thought it could be nothing less than some awful and horrible creature
sent from the shores of perdition to devour the whole land" (137). The
coming of John Knox astounds all Edinburgh "as if some dreadful apocalypse had been made" (67); his host appears to "the eye of faith" as "the
mustered armies of the dreadful God: —the angels of his wrath in their
burning chariots; the angels of his omnipotence, calm in their armour of
storms and flaming fires, and the Rider on the white horse" (69). This,
the heroic phase of the Reformation, is fulfilled in "the triumph of the
truth at St Andrews" (92).

Young Ringan imbibes his grandfather's prophetic energy: "while yet
a child, I was often worked upon by what he said, and felt my young
heart . . . kindled with the live coals of his godly enthusiasm" (22). He
carries on this apocalyptic insight into the truth of history:

> I beheld as it were a bright and shining hand draw aside the curtain of time,
> and disclose the blessings of truth and liberty that were ordained to rise from
> the fate of the oppressors . . . and I had a foretaste in that hour of my grandfa-
> ther's prophecy concerning the tasks that were in store for myself in the deliv-
> erance of my native land. So that . . . I yet had a blessed persuasion that the
> event would prove in the end a link in the chain, or a cog in the wheel, of the
> hidden enginery with which providence works good out of evil. (191)

Ringan's access to this allegorical clarity comes at a heavy cost. Where
his grandfather enacted a collective will in the heroic phase of the revolution, his part will be solitary and tragic.

To sustain the apocalyptic vision of a transparent history in which
human agency fulfils the work of Providence, Galt amplifies the narrative
technique of his imaginary autobiographies. The novel consists, remarkably, of a single monologue spanning three generations and a century and
a half of national history, in which Ringan fuses his memories of his own
experience, his father's deeds and his grandfather's recitals into a single,
seamless telling. Thus the speech act of the general will that commands a
revolutionary crisis, a calling, seeks to reproduce itself across the narrative
of history. The figure for that historical reproduction is the Covenant, the
figure of plot in *Ringan Gilhaize*. Like that figure in Galt's previous novel,
the entail, the Covenant signifies an inscription of agency into history
that assigns it the status of law. Binding in writing a relationship with
Providence, the Covenant invokes a divine causality which authorizes and
magnifies human acts—in effect, transferring agency from the divine to
the human. It is thus the opposite of the entail, a contract which transfers

human agency to property. If Galt (through Grandfather Gilhaize) represents the Reformation as a spontaneous social apocalypse, a universal synchronization of wills for which the tropes are unmediated vision and word of mouth, the Covenant is the series of contracts that must sustain that moment through the still fallen, secular history that resumes in the wake of the revolutionary moment. Ringan's narration, performing a genealogical unity of Gilhaize fathers, thus guarantees a formal unity of voice and writing, calling and covenant, through the authentic transmission of the word.[25]

The figure of historical agency as an agonized activity of reading and writing takes over the second half of the book, precipitating monological into monadic narration. Ringan announces the onset of his own story and the era of the Covenant by "[taking] up the avenging pen of history, and [dipping] it in the blood of martyrs" (162). Alone in prison, "I saw, as it were written in a book, that for my part and conduct I was doomed to die" (219). Not, however, before worse losses befall him. "But my task now is of vengeance and justice, not of sorrowing, and I must more sternly grasp the iron pen" (254). At the moment of trauma, when Ringan discovers his wife and daughters dead by suicide or murder after their rape by Claverhouse's dragoons,[26] voice and transparency fail: "But what these things import, I dare only guess, for *no one has ever told me* what became of my benign Sarah Lochrigg and our two blooming daughters; —all is phantasma that I recollect of the day of my return home" (263). Emerging from delirium, he prays to God to "make me an instrument to work out the purposes of thy dreadful justice" (264), and tells his son, "Open the Bible, and see what the Lord instructs us to do at this time" (265).

Ringan masters the movement of history by turning himself from sacrificial victim into sacerdotal agent who despatches victims: the structure of sacrifice remains. By turning it into writing the covenant, like the entail, predicates a tragic experience of history after all. The allegorical structure of history becomes fatal. Agency turns out to occupy the reflex between writing and being written, or writing out—rehearsing—an already-written script. Ringan takes up the iron pen, but to spell out a destiny prescribed for him. His tragic knowledge is that he is a character in the plot but not the author. The Covenanter recovers allegorical authenticity in a deadly implosion of his agency.

Galt figures this declension through the role of women in history, who exemplify different types of opposites to the protagonists' agency. At first, in the heroic era of Reformation, women's licentious and usurping will authorizes the uprising of a corrective masculine agency, in a resplendent allegorical expansion across universal, national, and domestic levels of history. The Reformation is figured as the mythic combat against the Scarlet Woman, variously represented by the Church of Rome, Queen Mary, and the adulteress Mrs. Kilspinnie. The sublime movement of a collective will keeps this revolution, in Galt's telling, comparatively bloodless—its violence is all spiritual, that is, ideological. But temporal history proceeds as the record of a local, bitter, dirty conflict in which women are rape victims. Galt's representation of the "killing time" reiterates a vision of civil war, not unlike Scott's and Hogg's, as a violation of common life. The difference lies (once again) in the ethical certainty with which Galt's protagonist resorts to violent action. Ringan must both suffer and perform the violence that Scott's heroes are protected from by the tropes of romance. If romance grants Scott's characters a mysterious freedom from causality, out of a history experienced as fatality and constraint, Galt's hero follows the reverse course, freely choosing his unfreedom, acting out a role already written, inflicting the death he will receive. The monologic narration conveys this ethical clarity, as an unbroken patrilineal transmission of the word, into the tragic theater of extermination. No children follow Ringan Gilhaize: like Ossian, he is the last of his race.[27] Instead, his posterity is constituted by the reader, who receives Galt's literary simulation of a patriarchal narration of the truth.

This last declension, from Ringan to reader, deadlocks the trope of authenticity—a deadlock which critics have read as the book's final production of the ethical conundrum of "fanaticism," in the narrator's fall into alienation and derangement.[28] *Ringan Gilhaize* amplifies the technique of Galt's earlier fictional autobiographies, which pretended not to be novels, by renouncing the irony that performed the work of fictionality in those earlier memoirs—unless, indeed, a tragic irony supervenes in the narrative's final stage. *Ringan Gilhaize* claims its moral and aesthetic power in a rhetorical cancellation of its status as work of fiction. Even as Ringan dissolves his individuality into the reported experience of his ancestors, in the early part of the work, his narrating presence is meant to remain opaque, "real"; he is not a self-evident persona, the conventional disguise of an author, in the manner of Scott. Proposing the author as medium in the spiritualist sense, channelling the Gilhaize voice, Galt reinstates a willed naïvete that covers up the gaps and mediations opened by Scott—between past and present, between history and fiction, between the tale and the machinery of telling, and between narrative and reader—in the last chapters of *Old Mortality*. *Ringan Gilhaize* challenges its reader with the rigorous fanaticism of its own narration.

PHILOSOPHICAL MELANCHOLY AND DELIRIUM

After dismissing his son to die in the crusade against the House of Stuart, Ringan Gilhaize languishes in a fever:

> I sat wondering if the things around me were not the substanceless imageries
> of a dream, and fancying that those terrible truths whereof I can yet only
> trust myself to hint, might be the fallacies of a diseased sleep. . . . At other
> times I felt all the loneliness of the solitude into which my lot was then cast,
> and it was in vain that I tried to appease my craving affections with the
> thought, that in parting with my son I had given him to the Lord. (278)

Ringan gives utterance to a typically Calvinist psychology of crisis. Fallen
from its divine origin, the soul endures a plight of metaphysical solitude
and epistemological uncertainty, in which the lonely glory of election may
always turn out to be its opposite, the outcast state of preterition. The
only certainty empirical knowledge yields is "the solitude into which my
lot was cast."

Susan Manning has demonstrated the recurrence of this Calvinist psychology, variously secularized and historicized, in Scottish moral philosophy and fiction, where it acquires the exemplary status of a modern structure of feeling. Hume's *Treatise of Human Nature* provides its definitive
apologia—giving it a comic rather than tragic narrativity, celebrating
ironical indeterminacy rather than uplifting it into a new faith. Manning
writes that "by adding *pleasurable* doubt to the Calvinist co-ordinates
[Hume] establishes a position which has profound affinities with the fiction of Scott."[29] At the end of the first book of *Treatise*, the author steps
back from his argument to complain:

> I am at first affrighted and confounded with that forelorn solitude, in which
> I am plac'd in my philosophy, and fancy myself some strange uncouth mon-
> ster, who not being able to mingle and unite in society, has been expell'd all
> human commerce, and left utterly abandon'd and disconsolate.[30]

Not only have the philosopher's heretical tenets made him a "monster"
in the view of society—a view that the pressure of sympathy obliges him
to share—but they bring an abysmal confusion within himself:

> Where am I, or what? From what causes do I derive my existence, and to
> what condition shall I return? Whose favour shall I court, and whose anger
> must I dread? What beings surround me? And on whom have I any influence,
> or who have any influence on me? I am confounded with all these questions,
> and begin to fancy myself in the most deplorable condition imaginable, invi-
> ron'd with the deepest darkness, and utterly depriv'd of the use of every mem-
> ber and faculty. (316)

The problem implies its solution. Hume has translated an epistemological
crisis, the evacuation of metaphysical relations from the world, into a
social crisis of exile and solitude. Society thus holds the cure for what
Hume calls his "philosophical melancholy and delirium." It constitutes

the illusory field of "custom" into which the alienated imagination will relax, not by choice but by a natural imperative. Finding himself "absolutely determin'd to live, and talk, and act like other people in the common affairs of life" (316), the philosopher may recruit his faculties—until nature, in the form of intellectual curiosity, urges him once more to resume his lonely ratiocination. Hume goes on to analyze the natural force that integrates us into common life in the second book of the *Treatise*, where he gives it the name of sympathy.

The protagonists of *Redgauntlet* and the *Confessions of a Justified Sinner* both find themselves in a Humean predicament of melancholy solitude. Appearing "an unaccountable monster" in others' view (19), Hogg's Robert Wringhim ends his story by fleeing across country, shunned by the common folk among whom he seeks refuge. Nature cannot cure him since no society will take him in. Instead of a destiny regulated by sociability and custom, the "Memoirs and Confessions" narrates the totalization of the sinner's solitude in a grim logic of extinction: the fall of the house of Colwan by serial murder, fratricide, suicide. *Redgauntlet* offers the comic narrative of socialization that the *Confessions of a Justified Sinner* refuses. Darsie Latimer, dejected stepbrother, complains of his exile from family:

> I am affected with a sense of loneliness, the more depressing, that it seems to me to be a solitude peculiarly my own. In a country where all the world have a circle of consanguinity, extending to sixth cousins at least, I am a solitary individual, having only one kind heart to throb in unison with my own. . . . I am in the world, as a stranger in the crowded coffee-house, where he enters, calls for what refreshments he wants, pays his bill, and is forgotten so soon as the waiter's mouth has pronounced his "Thank ye, sir." (4)

The simile of the crowded coffeehouse informs Darsie's melancholy with the historical and anthropological theme of modernization: he is exemplary in the very conviction that he is unique. The coffeehouse, prototypical site of the eighteenth-century public sphere, specifies its commercial ethos as well as the disappearance of an ancient web of "consanguinity."[31] Unlike Hogg and Galt, Scott accepts the wager of the republic of letters to make good the substitution. *Redgauntlet* will justify literature itself as the institution that provides a sentimental and aesthetic replenishment of traditional relations threatened with oblivion in modern society, but by advertising, rather than trying to conceal, the skeptical knowledge that these are imaginary and not real relations. Rather than being a false or imperfect substitute for some otherwise accessible reality, the work of fiction—advertising its condition as a work of fiction—authentically constitutes the field of customary representation, or socially accepted illusion, that accommodates modern consciousness.

Both *Redgauntlet* and the *Confessions of a Justified Sinner* novelize the Humean logic that a metaphysical relation, once skeptical reason has expelled it from the world, must reassert its lost authority in the fanatical mode of delusion, as the literalizing insistence of an obsolete sign system. The "cause" returns, in other words, as an ideology—Jacobite absolutism, Calvinist antinomianism—that justifies itself in a language of predestinarian fatalism. "The privilege of free action belongs to no mortal," sneers Redgauntlet: "our most indifferent actions are but meshes of the web of destiny by which we are all surrounded" (193). The classic scheme of historical romance identifies this lost Logos with the word of the father. Darsie Latimer and Robert Wringhim (in contrast to Ringan Gilhaize) are stepsons astray from a natural and social origin defined by biological paternity, divested now of its symbolic integrity. Ancient consanguinity, paternal authority, fatality, and literalism all predicate one another as constituents of a sublime but deathly cultural apparatus, an exploded illusion that reasserts itself as a sentence of extermination. "His skull is yet standing over the Rikargate," Redgauntlet ventriloquizes the dead father, "and even its bleak and mouldered jaws command you to be a man" (317).

Darsie's intimation of "one kind heart to throb in unison with my own" points toward the modern, sentimental solution of friendship, paradigmatically the customary relation that replaces kinship in commercial society. Hume's philosopher can forget his melancholy by being "merry with my friends"; the second book of the *Treatise* analyzes sympathy as the instinctual psychic motion by which one person assumes another's feelings; Smith's *Theory of Moral Sentiments* delineates social subjectivity as an imaginary economy of sympathetic exchange. *Redgauntlet* unfolds a complex meditation on friendship as the social connection that sustains individual identity against modern anomie, on the one hand, and against the primitive, "metaphysical" coercions of kinship, on the other. Scott's novel explores the ambivalent ascendancy of the new sociology of friendship, a voluntary, equal association among strangers, over the premodern usage of the term (in Scots) to designate extended, hierarchical kinship relations. Friendship, piety's successor, must bear the charge of an interactive, horizontal relation of sympathetic exchange through which both the desiring individual and the social group may reproduce themselves.

Redgauntlet sets friendship in schematic opposition to paternal authority. They form the modern (horizontal) and traditional (vertical) axes of the core ethical value of *pietas* or loyalty (flagged in the novel's epigraph from *As You Like It*). Alan Fairford equivocates between the claims of his father and his friend Darsie Latimer; Darsie yearns for Alan while his uncle commands him to embody his father's cause. At first glance the values of this opposition seem clear-cut. After the fall of the old regime, the word of the father can no longer reproduce the vital relations of culture. Modern friendship flourishes in sympathetic exchange, while the prescriptive, top-down vector of paternal authority threatens to provoke instead *antipathy*, the motor of an inhuman and mechanical conflict typified by the Redgauntlet family curse. By insisting on the subjective component of loyalty, in Smithian language of sympathy-based moral sentiment, Scott's first-person narration has already rewritten it as modern:

> I am, and have all along been, the exclusive object of my father's anxious hopes, and his still more anxious and engrossing fears; so what title have I to complain, although now and then these fears and hopes lead him to take a troublesome and incessant charge of all my motions? (11)

Alan Fairford uses the language of friendship to justify filial piety: his affections are bound to his father by the sympathetic insight into his "fears and hopes." Filial piety now relies on an imaginative apprehension of the father's vulnerability rather than his strength—investing the relation with a measure of sympathy's contractual charge, and founding sympathy on a shared affect of anxiety. Unmitigated strictness on the father's part, it is implied, would license the son's revolt. The novel does allow a brief idyll of father-son friendship, significantly a professional one, when the Fairfords collaborate to sort the chaotic archive of the Peebles lawsuit ("the specimen of all causes," 138) into a transparent narrative. But Alan deserts the lawsuit once he realizes that their collaboration has been resting on his father's betrayal of his friendship with Darsie. The anxious synthesis of paternal authority, filial piety, and mutual sympathy splinters under stress.[32]

At the same time, Darsie Latimer yearns for a lost world of kinship. This yearning drives the plot of *Redgauntlet* until it is overwhelmed by the reciprocal force of Redgauntlet's attempt to graft the dead cause onto a living heir. It seems that the new-modelled relations of friendship cannot by themselves assuage what the novel represents as a profound psychic need; their horizontality, covering a historyless present, is by definition superficial. The obliterated scutcheon of the Quaker Joshua Geddes expresses a willed sublimation of ancestral ties that is at once excessive and incomplete. We need those deep relations of kinship and fealty, but they must be recovered in the mode of friendship. In other words, they must be imaginary and sentimental relations before they can be "real" ones. (Heterosexual difference produces a strange inversion of this logic: Darsie's dangerous desire for Lilias is neutralized into friendship by the revelation that they are brother and sister.)

Darsie's adventures in the first volume, in what turns out to be an unwitting quest for origins, trace the pattern of a reconstitution of ancient friendship through the sentimental techniques of sympathy. Wandering across the countryside, he falls in with a series of countercultures outside civil society. As in *Rob Roy*, these map no unified temporal relation to modernity. The outlaw fiefdom of the Laird of the Lakes maintains its old ways in reactionary opposition to the state; Wandering Willie's Burnsian lifestyle of rural vagrancy and popular minstrelsy opens onto an underworld of the "folk"; while the official Society of Friends, the Quakers, represents a utopian exaggeration of modernity, constituted (no less than the Jacobite underground) in purely ideological terms. Darsie's dislocation from paternity seems to endow him with a compensatory talent for invoking sympathy. New friendships revive ancient relations—father, sister, feudal retainer—but in disguise, unrecognized. The plot withholds from them the logic of agency or causality. Joshua Geddes can indulge in a paternal kindness towards Darsie because he is not his father. Nor does the plot allow him to play the role: he cannot provide a home for Darsie, protect him from the rioters, or rescue him from captivity. The case of the popular minstrel Wandering Willie, who turns out to be Darsie's vassal, is still more instructive. In one of the novel's wonderful set pieces, Willie and the captive Darsie are able to exchange messages encoded in the titles of national airs that they play and whistle to one another. The narrative alludes to the story of Richard Coeur de Lion and Blondel, and it seems that a romance plot is being hatched: Darsie's sympathetic connoisseurship of popular tradition will surely bear fruit in a rescue attempt. Strikingly, though, no rescue follows. The episode, it seems, leads nowhere.

The plot of *Redgauntlet* establishes patterns of friendship in which the sentimental reconstitution of an ancient kinship relation follows its divorce from causality. Friendship is the subjective constituent of a tangled web of affiliations, coincidences, and recognitions that suspends narrative consequences, as we see in the final chapters at Father Crackenthorpe's inn, the maze into which all plots flow. The inn, like the coffeehouse, is a commercial space of hospitality, but this one lies outside civil society (on the margin between national and historical regimes), where it is presided over by false fathers—the carnivalesque Crackenthorpe, the pathetic Bonaventura. Everyone in the novel turns up, but in order that their diverse agencies *not* converge into a unified narrative engine. Bathos and confusion reign. Here Redgauntlet's invocation of a fatal, literal paternity can be emptied at last of its metaphysical charge. "Then, gentlemen, . . . the cause is lost for ever!" (373).

General Colin Campbell exorcizes "the cause" with the most powerful speech act in the Waverley novels. He designates the social regime of friendship with a set of interlocking recognitions and refusals of recognition:

> Amid this scene of confusion, a gentleman, plainly dressed in a riding habit, with a black cockade in his hat, but without any arms except a *couteau-de-chasse*, walked into their apartment without ceremony. . . . He had passed

through their guards, if in the confusion they now maintained any, without stop or question, and now stood, almost unarmed, among armed men, who, nevertheless, gazed on him as on the angel of destruction.

"You look coldly on me, gentlemen," he said. "Sir Richard Glendale—My Lord—we were not always such strangers. Ha, Pate-in-Peril, how is it with you? And you, too, Ingoldsby—I must not call you by any other name—why do you receive an old friend so coldly?" (371)

The angel of destruction assumes the form of a private gentleman who hails the conspirators as friends and at the same time refuses to recognize them as historical actors. The death this angel deals is a social death, that of Jacobitism's public, national status. Slavoj Žižek, paraphrasing Hegel's theory of historical repetition, invokes the model that Scott surely had in mind: "[W]hen Napoleon lost for the first time and was consigned to Elba, he did not know that he was already dead, that his historical role was finished, and he had to be reminded of it through his second defeat at Waterloo—at this point, when he died for the second time, he was really dead."[33] After Culloden not even the epic resonances of a Waterloo are attainable. Campbell dismisses the Jacobites to the oblivion of private life—unless they are willing to play the part of superfluous victims in an anachronistic theater of sacrifice:

Come, do not be fools, gentlemen; there was perhaps no harm meant or intended by your gathering together in this obscure corner, for a bear-baiting, or a cock-fighting, or whatever other amusement you may have intended . . . I have come here, of course, sufficiently supported both with cavalry and infantry, to do whatever might be necessary; but my commands are—and I am sure they agree with my inclination—to make no arrests, nay, to make no farther inquiry of any kind, if this good assembly will consider their own interest so far as to give up their immediate purpose, and return quietly home to their own houses. (372–73)

The General's authority does not rest solely on the army that backs his presence, since the modern state apparatus has permeated and colonized the lateral relations of friendship. This Charles Edward understands: "I bid you farewell, unfriendly friends—I bid you farewell, sir, (bowing to the General,) my friendly foe" (374). The paradoxes acknowledge that the Jacobite plot has already unravelled because of a failure to control the categories of friendship and authority by which historical agency is framed.[34]

TECHNOLOGIES OF SELF AND OTHER

Redgauntlet reaffirms the philosophical principles that have informed Scott's novels, not only the Humean skeptical-sentimental dialectic of fictional realism but the model of sympathy as the psychological basis for civil society formulated by Adam Smith in *The Theory of Moral Sentiments*. Sympathetic exchange becomes a crux in the *Confessions of a Justified Sinner*, where it is invested with the techniques of physiognomy and a Burkean politics of terror.

The Theory of Moral Sentiments represents sympathy as a work of the imagination that constitutes modern social bonds, regulating the boundaries of self and other, by the abstraction of feeling from its source in physical sensation. Sympathy arises not so much "from the view of the [other person's] passion, as from that of the situation which excites it."[35] It crafts itself upon "the shape and configuration of the imaginations" of other persons rather than upon the "passions which take their origin from the body" (27–29). In a studied and self-conscious rather than spontaneous performance, the (normatively male) spectator must "endeavour, as much as he can, to put himself in the situation of the other, and to bring home to himself every little circumstance of distress which can possibly occur to the sufferer"; but for that to happen the sufferer must first have sympathized with the spectator, moderating the expression of his joy or anguish to approximate a social norm of "insensibility," since people will be repelled by a violent outcry. Only then will the sufferer be able to receive the solace of the spectator's sympathy, the larger function of which is to maintain society as the cool or neutral medium of "propriety" (31–48). Thus sympathy "flattens" and "brings down" (in Smith's musical metaphor) the chaotic energy of the passions by passing them through the imaginary medium of the other. Reciprocally, we imagine ourselves as objects in the point of view of others: society is the "mirror" in which we observe and regulate our "countenance and behaviour" (110). "When I endeavour to examine my own conduct . . . I divide myself, as it were, into two persons," spectator and agent (110). The imaginative labor that appropriates other to self at the same time converts self to other. Social formation takes place through this strenuous, morally salutary and indeed necessary work of alienation and self-division.

Scott divides the first volume of *Redgauntlet* between two narrators who exchange letters, in a formal simulation of the "imaginary change of situation upon which," according to Smith, "sympathy is founded" (21). The traffic of letters, as it binds the reader into the structure of sympathetic exchange, highlights (via the allusion to Richardson and epistolary fiction) a distinctively novelistic tradition of sentimental reading. This mirror held up to our reading shows its participation in the cultural history that the novel represents, and we find ourselves obliged to reflect on how we too belong to civil society's by-now-ascendant liberal order. Scott's first volume models a formal equivalence between the techniques of sympathy and the romance trope of character doubling, familiar to readers of the Waverley novels. *Redgauntlet* narrates a progressive, adaptive technique of survival through sympathetic exchange. Darsie's assumption of multiple rather than binary sentimental connections means that antagonistic dualisms can be left behind. The kindly and inimical doubles who appear across the story, invoked by the hero's anxiety and desire, assume functions forbidden to him. *Redgauntlet* plays a deft joke on the formula with its initial doubling of the protagonists. Despite the intensity of their friendship, Alan Fairford not only fails to rescue Darsie but falls into the same supine state of disorientation and captivity as soon as he comes looking for him. The distinction between them—like the analogous aesthetic and ethical distinctions between romance and realism, sense and sensibility—was only maintained by the dialogue that produced it, in the opening letters. As soon as their condition changes they become the same. It is left to a third wayward son, the remorseful pirate Nanty Ewart, to supply the missing romantic double, and this time the topos works. Ewart's commission of the passionate, primitive acts of fornication and parricide, forbidden to the polite heroes, makes him fit to fill the vacuum of heroic action at the end of the story, in a last reactionary spasm that releases the structure of antagonism in his own death and that of his impious counterpart, the traitor Cristal Nixon. General Campbell, passing by, coolly disowns the secret agency by which his power is maintained: the "bodies blackening in the sun" (375) are so much waste matter, by-products of civil society's settlement. Here the sociological theme makes its last appearance. It is not that a modern, complex society has dispensed with an archaic, sacrificial deployment of virtuous or nefarious acts of violence. They have become specialized functions. In modern civil society, friendly foes and unfriendly friends are contracted out to kill, betray, and perish for you.

Notoriously, doubling takes the forms of fratricidal antipathy and schizophrenic fission in the *Confessions of a Justified Sinner*. The Reverend Wringhim's attempt at a purely doctrinal foundation of society (in Hume's phrase, on "abstract speculative principle") perpetuates its original act of schism, in a principle of "opposition" that sets Robert not only against his brother but against himself—producing the spectral emanation of the double, the further ideological declension of antinomianism, and the acts of extermination and suicide. The exchange between self and other brings a grievous confusion of both. "You think that I am your brother," the mysterious Gil-Martin introduces himself, "or that I am your second self" (117), immediately posing the problem of friendship as a relation that falls between (instead of subsuming) the terms of consanguinity and self-reflection. Ideology, or the imaginary relation of belief, provides the new bond: "I am indeed your brother, not according to the flesh, but in my belief of the same truths." The claim on an imaginary brotherhood founded on "belief of the same truths" cancels the skeptical basis of Smithian sympathy, which posits, after all, likeness rather than identity, harmonized difference rather than unison, as the sufficient condition of a social order. Identity through belief constitutes a fantasy of excessive socialization, called fanaticism by Enlightenment historiography, which postulates a community without otherness.

Confessions of a Justified Sinner unfolds a diabolical critique of the Smithian model of sympathy as socializing ethical discipline. Gil-Martin's "cameleon art of changing [his] appearance" (124) literalizes the "imaginary change of situation upon which sympathy is founded":

> I observed several times, when we were speaking of certain divines and their tenets, that his face assumed something of the appearance of theirs; and it struck me, that by setting his features to the mould of other people's, he entered at once into their conceptions and feelings. (119)

This reads like a parody of *The Theory of Moral Sentiments*: "By the imagination we place ourselves in his situation, . . . we enter as it were into his body, and become in some measure the same person with him, and thence form some idea of his sensations" (9). It echoes more closely, however, an anecdote about "the celebrated physiognomist Campanella" related by Edmund Burke in his *Philosophical Enquiry into the Origin of Our Ideas of the Sublime and Beautiful*:

> [T]his man, it seems, had not only made very accurate observations on human faces, but was very expert in mimicking such, as were any way remarkable. When he had a mind to penetrate into the inclinations of those he had to deal with, he composed his face, his gesture, and his whole body, as nearly as he could into the exact similitude of the person he intended to examine; and then carefully observed what turn of mind he seemed to acquire by this change. So that, says my author, he was able to enter into the dispositions and thoughts of people, as effectually as if he had been changed into the very men.[36]

Gil-Martin's "cameleon art" conflates sympathy with physiognomy, the Enlightenment science of interpreting facial forms. Physiognomy affirms a correspondence between material body and immortal soul in a sign system of gestures, vocal tones, and facial expressions imprinted on the body's surface. Johann Kaspar Lavater's monumental treatise on physiognomy, translated into English in the 1790s, defines its subject as "the Science of discovering the relation between the exterior and the interior—between the visible surface and the invisible spirit which it covers—between the animated, perceptible matter, and the imperceptible spirit which impresses this character of life upon it—between the apparent effect, and the concealed cause which produces it."[37] Lavater strives to weld together the religious and scientific epistemologies broken apart in the projects of Enlightenment by reforging the hermeneutic couplings—exterior and interior, appearance and essence, matter and spirit, effect and cause—deconstructed (for example) in Hume's experimental philosophy. Lavater's charge, accordingly, is not only hermeneutic but ethical. Physiognomy "is the soul of all our opinions, of our efforts, our actions, our expectations, our fears and our hopes. . . . It is our guide, and the rule of our conduct" (1:32–33). Lavater claims for his science the socializing function that the Scottish philosophers had allotted to sympathy: "Physiognomy unites hearts: it alone forms intimate and lasting connections; and friendship, that heavenly sentiment, has no foundation more solid" (2:51).

However physiognomy plays an ambiguous part in the Scottish technology of sympathy. It is more readily accommodated by Hume's account of sympathy (in the second book of the *Treatise*) as a natural, involuntary and contagious physiological reflex, than it is by Smith's program of imaginary abstraction, which not only followed Hume's account but sought to correct it. Sympathy, according to Hume, is the instinctive force that transforms the "idea" of another person's state of feeling, derived from the observation of expressive signs, into an equivalent state of feeling within the observer:

> This idea is presently converted into an impression, and acquires such a degree of force and vivacity, as to become the very passion itself, and produce an equal emotion, as any original affection. . . . This is the nature and cause of sympathy; and 'tis after this manner we enter so deep into the opinions and affections of others, whenever we discover them.[38]

The interpreted sign, that is, becomes the condition it signifies, in a reversal of the normal priority of impression and idea in Hume's argument.[39] This logic also reverses the dynamic of abstraction that will be insisted upon by Smith, since here the idea is reembodied. Reembodiment of the idea of the other as an impression of our own ("the very passion itself") produces the structure of penetration and appropriation ("we enter so deep into the opinions and affections of others") practised by Hogg's Gil-Martin.

Smith opens *The Theory of Moral Sentiments* with the recognition that sympathy involves the epistemological drive to "enter as it were into" another person's being:

> By the imagination we place ourselves in his situation, we conceive ourselves enduring all the same torments, we enter as it were into his body, and become in some measure the same person with him, and thence form some idea of his sensations, and even feel something which, though weaker in degree, is not altogether unlike them. (9)

However, Smith's insistence on the (Humean) principle that "it is by the imagination only that we can form any conception" of the other person's feelings attenuates the devilish scenario of body invasion and identity theft to a figure of speech ("as it were . . . in some measure . . . not altogether unlike"). Hume's wild sympathy—spontaneous, passionate, embodied—is the disciplinary target of *The Theory of Moral Sentiments.* Smith the civic moralist (in Nicholas Phillipson's phrase) seeks to domesticate the free-range model of sympathetic contagion, with its anarchic erasure of the boundaries of self and other (dissolving the individual into a mob), through a complex interactive labor of reflection that regulates those boundaries and produces the ethical subject of civil society. Smith forestalls the "conversion of an idea into an impression" that Hume calls "the nature and cause of sympathy" (*Treatise,* 370, 369) with his argument that sympathy can only be sustained upon the disembodiment of passion and sensation.[40] Physiognomy, with its fixation on the body's expressive surfaces, accordingly plays little or no part in the Smithian work of sympathy, which refines the "imaginary change of situation" through a conjectural reconstruction of "the whole case" of the other person's predicament (21).[41]

Some recent commentators have emphasized the national and imperial as well as civic arena of *The Theory of Moral Sentiments.* Smith's lectures and treatises, like Scott's historical novels, provided "an account of the union of Scotland and England which effected a conciliation between the two on the grounds of commerce, sociality, politeness, and aesthetics," as Smith sought "to found the notion of a civil society on a doctrine of social sympathy which was predicated on a concept of distance."[42] Seamus Deane and Luke Gibbons contrast Smith with his Irish contemporary Burke, whose *Philosophical Inquiry* (1757) "challenge[s] and disrupt[s] the integrationist narratives of the Scottish Enlightenment," conceptually based on tropes of distance, abstraction and exchange, with an "aesthetics of disintegration and terror." Instead of Smith's moral blueprint for Scottish assimilation into British civil society, Burke evokes the psycho-political regime of a "colonial sublime" constituted by passionate identification with distress and suffering. Where Smith would "purge the body and its discontents from the public sphere" to sustain the imaginary field of sympathetic exchange, Burke mobilizes "the contagion of our passions" for an ethical identification with oppressed and colonized peoples that Gibbons calls "the sympathetic sublime."[43] Burke's citation of the physiognomic skills of Campanella occurs in a discussion of the "cause of pain and fear": the physiognomist uses his skills of facial control to abstract himself from the agonies of torture by the Inquisition.

Burke's alternative declension of the Humean account of sympathy illuminates the crisis that shook the authority of *The Theory of Moral Sentiments* in the French Revolution controversy. It also suggests a genealogy for Hogg's recourse, in *Confessions of a Justified Sinner,* to what we might call Irish or colonial tropes of physiognomy and the sympathetic sublime that are starkly contrary to Scott's reaffirmation of Smithian codes of moral sentiment in *Redgauntlet*. Dugald Stewart, the main interpreter of Scottish Enlightenment thought to the generation of Scott and Jeffrey, reasserted Hume's emphasis on a physiologically determined, "inexplicable contagion of sympathetic imitation" in an explicit preference over Smith's moralization of "an illusion of the imagination" (in Stewart's dismissive phrase).[44] The historical context of Stewart's lectures—the French revolutionary wars—accounts not only for the reversion from Smith to Hume but for the Burkean associations with which the reversion is charged. Stewart, who cites Burke's anecdote about Campanella (2:186), grants the "mimical powers connected with our *bodily frame*" (2:154) a foundational role in the work of sympathy: "when we assume any strongly expressive look, and accompany it with appropriate gestures, some degree of the correspondent emotion is apt to arise within us" (2:185). He notes the "very close connection" between the "two talents, of mimickry and physiognomy" (2:186):

> [T]he effect of mimickry cannot fail, of itself, to present to the power of Conception, in the strongest and liveliest manner, the original which is copied; and therefore, it is not surprising, that, one such an occasion, the mimic should enter more completely into the ideas and feelings he wishes to seize, — to identify himself in imagination for the moment (if I may use the expression) with the archetype he has in view. (2:191)

But for Stewart, at the close of the revolutionary epoch, sympathetic imitation betrays the perilous vulnerability of the imagination to "the contagious nature of convulsions, of hysteric disorders, of panics, and of all the different kinds of enthusiasm" (2:195–96), especially "the infectious tendency of religious enthusiasm" (2:203) and the sublime energy of crowds (2:209). These topoi of the Burkean sublime are now stained by Burke's late politicization of them in the *Reflections on the Revolution in France*: they portend a frightening loss of identity and agency, rather than their enlargement through sympathetic solidarity with other oppressed subjects. Sympathy, promising fraternity, brings terror. Thus, in *Redgauntlet*, Scott dramatizes the association of a passionate, contagious sympathy, triggered by a physiognomic sign, with despotic coercion, biological fatality and the sublime, in the scene in which a resentful Darsie catches himself reflecting the horseshoe mark on his uncle's brow ("the fatal mark of our race," 189). This physiognomic revelation of a terrifying regression from the condition of modern socialized citizen to a hereditary, primitive, corporeal subjection is mediated to Darsie through reflection in a mirror—alluding to the Smithian sympathetic order that *Redgauntlet's* conspiracy aims to overthrow.

Confessions of a Justified Sinner narrates several instances of "convulsions, of hysteric disorders, of panics, and of all the different kinds of enthusiasm," animated by the "inexplicable contagion of sympathetic imitation," including the riot at the Black Bull inn (a satire of the Scott topos of civil war), the evangelical frenzies of the Wringhim household, and the bizarre scene in which Bell Calvert and Mrs. Logan, on catching sight of Robert accompanied by a figure who appears to be his dead brother, fall into a hysterical trance that spontaneously infects their landlady. Even Gil-Martin admits that he cannot exert "full control" over what he calls his "natural peculiarity"—although he is able to harness it, by a Smithian disciplinary exertion, to a will to power:

> "My countenance changes with my studies and sensations," said he. "It is a natural peculiarity in me, over which I have not full control. If I contemplate a man's features seriously, mine own gradually assume the very same appearance and character. And what is more, by contemplating a face minutely, I not only attain the same likeness, but, with the likeness, I attain the very same ideas as well as the same mode of arranging them, so that, you see, by looking at a person attentively, I by degrees assume his likeness, and by assuming his likeness I attain to the possession of his most secret thoughts." (86)

The invasive force of this physiognomy confounds the reciprocity tendered in Smith's "imaginary change of situation," just as it inverts the scenario of Burke's Campanella anecdote, which represented the philosopher as a torture victim. Gil-Martin, in the role of inquisitor, reads the other person's countenance with such skill that he takes over his "most secret thoughts." As it first assumes and then evacuates "likeness," interpretation cancels the category of interiority, making the self accessible through a detection of surface effects, erasing its integrity and uniqueness. This reading collapses the set of binary distinctions Lavater had claimed physiognomy would guarantee: surface and depth, inside and outside, likeness and identity, self and other.

With the surmise that his mysterious friend must be "the Czar Peter of Russia . . . travelling through Europe in disguise" (89; Peter the Great founded the most spectacular of eighteenth-century New Towns, built upon the corpses of his subjects), Wringhim names a fantasy of enlightened despotism haunting the politics of sympathy. The 1707 Treaty of Union, the political condition for modern civil society according to Scottish Whig historiography, is never mentioned in *The Private Memoirs and Confessions of a Justified Sinner*, even though it is the major national event that falls within this historical novel's precisely dated chronology—as, indeed, "union" is an impossible condition at every level of the representation.[45] If *Redgauntlet* reaffirms an Enlightenment cultural history in which the sympathetic imagination (instantiated in the work of fiction)

may replace archaic, authoritarian bonds with civil relations of sentimental exchange, *Confessions of a Justified Sinner* reduces Smithian sympathy
to the instrument of a distinctively modern politics of domination. Robert's initial act of looking, in which, moved by a desperate longing for
society, he views his own face reflected in the other, is swiftly overcome
by Gil-Martin's appropriation of the power to look, in a physiognomic
prowess that colonizes the selves it reads. At the same time Hogg's novel
recuperates, with shocking moral force, the Burkean "sympathetic sublime" of an involuntary identification with terror and anguish. The book
presents itself as a collection of documents comprising "the whole case"
of Robert Wringhim, a case so extreme that even his editor shares the
"detestation" in which he seems universally to be held (175). Yet the very
act of reading a first-person narration—a confession—forges the contagious link whereby we find ourselves in Robert's situation, beyond the
pale of civil society, "outcast in the world" (67).

AUTHENTICITY EFFECTS

An "Editor's Narrative" frames the first-person narrative, the "Private
Memoirs and Confessions of a Sinner, Written by Himself," that constitutes the core of Hogg's one-volume novel. At the end of the book the
editor confirms the authenticity of the memoirs with a circumstantial account of the discovery of the manuscript, complete with references to
contemporary literary figures (including Hogg himself), real locations in
Edinburgh and the Borders, the citation of "an authentic letter, published
in *Blackwood's Magazine*" describing the suicide's grave and its local
traditions (165), and even a "fac-simile" of a page from the original hand-
written document bound into the frontispiece. The "authentic letter,"
signed "JAMES HOGG," is printed in the August 1823 number of *Blackwood's*. The editor comments: "It bears the stamp of authenticity in every
line; yet, so often had I been hoaxed by the ingenious fancies displayed in
that Magazine, that when this relation met my eye, I did not believe it"
(169). Despite the Ettrick Shepherd's refusal to guide them, the editor and
his friends find and reopen the grave, and bring back a sodden roll of
printed and manuscript pages: the text of the "Private Memoirs and Confessions" we have been reading.

   Contemporary readers were soon in a position to know that Hogg was
the author of *Confessions of a Justified Sinner*, despite his attempts to keep
his identity secret. (He planted clues that it was the work of a Glasgow
or West Country author, only to have his name leaked in the "Noctes
Ambrosianae.")[46] The novel presents us with a combination of effects that
seems unprecedented even in the era of radical literary innovation and

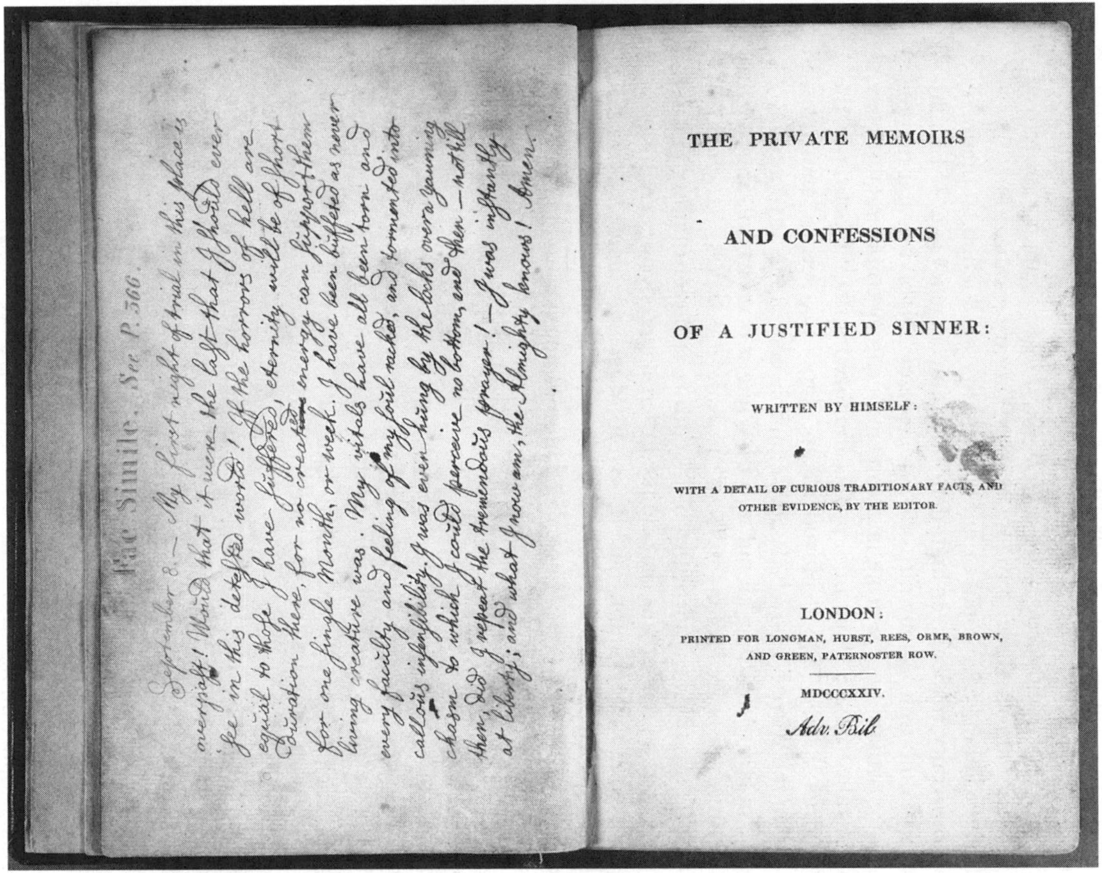

Figure 9.1. "It bears the stamp of authenticity in every line," *Private Memoirs and Confessions of a Justified Sinner* (1824), facsimile and title page. Courtesy of Trustees of the National Library of Scotland.

experimentation we call Romanticism. Here is a work of fiction that goes to unusual lengths to reproduce authenticating devices in the form of documentary evidence—the manuscript facsimile, the letter in *Blackwood's*—and at the same time to conceal the identity of its author, who then appears as a character in his own book, only to announce his refusal to have anything to do with the business of literary production.

Hogg combines two topoi of modern literary production, authenticity and anonymity, that enjoyed high-denomination currency in post-Enlightenment Edinburgh. Anonymity, the signature of "Nobody" that marked the potent volatility of writing in eighteenth-century commercial society, was installed as the trope of a professionalized author function in the *Edinburgh Review* and deployed in an elaborate, serial "anonymity game" in the Waverley novels. Scott's example encouraged a trend in Romantic fiction publishing: all but two of William Blackwood's thirty-five fiction titles appeared anonymously.[47] Raising the stakes, *Blackwood's Magazine* mystified the identities of its editors and contributors in a set of ciphers and pseudonyms that cloaked their aggressive interventions in the postwar Kulturkampf. The *London Magazine* blamed Scott for this bad declension: "The example given by the author of the Scotch Novels in this respect, is leading to a fashion of hoaxing and masquerade, in regard to authorship, which must degrade, and is degrading, the character of our literature."[48] Hogg himself achieved notoriety as both subject and object of *Blackwood's* hoaxes. The "Noctes Ambrosianae" pushed the game playing to saturnalian extremes: in an effective reversal of anonymity, other authors took over the Ettrick Shepherd and made him a mouthpiece for organic nationalist fantasias. By the early 1820s anonymity and its disreputable double, pseudonymity, occupied the scandalous, bellicose arena of party politics rather than an empyrean sphere of "literary authority."

Antiquarian discourse, meanwhile, had generated the authenticating conventions of documentation and editorial commentary since the seventeenth century. Mined for satire by the Augustan wits, its legitimacy was renewed in the modern nationalist collections of ancient poetry, ballads, and other organic literary and vernacular forms. Susan Stewart describes the "eighteenth-century crisis in authenticity" associated with Macpherson and Chatterton as a reaction formation of the modernization of literary production in Great Britain. As literature becomes a commercial object (a printed book for sale) it seeks to recuperate its "contexts," a lost world of organic relations of production, by representing itself as a relic of precapitalist origins. This recuperation takes place as a formal dynamic, a rhetoric of authentication, internal to the literary object: hence the series of eighteenth-century scandals in which a literary original turned out to be an invention, a writing grounded on nothing but its own act of writing. Stewart suggests that the novel—the modern, commercial, disenchanted genre par excellence—occupies an antithetical relation to the poetic project of a nostalgic simulation of origins, which it eventually subsumes. The mimetic and heteroglossic technology of novelistic realism, presumably, absorbs those attenuated shades of context within its more robustly secular, metonymic domain, rendering supererogatory a rhetoric of authentication.[49]

Scott's novels took over with a vengeance the authenticating devices of romance revival—editorial frames, antiquarian commentary, the citation of documentary sources—to establish the technical repertoire of what Fiona Robertson has called "fictions of authenticity."[50] Far from withering away under the inexorable rise of the novel, authenticity gains a heightened prominence in the tropes of authorial anonymity and self-representation that Hogg takes up in the *Confessions of a Justified Sinner.* Unusually for Scott, the editorial frame of *Redgauntlet* manifests itself at the close (rather than opening) of the novel in the form of a "Conclusion, by Dr Dryasdust, in a Letter to the Author of Waverley" (378–80). Dryasdust, an antiquarian persona invoked in earlier Waverley novels, reports several examples of what the title page of the *Confessions of a Justified Sinner* calls "traditionary facts and other evidence": an article in the *Whitehall Gazette,* a marriage contract in a family archive, the oral testimonies of an Edinburgh street porter and a Jacobite priest. This evidence flaunts its unreliability, its invented or fictive character, as it wraps up the novel's plots, emptying them into burlesque (the obsessive litigant who drops dead in court of a "perplexity fit") or generating a parodic, or maybe utopian, variant of the story we have been reading (instead of joining modern civil society, the feudal heir recedes into the folkloric world that has come to his rescue). Scott's editorial frame executes a set of strategies apparently opposite to Hogg's. His intervention insists on the narrative's fictional status, it makes urbane mockery of the structure of authentication, and it keeps the biographical figure of the author out of sight—even as Scott's identity as "the Author of *Waverley,*" although formally still a secret, was widely accepted by 1824.

If the original of the Author of *Waverley* is not visible in his own text (either in the fiction or the paratext), where might we find him? Lockhart's *Life of Scott* awards *Redgauntlet* a privileged place in the canon. Developing a strategy initiated by Scott himself in the editorial apparatus of the "Magnum Opus" edition, Lockhart casts *Redgauntlet* as the most autobiographical of the Waverley novels: "it contains perhaps more of the author's personal experiences than any other of them, or even than all the rest put together," featuring characters (including the author's father), events (his first love affair) and other details drawn from Scott's childhood and youth. Lockhart's detection of this vein of autobiographical reference proved decisive for later biographers, who base much of their information about Scott's early life on the evidence of the novel.[51] Indeed, the *Life of Scott* institutes the circular logic that sustains modern literary biography, whereby the works generate the meaning of the life supposed to be their explanatory ground.

Scott's and Hogg's novels thus represent themselves as occupying very different relations to the Romantic source topoi of authenticity (designating a cultural-historical origin behind the text) and the author (a personal origin behind the text). In *Redgauntlet*, Scott's topical apparatus insinuates itself, until the last few pages, largely through allusion to the prior canon of Waverley novels, while the author is likewise absorbed into a purely conventional figure—until his presence "behind" the text, guaranteed by never being named, becomes visible, after Scott's death, on the plane of biographical reference: after the novel chronologically, but before it etiologically. Literary biography establishes the tradition according to which the author is the origin of the work, subsuming other cultural, historical, and documentary sources, which are in any case flagged within the text as his own inventions. Fictionality guarantees, as it is guaranteed by, the author's invisible, informing "real presence." In the *Confessions of a Justified Sinner*, however, James Hogg is not only named but makes a formal appearance in the editorial frame. At the same time, this James Hogg—the Ettrick Shepherd who rebuffs the literati and holds fast to his georgic world—cannot be the same person as the nameless, alienated author of the book we are reading. The author does not occupy the station of an origin anterior to the novel's thematic of a metaphysically disastrous doubling and splitting.

The appearance of a work of fiction in mock-antiquarian disguise, as a found manuscript edited for modern readers, dates back at least to the origins of the modern novel in *Don Quixote*. Horace Walpole reinvented the convention in the *The Castle of Otranto*, where he made the historicizing feint—crucial for Scott—of invoking a premodern register of cultural difference.[52] Nor is the appearance of the author as a character in his own novel without precedent. Although there are earlier instances in (once again) *Don Quixote*, Aphra Behn's *Oroonoko* (1688), and Delarivier Manley's *New Atalantis* (1709), a Scottish example, Smollett's *Humphry Clinker* (1771), provides a closer precedent, splitting the figure of the author in two. He shows up embedded in the satirical milieu of metropolitan sophistication as one "S——," who, exhibiting none of "the outward signs of authorship," is able to live by his writing, free from "patronage" or "dependence." S——'s protoprofessional integrity is marked by an ambiguous blankness—he is literally a "character," a cipher. Later the story alights on the banks of Loch Lomond, "the Arcadia of Scotland," and quotes a poem by "Dr Smollett" celebrating the author's birthplace as a

"Pure stream"—literally (in the novel's topographical allegory) a source, unsullied and transparent.[53] The author of *Humphry Clinker* remains divided, between the name at home in the Highlands and the "S——" among fools and knaves in London.

Humphry Clinker alludes several times to the literary event that founded an invention of Scottish cultural origins on a scandalously disputed authenticity: the publication of James Macpherson's alleged translations of the ancient heroic poetry of the Highlands in the early 1760s. The "Poems of Ossian" effectively inaugurate the modern tradition of works of historical fiction supported by an antiquarian apparatus, with the crucial difference that in this case the authentication was meant to be taken literally. The "authenticity effect" (to adapt James Buzard's term) advertises a problematical, unstable boundary between history and fiction, evidence and invention, textual surface and ontological depth. Far from being anomalous, it is a cornerstone of modern Scottish national representation.[54] The controversy over the authenticity of Ossian exposed the predicament of tradition in modernity, with the first term conceptualized as a transmission of origins and the second as a radical break. What could reliably connect the present with a lost past? Samuel Johnson challenged Macpherson to exhibit the manuscript originals of the poems, and Macpherson's prevarication encouraged the verdict that he had faked them. Although Macpherson based his texts on oral traditions as well as manuscript remains, he lacked an adequate theorization of oral tradition in a modern culture aggressively committed to the authenticity of the written word. The Ossian affair has been read as expressing a critical relation between literary culture and a vanishing (or occluded) primitive orality.[55] It also brings into focus a categorical crisis in the material forms of writing as the medium or sublime substance of a modern national culture: in the relation between printed text, a mechanically reproduced and multiplied commodity, and manuscript, the trace of an authentic, unrepeatable act of invention.

It is to this crisis that the frontispiece of the *Private Memoirs and Confessions of a Justified Sinner* alludes. A printed simulation of a manuscript (the ghost of an original hand) confronts a title page that flaunts the categorical abstractions of an industrial print culture. Hogg's authenticity effects address not only, not even primarily, a residual, metaphysical nostalgia for orality, but an emergent, modern idealization of writing as a transfigured mode or medium of industrial production: one that closes the circuit of the human by securing, at one end, the purposeful labor of an individual author and, at the other, the corporate identity of a national public. Clifford Siskin has argued that this sublime circuit of writing—folding author, reader, and nation into a unified organic formation—comes decisively together in Romanticism under the disciplinary title of "literature." According to Siskin (and, in an analogous argument, to Friedrich Kittler), the Romantic emergence of "literature" marks the historical point at which the modern technology of writing is at once industrialized (turned into machinery) and naturalized (phantasmatically reattached to the body). Nothing less than the primary technology through which modernization realizes itself as a project, writing is made to seem an organic extension or function of human life. This naturalization takes place, crucially, in the Romantic-era novel, which identifies literacy with developmental narratives of individual and national subject formation.[56]

Scott's novels rehearse this very process: binding together the plots of personal, historical, and literary development, installing by example a national cultural formation. At the same time, the variety of fictions by Scottish authors opens up a set of critical disturbances in this cultural historiography. It makes a crucial difference to read them as products of a Scottish, not just an English or even a British, literary history, not least because "writing," "English," and "literature" occupied historically different relations for authors and readers in modern Scotland. The novels of Scott, notoriously, alienate post-Victorian readers through their resistance to naturalization at the level of style, in part because those readers have absorbed the achievement of Scott's contemporary Jane Austen, who perfected the stylistic technique of naturalization in free indirect discourse. Scott's English clings with a rigorous heaviness to the page, severed from the lively imitation of Scots speech and thus from a homological bonding of speaking, writing, and consciousness. Readers continue to read, that is, the burden of historical and institutional mediations—constituting the practice of literacy and the object of literature—that made English the language of an imperial political economy in Scotland. Writing, as English, continues to bear an excess (manifest in the work of reading) that keeps visible the machinery of a national subject formation which abstracts its users from a vernacular (organic) community.[57] The gap between speech and literacy remains evident, generative in its openness rather than through a naturalizing closure. (*Ringan Gilhaize*, with its monological narration in a "distressed" vernacular Scots, reimposes a metaphysical rather than naturalizing closure.) Penny Fielding has analyzed the structural contradictions of the figure of orality posited by Scottish Romantic writing as at once its abject other (popular illiteracy, symptom of modern social fragmentation) and lost origin (fantasia of an organic ancestral culture). Orality, that is, keeps reflecting back the aporia that constitutes the metaphysical and sociohistorical substance of writing.[58] Articulating this aporia, making it visible as the principle that at once drives and limits narrativity, *Redgauntlet* and *Confessions of a Justified Sinner* project functionally contrasting abstractions of their own work of writing, in the respective figures of fiction and textuality.

Stewart argues that figures of origin can only receive authentication through more writing, further textual production, in the form of editorial and documentary supplements.[59] Johnson's critique of Ossian exposed the circularity of such logic—the (at best) prematurity of its claim on cultural origins. The promoters of Ossian, he scoffed, "remember names, and perhaps some proverbial sentiments; and, having no distinct ideas, coin a resemblance without an original."[60] The strong solution to such a critique was to insist on the act of invention that coins a resemblance *as* an original. It would be Scott's solution. The first of Scott's metrical romances, *The Lay of the Last Minstrel*, and his first novel, *Waverley*, are allusively steeped in Ossian, which they swallow whole (scandal and all) by insisting on their status as inventions, works of fiction, even as they invoke historical evidence and traditionary sources. The effect is amplified in the more elaborate antiquarian framework of the "Magnum Opus" edition: "In Scott's notably fluid stratagems of authenticity and fictionality," writes Robertson, "source becomes story just as surely as, in the increasingly referential world of the first-edition frames, story becomes source."[61] The self-referencing rhetoric of fiction subsumes (but does not cancel) the burden of historical reference, perfecting a paradoxical logic of authentication.

In the wake of the Ossian scandal the modern nation could be recovered and circulated as a fiction, founded not in metaphysical properties, in causal connections, but in the shared associations—articulated in aesthetic categories, sustained through acts of commercial and sympathetic exchange—of its participating subjects: in other words, a reading public. This is the epochal invention of Scott's historical romances, far more consequential than their ideological reduction by his protégés at *Blackwood's*. The Nation-as-Romance assumed garish colours in the political spectacle that crowned civic life in postwar Edinburgh, the tartan-festooned state visit of George IV, discussed in the opening pages of this book. Scott's pageant exerted symbolic power precisely through the conspicuousness of its fictional devices: ideology, as Žižek reminds us, "*is not an illusion.*"[62] Seeing that it is only a show, the public is invited freely to take part, rather than coerced into believing in something "real." The viewer's and reader's assent to the representation takes place as an assent to—a recognition of—its fictional character. Such representations already assume their own demystification as a condition of access to them. In proffering the authenticity effect as the very device that yields the recognition of fictionality, Scott invokes a quintessentially modern, liberal ideology of reception, which relies upon recognition, consensus, and participation, rather than requiring a "primitive," naïve or fetishistic, subjectivity of belief—which will reassert itself in modern conditions, as we see in

Redgauntlet and *Confessions of a Justified Sinner,* in the antagonistic formation of fanaticism.

Nationalism theory tends to posit a more-or-less-unified reading public at this era of its inception, constituting the subjective field of the imagined community. Literary historians have described, in contrast, the fragmentation of the Romantic-era reading public along lines of political, religious, class, and gender difference in the periodicals that called it into being.[63] Certain Radical reviewers, reassessing Scott's achievement on the occasion of his death, gave him the credit—more forcefully for their opposition to his politics—for establishing the novel as the strong cultural form that absorbs and regulates such differences to produce a unified figure of the nation.[64] Scott's novels, however, mark this united reading public as itself a fiction, a provisional and experimental construct, as they continue to invoke a divided readership. The novels appeal to those who see through the fiction (of national cohesion, of historical progress, of liberal participation) as well as those who do not, who are in thrall to its illusions and accept it all as "real." Rather like Leo Strauss's formula for management of a liberal democracy, the novels invoke an elite readership, encoded in their dense texture of literary and historical allusion, and a naïve or popular readership that identifies with the characters and reads for the plot. Crucially, however, this distinction reflects a rhetorical or temporal difference within the subjectivity of reading more than it does actual, objectively different audiences. The "naïve reader" is a figure projected by these texts for our own indulgence, an aspect of ourselves, as we are doubled and divided between mental states of enlightened freedom and a primitive, irrational bondage. This structural doubling and division of the reader within the work of fiction necessarily destabilizes a specific ideological content, as Scott's reception history shows.[65]

Robert Mudie, afterwards the debunker of Edinburgh's metropolitan pretensions, describes one of the official banquets held during the king's visit: "Lord Ashburton proposed a toast, which was that of a national monument, —one that would last when a monument of stone and mortar had passed away—'The author of Waverley, whoever he may be, and his works.' "[66] The speaker identifies a real presence behind the pageant of sovereignty, the facsimile Jacobite King and his doubles, the National Monument, the Modern Athens: the transcendental figure of an author who covertly informs, as he is given a kind of immortality by, his works. Lockhart relates how Scott went walking in the streets with Home Secretary Peel during the royal visit, and despite his modest disclaimer was hailed by the crowd. If alderman Sir William Curtis mirrored a phony King of the Scots, Sir Walter Scott (at one point himself clad in Campbell tartans) appeared to be the sovereign's true shadow in a modern, postabsolutist and postnational age, poised equivocally between competing fictions of democracy and legitimacy—insofar as he was sovereignty's author.

The frontispiece of Robert Chambers's *Illustrations of the Author of Waverley* (1825) follows Scott's own self-representation, in the novel prefaces of the early 1820s, of "the Eidolon, or Representation, of the Author of Waverley," a figure as "closely veiled and wimpled" as the hermaphrodite Nature of Spenser's *Mutabilitie* Cantoes.[67] The difference between this veiled eidolon and its eighteenth-century precursors lies in the allusion to a celebrity whose identity has already been published and is now concealed. Astute readers would have recognized the bust behind the veil from Henry Raeburn's widely diffused portrait of Scott the minstrel (1808), whose signed productions preceded those of the Author of *Waverley*. The "Great Unknown" does not denote, in other words, a merely anonymous persona, a blank, but a known name's public reclamation of private cover—that "lair of the skull" which is the secret site of the imagination for author as well as for reader, behind the apparatus of the production, circulation and reception of printed books.[68] The veiled eidolon, his anonymity founded on his fame, crucially precedes the modern, Victorian cult of the author, which will offer instead (in the frontispiece to the Abbotsford Edition of the Waverley Novels, 1842)[69] a miraculous, metabiographical proliferation of Scott's visage, as though to make up for the years behind the veil. Jonah Siegel and David Brewer have argued that Scott's anonymity games provided for the strategic assertion of (respectively) authorial originality and proprietorship in an industrial print culture steeped in his inventions.[70] The veiled author is the emanation, I have been arguing, of the fictiveness of his own works, sustained and regulated by the social, consensual medium of a national reading public that recognizes and accepts the currency of their conventions, as the stock of an intimate human image—the face behind the veil—we hope may be our own.

Lockhart's authentication of an autobiographical presence in *Redgauntlet* gives body to the phantom of an original presence guaranteed by the veil of anonymity. It glosses the strategy by which *Redgauntlet* revisits the topoi of Scott's earlier Scottish novels in order to reaffirm, with scintillating prowess, their aesthetic and ideological principles: that history, nationality, and legitimacy are fictional constructions we fully possess in knowing them as such. Our recognition of their fictive status authenticates our privileged condition as liberal subjects who lend ourselves willingly to the discipline of illusion. The editorial conclusion of *Redgauntlet* enacts a terminal recession of the narrative into the condition of fiction, which it represents, hauntingly, as an essence of storytelling that precedes and outlasts the novel's material boundaries. Dr. Dryasdust, in his "Letter to the Author of Waverley," quotes one of his oral sources:

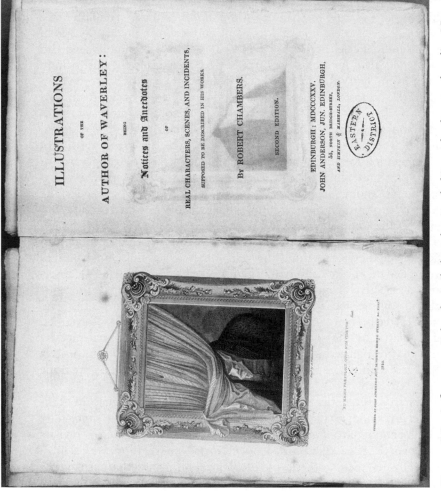

Figure 9.2. A figure as "closely veiled and wimpled" as the hermaphrodite Nature of Spenser's Mutability Cantoes, Robert Chambers, *Illustrations of the Author of Waverley* (2nd edition, 1825): frontispiece and title page. Courtesy of Trustees of the National Library of Scotland.

Figure 9.3. Astute readers would have recognized the bust behind the veil. Henry Raeburn's portrait of Scott (1808), commissioned by Constable and engraved by J. Horsburgh; trimmed version from *Peter's Letters to His Kinsfolk*, vol. 2. Author's collection.

"Willie, and a friend he had, they called Robin the Rambler, gae them warning, by playing tunes such as, 'the Campbells are coming,' and the like, whereby they got timeous warning to take the wing." I need not point out to your acuteness [*adds Dryasdust*] that this seems to refer to some inaccurate account of the transactions in which you seem so much interested. (379)

Oral tradition vindicates itself with this "inaccurate account," in which the feudal heir is absorbed into the Burnsian persona of "Rob the Rambler" instead of joining modern civil society, and popular minstrelsy comes to the rescue of the Jacobite conspirators. For rather than an "inaccurate account" this is surely a variant, a distinctive feature of oral tradition. Roberto Calasso makes a distinction between myth, kept alive in a culture by the proliferation of variants, and "the novel, *a narrative deprived of variants*," which "attempts to recover them by making the single text to which it is entrusted more dense, more detailed"—the familiar novelistic effects of heteroglossia, a referentially saturated social and historical mimesis, and so on.[71] *Redgauntlet* ends with the dissolution—the release—of its characters and plots into the unreliable but also, therefore, unconditional realm of popular tradition, which represents not so much an earlier historical stage as a pure, frictionless economy of storytelling. The novel draws upon this economy to entertain the very possibilities it is ostensibly, programmatically, shutting down; or rather, its pages provide the only place where we may catch the echoes and shadows of those possibilities, not so much shut down as subject to an interminable deferral. This at once melancholic and utopian domain is modern rather than ancient, in that it corresponds to the perpetual, profit-coining circulation of Scott's own tales in a culture (a reading public) that they themselves make up: fiction as inexhaustible surplus, cultural production as the sublime, redemptive double of an industrial political economy.

Such a conclusion is remote from that of *The Private Memoirs and Confessions of a Justified Sinner*, which leaves its reader with a baffling dissolution into the terminal literary condition not of fiction as a sublimated mode of production but of textuality, troped as a negative production of waste matter. Robert Wringhim is unable to inhabit history as though it were a fiction. Fanaticism stands for a fatal relation to history unmediated by aesthetic reflection. Robert's sense of his destiny is that above all it is written down: "written in the book of life" (69). In the antinarrative structure of predestinarian theology beginnings and ends are already scripted, finished, closed: "I was now a justified person, adopted among the number of God's children—my name written in the Lamb's book of life, and . . . no bypast transgression, nor any future act of my own, or of any other man, could be instrumental in altering the decree" (79). No variants are possible here.

If Robert is written down, his friend Gil-Martin is a reader, whose perspicuous scrutiny reduces persons to figures—to "characters" in the sense of inscriptions on a surface. This reading obliterates the ontological distinctions that the liberal programs of literacy are invoked to secure:[72]

[B]y contemplating a face minutely, I not only attain the same likeness, but, with the likeness, I attain the very same ideas as well as the same mode of arranging them, so that, you see, by looking at a person attentively, I by degrees assume his likeness, and by assuming his likeness I attain to the possession of his most secret thoughts. (86)

Gil-Martin's confession, relentlessly parsing the logic of sympathy, exposes its textual basis as well as the fantasy of Enlightenment despotism. We are not surprised to find him reading an actual book, the text of which provokes extraordinary sensations:

> I came up to him and addressed him, but he was so intent on his book, that, though I spoke, he lifted not his eyes. I looked on the book also, and still it seemed a Bible, having columns, chapters, and verses; but it was in a language of which I was wholly ignorant, and all intersected with red lines, and verses. A sensation resembling a stroke of electricity came over me, on first casting my eyes on that mysterious book, and I stood motionless. (85)

Illegibility is the point, the effect of writing viewed from outside itself. The electric shock Wringhim feels is the charge of an abstract textuality, a printed sign system unattached to human hand or voice. The Devil's book is a text for one reader only—it does not circulate in an economy, it does not constitute a culture. It is as though, in a blinding glimpse, Hogg's novel divines its own fate: a book of the damned, outcast from literary tradition, unreadable until an appropriately infernal later age.[73]

The editor of the *Memoirs and Confessions* complains that he cannot understand whether the document is a fable, an allegory, the ravings of a lunatic, or some other kind of writing:

> What can this work be? Sure, you will say, it must be an allegory; or (as the writer calls it) a religious PARABLE, showing the dreadful danger of self-righteousness? I cannot tell. (165)
>
> With regard to the work itself, I dare not venture a judgment, for I do not understand it. I believe no person, man or woman, will ever peruse it with the same attention that I have done, and yet I confess that I do not comprehend the writer's drift. (174–75)

The editor finds himself too in the position of one who confesses: here, the inadequacy of his binary categories—history or allegory, authenticity or hoax, reason or delusion—to interpret the story. In contrast to *Redgauntlet*, this access of dubiety across the frame narrative discredits rather than confirms the editor's mediating role. With the scenario of a document unearthed from the grave, Hogg literalizes, as we saw in chapter seven, the central metaphor of modern antiquarian revival: the recovery of "remains," "reliques," or "fragments" of a departed organic culture, registered in the style of a relentless empiricism:

> There was one thing I could not help remarking, that in the inside of one of the shoes there was a layer of cow's dung, about one eighth of an inch thick,

and in the hollow of the sole fully one fourth of an inch. It was firm, green, and fresh; and proved that he had been working in a byre. (172)

The sinner's body, reduced to a lower half that dissolves into slime, and its accessory, the manuscript "wrapped so close together, and so damp, rotten, and yellow, that it seemed one solid piece" (173), partake metaphorically as well as metonymically of that dung. The Calvinist doctrinal scheme invoked in the novel casts body and text as an excremental residue, like the reprobate sinner to whom they belong, like the material world itself: God's waste products.

The Confessions of a Justified Sinner predicts its own condition as an outcast text, not to be brought to life in a reader's imagination, circulated in a market or perpetuated in a tradition, as a perversely exhilarating gloss on its author's failure to emulate Sir Walter Scott's career as a wealthy and distinguished author of historical romances. Alert to the biographical resonance, commentators have underestimated the reach of the abyss opened at the end of the novel, suggesting a secure foundation in the reader's act of interpretation, or else in the traditional popular community of the author's origins.[74] The suicide's grave swallows author and reader as well as narrator and editor. We too, like "James Hogg," find ourselves doubled and split, without the Smithian consolation of induction into a society—at any rate, not until the twentieth century, when the canonization of accursed books brought *The Confessions of a Justified Sinner* to a public after all.[75] We could say that Hogg's novel adumbrates a condition outside literature—a perspective from which literature becomes visible as a political economy, a set of stratifying codes and practices, a material product and "remains."[76] But the conditions of that knowledge stay within the operations and devices of literacy and the subjectivity produced by it, revolving obsessively about the figures of its own production. Fiction, for Scott, reaffirms a social and ordinary reality, since fiction is the medium—the imaginary commerce—through which common life is sustained and reproduced. But textuality, in Hogg's novel, marks a lethal alienation from common life in its original condition of a traditional community, which, as the medium of natural belief, cannot be recovered in the commodity form of a fiction. For Hogg, as for ourselves, there is no access to that lost world except as another text.

Chapter 10

❧

A NEW SPIRIT OF THE AGE

A PAPER ECONOMY

Read *Elizth. de Bruce*—it is very clever but does not show much originality: the characters though very entertaining are in the manner of other authors and the finishd and filld up portraits of which the sketches are to be found elsewhere. One is too apt to feel on such occasions the pettied resentment that you might entertain against one who had poachd on your manor. But the case is quite different, and a claim set up on having been the first who betook himself to the illustration of some particular class of characters or department of life is no more a right of monopoly than that asserted by the old buccaneers by setting up a wooden cross and killing an Indian or two on some new discoverd Island. If they can make anything of their first discovery the better luck theirs; if not, let others come, penetrate further into the country, write descriptions, make drawings or settlements at their pleasure.
—Scott, *Journal*, 27 January 1827

In 1826 readers were puzzled, amused, and instructed by a new publication called *The Cook and Housewife's Manual; Containing the Most Approved Modern Receipts for Making Soups, Gravies, Sauces, Ragouts and Made-dishes*—puzzled, as well as amused and instructed, because the self-styled cookery book begins by posing as a sequel to a recent novel by the Author of *Waverley*. The title page ascribes the work to "Mrs Margaret Dods, of the Cleikum Inn, St Ronan's," the doughty, old-fashioned landlady in *Saint Ronan's Well* (1824). *The Cook and Housewife's Manual* picks up Scott's secondary characters where the end of his novel left them. Peregrine Touchwood, the vehement and fussy Nabob, continues to reside at the Cleikum Inn, consoling himself with an attempt to teach his hostess "an entirely new system . . . of rational practical cookery."[1] The arrival of a character from another Scottish novel, the gourmand Dr. Redgill from Susan Ferrier's *Marriage*, inspires Touchwood to convene "the CLEIKUM CLUB," a convivial society dedicated to gastronomic improvement.[2]

Touchwood's introductory address to the Club features a deft parody of Enlightenment stadial history. Proceeding from first principles ("Man is a cooking animal"), Touchwood traces the "ages of cookery" from "the hairy man of the woods . . . digging his roots with his claws" through the "ferocious hunter, gnawing the half-broiled bloody collop, torn from the still reeking carcass," the "pastoral" age of milk, broth, and barley, "the chivalrous or feudal age" of roast wild boars and swans, up to the present (32–35). When the lecture arrives at the first of the modernizing revolutions in Scottish history, however, it sticks at a formal and ideological crux: the intersection between this (Whig, Enlightenment) plot of universal improvement and a (Tory, Romantic) historiography that cherishes the relics of a vanishing past. The Reformation set back the development of British gastronomy by centuries, since monasteries had been seats of fine feeding: "Popery and made-dishes, Mr Cargill, —Episcopacy, roast-beef and plum-pudding, —and what is left to Presbytery, but its lang-kail brose and mashlum bannocks?" (22). Only quite recently have Oxford Colleges and Bishops' palaces initiated a culinary renaissance. This is a recognizeable burlesque, as Andrew Monnickendam notes, of cultural history according to the Waverley novels.[3]

"Meg Dods" follows this introductory matter with a chapter on "Scotch National Dishes" (48–58) in the sentimental-satiric vein of *Blackwood's* cultural nationalism: boasting the enrichment of Scots cuisine by French influence (thanks to the Auld Alliance), challenging English taste with details of the preparation of haggis and sheep's head. The second edition of *The Cook and Housewife's Manual* (1827) revised this nationalist emphasis. Scots dishes are demoted to a general chapter on "National Dishes, Scottish, Irish, Welsh, German, and Oriental," which now follows chapters on "Made-Dishes" and "French Cookery" in part 3. The recipe for haggis is expanded, however, with disgusting details:

> Clean a sheep's pluck thoroughly. Make incisions in the heart and liver to allow the blood to flow out, and parboil the whole, letting the wind-pipe lie over the side of the pot to permit the phlegm and blood to disgorge from the lungs; the water may be changed after a few minutes' boiling for fresh water.[4]

In an epilogue, Mrs. Dods defies her southern critics: "Set up their dainty gabs, to skunner at what SIR WALTER himsel, worthy auld MR CHRISTOPHER NORTH—a saunt on earth, —and many mair born gentlemen lick their lips after!" (514).

The author of *The Cook and Housewife's Manual* was Christian Isobel Johnstone, who reproduces Scott's and Ferrier's characters, and Scott's style, with scinitillating panache.[5] With the Cleikum Club Johnstone sets up a rival establishment to the "Noctes Ambrosianae," the famous symposium at Ambrose's tavern serialized in *Blackwood's Magazine*, in which lavish feasts fuel all kinds of conversation, from patriotic and sentimental songs to squibs, flytings, and homilies, attended by characters from contemporary novels as well as fictionalized versions of the Edinburgh literati. (The "Final Sederunt of the Cleikum Club," which closes the second edition of *The Cook and Housewife's Manual* [513–25], reverts to the dialogue form of the "Noctes.") Johnstone's techniques of formal parody (of Scottish novels and historiography) and of mixing kinds and discourses, blurring the boundaries between fiction and reference, are characteristic of the magazine genre of the symposium, a major forum for experimental writing in the 1820s.[6] Magazine reviewers applauded the experiment: "a system of domestic management, displayed on the favourite frame-work of a novel" (*Edinburgh Magazine*); "This alternation of grave and gay is exceedingly agreeable" (*Blackwood's*). Johnstone's 1826 preface defended her "novel attempt of endeavouring to conciliate the lovers of what is called 'light reading,' and to gain their attention, to that which they may consider a vulgar and unimportant art," since "it is the design of this Manual to promote the diffusion of useful knowledge" (7). Johnstone expanded the fictional framework in the second edition, with the addition of the "Final Sederunt," but in the fourth edition (1829) reduced it again (omitting the "Final Sederunt") and increased the book's didactic load. By casting the fictional symposium as framework for a cookery manual, Johnstone reverses the ideological project of the "Noctes"—a militantly masculine as well as Tory takeover of the feminized discourses of domesticity and sentiment—in addition to literalizing the aesthetic basis ("taste") of Blackwoodian cultural nationalism.[7] Johnstone's generic reversal also subsumes the strongest of contemporary national genres, the novel, folding it back into a didactic matrix, the manual of household economy. Not for nothing does Johnstone invoke Scott's sole experiment in what he himself identified as a female-authored genre of domestic national fiction. *Saint Ronan's Well* plays out a pessimistic, satirical and tragic narrative of contemporary manners, in which things fall apart between the vanity of a new dispensation and the decadence of the old.[8]

The Cook and Housewife's Manual was Johnstone's most successful book, running to a tenth edition by her death in 1857. The year after it came out Johnstone published her third and best novel, *Elizabeth de Bruce* (1827). Despite its superiority to *Clan-Albin*, *Elizabeth de Bruce* failed to meet the high expectations of its author and publisher. The vogue for Scottish novels was waning; the 1826 crash had destroyed one of the genre's principal publishers, Constable, as well as ruining its major author, and the book trade remained depressed well into the 1830s. Publishers were growing averse to the high-risk venture of a three-volume novel, especially since the market was showing signs of saturation—Scott, Hogg,

Galt, and Ferrier had produced their best work, and no major new talent or variant appeared on the horizon. After the disappointing reception of *Elizabeth de Bruce*, we find Johnstone resuming the cue of *The Cook and Housewife's Manual*, definitively abandoning the novel for the magazine genres of tale and essay and the instrumentality of "useful knowledge."

Elizabeth de Bruce, highly accomplished as it is, registers the exhaustion of Scottish fiction in the late 1820s. Narrated as though through a series of interlocking quotation marks, it too reads like a pastiche of Scott and Ferrier, with startling infusions from contemporary Irish fiction—a cross between *The Inheritance* and *Guy Mannering* with United Irishmen instead of gypsies. Both Scott and Hogg commented (privately) on what they saw as the novel's lack of originality (indeed, a German translation ascribed *Elizabeth von Bruce* to Scott).[9] Scott's more generous appraisal (quoted at the head of this chapter) acknowledges the work's connoisseurial finish, and reflects wryly on his own relationship to the phenomenon of secondary Scottish novels. The reflection turns on Scott's own conquest of terrain first opened up by women novelists, some of whom (adding piquancy to the colonization metaphor) were Irish.[10] Hogg's comment acknowledges that originality may be a gendered concern: "I have great faults to Mrs Johnston's work in which there is however great genius but the anachronisms are without end and the characters too much borrowed from Scott[.] Beyond all the story is forced and beyond all measures. Our ladies were pleased with it beyond measure so that it must have something very fascinating."[11]

The "cleverness" noted by contemporary readers refers to Johnstone's allusive play with the topoi of Scottish fiction, a dozen years after *Waverley* and the author's own "national tale" *Clan-Albin*. This retrospect takes account of the ascendancy of Scott and the house of Blackwood since 1815, as well as the catastrophe overshadowing production of the present novel, the 1826 crash. At the same time, Johnstone entangles her Scottish domestic scene and characters with a wild Irish romance plot, in a powerful reprise of the combination of Scottish and Irish characters, settings, and storylines with which she had experimented in *Clan-Albin*. In its reckoning with the impact of Scott and Blackwood on the development of national fiction after Waterloo, *Elizabeth de Bruce* revisits *Clan-Albin* as the marker of a path not taken, exploring the relations between Ireland and Scotland as historical and symbolic sites of literary Romanticism, even as Scottish fiction had appeared to go its separate way.[12] *Elizabeth de Bruce* joins not just settings and scenarios but, in a recombinatory logic, the different genres of Scottish and Irish national fiction, visible now as distinct yet intertwined national developments from the perspective of 1827. We read the diminishing possibilities of a genre that can no longer pretend to recommend a national future but scrutinizes instead the fragility of a present that is the uncertain product of an unfinished past. *Clan-Albin* had combined its Scottish and Irish themes within the Atlantic world horizon of the British empire and Napoleonic wars. The horizontal analogy between dispossessed Highlanders and Irish dialectically yielded—through the historical dynamic of their dispossession, war and empire—a utopian solution in the resettlement of the cleared glen by British veterans. *Elizabeth de Bruce* is darker in every sense: melancholy in tone, opaque and tortuous in the connections it draws between its Scottish domestic setting and British rule in Ireland, "a land of violence and blood—a land divided against itself . . . and the cold stranger trampling on both."[13] The combination of Scottish and Irish narratives yields a plot so "perplexed," "extravagant," and "convoluted" as to defy the reader's ability to follow it.[14] All the same, I attempt a selective summary, since *Elizabeth de Bruce* may be the most recondite of all the novels discussed in *Scott's Shadow*, unfamiliar even to specialists in Scottish and Romantic fiction.

Elizabeth de Bruce is a wild Irish girl fostered in Lowland Scotland, where she grows up amid the genial influences of nature and a postfeudal organic community populated by national-character types drawn from the Waverley novels and Blackwood tales: the sentimental Jacobite laird Monkshaugh, the true-blue Presbyterian minister Gideon Haliburton, the elvish changeling Francie Frisel, the veteran trooper Fugal, and a crowd of eccentric, vagrant, and crazy women (amounting to a burlesque of Scott's propensity for the type). Elizabeth and her friends worry that she has inherited the insanity of her father, a pathologically hypersensitive, opium-addicted Scottish nobleman: "She has the auld blood in her veins. Alas! that such malady should follow it!" (1:60). A kinsman, the financier Hutcheon, looks after Lord de Bruce and the estate, and plots to defraud Elizabeth of her inheritance. Halfway through the novel he dispossesses the organic community by calling in its debts.

Meanwhile Elizabeth's husband, gallant young officer Wolfe Grahame, crosses over to "the wild, broken world of Ireland" (3:132) to help put down the United Irishmen rising. This event, like Edward Waverley's departure for Scotland, sets the story in motion; like Waverley, Grahame will fall into rebel hands and be suspected of disloyalty. Grahame compares the Irish insurgents with those Scottish Jacobites who opposed the Union out of an honorable patriotism (1:221), and so fulfils the promise of his name—a compound of Scottish and Irish romantic rebels from both ends of the political spectrum: Grahame of Montrose (redeeming, no doubt, given the novel's reflections on the "Killing Time," Grahame of Claverhouse) with (beneath the official namesake, General Wolfe of Quebec) United Irishman leader Wolf Tone. In the most striking episodes of *Elizabeth de Bruce*, Wolfe's Irish expedition takes him into a colonial heart of darkness. Johnstone gives an unequivocally sympathetic representation of the Irish rebels, identifying them with the country's Gaelic and Catholic population, and dwells on the atrocities perpetrated by government forces. Wolfe and his party encounter a gruesome object nailed over the courtyard of an inn: "It was a human head, blackened and purpled, the eyes starting from their sockets, the muscles of the face strained as if in the last agony of violent suffocation. Such spectacles were at this period not uncommon in Ireland" (2:330–31). This is the handiwork of Justice O'Toole, "the Protestant flail." The local leader of the insurgents, patterned after the Milesian Prince in Owenson's *Wild Irish Girl*, is the dispossessed chieftain O'Connor of the West (another resonant name). He turns out to be the father of Elizabeth's tragic mother Aileen. Wolfe falls in with O'Connor's lieutenant, Dennis Slattery, who at first plays a national stereotype—the treacherous comic servant, like Joe Kelly in Edgeworth's *Ennui*—before acceding to heroic status. He is last seen striking down O'Toole with a "wild Irish whoop" of "Erin go bragh!" as he escapes from a party of redcoats.

We learn that the gentle lunatic de Bruce is not Elizabeth's father after all. De Bruce was betrothed to Aileen O'Connor; but Aileen's wicked aunt and uncle, having abjured their Catholic faith to gain legal title to the O'Connor estates, arranged for their son to carry off the bride on the eve of the wedding and marry her himself. Elizabeth is the issue of this forced marriage. She thus embodies, at the story's mysterious origins, a reversal of the standard national-tale plotting of Union: the daughter of a rape that exemplifies the traumatic dispossession of the native nobility, perpetuated in the anti-Catholic penal statutes. Elizabeth herself is untainted by the violence of her origin, just as the revelation of that origin frees her from the threat of the hereditary insanity of the de Bruces. (In an Edgeworthian insistence on the force of nurture over nature, the de Bruce hereditary taint is most threatening as an idea.) A concluding variation on the formula of Union pronounces her "a true-born native of Scotland, though an Irish heiress" (3:385).

Scotland, for the heroine, is the site of a beneficent Romantic fostering which heals the wounds of the past. The organic community itself performs the symbolic function allotted to the nurse in Scottish and Irish fiction, according to Katie Trumpener, the domestication and feminization of tradition.[15] Removal from her Irish origins, and from a turbulent Irish history, has endowed Elizabeth with a natural innocence and grace. It is as though Ireland has receded into the deep past of Celtic ancestral memory. Aileen O'Connor appears to her daughter in this kindly setting as the fairy queen of Lowland ballads: the figures of Irish history, consigned to a folkloric otherworld, maintain a liminal psychic presence in childhood if not (any more) in actual rural communities. Analogously, the bloody civil conflicts of Scottish history are sublimated into the interminable comic and sentimental talk—the substance of "national character"—that takes the place of action for entire chapters of *Elizabeth de Bruce*.

At the same time, the trope of hereditary insanity clarifies Scotland's function as site of a problematic forgetting, as much as a healing or purification, of an unfinished national history of injustice and cruelty. The matter of Ireland, metonymically and genetically proximate to provincial Scotland, is not in the end absorbed into the Scottish scene, tranquillized in legend and fiction. The novel closes with a grievous remembrance of loss, in the story of Elizabeth's parents, scarcely redeemed by the virtuous innocence that has blossomed in the ruins. The union between Elizabeth and Wolfe (already consummated at the novel's opening) can no longer bear, as it did in earlier national romances, the allegorical burden of a larger history; at best it offers a tentative, merely private hope for the future. "There was a prank," sniffs one of the heroine's de Bruce relatives, "to cross the breed of our ain family daftness with red-wode Irish madness!" (2:231). Elizabeth, no de Bruce at all, is entirely the offpsring of "red-wode Irish madness"—and her innocence exposes the true place of that madness outside the self, in imperial history. Johnstone demystifies the hackneyed theme of "Irish madness" by casting it as a material, historical, and political disorder, the name for a national experience of dispossession, struggle, and grief. And for that madness the novel foresees no cure.

The prominence of the United Irishmen rising in *Elizabeth de Bruce* does not so much look back to earlier Irish national tales (such as Edgeworth's *Ennui*, 1809, or Maturin's *The Milesian Chief*, 1812) as sideways and forward. In the years leading up to the 1829 Catholic Emancipation Act a spate of Irish novels revisited the events of 1798, including titles by John and Michael Banim, Sydney Morgan, and James McHenry. Johnstone's strong treatment of the rebellion declares an affiliation with these novels and recognizes Irish history as the contemporary political horizon of her own work. Ina Ferris has linked this late development of the national tale to the success of Daniel O'Connell's Catholic Association in "[forging] a new Irish public and a new hybrid politics of demand, bringing Ireland into the modern political arena":

Actively participating in this process, the national tale became the novel of insurgency, as writers deliberately summoned rankling memories of the 1798 rising as part of the emancipation campaign. Taking the form of engaged "recollection," such novels underline that on Irish ground the writing of history typically blocked both nostalgic "memorial" and impersonal "knowledge," so throwing off balance a British discourse that sought to sustain itself on an ethos of distance, moderation and impersonality.[16]

The wounds of the past—only thirty years since—are open and bleeding. "1798 was not part of a surmounted past in the Ireland of 1828 as was 1745, at least in Scott's reading of Scottish history, in the Scotland that saw the publication of *Waverley* in 1814." Against Scott's example, and against earlier national tales' invocation of Union as an "end of history," the late-1820s "novels of 1798 thus *summon* the past, specifically the insurrection, to enforce a present demand, and in so doing they draw attention to the way in which the matter of Ireland made it impossible to overlook the dependence of history (as representation of the past) on its status as an enunciation in and for the present."[17]

Elizabeth de Bruce brings this development back home to Scotland, as it takes up the Irish novel's "summoning of the past" for its critical reflection on the Scottish novel's uneasy reckoning with modernity. Scott's novels provided the dominant narrative form of that "ethos of distance, moderation and impersonality" in the post-Waterloo decade, with their performance of a "(tolerant) modern mediation of the heated differences of the (intolerant) past."[18] The introductory chapter of *Old Mortality* establishes the trope of a tranquil modern "distance" from civil strife in the elegiac setting of a country churchyard:

> Death has indeed been here, and its traces are before us; but they are softened and deprived of their horror by our distance from the period when they have been first impressed. Those who sleep beneath are only connected with us by the reflection that they have once been what we now are, and that, as their reliques are now identified with their mother earth, ours shall, at some future period, undergo the same transformation.[19]

The passage of time decomposes the social and political antagonisms that drive historical process into the universal, organic condition of death: old mortality. "O, rake not up the ashes of our fathers!" Scott's narrator appeals (quoting from John Home's *Douglas*) at the end of this introductory chapter. In the narrative that follows *Old Mortality* does exactly that. Scott's treatment of the late-seventeenth-century Covenanter insurgency reopened, rather than settled, debates about the status and legacy of Presbyterian radicalism in the postwar present. In the decade-long controversy that stormed around *Old Mortality*—in reviews and magazines, in rival fictions of the "Killing Time"—other writers followed Scott's novel in summoning the past to address the claims of the present, resisting what they saw as a Tory colonization of national memory.

Elizabeth de Bruce repeatedly invokes the 1679 Covenanter insurrection, the matter of *Old Mortality*, rather than the 1745 Jacobite rising, the matter of *Waverley*, as the Scottish analogue to its Irish history. The opening chapter cites "1679" as the cipher of a guilty secret history: as the de Bruce mansion burns to the ground, spectators imagine "the ghost of the Lady de Bruce who got foul play in that dark house" hovering above the flames (1:15). A couple of chapters later Gideon Haliburton compares the United Irishmen rebellion with the "Killing Time," when government troops persecuted the guardians of Scotland's religious and civil liberties: "Our ain brave auld Scotland, in her day of treading down and humiliation, felt this scourge, —when the red hand of the slayer was thrust into her peaceful bosom" (1:63). The violence consigned to Scotland's past, to the consolations of heritage, erupts in contemporary Ireland. Johnstone sustains the analogy between 1679 and 1798:

> Yet it is not wonderful if this dark period was marked by some authorized violence, and by atrocities which, if not authorized, were perchance necessarily winked at. Few generations have passed, even in this peaceful and happy land [Scotland], since torture itself was inflicted on the limbs of free men, not in secret, but as if the brutal office of the hangman had been an object of ambition to men of illustrious birth, who glutted their eyes with the sanguinary spectacles from which shame alone held back their hands. (2:362–63)

The narrator refers to the judicial torture of state prisoners after the defeat of the Covenanter army at Bothwell Bridge, vividly represented in one of the climactic scenes of *Old Mortality*. In Ireland such atrocities stain the threshold of the present. "Red-wode Irish madness" collapses the historical distance maintained in the novel's Scottish scenes, in which the conflicts of the past (the stuff of Waverley novels) inform harmless reminiscence and quirks of character. The collapse does not necessarily bring clarity: connections are baffled as soon as made, as, for instance, Johnstone obscures the historical and ideological links between Gideon's devout Presbyterianism and the bigotry of the "Protestant flail" (named O'Toole rather than, say, Macbriar).

Elizabeth de Bruce extends a literary bridge between the Scottish *Old Mortality* controversy and the late-1820s Irish novel of insurgency, across which symbolic traffic flows both ways. Johnstone's novel signals its historical relation to the *Old Mortality* controversy by depicting it within the narrative. At the opening of the third volume, in one of those "anachronisms" deplored by Hogg, Gideon Haliburton rides to Edinburgh to confront the editor of the newly published *Minstrelsy of the Scottish Border* over a libellous reference to one of the popular heroines of the Covenanting epoch: "he wished to appraise the calumniator of Janet Geddes . . . of his intention to take up the cudgels in her defence, and to have a regular 'Exchange of Flytings' anent her case" (3:5).[20] Marching into Scott's townhouse, Gideon finds himself hailed as an "original" by the assembled company, and charmed out of his grievance with effusions of wit and champagne. It is an "Ambrosian night" *avant la lettre* (3:24). Johnstone deftly (and, it must be said, affectionately) satirizes the ideological achievement ascribed to Scott's fiction and claimed by the *Blackwood's* set. Post-Enlightenment sociability overcomes partisan rancor, consigning it firmly to the past, by absorbing its discourses into the play and pleasure of literature. Gideon sets off to a flyting and returns chanting poetry.

Even so Johnstone consigns the *Old Mortality* controversy to the past. Her mock-heroic reduction empties the debate of its historical gravity, in a gesture that at once recognizes literature as the medium of national tradition and contextualizes its failure to cure history's "madness" by an aesthetic conversion into culture. *Elizabeth de Bruce* acknowledges its own late intervention in the story of Scottish Romantic fiction with its allusively insistent literariness, a stylization that advertises a retrospective meditation on the genre and its conditions. Literariness goes beyond the imitation of settings, characters, tropes, and incidents established by Scott and the Blackwood authors, beyond even the metafictional game playing of Gideon's Ambrosian night, to Johnstone's apparently gratuitous overcharging of her text with stray details and turns of phrase gleaned from modern Scottish fiction, especially Scott's. The description of Lady Tantallon's mantle, "lined and edged with the fur of the grey squirrel, the miniver of the old romance" (2:226), is taken from *Ivanhoe*; "*over crowed*" (2:304) is a Spenserian locution revived in *Rob Roy*; Deacon Daigh's "Is siller needed?" (3:80) echoes the Laird of Dumbiedikes's catchphrase in *The Heart of Mid-Lothian* (in an episode which takes place *at* Dumbiedikes).[21] These details, this burden of allusiveness, encourage the tautological insight that the novel's apparatus of mediation is, after all, literary; that a novel is, in the end, literature.

And literature, in a terminally materialist reduction, is not even words or letters but sign- and value-bearing printed paper. The Scottish plot of *Elizabeth de Bruce* carries a reflection on what Kevin Barry has called the "paper economy" of British Romanticism,[22] brought into painful focus (especially) for Scottish authors and publishers by the 1826 crash, which provides the economic horizon of Johnstone's retrospect on Scottish fiction. *Elizabeth de Bruce* appeared in the aftermath not only of the fall of Scott and Constable but of a public controversy over the government's attempt to restrict the circulation of paper money in Scotland, following a series of English bank failures. The fiercest intervention in the controversy came from Scott himself, whose "Letters of Malachi Malagrowther" defended the right to issue notes granted to the Scottish banks at the Union.[23] Scotland's modern economy, Scott claimed, had always been sustained by the exchange of paper, well before Pitt's wartime suspension of the gold standard and cash payments. Johnstone—again, following earlier novels by Scott—represents finance capitalism as the sublime historical force (at once real and fantastic) that threatens to disintegrate the modern domestic order; or rather, the threat of disintegration reveals the true scandal, that finance capitalism, rather than, say, a postfeudal, "enlightened" moral economy based on loyalty and sympathy, is the force that sustains that order. Johnstone also follows Scott in making her Scottish scene, charming as it is, dysfunctional: since nearly all the men are whimsical old bachelors or widowers, and nearly all the women are crazy, it cannot reproduce itself. As in its Scott prototypes (*The Antiquary, Saint Ronan's Well*), this community lives emotionally in the past, and the uncertainty of its tenure in the present is exposed when Hutcheon calls in his debts. The novel's kindly characters seek sanctuary from their creditor in the Canongate, as Scott was worrying he might have to in the same year as his own *Chronicles of the Canongate*. Providentially—that is, by an arbitrary flurry of plot reversals—the villain's machinations blow up in his face: there is a run on his bank, an angry mob burns down his house, he breaks his neck in an escape attempt. All the same the organic community stands revealed as an appearance, a precarious collective fiction, in perilous disavowal of its modern economic base. The community may be virtuous and spiritually nourishing, as a repository of memory and feeling, but it is also ontologically fragile, provisional, defenseless against the convulsions of the new economy. It is literally made of paper—in the sense, communicated by Johnstone's texture of allusion, that the fictions of Scott and the Blackwood authors, with their memorials of a traditional Scotland in the face of modernization, are made of paper. As the O'Connellite Irish novel yields its vexed political present, so *Elizabeth de Bruce* contemplates the recession of Scottish Romantic fiction into the past which is its setting.

THE SPIRIT OF THE TIME

> If Sir Walter Scott has gone to the grave in the belief that he is a Tory writer, no man was ever the dupe of so gross a self-delusion.
> —Christian Isobel Johnstone, "On the Political Tendency of
> Sir Walter Scott's Writings"

Elizabeth de Bruce was the fruit of Johnstone's brief career as a Blackwood's author, unremarked by the few critics who have written about her. For several years John Wilson had been inserting laudatory references to Johnstone's editorial regime at the *Inverness Courier* (with her husband, 1817–24) in the pages of *Blackwood's Magazine*. In 1824 the Johnstones opened negotiations with William Blackwood with a view to leaving Inverness for Edinburgh. Including some "stray pieces" in a letter to Blackwood on other business, Christian Johnstone makes the ritual protest (befitting her gender) of "a fine aversion to every species and degree of authorship," dropping into a mischievously flirtatious tone ("Mrs Johnstone is sorry to find upon search that her four moons are not to be seen to-night after all the talk of them").[24] The issue of this correspondence was *Elizabeth de Bruce*. Blackwood gave the novel a substantial print run (for a non-Scott title) of two thousand copies, but sales were disappointing. Johnstone's husband thought that potential readers might have been put off by Christopher North's failure to keep a public promise to review the novel in *Blackwood's*—after Wilson had privately expressed his admiration.[25] Meanwhile, Blackwood and John Johnstone engaged in a joint venture to buy the copyright of the *Edinburgh Weekly Chronicle*. Christian Johnstone was coeditor of the paper as well as a principal contributor, as she had been at the *Inverness Courier*. In 1831 her husband and Blackwood fell out, according to Blackwood because of Johnstone's irregular business habits and according to Johnstone because of their political differences; Johnstone released Blackwood from the agreement and bought his share.[26]

In August 1832 the Johnstones relaunched the *Edinburgh Weekly Chronicle* as the *Schoolmaster and Edinburgh Weekly Magazine*. Although John Johnstone's name appeared on the banner, the *Schoolmaster*, like its predecessor, was conceived, edited, and largely written by his wife.[27] The Johnstones were unable to keep up the weekly format, and in September 1833 the *Schoolmaster* morphed into a monthly, *Johnstone's Edinburgh Magazine*, retailing for the cheap price of eightpence (almost a quarter of the price, two shillings and sixpence, of an issue of *Blackwood's, Tait's,* or *Fraser's*). Mrs. Johnstone remained chief contributor and de facto editor. In May 1834 *Johnstone's* merged with *Tait's Edinburgh Magazine*, founded two years earlier; it seems the market could not support two Edinburgh liberal monthlies produced by the same publisher and printer. *Tait's* reduced its price from half-a-crown to a shilling, in a concession to the Johnstones' wish that their work be affordable to a mass public. Already a prominent contributor to *Tait's*, Christian Johnstone now became, according to Robert Chambers, "its chief contributor and director. Although she was nominally the editor, her authority was subject to the control of Mr Tait, who still retained the principal management, and thus she acted the same part for *Tait's Magazine* that Wilson did for *Blackwood's*."[28] Responsible for the selection and arrangement of contents, Johnstone effectively became, in Alexis Easley's words, "the first woman to serve as paid editor of a major Victorian periodical" (as *Tait's* would become). The literary and critical tone she brought to *Tait's*, Chambers adds, inspired it with fresh life and popularity.[29]

Thus Johnstone abandoned the three-volume novel to work in magazine genres: writing editorials, articles, and tales herself, and playing the more influential role of editor. She invested her fiction-writing skills in the genre of the tale as liberal-reformist didactic instrument, trained on social issues and intended for juvenile and working-class readers, as pioneered by Hannah More and Maria Edgeworth and now taken up by Harriet Martineau. (Johnstone reviewed Martineau's *Illustrations of Political Economy*, a set of exemplary fables, in 1832, and went on to publish her work in *Tait's*.)[30] Johnstone's own magazine tales for "youthful readers" were reissued in two collections, *The Diversions of Hollycot; or, The Mother's Art of Thinking* (1828) and *Nights of the Round Table; or, Stories of Aunt Jane and her Friends* (1832). The first number of the *Schoolmaster* includes a tale called "The Flogged Soldier. By Mrs Johnstone" (10–13), which turns out to be a redaction of the Phelim O'Bourke subplot from *Clan-Albin*, recycled to address a topical issue, the reform of military discipline. This was to be the first instalment in "The Story-Teller," a regular feature by Mrs. Johnstone, which would include—besides original work by herself and other British authors (including James Hogg)—translations and condensations of foreign fiction. "It is meant, in short, to do here, on a small scale, for Tales, what the *libraries* are doing for Voyages, Travels, Memoirs and Histories," Johnstone declared of "The Story-Teller": "to select and *condense*" literature for the working poor.[31] This project would be realized, fifteen years later, as *The Edinburgh Tales, Conducted by Mrs Johnstone*, an anthology combining "stories and novelettes" by British and foreign authors (including Carlyle, the Howitts, Mary Russell Mitford, and Robert Nicoll) with Johnstone's own work; it was first issued by Tait in weekly and monthly numbers and then in bound volumes (1845–46).[32]

This turn in Johnstone's career exemplifies a larger development of the late 1820s and 1830s well noted by literary and book historians, the slump in the novel and concomitant rise of the serial miscellany. "Our publishers of the proud northern metropolis seem to have lost all pluck since the lamented death of their great father, Mr Constable," commented *Fraser's Magazine*: "the vaunted Modern Athens is fast dwindling away into a mere spelling-book and primer manufactory."[33] Three-volume post-octavo novels were high-risk ventures in the wake of the 1826 crash; publishers preferred to invest in magazines, pamphlets, and works of fiction and "useful knowledge" serialized in monthly installments. "This is the age of periodicals; and, above all, of cheap periodicals. A revolution has taken place in the world of bookselling," boasted *Tait's Magazine*, reviewing its stablemate *Johnstone's* shortly before their merger. "The expensive quartos and octavos, which used to issue in such swarms from Albemarle Street, and the Row, and from the Edinburgh press in *Constable's* days, have given place to the *Waverley Novels*, *Lardner's Cyclopaedia*, *The Edinburgh Cabinet Library*, and some scores more of similar works, published in monthly parts, at cheap prices."[34] As well as the useful knowledge series that Johnstone calls "libraries," the reviewer includes Scott's "Magnum Opus" edition (1829–33) under the rubric of "cheap periodical": the novel thrived in the new economic climate by reconstituting itself in the serial medium, at first in reprint editions. The five-shilling monthly issue volume format of "Magnum Opus" was imitated in Colburn and Bentley's *Standard Novels* (1831–55), which set the pattern for fiction reprint publishing for most of the century. Hogg wanted his works reissued in serial format to compete with Scott's, a project that was realized after his death (in incomplete and compromised form, 1836) by the Glasgow publishers Blackie and Son, specialists in works of religious devotion and useful knowledge. Original fiction also gravitated to the periodical format, including the most innovative works of the 1830s, the *Blackwood's*-style philosophical mock-autobiography *Sartor Resartus* (serialized in *Fraser's*) and *Posthumous Papers of the Pickwick Club* (issued in monthly numbers).[35]

Reform and the attendant debates gave a boost to didactic genres and "useful knowledge," and helped bring into focus an emergent phenomenon, the industrial-era mass reading public. Even more than by the proliferation of monthly miscellanies and part issues, this public was represented in the early 1830s by the rise of the weekly magazine. The Johnstones' *Schoolmaster* followed the cue of *Chambers's Edinburgh Journal*, founded in February 1832 and conducted by the brothers William and Robert Chambers, which established a new kind of cheap but respectable weekly miscellany accessible to "the people." The failure of the Reform administration to repeal the stamp tax effectively prevented the issue of newspapers for working-class readers by keeping costs high (sevenpence a number). *Chambers's* sold for three halfpence, a price convenient to "*every man in the British dominions*," including laborers and schoolboys, by constituting itself as a miscellany of useful knowledge, a kind of occasional encyclopedia, variegated with stories and sketches.[36] An article in the second number, "Retrospective Review" (11 February 1832), justifies the cultural function of diffusing useful knowledge—troped as the stored contents of "an ancient library" (the ghostly repository of "thousands of disembodied authors")—throughout the lower ranks of society, in a process of literary and scientific enfranchisement that many progressive commentators regarded as a necessary condition for wider political enfranchisement.[37] *Chambers's* enthusiastically catered to—and helped realize—the phenomenon of mass literacy that had made the *Edinburgh Review* so uneasy earlier in the century. In doing so it founded what would become a typical Victorian genre, the cheap weekly miscellany of useful instruction and edifying entertainment for middle- and working-class families, the most famous example of which was Charles Dickens's (twopenny) *Household Words* (1850) and its successor *All the Year Round*.[38]

The *Schoolmaster* likewise identified itself as a "small Miscellany . . . intended for the *Many*—for the great mass of the *People*—that mighty class from which in every country the greatest men have arisen," driven to its present format by "the non-removal of the taxes on knowledge."[39] While professing a devotion to the "cheap and universal diffusion of really useful information of every kind" (2), the Johnstones also criticize what passes in most miscellanies as "really useful": "It is evidently thought better that [the people] should read of the growth of the tea-plant, than watch the progress of legislation, or inquire into *rights of industry*. . . . It is, therefore, the avowed purpose of this publication to be *political*, in so far as the science of politics is connected with the social well-being" (1). More outspokenly than *Chambers's*, the *Schoolmaster* invokes the political conditions in which the new Radical magazines appeared.

Tait's Edinburgh Magazine, founded as a champion of Reform against the Tory monthly *Blackwood's*, gives a polemically sharpened account of what it calls "the Spirit of the Time":

> A change has come over the Spirit of the Time; mighty questions have been stirred; deep interests have been created; vast masses of men, formerly inert and passive, have suddenly begun to heave to and fro with the force of a newly-inspired animation; old things are passing away—all things are becoming new.[40]

The reviewer traces a fitful, tempestuous half-century of political liberalization, from American Independence to the present Reform crisis. "I see you are half-inclined to be frightened by the popular croak of bad times, rivals, and overstocked markets," the publisher tells his interlocutor (Mr. Smith) in another editorial set piece, a Socratic dialogue archly titled "A Tete a tete with Mr Tait" (9). However, "there is a demand at this time for a magazine of liberal principles, of independent spirit, bearing upon the times, bringing out the sympathies of mankind"—those principles, in the year of the Reform Bill, being identified as "Liberality, Spirit, Utility" (10). The motto of the magazine, *Fiat Justitia* (let justice be done), issues a challenge to the *Edinburgh Review* (correcting its minatory motto, *Judex damnatur cum nocens absolvitur*) as well as a rebuke to *Blackwood's*, its precursor and local antagonist. Mr. Tait welcomes conflict, which invigorates and clarifies; he primes his new magazine against the anti-Reform arsenal of "Toryism, toad-eatery and . . . cock-and-bull stories all about the abominations of the French Revolution, as if every movement in favour of liberty and equal laws were necessarily and inseparably connected with bloodshed and brutality," and denounces the tactics of "personality, scurrility, scandal, and defamation" with which *Blackwood's* had burst onto the scene fifteen years earlier (11–14). In contrast, *Tait's* reclaims the spirit of liberalism for a new era, characterized in a language of Romantic idealism drawn from the London Radical journals: "gladness of soul, elasticity of heart, truth of thought, clearness of expression, and that dexterity of mental distillation which draws from the chaotic wash of an agitated world the essence of truth, of beauty, and of goodness" (13). Mr. Tait's appeal to aesthetic principles is especially striking. He lays claim to the (Blackwoodian) term of "ornament" as well as to a radical "utility": "I am delighted to hear you talk of utility and ornament in one breath," says Mr. Smith (14). "Ornament is the perfection, the refinement, the acme of utility," avers Mr. Tait: "what is life without beauty and embellishment? . . . [I]f it be useful, it will be beautiful, for use and beauty are inseparable" (14).

Tait's sounds a rhetoric of dialectical surmounting in the first number of the third volume (February 1833). An opening address "To Our Readers" ("We have fought the people's battles with all our might") culminates in the slogan, "JUSTICE TO ALL CLASSES—MONOPOLIES AND EXCLUSIVE PRIVILEGES TO NONE." A major article, "The Whig Coterie of Edinburgh," broadens the critique beyond Blackwood's Toryism to address the general literary establishment of post-Enlightenment Edinburgh:

> The old parties have been broken up with the old system, and new ones are forming. Not to speak it profanely, "all old things have passed away." The Tory party is an unreal shade. . . . The Whig party is a mere name bestowed upon all that worthy class of the community who wish to have matters amended, without well knowing how to set about it.[41]

In its early numbers the *Edinburgh Review* was "if anything, a Tory publication." In a climate of general repression, its editors "avoided the expression of any decided opinions, preferring the eclectic or sceptical tone," to the extent of inadvertently collaborating in the anti-Jacobin hysteria of the day; they were "theoretical, not practical statesmen," aloof from the hurly-burly of politics and deaf to "the voice of the people" (59). This unkind cut neglects, to be sure, the generous exertions of Jeffrey and his colleagues in defense of prominent Radicals at government treason trials, in the zeal to indict them for belonging to the Reform-era political establishment. *Tait's* picks up a Radical critique already levelled at Edinburgh by the London magazines, earlier imitators and adversaries of *Blackwood's*, in the 1820s.[42] That such a critique can now be made by a pro-Reform monthly in Edinburgh is indeed a sign of the times. Reform has opened a new horizon, and a perspective beyond the old contest between Whig and Tory elites, from which—dialectically surmounted—they appear as two arms of the same sickly body politic, a Scottish Old Corruption whose days are surely numbered.

"All old things have passed away." The sense of a transition between eras in Scotland, the passing of an ancien régime, was marked not only by the Reform Bill, which bore with particular force on the institutions of the "Dundas Despotism,"[43] but by the death of the regime's most distinguished representative—and bitter opponent of the new order—Sir Walter Scott.

Beneath the black-bordered announcement of Scott's death in the *Schoolmaster* Christian Johnstone calls for a biographer worthy of the subject. She names the intimate members of Scott's circle, Lockhart, William Laidlaw, and James Ballantyne, as fittest for the task, "until some master-mind shall arise, who . . . may, in the memoirs of SIR WALTER SCOTT, embody the Philosophy of Humanity, and the spirit of our own national history, with that finer spirit, expansive as Life, and enduring as Time, which pervades all that he has written."[44] In the five years before the publication of Lockhart's authorized version several rival biographies appeared, some of them merely opportunistic, and some attempting a reassessment of Scott in the light of the new dispensation he had gone to the grave opposing. Johnstone raises the key ideological terms—"Philosophy of Humanity" and "spirit of our own national history"—that should inform such a reassessment: the first carrying Radical overtones, the latter Blackwoodian. In the dawn of a Reformed Age the terms may at last converge, since the spirit of national history has changed its political form. How then to read what was now the manifest contradiction between Scott's political commitments and his iconic status as national author?

"He was led to give up for party what was meant for mankind," lamented a sympathetic Whig biographer, quoting a phrase heavy with allusive freight: Goldsmith had coined it against Burke, Lockhart applied it to Jeffrey in *Peter's Letters to His Kinsfolk*, and Hazlitt turned it against Scott in *The Spirit of the Age*.[45] Weir restates the Radical critique of Scott (discussed in chapter 1) made by John Scott and Hazlitt ten years earlier. The paradox that will be most powerfully rationalized by Georg Lukács, one hundred years later, is already in place: the "extraordinary inconsistency in his character" between Scott's "*aristocratic*" personal culture ("his habits, his demeanour, and his desires") and the "spirit of what is termed 'liberalism' " in his fiction (314). "If it be true what Byron said of him, 'that he was the *poet* of princes,' it is as unquestionably true, that he was the *chronicler* of the people, and may be said, in this respect, to be in prose what Burns was in rhyme" (315). Scott's political opponents readily grant his literary works a universal cultural value that secures its central place in a national tradition, rooted in "the people." In contrast to Lockhart (in *Peter's Letters*), and following Hazlitt, the Whig biographer insists upon Scott's partisan embroilment; and in order to keep that from compromising the expression of "national spirit," he reinstates the biographical split between Sir Walter and the Author of *Waverley*—between the narrow politics of party and personality, and the universal sympathy of art.

The Edinburgh Radical journals also address the crux between Scott's politics and his fiction.[46] In her leading article in the *Schoolmaster*, "On the Political Tendency of Sir Walter Scott's Writings," Johnstone mounts the most generous attempt to reclaim Scott for the spirit of the age.

> Convinced that in heart and mind, in principle and affection, and (with a few incidental and casual aberrations into which he was hurried or betrayed) in conduct also, this illustrious person belonged to no state party, we would fain redeem his venerable and beloved name from the political party which claims it—and sound to a Crusade which should "conquer his tomb from the infidels." (129)

Johnstone appropriates a key topos of "Holy Alliance" Toryism, the Crusade, in order to rescue "what was meant for mankind" from the thrall of "party" (129).[47] Scott's genius is rooted in a natural magnanimity:

> [W]ith this large natural character, it will not be difficult to show that he essentially belonged to the *People*—to *Mankind*; and that the tendency of all his writings has been to enlighten and expand the minds of men, by enlarging their affections; by making them neither Whig nor Tory, but something infinitely better than both. . . . He could neither long resist, nor ever once conquer that power which struggled in his understanding, and triumphed in his heart, and made him what he is, always a *Liberal*, and often a *Radical* writer, differing only in shadows and modes from many who are avowedly so. (129–30)

Johnstone's gestures of redemption grow increasingly audacious: "Has the railing of the most violent Radical, or the strongest arguments of Paine, struck a more fatal blow at monarchy than the popular narratives of Scott?" (131); they have done "more to spread true *Liberalism* . . . than the most elaborate discourses of the Whig teachers" (132). Scott's kings are weak or vicious, his common folk righteous and generous, his Covenanters nobler than his Jacobites, and "Sir WALTER's heroines are all Revolutionists, or in the Opposition" (133).[48]

Three months later, writing in *Tait's*, Harriet Martineau develops and qualifies Johnstone's radical reclamation. Anticipating Carlyle's more famous reassessment, and amplifying John Scott's earlier panegyric on the "health and manliness" inculcated by the Scotch novels, Martineau proposes to analyse the "peculiarly healthy" social and psychological conditions that provided "the discipline of the genius of Scott" and to "attempt an estimate of the services that genius has rendered to society."[49] Raised in "a kindly moral atmosphere," tempered by childhood affliction and the influence of natural surroundings (305), Scott became a man of the people as well as a Tory antiquary. His character encompasses all ranks and both genders: "robust as a ploughman, able to walk like a pedlar, and to ride like a knight-errant, and to hunt like a squire; industrious as a handicraftsman; . . . gentle as a woman; intrepid as the bravest hero of his own immortal works" (305–6). This protean capacity brings readers together in a unified national community, at least while they are reading (446–48). Martineau praises the commercial and moral benefits Scott's writings have brought to his country. "Is this a slight service to have rendered? —to have, perhaps unconsciously, taught human equality, while professing to exhibit human inequality? . . . The fictions of Scott have done more towards exposing priestcraft and fanaticism than any influence of our time, short of actual observation" (449). Above all: "Much has Walter Scott done, and done it also unconsciously, for woman," with his depictions of great-hearted heroines in restrictive social conditions—Flora MacIvor, Die Vernon, Rebecca, and Jeanie Deans (455–56).

The key word in this assessment turns out to be "unconsciously." Scott's fiction expresses an organic movement of sympathy beneath and counter to the misguided current of its author's intentions—which are nevertheless, in Martineau's account, decisive. Taking up the earlier radical critique, Martineau confronts Scott's deficiencies. He lacked "sympathy for the race," for the people as a collective body (453–54). Most crucially, he failed to understand the new social function of works of fiction that his own success had made possible. He took literature "lightly," seemingly unaware that it might serve a serious purpose, even though his practice might have "taught us the power of fiction as an agent of morals and philosophy" (458). Scott "has indicated, by his own achievements, the way to larger and higher achievements" (459). Martineau seems to have in mind an amplified, industrial-age version of the Jacobin novels of the 1790s: "We have yet to wait for the philosophical romance, for the novels which shall relate to other classes beside the aristocracy. . . . [W]e must have, in a new novelist, the graver themes—not the less picturesque, perhaps, for their reality—which the present condition of society suggests" (458–59). That present condition—of political struggle and social transformation—demands a fittingly heroic representation: "What can afford finer moral scenery, than the transition state in which society now is?" (459). Nor was Martineau mistaken, as she pointed the way from Scott to the "Condition of England" fiction of the coming decade.

RECESSIONAL

[H]ow shall we domesticate ourselves in this spectral Necropolis, or rather
City both of the Dead and of the Unborn, where the present seems little
other than an inconsiderable Film dividing the Past and the Future?
                              —Carlyle, *Sartor Resartus*

There would be no early-Victorian "Condition of Scotland" novel. Large-
scale economic, political and social changes broke up the infrastructure
of Edinburgh's literary culture after 1832. Modernizing transport and
financial technologies brought the city too close to London for it to retain
the gravity of a rival center, so that when the British book trade recovered
from the post-1826 slump, it was decisively London-based. Reform legislation rationalized Scottish institutions, bringing them into line with English models and eroding their regional autonomy. London consolidated
its primacy as world city, the undisputed capital of literary as of other
markets, and the great Scottish periodicals and publishing houses went
south, along with ambitious intellectuals like Thomas Carlyle.[50] The reviewers of 1832 were not wrong to read Scott's death and the Reform
Bill as signs of the times, the end of the Edinburgh post-Enlightenment.

Carlyle's 1838 review of Lockhart's *Life of Scott* issued the first major
challenge to Scott's reputation after his death, setting the terms for its
modern depreciation.[51] Carlyle takes up the salient themes of Martineau's
article in *Tait's* (Scott's "health," his invocation of a national reading
public, his failure to take his art seriously) and presses them into the more
stringent censure of a disabling worldliness. The subjection of Scott's genius to commercial conditions is symptomatic not just of a fatal character
flaw, but (by implication) of the inadequacy of his preferred genre, the
novel, so relentlessly preoccupied with the surfaces of life—manners, cos-
tumes, setting, business, talk. Carlyle's foundation of his own literary career on a repudiation of fiction is well known. In 1822, at the height of
the Scottish fiction boom, the young Carlyle started writing several tales
of his own, including one set in 1745, in addition to translating Goethe's
Wilhelm Meister's Apprenticeship. His dissatisfactions with the form coincided with its crisis and decline through the late 1820s and issued in
a denunciation of "the whole class of Fictitious Narratives" in *Fraser's
Magazine* in 1832. There Carlyle opposes fiction, no better after all than
"*lying*," to "*Reality*" and "*fact*."[52] The reinstatement of an old dichotomy
dismisses not only the novel's claims on the representation of reality but
the philosophical basis of those claims in Hume's discovery of the fictionality of common life. Carlyle's decade-long turn to a literary career articulates, in short, a turn away from the Scottish empiricist tradition, issuing

in Scott's novels, that dominated the scene when he began writing, even as that scene and tradition were beginning to disintegrate. Nor was Carlyle the only rising author to abandon an early commitment to fiction in Scott's shadow. Robert Chambers, who began a historical novel on the life of Montrose before publishing *Illustrations of the Author of Waverley* in 1823, found his feet as coeditor of *Chambers's Edinburgh Journal* in the early 1830s, embraced "physiology" in the 1840s, and went on to produce one of the sensational books of the age, *Vestiges of the Natural History of Creation* (1844). Chambers followed a path opposite to Carlyle's, developing the Enlightenment genre of conjectural history to extreme conclusions.[53] Meanwhile Carlyle undertook a more complex and rigorous rejection of the Edinburgh post-Enlightenment in his great works of the 1830s, *Sartor Resartus* and *The French Revolution*. These works perform, in the prescriptive mode of critique, the disintegration of the literary field that a modern tradition of Scottish criticism has read as an organic or metaphysical disaster, a national cultural extinction, the main symptom of which is the disappearance of an indigenous tradition of the novel after Scott's death.[54]

The experience of translating *Wilhelm Meister* impressed Carlyle with the futility of a metonymy-based novelistic realism rather than his own lack of command of the genre. All that circumstantial detail was a distraction from what was really important—the view to a more exalted, permanent reality. Thus Carlyle admitted (and by no Kantian ingress, despite his claims on German Romanticism) a return of the transcendental dimension exorcized by Hume, and a reopening of mystical dualisms between appearance and essence, surface and depth, illusion and reality. What took the place of common life in his own writing would be the abstract scheme of an alienation from it, in the conventional form of a Puritan conversion narrative; and what took the place of metonymy, conversely, would be metaphor. Carlyle realized these substitutions in his first masterpiece, *Sartor Resartus*, conceived in 1830 as a magazine article, composed as a three-volume book, and published as a magazine serial in 1833–34.[55] *Sartor Resartus* presents a systematic antithesis of the novelistic realism projected in Humean empiricism and practiced in Scott's historical romances. Instead it assumes the mixed genre of modern Menippean satire, the hotchpotch of periodical review, fantastic autobiography, literary hoax, and philosophical parody, cooked up (above all) in *Blackwood's Magazine* in the decade and a half since Waterloo.

Indeed, although serialized in *Fraser's* (a London-based imitation of *Blackwood's*, edited by former *Blackwood's* man William Maginn), *Sartor Resartus* can be viewed as the ultimate *Blackwood's* article—the most hyperbolic of those experimental fusions of cultural criticism with fictional form and the most drastic alternative to the Scottish historical novel to emerge from the Blackwoodian crucible. Discussions of *Sartor Resartus* as a work of fiction tend to overlook its Scottish genealogy and emphasize instead the Anglo-Irish and German traditions Carlyle himself alludes to, thus repeating the work's own, programmatic suppression of its local literary circumstances.[56] The German philosophical masquerade was a *Blackwood's* device (pioneered by Lockhart), while the work's form, a radical metaphysical treatise embedded in a memoir of the author and relayed to the public via a set of manuscript fragments and a baffled Tory editor, recalls Hogg's *Confessions of a Justified Sinner* as well as Scott's *Tales of My Landlord* and other antiquarian-framed Scottish fictions.

Sartor Resartus begins as a conjectural anthropology of the matter of the novel, common life, which it materializes in the synecdoche of "Clothes" (Carlyle obligingly puns on "custom" and "costume")[57] and then submits to a paradigmatic abstraction. Clothes, of course, are a prominent topos of historical fiction, which establishes the distance between past and present through a defamiliarizing description of the surfaces of everyday life. *Ivanhoe* (an important novel for Carlyle), one source of which was Joseph Strutt's treatise *A Complete View of the Dress and Habits of the People of England*, introduces its characters through detailed inventories of their costume.[58] Carlyle repeatedly cites vivid historical or anthropological instances of the semiosis of clothing, only to resist the narrative pull of anecdote for a paradigmatic gloss ("German fashionable dress of the Fifteenth Century," 1:7; George Fox's leather suit, 3:1). Teufelsdröckh's philosophy shifts the significance of clothes from metonymy to metaphor. Clothes represent the veil of appearances that a visionary realism will tug aside.

That unclothing takes place in the biographical narrative of book 2. Carlyle progressively abstracts the materials of the bildungsroman, from the allegorically generalized notations of setting, character, and incident in the early chapters, to the bare binary scheme (denial/affirmation) of the climactic conversion sequence. This schematic insistence enacts a diametric opposition to the Humean dialectic, of skeptical alienation followed by a sentimental return to common life, that structured Scott's seminal novel of development *Waverley*. *Sartor Resartus* yields at its core a counter-Enlightenment reversion to the alienation plot of Puritan progress that invested the English novel at its origins, stripped now of accreted realist trappings and represented in paradigmatic glory. The treatment of the affirmative turn in the conversion scheme, "The Everlasting Yea," is notoriously problematic, since Teufelsdröckh's revelation lacks not only metonymic but doctrinal and metaphysical substance. What prevails is the formal authority of the scheme itself. German idealist philosophy provides (after all) a fashionable disguise for the old Calvinist conversion plot, which stands in for the visionary reality to which it is supposed to give access.

The stylistic vehicle for this program of paradigmatic abstraction is metaphor, theorized in *Sartor Resartus* as the organic medium of symbol making (the "muscles and tissues and living integuments" of "the Flesh-garment, Language," 57) and flexed as rhetorical substitute for a metonymic realism. Metaphor, the trope of depth not surface, rescues language from sublimation in the work's ascetic drive to abstraction and constitutes the pleasurably thick, impure, savory stylistic texture of *Sartor Resartus*. The resulting tension between schematic abstraction and a "pie-bald, entangled, hyper-metaphorical style of writing" (221) keeps the book alive. Maginn's catchphrase for Carlylean style, "Allgemeine-Mid-Lothianish of Auld Reekie," brilliantly renders its character as a mode of translation, a Scottish writing that alienates English through the mock-philological "deep" medium of a Northern linguistic analogue, German, standing in a metaphoric relation to English—rather than through those metonymically proximate forms of vernacular Scots that have arguably, thanks to Burns and Scott, become a homely dialect to all nineteenth-century British readers.[59] *Sartor Resartus* thus marks a highlight of that modern Scottish series of pseudoantiquarian hoaxes and experiments in the alienation of English that began with Macpherson's translations of "Ossian." More thoroughly even than the *Poems of Ossian*, since an archaeology of Scottish origins is emphatically not part of its project, Carlyle's text evacuates the literary-historical habitus of its production, post-Enlightenment Edinburgh.

The program of schematic sublimation and metaphoric condensation in *Sartor Resartus* is aimed not just at the novel, then, but at Scotland too: at the idea of the nation projected in Scottish historical fiction as well as at the work's own literary-historical conditions. Paradoxically, the return to a Puritan conversion plot fulfils the project of disciplinary attenuation of a metonymically "thick" national character that we saw rehearsed in the earlier tradition of Scottish domestic fiction (in chapter 3), all the more thoroughly now for the plot's Germanic disguise. In the last chapter of *Sartor Resartus*, in an image that might have come from *The Cook and Housewife's Manual*, the editor characterizes the work we have been reading as an "enormous, amorphous Plumpudding, more like a Scottish Haggis, which Herr Teufelsdröckh had kneaded for his fellow mortals" (221). That is to say, *Sartor Resartus* is not just a satirical miscellany (Carlyle alludes to the etymology *satura lanx*): it is a Scottish satirical miscellany. Its Scottishness inheres in a formal and stylistic, mixed-metaphorical heterogeneity that articulates a radical revulsion from the ideological topoi of national character and common life, for which, after 1832, a social consensus can no longer plausibly be said to hold. New forces are at work "in the secret depths of English [*sic*] national Existence," warns Teufelsdröckh, "striving to separate and isolate it into two contradictory, uncommunicating masses" (216), embodied by the West-End Dandy and Irish "Poor-Slave." These antinational figures reinstate, with a coming vengeance, the antithesis between decadent cosmopolitan aristocrat and rude Hibernian peasant that framed Edgeworth's Irish tales. Carlyle sets the theme for the "Condition of England" novel, called for by Martineau, that would emerge in the ensuing decade, splitting the old form of the nation along the industrial fault line of class.

Sartor Resartus closes with Teufelsdröckh's cryptic disappearance, a mock-mystifying withdrawal of the author function, in an elegiac complex of partings. In the penultimate chapter we glimpse a unique if unreliable acknowledgment of the work's Scottish origins (earlier, we have been told that Teufelsdröckh first thought of it in Monmouth Street, in London):

> [T]urning the corner of a lane, in the Scottish Town of Edinburgh, I came upon a Signpost, whereon stood written that such and such a one was "Breeches-Maker to his Majesty;" and stood painted the Effigies of a Pair of Leather Breeches, and between the knees these memorable words, SIC ITUR AD ASTRA. Was not this the martyr prison-speech of a Tailor sighing indeed in bonds, yet sighing towards deliverance; and prophetically appealing to a better day? A day of justice, when the worth of Breeches would be revealed to man, and the Scissors become for ever venerable.
>
> Neither, perhaps, may I now say, has his appeal been altogether in vain. It was in this high moment, when the soul, rent, as it were, and shed asunder, is open to inspiring influence, that I first conceived this Work on Clothes[.] (220)

The author conceives his great work in Edinburgh amid reminiscences of the suffering Covenanters and—in a fainter, allusive echo—the stricken Walter Scott. "Sic itur ad astra," adorning the grotesque image of the empty breeches, supplies the motto of the Canongate coat of arms—locating Teufelsdröckh's epiphany in that precinct—as well as the epigraph of *Chronicles of the Canongate*, Scott's first work of fiction conceived and written after the crash. The pretended author of the *Chronicles*, Chrystal Croftangry, is a ruined laird and advocate who seeks refuge from his creditors in the Canongate.[60] Scott's own crisis has abraded the once-dense layers of fiction to a biographical transparency: empty breeches indeed. Meanwhile Carlyle, acknowledging the source of his devices of transcendence (the conversion plot, the rhetoric of prophecy), redeems the Radical Presbyterian tradition from the historical novel more drastically than Hogg or Galt had been able to, by jettisoning the genre altogether. By the time this final instalment appeared in *Fraser's Magazine* the Carlyles had left Craigenputtock for London. Not the least resonant of the farewells posed in *Sartor Resartus* is its farewell to Scotland.

Notes

❧

Preface

1. See, e.g., Reiss, *Meaning of Literature*; Guillory, *Cultural Capital*; Siskin, *Work of Writing*. On the eighteenth-century Scottish literary field see Potkay, *Fate of Eloquence in the Age of Hume*; Phillips, *Society and Sentiment*; Sher, *Enlightenment and the Book*.

2. Garside, "English Novel in the Romantic Period," 44–47, 64; St Clair, *Reading Nation in the Romantic Period*, 170, 220–22, 245–46; Ferris, *Achievement of Literary Authority*, 237–47; Sutherland, *Life of Walter Scott*, 109–11, 139, 240–47.

3. Recent studies of history and fiction in Scott's novels include Kerr, *Fiction Against History*; Ferris, *Achievement of Literary Authority*; Robertson, *Legitimate Histories*; Zimmerman, *Boundaries of Fiction*; Rigney, *Imperfect Histories*. If fiction tends to be history's inauthentic antithesis in Rigney's account, and history fiction's in Kerr's, Zimmerman renders most clearly their dialectical conjunction.

4. This is the argument of my first book, *Modern Romance and Transformations of the Novel*.

5. Gallagher and Greenblatt, *Practicing New Historicism*, 169.

6. Scott, "Introductory Epistle" to *Fortunes of Nigel* (1821), 8. Future references are given in the text.

7. See Kathryn Sutherland's analysis of this scene and Scott's "model Smithian economy" of the imagination: "Fictional Economies," 99–107, 110.

8. Bourdieu, *Rules of Art*, especially 47–173, 214–77. Bourdieu reproduces Marx's "camera obscura" model of ideology ("in all ideology men and their circumstances appear upside-down as in a *camera obscura*" [*The German Ideology*, 14]); see also McGann, *Romantic Ideology*, 9.

9. Bourdieu, *Rules of Art*, 254. McCracken-Flesher's *Possible Scotlands* is the recent study most alert to this convergence.

10. The view is especially current among historians, e.g., Brewer, *Pleasures of the Imagination*, 657–58; Devine, *Scottish Nation*, 292, and *Scotland's Empire*, 354–56; Buchan, *Capital of the Mind*, 339–40.

11. See, e.g., Lee, *Nationalism and Irony*; McGann, "Walter Scott's Romantic Postmodernity."

12. Lynch, "Gothic Libraries and National Subjects," 41.

13. Lauder, *Wolfe of Badenoch*, 1:v–vi.

14. Bourdieu, *Rules of Art*, 213–34.

15. Thanks to the Stirling/South Carolina Research Edition of the Collected Works of James Hogg (ongoing since 1995) and the scholarship attending it.

16. On the absence of Scotland in Romanticism and the absence of Romanticism in Scotland, see Davis, Duncan, and Sorensen, introduction to *Scotland and the Borders of Romanticism*, 1–10. Studies of the interplay between English and Scottish writing in post-Union British literature and "four nations" and transatlantic approaches to literary history include Manning, *Puritan-Provincial Vision*; Ferris, *Achievement of Literary Authority*; Crawford, *Devolving English Literature*; Pittock, *Poetry and Jacobite Politics*; Trumpener, *Bardic Nationalism*; Davis, *Acts of Union*; Manning, *Fragments of Union*; Sorensen, *Grammar of Empire*; Carruthers and Rawes, *English Romanticism and the Celtic World*. For the contribution of the Scottish Enlightenment philosophers and Scott to Romantic historicism see Chandler, *England in 1819*. Other recent studies in Romanticism that enlarge the role of Scottish writing beyond the token appearance of *Waverley* include Lee, who groups Scott and Carlyle with Irishman Burke as architects of an irony-based conservative Romantic nationalism, in *Nationalism and Irony*; Russett, who attends to "the gothic exorbitance of Scottish literary Romanticism"—Scott, Hogg, and *Blackwood's*—in *Fictions and Fakes* (155); and Christensen, for whom, however, the *Edinburgh Review* and *Waverley* install an anti-Romantic ideology of "normal change," in *Romanticism at the End of History*.

17. Other recent book-length studies of Scott and his contexts in Romantic-period and eighteenth-century writing include Robertson, *Legitimate Histories*; Irvine, *Enlightenment and Romance*; Jones, *Literary Memory*. Scott plays a key role in recent historicist studies of the Gothic: Gamer, *Romanticism and the Gothic*; Watt, *Contesting the Gothic*. For Scottish Romantic fiction in the long nineteenth century see Fielding, *Writing and Orality*; Mack, *Scottish Fiction and the British Empire*. The only prior monograph devoted to early-nineteenth-century Scottish fiction is MacQueen, *Rise of the Historical Novel*.

18. A short canon of recently recovered national and historical fictions occluded by Scott's "originality" would include Sophia Lee's *The Recess* (1783), Sydney Owenson's *The Wild Irish Girl* (1806), Sophie Cottin's *Elizabeth* (translated 1807), Jane Porter's *The Scottish Chiefs* (1810), and Charles Maturin's *The Milesian Chief* (1812). For a stimulating recent account of Scott's originality, see Maxwell, "Inundations of Time."

Chapter 1: Edinburgh, Capital of the Nineteenth Century

1. Mudie, *Historical Account of His Majesty's Visit*, 88.
2. For detailed accounts of the visit see Prebble, *King's Jaunt*; McCracken-Flesher, *Possible Scotlands*, 73–107.
3. See Trevor-Roper, "Invention of Tradition"; for a recent reaffirmation of the consensus, Devine, *Scotland's Empire*, 354–56. On Scott's Jacobite revivalism see Pittock, *Invention of Scotland*, 84–90.
4. See Hughes, "James Hogg and Edinburgh's Triumph over Napoleon."
5. Hazlitt, "What Is the People?" *Examiner*, 7 March 1818; cited in Burgess, *British Fiction*, 214.
6. *Blackwood's* 12 (September 1822): 387.
7. Ibid., 310. Future references to this article will be given in the text.

8. On the political struggle to define the Jaunt see McCracken Flesher, "Great Disturber of the Age"; *Possible Scotlands*, 81–86, 101–7.

9. Lockhart, *Life of Scott*, 7:48. Future references to this edition will be given in the text.

10. On theatricality and nationalism see Craig, "Scott's Staging of the Nation."

11. "Sir Billy Blubberlips, the fidus Achates of the hero of modern romance," as he is called in Felix MacDonogh's *Hermit in Edinburgh*, 3:215.

12. For Scott's account of the Coronation, see Lockhart, *Life of Scott*, 7:345–67. For modern accounts see Girouard, *Return to Camelot*, 26–28.

13. Cf. Arata, "Scott's Pageants," 105–7: "The very self-consciousness of its antiquarianism . . . helped make the Royal Jaunt into a peculiarly modern type of spectacle" (107); McCracken-Flesher, *Possible Scotlands*, 74–76: "By entering circulation the King revealed the constructedness of his role" (75).

14. See Youngson, *Making of Classical Edinburgh*, 259–62.

15. Ibid., 148–56.

16. Cockburn, *Memorials of His Time*, 277, 279–80. See also Daiches, *Edinburgh*, 195–97.

17. In Stuart's *Antiquities of Athens*; see Daiches, *Edinburgh*, 195.

18. Peacock, *Novels*, 2:657. MacQuedy is based on J. R. McCulloch, former editor of the *Scotsman*, professor of political economy at the University of London, and a leading contributor to the *Edinburgh Review*.

19. *Blackwood's* 11 (April 1822): 484.

20. MacDonogh, *Hermit in Edinburgh*, 1:1; the book distances itself from "a novel written, called Edinburgh" from the same publisher. Tory in politics, intermittently satirical, it confines itself to general observations, apart from a swing at Lady Morgan ("Lady Mordante") and a few other targets. As for *Edinburgh*, its most notable feature—apart from the lampoon of Edinburgh worthies, from "Sir Walter Jokeby" (1:64) and "Mr Blight-all" (Jeffrey, 1:163) to the whisky baronet Sir William Fettes (1:136)—is its vestigial plot: Miss S., the mysterious belle at Lord Ossian's soiree, turns out to be a "Cyprian" from "the shades below, where the Edinburgh Paphos, more like to Erebus, exists" (2:252).

21. *Glenfergus* begins vigorously, with sharp vignettes of sentimental old maids and female quixotes, but soon succumbs to the deadweight of un-reimagined stock conventions. Its most bizarre character is Dr. Wild, an "experimental philosopher" in the style of Frankenstein, who turns dogs and sheep into one another by transfusing their blood (2:13–15).

22. Mudie, *Modern Athens*, 124. Future references will be given in the text.

23. Devine, *Scotland's Empire*, xxvi and passim.

24. See Clifford, McWilliam, and Walker, *Buildings of Scotland*, 437; Youngson, *Making of Classical Edinburgh*, 159–60.

25. "On the Proposed National Monument at Edinburgh," *Blackwood's* 5 (July 1819): 377–87. Future references to this article will be given in the text. The other articles in the series are "Restoration of the Parthenon in the National Monument," *Blackwood's* 5 (August 1819): 509–12 and 6 (November 1819): 137–48; "Public Buildings of Edinburgh," 6 (January 1820): 370–75; "On the Proposed Monument for Lord Melville," 6 (January 1820): 562–67.

26. On Barker and the Romantic panorama see Chandler and Gilmartin, introduction to *Romantic Metropolis*, 7–11.

27. Stoddart, *Remarks on Local Scenery and Manners*, 1:39–40. Stoddart praises the view of Queen Street at sunset from "the fields on the north" for the sublime architectural effect of "uninterrupted succession, which constitutes what Mr Burke calls the artificial infinite," 1:43; see also his comparison of the eastward and westward views from the North Bridge, 1:45–48.

28. Lockhart, *Peter's Letters to His Kinsfolk*, 1:6–7, 8–9. Further citations will be given in the text.

29. Cf. Burke, *Reflections on the Revolution in France*: "We see, that the parts of the system do not clash. . . . We compensate, we reconcile, we balance. We are enabled to unite into a consistent whole the various anomalies and contending principles that are found in the minds and affairs of men. From hence arises, not an excellence in simplicity, but one far superior, an excellence in composition. . . . It is from this view of things that the best legislators have often been satisfied with the establishment of some sure, solid, and ruling principle in government; a power like that which some of the philosophers have called a plastic nature; and having fixed the principle, they have left it afterwards to its own operation" (281–82).

30. Cockburn, *Memorials*, 159, 163, 196–97.

31. Scott, *Fortunes of Nigel*, 4.

32. See, e.g., Collins, *Profession of Letters*, 129–33; Sutherland, *Life of Walter Scott*, 122–24. See also, however, Richard Sher's recent challenge to "the myth of Constable as a revolutionary publisher," *Enlightenment and the Book*, 429–31, 438–40.

33. In September 1807 John Murray Jr. sounded out George Canning, Secretary of Foreign Affairs, on the possibility of establishing a pro-government rival to the *Edinburgh Review*. Scott and Murray were already conferring when the October 1808 *Edinburgh Review* precipitated their plans by coming out in opposition to the British campaign on the continent. Although he declined to be editor Scott became the main strategist in setting up the new *Quarterly Review*, defining its editorial principles, canvassing major contributors and contributing articles himself. See Hayden, *Romantic Reviewers*, 22–34.

34. Parker, *Literary Magazines and British Romanticism*, 2; on *Blackwood's* see 106–11, 124, 136–37.

35. "Edinburgh Novels," *Edinburgh Magazine* 3 (June 1819): 60.

36. "Thoughts on Novel Writing," *Blackwood's* 4 (January 1819): 394–96.

37. St Clair, *Reading Nation in the Romantic Period*, 216–17, 221.

38. Garside, "English Novel in the Romantic Era," 15.

39. These and subsequent figures come from ibid., 76.

40. Blackwood was the fifth largest publisher of fiction in the United Kingdom: see also Garside, "Hogg and the Blackwoodian Novel," 7.

41. See Hart, *Scottish Novel*, 31–84; Garside, "Hogg and the Blackwoodian Novel," 8–11.

42. See Chandler, *England in 1819*, 105–40; Christensen, *Romanticism at the End of History*, 3–8.

43. On Scott's exploration of periodicity and "the past as present" in the early Waverley novels see Maxwell, "Inundations of Time," 437–58.

44. Scott, "Works of John Home," 168.

45. Blackwood, who weathered the crash, published only eight new novels from 1827 to 1829: see Garside, "English Novel in the Romantic Era," 89–90.

46. Cockburn, *Life of Lord Jeffrey*, 1:74, 76–77, 78. See also *Memorials*, 74–88.

47. Cockburn, *Memorials of his Time*, 81. On Stewart, Millar and the anti-Jacobin reaction see Donald Winch, "System of the North," 32–33.

48. Cockburn, *Life of Lord Jeffrey*, 1:126. On the Peace of Amiens and the *Edinburgh Review* see Christensen, *Romanticism at the End of History*, 107–28.

49. For England, see Brewer, *Pleasures of the Imagination*, 44–50, 125–66.

50. Griffin, *Literary Patronage in England*, 10.

51. Sher, "Book in the Scottish Enlightenment," 42. For a full discussion, see Sher, *Enlightenment and the Book*, 265–400.

52. See Ferris, *Achievement of Literary Authority*, 19–23.

53. Scott, *Provincial Antiquities*, 1:81.

54. See Fontana, *Rethinking the Politics of Commercial Society*.

55. See Sher, *Church and University in Enlightenment Scotland*: on the Moderates' ideology, 151–74, 324–28; on the political and social determinants of the decline of the "Moderate Enlightenment," 304–22.

56. See Cockburn, *Memorials*, 271–72, 336–37, 353–55, 398.

57. Klancher, *Making of English Reading Audiences*, 18–46; see also Butler, "Culture's Medium," 131–47.

58. Ferris, *Achievement of Literary Authority*, 10–11, 79–86. See also Garside, "Scott and the 'Common Novel.' "

59. Siskin, *Work of Writing*, 172–90.

60. Jeffrey's review (*Edinburgh Review* 12 [1808]: 1–35) is reprinted in Haydn, *Scott: The Critical Heritage*, 35–51.

61. Hazitt, *Spirit of the Age*, 230. Hazlitt develops John Scott's "panegyric" in the first issue of the *London Magazine* (1820).

62. Ibid., 232–33. The passage in *Ivanhoe*, at the beginning of chapter 43, reads: "Even in our own day, when morals are better understood, an execution, a bruising-match, a riot, or a meeting of radical reformers, collects, at considerable hazard to themselves, immense crowds of spectators, otherwise little interested, except to see how matters are to be conducted, or whether the heroes of the day are, in the heroic language of insurgent tailors, 'flints' or 'dunghills' " (382). "Flints" and "dunghills" are cant terms meaning strikers and scabs.

63. Hazlitt refers to Scott's involvement with the the *Beacon* and the *Sentinel* in 1821–22. For a while it had seemed as though Scott might have to fight a duel when his name was revealed as one of the financial backers of the *Beacon*. Its no less scurrilous successor the *Sentinel* provoked the duel in which Stuart of Dunearn killed Boswell; Hazlitt visited Edinburgh during Stuart's trial and acquittal.

64. These critiques are discussed in the last chapter of *Scott's Shadow*.

65. "Author of the Scotch Novels," *London Magazine* 1 (1820): 17–18.

66. St. Clair, *Reading Nation in the Romantic Period*, 170.

67. Scott, *Fortunes of Nigel*, 8, 4–5; Scott's MS reading, "Representation," is restored in the new Edinburgh Edition; the phrase was published as "Representative Vision."

68. Scott, *Monastery*, 360–61. On this episode in the context of Scott's long-range effort to establish "absolute proprietorship" over his works see Brewer, *Afterlife of Character*, 195–201.

69. Green, *Scotch Novel Reading*, 1:4, 5. Green's heroine is eventually cured of her infatuation with Scottish romances when her enterprising lover masquerades as a Highland chief, in a burlesque of the conclusions of Mary Brunton's *Discipline* and Susan Ferrier's *Marriage*.

70. *Scotch Novel Reading*, 1:7–9, 236; 2:112–13; Hogg vindicated, 2:111. For a fuller discussion see Robertson, *Legitimate Histories*, 123–24.

71. For the rumor see *Archibald Constable and his Literary Correspondents*, 2:371 (letter from J. R. McCulloch, 9 December 1821).

72. [Jeffrey], "Secondary Scottish Novels," 160. The two-part review of "Scottish Novels of the Second Class" which appeared contemporaneously in Constable's *Edinburgh Magazine* performs a cruder hatchet job on the chief Blackwood authors, devoting most of the first part (13 [July 1823]: 1–9) to a demolition of Galt's *Ringan Gilhaize*, and the second (13 [October 1823]: 485–91) to an attack on the prose fiction oeuvre of Hogg.

73. [John Scott], "Blackwood's Magazine," *London Magazine* 2 (November 1820): 517; for the "Veiled Conductor of Blackwood's Magazine" see also *Blackwood's* 3 (May 1818): 211–15 (in an issue that also includes "Phantasmagoria," an apparition narrative by "Simon Shadow").

74. [John Scott], "Living Authors; No. I. The Author of the Scotch Novels," *London Magazine* 1 (January 1820): 16, 18.

75. Jane Porter's *The Scottish Chiefs* (1810) (a hectic romance of William Wallace) helped popularize Scottish historical fiction four years before *Waverley*. Critics who make much of *The Scottish Chiefs* as a disavowed precursor of *Waverley* tend to overlook Scott's own sensationally successful Highland romance of the same year, *The Lady of the Lake*. Other pre-*Waverley* novels with Scottish settings were produced in London, such as *Caledonia; or, the Stranger in Scotland: A National Tale* (1810), *Glencarron: A Scottish Tale* (1811) by Sarah Wigley, and several novels by Honoria Scott, including *The Vale of Clyde: A Tale* (1810), *A Winter in Edinburgh* (1810), and *Strathmay: Or Scenes in the North, Illustrative of Scottish Manners* (1813). See Garside, "Scott and the 'Common Novel,' " and the listings in Garside and Schöwerling, *English Novel*.

76. "Remarks on the Character and Writings of the late Mrs Brunton," *Edinburgh Magazine* 3 (January 1819): 45–49. For Scottish fiction before Scott and the "moral-evangelical" tradition see Garside, "English Novel in the Romantic Era," 59–61.

77. See Scott's epilogue to *Tales of My Landlord: Third Series* (1819): "if the present author, himself a phantom, may be permitted to distinguish a brother, or perhaps a sister shadow, he would mention, in particular, the author of the very lively work, entitled 'Marriage' " (*A Legend of the Wars of Montrose*, 183); and the 1830 introduction to *St. Ronan's Well*: "The ladies, in particular, gifted by nature with keen powers of observation and light satire, have been so distinguished by these works of talent, that, reckoning from the authoress of *Evelina* to her of *Marriage*, a catalogue might be made, including the brilliant and talented names of Edgeworth, Austen, Charlotte Smith, and others, whose success seems

to have appropriated [the domestic] province of the novel as exclusively their own" (1894 ed., ix). On Ferrier see Doyle, *Memoir and Correspondence of Susan Ferrier*, 55, 65–66, 125.

78. Scott, *Tale of Old Mortality*, 3. See Mack's illuminating discussion of the Clydesdale setting of Scott's "Tale of the West": Introduction (1999), xiii–xxi.

79. On Scottish tale collections in the 1820s see Killick, "Hogg and the Collection of Short Fiction," 23–24.

80. On *Walladmor*, and the wider phenomenon of Scott impostures, see Russett, *Fictions and Fakes*, 158–64.

81. *Lochandhu*—a farrago involving Highlanders, outlaws, smugglers, a dwarf and a legless blind minstrel—is enlivened by bouts of violent slapstick in the manner of Smollett. Advertised in 1825, *The Wolfe of Badenoch* was stalled in press during the crash and finally published by Constable's erstwhile partner Robert Cadell. The action culminates in the Battle of Otterbourne; the tale is otherwise notable for a burlesque of the death scene of Ulrica in *Ivanhoe*. The Border minstrel Adam o' Gordon plucks his harp while the castle burns around him: "I do but work myself into proper bardic enthusiasm, that I may better describe the grandeur of this terrific scene. Trust me, this is the minstrel's golden moment—" His afflatus is interrupted by the hero Sir Patrick Hepborne, who carries him off bodily, and an ignominious outbreak of coughing (2:162).

82. Lauder, *Wolfe of Badenoch*, 1:v–vi.

83. Galt to Blackwood, 30 January 1821; NLS MS 4006 fols. 219–20. Printed in Oliphant, *Annals of a Publishing House*, 1:452 (where it is misdated 1822). The "Legatees" is *The Ayrshire Legatees*; "The Pastor" is *Annals of the Parish*.

84. Galt, *Autobiography*, 2:227–28; see Scott, "General Preface" (1829), *Waverley*, 352. On the topos see Robertson, *Legitimate Histories*, 123–42; Russett, *Fictions and Fakes*, 161–63.

85. *Constable and his Literary Correspondents*, 3:151–52.

86. Brunton, *Emmeline*, lxxvi (letter to Mrs. Craigie, 10 December 1814).

87. Johnstone, *Clan-Albin*, 1.

88. Johnston, *Lairds of Glenfern*, 1:v–vi. If the claim echoes Johnstone's in *Clan-Albin*, so too does the novel's geography, which ranges from the Highlands to Edinburgh, London, Spain during Wellington's campaign, and even the West Indies, where the heroine is rescued by a "faithful negro slave."

89. Ferrier, *Inheritance*, 2:306–7. Did Virginia Woolf remember Ferrier's novel when she named the Scott-loving patriarch of *To the Lighthouse* Mr. Ramsay?

90. *Blackwood's* 7 (June 1820): 265.

91. Mudie, *Glenfergus*, 1:75.

92. See "Letter to the Author of Rob Roy," *Blackwood's* 2 (March 1818): 662–64. The author signed himself "Nicol Jarvie, *tertius*."

93. *Blackwood's* 10 (August 1821): 5–7.

94. Galt, *Bogle Corbet*, 1:102; Hamilton, *Cyril Thornton*, 73.

95. See Hughes, "Recovering Hogg's Personal Manuscript."

96. *Blackwood's* 10 (August 1821): 25; 10 (December 1821): 655.

97. On the *Old Mortality* controversy see, especially, Ferris, *Achievement of Literary Authority*, 137–94; Rigney, *Imperfect Histories*, 31–52. The reviewers were Thomas McCrie, the distinguished biographer of John Knox, writing in the

Edinburgh Christian Instructor 14 (1817): 41–73, 100–140, 170–201; Josiah Conder, in the *Eclectic Review* 7 (1817): 309–36. For Scott's response (with William Erskine and William Gifford) see the *Quarterly Review* 16 (1817): 430–80. By no means all of Scott's political opponents agreed with the evangelical critique. Radical reviewers John Scott (*London Magazine*) and Christian Johnstone (*Johnstone's Magazine*) applauded Scott for his depictions of virtuous Presbyterian characters.

98. See Ferris, *Achievement of Literary Authority*, 161–94. On Hogg, Galt, and *Old Mortality* see also Mack, *Scottish Fiction and the British Empire*, 135–66.

99. Mack, "Rage of Fanaticism"; *Scottish Fiction and the British Empire*, 69–70. In a paper read at the 1999 International Scott Conference, Mack suggests that *Redgauntlet* is also influenced by Hogg's critique of Scott's historical fiction in *The Three Perils of Woman*. See also Catherine Jones's argument that *Redgauntlet* "owes much to the example of [Galt's] *The Entail*," *Literary Memory*, 105.

100. Hamilton, *Metaromanticism*, 128–38.

101. For a full discussion see Duncan, *Modern Romance*, 146–76.

102. Bourdieu, *Rules of Art*, 232.

103. Craciun, "Romantic Spinstrelsy," 207–8, 219.

104. On eighteenth-century clubs see McElroy, *Scotland's Age of Improvement*; Crawford, "Robert Fergusson's Robert Burns." On the "Noctes Ambrosianae" as "the great Romantic professional carnivalesque novel" see Kelly, *English Fiction of the Romantic Period*, 256–57.

105. Garside, "English Novel in the Romantic Era," 72–75, 90.

106. Ferris, *Achievement of Literary Authority*, 79–104; Duncan, *Modern Romance*, 128–67.

107. The term, originally affixed to Eliza Montagu's circle in the 1750s and '60s, was revived as a pejorative term for literary or intellectual women: "Much used by reviewers of the first quarter of the 19th c.," according to the *OED*, which cites the *Edinburgh Review*, Hazlitt, and De Quincey (s.v. "Blue-stocking," 2).

108. Middle- and professional-class women in eighteenth-century Edinburgh enjoyed greater access to work (and greater social acceptance as workers) than their counterparts in England, according to Elizabeth Sanderson, who notes anecdotal evidence for a cultural change sometime after the 1780s and the relegation of women to the domestic sphere by the mid-nineteenth century: *Women and Work in Eighteenth-Century Edinburgh*, 106, 117–35, 168–72. Sanderson does not discuss literature, dominated by the academic, clerical, and legal professions in Enlightenment Edinburgh.

109. Brunton, *Emmeline*, xxxvi (letter to Eliza Izett, 30 August 1810).

110. On Izett and her circle (which included James Hogg and Anne Grant besides Mary Brunton) see Currie, "James Hogg's Literary Friendships," xliii–lvii.

111. Doyle, *Memoirs and Correspondence of Susan Ferrier*, 145–46. See also Copeland, *Women Writing about Money*, 194–95, 200–202.

112. Scott, *Journal*, 734; see also 736 and *Letters*, 2:2–3, 8:356–57.

113. De Quincey, *Recollections of the Lakes*, 205 (first published in *Tait's Edinburgh Magazine*, April 1839).

114. On Johnstone and Galt see Gordon, *John Galt*, 127–29.

115. "There are two John Galts" (Gordon, "Galt's Politics," 119); "Scott was two men" (Daiches, "Scott's Achievement as a Novelist," 36); for the two Hoggs, see Gifford, *James Hogg*.

Chapter 2: The Invention of National Culture

1. Phillips, *Society and Sentiment*, 310–20 (310, 320). See also Miller, *Cockburn's Millennium*. Catherine Jones's *Literary Memory* discusses the diversity of the styles and genres of memory in Enlightenment and post-Enlightenment writing.
2. Cockburn, *Memorials of His Time*, 25–26.
3. Galt, *Glenfell*, 53.
4. Chambers, *Traditions of Edinburgh*, 1:1.
5. The most detailed and perceptive account of *Peter's Letters* remains that of Hart, who reads it as an experiment in "national biography": *Lockhart as Romantic Biographer*, 49–75.
6. Lang, *Life and Letters*, 1:57–58.
7. De Staël's *De l'Allemagne* was translated into English in 1813. Lockhart attended Fichte's lectures, and met Goethe: Lang, *Life and Letters*, 1:118–19.
8. See Craig, *Out of History*, 82–118; Duncan, "North Britain, Inc."
9. On the Romantic discourse of periodization or "the Spirit of the Age," see Chandler, *England in 1819*, 105–14.
10. "On the Revival of a Taste for our Ancient Literature," *Blackwood's* 4 (December 1818): 264–66; Schlegel, *Lectures in the History of Literature*, 1:2.
11. Scott advised and encouraged Lockhart in the composition of *Peter's Letters*, applauding "the exquisite Dr Morris and his compeers" and supplying information on "the state of our Scottish literature about twenty five years since." On the book's publication he acknowledged Lockhart's "kind and delicate account of his visit to Abbotsford" (Scott, *Letters*, 5:323, 332, 431). At the beginning of 1820 Lockhart was formally engaged to Scott's daughter Sophia, and shortly afterwards appointed his father-in-law's literary executor.
12. On the Romantic opening of the opposition see Connell, *Romanticism, Economics and the Question of 'Culture'*: "early nineteenth-century political economy, and the debate on its legitimacy, scope, and function, played a formative role in the emergence of the idea of 'culture' itself, as a humanistic or spiritual resource resistant to the intellectual enervation produced by modern, commercial societies" (7). See also Gallagher, *Body Economic*, 7–34, who argues that both discourses share a conceptual common ground of "corporeal and sensational experience" (8).
13. Nairn, *Break-up of Britain*, 105–12.
14. Habermas, *Structural Transformation of the Public Sphere*, 27–43, 51–56.
15. See Trumpener, *Bardic Nationalism*, 28–30, 78–79; Manning, "Antiquarianism, the Scottish Science of Man"; Ferris, "Pedantry and the Question of Enlightenment History."
16. Chandler, *England in 1819*, 127–35.
17. Cockburn, *Memorials of his Time*, 73.
18. Burke, *Reflections on the Revolution*, 211–14.

19. Jeffrey, "Mounier," 13. Further references to this article will be given in the text.

20. Fontana, *Rethinking the Politics of Commercial Society*, 11–25, 79–96, 112–46. See also Christensen's analysis of Jeffrey's review as representative of the general project of the *Edinburgh Review*: "it was necessary to shift from a revolutionary ideology that misconstrued beneficial social change as violent and discontinuous to a political economy that redescribed change as continuous, systematic, and, therefore, predictable" (*Romanticism at the End of History*, 108). On Jeffrey's intellectual background see Flynn, "Francis Jeffrey and the Scottish Critical Tradition."

21. Jeffrey, "De la littérature," 18. Jeffrey construes as a threat what Diderot had offered as the promise of the *Encyclopédie*, in 1781.

22. Jeffrey expresses a muted hope that new institutions of popular education, such as Friendly Societies, may counter the process ("De la littérature," 23–24). Connell reads Jeffrey as divided between the conservative, Fergusonian analysis of the modern fragmentation of the public sphere and the ameliorative account of the diffusion of literature in commercial society that he inherited from his teacher, Dugald Stewart (*Romanticism, Economics and the Question of 'Culture,'* 70–76, 92–101). On the trope of "illiteracy" in Scotland in the first half of the nineteenth century see Fielding, *Writing and Orality*, 19–42.

23. Ferris, *Achievement of Literary Authority*, 19–34; Klancher, *Making of English Reading Audiences*, 47–75.

24. See Stafford, "*Edinburgh Review* and the Representation of Scotland."

25. Peter Williamson's *Edinburgh Directory for 1773–74* placed the Lords (Judges) of Session in the top rank of citizens, followed by Advocates; cited in Daiches, *Edinburgh*, 153–54. On the Scottish legal profession in the early nineteenth century see Michie, *Enlightenment Tory in Victorian Scotland*, 37–44.

26. See Shattock, *Politics and Reviewers*, 5–7.

27. Curry, *Scott's Edinburgh Annual Register*, 136, 139. Further references to this article are given in the text. Scott's sociological analysis—taken up by Lockhart in *Peter's Letters*—proved influential. For a refutation see Roper, *Reviewing before the Edinburgh*.

28. Parodying Southey's Oriental romance *The Curse of Kehama* (1810), canto 23, stanza 5: "Even over Veeshnoo's empyreal seat / They trust the Rajah shall extend their sway, / And that the seven-headed Snake, whereon / The strong Preserver sets his conquering feet, / Will rise and shake him headlong from his throne, / When, in their irresistible array, / Amid the milky Sea they force their way."

29. "Remarks on the Periodical Criticism of England," 671. Further references to this article are given in the text. In *Peter's Letters* Lockhart defends it as "the first regular attack" on the hegemony of the quarterlies (2:215).

30. Blackwood did for the magazine what Constable had done for the review, paying his top contributors 10 guineas per sheet—more than double the standard rate at miscellanies, if still less than half of what an author could expect to earn at the *Edinburgh Review*. See Polsgrove, "They Made it Pay," 418–19.

31. For some other recent accounts of this genealogy, see Chandler, *England in 1819*, 127–47; Siskin, *Work of Writing*, 79–99; and Connell, *Romanticism, Economics*.

32. Chandler, *England in 1819*, 67.

33. Butler, "Culture's Medium," 136–37; *Tait's Edinburgh Magazine* 11 (1833): 58–59. See Shattock, *Politics and Reviewers*, 3–15.

34. *Blackwood's* 3 (June 1818): 257. On Buchanan and Scottish Radical and Whig traditions see Kidd, *Subverting Scotland's Past*, 92–94, 214, 271; McIlvanney, *Burns the Radical*, 17–24; Snodgrass, "*Blackwood's* Subversive Scottishness," 102–6.

35. Klancher, *Making of English Reading Audiences*, 52–53.

36. Jeffrey, "De la Littérature," 17.

37. *Edinburgh Monthly Magazine* 1 (1817): 39, 13.

38. Lockhart, "Remarks on the Periodical Criticism of England," 672.

39. Schlegel, *History of Literature*, 1:6. Further references to this edition are given in the text.

40. "Remarks on Schlegel's History of Literature," *Blackwood's* 3 (1818): 510.

41. "Observations on 'Peter's Letters to His Kinsfolk,' " *Blackwood's* 4 (1819): 612–21, 745–52.

42. John Scott saw the relation between *Peter's Letters* and *Blackwood's* as the crux of the Blackwoodian "system of fraud and scandal": *London Magazine* (November, 1820): 509–21. "Peter is the Editors, puffing their own magazine in the style of the quack-doctor's stage, and professing contrition while hatching fresh offences!" (511); "Peter Morris, the hypocrite in front, and Christopher North, the ruffian behind" (514).

43. Buzard, *Disorienting Fiction*, 8–12; on "autoethnography" in the national tale and Scott, 41, 63–68. See also Herbert, *Culture and Anomie*, 1–28.

44. Lockhart, *Peter's Letters to His Kinsfolk*, 2:206 (emphasis mine). Future references will be cited in the text.

45. On the role of "the English constitution" in the Enlightenment tradition of Scottish historiography that Lockhart is adapting here, see Kidd, *Subverting Scotland's Past*, 101–28, 254–55.

46. The diagnostic term "Caledonian Antisyzygy," coined in 1919 by G. Gregory Smith and taken up by Hugh MacDiarmid, signified the internal contradictoriness of Scottish national character. For its literary-historical manifestation as a "dissociation of sensibility" see Muir, *Scott and Scotland*. For critiques see Tom Nairn, *Break-Up of Britain*, 119–23; Craig, *Out of History*, 82–118; Crawford, "Scottish Literature and English Studies," 233–37.

47. Compare Schlegel's argument that Hume's philosophical skepticism, "by no means becoming in a great national historian," undermined his literary influence: *History of Literature*, 2:221.

48. Schlegel, *History of Literature*, 1:16.

49. This scene, with its touristic-aesthetic descriptive technique, is indebted to the cathedral crypt episode in chapter 20 of Scott's *Rob Roy* (242–45).

50. Lockhart, *Life of Robert Burns* (1828); reprinted in Low, *Robert Burns*, 343. On Burns's reputation in the generation following his death see Davis, *Acts of Union*, 124–48.

51. Scott, *Tale of Old Mortality*, 14.

52. Lockhart's later, more circumstantial account of his visit to Abbotsford, in the *Life of Scott*, conveys even more of the atmosphere of a visit to a theme park (5:368–80). Lockhart sets off his insider's status as private guest against two American tourists, "rich specimens" wearing "new jackets and trowsers of the Macgregor tartan" (5:387).

53. Compare Lockhart's account with Washington Irving's, in a series of letters written during his 1817 visit to Abbotsford but not published until nearly twenty years later (reprinted in the *Life of Scott*, 5:243–52). Irving, more radically a stranger, is disconcerted by the monotony and bareness of a landscape that he had imagined through Scott's poetry as a lush ancestral homeland (5:248–49). On Scottish philosophical associationism and Scott's rhetoric of place see Craig, "Scotland and the Regional Novel," 240–48.

54. Lang reproduces a watercolor sketch of Sophia by Lockhart that shows her in the classic harp-playing pose of the national heroine: *Life and Letters*, vol. 1, facing 288. For the convention see Trumpener, *Bardic Nationalism*, 18–19.

55. St Clair, *Reading Nation*, 170.

56. See Hayden, *Scott: The Critical Heritage*, 38–39.

57. See Scott's comments on "The Scottish Edition": *Minstrelsy of the Scottish Border*, 123–26.

58. See Buzard, *Beaten Track*, 172–92.

59. Compare Lockhart on Burns: "The political circumstances of Scotland were, and had been, such as to starve the flame of patriotism; the popular literature had striven, and not in vain, to make itself English; and, above all, a new and cold system of speculative philosophy had begun to spread widely among us. A peasant appeared, and set himself to check the creeping pestilence of this indifference" (Low, *Burns: The Critical Heritage*, 345).

60. "I thought ten thousand swords must have leaped from their scabbards to avenge even a look that threatened her with insult.—But the age of chivalry is gone" (Burke, *Reflections*, 170).

61. Žižek, *Tarrying with the Negative*, 222.

Chapter 3: Economies of National Character

1. Earlier Scottish tales, e.g., by Elizabeth Helme, were published in London: *Duncan and Peggy: A Scottish Tale* (1794), *Albert: or, The Wilds of Strathnavern* (1799), *St. Clair of the Isles: or, The Outlaws of Barra; A Scottish Tradition* (1803). Robert Couper's *The Tourifications of Malachi Meldrum, Esq., of Meldrum-Hall* was published in 1803 in Aberdeen; Joseph Strutt's antiquarian romance *Queenhoo-Hall*, completed by Scott, was published in Edinburgh contemporaneously with *Cottagers of Glenburnie*.

2. Hamilton, *Cottagers of Glenburnie*, 137. Future references will be given in the text.

3. *Critical Review*, 3rd ser., 15 (December 1808): 421, 430.

4. Boswell, *Journal of a Tour to the Hebrides*, 166.

5. Douglas, *Purity and Danger*, 36; Barthes, "Reality Effect."

6. See Kelly, *English Fiction of the Romantic Period*, 89–91; Copeland, *Women Writing about Money*, 65–67.

7. Galt, *Voyages and Travels*, 105.

8. Moretti, *Atlas of the Euopean Novel*, 40.

9. Buzard, *Disorienting Fiction*, 161.

10. Copeland, *Women Writing about Money*, includes Hamilton, Brunton, and Ferrier among Romantic-era women novelists who promote improvement and "stress the respectability of female employment" for gentlewomen (163).

11. Trumpener, *Bardic Nationalism*, 137–52. On *The Wild Irish Girl* as origin of the national tale "rooted in [national] grievance" see Ferris, *Romantic National Tale*, 51. On Edgeworth and Owenson see Robert Tracy, "Maria Edgeworth and Lady Morgan."

12. For the postcolonial tradition of reading *Castle Rackrent* see Eagleton, *Heathcliff and the Great Hunger*, 166– 68; Dunne, *Maria Edgeworth and the Colonised Mind*; Graham, "History, Gender and the Colonial Moment"; Connolly, "Reading Responsibility in *Castle Rackrent*."

13. Butler, general introduction, VIII.

14. Edgeworth, *Castle Rackrent and Ennui*, 63. Future references to both novels will be given in the text.

15. On irony in *Castle Rackrent* see Gallagher, *Nobody's Story*, 298–99; Moore, "Acts of Union," 121–28.

16. See Duncan, "Pathos of Abstraction," 40–46.

17. See Crawford, *Devolving English Literature*, 22–27; Sorensen, *Grammar of Empire*, 138–52.

18. Hume, "Of National Characters," 207.

19. Millar, *Origin of the Distinction of Ranks*, 5.

20. On the close of *Ennui* see Gallagher, *Nobody's Story*, 300–305; Ó Gallchoir, "Maria Edgeworth's Revolutionary Morality," who analyses "a tension between the stasis of domestic realism, which purports to describe things as they are, and a desire to propose models of change," 89.

21. Buzard, *Disorienting Fiction*, 163.

22. Dennis, *Nationalism and Desire*, 47; see also Connolly, "Politics of Love in *The Wild Irish Girl*"; Ferris, *Romantic National Tale*, 54–66.

23. The plot has a long afterlife in popular romance; its most brilliant twentieth-century redaction can be seen in the 1945 film by Michael Powell and Emeric Pressburger, *I Know Where I'm Going*.

24. The ambivalence informs the critical discussion. Peter Womack coins the terms "Gaelic idyll" and "women's Highlands" for a tradition that includes—besides Brunton and Ferrier—novelists Elizabeth Helme, Mary Johnston, and Jane Porter; poet Anne Grant; and playwright Joanna Baillie in a conservative ideological project, the fantasy of a privatized reconstitution of the organic community that reproduces the "immanent principle of a total structure of subordination": *Improvement and Romance*, 135–39. Feminist critics emphasize reformation within the domestic enclave: Brunton's Highlands are the setting for "a quiet sexual radicalism" and the depiction of "women as fully social beings" (Smith,

"Men, Women, and Money," 53–54); the close of *Discipline* instantiates a "haven where the relationship between man and woman is companionate rather than hierarchical" (Green, *Courtship Novel*, 133); *Marriage*, "a fictional transformation of Wollstonecraft's *Vindication*" (Mellor, *Romanticism and Gender*, 49), "opens up a radically new concept of an egalitarian marriage in which the wife has as much power as her husband" (9). The most recent criticism argues that these novels model the integration of the Highlands into the modern British economy: "In *Discipline*, British commerce underpins the preservation of Highland tradition" (Alker, "The Business of Romance," 200); Scottish national tales advocate "a second kind of domestication: Highlanders' integration into a commercial British nation-state. These novels prescribed a national division of moral labor according to which the Highlands would provide a refuge from, and a moral antidote to, the corruption engendered by southern metropolitan Britain's imperial activities" (Shields, "From Family Roots to the Routes of Empire," 923).

25. Brunton, *Discipline*, 3:291 n. G. Subsequent references will be given in the text.

26. On the shift from "a novel of manners" to a new "regional realism," see Bour, "Mary Brunton's Novels," 30–31.

27. Innes-Smith and Hughes-Hartman, *Inveraray Castle*, 6. Johnstone makes "smokes" the sign of a healthy community in *Clan-Albin*—their extinction means clearance.

28. See Trumpener, *Bardic Nationalism*, 194–241. On the regime of extended or "total domesticity" see Womack, *Improvement and Romance*, 136–37; Shields, "From Family Roots to the Routes of Empire."

29. See Devine, *Scotland's Empire*, 224–26, 244–49.

30. Scott, "Culloden Papers," 333.

31. See Lenman, *Integration, Enlightenment, and Industrialization*, 151.

32. Ferrier, *Marriage* (1818), 97–98. Subsequent references to this edition are given in the text.

33. On the formation of taste as a global project in Ferrier's fiction, see Price, "Politics of Pedantry": "Less concerned to express a subjectivity than to exercise readers' taste, Ferrier's novels . . . become legible if we situate them . . . within a competing contemporary culture of the anthology-piece" (76).

34. While the name "Glenfern" may seem generic, this passage resonates with the early description of Mrs. Grant's first view of the tower of Clathan—"her heart sank at the sight of its square grey walls and desolate situation"—in Mary Johnston's *Lairds of Glenfern* (1:33).

35. Despite the assertion that this scenery exceeds poetic powers of description, Ferrier's 1841 revision of *Marriage* for *Bentley's Standard Novels* inserts "the well-known lines" from Scott's *Lay of the Last Minstrel* ("Land of brown heath and shaggy wood!") just before this passage (510–11).

36. Ferrier's Scots characters carry more vivid detailing—more reality effect—than her English ones: national fiction renders its types as "thick" or "thin," in contrast to E. M. Forster's distinction between "round" and "flat" characters (in *Aspects of the Novel*, 65–75). The English tend to thinness, with the notable exception of the gourmand Dr. Redgill, thickened through Ferrier's satire of unsublimated taste as appetite. Sensuous attention to the particularities of his diet

endows Redgill, rhetorically as well as physiologically, with bulk and texture. On food and national allegory in Ferrier, see Moss, "Recipes for Disaster"; on the disjunction between taste and appetite in Regency writing, see Gigante, *Taste*, 160–72. On the neoclassical hierarchy of abstract (polite) over particular (low) character depiction, see Lynch, *Economy of Character*, 58–67.

37. See Price, "Politics of Pedantry": " 'Taste' differentiates good from bad characters (and writers), but also provides so much common ground for the former as to call the very possibility of psychic depth into question. Quotation makes Ferrier's readers just as interchangeable" (79).

38. Ferrier, *Inheritance*, 1:207–8. Further references are given in the text.

39. On the writing and publication of *Marriage* see Doyle, *Memoir and Correspondence of Susan Ferrier*, 55, 138–45.

40. Scott, *Waverley*, 33.

41. See Duncan, *Modern Romance*, 87–105; Buzard, *Disorienting Fiction*, 81–98. On the "allegory of salvage" see Clifford, "Ethnographic Allegory."

42. Scott, *Antiquary*, 3. Subsequent references will be given in the text.

43. Žižek, *Tarrying with the Negative*, 201.

44. Doyle, *Memoir and Correspondence of Susan Ferrier*, 157.

45. Drescher, ed., *Literature and Literati*, 329.

46. Lynch, *Economy of Character*, 132.

47. Galt, *Sir Andrew Wylie*, 1:1. Subsequent references will be given in the text.

48. Sorensen, *Grammar of Empire*, 137; on Smith and linguistic self-fashioning, 138–52.

49. Hart, *Scottish Novel*, 35.

50. See Girard, *Deceit, Desire and the Novel*; Dennis, *Nationalism and Desire*.

Chapter 4: Modernity's Other Worlds

1. For recent discussions of Scott's fiction and tourism see Dekker, *Fictions of Romantic Tourism*, 126–99; Buzard, *Disorienting Fiction*, 63–104; Pittock, "Scott and the British Tourist."

2. Hogg, *Spy*, 401.

3. *Edinburgh Magazine* 2 (1818): 149, 41.

4. For these influential concepts see Trevor-Roper, "Invention of Tradition"; Pittock, *Invention of Scotland*; Hechter, *Internal Colonialism*.

5. See Pittock, *Invention of Scotland*, 84–90; Kidd, *Subverting Scotland's Past*, 256–67; Brewer, *Pleasures of the Imagination*, 657–58; Devine, *Scottish Nation*, 292.

6. Anderson, *Imagined Communities*, 30–37. Anderson derives the phrase "homogeneous, empty time" from Walter Benjamin's *Theses on the Philosophy of History*. For a suggestive summary see Moretti, *Atlas of the European Novel*, 16–17.

7. Makdisi, *Universal Empire*, 9–10. See also Trumpener, *Bardic Nationalism*; Mack, *Scottish Fiction and the British Empire*.

8. Ernest Gellner's phrase, cited in Nairn, *Break-Up of Britain*, 96.

9. Moretti, *Atlas of the European Novel*, 40.

10. This critical tendency culminates in William St Clair's claim (recklessly amplifying Mark Twain's) that Scott's dominance of the nineteenth-century transatlantic "reading nation" issued not only in the American Civil War but in the First World War: *Reading Nation*, 390, 427.

11. Koselleck, *Futures Past*, 148.

12. See Makdisi, *Universal Empire*, 70–99; Trumpener, *Bardic Nationalism*, 128–57; Christensen, *Romanticism at the End of History*, 153–75; Mack, *Scottish Fiction*, 8–12, 99–101. On the elegiac and aesthetic reconstitution of historical space, see Duncan, *Modern Romance*, 79–105; on Scott's "temporalization of space" as autoethnographic technique, see Buzard, *Disorienting Fiction*, 85–98. For a complication of these accounts, see Ferris, "Translation from the Borders," 214–20. Cairns Craig cites world-system theory and the work of Henri Lefebvre to argue that the Scottish romance tradition founded by Scott tropes the irreducibility of spatial difference in order to maintain a distinctively Scottish construction of cultural identity: *Out of History*, 113–18. See also Craig's critique of Anderson, "Scott's Staging of the Nation."

13. Scott, "Culloden Papers," 333.

14. Ferris, "Translation from the Borders," 221–22. See also Trumpener, *Bardic Nationalism*, 217–18; Shields, "From Family Roots to the Routes of Empire," 926–32.

15. Johnstone, *Clan-Albin*, 62.

16. Scott takes up the utopian solution of *Clan-Albin* in *The Heart of Midlothian* (1818), which represents the settlement of Lowland farmers on a Highland estate: see Sussman, "Emptiness at *The Heart of Midlothian*."

17. See, e.g., Davie, *Heyday of Sir Walter Scott*, 56–64; Hart, *Scott's Novels*, 33–48; Cockshutt, *Achievement of Walter Scott*, 153–70. See Lincoln, "Rob Roy and Empire," for a recent argument convergent with the present chapter's.

18. Millgate, *Walter Scott*, 133.

19. For this tradition see Forbes, "Rationalism of Sir Walter Scott"; Garside, "Scott and the 'Philosophical' Historians"; McMaster, *Scott and Society*, 49–77; Sutherland, "Fictional Economies"; Vakil, "Walter Scott and the Historicism of Scottish Enlightenment Philosophical History"; Kaufmann, *Business of Common Life*, 101–9.

20. Chandler, *England in 1819*, 107, 127–35.

21. Ibid., 129 (glossing a passage in Millar's *Origin of the Distinction of Ranks*).

22. The passage is cited by several recent commentators, e.g., Craig, *Out of History*, 38; Chandler, *England in 1819*, 132; Kaufmann, *Business of Common Life*, 107; Villari, "Romance and History in *Waverley*"; Makdisi, *Universal Empire*, 73; Moretti, *Atlas of the European Novel*, 39.

23. Scott, *Waverley*, 340.

24. See Pittock, *Invention of Scotland*, 85.

25. See Buzard, *Disorienting Fiction*, 71.

26. Lukács, *Historical Novel*, 57; the phrase is Cockshutt's, *Achievement of Walter Scott*, 159 n. 2.

27. Millgate, *Walter Scott*, 149–50; see also Hewitt, "*Rob Roy* and First-Person Narratives."

28. Scott, *Rob Roy*, 387. Further references will be given in the text.

29. See Micale, *Approaching Hysteria*, 22–23. On sexuality, gender and "politeness" in *Rob Roy*, see Irvine, *Enlightenment and Romance*, 153–74.

30. Womack, *Improvement and Romance*, 147–48.

31. Smith, *Wealth of Nations*, 22. Future references are given in the text.

32. Poovey, *History of the Modern Fact*, 217.

33. Smith notes that the monopolistic profits of the sugar and tobacco plantations were largely responsible for sustaining slavery within the British empire: *Wealth of Nations*, 388–89. See Devine and Jackson, *Glasgow*, on the tobacco trade, 139–83, and the Caribbean sugar and rum trades: 79, 189–90, 216–18; also Devine, *Scotland's Empire*, 75–76, 221–49.

34. For Scott's role in canonizing Defoe see Brown, *Institutions of the English Novel*, 179–92.

35. As Mack insists: *Scottish Fiction*, 121–22.

36. On Gothic motifs in *Rob Roy* see Robertson, *Legitimate Histories*, 178–87.

37. See Moretti, *Atlas of the European Novel*, 35–47.

38. See Womack, *Improvement and Romance*, 20–24; Crawford, *Devolving English Literature*, 16–17.

39. On Scott, Highlanders, and violence see McNeil, "Inside and Outside the Nation."

40. Burt, *Letters from a Gentleman*, 1:xxii—xxiii.

41. See Simmons, "Man of Few Words." In Hogg's "The Pongos" the apes are more humane than European colonists: *Altrive Tales*, 160–71.

42. See the classic account by Fabian, *Time and the Other*.

43. Womack, *Improvement and Romance*, 60.

44. Originally published in the *Quarterly Review* 26 (October 1821): 109–48; reprinted in Hayden, *Scott: The Critical Heritage*, 215. Senior alludes to Scott's discussion of the contract between author and reader at the opening of vol. 2 of *Waverley*: "Shall this be a short or a long chapter? —This is a question in which you, gentle reader, have no vote. . . . [T]hough it lies within my arbitrary power to extend my materials as I think proper, I cannot call you into the Exchequer if you do not think proper to read my narrative" (115).

45. Mill, *On Liberty*, 69.

Chapter 5: The Rise of Fiction

1. Hume, "Of National Character," 207.

2. See Simpson, *Romanticism, Nationalism and the Revolt against Theory*, 4 and passim.

3. Hume, *Treatise of Human Nature*, 234. Further references to this edition will be given in the text.

4. *Jane Austen's Letters*, 274 (9 September 1814); see Moretti, *Atlas of the European Novel*, 17–24; Duncan, "Regional or Provincial Novel," 329–32.

5. Scott, "*Emma; a Novel*," 230. Future references are given in the text. The essay was published in the *Quarterly Review* 14 (October 1815): 188–201.

6. Miranda Burgess discusses Scott's review of *Emma* in the light of both authors' investment in a national public sustained by novel reading: "Domesticating Gothic," 392–95.

7. Austen, *Emma*, 355. Further references will be cited in the text.

8. Miller, *Jane Austen*, 60.

9. Smith, *Theory of Moral Sentiments*, 41–42.

10. See Manning, *Fragments of Union*, 32–52.

11. Livingston, *Hume's Philosophy of Common Life*, 30.

12. "The Pyrrhonian illumination shows that there is no Archimedean point outside common life as a whole from which it can be either certified or criticized. We have no alternative, then, but to *use* the prejudices and customs of common life as a framework for understanding the real, with no guarantee that we shall understand things as they really are" (Livingston, *Hume's Philosophy*, 30–31).

13. Miller, *Philosophy and Ideology in Hume's Political Thought*, 36–39; see also Damrosch, *Fictions of Reality*, 17–23; François, "To Hold in Common and Know by Heart."

14. Hume, "both a naturalist and a skeptic," does not "[represent] his consequent naturalism as simply a re-occupation of the perspective of antecedent naturalism"; its mode, instead, is that of a "rueful belief of post-skeptical self-understanding," according to Janet Broughton in "The Inquiry in Hume's *Treatise*": "Irony is Hume's way of representing a special self-consciousness, detachment, or doubling." For a contrasting view see Vermeule, who contends that the Humean account of belief is finally nondialectical, as Hume maintains a dualistic oscillation between the insupportable melancholia of "reflection" and an irrational absorption in "common life" that reconstitutes the fanaticism it abhors (*Party of Humanity*, 205–7).

15. Gallagher, *Nobody's Story*, 173. Robert Alter's *Partial Magic* shows us what an alternative history of the novel as defined by the principle of fictionality, rather than by the referential function of "formal realism," might look like: it recasts the nineteenth century—the telos of realist-inflected "rise of the novel" narratives—as anomalous rather than normative, an "eclipse" rather than a zenith.

16. Hunter, *Before Novels*, 27.

17. Davis, *Factual Fictions*, 70, 36.

18. Ibid., 210–11.

19. Defined, according to Michael McKeon, in the debate between Fielding and Richardson (*Origins of the English Novel*, 39–64, 118–28).

20. Gallagher, *Nobody's Story*, 164, 174.

21. Bender, "Enlightenment Fiction and the Scientific Hypothesis," 6.

22. Gallagher, *Nobody's Story*, 173.

23. Iser, *Fictive and the Imaginary*, xiv–xv. Compare Gallagher and Greenblatt: novels "limber us up to cross ontological levels with ease, to poise ourselves on provisional ground, to assent for the moment while keeping our readiness to depart from the fictional world" (*Practicing New Historicism*, 170).

24. Iser, *Fictive and the Imaginary*, xvi, 87, 111.

25. See Craig, "Coleridge, Hume, and the Chains of the Romantic Imagination."

26. Iser, *Fictive and the Imaginary*, 111, 112–30. Bender contrasts Hume's philosophical account with Bentham's separation of "the fictionality of poetic inventions from harmless natural fictions on the one hand and from the dangerous mystifications of priests and lawyers on the other" (*Imagining the Penitentiary*, 36). Compare also Bender, "Enlightenment Fiction and the Scientific Hypothesis," 8–9, 14.

27. Zimmerman, *Boundaries of Fiction*, 43–44.

28. Ibid., 239. David Wootton argues that Hume conceived his *History* as competing with the novel for a reading public ("David Hume, 'the Historian,' " 281–84).

29. For these see Bender, "Enlightenment Fiction and the Scientific Hypothesis"; Kaufmann, *Business of Common Life*; Burgess, *British Fiction and the Production of Social Order*.

30. Phillips, *Society and Sentiment*, 126.

31. See, e.g., Gallagher, *Nobody's Story*; 167–74; Mullan, *Sentiment and Sociability*,18–44; Burgess, *British Fiction and the Production of Social Order*, 100–102; Pinch, *Strange Fits of Passion*, 19–35.

32. See Duncan, "Adam Smith, Samuel Johnson and the Institutions of English," 46–51. Although Smith's lectures were not published, their argument was widely diffused; and although Smith does not recommend the novel as a model, it was there that his prescriptions would be fully applied.

33. Gossman, *Between History and Literature*, 227–30.

34. See Zimmerman, *Boundaries of Fiction*, 237.

35. Clifford Siskin identifies the novel rather than poetry as the Romantic discourse where this takes place (*Work of Writing*, 172–90).

36. Zimmerman, *Boundaries of Fiction*, 4, 222.

37. Bender, "Enlightenment Fiction and the Scientific Hypothesis," 21.

38. Scott, "Works of John Home," 193–94.

39. See Manning, *Fragments of Union*, 27, 47–52: "Reid's and Beattie's 'refutations' of Hume . . . effectively propagated the union-fragmentation tensions in his thought in the very form of their negations, at the same time as their stories of the self extended the implications of his analogy between identity and grammar" (48). See also Jones, *Literary Memory*, 38–39; Stewart, *Elements of Philosophy*, vol. 1 (1792), 71, 87–88.

40. Vermeule calls Hume "the pre-eminent eighteenth-century theorist of belief" and contends that his engagement with the category yields "a theory of the literary itself" (*Party of Humanity*, 205, 183).

41. Hume's argument is consistent with the didactic conception of history, informing his later turn to the genre, as an efficacious genre for instilling moral sentiment: see Wootton, "David Hume, 'the Historian,' " 281–84.

42. Blair, *Lectures on Rhetoric*, 421.

43. Home (Kames), *Elements of Criticism*, 1:71. Subsequent references given in the text.

44. However Kames also says that "reading and acting have greatly the advantage" over painting in that the "succession of impressions" better represents the temporality of passion (*Elements*, 1:72).

45. Reid, *Inquiry into the Human Mind*, 23, 22. Future references will be cited in the text.

46. Reid, *Essays on the Intellectual Powers*, 44.

47. On Stewart's influence, see Phillipson, "Pursuit of Virtue in Scottish University Education"; Winch, "System of the North," 25–61; Connell, *Romanticism, Economics and the Question of "Culture,"* 70–76. On the Edinburgh moral philosophy chair, see Sher, "Professors of Virtue."

48. Reid, *Essays on the Intellectual Powers*, 44.

49. See Poovey, *History of the Modern Fact*, 14, 173–77, 201–3.

50. Cockburn, *Memorials of His Time*, 187.

51. Ibid., 188.

52. Brown, *Observations*, 95. Future references will be given in the text.

53. Brown, *Lectures*, 1:327. Future references will be given in the text. On the controversy surrounding Brown's appointment see Cockburn, *Memorials*, 237.

54. Stewart, who outlived his student, would insert a critique of Brown in the last volume (1827) of *Elements of the Philosophy of the Human Mind*: he deplores Brown's "severe, and not very respectful strictures on Dr Reid" and complains that his poetic temperament compromised the patience and accuracy necessary for philosophical enquiry (3:310, 501–5). Cockburn surmises "that Stewart, angry at Brown's rejection of the *Common Sense* of Reid and of himself, wrote this Note in a state of personal irritation" (*Memorials*, 347).

55. Gossman, *Between History and Literature*, 233.

56. Benjamin, *Illuminations*, 261. Future references will be given in the text.

57. I review my discussion of *Waverley* in *Modern Romance*, 73–105. For *Waverley*, 1745, and *Tom Jones* see Brown, *Institutions of the English Novel*, 138–40.

58. On Hume as source of a modern British "moderate" conservative tradition see Bongie, *David Hume, Prophet of the Counter-Revolution*; Livingston, *Hume's Philosophy of Common Life*; Miller, *Philosophy and Ideology in Hume's Political Thought*: "a revolutionary philosophy is wedded to an establishment ideology to yield what is probably the best example we have of a secular and sceptical conservative political theory," 187.

59. Wootton, "David Hume 'the Historian,' " 301–2. On the juridical-ethical tradition of casuistry in Smith and Scott see Chandler, *England in 1819*, 309–20.

60. Phillips, *Society and Sentiment*, 34, 36–37.

61. Cf. Hamilton: "Consistent with *Waverley*'s Burkean grasp of the history of revolution is its relinquishing of Kant's supposed advance on Humean philosophy: it reverts from the logical necessity of believing in valid representation to Hume's strictly psychological explanation of why we do so" (*Metaromanticism*, 121). On Hume and Scott see also Lincoln, "Sentimental and Accountable Reading": Lincoln argues that Scott uses romance conventions as a conservative, stabilizing counterweight to the skeptical knowledge of history. On Scott's conservatism and Romantic irony, see Chase, "Walter Scott"; Lee, *Nationalism and Irony*, 19–24.

62. Scott, *Antiquary*, 35, 277. Subsequent references will be cited in the text.

63. Christensen, *Romanticism at the End of History*, 7, citing Wallerstein, *Unthinking Social Science*, 16–17.

64. Notoriously, E. M. Forster reduced *The Antiquary* to a plot summary in order to expose the aesthetic vacuum covered by Scott's reputation (*Aspects of the Novel*, 31–38). See also Hart, *Scott's Novels*, 247; Brown, *Walter Scott and the Historical Imagination*, 66–67.

65. Forster, *Aspects of the Novel*, 34. Even this remark betrays the slovenliness with which Forster reads Scott: in *Guy Mannering*, Scott's previous novel, the young gentleman who appears at the opening of the narrative conspicuously fails to make his spouse happy.

66. David Hewitt demonstrates that "the action of *The Antiquary* starts on 15 July 1794 and concludes a little before 12 August of that year" (Scott, *Antiquary*, 444). Previous commentators had tended to accept a date around 1797–98.

67. E.g., Hart, *Scott's Novels*, 248; Wilt, *Secret Leaves*, 156–70; Millgate, *Walter Scott*, 89–104.

68. See Burgess, "Scott, History, and the Augustan Public Sphere"; Ferris, "Pedantry and the Question of Enlightenment History," 277–81; Lee, *Nationalism and Irony*, 78–79, 90–101; McCracken-Flesher, *Possible Scotlands*, 36–43.

69. Cf. Kaufmann, *Business of Common Life*: "Manners, recognition, and respect serve as the glue that keeps the state together and binds the castes in such a way as to create a positive sense of mutual dependence. . . . *The Antiquary* deploys manners against the disruptions that Scott has considered as the necessary preconditions of narrativity itself" (121).

70. Scott, *Tale of Old Mortality*, 7. Future references to this edition will be cited in the text. Mack restores the novel's manuscript title, *The Tale of Old Mortality*; the present discussion will refer to it by the title under which it was published in Scott's lifetime.

71. Agamben, *State of Exception*, 1–5, 50–52. On *Old Mortality* as a "model of revolution," see Welsh, *Hero of the Waverley Novels*, 196–208.

Chapter 6: Hogg's Body

1. Lockhart, *Peter's Letters*, 1:129. See also "Triennial Commemoration of Burns," *Edinburgh Weekly Journal* 22 (24 February 1819): 60–62; (3 March 1819): 69. Against these Tory accounts see Cockburn: "This was long remembered as the first public dinner at which any of the Whigs of Edinburgh had spoken. It was the first that showed them the use to which such meetings could be turned, and was the immediate cause of the political dinners that soon after made such an impression" (*Memorials of His Time*, 336–37).

2. Scott, *Letters*, 3:373; Laidlaw, *Recollections of Sir Walter Scott*, 4.

3. Hogg, "Journey through the Highlands of Scotland" (1802), 815–16.

4. Hogg, *Queen's Wake*, 37. Future references will be noted in the text.

5. See Hogg, *Letters*, 1:300–301, 303, 305, 378. For the Blackwoodian claim on Hogg, see Wilson, "Some Observations on the Poetry . . . of Scotland."

6. "The True and Authentic Account of the Twelfth of August, 1819," *Blackwood's* 4 (1819): 597; Hogg, *Letters*, 1:421.

7. "Mr Hogg and Blackwood's Magazine," *Scotsman*, no. 190 (11 November 1820): 367; see also John Scott, "Mohock Magazine," 677–81.

8. See Mergenthal, *"Naturae Donum"*; Schoenfield, "Butchering James Hogg"; McLachlan, "Hogg and the Art of Brand Management"; on Hogg's late attempt to reclaim his authorial persona see Hughes's introduction to Hogg, *Lay Sermons*, xix–xxvii.

9. Hogg's claim is supported by a letter to Blackwood of 24 September 1817: see Hogg, *Letters*, 1:300–301.

10. Scott, *Letters*, 5:156–57 (25 May 1818). For the affair see also Hogg, *Letters*, 1:349–51.

11. Miller, *Electric Shepherd*, 38.

12. For these attacks, see Ferris, *Achievement of Literary Authority*, 137–94; Rigney, *Imperfect Histories*, 31–52.

13. See Lockhart, *Life of Scott*, 2:134–80; Hogg, *Letters*, 1:39–41.

14. See, e.g., Oliphant, *Annals of a Publishing House*, 1:318–57; Gifford, *James Hogg*, 17–21, 83–85, 124–26. For nuanced accounts of a friendship and its tensions see MacLachlan, "Scott and Hogg"; Miller, *Electric Shepherd*, 31–33, 38–39, 46, 51–52, 86–87, 138, 324–25.

15. See Alexander, *"Anecdotes to Familiar Anecdotes"*; Mergenthal, "James Hogg and his 'Best Benefactor.' "

16. Hogg, *Anecdotes of Scott*, 60. Subsequent references will be noted in the text.

17. Hogg, "Memoir of the Author's Life," 48. Subsequent references will be noted in the text.

18. Scott, *Poetical Works*, 51.

19. Hogg, *Spy*, 119–20. Hogg had recently farmed in Nithsdale.

20. Gillian Hughes, introduction to Hogg, *Spy*, xxx.

21. Hogg, *Spy*, 556–71; the cited phrases are from Manning's review of the edition, *Studies in Hogg and His World* 11 (2000): 135.

22. Douglas S. Mack, introduction to Hogg, *Queen's Wake*, xxiv. Mack makes the most thorough case for interpreting a "radical Hogg" in opposition to the standard view of him as a *Blackwood's* Tory, xv–xxv; see also, more broadly, Mack's *Scottish Fiction and the British Empire*, 120–30; Currie, "James Hogg's Literary Friendships."

23. Hogg, *Spy*, 515–16; subsequent references will be noted in the text.

24. Currie, *Sir Walter Scott's Edinburgh Annual Register*, 132–70.

25. Hughes, introduction to Hogg, *Spy*, xxxvi–xxxvii.

26. St. Clair, *Reading Nation in the Romantic Period*, 170.

27. See Lockhart, *Life of Scott*, 7:379–84; *Constable and his Literary Correspondents*, 3:303–32.

28. See Scott's analyses of the trade in his correspondence, e.g., to Joanna Baillie, 17 March 1817 (*Letters*, 4:410–12).

29. Scott, *Letters*, 4:431.

30. Oliphant, *Annals of a Publishing House*, 1:51–52.

31. Lockhart, *Life of Scott*, 6:266–67.

32. Scott, *Letters*, 4:462 (to the aristocratic amateur Lady Louisa Stuart).

33. Garside, "Three Perils in Publishing," 45–63.

34. Hogg, "Odd Characters," 140; Hogg, *Letters*, 1:15. On their early relation see Miller, *Electric Shepherd*, 28–38.

35. Hogg, *Anecdotes of Scott*, 38.

36. Laidlaw, *Recollections of Sir Walter Scott*, 6.

37. Hogg, *Letters*, 1:15.

38. Scott, *Letters*, 1:158–59.

39. Maclachlan, "Scott and Hogg," 332.

40. Hogg, *Letters*, 1:80.

41. Hogg, "Journey through the Highlands of Scotland," *Scots Magazine* (1803): 89.

42. Ibid., 383–84. See Hasler, "Reading the Land," 71–72.

43. Hogg, *Tour in the Highlands in 1803*, 19–20.

44. Hogg, *Letters*, 1:40.

45. Ibid., 1:48.

46. Hogg, *Mountain Bard*, 66.

47. Hogg, *Letters*, 1:256–61; Scott, *Letters*, 3:123–28, 132, 141–43.

48. See Johnson, *Sir Walter Scott*, 1:205–6. On the talismanic function of Scott's name in Scottish Romanticism see Russett, *Fictions and Fakes*, 157–72.

49. Hogg, *Mountain Bard*, 49. Subsequent references will be noted in the text.

50. Hogg revised the final stanza of "Gilmanscleuch" for the 1821 edition of *The Mountain Bard*:

> A Scott muste aye support ane Scott,
> When as he synketh low;
> But he that proudlye lifts his heide
> Muste learne his place to knowe.

Douglas Mack suggests that "this bitter and defiant change" reflects Hogg's disillusionment with Scott as literary patron over the intervening years ("Hogg, Scott, Byron and John Murray").

51. See Mack, introduction to Hogg, *Queen's Wake*, xxvi–xxxviii. On the "minstrel contest" in *The Queen's Wake* see Simpson, "Minstrelsy Goes to Market," 697–704.

52. Hogg, *Queen's Wake*, 7. Subsequent references are noted in the text.

53. The bard is in fact based on Hogg's friend John Grieve: see *Queen's Wake*, 428.

54. Wordsworth to R. P. Gillies, 23 November 1814; cited in Groves, *James Hogg*, 51.

55. Scott, *Poetical Works*, 592.

56. Hogg, *Anecdotes of Scott*, 59.

57. Hogg, *Letters*, 1:137 (3 April 1813).

58. See Hogg, *Queen's Wake*, lxviii–lxx.

59. Scott, *Poetical Works*, 592.

60. Hogg pursues his poetic rivalry with Scott in *Mador of the Moor* (1816), a revisionist parody of *The Lady of the Lake*: see James Barcus's introduction, Hogg, *Mador of the Moor*, xxii–xxvi.

61. Scott, *Letters*, 8:65.

62. Hogg, *Three Perils of Woman*, 11. Future references will be noted in the text. See also Mack, *Scottish Fiction and the British Empire*, 28–29.

63. See Mack's introduction to Hogg, *Brownie of Bodsbeck*, xvi–xvii; Garside, "Three Perils in Publishing," 45–63; Duncan, introduction to Hogg, *Winter Evening Tales*, xvi–xvii.

64. "Lines to Sir Walter Scott, Bart." (24 April 1820), in Hogg, *Selected Poems*, 96.

65. Hogg's figural multiplication, in Caroline McCracken-Flesher's sophisticated reading of the novel's economic allegory, "locks Sir Walter within the devaluing play of equivalence" ("The Fourth Peril of James Hogg," 49).

66. Hogg, *Letters*, 1:428.

67. Hogg, *Letters*, 2:91–92 (Hogg to Scott, 26 June 1821). See Hughes, "Recovering Hogg's Personal Manuscript of *The Three Perils of Man*," 109–11.

68. Hogg, *Three Perils of Man*, 467–69. Subsequent references will be noted in the text.

69. *Blackwood's* 2 (October 1817): 89–96.

70. *Letters of Sir Walter Scott*, 7:23.

71. Nietzsche, *On the Genealogy of Morals*, 97.

72. Hasler, introduction to Hogg, *Three Perils of Woman*, xiv.

73. See, e.g., Groves, "Edinburgh Prostitution Scandal of 1823"; Mack, "Gatty's Illness in *The Three Perils of Woman*."

74. See Hasler's articles "Reading the Land," 73–76, and "*Three Perils of Woman* and John Wilson's *Lights and Shadows of Scottish Life*," 43; see also Barrell, "Putting Down the Rising," 130–38.

75. See Mack, "Lights and Shadows of Scottish Life" and *Scottish Fiction and the British Empire*, 21–25; Hasler, "*Three Perils of Woman* and John Wilson's *Lights and Shadows of Scottish Life*," 30–45, and introduction to Hogg, *Three Perils of Woman*, xviii–xxiii.

76. Other examples include Lockhart's *Matthew Wald* and Galt's *The Omen*. On *Confessions* as an "attempted neo-Blackwoodian novel" that "turned in its closing stages into an anti-Blackwoodian novel" see Garside, introduction to Hogg, *Confessions of a Justified Sinner*, xli–xliii, and Garside, "Hogg and the Blackwoodian Novel," 17. For Wilson and Lockhart in the novel, see Bloedé, "Genesis of the Double," 186; Gifford, *James Hogg*, 142–43.

77. Hogg, *Confessions of a Justified Sinner*, 89. Subsequent references will be cited in the text.

78. One of the shadows, Douglas Mack has convincingly argued, is that of Robert Burns, whose body suffered a pious exhumation in 1815 ("Body in the Opened Grave").

79. Hogg to Alexander Blackwood, 3 July 1834: NLS MS 4039, fols. 31–32.

80. "Hogg's Three Perils of Woman," *Blackwood's* 14 (October 1823): 427. Subsequent references are cited in the text. On the novel's reception history see David Groves, afterword to Hogg, *Three Perils of Woman*, 409–20.

81. On the emergent "Romantic notion of monstrosity as too much life . . . the principle of life propagating itself to excess from within," see Gigante, "Monster in the Rainbow," 434.

82. Lockhart, *Peter's Letters to His Kinsfolk*, 1:139.

83. Green, *Scotch Novel Reading*, 1:10–11.

84. Scott, *Quentin Durward*, 237.

85. On Burke and swine, see Gigante, *Taste*, 62–67.

86. Alexander, "Hogg in the *Noctes Ambrosianae*," 40, 42.

87. *Blackwood's* 22 (July 1827): 105. Subsequent references to this article are noted in the text.

88. *Blackwood's* 27 (July 1830): 670. Subsequent references to this article are noted in the text.

89. *Blackwood's* 22 (July 1827): 110.

90. "Hogg's Three Perils of Woman," *Blackwood's* 14 (October 1823): 428.

91. Gordon, "*Christopher North*"; for an entertaining demolition see Carswell, *Sir Walter*, 221.

92. Noble, "John Wilson (Christopher North)," 126.

93. Wilson, *Lights and Shadows of Scottish Life*, 5–6.

94. According to Hasler, "no fewer than eighteen of the stories [in *Lights and Shadows of Scottish Life*] involve death, near approaches to it or funerals" ("*The Three Perils of Woman* and John Wilson's *Lights and Shadows of Scottish Life*," 31). See also Hasler's introduction to Hogg, *Three Perils of Woman*, xxi–xxiii.

95. Cited in Noble, "John Wilson (Christopher North)," 138.

96. Cockburn, *Memorials of his Time*, 304.

97. Noble, "John Wilson (Christopher North)," 127.

98. See, e.g., Groves, *James Hogg*, 126.

99. See Sorensen, *Grammar of Empire*, 138–71.

100. For early-nineteenth-century discussions of Burns see Low, *Robert Burns*, 178–426.

Chapter 7: The Upright Corpse

1. Hogg, *Anecdotes of Scott*, 61.

2. Hogg, "Mysterious Bride," 943.

3. Scott, *Letters on Demonology and Witchcraft*, 389–90.

4. Scott, "Ann Radcliffe" (preface to vol. 10 of *Ballantyne's Novelist's Library*), reprinted in Williams, *Scott on Novelists and Fiction*, 115–16; in the same volume, see also Scott's reviews of *Frankenstein*, 260–62, Galt's *Omen*, 301, 309–11, and Hoffmann ("On the Supernatural in Fictitious Composition"), 312–26, 335–36, 352–53.

5. Hogg, *Winter Evening Tales*, 78. Future citations will be noted in the text. On the clash of explanatory models in Hogg's tales see Rubenstein, "Varieties of Explanation in *The Shepherd's Calendar*."

6. Durkheim, *Elementary Forms of the Religious Life*, 39, 41.

7. Freud, "Uncanny," 226, 234, 244, 241. Future citations will be given in the text.

8. See Burrow, *Evolution and Society*, 240–41; Bann, *Romanticism and the Rise of History*, 7–8; Kaufmann, "Thanks for the Memory," 144–46.

9. On romance revival and national culture, see Duncan, *Modern Romance*, 2–4, 21–27, 54–59.

10. For the "natural historical" paradigm of social development and the eighteenth-century Scottish contribution to it, see Nisbet, *Social Change and History*, 137–208.

11. Freud's recourse to a "Scottish" stadial scheme of cultural history makes his analysis of the uncanny more illuminating of Scottish Romanticism, with the thematic prominence awarded to culture and history, than Todorov's "fantastic," the other major theoretical account of the representation of the supernatural within a modern scientific "world of common reality." Todorov locates the fantastic, the subjective effect of a "hesitation experienced by a person who knows only the laws of nature, confronting an apparently supernatural event," with the period of European Romanticism, in the cultural interim between Enlightenment rationalism and the explanations of psychoanalysis (*Fantastic*, 25).

12. For modern discussions, see, especially, Simpson, *Protean Scot*; Miller, *Doubles*.

13. Murray Pittock argues that Hogg's uncanny iterates "the cultural opacity of the lived life of Scotland's communities" to the enlightened gaze ("Hogg's Gothic," 72).

14. Hogg, *Anecdotes of Scott*, 50–51.

15. Ferris, *Achievement of Literary Authority*, 185–94.

16. Scott, *Black Dwarf*, 5.

17. Hogg, *Brownie of Bodsbeck*, 53. Future citations will be given in the text.

18. Scott, *Old Mortality*, ed. Davidson and Stevens, 466 (note to the 1830 edition).

19. Scott, *Tale of Old Mortality*, 37, 47.

20. See Hogg, *Winter Evening Tales*, 372–92.

21. Cf. Mack, *Scottish Fiction and the British Empire*: "The narrative voice of the *Brownie* . . . is located both inside and outside the traditional oral culture of the Ettrick community" (130).

22. "The miniature, linked to nostalgic versions of childhood and history, presents a diminutive, and thereby manipulable, version of experience, a version which is domesticated and protected from contamination" (Stewart, *On Longing*, 69).

23. See Scott's 1830 introduction to *The Monastery* (1893), xiii–xv; Hogg, "Memoir of the Author's Life," 55. On *The Three Perils of Man* and Scott's novels, see Tulloch, "Writing 'by Advice,' " 33–35.

24. Hogg, *Three Perils of Man*, 323. Future references to this edition will be given in the text.

25. Fielding, *Writing and Orality*, 4.

26. See Tulloch, "Writing 'by Advice,' " 40–42. On sexual conquest in *Ivanhoe*, see Duncan, introduction to Scott, *Ivanhoe* (1996), xxi–xxii.

27. Fielding, *Writing and Orality*, 81–98.

28. The name of the poet in *Perils of Man* burlesques the role: "Colley Carroll" is a cross between the Ossianic Bard, "Carril of other times," and the Laureate of Pope's *Dunciad*.

29. Kilgour, *From Communion to Cannibalism*, 3–18.

30. Abraham and Torok, "Mourning *or* Melancholia." Future citations are given in the text. For another discussion of Abraham and Torok in Hogg, see MacKenzie, "Confessions of a Gentrified Sinner."

31. "On the Late National Calamity," *Blackwood's* 1 (December 1817): 249–52. See Esther Schor, *Bearing the Dead*, 196–28.

32. Anderson, *Imagined Communities*, 17–18.

33. On the relations between the poem's frame and plot, the minstrel's lay and the wizard's book, see Goslee, *Scott the Rhymer*, 18–40; Russett, *Fictions and Fakes*, 165–72.

34. Stewart, *Crimes of Writing*, 66–101, 102–32.

35. All quotations from *The Lay of the Last Minstrel* are taken from Scott, *Poetical Works*, 1–48.

36. For this cultural history, see Percy's "Essay on the Ancient Minstrels in England" and Scott's own "Remarks on Popular Poetry," added to the 1830 edition of *Minstrelsy of the Scottish Border*, 503–20.

37. On Scott's fashioning of a modern-yet-antique poetic function in the *Lay*, see Murphy, *Poetry as an Occupation and an Art*, 142–70; McLane, "Figure Minstrelsy Makes," 442–43. On the historical present and futurity in the *Poems of Ossian* see Duncan, "Pathos of Abstraction," 48–51.

38. On the goblin-page as romance reader see Goslee, *Scott the Rhymer*, 17–20, 35–39; Russett, *Fictions and Fakes*, 167–71.

39. On the poem's "multimedia" effects see Langan, "Understanding Media in 1805."

40. For contrasting views, see Moretti, who draws an antithesis between the nineteenth-century novel and the "world literature" realized in twentieth-century magic realism (*Modern Epic*, 56–88, 233–50), and Moses, who argues for the ideological continuity of a common project of imperialist nostalgia across historical epochs ("Magical Realism at World's End").

41. See W. G. Shepherd, "Fat Flesh," for a fine discussion of this episode.

42. For a humanist reading of Hogg's use of the inset tales, see Groves, *James Hogg*, 101–2.

43. Manning, *Fragments of Union*, 97–106. Manning's fascinating discussion of the "Dutch" topos (of satiation and constancy) in Scottish writing also draws on psychoanalytic themes of incorporation and the boundaries of identity, but to very different effect.

44. See De Groot, "Imperilled Reader in *The Three Perils of Man*."

45. Boston, *Human Nature in its Fourfold State*, 34. Hogg featured the Rev. Boston in an unfinished tale, "The Two Drovers" (which has nothing to do with Scott's story of the same title).

46. Boston, *Human Nature in its Fourfold State*, 55.

47. See Schoenfield's discussion of Hogg's fate in the magazine market and the cannibalistic puns on his name made by the *Blackwood's* literati, "Butchering James Hogg," 213–14.

48. On this figure see, especially, John Barrell, "Putting Down the Rising," 132–37.

49. See the discussion of sympathetic contagion in the "Technologies of Self and Other" section in chap. 9 of this book.

50. Hogg, *Three Perils of Woman*, 53. Future references will be cited in the text.

51. Aldini, *Account of the Late Improvements in Galvanism*, 82. See also *Edinburgh Review* 3 (October 1803): 194–98.

52. Aldini, *General View of the Application of Galvanism to Medical Purposes, Principally in Cases of Suspended Animation* (London, 1819), 47, 65; M. La Beaume, *Observations on the Properties of the Air-Pump Vapour Bath* (London, 1819), 70: cited in Jackson, "Gatty Bell's Illness," 21–22.

53. On scientific materialism in Edinburgh and London and the new morphology, see Desmond, *Politics of Evolution*, 25–81; on the controversies around vitalism, see Jacyna, "Immanence or Transcendence"; on phrenology, see Cooter, *Cultural Meaning of Popular Science*, 22–28, 101–3.

54. *Blackwood's* 37 (February 1835): 261.

55. On Hogg's membership in the Forum, a literary and scientific debating club, and its successor, the Edinburgh Forum, between 1811 and 1813, see Hughes, "James Hogg and the Forum." The Forum had links with the Edinburgh Institution and included a number of physicians among its officers and board members. For Hogg's connection with Robert Macnish, author and phrenologist, see Miller, *Cockburn's Millennium*, 204–8.

56. On *Frankenstein* and physiology, see Mellor, "Making a 'Monster,' " 17–22; Hindle, "Vital Matters"; Butler, "*Frankenstein* and Radical Science."

57. Foucault, *Order of Things*, 226–32.

58. Bold, "Traditional Narrative Elements in *The Three Perils of Woman*," 56 n.17.

59. The critical debate over Gatty's coma and its issue, in which divine conception and spontaneous organic generation are pitted in explanatory opposition, charts a perplexity about how to read *The Three Perils of Woman* as much as about its content. See the exchanges between Groves and Bloedé in *Wordsworth Circle* and *Studies in Hogg and his World* (1987–92); Mack, "Gatty's Illness in *The Three Perils of Woman*"; Jackson, "Gatty Bell's Illness" (diagnosing catalepsy).

60. Trumpener, "National Character, Nationalist Plots," 709–12. On Wilson, see Hasler, "*Three Perils of Woman* and John Wilson's *Lights and Shadows of Scottish Life*"; on *The Heart of Mid-Lothian*, see Duncan, *Modern Romance*, 146–76.

61. See Hasler's introduction to *The Three Perils of Woman*, xvi–xxvi: "the living corpse affronts [the] imaginary continua" (xxiii–xxiv) of historical time "accorded literary canonisation in the novels of Scott" (xxv). See also Barrell's discussion of the upright corpse as figure for the recalcitrance of a disavowed history of atrocity: "The figure of the upright corpse, of the resurrection of what we think—even wish—safely consigned to the past, becomes the main means by which the novella conducts its ambiguous meditations on how modern Scotland should regard its violent history" ("Putting Down the Rising," 135).

62. *Blackwood's* 25 (March 1827): 389.

63. Hogg, *Confessions of a Justified Sinner*, 168. Future references will be given in the text.

64. On the Romantic trope of exhumation and its contexts, see Russett, *Fictions and Fakes*, 184–91; Manning, "That Exhumation Scene Again."

65. Lockhart, *Peter's Letters to His Kinsfolk*, 2:314.

66. Scott, *Ivanhoe*, 7; Chandler, *England in 1819*, 167–70.

67. Benjamin, *Origin of the German Tragic Drama*, 217.

Chapter 8: Theoretical Histories of Society

1. Galt, *Literary Life and Miscellanies*, 1:262.

2. Gillies, *Memoirs of a Literary Veteran*, 3:58–59.

3. Galt, *Autobiography*, 2:219–20. Future references will be given in the text.

4. See, especially, Costain, "Theoretical History and the Novel" (arguing that only *Annals of the Parish* rigorously fits the category) and "Scottish Fiction of John Galt" (the entire "Tales of the West" constitutes "an extended theoretical history," 121 n. 21).

5. Stewart, "Life and Writings of Adam Smith," 293.

6. Poovey, *History of the Modern Fact*, 232; on probability and the novel, see Bender, "Enlightenment Fiction and the Scientific Hypothesis"; Patey, *Probability and Literary Form*.

7. On the interest in these noncanonical forms by eighteenth-century historians—especially in Scotland—see Phillips, *Society and Sentiment*, 131–61.

8. Galt, *Provost*, 34. Future references to this edition will be cited in the text.

9. Effie Deans gives birth and is committed to prison before the Porteous riot; her trial takes place afterwards.

10. See Duncan, *Modern Romance*, 151–61.

11. *Ringan Gilhaize*—in the course of its more extensive quarrel with *Old Mortality*—features a *Brownie of Bodsbeck*–like interlude (178–81). Douglas Gifford and Gillian Hughes have commented on Hogg's imitation of *The Provost* in his late fictional memoir "Some Remarkable Passages in the Life of an Edinburgh Baillie": see Gifford, *James Hogg*, 189–92, and Hughes's introduction to Hogg, *Tales of the Wars of Montrose*, xxv–xxvii.

12. Galt, *Literary Life and Miscellanies*, 1:226.

13. Reid, *Inquiry*, 190; *Essays on the Intellectual Powers*, 44.

14. Poovey, *History of the Modern Fact*, 176–77.

15. Galt, *Literary Life and Miscellanies*, 1:155.

16. Scott, *Letters*, 6:468 (11 June 1821).

17. One such reader was John Wilson's mother, who expressed her annoyance when told the work was fictitious. Wilson himself commented that it "was not a book but a fact." G. M. Trevelyan cites *Annals of the Parish* as a documentary source in his *English Social History* (1951). See Oliphant, *Annals of a Publishing House*, 1:451, 452; Gordon, *John Galt*, 38. For a critique of Galt's historical accuracy see Whatley, "*Annals of the Parish* and History."

18. *Blackwood's* 7 (June 1820): 265.

19. Hogg, *Letters*, 2:78–79 (Hogg to Blackwood).

20. See Gordon, *John Galt*: on *Sir Andrew Wylie*, 42, 44–48; on *The Entail*, 57.

21. Galt, *Annals of the Parish*, 1. Further references will be cited in the text.

22. On Galt's development of conjectural history to create "the novel of provincial life as the index of historical change," see Craig, "Scotland and the Regional Novel," 248–51.

23. See MacQueen's account of the novel's combination of "the intensely local . . . with the universal" through the interplay of Balwhidder's narration and Galt's irony, *Rise of the Historical Novel*, 115–28. See also Simpson, "Ironic Self-Revela-

tion in *Annals of the Parish*": "the final effect, though plainly reductive, is not destructive. The reader is drawn close to Mr Balwhidder and kept there" (87).

24. Deidre Lynch, "Transformations of the Novel—I," argues that the revival of Defoe's techniques of variably reliable first-person narration, for experiments in the representation of ideology, took place in 1790s Jacobin novels (e.g., Godwin's *Caleb Williams*).

25. For views of the "Thady problem" see, e.g., Newcomer, "Disingenuous Thady Quirk"; Dunne, *Maria Edgeworth and the Colonial Mind*, 7–8; Hack, "Inter-Nationalism," 158–61; Moore, "Acts of Union," 121–28; Connolly, "Reading Responsibility in *Castle Rackrent*."

26. Trumpener, *Bardic Nationalism*, 155–56.

27. Coleridge, *Marginalia*, 12:2, 840.

28. Cf. Bardsley, "Your Local Representative": "Neither history nor novel, in its content and its form [*The Provost*] expresses and enforces a scepticism about the shape of history and any event's place in it, about individuals' roles in political institutions and their reform, and of the possibility of any account's being adequate to the most local of events and issues, much less anything beyond them" (76).

29. See Gordon, *John Galt*, 57, and introduction to Galt, *Entail*, x–xiv.

30. A minor verbal echo recurs to the most Galtian section of Scott's novel, its comic local history of the dealings among the Deans, Butler, and Dumbiedikes families: "Widow Butler and Widower Deans struggled with poverty, and the hard and sterile soil of those 'parts and portions' of the lands of Dumbiedikes which it was their lot to occupy" (Scott, *The Heart of Mid-Lothian*, 72); compare "the deep and greedy satisfaction with which the persevering pedlar received the earth and stone that gave him infeftment of that cold and sterile portion of his forefathers' estate" (Galt, *Entail*, 12). Future references will be cited in the text.

31. Bardsley, "Novel and Nation Come to Grief," 547–52, 554–55.

32. Schoenfield, "Family Plots," 62.

33. See Rajit S. Dosanjh, " 'Eloquence of the Bar.' "

34. Schoenfield, "Family Plots," 62–63.

35. Galt, *Glenfell*, vi, 34.

36. On the dynastic plot, see Bardsley, "Novel and Nation Come to Grief," 543. Bardsley argues that Galt's emptying of dialectical alternatives discredits allegory as a system of correspondences that subjects the particularity of human lives to ideological abstraction (544, 562).

37. On the British state's recuperation of Jacobitism and the Highland clans as icons of patriotic valor in the French wars, see Devine, *Scotland's Empire*, 307–8, 353–59.

38. For the topos, see Blumenberg, *Shipwreck with Spectator* (1997), 26–73. I am indebted to Kevis Goodman's discussion, *Georgic Modernity*, 91–93. Compare Galt's treatment—powerfully juxtaposing irony and sentiment—in *The Provost*, 75–78.

39. This recalls a grotesque anecdote Boswell tells about himself: "in the pit of Drury-lane play-house, in a wild freak of youthful extravagance, I entertained the audience prodigiously, by imitating the lowing of a cow" (*Journal of a Tour to the Hebrides*, 406).

40. On "the Leddy's triumphs of 'character,' " see Hart, *Scottish Novel*, 48–49.

41. *Blackwood's* 13 (June 1823): 723. In *The Afterlife of Character*, David Brewer shows that "character migration" was a phenomenon already well established in eighteenth-century British fiction, 78–164.

Chapter 9: Authenticity Effects

1. On fiction and history in *Redgauntlet* see Kerr, *Fiction Against History*, 102–23; de Groot, "Fiction and History"; Brown, *Institutions of the English Novel*, 145–70. See also Sutherland's introduction: "the novel's 'true centre' turns out to be story-telling itself—how stories are told and received" (xv).

2. On the "anthological" quality of *Redgauntlet* see Price, *Anthology and the Rise of the Novel*, 54–66; Watson, *Revolution and the Form of the British Novel*, 149–53.

3. See, e.g., Kerr, *Fiction Against History*; Redekop, "Beyond Closure."

4. Robertson, *Legitimate Histories*, 248. See also Watson, who links Hogg's novel to Maturin's *Melmoth the Wanderer* (1820) and Hazlitt's *Liber Amoris* (1823): *Revolution and the Form of the British Novel*, 155–76. All three novels, of course, develop thematic and formal devices (framed and intercalated narratives) from Shelley's *Frankenstein* (1818).

5. *Redgauntlet*, 381–83; Garside, "Printing *Confessions*" and introduction to Hogg, *Confessions of a Justified Sinner*, lv–lxvi. In a letter to Lady Abercorn, 4 June 1824, Scott refers to a novel by Lockhart as "the Confessions of Adam Blair"—a slip that suggests he might have had Hogg's new work in mind. See Scott, *Letters*, 8:293. Lockhart published his own novel of Presbyterian psychosis, *The History of Matthew Wald*, in 1824. On the 1823–24 vogue for the one-volume "Blackwood novel," see Garside, "Hogg and the Blackwood Novel," 11.

6. McGann, "Walter Scott's Romantic Postmodernity."

7. See Gallagher, *Nobody's Story*, 96–131.

8. Chandler, *England in 1819*, 105–9, 127–35.

9. Christensen, *Romanticism at the End of History*, 10–13. On Scott, see Welsh, *Hero of the Waverley Novels*, 191–96; Duncan, *Modern Romance*, 51–54, 87–92.

10. Thus Scott's and Hogg's novels articulate a logic dialectically opposite to the postmodern genre Linda Hutcheon calls "historiographic metafiction," "novels that are intensively self-reflexive but that also both re-introduce historical context into metafiction and problematize the entire question of historical knowledge" ("The Pastime of Past Time," 481). On *The Antiquary*, Scott's "first trilogy," and the historical present, see Maxwell, "Inundations of Time," 437–58.

11. Catherine Jones argues that *Redgauntlet* (also) "owes much to the example of [Galt's] *Entail*" (*Literary Memory*, 105, 108); Douglas Mack has argued that Scott's novel also responds to Hogg's *Three Perils of Woman*, in a paper delivered at the 1999 International Scott Conference at the University of Oregon.

12. 1824 also saw Hogg's last exercise in the long narrative poem, *Queen Hynde*, bowdlerized and otherwise disfigured in press. The following year he started work on a series of tales to be called *Lives of Eminent Men*, a return to

the Blackwoodian genre of fictional memoir of which Galt was the master, and which Hogg had essayed in the two best tales in *Winter Evening Tales*. A general recession in the book trade following the 1826 crash contributed to the abandonment of large-scale works. Hogg's later ambitions for his prose fiction included a collected edition of his tales to compete with Scott's "Magnum Opus" and a return to Scottish historical fiction, after Scott's death, in the series of *Tales of the Wars of Montrose* (1835; although the two strongest items in the collection were written in 1826). See Gillian Hughes's introduction to Hogg, *Tales of the Wars of Montrose*, xi–xxix.

13. Kelly, *English Fiction of the Romantic Period*, 260–73; Garside, introduction to Hogg, *Confessions of a Justified Sinner*, xvii–xix, xxxiii.

14. See Mack, *Scottish Fiction and the British Empire*, 159–66.

15. On *Confessions of a Justified Sinner* in this light, see Sedgwick, *Between Men*, 97–117; on *Redgauntlet*, Whyte, "Queer Readings, Gay Texts," 152–59.

16. "Fairford, still following Job, was involved in another tortuous and dark passage, which involuntarily reminded him of Peter Peebles's lawsuit" (*Redgauntlet*, 240). Future references will be cited in the text. For "grammar of the imagination," see Manning, *Fragments of Union*, 32–52.

17. See Manning, *Puritan-Provincial Vision*, 80–83.

18. Hogg, *Confessions of a Justified Sinner*, 90. Future references will be cited in the text.

19. As Gary Kelly notes, the novel's Scots-speaking characters show an intuitive ability to sense the true case of a character or situation (*English Fiction of the Romantic Period*, 266).

20. Hume, "Of Parties in General," 60.

21. Galt, *Rothelan*, vol. 2, chap. 2. Future references will be given in the text.

22. Hogg also burlesques the scenario of sympathetic imprinting, in the elder Wringhim's anecdote of a lady "who was delivered of a blackamoor child, merely from the circumstance of having got a start by the sudden entrance of her negro servant" (*Confessions of a Justified Sinner*, 73).

23. See Hart, *Scottish Novel*, 143–81.

24. Galt, *Ringan Gilhaize*, 53. Future references will be cited in the text.

25. See Ferris, *Achievement of Literary Authority*, 176–85: on the narratological "rage for continuity" (183) that "makes time monolithic" (221), and on the diffusion of the Covenant as a historical event (180–82).

26. On this theme see Bardsley, "Trauma of Breaking, and of Making, Covenants."

27. On the figure and its Romantic currency see Fiona Stafford, *Last of the Race*, especially 197–232 ("The year 1826 was something of an *annus mirabilis* for the last of the race," 232).

28. Some commentators (e.g., the novel's editor, Patricia Wilson) suggest a pathological interpretation of Ringan's monologue, after the ironical mode of Galt's earlier autobiographies. In the last part of the tale Ringan is not just heartbroken but deranged, "alienated . . . from reality" (introduction to *Ringan Gilhaize*, xviii); see also Wilson, "*Ringan Gilhaize*: A Neglected Masterpiece?" 142–50. On Galt's ironic technique see MacQueen, *Rise of the Historical Novel*, 130–39.

29. Manning, *Puritan-Provincial Vision*, 44.

30. Hume, *Treatise of Human Nature*, 311.

31. See Habermas, *Structural Transformation of the Public Sphere*, 32–33, 43–51.

32. On Scott's treatment of patriarchy and contract see Welsh, *Hero of the Waverley Novels*, 213–41 (on *Redgauntlet*, 227–31).

33. Žižek, *Sublime Object of Ideology*, 134. For a reading of this scene as a paradigmatic accession of the "real" see Shaw, *Narrating Reality*, 1–2.

34. Charles Edward Stuart cannot sustain either the paternal Logos, in its ideological form of Divine Right absolutism, or the new ethos of homosocial friendship, to both of which he appeals in vain. These, and their supporting terms, are hopelessly scrambled. Charles invokes the doctrine of the king's two bodies to defend his dalliance with Clementina Walkinshaw: a private indulgence of the sexual body should not compromise the public authority of the sovereign body. But the appeal fails through its contamination by the modern relation it actually invokes, the distinction between public and private life: in fact Charles's liaison does compromise his role as father of the nation, since his mistress is betraying him to the government (*Redgauntlet*, 355–58). See also Judith Wilt's argument that the liaison terminates a fatal feminization of Stuart patriarchy ("a feminine influence predominates"): *Secret Leaves*, 126–29.

35. Smith, *Theory of Moral Sentiments*, 10. Future references will be given in the text.

36. Burke, *Philosophical Enquiry*, 120. Burke's source is Jacob Spon, *Recherches curieuses d'antiquité, contenues en plusieurs dissertations* (Lyon, 1683), 358. The Gil-Martian formulation, "to enter into the disposition and thoughts of people," alters the original, "pour juger . . . ce que ces personnes avoient dans le coeur" [to judge . . . what people had in their hearts].

37. Lavater, *Essays on Physiognomy*, 1:20. Future references will be given in the text.

38. Hume, *Treatise of Human Nature*, 367, 369. Future references will be given in the text.

39. Pinch, *Strange Fits of Passion*, 34; on Hume's contagious, "transpersonal" model of the feelings, see 3–7, 17–44.

40. See Mullan's (*Sentiment and Sociability*, 25–56) comparison between Hume's contagious model of sympathy and Smith's version predicated upon "spectatorial aloofness" (43); and Phillipson, "Adam Smith as Civic Moralist."

41. For the resonance of this term in Smith and Scott, see Chandler, *England in 1819*, 229–30, 307–20.

42. Deane, *Strange Country*, 37.

43. Gibbons, *Edmund Burke and Ireland*, 11, 84, 105–6.

44. Stewart, *Elements of Philosophy*, 2:208, 171–72. Future citations will be given in the text.

45. On the Union and Scottish historiography, see Kidd, *Subverting Scotland's Past*, 98–99.

46. See Garside's introduction, *Confessions of a Justified Sinner*, lxvi–lxviii.

47. Gallagher, *Nobody's Story*, 60–65, 122–23, 142–44; Ferris, *Achievement of Literary Authority*, 19–29; Millgate, *Walter Scott*, 107; Griffin, "Anonymity

344 NOTES TO PAGES 274-280

and Authorship"; Garside, "English Novel in the Romantic Era," 66–67, "Hogg and the Blackwood Novel," 10.

48. "Blackwood's Magazine," *London Magazine* (November 1820): 517. See Russett, *Fictions and Fakes*, 172–79.

49. Stewart, *Crimes of Writing*, 35–38, 68–74, 102–31.

50. Robertson reads Scott's editorial apparatus as a Gothic convention that destabilizes the historicist certainties it ostensibly serves (*Legitimate Histories*, 117–60). She argues that even the ostensibly sober antiquarian and biographical "paratexts of the Magnum Opus continue rather than expiate the 'liberties' taken under the guise of anonymity in the first editions" (160).

51. Lockhart, *Life of Scott*, 7:214; see also Sutherland, *Life of Walter Scott*, 269–71. On the autobiographical content of the "Magnum Opus" apparatus, see Millgate, *Scott's Last Edition*, 111–14.

52. See Trumpener, *Bardic Nationalism*, 109–12. On Scott and the topos, see Robertson, *Legitimate Histories*, 123–42, and Russett, *Fictions and Fakes*, 23–25, 158–64.

53. Smollett, *Humphry Clinker*, 118, 230–32.

54. Buzard adapts the phrase "authenticity effect" from Barthes's "reality effect," to denote a more straightforwardly "ideological" usage than I do here (*Beaten Track*, 172–92). On Ossian and national origins see Davis, *Acts of Union*, 77–88.

55. See Trumpener, *Bardic Nationalism*, 74–76; Fielding, *Writing and Orality*, 9–10. See also Stafford, "Blair's Ossian, Romanticism, and the Teaching of Literature," 76–81.

56. Siskin, *Work of Writing*, 172–90; Kittler, *Discourse Networks 1800/1900*. On "developmental narratives," see also Siskin's *Historicity of Romantic Discourse*.

57. On the leading part played by eighteenth-century Scots intellectuals in the standardization of English as a national language and in the disciplinary invention of English literature, see Crawford, *Devolving English Literature*, 16–44; Crawford, *Scottish Invention of English Literature*, 37–132; Sorensen, *Grammar of Empire*, 138–52; Siskin, *Work of Writing*, 79–94.

58. Fielding, *Writing and Orality*, 3–42; see also Fielding, "Writing at the North."

59. Stewart, *Crimes of Writing*, 102–31.

60. Johnson, *Journey to the Western Islands of Scotland*, 118.

61. Robertson, *Legitimate Histories*, 120.

62. Žižek, *Tarrying with the Negative*, 230.

63. See Klancher, *Making of English Reading Audiences*, 18–46.

64. See the discussion of these assessments in the next chapter. For a contemporary account of the novel's triumph over the periodical as national form, see Siskin, *Work of Writing*, 155–71.

65. On Scott and liberalism, see Kaufmann, *Business of Common Life*, 93–137; Christensen, *Romanticism at the End of History*, 168–75. On *Redgauntlet* and state formation, see Irvine, *Enlightenment and Romance*, 214–15; Lee, "Giants in the North," 120.

66. Mudie, *Historical Account of His Majesty's Visit to Scotland*, 243.

67. Scott, *Fortunes of Nigel*, 4–5. The veiled eidolon of the author appears in the second edition (1825) of *Illustrations of the Author of Waverley*; the frontispiece of the rare 1823 first edition is a portrait of Rob Roy.

68. Anderson, *Imagined Communities*, 35.

69. On the Abbotsford Edition and its influence, see Maxwell, "Scott and the Genesis of the Victorian Illustrated Book," 28–46.

70. Siegel, *Desire and Excess*, 93–97; Brewer, *Afterlife of Character*, 192–201.

71. Calasso, *Marriage of Cadmus and Harmony*, 281.

72. And in doing so reverses the history of novelistic character, supposed to have attained "depth" in the Romantic period: see Lynch, *Economy of Character*, 123–33.

73. The form of Hogg's novel—a book divided between two narratives, set in an abysmal relation of glossing one another—casts it as a parody-bible. See Stallybrass's reflections on the physical status of the codex and the conditions of biblical interpretation, "Books and Scrolls."

74. For the former—striking the balance achieved by neither sinner nor editor—see Manning, *Puritan-Provincial Vision*, 84; for the latter, see Kelly, *English Fiction of the Romantic Period*, 261–73. On the disruptive force of oral storytelling within a literary narrative, see Mack, *Scottish Fiction and the British Empire*, 159–64.

75. See Hughes, "Critical Reception of *The Confessions of a Justified Sinner*"; Campbell, "Literary Criticism and *Confessions of a Justified Sinner.*"

76. Polemically staked out, e.g., by Tony Bennett in *Outside Literature*.

Chapter 10: A New Spirit of the Age

1. Johnstone, *Cook and Housewife's Manual* (1826), 14. Future references will be given in the text.

2. Scott based his fictional town of St. Ronan's on Innerleithen, near Peebles. The Cleikum Inn took on a life of its own in local tradition. In May 1835 James Hogg (who founded the St. Ronan's Border Games, still extant, in 1827) was inducted into the freemasons' Lodge Canongate Kilwinning, No. 2, and elected Poet Laureate, in a special sederunt at "the Cleikum Inn, kept by Meg Dods." See Anderson, *At the Sign of the Cleikum*, 181.

3. Monnickendam, "Eating Your Words," 37; see also Perkins, "Taste for Scottish Fiction," who reads the Scott and Ferrier parodies as responses to the industrial-scale commodification of Scottish fiction.

4. *Cook and Housewife's Manual*, 2nd ed. (1827), 354. Future references will be given in the text.

5. Johnstone based her book on material originally serialized in the *Inverness Courier*.

6. See Kelly, *English Fiction of the Romantic Period*, 256–57.

7. This period sees a critical desublimation of the aesthetic trope of taste, reflecting claims on it by a rising middle class (Gigante, *Taste*, 60–67, 170–73).

8. See Burgess, *British Fiction and the Production of Social Order*, 217–34; Irvine, "Gender and the Place of Culture in Scott's *Saint Ronan's Well.*"

9. *Elizabeth von Bruce*, "nach Walter Scott" (3 vols.; Stuttgart, 1827). The German version of *Clan-Albin* had also been ascribed to Scott.

10. All the more so, perhaps, in that Scott's metaphor echoes the famous denunciation of European colonialism at the end of Swift's *Gulliver's Travels*, 286.

11. Scott, *Journal*, 306. Hogg, *Letters*, 2:261 (to William Blackwood, 5 April 1827).

12. "In the early nineteenth century . . . the constant copying and cross-pollination between the Scottish and Irish novel amount almost to a transperipheral literary life" (Trumpener, *Bardic Nationalism*, 17); see also 151–52.

13. Johnstone, *Elizabeth de Bruce*, 1:89. Future references will be given in the text.

14. "Its plot . . . is so exceedingly complex and intricate" (*La Belle Assemblée*, 3rd ser., 5 (March 1827): 130; "it is perplexed, and often extravagant—and sometimes tedious—but full of fancy and spark and cleverness" (Henry Thomson, letter to William Blackwood, 30 January 1827): see Garside et al., *British Fiction 1800–1829*, www.british-fiction.cf.ac.uk/publishing/eliz27-44.html. In his introduction to *Clan-Albin* Andrew Monnickendam comments on the "extraordinarily convoluted plot" of *Elizabeth de Bruce* (vi).

15. Trumpener, *Bardic Nationalism*, 197–98, 211–30.

16. Ferris, *Romantic National Tale*, 17; see the general discussion of these late novels, 127–54.

17. Ibid., 135, 139.

18. Ibid., 135–36.

19. Scott, *Tale of Old Mortality*, 7.

20. Gideon specifies the offensive note as appearing in vol. 2, p. 7 of the *Minstrelsy* (2:9–81). Scott's first two volumes were published in 1802, so that this episode appears to conflate the United Irishman and Robert Emmet risings.

21. See Scott, *Ivanhoe*, 34; *Rob Roy*, 221, 484; *Heart of Mid-Lothian*, 94, 114.

22. Barry, "Aesthetic Formation of a 'Man of Credit.' "

23. See Rowlinson, "Scotch Hate Gold"; McCracken-Flesher, *Possible Scotlands*, 142–53.

24. Christian Johnstone to Blackwood, 5 October 1824: NLS Blackwood's MS 4012, fol. 210.

25. John Johnstone to Blackwood, 5 May 1828: NLS MS 4019, fol. 59.

26. See the correspondence between Blackwood and Johnstone, January–February 1831, in NLS MS 4030 fols. 55, 65, 67, 69; MS 30,004 fols. 140, 142.

27. Chambers, *Biographical Dictionary*, 2:405; *DNB*, s.v. "Johnstone, Christian."

28. Chambers, *Biographical Dictionary*, 2:405–6.

29. Easley, *First-Person Anonymous*, 62; see also Easley, "*Tait's Edinburgh Magazine* in the 1830s," 263–67. According to the *Wellesley Index of Victorian Periodicals*, Johnstone wrote four hundred articles or 20 percent of *Tait's* during her tenure as editor, 1834–46.

30. "Miss Martineau's Illustrations of Political Economy," *Tait's Edinburgh Magazine*, o.s., 1 (1832): 612–18. On Hannah More as "a model of the new socially concerned woman writer" in the liberal periodicals of the 1830s, see Eas-

ley, *First-Person Anonymous*, 21–23. See also Easley, "*Tait's Edinburgh Magazine* in the 1830s."

31. *Schoolmaster* 1, no. 2 (September 1832): 25.

32. See Easley, *First-Person Anonymous*, 72–77.

33. *Fraser's Magazine* 1, no. 2 (March 1830): 236.

34. "Johnstone's Edinburgh Magazine," *Tait's*, o.s., 3 (September 1833): 783; "The Cheap and Dear Periodicals," *Tait's*, n.s., 1 (January 1834): 392.

35. For useful overviews of these developments see Altick, *English Common Reader*, 332–39; Chittick, *Dickens and the 1830s*, 28–30.

36. *Chambers's Edinburgh Journal* 1 (4 February 1832): 1.

37. Chambers democratizes one of the potent Romantic-era topoi of the literary tradition: see Lynch, "Gothic Libraries and National Subjects."

38. On *Chambers's Edinburgh Journal* and its contexts, see Scholnick, "Fiery Cross of Knowledge"; Secord, *Victorian Sensation*, 67–69.

39. *Schoolmaster*, 1 (4 August 1832): 1–2; future references to this article are given in the text. To mitigate the charge of copying *Chambers's*, the Johnstones cite a genealogy of "Cheap Periodicals" from Defoe's the *Review* to Hogg's the *Spy* (2). The weekly periodical was not in itself a new phenomenon; what took hold, and effectively constituted a new genre, was its adaptation of the monthly magazine format of encyclopedic miscellany, pioneered in more expensive serial volume and number publications such as *Constable's Miscellany* as well as in the monthlies themselves. The miscellany's didactic function is explicit in its title, from a speech by Henry Brougham on the diffusion of education (29 January 1828): "The schoolmaster is abroad; and I trust to him, armed with his primer, against the soldier in full military array."

40. *Tait's*, o.s., 1 (April 1832), 57. Future references to this issue are given in the text.

41. *Tait's*, o.s., 3 (February 1833): 58. Future references to this issue are given in the text.

42. See Butler, "Culture's Medium," 136–37; Parker, *Literary Magazines and British Romanticism*, 3.

43. On the regime's crisis and fall see Lenman, *Integration, Enlightenment and Industrialization*, 154–67; Fry, *Dundas Despotism*, 370–84.

44. Johnstone, "On the Political Tendency of Sir Walter Scott's Writings," 129.

45. Weir and Allan, *Life of Sir Walter Scott*, 145. Future references will be given in the text. For the phrase see Lonsdale, *Poems of Gray, Collins and Goldsmith*, 749; Lockhart, *Peter's Letters to His Kinsfolk*, 1:124; Hazlitt, *Spirit of the Age*, 233.

46. The commemorative supplement of *Chambers's* joins in the general praise for Scott, mildly deplores his political stance in 1819–20, and says that despite his kindness to individual commoners, Scott had "no affection for the people as a body": *Chambers's Edinburgh Journal*, 1, no. 36 (6 October 1832).

47. Johnstone allusively pits Scott's usage of the topos in his *Tales of the Crusaders* (1825), informed by the skeptical historicism of Robertson and Gibbon, against the fanatical Christian revivalism of Southey's *Roderick, The Last of the Goths* (1814). See Watt, "Scott, the Scottish Enlightenment and Romantic Orientalism," 107–8.

48. Andrew Monnickendam sees Johnstone's "liberal appropriation" of Scott as anticipating Lukács and licensing a "deconstruction" of Lockhart's Tory hagiography ("The Odd Couple," 30–36).

49. Martineau, "Characteristics of the Genius of Scott," 301. Future references will be given in the text. Cf. John Scott, "The Author of the Scotch Novels," *London Magazine* 1 (1820): "his mind appears to possess, in a degree peculiar to itself, the admirable property of digesting all its food into *healthy chyle*," 12.

50. On Carlyle's departure from Scotland as a symptom of national literary decline see Craig, *Scottish Literature and the Scottish People*, 282–87.

51. Carlyle's essay appeared in the *London and Westminster Review* 28 (January 1838): 293–345. See Hayden, *Scott: The Critical Heritage*, 345–73; Hillhouse, *Waverley Novels and Their Critics*, 214–17. On Carlyle and Scott, see Crawford, *Devolving English Literature*, 135–42; Frye, "Romancing the Past"; Lee, *Nationalism and Irony*, 105–7.

52. "Biography," *Fraser's Magazine* 27 (1832): 253–60. See Moore, "Thomas Carlyle and Fiction"; Schor, "Stupidest Novel in London," 120–22.

53. See Secord, *Victorian Sensation*, 82, 88–89.

54. See Muir, *Scott and Scotland*; Craig, *Scottish Literature and the Scottish People*, 161–65, 227–31; Nairn (who ends up reiterating the nationalist historiography he is criticizing), *Break-Up of Britain*, 118–23. For a critique see Craig, *Out of History*, 65–67, 88–105.

55. On the genesis of *Sartor Resartus* and its magazine characteristics, see Parker, *Literary Magazines and British Romanticism*, 158–62.

56. The major exception is Robert Crawford in *Devolving English Literature*, 134–51. See also Jessop, *Carlyle and Scottish Thought*.

57. Carlyle, *Sartor Resartus*, 28. Future references will be given in the text.

58. Maginn's burlesque historical romance *Whitehall: or, The Days of George IV* (1827) anticipates the last chapters of *Sartor Resartus* in applying Scott's descriptive technique to contemporary fashions. For an excerpt see Hayden, *Scott: The Critical Heritage*, 302–3.

59. *Fraser's Magazine*, June 1833; reprinted in *Sartor Resartus*, 228–29. Maginn is referring to Carlyle's translation of Goethe. See Crawford, *Devolving English Literature*, 139–40.

60. Scott, *Chronicles of the Canongate*, 1, 13. See Jordan, "Chrystal Croftangry, Scott's Last and Best Mask."

Bibliography

Early Nineteenth-Century Periodicals

La Belle Assemblée
Blackwood's Edinburgh Magazine
Chambers's Edinburgh Journal
Critical Review, 3rd ser.
Edinburgh Annual Register
Edinburgh Magazine, and Literary Miscellany
Edinburgh Monthly Magazine
Edinburgh Review
Edinburgh Weekly Journal
The Examiner
Fraser's Magazine for Town and Country
Johnstone's Edinburgh Magazine
London Magazine
Quarterly Review
The Schoolmaster
Scots Magazine
The Scotsman
The Spy
Tait's Edinburgh Magazine

Sources Published before 1900

Aldini, John. *An Account of the Late Improvements in Galvanism, with a Series of Curious and Interesting Experiments*. London: Cuthell & Martin, 1803.

Austen, Jane. *Emma*. Ed. Ronald Blythe. Harmondsworth: Penguin, 1966.

———. *Jane Austen's Letters*. Ed. Deirdre Le Faye. Oxford: Oxford University Press, 1995.

Blair, Hugh. *Lectures on Rhetoric and Belles Lettres*. 2nd ed., 1785. Ed. Linda Ferreira-Buckley and S. Michael Halloran. Carbondale: Southern Illinois University Press, 2005.

Boston, Thomas. *Human Nature in its Fourfold State*. 19th ed. Edinburgh: Clark, 1776.

Boswell, James. *Journal of a Tour to the Hebrides with Samuel Johnson, Ll.D.*, with Samuel Johnson, *A Journey to the Western Islands of Scotland*. Ed. Peter Levi. Harmondsworth: Penguin, 1984.

Brown, Thomas. *Lectures on the Philosophy of the Human Mind*. 3 vols. Philadelphia: John Grigg, 1824.

———. *Observations on the Nature and Tendency of the Doctrine of Mr Hume, Concerning the Relation of Cause and Effect*. 1806. New York: Garland, 1983.

Brunton, Mary. *Discipline: A Novel*. 3 Vols. Edinburgh: Manners and Miller, 1814.

———. *Emmeline; with Some Other Pieces*. Edinburgh: Manners and Miller, Constable, 1819.

Burke, Edmund. *A Philosophical Enquiry into the Origin of our Ideas of the Sublime and Beautiful*. 1759. Ed. Adam Phillips. Oxford: Oxford University Press, 1990.

———. *Reflections on the Revolution in France*. 1790. Ed. Conor Cruise O'Brien. London: Penguin, 1968.

Burt, Edmund. *Letters from a Gentleman in the North of Scotland to his Friend in London*. 1754. Ed. Robert Jamieson. 5th ed. 2 vols. London: Ogle, Duncan, and Co., 1818.

Carlyle, Thomas. *Sartor Resartus*. Ed. Kerry McSweeney and Peter Sabor. Oxford: Oxford University Press, 1987.

Chambers, Robert. *A Biographical Dictionary of Eminent Scotsmen*. 6 vols. London: Blackie, 1875.

———. *Illustrations of the Author of Waverley*. 2nd ed. Edinburgh: Anderson, 1825.

———. *Traditions of Edinburgh*. 2 vols. Edinburgh: W. & C. Tait, 1825.

Cockburn, Henry. *The Life of Lord Jeffrey; With a Selection from his Correspondence*. 2 vols. Edinburgh: A & C Black, 1852.

———. *Memorials of His Time*. Ed. Karl Miller. Chicago: University of Chicago Press, 1974.

Coleridge, Samuel Taylor. *Collected Works of Samuel Taylor Coleridge*. Vol. 12, *Marginalia*. Ed. George Whalley. Princeton: Princeton University Press, 1980.

Constable, Thomas. *Archibald Constable and His Literary Correspondents*. 3 vols. Edinburgh: Edmonston & Douglas, 1873.

De Quincey, Thomas. *Recollections of the Lakes and the Lake Poets*. Ed. David Wright. Harmondsworth: Penguin, 1970.

Doyle, John A. *Memoir and Correspondence of Susan Ferrier, 1782–1854*. London: Eveleigh Nash & Grayson, 1929.

Drescher, Horst W., ed. *Literature and Literati: The Literary Correspondence and Notebooks of Henry Mackenzie*. Vol. 1, *Letters 1766–1827*. Frankfurt am Main: Peter Lang, 1989.

Edinburgh; A Satirical Novel. By the Author of London: or, a Month at Steven's. 3 vols. London: Sherwood, Neely, and Jones, 1820.

Edgeworth, Maria. *Castle Rackrent and Ennui*. Ed. Marilyn Butler. Harmondsworth: Penguin, 1993.

Ferrier, Susan. *The Inheritance*. 3 vols. Edinburgh: Blackwood, 1824.

———. *Marriage*. 1818. Ed. Herbert Foltinek. Oxford: Oxford University Press, 1986.

———. *Marriage*. 1841. New York: Penguin, 1986.

Galt, John. *Annals of the Parish; or, The Chronicle of Dalmailing*. Ed. James Kinsley. Oxford: Oxford University Press, 1986.

———. *The Autobiography of John Galt*. 2 vols. London: Cochrane, 1833.

———. *Bogle Corbet; or, The Emigrants*. 3 vols. London: Colburn, 1831.

———. *The Entail, or, The Lairds of Grippy*. Ed. Ian A. Gordon. Oxford: Oxford University Press, 1970.

————. *Glenfell; or, Macdonalds and Campbells. An Edinburgh Tale of the Nineteenth Century*. London: Sir Richard Phillips, 1820.

————. *The Literary Life and Miscellanies of John Galt*. 3 vols. Edinburgh: Blackwood, 1834.

————. *The Omen*. Edinburgh: Blackwood, 1825.

————. *The Provost*. Ed. Ian A. Gordon. Oxford: Oxford University Press, 1973.

————. *Ringan Gilhaize, or, The Covenanters*. Ed. Patricia J. Wilson. Edinburgh: Scottish Academic Press, 1984.

————. *Rothelan; A Romance of the English Chronicles*. 3 vols. Edinburgh: Oliver & Boyd, 1824.

————. *Sir Andrew Wylie of That Ilk*. 3 vols. Edinburgh: Blackwood, 1822.

————. *The Spae-Wife: A Tale of the Scottish Chronicles*. Edinburgh: Oliver & Boyd, 1823.

————. *Voyages and Travels, in the Years 1809, 1810, and 1811; Containing Statistical, Commercial, and Miscellaneous Observations on Gibraltar, Sardinia, Sicily, Malta, Serigo, and Turkey*. London: Cadell & Davies, 1812.

Gillies, Robert Pearse. *Memoirs of a Literary Veteran; Including Sketches and Anecdotes of the Most Distinguished Literary Characters from 1794 to 1849*. 3 vols. London: Bentley, 1851.

Gordon, Mary Wilson. *"Christopher North": A Memoir of John Wilson, Late Professor of Moral Philosophy in the University of Edinburgh*. New York: Hagemann, 1894.

Green, Sarah. *Scotch Novel Reading; or, Modern Quackery. A Novel Really Founded on Facts. By a Cockney*. 3 vols. London: A. K. Newman & Co., 1824.

Hamilton, Elizabeth. *The Cottagers of Glenburnie; A Tale for the Farmer's Ingle-Nook*. Edinburgh: Manners and Miller, 1808.

Hamilton, Thomas. *The Youth and Manhood of Cyril Thornton*. Ed. Maurice Lindsay. Aberdeen: Association for Scottish Literary Studies, 1990.

Hazlitt, William. *Lectures on English Poets and The Spirit of the Age*. London: Dent, 1967.

Hogg, James. *Altrive Tales*. Ed. Gillian Hughes. Edinburgh: Edinburgh University Press, 2003.

————. *Anecdotes of Scott*. Ed. Jill Rubenstein. Edinburgh: Edinburgh University Press, 1999.

————. *The Brownie of Bodsbeck*. Ed. Douglas Mack. Edinburgh: Scottish Academic Press, 1976.

————. *The Collected Letters of James Hogg*. Vol. 1, *1800–1819*. Ed. Gillian Hughes. Edinburgh: Edinburgh University Press, 2004.

————. *The Collected Letters of James Hogg*. Vol. 2, *1820–1831*. Ed. Gillian Hughes. Edinburgh: Edinburgh University Press, 2006.

————. "A Journey through the Highlands of Scotland, in the months of July and August 1802, in a series of letters to — —, esq." *Scots Magazine* 64 (1802): 813–18, 956–63; 65 (1803): 89–95, 251–54, 312–14, 382–86.

————. *Mador of the Moor*. Ed. James Barcus. Edinburgh: Edinburgh University Press, 2005.

————. "Memoir of the Author's Life." In Hogg, *Altrive Tales*, 11–78.

————. *The Mountain Bard*. Edinburgh: Constable, 1807.

Hogg, James. "The Mysterious Bride, by the Ettrick Shepherd," *Blackwood's Edinburgh Magazine* 28 (December 1830): 943–50.

———. "Odd Characters," *Studies in Hogg and His World* 1 (1990): 136–52.

———. *The Private Memoirs and Confessions of a Justified Sinner.* Ed. Peter Garside. Edinburgh: Edinburgh University Press, 2002.

———. *Queen Hynde.* Ed. Suzanne Gilbert and Douglas S. Mack. Edinburgh: Edinburgh University Press, 1998.

———. *The Queen's Wake: A Legendary Poem.* Ed. Douglas S. Mack. Edinburgh: Edinburgh University Press, 2004.

———. *A Queer Book.* Ed. Gillian Hughes. Edinburgh: Edinburgh University Press, 1995.

———. "A Scots Mummy: To Sir Christopher North," *Blackwood's Edinburgh Magazine* 14 (August 1823): 188–90.

———. *Selected Poems.* Ed. Douglas Mack. Oxford: Clarendon Press, 1970.

———. *The Spy.* Ed. Gillian Hughes. Edinburgh: Edinburgh University Press, 2000.

———. *Tales of the Wars of Montrose.* Ed. Gillian Hughes. Edinburgh: Edinburgh University Press, 2002.

———. *The Three Perils of Man: War, Women, and Witchcraft.* Ed. Douglas Gifford. Edinburgh: Scottish Academic Press, 1972.

———. *The Three Perils of Woman; or, Love, Leasing, and Jealousy. A Series of Domestic Scottish Tales.* Ed. Antony J. Hasler and Douglas S. Mack. Edinburgh: Edinburgh University Press, 1995.

———. *A Tour in the Highlands in 1803.* Paisley: Gardner, 1888.

———. *Winter Evening Tales.* Ed. Ian Duncan. Edinburgh: Edinburgh University Press, 2002.

Home, Henry, Lord Kames. *Elements of Criticism.* Ed. Peter Jones. 2 vols. Indianapolis: Liberty Fund, 2005.

Hume, David. "Of National Characters." In *Essays: Moral, Political and Literary,* ed. Eugene F. Miller, 197–215. Indianapolis: Liberty Fund, 1985.

———. "Of Parties in General." In *Essays: Moral, Political and Literary,* ed. Eugene F. Miller, 54–63. Indianapolis: Liberty Fund, 1985.

———. *A Treatise of Human Nature.* Ed. Ernest C. Mossner. Harmondsworth: Penguin, 1969.

Jeffrey, Francis. "Mad. de Staël, De la Littérature considérée dans ses rapports avecs les institutions sociales." *Edinburgh Review* 21 (1813): 1–44.

———. "Mounier, de l'influence des Philosophes, Francs-Maçons, et Illuminées, sur la Revolution de France." *Edinburgh Review* 1 (1802): 1–18.

———. "Secondary Scottish Novels." *Edinburgh Review* 39 (1823): 158–79.

Johnson, Samuel. *A Journey to the Western Islands of Scotland.* In Boswell, *Tour to the Hebrides.*

Johnston, Mary. *The Lairds of Glenfern; or, Highlanders of the Nineteenth Century. A Tale.* 2 vols. London: Newman, 1816.

Johnstone, Christian Isobel. *Clan-Albin: A National Tale.* Ed. Andrew Monnickendam. Glasgow: Association for Scottish Literary Studies, 2003.

—— [Mrs Margaret Dods, pseud.]. *The Cook and Housewife's Manual*. Edinburgh: Oliver & Boyd, 1826; 2nd ed., 1827.

——. *Elizabeth de Bruce*. 3 vols. Edinburgh: Blackwood, 1827.

——. "On the Political Tendency of Sir Walter Scott's Writings." *Schoolmaster, and Edinburgh Weekly Magazine* 1, no. 9 (29 September 1832): 129–33.

——. *The Saxon and the Gaël; or, The Northern Metropolis*. 4 vols. London: Tegg, 1814

Laidlaw, William. *Recollections of Sir Walter Scott (1802–1804)*. Hawick: Transactions of the Hawick Archeological Society, 1905.

Lang, Andrew. *The Life and Letters of John Gibson Lockhart*. 2 vols. London: Nimmo, 1897.

Lauder, Sir Thomas Dick. *Lochandhu: A Tale of the Eighteenth Century*. 3 vols. Edinburgh: Constable, 1825.

——. *The Wolfe of Badenoch: A Historical Romance of the Fourteenth Century*. 3 vols. London: Cadell, 1827.

Lavater, John Caspar. *Essays on Physiognomy, Designed to Promote the Knowledge and the Love of Mankind*. Trans. Henry Hunter. 3 vols. London: John Murray, 1789–92.

Lockhart, John Gibson, *Memoirs of the Life of Sir Walter Scott, Bart*. 2nd ed. 10 vols. London: Cadell, 1839.

——. "On the Revival of a Taste for Our Ancient Literature," *Blackwood's Edinburgh Magazine* 4 (1818): 264–66.

——. *Peter's Letters to His Kinsfolk*. 3 vols. Edinburgh: Blackwood, 1819.

——. "Remarks on the Periodical Criticism of England, by the Baron von Lauerwinkel." *Blackwood's Edinburgh Magazine* 12 (1818): 670–79.

Lonsdale, Roger, ed. *The Poems of Gray, Collins and Goldsmith*. London: Longman, 1969.

MacDonogh, Felix. *The Hermit in Edinburgh: or, Sketches of Manners and Real Characters and Scenes in the Drama of Life in Edinburgh*. 3 vols. London: Sherwood, Jones, 1824.

Martineau, Harriet. "Characteristics of the Genius of Scott." *Tait's Edinburgh Magazine* 2, no. 9 (1832): 301–14; 2, no. 10 (1833): 445–60.

Marx, Karl, and Friedrick Engels. *The German Ideology*. Ed. R. Pascal. New York: International Publishers, 1947.

Mill, John Stuart. *On Liberty*. Ed. Gertrude Himmelfarb. Harmondsworth: Penguin, 1982.

Millar, John. *The Origin of the Distinction of Ranks*. 4th ed., 1806. Bristol: Thoemmes, 1990.

Mudie, Robert. *Glenfergus*. 3 vols. Edinburgh: Oliver & Boyd, 1820.

——. *A Historical Account of His Majesty's Visit to Scotland*. Edinburgh: Oliver & Boyd, 1822.

——. *The Modern Athens: A Dissertation and Demonstration of Men and Things in the Scotch Capital. By a Modern Greek*. London: Knight & Lacey, 1825.

Nietzsche, Friedrich. *On the Genealogy of Morals*. Trans. Walter Kaufman and R. J. Hollingdale. New York: Vintage, 1969.

Oliphant, Margaret. *Annals of a Publishing House: William Blackwood and Sons, Their Magazine and Friends*. 2 vols. Edinburgh: Blackwood, 1897.

Owenson, Sydney. *The Wild Irish Girl*. Ed. Claire Connolly and Stephen Copley. London: Pickering & Chatto, 2000.

Peacock, Thomas Love. *Novels*. Ed. David Garnett. 2 vols. London: Hart-Davis, Macgibbon, 1963.

Percy, Thomas. Appendix 1, "An Essay on the Ancient Minstrels in England." In *Reliques of Ancient English Poetry, Consisting of old heroic ballads, songs, and other pieces of our earlier poets*. 3 vols. London: Dodsley, 1765.

Porter, Jane. *The Scottish Chiefs: A Romance*. 5 vols. London: Longman, 1810.

Reid, Thomas. *Essays on the Intellectual Powers of Man*. Ed. Derek R. Brookes. Edinburgh: Edinburgh University Press, 2002.

———. *An Inquiry into the Human Mind, On the Principles of Common Sense*. Ed. Derek R. Brookes. Edinburgh: Edinburgh University Press, 1997.

Schlegel, Frederick. *Lectures in the History of Literature, Ancient and Modern*. Trans. J. G. Lockhart. Philadelphia: Dobson, 1818.

Scott, John. "Blackwood's Magazine," *London Magazine* 1 (June 1820): 509–21.

———. "Living Authors (Being a Series of Critical Sketches.) No. 1. The Author of the Scotch Novels." *London Magazine* 1 (January 1820): 11–22

———. "The Mohock Magazine," *London Magazine* 2 (December 1820): 666–85.

Scott, Walter. "Ann Radcliffe." in *Sir Walter Scott on Novelists and Fiction*, ed. Ioan Williams, 102–19. London: Routledge & Kegan Paul, 1968.

———. *The Antiquary*. Ed. David Hewitt. Edinburgh: Edinburgh University Press, 1995.

———. *The Black Dwarf*. Ed. Peter Garside. Edinburgh: Edinburgh University Press, 1993.

———. *Chronicles of the Canongate*. Ed. Claire Lamont. Edinburgh: Edinburgh University Press, 2000.

———. "Culloden Papers." *Quarterly Review* 14, no. 28 (January 1816): 284–333.

———. "Emma; a Novel." In Williams, *Scott on Novelists and Fiction*, 225–36.

———. *The Fortunes of Nigel*. Ed. Frank Jordan. Edinburgh: Edinburgh University Press, 2004.

———. *The Heart of Mid-Lothian*. Ed. David Hewitt and Alison Lumsden. Edinburgh: Edinburgh University Press, 2004.

———. *Ivanhoe*. Ed. Graham Tulloch. Edinburgh: Edinburgh University Press, 1998.

———. *The Journal of Sir Walter Scott*. Ed. W.E.K. Anderson. Edinburgh: Canongate, 1998.

———. *A Legend of the Wars of Montrose*. Ed. J. H. Alexander. Edinburgh: Edinburgh University Press, 1995.

———. *Letters of Sir Walter Scott*. Ed. H.J.C. Grierson. 12 vols. London: Constable, 1932.

———. *Letters on Demonology and Witchcraft, Addressed to J. G. Lockhart, Esq.* 2nd ed. London: Murray, 1831.

———. *Minstrelsy of the Scottish Border.* Ed. Thomas Henderson. London: Harrap, 1931.

———. *The Monastery.* 1830. London: A. & C. Black, 1893.

———. *The Monastery.* Ed. Penny Fielding. Edinburgh: Edinburgh University Press, 2000.

———. *Old Mortality.* 1830. Ed. Peter Davidson and Jane Stevens. Oxford: Oxford University Press, 1993.

———. "On the Present State of Periodical Criticism." *Edinburgh Annual Register* 2 (1811): 546-81. Reprinted in Curry, *Sir Walter Scott's Edinburgh Annual Register,* 132–70.

———. *Poetical Works.* Ed. J. Logie Robertson. London: Oxford University Press, 1971.

———. *Provincial Antiquities and Picturesque Scenery of Scotland.* 2 vols. London: Rodwell & Martin, 1826.

———. *Quentin Durward.* Ed. J. H. Alexander and G.A.M. Wood. Edinburgh: Edinburgh University Press, 2001.

———. *Redgauntlet.* Ed. G.A.M. Wood and David Hewitt. Edinburgh: Edinburgh University Press, 1997.

———. *Rob Roy.* Ed. Ian Duncan. Oxford: Oxford University Press, 1998.

———. *St Ronan's Well.* 1830. London: A. & C. Black, 1894.

———. *The Tale of Old Mortality.* Ed. Douglas Mack. Edinburgh: Edinburgh University Press, 1993.

———. *Waverley; or, 'Tis Sixty Years Since.* Ed. Claire Lamont. Oxford: Clarendon Press, 1981.

———. "The Works of John Home . . . to Which Is Affixed an Account of His Life and Writings. By Henry Mackenzie." *Quarterly Review* 36, no. 71 (June 1827): 167–216.

"Scottish Novels of the Second Class," *Edinburgh Magazine* 13 (1823): 1–13, 485–91.

Sinclair, Sir John. *The Statistical Account of Scotland: Drawn Up From the Communications of Different Parishes.* 21 vols. Edinburgh: W. Creech, 1791–99.

Smith, Adam. *An Inquiry into the Nature and Causes of the Wealth of Nations.* Ed. R. H. Campbell and A. S. Skinner. 2 vols.; Oxford: Clarendon Press, 1976.

———. *Lectures on Rhetoric and Belles Lettres.* Ed. J. C. Bryce. Oxford: Clarendon Press, 1983.

———. *The Theory of Moral Sentiments.* Ed. D. D. Raphael and A. L. Macfie. Oxford: Clarendon Press, 1976.

Smollett, Tobias. *Humphry Clinker.* Ed. James L. Thorson. New York: Norton, 1983.

Southey, Robert. *Poems of Robert Southey.* Ed. Maurice H. Fitzgerald. London: Oxford University Press, 1909.

Spon, Jacob. *Recherches curieuses d'antiquité, contenues en plusieurs dissertations.* Lyon: T. Amaulry, 1683.

Stewart, Dugald. "Account of the Life and Writings of Adam Smith, LL.D." Ed. I. S. Ross. In Adam Smith, *Essays on Philosophical Subjects,* ed. W.P.D. Wightman and J. C. Bryce, 269–351. Oxford: Clarendon Press, 1980.

Stewart, Dugald. *Elements of Philosophy of the Human Mind*. 3 vols. London: Strahan, 1792; Edinburgh: Ramsay, 1814; London: Murray, 1827.

Stoddart, Sir John. *Remarks on Local Scenery and Manners in Scotland during the Years 1799 and 1800*. 2 vols. London: W. Miller, 1801.

Swift, Jonathan. *Gulliver's Travels*. Ed. Paul Turner. Oxford: Oxford University Press, 1971.

Weir, William, and George Allan, *Life of Sir Walter Scott, W.S., Bart., with Critical Notices of His Writings*. Edinburgh: Thomas Ireland, Jr., 1832.

Wilson, John. *Lights and Shadows of Scottish Life: A Selection from the Papers of the Late Arthur Austin*. 2nd ed. Edinburgh: Blackwood, 1822.

————. "On the Late National Calamity," *Blackwood's Edinburgh Magazine* 1 (December 1817): 249–52.

————. "Some Observations on the Poetry of the Agricultural and that of the Pastoral Districts of Scotland, Illustrated by a Comparative View of the Genius of Burns and That of the Ettrick Shepherd," *Blackwood's Edinburgh Magazine* 4 (1819): 521–29.

Sources Published after 1900

Abraham, Nicolas, and Maria Torok. "Mourning *or* Melancholia: Introjection *versus* Incorporation." 1972. In *The Shell and the Kernel*, ed. Nicholas T. Rand. Chicago: University of Chicago Press, 1994.

Agamben, Giorgio. *State of Exception*. Trans. Kevin Attell. Chicago: University of Chicago Press, 2005.

Alexander, J. H. "Anecdotes to Familiar Anecdotes." *Studies in Hogg and his World* 13 (2002): 5–15.

————. "Hogg in the *Noctes Ambrosianae*." *Studies in Hogg and His World* 4 (1993): 37–47.

————, ed. *The Tavern Sages: Selections from the Noctes Ambrosianae*. Aberdeen: Association for Scottish Literary Studies, 1992.

Alexander, J. H., and David Hewitt, eds. *Scott and His Influence: The Papers of the Aberdeen Scott Conference, 1982*. Aberdeen: Association for Scottish Literary Studies, 1983.

————. *Scott in Carnival: Selected Papers from the Fourth International Scott Conference*. Aberdeen: Association for Scottish Literary Studies, 1993.

Alker, Sharon. "The Business of Romance: Mary Brunton and the Virtue of Commerce." *European Romantic Review* 13, no. 2 (2002): 199–205.

Alter, Robert. *Partial Magic: The Novel as a Self-Conscious Genre*. Berkeley: University of California Press, 1975.

Altick, Richard D. *The English Common Reader: A Social History of the Mass Reading Public, 1800–1900*. Chicago: University of Chicago Press, 1957.

Anderson, Benedict. *Imagined Communities: Reflections on the Origin and Spread of Nationalism*. London: Verso, 1983.

Anderson, J. A. *At the Sign of the Cleikum: Reminiscences of Innerleithen, 1926–1932*. Ed. Olive M. W. Russell. Selkirk: Bordersprint Ltd., 1996.

Arata, Steven. "Scott's Pageants: The Example of *Kenilworth*." *Studies in Romanticism* 40, no. 1 (Spring 2001): 99–107.

Bann, Stephen. *Romanticism and the Rise of History.* New York: Twayne, 1995.

Bardsley, Alyson. "Novel and Nation Come to Grief: The Dead's Part in John Galt's *The Entail.*" *Modern Philology* 99, no. 4 (2002): 540–63.

———. "The Trauma of Breaking, and of Making, Covenants: John Galt's *Ringan Gilhaize.*" Paper read at the Scotland, Ireland, and the Romantic Aesthetic Conference, University of Aberdeen, 2002.

———. "Your Local Representative: John Galt's *The Provost.*" *Scottish Literary Journal* 24, no. 1 (1997): 72–76.

Barrell, John. "Putting Down the Rising." In Davis, Duncan, and Sorensen, *Scotland and the Borders of Romanticism*, 130–38.

Barry, Kevin. "The Aesthetic Formation of a 'Man of Credit' in the Period of Enlightenment and Romanticism." In *Scotland, Ireland and the Romantic Aesthetic*, ed. David Duff and Catherine Jones. Lewisburg, Pa.: Bucknell University Press, 2007.

Barthes, Roland. "The Reality Effect." In *The Rustle of Language*, trans. Richard Howard, 141–48. New York: Farrar, Straus and Giroux, 1986.

Bender, John. "Enlightenment Fiction and the Scientific Hypothesis." *Representations* 61 (1998): 6–28.

———. *Imagining the Penitentiary: Fiction and the Architecture of Mind in Eighteenth-Century England.* Chicago: University of Chicago Press, 1987.

Benjamin, Walter. *Illuminations.* Trans. Harry Zohn. New York: Schocken Books, 1969.

———. *The Origin of German Tragic Drama.* Trans. John Osborne. London: NLB, 1977.

Bennett, Tony. *Outside Literature.* New York: Routledge, 1990.

Bloch, Ernst. *Heritage of Our Times.* Oxford: Polity Press, 1991.

Bloedé, Barbara. "Hogg and the Edinburgh Prostitution Scandal," *Newsletter of the James Hogg Society* 8 (1989): 15–18.

———. "James Hogg's *Private Memoirs and Confessions of a Justified Sinner*: The Genesis of the Double," *Etudes Anglaises* 26, no. 2 (1973): 174–86

———. "*The Three Perils of Woman* and the Edinburgh Prostitution Scandal of 1823: A Reply to Dr Groves." *Studies in Hogg and His World* 3 (1992): 88–94.

Bloom, Harold. *The Anxiety of Influence: A Theory of Poetry.* New York: Oxford University Press, 1973.

Blumenberg, Hans. *Shipwreck with Spectator: Paradigms of a Metaphor for Existence.* Trans. Steven Rendall. Cambridge, Mass.: MIT Press, 1997.

Bold, Valentina. "Traditional Narrative Elements in *The Three Perils of Woman.*" *Studies in Hogg and His World* 3 (1992): 42–56.

Bongie, Laurence L. *David Hume, Prophet of the Counter-Revolution.* Oxford: Clarendon Press, 1965.

Bour, Isabelle. "Mary Brunton's Novels, or, The Twilight of Sensibility." *Scottish Literary Journal* 24, no. 2 (1997): 24–35.

Bourdieu, Pierre. *The Rules of Art: Genesis and Structure of the Literary Field.* Trans. Susan Emanuel. Stanford: Stanford University Press, 1996.

Brewer, David. *The Afterlife of Character, 1726–1825.* Philadelphia: University of Pennsylvania Press, 2005.

Brewer, John. *The Pleasures of the Imagination: English Culture in the Eighteenth Century*. London: HarperCollins, 1997.

Broughton, Janet. "The Inquiry in the *Treatise*." *Philosophical Review* 113, no. 4 (2004): 537–56.

Brown, David. *Walter Scott and the Historical Imagination*. London: Routledge & Kegan Paul, 1979.

Brown, Homer O. *Institutions of the English Novel: From Defoe to Scott*. Philadelphia: University of Pennsylvania Press, 1997.

Buchan, James. *Capital of the Mind: How Edinburgh Changed the World*. London: John Murray, 2003.

Burgess, Miranda J. *British Fiction and the Production of Social Order, 1740–1830*. Cambridge: Cambridge University Press, 2000.

———. "Domesticating Gothic: Jane Austen, Ann Radcliffe, and National Romance." In *Lessons of Romanticism: A Critical Companion*, ed. Thomas Pfau and Robert F. Gleckner, 392–412. Durham, N.C.: Duke University Press, 1998.

———. "Scott, History, and the Augustan Public Sphere." *Studies in Romanticism* 40, no. 1 (2001): 123–35.

Burrow, J. W. *Evolution and Society: A Study in Victorian Social Theory*. Cambridge: Cambridge University Press, 1966.

Butler, Marilyn. "Culture's Medium: The Role of the Review." In *The Cambridge Companion to British Romanticism*, ed. Stuart Curran, 120–47. Cambridge: Cambridge University Press, 1993.

———. "*Frankenstein* and Radical Science." In Mary Shelley, *Frankenstein*, ed. J. Paul Hunter, 302–13. New York: Norton, 1996.

———. General introduction to *Novels and Selected Works of Maria Edgeworth*, vol. 1, *Castle Rackrent; Irish Bulls; Ennui*, ed. Jane Desmarais, Tim McLoughlin and Marilyn Butler. London: Pickering and Chatto, 1999.

Buzard, James. *The Beaten Track: Tourism and the Ways to "Culture," 1800–1918*. Oxford: Clarendon Press, 1993.

———. *Disorienting Fiction: The Autoethnographic Work of Nineteenth-Century British Novels*. Princeton: Princeton University Press, 2005.

———. "Translation and Tourism: Scott's *Waverley* and the Rendering of Culture." *Yale Journal of Criticism* 8, no. 2 (1995): 31–59.

Calasso, Roberto. *The Marriage between Cadmus and Harmony*. Trans. Tim Parks. New York: Knopf, 1993.

Campbell, Ian. "Afterword: Literary Criticism and *Confessions of a Justified Sinner*." In Hogg, *Private Memoirs and Confessions of a Justified Sinner*, 177–94.

———. "James Hogg and the Bible." In *The Bible and Scottish Literature*, ed. David F. Wright, 94–109. Edinburgh: St Andrew Press, 1988.

Carruthers, Gerard, and Alan Rawes, eds. *English Romanticism and the Celtic World*. Cambridge: Cambridge University Press, 2003.

Carswell, Donald. *Sir Walter: A Four Part Study in Biography*. London: J. Murray, 1930.

Chandler, James. *England in 1819: The Politics of Literary Culture and the Case of Romantic Historicism*. Chicago: University of Chicago Press, 1998.

Chandler, James, and Kevin Gilmartin, eds. *Romantic Metropolis: The Urban Scene of British Culture, 1780–1840*. Cambridge: Cambridge University Press, 2005.

Chase, Bob. "Walter Scott: A New Historical Paradigm." In *The Expansion of England: Race, Ethnicity and Cultural History*, ed. Bill Schwartz, 92–129. London: Routledge, 1996.

Chittick, Kathryn. *Dickens and the 1830s*. Cambridge: Cambridge University Press, 1990.

Christensen, Jerome. "The Detection of the Romantic Conspiracy in Britain." *SAQ* 95, no. 3 (1996): 603–27.

———. *Romanticism at the End of History*. Baltimore: Johns Hopkins University Press, 2000.

Clifford, James. "On Ethnographic Allegory." In *Writing Culture: The Poetics and Politics of Ethnography*, ed. James Clifford and George E. Marcus, 98–121. Berkeley: University of California Press, 1986.

Clifford, John, Colin McWilliam, and David Walker. *The Buildings of Scotland: Edinburgh*. Harmondsworth: Penguin, 1984.

Clive, John. *Scotch Reviewers: The Edinburgh Review 1802–1815*. Cambridge, Mass.: Harvard University Press, 1957.

Cockshut, A.O.J. *The Achievement of Walter Scott*. London: Collins, 1969.

Colley, Linda. *Britons: Forging the Nation 1707–1837*. New Haven: Yale University Press, 1992.

Collini, Stefan, Donald Winch, and John Burrow. *That Noble Science of Politics: A Study in Nineteenth-Century Intellectual History*. Cambridge: Cambridge University Press, 1983.

Collins, A. S. *The Profession of Letters: A Study of the Relation of Author to Patron, Publisher, and Public, 1780–1832*. London: G. Routledge & Sons, 1928.

Connell, Philip. *Romanticism, Economics and the Question of "Culture."* Oxford: Oxford University Press, 2001.

Connolly, Claire, "Introduction: The Politics of Love in *The Wild Irish Girl*." In Sydney Owenson, *The Wild Irish Girl*, ed. Claire Connolly and Stephen Copley, xxv–lxvi. London: Pickering and Chatto, 2000.

———. "Reading Responsibility in *Castle Rackrent*." In *Ireland and Cultural Theory: The Mechanics of Authenticity*, ed. Richard Kirkland and Colin Graham, 136–61. Basingstoke: Macmillan, 1999.

Cooter, Roger. *The Cultural Meaning of Popular Science: Phrenology and the Organization of Consent in Nineteenth-Century Britain*. Cambridge: Cambridge University Press, 1984.

Copeland, Edward. *Women Writing about Money: Women's Fiction in England, 1790–1820*. Cambridge: Cambridge University Press, 1995.

Costain, Keith M. "The Scottish Fiction of John Galt." In Gifford, *History of Scottish Literature*, 3:107–22.

———. "Theoretical History and the Novel: The Scottish Fiction of John Galt." *ELH* 43, no. 3 (1976): 342–65.

Craciun, Adriana. "Romantic Spinstrelsy: Anne Bannerman and the Sexual Politics of the Ballad." In Davis, Duncan, and Sorensen, *Scotland and the Borders of Romanticism*, 204–24.

Craig, Cairns. "Coleridge, Hume, and the Chains of the Romantic Imagination." In Davis, Duncan, and Sorensen, *Scotland and the Borders of Romanticism*, 20–37.

———. *Out of History: Narrative Paradigms in Scottish and English Culture.* Edinburgh: Polygon, 1996.

Craig, Cairns. "Scotland and the Regional Novel." In *The Regional Novel in Britain and Ireland 1800–1990*, ed. K. Snell, 221–56. Cambridge: Cambridge University Press, 1998.

———. "Scott's Staging of the Nation." *Studies in Romanticism* 40, no. 1 (Spring 2001): 13–28.

Craig, David. *Scottish Literature and the Scottish People, 1680–1830.* London: Chatto & Windus, 1961.

Crawford, Robert. *Devolving English Literature.* Oxford: Clarendon Press, 1992.

———. "Robert Fergusson's Robert Burns." In *Robert Burns and Cultural Authority*, ed. Robert Crawford, 1–22. Edinburgh: University of Edinburgh Press, 1997.

———, ed. *The Scottish Invention of English Literature.* Cambridge: Cambridge University Press, 1998.

———. "Scottish Literature and English Studies." In Crawford, *Scottish Invention of English Literature*, 225–46.

Currie, Janet. "James Hogg's Literary Friendships with John Grieve and Eliza Izett." In James Hogg, *Mador of the Moor*, ed. J. Barcus, xliii–lvii.

Curry, Kenneth. *Sir Walter Scott's Edinburgh Annual Register.* Knoxville: University of Tennessee Press, 1977.

Daiches, David. *Edinburgh.* London: Hamish Hamilton, 1978.

———. "Scott's Achievement as a Novelist." In *Modern Judgements: Walter Scott*, ed. D. D. Devlin, 33–62. London: Macmillan, 1968.

Damrosch, Leo. *Fictions of Reality in the Age of Hume and Johnson.* Madison: University of Wisconsin Press, 1989.

Davie, Donald. *The Heyday of Sir Walter Scott.* London: Routledge & Kegan Paul, 1961.

Davis, Leith. *Acts of Union: Scotland and the Literary Negotiation of the British Nation, 1707–1830.* Stanford: Stanford University Press, 1998.

Davis, Leith, Ian Duncan, and Janet Sorensen, eds. *Scotland and the Borders of Romanticism.* Cambridge: Cambridge University Press, 2004.

Davis, Lennard. *Factual Fictions: The Origins of the English Novel.* New York: Columbia University Press, 1983.

Deane, Seamus. *Strange Country: Modernity and Nationhood in Irish Writing since 1790.* Oxford: Clarendon Press, 1997.

De Groot, H. B. "Fiction and History: The Case of *Redgauntlet*." In Alexander and Hewitt, *Scott in Carnival*, 358–69.

———. "The Imperilled Reader in *The Three Perils of Man*." *Studies in Hogg and His World* 1 (1990): 114–25.

Dekker, George. *The Fictions of Romantic Tourism: Radcliffe, Scott, and Mary Shelley.* Stanford: Stanford University Press, 2005.

Demata, Massimiliano, and Duncan Wu, eds. *British Romanticism and the Edinburgh Review: Bicentenary Essays.* New York: Palgrave, 2002.

Dennis, Ian. *Nationalism and Desire in Early Historical Fiction.* Basingstoke: Macmillan, 1997.

Desmond, Adrian. *The Politics of Evolution: Morphology, Medicine, and Reform in Radical London.* Chicago: University of Chicago Press, 1989.

Devine, T. M. *Scotland's Empire, 1600–1815.* London: Allen Lane, 2003.

———. *The Scottish Nation: A History, 1700–2000.* New York: Viking, 1999.

Devine, T. M., and Gordon Jackson, eds. *Glasgow: Beginnings to 1830.* Manchester: Manchester University Press, 1995.

Dosanjh, Rajit S. "The 'Eloquence of the Bar': Hugh Blair's Lectures, Professionalism and Scottish Legal Education." In Crawford, *Scottish Invention of English Literature,* 55–67.

Douglas, Mary. *Purity and Danger: An Analysis of Concepts of Pollution and Taboo.* London: Routledge & Kegan Paul, 1966.

Duncan, Ian. "Adam Smith, Samuel Johnson and the Institutions of English." In Crawford, *Scottish Invention of English Literature,* 37–54.

———. Introduction to Walter Scott, *Ivanhoe,* ed. Ian Duncan, vi–xxvi. Oxford: Oxford University Press, 1996.

———. *Modern Romance and Transformations of the Novel: The Gothic, Scott, Dickens.* Cambridge: Cambridge University Press, 1992.

———. "North Britain, Inc." *Victorian Literature and Culture* 23 (1995): 339–50.

———. "The Pathos of Abstraction: Adam Smith, Ossian, and Samuel Johnson." In Davis, Duncan, and Sorensen, *Scotland and the Borders of Romanticism,* 38–56.

———. "The Regional or Provincial Novel." In *A Companion to the Victorian Novel,* ed. Patrick Brantlinger and William B. Thesing, 318–35. Oxford: Blackwell, 2002.

———. "Scott, Hogg, Orality, and the Limits of Culture." *Studies in Hogg and His World* 8 (1997): 56–74.

———. "The Upright Corpse: Hogg, National Literature, and the Uncanny." *Studies in Hogg and His World* 5 (1994): 29–54.

Durkheim, Emile. *The Elementary Forms of the Religious Life.* New York: Free Press, 1965.

Eagleton, Terry. *Heathcliff and the Great Hunger: Studies in Irish Culture.* London: Verso, 1995.

Easley, Alexis. *First Person Anonymous: Women Writers and Victorian Print Media, 1830–1870.* Aldershot: Ashgate, 2004.

———. "*Tait's Edinburgh Magazine* in the 1830s: Dialogues on Gender, Class, and Reform." *Victorian Periodicals Review* 38, no. 3 (2005): 263–79.

Fabian, Johannes. *Time and the Other: How Anthropology Makes Its Object.* New York: Columbia University Press, 1983.

Ferris, Ina. *The Achievement of Literary Authority: Gender, History, and the Waverley Novels.* Ithaca: Cornell University Press, 1991.

Ferris, Ina. "Pedantry and the Question of Enlightenment History: The Figure of the Antiquary in Scott." *European Romantic Review* 13, no. 3 (2002): 273–83.

———. *The Romantic National Tale and the Question of Ireland*. Cambridge: Cambridge University Press, 2002.

———. "Translation from the Borders: Encounter and Recalcitrance in *Waverley* and *Clan-Albin*." *Eighteenth-Century Fiction* 9, no. 2 (1997): 203–22.

Fielding, Penny. "Jane Austen's Dirty Realism." Lecture, University of Oregon, Eugene, 1999.

———. *Writing and Orality: Nationality, Culture, and Nineteenth-Century Scottish Fiction*. Oxford: Clarendon Press, 1996.

———. "Writing at the North: Rhetoric and Dialect in Eighteenth-Century Scotland." *Eighteenth Century: Theory and Interpretation* 39, no. 1 (1998): 25–43.

Flynn, Philip. "Francis Jeffrey and the Scottish Critical Tradition." In Demata and Wu, *British Romanticism and the Edinburgh Review*, 13–32.

Fontana, Biancamaria. *Rethinking the Politics of Commercial Society: The Edinburgh Review, 1802–1832*. Cambridge: Cambridge University Press, 1985.

Forbes, Duncan. "The Rationalism of Sir Walter Scott." *Cambridge Journal* 7 (1953): 20–35.

Forster, E. M. *Aspects of the Novel*. London: E. Arnold, 1949.

Foucault, Michel. *The Order of Things: An Archaeology of the Human Sciences*. New York: Vintage, 1970.

François, Anne-Lise. "To Hold in Common and Know by Heart: The Prevalence of Gentle Forces in Humean Empiricism and Romantic Experience." *Yale Journal of Criticism* 7, no. 1 (1994): 139–62.

Freud, Sigmund. "The Uncanny." In *The Standard Edition of the Complete Psychoanalytic Works of Sigmund Freud*, trans. James Strachey, 17:219–52. London: Hogarth Press, 1955.

Fry, Michael. *The Dundas Despotism*. Edinburgh: Edinburgh University Press, 1992.

Frye, Lowell T. "Romancing the Past: Walter Scott and Thomas Carlyle." *Carlyle Studies Annual* 16 (1996): 37–49.

Gallagher, Catherine. *The Body Economic: Life, Death, and Sensation in Political Economy and the Victorian Novel*. Princeton: Princeton University Press, 2006.

———. *Nobody's Story: The Vanishing Acts of Women Writers in the Marketplace, 1670–1820*. Berkeley: University of California Press, 1994.

Gallagher, Catherine, and Stephen Greenblatt. *Practicing New Historicism*. Chicago: University of Chicago Press, 2000.

Gamer, Michael. *Romanticism and the Gothic: Genre, Reception, and Canon Formation*. Cambridge: Cambridge University Press, 2000.

Garside, P. D. "Scott and the 'Philosophical' Historians." *Journal of the History of Ideas* 36 (1975): 497–512.

Garside, Peter. "The English Novel in the Romantic Period." In Garside and Schöwerling, *English Novel, 1770–1829*, 15–103.

———. "Hogg and the Blackwoodian Novel." *Studies in Hogg and His World* 15 (2004): 5–20.

————. "Popular Fiction and National Tale: Hidden Origins of Scott's *Waverley*." *Nineteenth-Century Literature* 46, no. 1 (1991): 30–53.

————. "Printing *Confessions*." *Studies in Hogg and His World* 9 (1998): 16–31

————. "Three Perils in Publishing: Hogg and the Popular Novel," *Studies in Hogg and His World* 2 (1991): 45–63.

————. "Walter Scott and the 'Common Novel,' 1808–1819." *Cardiff Corvey: Reading the Romantic Text* 3 (September 1999), http://www.cf.ac.uk/encap/corvey/articles/cc03_n02.html.

Garside, Peter, and Rainer Schöwerling, eds. *The English Novel, 1770–1829: A Bibliographical Survey of Prose Fiction Published in the British Isles*. Vol. 2, *1800–1829*. Oxford: Oxford University Press, 2000.

Garside, Peter, Jacqueline Belanger, and Sharon Ragaz. *British Fiction 1800–1829: A Database of Production, Circulation, and Reception*. Centre for Editorial and Intertextual Research, Cardiff University, www.british-fiction.cf.ac.uk

Gibbons, Luke. *Edmund Burke and Ireland: Aesthetics, Politics and the Colonial Sublime*. Cambridge: Cambridge University Press, 2003.

Gifford, Douglas, ed. *The History of Scottish Literature*. Vol. 3, *The Nineteenth Century*. Aberdeen: Aberdeen University Press, 1988.

————. *James Hogg*. Edinburgh: Ramsay Head, 1976.

Gigante, Denise. "The Monster in the Rainbow: Keats and the Science of Life." *PMLA* 117, no. 3 (2002): 433–48.

————. *Taste: A Literary History*. New Haven: Yale University Press, 2005.

Girard, Rene. *Deceit, Desire, and the Novel: Self and Other in Literary Structure*. Trans. Yvonne Freccero. Baltimore: Johns Hopkins University Press, 1965.

Girouard, Mark. *The Return to Camelot: Chivalry and the English Gentleman*. New Haven: Yale University Press, 1981.

Goodman, Kevis. *Georgic Modernity and British Romanticism: Poetry and the Mediation of History*. Cambridge: Cambridge University Press, 2004.

Gordon, Ian A. "Galt's Politics." In *John Galt: Reappraisals*, ed. Elizabeth Waterson, 119–26. Guelph: University of Guelph, 1985.

————. *John Galt: The Life of a Writer*. Edinburgh: Oliver & Boyd, 1972.

Gordon, Robert C. *Under Which King? A Study of the Scottish Waverley Novels*. Edinburgh: Oliver & Boyd, 1969.

Goslee, Nancy Moore. *Scott the Rhymer*. Lexington: University Press of Kentucky, 1988.

Gossman, Lionel. *Between History and Literature*. Cambridge, Mass.: Harvard University Press, 1990.

Graham, Colin. "History, Gender and the Colonial Moment: *Castle Rackrent*." *Irish Studies Review* 14 (1996): 21–24.

Green, Katherine Sobba. *The Courtship Novel, 1740–1820: A Feminized Genre*. Lexington: University Press of Kentucky, 1991.

Griffin, Dustin. *Literary Patronage in England, 1650–1800*. Cambridge: Cambridge University Press, 1996.

Griffin, Robert. "Anonymity and Authorship." *New Literary History* 30, no. 4 (1999): 877–95.

Groves, David. *James Hogg: The Growth of a Writer*. Edinburgh: Scottish Academic Press, 1988.

Groves, David. "James Hogg's *Confessions* and *The Three Perils of Woman* and the Edinburgh Prostitution Scandal of 1823." *Wordsworth Circle* 18 (1987): 127–31

———. "*The Three Perils of Woman* and the Edinburgh Prostitution Scandal of 1823." *Studies in Hogg and His World* 2 (1991): 95–102.

Guillory, John. *Cultural Capital: The Problem of Literary Canon Formation.* Chicago: University of Chicago Press, 1993.

Habermas, Jürgen. *The Structural Transformation of the Public Sphere: An Inquiry into a Category of Bourgeois Society.* Trans. Thomas Burger. Cambridge, Mass.: MIT Press, 1991.

Hack, Daniel. "Inter-Nationalism: *Castle Rackrent* and Anglo-Irish Union." *Novel* 29, no. 2 (1996): 145–64.

Hamilton, Paul. *Metaromanticism: Aesthetics, Literature, Theory.* Chicago: University of Chicago Press, 2003.

Hart, Francis Russell. *Lockhart as Romantic Biographer.* Edinburgh: Edinburgh University Press, 1971.

———. *The Scottish Novel: From Smollett to Spark.* Cambridge, Mass.: Harvard University Press, 1978.

———. *Scott's Novels: The Plotting of Historic Survival.* Charlottesville: University Press of Virginia, 1966.

Hasler, Antony J. "Reading the Land: James Hogg and the Highlands." *Studies in Hogg and His World* 4 (1993): 57–82.

———. "*The Three Perils of Woman* and John Wilson's *Lights and Shadows of Scottish Life.*" *Studies in Hogg and His World* 1 (1990): 30–45.

Hayden, John O. *The Romantic Reviewers, 1802–1824.* Chicago: University of Chicago Press, 1969.

———, ed. *Scott: The Critical Heritage.* New York: Barnes & Noble, 1970.

Hechter, Michael. *Internal Colonialism: The Celtic Fringe in British National Development, 1536–1966.* Berkeley: University of California Press, 1975.

Herbert, Christopher. *Culture and Anomie: Ethnographic Imagination in the Nineteenth Century.* Chicago: University of Chicago Press, 1991.

Hewitt, David. "*Rob Roy* and First-Person Narratives." In Alexander and Hewitt, *Scott and his Influence*, 372–81.

Hillhouse, James T. *The Waverley Novels and their Critics.* Minneapolis: University of Minnesota Press, 1936.

Hindle, Maurice. "Vital Matters: Mary Shelley's *Frankenstein* and Romantic Science." *Critical Survey* 2, no. 1 (1990): 29–35.

Hughes, Gillian. "The Critical Reception of *The Confessions of a Justified Sinner.*" *Newsletter of the James Hogg Society* 1 (1982): 11–14.

———. "James Hogg and Edinburgh's Triumph over Napoleon." *Scottish Studies Review* 4, no. 1 (2003): 98–111.

———. "James Hogg and the Forum." *Studies in Hogg and His World* 1 (1990): 57–70.

———. "Recovering Hogg's Personal Manuscript for *The Three Perils of Man.*" *Studies in Hogg and His World* 13 (2002): 104–26.

Hughes-Hartman, George, and Robert Innes-Smith. *Inveraray Castle.* Derby: Heritage House Group, 2002.

Hunter, J. Paul. *Before Novels: The Cultural Contexts of Eighteenth-Century English Fiction.* New York: Norton, 1990.

Hutcheon, Linda. " 'The Pastime of Past Time': Fiction, History, Historiographical Metafiction." In *Essentials of the Theory of Fiction,* ed. Michael J. Hoffman and Patrick D. Murphy, 472–95. Durham, N.C.: Duke University Press, 1996.

Irvine, Robert. *Enlightenment and Romance: Gender and Agency in Smollett and Scott.* Oxford: Peter Lang, 2000.

———. "Gender and the Place of Culture in Scott's *St Ronan's Well.*" *Scottish Studies Review* 2, no. 1 (2001): 46–64.

Iser, Wolfgang. *The Fictive and the Imaginary: Charting Literary Anthropology.* Baltimore: Johns Hopkins University Press, 1993.

Jackson, Richard. "Gatty Bell's Illness in James Hogg's *The Three Perils of Woman.*" *Studies in Hogg and His World* 14 (2003): 16–29.

Jacyna, L. S. "Immanence or Transcendence: Theories of Life and Organization in Britain, 1790–1835." *Isis* 74, no. 3 (1983): 311–29.

Jessop, Ralph. *Carlyle and Scottish Thought.* Houndmills: Macmillan, 1997.

Johnson, Edgar. *Sir Walter Scott: The Great Unknown.* 2 vols. New York: Macmillan, 1970.

Jones, Catherine. *Literary Memory: Scott's Waverley Novels and the Psychology of Narrative.* Lewisburg, Pa.: Bucknell University Press, 2003.

Jordan, Frank. "Chrystal Croftangry, Scott's Last and Best Mask." *Scottish Literary Journal* 7 (1980): 185–92.

Kaufmann, David. *The Business of Common Life: Novels and Classical Economics between Revolution and Reform.* Baltimore: Johns Hopkins University Press, 1995.

———. "Thanks for the Memory: Bloch, Benjamin, and the Philosophy of History." *Yale Journal of Criticism* 6, no. 1 (Spring 1993): 143–62.

Kelly, Gary. *English Fiction of the Romantic Period, 1789–1830.* London: Longman, 1989.

Kerr, James. *Fiction Against History: Scott as Storyteller.* Cambridge: Cambridge University Press, 1989.

Kidd, Colin. *Subverting Scotland's Past: Scottish Whig Historians and the Creation of an Anglo-British Identity, 1689–c. 1830.* Cambridge: Cambridge University Press, 1993.

Kilgour, Maggie. *From Communion to Cannibalism: An Anatomy of Metaphors of Incorporation.* Princeton: Princeton University Press, 1990.

Killick, Tim. "Hogg and the Collection of Short Fiction in the 1820s." *Studies in Hogg and His World* 15 (2004): 21–31.

Kittler, Friedrich A. *Discourse Networks 1800/1900.* Trans. Michael Metteer. Stanford: Stanford University Press, 1990.

Klancher, Jon. *The Making of English Reading Audiences, 1790–1832.* Madison: University of Wisconsin Press, 1987.

Koselleck, Reinhart. *Futures Past: On the Semantics of Historical Time.* Cambridge, Mass.: MIT Press, 1985.

Langan, Celeste. "Understanding Media in 1805: Audovisual Hallucination in *The Lay of the Last Minstrel.*" *Studies in Romanticism* 40, no. 1 (Spring 2001): 49–70.

Lee, Yoon Sun. "Giants in the North: *Douglas*, the Scottish Enlightenment, and Scott's *Redgauntlet.*" *Studies in Romanticism* 40, no. 1 (2001): 109–21.

———. *Nationalism and Irony: Burke, Scott, Carlyle.* New York: Oxford University Press, 2004.

Lincoln, Andrew. "Scott and Empire: The Case of *Rob Roy.*" *Studies in the Novel* 34, no. 1 (2002): 43–59.

———. "Sentimental and Accountable Reading: Scott, Romance and History" Paper read at the Reason and Romance Conference, University of Sheffield, May 2004.

———. "Walter Scott and the Birth of the Nation." *Romanticism: The Journal of Romantic Culture & Criticism* 8, no. 1 (2002): 1–17.

Livingston, Donald W. *Hume's Philosophy of Common Life.* Chicago: University of Chicago Press, 1984.

Low, Donald A., ed. *Robert Burns: The Critical Heritage.* London: Routledge & Kegan Paul, 1974.

Lukács, Georg. *The Historical Novel.* Trans. Hannah Mitchell and Stanley Mitchell. Lincoln: University of Nebraska Press, 1983.

Lynch, Deidre Shauna. *The Economy of Character: Novels, Market Culture, and the Business of Inner Meaning.* Chicago: University of Chicago Press, 1998.

———. "Gothic Libraries and National Subjects." *Studies in Romanticism* 40, no. 1 (2001): 29–48.

———. "Transformations of the Novel—I." In *The New Cambridge History of British Literature: The Romantic Period*, ed. James Chandler. Cambridge: Cambridge University Press, 2008.

Mack, Douglas S. "The Body in the Opened Grave: Robert Burns and Robert Wringhim." *Studies in Hogg and His World* 7 (1996): 70–79.

———. "Gatty's Illness in *The Three Perils of Woman*," *Studies in Hogg and His World* 1 (1990): 133–35.

———. "Hogg, Scott, Byron and John Murray of Albermarle Street." *Studies in Scottish Literature* 35–36 (2007): 1–19.

———. Introduction to *The Tale of Old Mortality*, by Walter Scott, xii–xxix. Harmondsworth: Penguin, 1999.

———. "Lights and Shadows of Scottish Life: James Hogg's *The Three Perils of Woman.*" In *Studies in Scottish Fiction: Nineteenth Century*, ed. Horst W. Drescher and Joachim Schwend, 15–27. Frankfurt-am-Main: Publications of the Scottish Studies Centre of the Universitat Mainz 3, 1985.

———. " 'The Rage of Fanaticism in Former Days': James Hogg's *Confessions of a Justified Sinner* and the Controversy over *Old Mortality.*" In *Nineteenth-Century Scottish Fiction: Critical Essays*, ed. Ian Campbell, 37–50. Manchester: Carcanet, 1979.

———. *Scottish Fiction and the British Empire.* Edinburgh: Edinburgh University Press, 2006.

MacKenzie, Scott. "Confessions of a Gentrified Sinner: Secrets in Scott and Hogg." *Studies in Romanticism* 41, no. 1 (2002): 3–32.

MacLachlan, Robin. "Hogg and the Art of Brand Management." *Studies in Hogg and his World* 14 (2003), 5-15.

———. "Scott and Hogg: Friendship and Literary Influence." In Alexander and Hewitt, *Scott and His Influence*, 331–40.

MacQueen, John. *The Enlightenment and Scottish Literature*. Vol. 2, *The Rise of the Historical Novel*. Edinburgh: Scottish Academic Press, 1989.

Makdisi, Saree. *Romantic Imperialism: Universal Empire and the Culture of Modernity*. Cambridge: Cambridge University Press, 1998.

Manning, Susan. "Antiquarianism, the Scottish Science of Man, and the Emergence of Modern Disciplinarity." In Davis, Duncan, and Sorensen, *Scotland and the Borders of Romanticism*, 57–76.

———. *Fragments of Union: Making Connections in Scottish and American Writing*. Houndmills: Palgrave, 2002.

———. *The Puritan-Provincial Vision: Scottish and American Literature in the Nineteenth Century*. Cambridge: Cambridge University Press, 1990.

———. "That Exhumation Scene Again: Transatlantic Hogg." *Studies in Hogg and His World* 16 (2005): 86–111.

Maxwell, Richard. "Inundations of Time: A Definition of Scott's Originality." *ELH* 68, no. 2 (2001): 419–68.

———. "Scott and the Genesis of the Victorian Illustrated Book." In *The Victorian Illustrated Book*, ed. Richard Maxwell, 1–51. Charlottesville: University Press of Virginia, 2002.

McCracken-Flesher, Caroline. "The Fourth Peril of James Hogg: Walter Scott and the Demonology of Minstrelsy." *Studies in Hogg and His World* 11 (2000): 39–55.

———. " 'The great disturber of the age': James Hogg at the King's Visit, 1822." *Studies in Hogg and His World* 9 (1998): 64–83.

———. *Possible Scotlands: Walter Scott and the Story of Tomorrow*. New York: Oxford University Press, 2005.

McElroy, Davis D. *Scotland's Age of Improvement: A Survey of Eighteenth Century Literary Clubs and Societies*. Pullman: Washington State University Press, 1969.

McGann, Jerome. *The Romantic Ideology: A Critical Investigation*. Chicago: Chicago University Press, 1983.

———. "Walter Scott's Romantic Postmodernity." In Davis, Duncan, and Sorensen, *Scotland and the Borders of Romanticism*, 113–29.

McIlvanney, Liam. *Burns the Radical: Poetry and Politics in Late Eighteenth-Century Scotland*. East Linton: Tuckwell, 2002.

McKeon, Michael. *The Origins of the English Novel, 1600–1740*. Baltimore: Johns Hopkins University Press, 1987.

McLane, Maureen. "The Figure Minstrelsy Makes: Poetry and Historicity." *Critical Inquiry* 29, no. 3 (2003): 429–52.

McMaster, Graham. *Scott and Society*. Cambridge: Cambridge University Press, 1981.

McMillan, Dorothy. "Figuring the Nation: Christian Isobel Johnstone as Novelist and Editor." *Études écossaises* 9 (2003): 27–41.

McNeil, Ken. "Inside and Outside the Nation: Highland Violence in Walter Scott's *Tales of a Grandfather*." *Literature and History* 8, no. 2 (1999): 1–17.

Mellor, Anne K. "Making a 'Monster': An Introduction to *Frankenstein*." In *The Cambridge Companion to Mary Shelley*, ed. Esther Schor, 9–25. Cambridge: Cambridge University Press, 2003.

———. *Romanticism and Gender*. New York: Routledge, 1993.

Mergenthal, Silvia. "James Hogg and his 'Best Benefactor': Two Versions of Hogg's Anecdotes of Scott." *Studies in Hogg and His World* 4 (1993): 26–36.

———. "*Naturae Donum*: Comments on Hogg's Self-Image and Image." *Studies in Hogg and His World* 1 (1990): 71–79.

Micale, Mark. *Approaching Hysteria: Disease and Its Interpretations.* Princeton: Princeton University Press, 1995.

Michie, Michael. *An Enlightenment Tory in Victorian Scotland: The Career of Sir Archibald Alison.* Montreal: McGill-Queen's University Press, 1997.

Miller, D. A. *Jane Austen, or The Secret of Style.* Princeton: Princeton University Press, 2003.

Miller, David. *Philosophy and Ideology in Hume's Political Thought.* Oxford: Clarendon Press, 1981.

Miller, Karl. *Cockburn's Millennium.* Cambridge, Mass.: Harvard University Press, 1976.

———. *Doubles: Studies in Literary History.* Oxford: Oxford University Press, 1985.

———. *Electric Shepherd: A Likeness of James Hogg.* London: Faber & Faber, 2004.

Millgate, Jane. *Scott's Last Edition: A Study in Publishing History.* Edinburgh: Edinburgh University Press, 1987.

———. *Walter Scott: The Making of the Novelist.* Edinburgh: Edinburgh University Press, 1984.

Monnickendam, Andrew. "Eating Your Words: Plate and Nation in Meg Dods's *The Cook and Housewife's Manual.*" *Scottish Studies Review* 6, no. 1 (2005): 33–42.

———. "The Odd Couple: Christian Isobel Johnstone's Reviews of Maria Edgeworth and Sir Walter Scott." *Scottish Literary Journal* 27, no. 1 (2000): 22–38.

Moore, Carlisle. "Thomas Carlyle and Fiction: 1822–1834." *Nineteenth Century Studies* (1940): 131–77.

Moore, Lisa L. "Acts of Union: Sexuality and Nationalism, Romance and Realism in the Irish National Tale." *Cultural Critique* 44 (2000): 113–44.

Moretti, Franco. *Atlas of the European Novel, 1800–1900.* London: Verso, 1998.

———. *Modern Epic: The World System from Goethe to Garcia Marquez.* London: Verso, 1996.

———. *The Way of the World: The Bildungsroman in European Culture.* London: Verso, 1987.

Moses, Michael Valdez. "Magical Realism at World's End." *Literary Imagination* 3, no. 1 (2001): 105–33.

Moss, Sarah. "Recipes for Disaster: Eating and Gender in the Novels of Susan Ferrier." *Scottish Studies Review* 5, no. 2 (2004): 27–40.

Muir, Edwin. *Scott and Scotland: The Predicament of the Scottish Writer.* Edinburgh: Polygon, 1982.

Mullan, John. *Sentiment and Sociability: The Language of Feeling in the Eighteenth Century.* Oxford: Clarendon Press, 1988.

Murphy, Peter. *Poetry as an Occupation and an Art in Britain, 1760–1830.* Cambridge: Cambridge University Press, 1993.

Nairn, Tom, *The Break-Up of Britain: Crisis and Neo-Nationalism.* London: NLB, 1981.

Newcomer, James. "Castle Rackrent: The Disingenuous Thady Quirk." In *Family Chronicles: Maria Edgeworth's Castle Rackrent*, ed. Coílín Owens, 79–85. Totowa, N.J.: Barnes and Noble, 1987.

Nisbet, Robert A. *Social Change and History: Aspects of the Western Theory of Development*. New York: Oxford University Press, 1969.

Noble, Andrew. "John Wilson (Christopher North) and the Tory Hegemony." In Gifford, *History of Scottish Literature*, 125–51.

Ó Gallchoir, Clíona. "Maria Edgeworth's Revolutionary Morality and the Limits of Realism." *Colby Library Quarterly* 36, no. 2 (June 2000): 87–97.

Parker, Mark Louis. *Literary Magazines and British Romanticism*. Cambridge: Cambridge University Press, 2000.

Patey, Douglas Lane. *Probability and Literary Form: Philosophical Theory and Literary Practice in the Augustan Age*. Cambridge: Cambridge University Press, 1984.

Perkins, Pam. "A Taste for Scottish Fiction: Christian Johnstone's *Cook and Housewife's Manual*." *European Romantic Review* 11, no. 2 (2000): 248–58.

Phillips, Mark Salber. *Society and Sentiment: Genres of Historical Writing in Britain, 1740–1820*. Princeton: Princeton University Press, 2000.

Phillipson, Nicholas. "Adam Smith as Civic Moralist." In *Wealth and Virtue: The Shaping of Political Economy in the Scottish Enlightenment*, ed. Istvan Hont and Michael Ignatieff, 179–202. Cambridge: Cambridge University Press, 1983.

———. "The Pursuit of Virtue in Scottish University Education: Dugald Stewart and Scottish Moral Philosophy in the Enlightenment." In *Universities, Society and the Future*, ed. Nicholas Phillipson, 81–109. Edinburgh: Edinburgh University Press, 1983.

Pinch, Adela. *Strange Fits of Passion: Epistemologies of Emotion, Hume to Austen*. Stanford: Stanford University Press, 1996.

Pittock, Murray G. H. "Hogg's Gothic and the Transformation of Genre: Towards a Scottish Romanticism." *Studies in Hogg and His World* 15 (2004): 67–75.

———. *The Invention of Scotland: The Stuart Myth and the Scottish Identity, 1638 to the Present*. London: Routledge, 1991.

———. *Poetry and Jacobite Politics in Eighteenth-Century Britain and Ireland*. Cambridge: Cambridge University Press, 1994.

———. "Scott and the British Tourist." In Carruthers and Rawes, *English Romanticism and the Celtic World*, 151–66.

Polsgrove, Carol. " 'They Made it Pay': British Short Fiction Writers, 1820-1840." *Studies in Short Fiction* 11, no. 4 (1974): 417–21.

Poovey, Mary. *A History of the Modern Fact: Problems of Knowledge in the Sciences of Wealth and Society*. Chicago: University of Chicago Press, 1998.

Potkay, Adam. *The Fate of Eloquence in the Age of Hume*. Ithaca: Cornell University Press, 1994.

Prebble, John. *The King's Jaunt: George IV in Scotland, August 1822*. London: Collins, 1988.

Price, Leah. *The Anthology and the Rise of the Novel: From Richardson to George Eliot*. Cambridge: Cambridge University Press, 2000.

Price, Leah. "The Politics of Pedantry from Thomas Bowdler to Susan Ferrier." *Women's Writing* 7, no. 1 (2000): 75–88.

Redekop, Magdalene. "Beyond Closure: Buried Alive with Hogg's *Justified Sinner.*" *ELH* 52, no. 1 (Spring 1985): 159–84.

Reiss, Timothy J. *The Meaning of Literature.* Ithaca: Cornell University Press, 1992.

Rigney, Anne. *Imperfect Histories: The Elusive Past and the Legacy of Romantic Historicism.* Ithaca: Cornell University Press, 2001.

Robertson, Fiona. *Legitimate Histories: Scott, Gothic and the Authorities of Fiction.* Oxford: Clarendon Press, 1994.

Roper, Derek. *Reviewing before the Edinburgh, 1788–1802.* London: Methuen & Co., 1978.

Rowlinson, Matthew. " 'The Scotch Hate Gold': British Identity and Paper Money." In *Nation States and Money: The Past, Present and Future of National Currencies,* ed. Emily Gilbert and Eric Hellreiner, 47–67. London: Routledge, 1999.

Rubenstein, Jill. "Varieties of Explanation in *The Shepherd's Calendar.*" *Studies in Hogg and His World* 4 (1993): 1–11.

Russett, Margaret. *Fictions and Fakes: Forging Romantic Authenticity, 1760–1845.* Cambridge: Cambridge University Press, 2006.

Sanderson, Elizabeth. *Women and Work in Eighteenth-Century Edinburgh.* New York: St. Martin's, 1996.

Schoenfield, Mark L. "Butchering James Hogg: Romantic Identity in the Magazine Market." In *At the Limits of Romanticism: Essays in Cultural, Feminist, and Materialist Criticism,* ed. Mary Favret and Nicola Watson, 207–24. Bloomington: Indiana University Press, 1994.

———. "The Family Plots: Land and Law in John Galt's *The Entail.*" *Scottish Literary Journal* 24, no. 1 (1997): 60–65.

Scholnick, Robert. " 'The Fiery Cross of Knowledge': *Chambers's Edinburgh Journal,* 1832–1843." *Victorian Periodicals Review* 32, no. 4 (1999): 324–58.

Schor, Esther. *Bearing the Dead: The British Cult of Mourning from the Enlightenment to Victoria.* Princeton: Princeton University Press, 1994.

Schor, Hilary M. "The Stupidest Novel in London: Thomas Carlyle and the Sickness of Victorian Fiction." *Carlyle Studies Annual* 16 (1996): 117–31.

Secord, James A. *Victorian Sensation: The Extraordinary Publication, Reception, and Secret Authorship of Vestiges of the Natural History of Creation.* Chicago: University of Chicago Press, 2000.

Segwick, Eve Kosofsky. *Between Men: English Literature and Male Homosocial Desire.* New York: Columbia University Press, 1985.

Shaw, Harry E. *Narrating Reality: Austen, Scott, Eliot.* Ithaca: Cornell University Press, 1999.

Shepherd, W. G. "Fat Flesh: The Poetic Theme of *The Three Perils of Man.*" *Studies in Hogg and His World* 3 (1992): 1–9.

Sher, Richard B. "The Book in the Scottish Enlightenment." In *The Culture of the Book in the Scottish Enlightenment,* ed. Paul Wood, 40–60. Toronto: Thomas Fisher Rare Book Library, University of Toronto Press, 2000.

————. *Church and University in the Scottish Enlightenment: The Moderate Literati of Edinburgh*. Princeton: Princeton University Press, 1985.

————. *The Enlightenment and the Book: Scottish Authors and Their Books in Eighteenth-Century Britain, Ireland, and America*. Chicago: University of Chicago Press, 2006.

————. "Professors of Virtue: The Social History of the Edinburgh Moral Philosophy Chair in the Eighteenth Century." In *Studies in the Philosophy of the Scottish Enlightenment,* ed. M. A. Stewart, 87–126. Oxford: Oxford University Press, 1990.

Shields, Juliet. "From Family Roots to the Routes of Empire: National Tales and the Domestication of the Scottish Highlands." *ELH* 72, no. 4 (2005): 919–40.

Shattock, Joanne. *Politics and Reviewers: The Edinburgh and the Quarterly in the Early Victorian Age*. London: Leicester University Press, 1989.

Siegel, Jonah. *Desire and Excess: The Nineteenth-Century Culture of Art*. Princeton: Princeton University Press, 2000.

Simmons, Clare A. "A Man of Few Words: The Romantic Orang-Outang and Scott's *Count Robert of Paris*." *Scottish Literary Journal* 17, no. 1 (May 1990): 21–34.

Simpson, David. *Romanticism, Nationalism and the Revolt against Theory*. Chicago: University of Chicago Press, 1993.

Simpson, Erik. "Minstrelsy Goes to Market: Prize Poems, Minstrel Contests and Romantic Poetry." *ELH* 71, no. 3 (2004): 691–718.

Simpson, Kenneth G. "Ironic Self-Revelation in *Annals of the Parish*." In Whatley, *John Galt 1779–1979*, 64–91.

————. *The Protean Scot: The Crisis of Identity in Eighteenth-Century Scottish Literature*. Aberdeen: Aberdeen University Press, 1988.

Siskin, Clifford. *The Historicity of Romantic Discourse*. New York: Oxford University Press, 1988.

————. *The Work of Writing: Literature and Social Change in Britain, 1700–1830*. Baltimore: Johns Hopkins University Press, 1998.

Smith, Sarah W. R. "Men, Women, and Money: The Case of Mary Brunton." In *Fetter'd or Free? British Women Novelists, 1670–1815,* ed. Mary Anne Schofield and Cecilia Macheski, 40–58. Athens: Ohio University Press, 1986.

Snodgrass, Charles. "*Blackwood's* Subversive Scottishness." In *Print Culture and the Blackwood Tradition, 1805–1930,* ed. David Finkelstein, 90–116. Toronto: University of Toronto Press, 2006.

Sorensen, Janet. *The Grammar of Empire in Eighteenth-Century British Writing*. Cambridge: Cambridge University Press, 2000.

St. Clair, William. *The Reading Nation in the Romantic Period*. Cambridge: Cambridge University Press, 2004.

Stafford, Fiona. "Blair's Ossian, Romanticism, and the Teaching of Literature," in Crawford, *Scottish Invention of English Literature*, 68–88.

————. "*The Edinburgh Review* and the Representation of Scotland." In Demata and Wu, *British Romanticism and the Edinburgh Review*, 33–57.

————. *The Last of the Race: The Growth of a Myth from Milton to Darwin*. Oxford: Clarendon Press, 1994.

Stallybrass, Peter. "Books and Scrolls: Navigating the Bible." In *Books and Readers in Early Modern England*, ed. Jennifer Andersen and Elizabeth Sauer, 42–79. Philadelphia: University of Pennsylvania Press, 2002.

Stewart, Susan. *Crimes of Writing: Problems in the Containment of Representation*. New York: Oxford University Press, 1991.

———. *On Longing: Narratives of the Miniature, the Gigantic, the Souvenir, the Collection*. Durham: Duke University Press, 1993.

Strout, Alan Lang. *A Bibliography of Articles in Blackwood's Magazine, Volumes I through XVIII: 1817–1825*. Lubbock: Texas Technical College Library Bulletin, 1959.

Sussman, Charlotte. "The Emptiness at *The Heart of Midlothian*: Nation, Narration, and Population." *Eighteenth-Century Fiction* 15, no. 1 (2002): 103–26.

Sutherland, John. *The Life of Walter Scott: A Critical Biography*. Oxford: Blackwell, 1995.

Sutherland, Kathryn. Introduction to Walter Scott, *Redgauntlet*, ed. Kathryn Sutherland, vii–xxxiii. Oxford: Oxford University Press, 1985.

———. "Fictional Economies: Adam Smith, Sir Walter Scott and the Nineteenth Century Novel." *ELH* 54, no. 1 (1987): 97–127.

Todorov, Tzvetan. *The Fantastic: A Structural Approach to a Literary Genre*. Trans. Richard Howard. Cleveland: Case Western University, 1973.

Tracy, Robert. "Maria Edgeworth and Lady Morgan: Legality versus Legitimacy." *Nineteenth-Century Fiction* 40, no. 1 (1985): 1–22.

Tracy, Thomas. "The Mild Irish Girl: Domesticating the National Tale." *Éire-Ireland* 39, nos. 1 & 2 (2004): 81–109.

Trevor-Roper, Hugh. "The Invention of Tradition: The Highland Tradition of Scotland." In *The Invention of Tradition*, ed. Eric Hobsbawm and Terence Ranger, 15–42. Cambridge: Cambridge University Press, 1983.

Trumpener, Katie, *Bardic Nationalism: The Romantic Novel and the British Empire*. Princeton: Princeton University Press, 1997.

———. "National Character, Nationalist Plots: National Tale and Historical Novel in the Age of *Waverley*, 1806–1830." *ELH* 60 (1993): 685–731.

Tulloch, Graham. "Writing 'By Advice': *Ivanhoe* and *The Three Perils of Man*." *Studies in Hogg and His World* 15 (2004): 32–52.

Vakil, Cyrus. "Walter Scott and the Historicism of Scottish Enlightenment Philosophical History." In Alexander and Hewitt, *Scott in Carnival*, 404–18.

Vermeule, Blakey. *The Party of Humanity: Writing Moral Psychology in Eighteenth-Century Britain*. Baltimore: Johns Hopkins University Press, 2000.

Villari, Enrica. "Romance and History in *Waverley*." In *Athena's Shuttle: Myth, Religion, Ideology from Romanticism to Modernism*, ed. F. Marucci and E. Sdegno, 93–111. Milan: Cisalpino, 2000.

Wallerstein, Immanuel. *The Modern World-System III: The Second Era of Great Expansion of the Capitalist World-Economy, 1730–1840s*. San Diego: Academic Press, 1989.

———. *Unthinking Social Science: The Limits of Nineteenth-Century Paradigms*. Cambridge, Mass.: Polity Press, 1991.

Ward, J. R. "The British West Indies in the Age of Abolition, 1748–1815." In *The Oxford History of the British Empire*, vol. 2, *The Eighteenth Century*, ed. P. J. Marshall, 415–39. Oxford: Oxford University Press, 1998.

Watson, Nicola. *Revolution and the Form of the British Novel, 1790–1805: Intercepted Letters, Interrupted Seductions.* Oxford: Clarendon, 1994.

Watt, Ian. *The Rise of the Novel: Studies in Defoe, Richardson and Fielding.* London: Chatto & Windus, 1957.

Watt, James. *Contesting the Gothic: Fiction, Genre, and Cultural Conflict, 1764–1832.* Cambridge: Cambridge University Press, 1999.

———. "Scott, the Scottish Enlightenment, and Romantic Orientalism." In Davis, Duncan, and Sorensen, *Scotland and the Borders of Romanticism*, 94–112.

Welsh, Alexander. *The Hero of the Waverley Novels: With New Essays on Scott.* Princeton: Princeton University Press, 1992.

Whatley, Christopher A. "*Annals of the Parish* and History." In Whatley, *John Galt 1779–1979*, 51–63.

———, ed. *John Galt 1779–1979.* Edinburgh: Ramsay Head, 1979.

Whyte, Christopher. "Queer Readings, Gay Texts: From *Redgauntlet* to *The Prime of Miss Jean Brodie*." In *Scotland in Theory: Reflections on Culture and Literature*, ed. Eleanor Bell and Gavin Miller, 147–65. Amsterdam: Rodopi, 2004.

Williams, Ioan, ed. *Sir Walter Scott on Novelists and Fiction.* New York: Barnes and Noble, 1970.

Wilson, Patricia J. "*Ringan Gilhaize*: A Neglected Masterpiece?" In Whatley, *John Galt 1779–1979*, 120–50.

Wilt, Judith. *Secret Leaves: The Novels of Walter Scott.* Chicago: University of Chicago Press, 1985.

Winch, Donald. "The System of the North: Dugald Stewart and his Pupils." In Collini, Winch, and Burrow, *That Noble Science of Politics*, 23–61.

Womack, Peter. *Improvement and Romance: Constructing the Myth of the Highlands.* Basingstoke: Macmillan, 1989.

Wootton, David. "David Hume, 'The Historian.'" In *The Cambridge Companion to Hume*, ed. David Fate Norton, 281–312. Cambridge: Cambridge University Press, 1993.

Youngson, A. J. *The Making of Classical Edinburgh, 1750–1840.* Edinburgh: Edinburgh University Press, 1966.

Zimmerman, Everett. *The Boundaries of Fiction: History and the Eighteenth-Century British Novel.* Ithaca: Cornell University Press, 1996.

Žižek, Slavoj. *The Sublime Object of Ideology.* London: Verso, 1989.

———. *Tarrying with the Negative: Kant, Hegel, and the Critique of Ideology.* Durham, N.C.: Duke University Press, 1993.

Index